Hard Press

PROLEGOMENA

to the

HISTORY OF ISRAEL.

PREFACE.

The work which forms the greater part of the present volume first
appeared in 1878 under the title "History of Israel. By J.
Wellhausen. In two volumes. Volume I." The book produced a great
impression throughout Europe, and its main thesis, that "the Mosaic
history is not the starting-point for the history of ancient
Israel, but for the history of Judaism," was felt to be so
powerfully maintained that many of the leading Hebrew teachers of
Germany who had till then stood aloof from the so-called "Grafian
hypothesis"—the doctrine, that is, that the Levitical Law and
connected parts of the Pentateuch were not written till after the
fall of the kingdom of Judah, and that the Pentateuch in its
present compass was not publicly accepted as authoritative till
the reformation of Ezra—declared themselves convinced by
Wellhausen's arguments. Before 1878 the Grafian hypothesis was
neglected or treated as a paradox in most German universities,
although some individual scholars of great name were known to have
reached by independent inquiry similar views to those for which
Graf was the recognised sponsor, and although in Holland the
writings of Professor Kuenen, who has been aptly termed Graf's
goel, had shown in an admirable and conclusive manner that the
objections usually taken to Graf's arguments did not touch the
substance of the thesis for which he contended.
Since 1878, partly through the growing influence of Kuenen, but
mainly through the impression produced by Wellhausen's book, all
this has been changed. Almost every younger scholar of mark is on
the side of Vatke and Reuss, Lagarde and Graf, Kuenen and
Wellhausen, and the renewed interest in Old Testament study which
is making itself felt throughout all the schools of Europe must be
traced almost entirely to the stimulus derived from a new view of
the history of the Law which sets all Old Testament problems in a
new light.

Our author, who since 1878 had been largely engaged in the study
of other parts of Semitic antiquity, has not yet given to the world
his promised second volume. But the first volume was a complete
book in itself; the plan was to reserve the whole narrative of the
history of Israel for vol.ii., so that vol.i. was entirely

occupied in laying the critical foundations on which alone a real history of the Hebrew nation could be built. Accordingly, the second edition of the History, vol.i., appeared in 1883 (Berlin, Reimer), under the new title of "Prolegomena to the History of Israel." In this form it is professedly, as it really was before, a complete and self-contained work; and this is the form of which a translation, carefully revised by the author, is now offered to the public.

All English readers interested in the Old Testament will certainly be grateful to the translators and publishers for a volume which in its German garb has already produced so profound an impression on the scholarship of Europe; and even in this country the author's name is too well known to make it necessary to introduce him at length to a new public. But the title of the book has a somewhat unfamiliar sound to English ears, and may be apt to suggest a series of dry and learned dissertations meant only for Hebrew scholars. It is worth while therefore to point out in a few words that this would be quite a false impression; that the matters with which Professor Wellhausen deals are such as no intelligent student of the Old Testament can afford to neglect; and that the present volume gives the English reader, for the first time, an opportunity to form his own judgment on questions which are within the scope of any one who reads the English Bible carefully and is able to think clearly, and without prejudice, about its Contents. The history of Israel is part of the history of the faith by which we live, the New Testament cannot be rightly understood without understanding the Old, and the main reason why so many parts of the Old Testament are practically a sealed book even to thoughtful people is simply that they have not the historical key to the interpretation of that wonderful literature.

The Old Testament does not furnish a history of Israel, though it supplies the materials from which such a history can be constructed. For example, the narrative of Kings gives but the merest outline of the events that preceded the fall of Samaria; to understand the inner history of thc time we must fill up this outline with the aid of the prophets Amos and Hosea. But the more the Old Testament has been studied, the more plain has it become that for many parts of the history something more is needed than merely to read each part of the narrative books in connection with the other books that illustrate the same period. The Historical Books and the Pentateuch are themselves very composite structures, in which old narratives occur imbedded in later compilations, and groups of old laws are overlaid by ordinances of comparatively recent date. Now, to take one point only, but that the most important, it must plainly make a vast difference to our whole view of the providential course of Israel's history if it appear

4

that instead of the whole Pentateuchal law having been given to Israel before the tribes crossed the Jordan, that law really grew up little by little from its Mosaic germ, and did not attain its present form till the Israelites were the captives or the subjects of a foreign power. This is what the new school of Pentateuch criticism undertakes to prove, and it does so in a way that should interest every one. For in the course of the argument it appears that the plain natural sense of the old history has constantly been distorted by the false presuppositions with which we have been accustomed to approach it—that having a false idea of the legal and religious culture of the Hebrews when they first entered Canaan, we continually miss the point of the most interesting parts of the subsequent story, and above all fail to understand the great work accomplished by the prophets in destroying Old Israel and preparing the way first for Judaism and then for the Gospel. These surely are inquiries which no conscientious student of the Bible can afford to ignore.

The process of disentangling the twisted skein of tradition is necessarily a very delicate and complicated one, and involves certain operations for which special scholarship is indispensable. Historical criticism is a comparatively modern science, and in its application to this, as to other histories, it has made many false and uncertain steps. But in this, as in other sciences, when the truth has been reached it can generally be presented in a comparatively simple form, and the main positions can be justified even to the general reader by methods much less complicated, and much more lucid, than those originally followed by the investigators themselves. The modern view as to the age of the Pentateuchal law, which is the key to the right understanding of the History of Israel, has been reached by a mass of investigations and discussions of which no satisfactory general account has ever been laid before the English reader. Indeed, even on the Continent, where the subject has been much more studied than among us, Professor Wellhausen's book was the first complete and sustained argument which took up the question in all its historical bearings.

More recently Professor Kuenen of Leyden, whose discussions of the more complicated questions of Pentateuch analysis are perhaps the finest things that modern criticism can show, has brought out the second edition of the first volume of his Onderzoek, and when this appears in English, as it is soon to do, our Hebrew students will have in their hands an admirable manual of what I may call the anatomy of the Pentateuch, in which they can follow from chapter to chapter the process by which the Pentateuch grew to its present form. But for the mass of Bible-readers such detailed analysis will always be too difficult. What every one can understand and ought to try to master, is the broad historical aspect of the matter. And this the present volume sets forth in a way that must be full of interest to every one who has tasted the intense pleasure of following institutions and ideas in their growth, and who has faith enough to see the hand of God as clearly in a long providential development as in a sudden miracle.

The reader will find that every part of the "Prolegomena" is instinct with historical interest, and contributes something to a vivid realisation of what Old Israel really was, and why it has so great a part in the history of spiritual faith. In the first essay of the Prolegomena a complete picture is given of the history of the ordinances of worship in Israel, and the sacrifices, the feasts, the priesthood, are all set in a fresh light. The second essay, the history of what the Israelites themselves believed and recorded about their past, will perhaps to some readers seem less inviting, and may perhaps best be read after perusal of the article, reprinted from the "Encyclopaedia Britannica", which stands at the close of the volume and affords a general view of the course of the history of Israel, as our author constructs it on the basis of the researches in his Prolegomena. The essay on Israel and Judaism with which the Prolegomena close, may in like manner be profitably compared with sect. II of the appended sketch—a section which is not taken directly from the "Encyclopaedia", but translated from the German edition of the article "Israel", where the subject is expanded by the author. Here the reader will learn how close are the bonds that connect the critical study of the Old Testament with the deepest and unchanging problems of living faith.

W. ROBERTSON SMITH.

TRANSLATORS' NOTE.

Pages 237 [chapter IV . 3] to 425 [end] of the "Prolegomena" and section II of "Israel" are translated by Mr. Menzies; for the rest of the volume Mr. Black is responsible. Both desire to express their indebtedness to Professor Robertson Smith for many valuable suggestions made as the sheets were passing through the press.

TABLE OF CONTENTS.

PROLEGOMENA.

INTRODUCTION—

1. Is the Law the starting-point for the history of ancient Israel or for that of Judaism ? The latter possibility is not precluded a priori by the history of the Canon. Reasons for considering it. De Wette, George, Vatke, Reuss, Graf

2. The three strata of the Pentateuch: Deuteronomy, Priestly Code, Jehovist

3. The question is as to the Priestly Code and its historical position. Method of the investigation

A. HISTORY OF WORSHIP.

CHAPTER I. THE PLACE OF WORSHIP—

I.I.1. The historical and prophetical books show no trace in Hebrew antiquity of a sanctuary of exclusive legitimacy

I.I.2. Polemic of the prophets against the sanctuaries. Fall of Samaria. Reformation of Josiah

I.I.3. Influence of the Babylonian exile

I.*Ii*.1. The Jehovist (*je*) sanctions a multiplicity of altars

I.*Ii*.2. Deuteronomy (D) demands local unity of worship

I.*Ii*.3. The Priestly Code (RQ) presupposes that unity, and transfers it, by means of the Tabernacle, to primitive times

I.III.1. The tabernacle, as a central sanctuary and dwelling for the ark, can nowhere be found in the historical tradition

I.III.2. Noldeke's view untenable

CHAPTER II. SACRIFICE—

Ii.I.1. The ritual is according to RQ the main subject of the Mosaic legislation, according to *je* it is pre-Mosaic usage; in RQ the point is How, according to *je* and D To Whom, it is offered

Ii.I.2. The historical books agree with *je*; the prophets down to Ezekiel contradict RQ

Ii.Ii.1. Material innovations in RQ. Preliminary remarks on the notion, contents, mode of offering, and propitiatory effects of sacrifice.

Ii.Ii.2. Material and ideal refinement of the offerings in RQ

Ii.Ii.3. The sacrificial meal gives way to holocausts

Ii.Ii.4. Development of the trespass-offering.

Ii.III.1. The centralisation of worship at Jerusalem destroyed the connection of sacrifice with the natural occasions of life, so that it lost its original character

CHAPTER III. THE SACRED FEASTS—

III.I.1. In *je* and D there is a rotation of three festivals. Easter and Pentecost mark the beginning and the end of the corn-harvest, and the autumn feast the vintage and the bringing home the corn from the threshing-floor. With the feast of unleavened bread (Massoth) is conjoined, especially in D, the feast of the sacrifice of the male firstborn of cattle (Pesah).

III.I.2. The feasts based on the offering of firstlings of the field and of the herd. Significance of the land and of agriculture for religion

III.*Ii*.1. In the historical and prophetical books, the autumn feast only is distinctly attested, and it is the most important in *je* and D also: of the others there are only faint traces .

III.*Ii*.2. But the nature of the festivals is the same as in *je* and D

III.III.1. In RQ the feasts have lost their reference to harvest and the first fruits; and this essentially changes their nature

III.III.2. The metamorphosis was due to the centralisation of worship, and may he traced down through Deuteronomy and Ezekiel to RQ,

III.III.3. To the three festivals RQ adds the great day of atonement, which arose out of the fast-days of the exile

III.IV.1. The Sabbath, which is connected with the new moon, was originally a lunar festival Exaggeration of the Sabbath rest in the Priestly Code

III.IV.2. Sabbatical year, and year of Jubilee

CHAP. IV. THE PRIESTS AND THE LEVITES—

IV.I.1. According to Ezek. xliv., only the Levites of Jerusalem, the sons of Zadok, are to continue priests in the new Jerusalem; the other Levites are to be degraded to their servants and denuded of their priestly rights. According to RQ the Levites never possessed the priestly right, but only the sons of Aaron

IV.I.2. These answer to the sons of Zadok

IV.*Ii*.1. In the earliest period of the history of Israel there is no distinction between clergy and laity. Every one may slaughter and sacrifice; there are professional priests only at the great sanctuaries. Priestly families at Sihiloh and Dan.

No setting apart of what is holy

IV.*Ii*.2. Royal temples of the kings; priests at them as royal officials

IV.*Ii*.3. Importance of the North-Israelite priesthood in the time of the kings

IV.*Ii*.4. The family of Zadok at Jerusalem

IV.III.1. In the oldest part of *je* there are no priests; no Aaron by the side of Moses

IV.III.2. In D the Levites are priests. They occur in that character, not to speak of Judges xviii. seq., only in the literature of the exile. Their descent from Moses or Aaron. The spiritual and the secular tribe of Levi. Difficulty of bringing them together

IV.III.3. Consolidation of the spiritual tribe in RQ; separation of priests and Levites. Further development of the clergy after the exile. The high priest as head of the theocracy

CHAPTER V. THE ENDOWMENT OF THE CLERGY—

V.I.1. The sacrificial dues raised in RQ

V.I.2. The firstlings were turned into contributions to the priests, and doubled in amount

V.*Ii*.1. Levitical towns

V.*Ii*.2. The historical situation underlying the priestly pretensions in RQ

B. HISTORY OF TRADITION.

CHAPTER VI. CHRONICLES—

VI.I.1. David becomes Saul's successor without any exertion, all Israel being already on his side, namely, the priests and Levites

Distortion of the original story of the bringing of the ark to Jerusalem. Omission of unedifying incidents in David's life

VI.I.2. Preparation for the building of the temple. Delight of the narrator in numbers and names. Inconsistency with 1Kings i, ii.

Picture of David in Chronicles

VI.I.3. Solomon's sacrifice at the tabernacle at Gibeah. Building of the temple. Retouching of the original narrative

VI.*Ii*.1. Estimate of the relation between Judah and Israel; the Israelites do not belong to the temple, nor, consequently, to the theocracy

VI.*Ii*.2. Levitical idealising of Judah. View taken of those acts of rulers in the temple-worship which the books of Kings condemn or approve. Inconsistencies with the narrative of the sources; importation of priests and Levites.

VI.*Ii*.3. Divine pragmatism of the sacred history, and its results

VI.*Ii*.4. The books of Kings obviously present throughout

VI.III.1. The genealogical registers of I Chron.i-ix The ten tribes

VI.III.2. Judah and Levi

VI.III.3. Chronicles had no other sources for the period before the exile than the historical books preserved to us in the Canon. The diversity of historical view is due to the influence of the law, especially the Priestly Code. The Midrash

CHAPTER VII. JUDGES, SAMUEL, AND KINGS—

VII.I.1. The formula on which the book of Judges is constructed in point of chronology and of religion

VII.I.2. Its relation to the stem of the tradition. Judg. xix.-xxi.

VI.*Ii*.3. Occasional additions to the original narratives

VII.I.4. Difference of religious attitude in the latter

VII.*Ii*.1. Chronological and religious formulas in the books of Samuel

VII.*Ii*.2. The stories of the rise of the monarchy and the elevation of Saul entirely recast

VII.*Ii*.3. Saul's relation to Samuel

VII.*Ii*.4. The narrative of David's youth The view taken of Samuel may be regarded as a measure of the growth of the tradition Saul and David

VII.III.1. The last religious chronological revision of the books of Kings. Similar in kind to that of Judges and Samuel Its standpoint Judaean and Deuteronomistic

VII.III.2. Its relation to the materials received from tradition

VII.III.3. Differences of sentiment in the sources

VII.III.4. In Chronicles the history of ancient Israel is recast in accordance with the ideas of the Priestly Code; in the older historical books it is judged according to the standard of Deuteronomy

CHAPTER VIII. THE NARRATIVE OF THE HEXATEUCH—

C. ISRAEL AND JUDAISM.

CHAPTER IX. CONCLUSION OF THE CRITICISM OF THE LAW—

IX.I.1. The veto of critical analysis

IX.I.2. The historical presuppositions of Deuteronomy

IX.I.3. The Deuteronomistic revision does not extend over the Priestly Code

IX.*Ii*.1. The final revision of the Hexateuch proceeds from the Priestly Code, as we see from Leviticus xvii. seq.

IX.*Ii*.2. Examination of Leviticus xxvi.

IX.*Ii*.3. R cannnot be separated from RQ

IX.III<.1.> The language of the Priestly Code

IX.III.2. ?

CHAPTER X. THE ORAL AND THE WRITTEN TORAH—

X.I.1. No written law in ancient Israel. The Decalogue

X.I.2. The Torah of Jehovah in the mouth of priests and prophets

X.I.3. View of revelation in Jeremiah, Zechariah, and the writer of Isa. xl.-lxvi.

X.II.1. Deuteronomy was the first law in our sense of the word. It obtains authority during the exile. End of prophecy

X.*Ii*.2. The reforming legislation supplemented by that of the restoration. The usages of worship codified and systematised by Ezekiel and his successors. The Priestly Code—its introduction by Ezra

X.*Ii*.3. The Torah the basis of the Canon. Extension of the notion originally attached to the Torah to the other books

CHAPTER XI. THE THEOCRACY AS IDEA AND AS INSTITUTION—

XI.I.1. Freshness and naturalness of early Israelite history

XI.I.2. Rise of the state. Relation of Religion and of the Deity to the life of state and nation.

XI.I.3. The Messianic theocracy of the older prophets is built up on the foundations afforded by the actual community of their time

XI.I.4. The idea of the covenant

XI.*Ii*.1. Foundation of the theocratic constitution under the foreign domination

XI.*Ii*.2. The law and the prophets.

_-*-*-*-*-*-*-*-*-*

ISRAEL.

1. The beginnings of the nation

2. The settlement in Palestine.

3. The foundation of the kingdom, and the first three kings

4. From Jeroboam I. to Jeroboam *ii.*

5. God, the world, and the life of men in Old Israel

6. The fall of Samaria

7. The deliverance of Judah

8. The prophetic reformation .

9. Jeremiah and the destruction of Jerusalem .

10. The captivity and the restoration

11. Judaism and Christianity

12. The Hellenistic period

13. The Hasmonaeans

14. Herod and the Romans

15. The Rabbins

16. The Jewish Dispersion

INTRODUCTION.

In the following pages it is proposed to discuss the place in history of the "law of Moses;" more precisely, the question to be considered is whether that law is the starting-point for the history of ancient Israel, or not rather for that of Judaism, *ie.*, of the religious communion which survived the destruction of the nation by the Assyrians and Chaldaeans.

I. It is an opinion very extensively held that the great mass of the books of the Old Testament not only relate to the pre-exilic period, but date from it. According to this view, they are remnants of the literature of ancient Israel which the Jews rescued as a heritage from the past, and on which they continued to subsist in the decay of independent intellectual life. In dogmatic theology Judaism is a mere empty chasm over which one springs from the Old Testament to the New; and even where this estimate is modified, the belief still prevails in a general way that the Judaism which received the books of Scripture into the canon had, as a rule, nothing to do with their production. But the exceptions to this principle which are conceded as regards the second and third divisions of the Hebrew canon cannot be called so very slight. Of the Hagiograpba, by far the larger portion is demonstrably post-exilic, and no part demonstrably older than the exile. Daniel comes as far down as the Maccabaean wars, and Esther is perhaps even later. Of the prophetical literature a very appreciable fraction is later than the fall of the Hebrew kingdom; and the associated historical books (the "earlier prophets" of the Hebrew canon) date, in the form in which we now possess them, from a period subsequent to the death of Jeconiah, who must have survived the year 560 B.C. for some time. Making all allowance for the older sources utilised, and to a large extent transcribed word for word, in Judges, Samuel, and Kings, we find that apart from the Pentateuch the preexilic portion of the Old Testament amounts in bulk to little more than the half of the entire volume. All the rest belongs to the later period, and it includes not merely the feeble after-growths of a failing vegetation, but also productions of the vigour and originality of Isa. xl.lxvi. and Ps.lxxiii.

We come then to the Law. Here, as for most parts of the Old Testament, we have no express information as to the author and date of composition, and to get even approximately at the truth we are shut up to the use of such data as can be derived from an analysis of the contents, taken in conjunction with what we may happen to know from other sources as to the course of Israel's history. But the habit has been to assume that the historical period to be considered in this connection ends with the Babylonian exile as certainly as it begins with the exodus from Egypt. At first sight this assumption seems to be justified by the history of the canon; it was the Law that first became canonical through the influence of Ezra and Nehemiah; the Prophets became so considerably later, and the Hagiographa last of all. Now it is not unnatural, from the chronological order in which these writings were received into the canon, to proceed to an inference as to their approximate relative age, and so not only to place the Prophets before the Hagiographa, but also the five books of Moses before the Prophets. If the Prophets are for the most part older than the exile, how much more so the Law! But however trustworthy such a mode of comparison may

23

be when applied to the middle as contrasted with the latest portion of the canon, it is not at all to be relied on when the first part is contrasted with the other two. The very idea of canonicity was originally associated with the Torah, and was only afterwards extended to the other books, which slowly and by a gradual process acquired a certain measure of the validity given to the Torah by a single public and formal act, through which it was introduced at once as the Magna Charta of the Jewish communion (Nehemiah viii.-x.) In their case the canonical— that is, legal—character was not intrinsic, but was only subsequently acquired; there must therefore have been some interval, and there may have been a very long one, between the date of their origin and that of their receiving public sanction. To the Law, on the other hand, the canonical character is much more essential, and serious difficulties beset the assumption that the Law of Moses came into existence at a period long before the exile, aml did not attain the force of law until many centuries afterwards, and in totally different circumstances from those under which it had arisen. At least the fact that a collection claiming public recognition as an ecclesiastical book should have attained such recognition earlier than other writings which make no such claim is no proof of superior antiquity.

We cannot, then, peremptorily refuse to regard it as possible that what was the law of Judaism may also have been its product; and there are urgent reasons for taking the suggestion into very careful consideration. It may not be out of place here to refer to personal experience. In my early student days I was attracted by the stories of Saul and David, Ahab and Elijah; the discourses of Amos and Isaiah laid strong hold on me, and I read myself well into the prophetic and historical books of the Old Testament. Thanks to such aids as were accessible to me, I even considered that I understood them tolerably, but at the same time was troubled with a bad conscience, as if I were beginning with the roof instead of the foundation; for I had no thorough acquaintance with the Law, of which I was accustomed to be told that it was the basis and postulate of the whole literature. At last I took courage and made my way through Exodus, Leviticus, Numbers, and even through Knobel's Commentary to these books. But it was in vain that I looked for the light which was to be shed from this source on the historical and prophetical books. On the contrary, my enjoyment of the latter was marred by the Law; it did not bring them any nearer me, but intruded itself uneasily, like a ghost that makes a noise indeed, but is not visible and really effects nothing. Even where there were points of contact between it and them, differences also made themselves felt, and I found it impossible to give a candid decision in favour of the priority of the Law. Dimly I began to perceive that throughout there was between them all the difference that separates two wholly distinct worlds. Yet, so far from attaining clear conceptions, I only fell into deeper confusion, which was worse confounded by the explanations of Ewald in the second volume of history of Israel. At last, in the course of a casual visit in Gottingen in the summer of 1867, I learned through Ritschl that Karl Heinrich Graf placed the law later than the Prophets, and, almost without knowing his reasons for the hypothesis, I was prepared to accept it; I readily acknowledged to myself thc possibility of understanding Hebrew antiquity without the book of the Torah.

The hypothesis usually associated with Graf's name is really not his, but-that of his teacher, Eduard Reuss. It would be still more correct to call it after Leopold Gcorge

24

and Wiihelm Vatke, who, independent alike of Reuss and of each other, were the first to give it literary currency. All three, again, are disciples of Martin Lebrecht de Wette, the epochmaking pioneer of historical criticism in this field./1/

******************************* 1. M. W. L. de Wette, Beitraege zur Einleitung in das A. T. (Bd. I. Kritischer Versuch ueber die Glaubwuerdigkeit der Buecher der Chronik; Bd. *Ii*. Kritik der Mosaischen Geschichte, Halle, 1806-07); J. F. L. George, Die alterer Juedischen Feste mit einer Kritik der Gesetzgebung des Pentateuch (Berlin, 1835; preface dated 12th October); W. Vatke, Die biblische Theologie wissenschaftlich dargestellt (Berlin, 1835; preface dated 18th October; publication did not get beyond first part of the first volume); K. H. Graf, Die geschichtlicher Buecher des Alten Testaments (Leipsic, 1866). That Graf as well as J. Orth (Nouv. Rev. de Theol., iii. 84 sqq., iv. 350 sqq., Paris, 1859-60) owed the impulse to his critical labours to his Strassburg master was not unknown; but how great must have been the share of Reuss in the hypothesis of Graf has only been revealed in 1879, by the publication of certain theses which he had formulated as early as 1833, but had hesitated to lay in print before the general theological public. These are as follows:— "1. L'element historique du Pentateuque peut et doit etre examine a part et ne pas etre confondu avec l'element legal. 2. L'un et l'autre ont pu exister sans redaction ecrite. La mention, chez d'anciens ecrivains, de certaines traditions patriarcales ou mosaiques, ne prouve pas l'existence du Pentateuque, et une nation peut avoir un droit coutumier sans code ecrit. Les traditions nationales des Israelites remontent plus haut que les lois du Pentateuque et la redaction des premieres est anterieure a celle des secondes. 4. L'interet principal de l'historien doit porter sur la date des lois, parce que sur ce terrain il a plus de chance d'arriver a des resultats certains. *Ii* faut en consequence proceder a l'interrogatoire des temoins. 5. L'histoire racontee, dans les livres des Juges et de Samuel, et meme en partie celle comprise dans les livres des Rois, est en contradiction avec des lois dites mosaiques; donc celles-ci etaient inconnues a l'epoque de la redaction de ces livres, a plus forte raison elles n'ont pas existe dans les temps qui y vent decrits. 6. Les prophetes du 8e et du 7e siecle ne savent rien du code mosaique. 7. Jeremie est le premier prophete qui connaisse une loi ecrite et ses citations rapportent au Deuteronome. 8. Le Deuteronome (iv.45-xxviii.68) est le livre que les pretres pretendaient avoir trouve dans le temple du temps du roi Josias. Ce code est la partie la plus ancienne de la legislation (redigee) comprise dans le Pentateuque. 9. L'histoire des Israelites, en tant qu'il s'agit du developpement national determine par des lois ecrites, se divisera en deux periodes, avant et apres Josias. 10. Ezechiel est anterieur a la redaction du code rituel et des lois qui ont definitivement organise la hierarchie. 11. Le livre du Josue n'est pas, tant s'en faut, la partie la plus recente de l'ouvrage entier. 12. Le redacteur du Pentateuque se distingue clairement de l'ancien prophete Moyse." —L'Histoire Sainte et la Loi, Paris, 1879, pp. 23, 24.

****

He indeed did not himself succeed in reaching a sure position, but he was the first clearly to perceive and point out how disconnected are the alleged starting-point of Israel's history and that history itself. The religious community set up on so broad a basis in the wilderness, with its sacred centre and uniform organisation, disappears and leaves no trace as soon as Israel settles in a land of its own, and becomes, in any proper sense, a nation. The period of the Judges presents itself to us as a confused chaos, out of which order and coherence are gradually evolved under the pressure of external circumstances, but perfectly naturally and without the faintest reminiscence of a sacred unifying constitution that had formerly existed. Hebrew antiquity shows absolutely no tendencies towards a hierocracy; power is wielded solely by the heads of families and of tribes, and by the kings, who exercise control over religious worship also, and appoint and depose its priests. The influence possessed by the latter is purely moral; the Torah of God is not a document in their hands which guarantees their own position, but merely an instruction for others in their mouths; like the word of the prophets, it has divine authority but not political sanction, and has validity only in so far as it is voluntarily accepted. And as for the literature which has come down to us from the period of the Kings, it would puzzle the very best intentions to beat up so many as two or three unambiguous allusions to the Law, and these cannot be held to prove anything when one considers, by way of contrast, what Homer was to the Greeks.

To complete the marvel, in post-exile Judaism the Mosaism which until then had been only latent suddenly emerges into prominence everywhere. We now find the Book regarded as the foundation of all higher life, and the Jews, to borrow the phrase of the Koran, are "the people of the Book;" we have the sanctuary with its priests and Levites occupying the central position, and the people as a congregation encamped around it; the cultus, with its burnt-offerings and sin-offerings, its purifications and its abstinences, its feasts and Sabbaths, strictly observed as prescribed by the Law, is now the principal business of life. When we take the community of the second temple and compare it with the ancient people of Israel, we are at once able to realise how far removed was the latter from so-called Mosaism. The Jews themselves were thoroughly conscious of the distance. The revision of the books of Judges, Samuel, and Kings, undertaken towards the end of the Babylonian exile, a revision much more thorough than is commonly assumed, condemns as heretical the whole age of the Kings. At a later date, as the past became more invested with a certain nimbus of sanctity, men preferred to clothe it with the characters of legitimacy rather than sit in judgment upon it. The Book of Chronicles shows in what manner it was necessary to deal with the history of bygone times when it was assumed that the Mosaic hierocracy was their fundamental institution.

2. The foregoing remarks are designed merely to make it plain that the problem we have set before us is not an imaginary one, but actual and urgent. They are intended to introduce it; but to solve it is by no means so easy. The question what is the historical place of the Law does not even admit of being put in these simple terms. For the Law, If by that word we understand the entire Pentateuch, is no literary unity, and no simple historical quantity./1/

*********************** 1. Compare the article "Pentateuch" in the Ninth edition of the Encyclopædia Britannica, vol. xviii. *************************

26

Since the days of Peyrerius and Spinoza, criticism has acknowledged the complex character of that remarkable literary production, and from Jean Astruc onwards has laboured, not without success, at disentangling its original elements. At present there are a number of results that can be regarded as settled. The following are some of them. The five Books of Moses and the Book of Joshua constitute one whole, the conquest of the Promised Land rather than the death of Moses forming the true conclusion of the patriarchal history, the exodus, and the wandering in the wilderness. From a literary point of view, accordingly, it is more accurate to speak of the Hexateuch than of the Pentateuch. Out of this whole, the Book of Deuteronomy, as essentially an independent law-book, admits of being separated most easily. Of what remains, the parts most easily distinguished belong to the so-called "main stock" ("Grundschrift"), formerly also called the Elohistic document, on account of the use it makes of the divine name Elohim up to the time of Moses, and designated by Ewald, with reference to the regularly recurring superscriptions in Genesis, as the Book of Origins. It is distinguished by its liking for number, and measure, and formula generally, by its stiff pedantic style, by its constant use of certain phrases and turns of expression which do not occur elsewhere in the older Hebrew; its characteristics are more strongly marked than those of any of the others, and make it accordingly the easiest to recognise with certainty. Its basis is the Book of Leviticus and thc allied portions of the adjoining books,— Exodus xxv.-xl., with the exception of chaps. xxxii.-xxxiv., and Num.i.-x., xv.-xix., xxv.-xxxvi., with trifling exceptions. It thus contains legislation chiefly, and, in point of fact, relates substantially to the worship of the tabernacle and cognate matters. It is historical only in form; the history serves merely as a framework on which to arrange thc legislative material, or as a mask to disguise it. For the most part, the thread of the narrative is extremely thin, and often serves merely to carry out the chronology, which is kept up without a hiatus from the Creation to the Exodus; it becomes fuller only on the occasions in which other interests come into play, as, for example, in Genesis, with regard to the three preludes to the Mosaic covenant which are connected with the names of Adam, Noah, and Abraham respectively. When this fundamental document is also separated out as well as Deuteronomy, there remains the Jehovistic history-book, which, in contrast with the two others, is essentially of a narrative character, and sets forth with full sympathy and enjoyment the materials handed down by tradition. The story of the patriarchs, which belongs to this document almost entirely, is what best marks its character; that story is not here dealt with merely as a summary introduction to something of greater importance which is to follow, but as a subject of primary importance, deserving the fullest treatment possible. Legislative elements have been taken into it only at one point, where they fit into the historical connection, namely, when the giving of the Law at Sinai is spoken of (Exodusxx.-xxiii., xxxiv.)

Scholars long rested satisfied with this twofold division of the non-Deuteronomic Hexateuch, until Hupfeld demonstrated in certain parts of Genesis, which until then had been assigned partly to the "main stock" and partly to the Jehovist, the existence of a third continuous source, the work of the so-called younger Elohist. The choice of this name was due to the circumstance that in this document also Elohim is the ordinary name of the Deity, as it is in the "main stock" up to Exodus vi.; the epithet "younger," however, is better left out, as it involves an unproved assumption, and besides, is no longer required for distinction's sake, now that the "main stock" is no longer referred to under so unsuitable a name as that of Elohist. Hupfeld further assumed that all the three sources continued to exist separately until some one at a later date brought them together simultaneously into a single whole. But this is a view that cannot be maintained: not merely is the Elohist in his matter and in his manner of looking at things most closely akin to the Jehovist; his document has come down to us as Noldeke was the first to perceive, only in extracts embodied in the Jehovist narrative./1/

************************** Hermann Hupfeld, Die Quellen der Genesis u. die Art ihrer Zusammersetzung, Berlin, 1853; Theodor Noldeke, Die s. g. Grundschrift des Pentateuch, in Untersuchungen zur Kritik des Alten Testaments, Kiel, 1869. *************************

Thus, notwithstanding Hupfeld's discovery, the old division into two great sections continues to hold good, and there is every reason for adhering to this primary distinction as the basis of further historical research, in spite of the fact, which is coming to be more and more clearly perceived, that not only the Jehovistic document, but the "main stock" as well, are complex products, and that alongside of them occur hybrid or posthumous elements which do not admit of being simply referred to either the one or the other formation. 2

********************* 2. J. Wellhausen, Die Composition des Hexateuchs, in Jahrb. f. Deutsche Theologie, 1876, pp. 392-450, 531-602; 1877, pp. 407-479. I do not insist on all the details, but, as regards the way in which the literary process which resulted in the formation of the Pentateuch is to be looked at in general, I believe I had indicated the proper line of investigation. Hitherto the only important corrections I have received have been those of Kuenen in his Contributions to the Criticism of the Pentateuch and Joshua, published in the Leyden Theologisch Tijdschrift; but these are altogether welcome, inasmuch as they only free my own fundamental view from some relics of the old leaven of a mechanical separation of sources which had continued to adhere to it. For what Kuenen points out is, that certain elements assigned by me to the Elohist are not fragments of a once independent whole, but interpolated and parasitic additions. What effect this demonstration may have on the judgment we form of the Elohist himself is as yet uncertain. In the following pages the Jehovistic history-book is denoted by the symbol *je*, its Jehovistic part by J, and the Elohistic by E; the "main stock" pure and simple, which is distinguished by its systematising history and is seen unalloyed in Genesis, is called the Book of the Four Covenants and is symbolised by Q; for the "main stock" as a whole (as modified by an editorial process) the title of Priestly Code and the symbol RQ (Q and Revisers) are employed. ************************

Now the Law, whose historical position we have to determine, is the so-called "main stack," which, both by its contents and by its origin, is entitled to be called the Priestly Code, and will accordingly be so designated. The Priestly Code preponderates over the rest of the legislation in force, as well as in bulk; in all matters of primary importance it is the normal and final authority. It was according to the mode furnished by it that the Jews under Ezra ordered their sacred community, and upon it are formed our conceptions of the Mosaic theocracy, with the tabernacle at its centre, the high priest at its head, the priests and Levites as its organs, the legitimate cultus as its regular function. It is precisely this Law, so called par excellence, that creates the difficulties out of which our problem rises, and it is only in connection with it that the great difference of opinion exists as to date. With regard to the Jehovistic document, all are happily agreed that, substantially at all events, in language, horizon, and other features, it dates from the golden age of Hebrew literature, to which the finest parts of Judges, Samuel, and Kings, and the oldest extant prophetical writings also belong,—the period of the kings and prophets which preceded the dissolution of the two Israelite kingdoms by the Assyrians. About the origin of Deuteronomy there is still less dispute; in all circles where appreciation of scientific results can be looked for at all, it is recognised that it was composed in the same age as that in which it was discovered, and that it was made the rule of Josiah's reformation, which took place about a generation before the destruction of Jerusalem by the Chaldaeans. It is only in the case of the Priestly Code that opinions differ widely; for it tries hard to imitate the costume of the Mosaic period, and, with whatever success, to disguise its own. This is not nearly so much the case with Deuteronomy, which, in fact, allows the real situation (that of the period during which, Samaria having been destroyed, only the kingdom of Judah continued to subsist) to reveal itself very plainly through that which is assumed (xii.8, xix.8). And the Jehovist does not even pretend to being a Mosaic law of any kind; it aims at being a simple book of history; the distance between the present and the past spoken of is not concealed in the very least. It is here that all the marks are found which attracted the attention of Abenezra and afterwards of Spinoza, such as Gen. xii. 6 ("And the Canaanite was then in the land"), Gen.xxxvi.31 ("These are the kings who reigned in Edom before the children of Israel had a king"), Num. xii.6, 7, Deut. xxxiv.10 ("There arose not a prophet since in Israel like unto Moses"). The Priestly Code, on the other hand, guards itself against all reference to later times and settled life in Canaan, which both in the Jehovistic Book of the Covenant (Exodus xxi.-xxiii.) and in Deuteronomy are the express basis of the legislation: it keeps itself carefully and strictly within the limits of the situation in the wilderness, for which in all seriousness it seeks to give the law. It has actually been successful, with its movable tabernacle, its wandering camp, and other archaic details, in so concealing the true date of its composition that its many serious inconsistencies with what we know, from other sources, of Hebrew antiquity previous to the exile, are only taken as proving that it lies far beyond all known history, and on account of its enormous antiquity can hardly be brought into any connection with it. It is the Priestly Code, then, that presents us with our problem.

3. The instinct was a sound one which led criticism for the time being to turn aside from the historical problem which had originally presented itself to De Wette, and afterwards had been more distinctly apprehended by George and Vatke, in order, in the first instance, to come to some sort of clear understanding as to the composition of the Pentateuch. But a mistake was committed when it was supposed that by a separation of the sources (in which operation attention was quite properly directed chiefly to Genesis) that great historical question had been incidentally answered.

The fact was, that it had been merely put to sleep, and Graf has the credit of having, after a considerable interval, awakened it again. In doing so, indeed, he in turn laboured under the disadvantage of not knowing what success had been achieved in separating the sources, and thereby he became involved in a desperate and utterly untenable assumption. This assumption, however, had no necessary connection with his own hypothesis, and at once fell to the ground when the level to which Hupfeld brought the criticism of the text had been reached. Graf originally followed the older view, espoused by Tuch in particular, that in Genesis the Priestly Code, with its so obtrusively bare skeleton, is the "main stock," and that it is the Jehovist who supplements, and is therefore of course the later. But since, on the other hand, he regarded the ritual legislature of the middle books as much more recent than the work of the Jehovist, he was compelled to tear it asunder as best he could from its introduction in Genesis, and to separate the two halves of the Priestly Code by half a millennium. But Hupfeld had long before made it quite clear that the Jehovist is no mere supplementer, but the author of a perfectly independent work, and that the passages, such as Gen. xx.-xxii., usually cited as examples of the way in which the Jehovist worked over the "main stock," really proceed from quite another source,— the Elohist. Thus the stumbling-block of Graf had already been taken out of the way, and his path had been made clear by an unlooked-for ally. Following Kuenen's suggestion, he did not hesitate to take the helping-hand extended to him; he gave up his violent division of the Priestly Code, and then had no difficulty in deducing from the results which he had obtained with respect to the main legal portion similar consequences with regard to the narrative part in Genesis. *1*

*************************** 1. K. H. Graf, Die s. g. Grundschrift des Pentateucks, in Merx's Archiv (1869), pp. 466-477. As early as 1866 he had already expressed himself in a letter to Kuenen November 12) as follows:— "Vous me faites pressentir une solution de cette enigme...c'est que les parties elohistiques de la Genese seraient posterieures aux parties jehovistiques." Compare Kuenen, Theol. Tijdschrift (1870), p.412. Graf had also in this respect followed Reuss, who (ut supra, p. 24) says of himself: "Le cote faible de ma critique a ete que, a l'egard de tout ce qui ne rentrait pas dans les points enumeres ci-dessus, je restais dans l'orniere tracee par mes devanciers, admettant sans plus ample examen que le Pentateuque etait l'ouvrage de l'HISTORIEN elohiste, complete par l'HISTORIEN jehoviste, et ne me rendant pas compte de la maniere dont l'element legal, dont je m'etais occupe exclusivement, serait venu se joindre a l'element historique. ***************************

The foundations were now laid; it is Kuenen who has since done most for the further development of the hypothesis./2/

*************************** 2. A. Kuenen, Die Godsdienst van Israel, Haarlem, 1869-70 (Eng. transl. Religion of Israel, 1874-5), and De priesterlijke Bestanddeelen van Pentateuch en Josua, in Theol. Tijdschr.(1870), pp. 391-426. ***************************

The defenders of the prevailing opinion maintained their ground as well as they could, but from long possession had got somewhat settled on their lees. They raised against the assailants a series of objections, all of which, however, laboured more or less under the disadvantage that they rested upon the foundation which had already been shattered. Passages were quoted from Amos and Hosea as implying an acquaintance with the Priestly Code, but they were not such as could make any impression on those who were already persuaded that the latter was the more recent. Again it was asserted, and almost with violence, that the Priestly Code could not be later than Deuteronomy, and that the Deuteronomist actually had it before him. But the evidences of this proved extremely problematical, while, on the other hand, the dependence of Deuteronomy, as a whole, on the Jehovist came out with the utmost clearness. Appeal was made to the latest redaction of the entire Hexateuch, a redaction which was assumed to be Deuteronomistic; but this yielded the result that the deuteronomistic redaction could nowhere be traced in any of the parts belonging to the Priestly Code. Even the history of the language itself was forced to render service against Graf: it had already been too much the custom to deal with that as if it were soft wax. To say all in a word, the arguments which were brought into play as a rule derived all their force from a moral conviction that the ritual legislation must be old, and could not possibly have been committed to writing for the first time within the period of Judaism; that it was not operative before then, that it did not even admit of being carried into effect in the conditions that prevailed previous to the exile, could not shake the conviction— all the firmer because it did not rest on argument—that at least it existed previously.

The firemen never came near the spot where the conflagration raged; for it is only within the region of religious antiquities and dominant religious ideas,—the region which Vatke in his Biblische Theologie had occupied in its full breadth, and where the real battle first kindled—that the controversy can be brought to a definite issue. In making the following attempt in this direction, I start from the comparison of the three constituents of the Pentateuch,—the Priestly Code, Deuteronomy, and the work of the Jehovist. The contents of the first two are, of course, legislation, as we have seen; those of the third are narrative; but, as the Decalogue (Exodus xx.), the Law of the two Tables (Exodus xxxiv.), and the Book of the Covenant (Exodus xxi.-xxiii.) show, the legislative element is not wholly absent from the Jehovist, and much less is the historical absent from the Priestly Code or Deuteronomy. Further, each writer's legal standpoint is mirrored in his account of the history, and conversely; thus there is no lack either of indirect or of direct points of comparison. Now it is admitted that the three constituent elements are separated from each other by wide intervals; the question then arises, In what order? Deuteronomy stands in a relation of comparative nearness both to the Jehovist and to the Priestly Code; the distance between the last two is by far the greatest,—so great that on this ground alone Ewald as early as the year 183I (Stud. u. Krit., p. 604) declared it impossible that the one could have been written to supplement the other. Combining this observation with the undisputed priority of the Jehovist over Deuteronomy, it will follow that the Priestly Code stands last in the series. But such a consideration, although, so far as I know, proceeding upon admitted data, has no value as long as it confines itself to such mere generalities. It is necessary to trace the succession of the three elements in detail, and at once to test and to fix each by reference to an independent standard, namely, the inner development of the history of Israel so far as that is known to us by trustworthy testimonies, from independent sources.

The literary and historical investigation on which we thus enter is both wide and difficult. It falls into three parts. In the first, which lays the foundations, the data relating to sacred archaeology are brought together and arranged in such a way as to show that in the Pentateuch the elements follow upon one another and from one another precisely as the steps of the development demonstrably do in the history. Almost involuntarily this argument has taken the shape of a sort of history of the ordinances of worship. Rude and colourless that history must be confessed to be,—a fault due to the materials, which hardly allow us to do more than mark the contrast between pre-exilic and post-exilic, and, in a secondary measure, that between Deuteronomic and pre-Deuteronomic. At the same time there is this advantage arising out of the breadth of the periods treated: they cannot fail to distinguish themselves from each other in a tangible manner; it must be possible in the case of historical, and even of legal works, to recognise whether they were written before or after the exile. The second part, in many respects dependent on the first, traces the influence of the successively prevailing ideas and tendencies upon the shaping of historical tradition, and follows the various phases in which that was conceived and set forth. It contains, so to speak, a history of tradition. The third part sums up the critical results of the preceding two, with some further determining considerations, and concludes with a more general survey.

The assumptions I make will find an ever-recurring justification in the course of the investigation; the two principal are, that the work of the Jehovist, so far as the nucleus of it is concerned, belongs to the course of the Assyrian period, and that Deuteronomy belongs to its close. Moreover, however strongly I am convinced that the latter is to be dated in accordance with 2Kings xxii., I do not, like Graf, so use this position as to make it the fulcrum for my lever. Deuteronomy is the starting-point, not in the sense that without it it would be impossible to accomplish anything, but only because, when its position has been historically ascertained, we cannot decline to go on, but must demand that the position of the Priestly Code should also be fixed by reference to history. My inquiry proceeds on a broader basis than that of Graf, and comes nearer to that of Vatke, from whom indeed I gratefully acknowledge myself to have learnt best and most.

A. HISTORY OF THE ORDINANCES OF WORSHIP.

" Legem non habentes natura faciunt legis opera."—Romans ii.

["(When Gentiles) who do not have the law, do instinctively what the law requires...." Romans 2:14 NRSV]

CHAPTER I. THE PLACE OF WORSHIP.

As we learn from the New Testament, the Jews and the Samaritans in the days of Jesus were not agreed on the question which was the proper place of worship, but that there could be only one was taken to be as certain as the unity of God Himself. The Jews maintained that place to be the temple at Jerusalem, and when it was destroyed they ceased to sacrifice. But this oneness of the sanctuary in Israel was not originally recognised either in fact or in law; it was a slow growth of time. With the help of the Old Testament we are still quite able to trace the process. In doing so, it is possible to distinguish several stages of development. We shall accordingly proceed to inquire whether the three constituent parts of the Pentateuch give tokens of any relationship to one or other of these; whether and how they fall in with the course of the historical development which we are able to follow by the aid of the historical and prophetic books from the period of the Judges onwards.

I.I.1. For the earliest period of the history of Israel, all that precedes the building of the temple, not a trace can be found of any sanctuary of exclusive legitimacy. In the Books of Judges and Samuel hardly a place is mentioned at which we have not at least casual mention of an altar and of sacrifice. In great measure this multiplicity of sanctuaries was part of the heritage taken over from the Canaanites by the Hebrews; as they appropriated the towns and the culture generally of the previous inhabitants, so also did they take possession of their sacred piaces. The system of high places (Bamoth), with all the apparatus thereto belonging, is certainly Canaanite originally (Deut. xii.2, 30; Num. xxxiii.52; Exodus xxxiv.12 seq.), but afterwards is of quite general occurrence among the Hebrews. At Shechem and Gibeon the transition takes place almost in the full light of history; some other old-Israelite places of worship, certain of which are afterwards represented as Levitical towns, betray their origin by their names at least, *e.g.*, Bethshemesh or Ir Heres (Sun-town), and Ashtaroth Karnaim (the two-horned Astarte). In the popular recollection, also, the memory of the fact that many of the most prominent sacrificial seats were already in existence at the date of the immigration continues to survive. Shechem, Bethel, Beersheba, figure in Genesis as instituted by the patriarchs; other equally important holy sites, not so. The reason for the distinction can only lie in a consciousness of the more recent origin of the latter; those of the one class had been found by the people when they came, those of the other category they had themselves established. For of course, if the Hebrews did not hesitate to appropriate to themselves the old holy places of the country, neither did they feel any difficulty in instituting new ones. In Gilgal and Shiloh, in the fixed camps where, in the first instance, they had found a permanent foothold in Palestine proper, there forthwith arose important centres of worship; so likewise in other places of political importance, even in such as only temporarily come into prominence, as Ophrah, Ramah, and Nob near Gibeah. And, apart from the greater cities with their more or less regular religious service, it is perfectly permissible to erect an altar extempore, and offer sacrifice wherever an occasion presents itself. When, after the battle of Michmash, the people, tired and hungry, fell upon the cattle they had taken, and began to devour the flesh with the blood (that is, without pouring out the blood on the altar), Saul caused a great stone to be erected, and ordered that every man should slaughter his ox or his sheep there.

This was the first altar which Saul erected to Jehovah, adds the narrator, certainly not as a reproach, nor even to signalise his conduct as anything surprising or exceptional. The instance is all the more instructive, because it shows how the prohibition to eat flesh without rendering the blood back to God at a time when the people did not live crowded together within a quite limited area necessarily presupposed liberty to sacrifice anywhere—or to slaughter anywhere; for originally the two words are absolutely synonymous.

It need not be said that the sacrificial seats (even when the improvised ones are left out of account) were not all alike in the regard in which they were held, or in the frequency with which they were resorted to. Besides purely local ones, there were others to which pilgrimages were made from far and near. Towards the close of the period of the judges, Shiloh appears to have acquired an importance that perhaps extended even beyond the limits of the tribe of Joseph. By a later age the temple there was even regarded as the prototype of the temple of Solomon, that is, as the one legitimate place of worship to which Jehovah had made a grant of all the burnt-offerings of the children of Israel (Jer. vii.12; 1Samuel ii. 27-36). But, in point-of-fact, if a prosperous man of Ephraim or Benjamin made a pilgrimage to the joyful festival at Shiloh at the turn of the year, the reason for his doing so was not that he could have had no opportunity at his home in Ramah or Gibeah for eating and drinking before the Lord. Any strict centralisation is for that period inconceivable, alike in the religious as in every other sphere. This is seen even in the circumstance that the destruction of the temple of Shiloh, the priesthood of which we find officiating at Nob a little later, did not exercise the smallest modifying influence upon the character and position of the cultus; Shiloh disappears quietly from the scene, and is not mentioned again until we learn from Jeremiah that at least from the time when Solomon's temple was founded its temple lay in ruins.

For the period during which the temple of Jerusalem was not yet in existence, even the latest redaction of the historical books (which perhaps does not everywhere proceed from the same hand, but all dates from the same period—that of the Babylonian exile—and has its origin in the same spirit) leaves untouched the multiplicity of altars and of holy places. No king after Solomon is left uncensured for having tolerated the high places, but Samuel is permitted in his proper person to preside over a sacrificial feast at the Bamah of his native town, and Solomon at the beginning of his reign to institute a similar one at the great Bamah of Gibeon, without being blamed. The offensive name is again and again employed in the most innocent manner in 1Samuel ix., x., and the later editors allow it to pass unchallenged. The principle which guides this apparently unequal distribution of censure becomes clear from 1Kings iii. 2: "The people sacrificed upon the high places, for as yet no house to the name of Jehovah had been built." Not until the house had been built to the name of Jehovah—such is the idea—did the law come into force which forbade having other places of worship besides./1/

******************************** 1. Compare 1Kings viii. 16. According to Deut. xii.10 seq., the local unity of worship becomes law from the time when the Israelites have found rest (menuha). Comparing 2Samuel vii.11 and 1Kings v. 18

(A.V., v.4), we find that "menuha" first came in with David and Solomon. The period of the judges must at that time have been regarded as much shorter than appears in the present chronology. **************************************

From the building of the temple of Solomon, which is also treated as a leading epoch in chronology, a new period in the history of worship is accordingly dated,—and to a certain extent with justice. The monarchy in Israel owed its origin to the need which, under severe external pressure, had come to be felt for bringing together into the oneness of a people and a kingdom the hitherto very loosely connected tribes and families of the Hebrews; it had an avowedly centralising tendency, which very naturally laid hold of the cultus as an appropriate means for the attainment of the political end. Gideon even, the first who came near a regal position, erected a costly sanctuary in his city, Ophrah. David caused the ark of Jehovah to be fetched into his fortress on Mount Sion, and attached value to the circumstance of having for its priest the representative of the old family which had formerly kept it at Shiloh. Solomon's temple also was designed to increase the attractiveness of the city of his residence. It is indubitable that in this way political centralisation gave an impulse to a greater centralisation of worship also, and the tendency towards the latter continued to operate after the separation of the two kingdoms,—in Israel not quite in the same manner as in Judah. Royal priests, great national temples, festal gatherings of the whole people, sacrifices on an enormous scale, these were the traits by which the cultus, previously (as it would seem) very simple, now showed the impress of a new time. One other fact is significant: the domestic feasts and sacrifices of single families, which in David's time must still have been general, gradually declined and lost their importance as social circles widened and life became more public.

But this way of regarding the influence of the monarchy upon the history of the worship is not that of the author of the Books of Kings. He views the temple of Solomon as a work undertaken exclusively in the interests of pure worship, and as differing entirely in origin from the sacred buildings of the kings of Israel, with which accordingly it is not compared, but contrasted as the genuine is contrasted with the spurious. It is in its nature unique, and from the outset had the design of setting aside all other holy places,—a religious design independent of and unconnected with politics. The view, however, is unhistorical; it carries back to the original date of the temple, and imports into the purpose of its foundation the significance which it had acquired in Judah shortly before the exile. In reality the temple was not at the outset all that it afterwards became. Its influence was due to its own weight, and not to a monopoly conferred by Solomon. We nowhere learn that that king, like a forerunner of Josiah, in order to favour his new sanctuary sought to abolish all the others; there is not the faintest historical trace of any such sudden and violent interference with the previously existing arrangements of worship. Never once did Solomon's successors, confined though they were to the little territory of Judah, and therefore in a position in which the experiment might perhaps have been practicable, make the attempt (which certainly would have been in their interest) to concentrate all public worship within their own temple, though in other directions we find them exercising a very arbitrary control over affairs of religion. The high places were not removed; this is what is regularly told us in the case of them all. For Israel properly so called, Jerusalem was at no time, properly speaking, the place which Jehovah had chosen; least of all was it so after the division of the kingdom.

The Ephraimites flocked in troops through the entire length of the southern kingdom as pilgrims to Beersheba, and, in common with the men of Judah, to Gilgal on the frontier. Jerusalem they left unvisited. In their own land they served Jehovah at Bethel and Dan, at Shechem and Samaria, at Penuel and Mizpah, and at many other places. Every town had its Bamah, in the earlier times generally on an open site at the top of the hill on the slopes of which the houses were. Elijah, that great zealot for purity of worship, was so far from being offended by the high places and the multiplicity of altars to Jehovah that their destruction brought bitterness to his soul as the height of wickedness, and with his own hand he rebuilt the altar that had fallen into ruins on Mount Carmel. And that the improvised offering on extraordinary occasions had also not fallen into disuse is shown by the case of Elisha, who, when his call came as he was following the plough, hewed his oxen to pieces on the spot and sacrificed. In this respect matters after the building of Solomon's temple continued to be just as they had been before. If people and judges or kings alike, priests and prophets, men like Samuel and Elijah, sacrificed without hesitation whenever occasion and opportunity presented themselves, it is manifest that during the whole of that period nobody had the faintest suspicion that such conduct was heretical and forbidden. If a theophany made known to Joshua the sanctity of Gilgal, gave occasion to Gideon and Manoah to rear altars at their homes, drew the attention of David to the threshing-floor of Araunah, Jehovah Himself was regarded as the proper founder of all these sanctuaries,—and this not merely at the period of the Judges, but more indubitably still at that of the narrator of these legends. He rewarded Solomon's first sacrifice on the great Bamah at Gibeon with a gracious revelation, and cannot, therefore, have been displeased by it. After all this, it is absurd to speak of any want of legality in what was then the ordinary practice; throughout the whole of the earlier period of the history of Israel, the restriction of worship to a single selected place was unknown to any one even as a pious desire. Men believed themselves indeed to be nearer God at Bethel or at Jerusalem than at any indifferent place, but of such gates of heaven there were several; and after all, the ruling idea was that which finds its most distinct expression in 2Kings v.17,—that Palestine as a whole was Jehovah's house, His ground and territory. Not outside of Jerusalem, but outside of Canaan had one to sojourn far from His presence, under the dominion and (cujus regio ejus religio) in the service of strange gods. The sanctity of the land did not depend on that of the temple; the reverse was the case. *1*

*********************************** 1. Gen. iv.14, 16: when Cain is driven out of the land (Canaan), he is driven from the presence of Jehovah (Jonah i.3, 10). Gen. xlvi.4: Jacob is not to hesitate about going down into Egypt, for Jehovah will, by a special act of grace, change His dwelling-place along with him. Exodus xv.17: "Thou broughtest thy people to the mountain of thine inheritance, to the place which thou hadst prepared for thyself to dwell in," the explanation which follows, "to the sanctuary which thy hand had established," is out of place, for the mountain of the inheritance can only be the mountainous land of Palestine. 1Samuel xxvi.19: David, driven by Saul into foreign parts, is thereby violently sundered from his family share in the inheritance of Jehovah, and compelled to serve other gods. Hos. viii.1: one like an eagle comes against the house of Jehovah, *i.e.*, the Assyrian comes against Jehovah's land. Hos. ix.15: "I will drive them out of mine house," *i.e.*, the Israelites out of their land. Most distinct is the language of Hos. ix.3-5: "They shall not continue to dwell in Jehovah's land; Ephraim must back to Egypt, and must eat that which is unclean in Assyria. They shall not any more offer wine-offerings to Jehovah, or set forth offerings [read with Kuenen Y(RKW for Y(RBW] before Him; their bread is as the bread of mourners; whosoever eats of it is polluted, for their bread shall be only for the staying of hunger, and shall not be brought into the house of Jehovah. What indeed will ye do in the time of the solemn assembly and in the day of the feast of Jehovah? "Compare Jer. xvi.13; Ezek. iv.13; Mal. ii.11; 2Kings xvii.25 seq. It is also possible that the "great indignation" of 2Kings iii.27 is regarded less as Jehovah's than as that of Chemosh, in whose land the army of Israel is at the time. ***

I.I.2. A change in this respect first begins to be prepared at that important epoch of the religious history of Israel which is marked by the fall of Samaria and the rise of the prophets connected therewith. Amos and Hosea presuppose a condition of matters just such as has been described: everywhere—in the towns, on the mountains, under green trees—a multitude of sanctuaries and altars, at which Jehovah is served in good faith, not with the purpose of provoking Him, but in order to gain His favour. The language held by these men was one hitherto unheard of when they declared that Gilgal, and Bethel, and Beersheba, Jehovah's favourite seats, were an abomination to Him; that the gifts and offerings with which He was honoured there kindled His wrath instead of appeasing it; that Israel was destined to be buried under the ruins of His temples, where protection and refuge were sought (Amos ix.). What did they mean ? It would be to misunderstand the prophets to suppose that they took offence at the holy places— which Amos still calls Bamoth (vii.9), and that too not in scorn, but with the deepest pathos—in and by themselves, on account of their being more than one, or not being the right ones. Their zeal is directed, not against the places, but against the cultus there carried on, and, in fact not merely against its false character as containing all manner of abuses, but almost more against itself, against the false value attached to it. The common idea was that just as Moab showed itself to be the people of Chemosh because it brought to Chemosh its offerings and gifts, so Israel proved itself Jehovah's people by dedicating its worship to Him, and was such all the more surely as its worship was zealous and splendid; in times of danger and need, when His help was peculiarly required, the zeal of the worshippers was doubled and trebled. It is against this that the prophets raise their protest while they demand quite other performances as a living manifestation of the relation of Israel to Jehovah. This was the reason of their so great hostility to the cultus, and the source of their antipathy to the great sanctuaries, where superstitious zeal outdid itself; it was this that provoked their wrath against the multiplicity of the altars which flourished so luxuriantly on the soil of a false confidence. That the holy places should be abolished, but the cultus itself remain as before the main concern of religion, only limited to a single locality was by no means their wish; but at the same time, in point of fact, it came about as an incidental result of their teaching that the high place in Jerusalem ultimately abolished all the other Bamoth. External circumstances, it must be added, contributed most essentially towards the result.

38

As long as the northern kingdom stood, it was there that the main current of Israelite life manifested itself; a glance into the Books of Kings or into that of Amos is enough to make this clear. In Jerusalem, indeed, the days of David and of Solomon remained unforgotten; yearning memories went back to them, and great pretensions were based upon them, but with these the actual state of matters only faintly corresponded. When Samaria fell, Israel shrivelled up to the narrow dimensions of Judah, which alone survived as the people of Jehovah. Thereby the field was left clear for Jerusalem. The royal city had always had a weighty preponderance over the little kingdom, and within it, again, the town had yielded in importance to the temple. From the few narratives we have relating to Judah one almost gathers an impression as if it had no other concern besides those of the temple; the kings in particular appear to have regarded the charge of their palace sanctuary as the chief of all their cares./1/

** 1. Nearly all the Judaean narratives in the Books of Kings relate to the temple and the measures taken by the ruling princes with reference to this their sanctuary. **

In this way the increased importance of Judah after the fall of Samaria accrued in the first instance to the benefit of the capital and its sanctuary, especially as what Judah gained by the fall of her rival was not so much political strength as an increase of religious self-consciousness. If the great house of God upon Mount Zion had always overtopped the other shrines in Judah, it now stood without any equal in all Israel. But it was the prophets who led the way in determining the inferences to be drawn from the change in the face of things. Hitherto they had principally had their eyes upon the northern kingdom, its threatened collapse, and the wickedness of its inhabitants, and thus had poured out their wrath more particularly upon the places of worship there. Judah they judged more favourably, both on personal and on substantial grounds, and they hoped for its preservation, not concealing their sympathies for Jerusalem (Amos i.2). Under the impression produced by their discourses accordingly, the fall of Samaria was interpreted as a judgment of God against the sinful kingdom and in favour of the fallen house of David, and the destruction of the sanctuaries of Israel was accepted as an unmistakable declaration on Jehovah's part against His older seats on behalf of His favourite dwelling on Zion. Finally, the fact that twenty years afterwards Jerusalem made her triumphant escape from the danger which had proved fatal to her haughty rival, that at the critical moment the Assyrians under Sennacherib were suddenly constrained to withdraw from her, raised to the highest pitch the veneration in which the temple was held. In this connection special emphasis is usually laid— and with justice—upon the prophetical activity of Isaiah, whose confidence in the firm foundation of Zion continued unmoved, even when the rock began to shake in an alarming way. Only it must not be forgotten that the significance of Jerusalem to Isaiah did not arise from the temple of Solomon, but from the fact that it was the city of David and the focus of his kingdom, the central point, not of the cultus, but of the sovereignty of Jehovah over His people. The holy mount was to him the entire city as a political unity, with its citizens, councillors, and judges (xi.9); his faith in the sure foundation on which Zion rested was nothing more than a faith in the living presence of Jehovah in the camp of Israel. But the contemporaries of the prophet interpreted otherwise his words and the events which had occurred. In their view Jehovah dwelt on Zion because His house was there; it was the temple that had been shown by history to be His true seat, and its inviolability was accordingly the pledge of the indestructibility of the nation. This belief was quite general in Jeremiah's time, as is seen in the extremely vivid picture of the seventh chapter of his book; but even as early as the time of Micah, in the first third of the seventh century, the temple must have been reckoned a house of God of an altogether peculiar order, so as to make it a paradox to put it on a level with the Bamoth of Judah, and a thing unheard of to believe in its destruction.

At the same time, notwithstanding the high and universal reverence in which the temple was held, the other sanctuaries still continued, in the first instance, to subsist alongside of it. King Hezekiah indeed is said to have even then made an attempt to abolish them, but the attempt, having passed away without leaving any trace, is of a doubtful nature. It is certain that the prophet Isaiah did not labour for the removal of the Bamoth. In one of his latest discourses his anticipation for that time of righteousness and the fear of God which is to dawn after the Assyrian crisis is: "Then shall ye defile the silver covering of your graven images and the golden plating of your molten images—ye shall cast them away as a thing polluted; Begone! shall ye say unto them" (xxx.22). If he thus hopes for a purification from superstitious accretions of the places where Jehovah is worshipped, it is clear that he is not thinking of their total abolition. Not until about a century after the destruction of Samaria did men venture to draw the practical conclusion from the belief in the unique character of the temple at Jerusalem. That this was not done from a mere desire to be logical, but with a view to further reforms, need not be said. With the tone of repudiation in which the earlier prophets, in the zeal of their opposition, had occasionally spoken of practices of worship at large, there was nothing to be achieved; the thing to be aimed at was not abolition, but reformation, and the end it was believed would be helped by concentration of all ritual in the capital. Prophets and priests appear to have made common cause in the prosecution of the work. It was the high priest Hilkiah who in the first instance called attention to the discovered book which was to be made the basis of action; the prophetess Huldah confirmed its divine contents; the priests and prophets were a prominent element in the assembly at which the new law was promulgated and sworn to. Now an intimate fellowship between these two leading classes appears to be characteristic of the whole course of the religious movement in Judah, and to have been necessarily connected with the lines on which that movement advanced; *1*

**************************** 1. While Hosea, the man of northern Israel, frequently assails the clergy of his home, and lays upon them the chief share of the blame for the depraved and blinded condition of the people, Isaiah even in his fiercest declamation against the superstitious worship of the multitude, has not a word to say against the priests, with whose chief, Uriah, on the contrary, he stands in a relation of great intimacy. But it is from the Book of Jeremiah, the best mirror of the contemporary relations in Judah, that the close connection between priests and prophets can be gathered most particularly. To a certain extent they shared the

possession of the sanctuary between them. (Compare Lam. ii.20.)
****

we shall be justified therefore in assuming that the display of harmony between them on this occasion was not got up merely for the purposes of scenic effect, but that the change in the national cultus now proposed was really the common suggestion of prophets and priests. In point of fact, such a change was equally in accordance with the interests of the temple and with those of the prophetic party of reform. To the last named the restriction of the sacrificial worship must have in itself seemed an advantage; to it in later times the complete abolition of sacrifice was mainly due, and something of the later effect doubtless lay in the original intention. Then, too, the Jehovah of Hebron was only too easily regarded as distinct from the Jehovah of Bethshemesh or of Bethel, and so a strictly monarchical conception of God naturally led to the conclusion that the place of His dwelling and of His worship could also only be one. All writers of the Chaldaean period associate monotheism in the closest way with unity of worship (Jer. ii.28, xi.13). And the choice of the locality could present no difficulty; central point of the kingdom had of necessity also to become the central point of the worship. Even Jerusalem and the house of Jehovah there might need some cleansing, but it was clearly entitled to a preference over the obscure local altars. It was the seat of all higher culture, lying under the prophets' eyes, much more readily accessible to light and air, reform and control. It is also possible, moreover, that the Canaanite origin of most of the Bamoth, which is not unknown, for example, to Deuteronomy, may have helped to discredit them, while, on the other hand, the founding of Jerusalem belonged to the proudest memories of Israelite history, and the Ark, which had been the origin of the temple there, had a certain right to be considered the one genuine Mosaic sanctuary. *1*

************************************ 1. Luther in his address to the princes of Germany counsels in the twentieth place that the field chapels and churches be destroyed, as devices of the devil used by him to strengthen covetousness, to set up a false and spurious faith, to weaken parochial churches, to increase taverns and fornication, to squander money and labour to no purpose, and merely to lead the poor people about by the nose. (Niemeyer's Reprint, p. 54)
****

In the eighteenth year of Josiah, 601 B.C., the first heavy blow fell upon the local sacrificial places. How vigorously the king set to work, how new were the measures taken, and how deeply they cut, can be learned from the narrative of 2Kings xxiii. Yet what a vitality did the green trees upon the high mountains still continue to show! Even now they were but polled, not uprooted. After Josiah's death we again see Bamoth appearing on all hands, not merely in the country, but even in the capital itself. Jeremiah has to lament that there are as many altars as towns in Judah. All that had been attained by the reforming party was that they could now appeal to a written law that had been solemnly sworn to by the whole people, standing ever an immovable witness to the rights of God. But to bring it again into force and to carry it out was no easy matter, and would certainly have been impossible to the unaided efforts of the prophets—a Jeremiah or an Ezekiel.

I.3 Had the people of Judah remained in peaceful possession of their land, the reformation of Josiah would hardly have penetrated to the masses; the threads uniting the present with the past were too strong. To induce the people to regard as idolatrous and heretical centres of iniquity the Bamoth, with which from ancestral times the holiest memories were associated, and some of which, like Hebron and Beersheba, had been set up by Abraham and Isaac in person, required a complete breaking-off of the natural tradition of life, a total severance of all connection with inherited conditions. This was accomplished by means of the Babylonian exile, which violently tore the nation away from its native soil, and kept it apart for half a century,—a breach of historical continuity than which it is almost impossible to conceive a greater. The new generation had no natural, but only an artificial relation to the times of old; the firmly rooted growths of the old soil, regarded as thorns by the pious, were extirpated, and the freshly ploughed fallows ready for a new sowing. It is, of course, far from being the case that the whole people at that time underwent a general conversion in the sense of the prophets. Perhaps the majority totally gave up the past, but just on that account became lost among the heathen, and never subsequently came into notice. Only the pious ones, who with trembling followed Jehovah's word, were left as a remnant; they alone had the strength to maintain the Jewish individuality amid the medley of nationalities into which they had been thrown. From the exile there returned, not the nation, but a religious sect,—those, namely, who had given themselves up body and soul to the reformation ideas. It is no wonder that to these people, who, besides, on their return, all settled in the immediate neighbourhood of Jerusalem, the thought never once occurred of restoring the local cults. It cost them no struggle to allow the destroyed Bamoth to continue lying in ruins; the principle had become part of their very being, that the one God had also but one place of worship, and thenceforward for all time coming this was regarded as a thing of course.

I.II

Such was the actual historical course of the centralisation of the cultus, and such the three stadia which can be distinguished. The question now presents itself, whether it is possible to detect a correspondence between the phases of the actual course of events and those of the legislation relating to this subject. All three portions of the legislation contain ordinances on the subject of sacrificial places and offerings. It may be taken for granted that in some way or other these have their roots in history, and do not merely hang in the air, quite away from or above the solid ground of actuality.

I.*Ii*.1. The main Jehovistic law, the so-called Book of the Covenant, contains (Exodus xx.24-26) the following ordinance: "An altar of earth shalt thou make unto me, and thereon shalt thou sacrifice thy burnt offerings and thy peace-offerings, thy sheep and thine oxen; in place where I cause my name to be honoured will I come unto and will bless thee. Or if thou wilt make me an altar of stones, thou shalt not build it of hewn stones, for if thou hast lifted up thy tool upon it thou hast polluted it. And thou shalt not go up to mine altar by steps, that thy nakedness be not discovered before it." Unquestionably it is not the altar of the tabernacle, which was made of wood and plated over with brass, nor that of Solomon's temple, which on its eastern side had a flight of steps, *1*

*************************************** 1. The altar of the second temple had no steps, but a sloping ascent to it, as also, according to the belief of the Jews, had that of the tabernacle. The reason, moreover, for which in Exodus xx.26 steps are forbidden, disappears when the priests are provided with breeches (Exodus xxviii.42). **************************************

and had a passage right round it at half its height, that is here described as the only true one. On the other hand, it is obvious that a multiplicity of altars is not merely regarded as permissible, but assumed as a matter of course. For no stress at all is laid upon having always the same sacrificial seat, whether fixed or to be moved about from place to place; earth and unhewn stones *2* of the field

************************************** 2. The plural "stones" is perhaps worthy of note. There were also sacrificial places consisting of one great stone (1Samuel xiv.33, vi.14, 15; 2Samuel xx.8; Judges vi.20, xiii.19, 20; 1Kings i.9); to the same category also doubtless belongs originally the threshing-floor of Araunah, 2Samuel xxiv.21; compare Ezra iii.3, [L MKWNTW]. But inasmuch as such single sacred stones easily came into a mythological relation to the Deity, offence was taken at them, as appears from Judges vi.22-24, where the rock altar, the stone under the oak which was conceived of as the seat of the theophany, upon which Gideon offers, and out of which the flame issues (vi.19-21), is corrected into an altar upon the rock. The macceboth are distinguished from the altar in Exodus xxiv.4, yet elsewhere clearly put on the same plane with it (Gen. xxxiii.20), and everywhere more   or   less   identified   with   the   Deity   (Gen.   xxviii.). **************************************

can be found everywhere, and such an altar falls to pieces just as readily as it is built. A choice of two kinds of material is also given, which surely implies that the lawgiver thought of more than one altar; and not at the place, but at every place where He causes His name to be honoured will Jehovah come to His worshippers and bless them. Thus the law now under consideration is in harmony with the custom and usage of the first historical period, has its root therein, and gives sanction to it. Certainly the liberty to sacrifice everywhere seems to be somewhat restricted by the added clause, "in every place where I cause my name to be honoured." But this means nothing more than that the spots where intercourse between earth and heaven took place were not willingly regarded as arbitrarily chosen, but, on the contrary, were considered as having been somehow or other selected by the Deity Himself for His service.

In perfect correspondence with the Jehovistic law is the Jehovistic narrative of the Pentateuch, as, in particular, the story of the patriarchs in J and E very clearly shows. At every place where they take up their abode or make a passing stay, the fathers of the nation, according to this authority, erect altars, set up memorial stones, plant trees, dig wells. This does not take place at indifferent and casual localities, but at Shechem and Bethel in Ephraim, at Hebron and Beersheba in Judah, at Mizpah, Mahanaim, and Penuel in Gilead; nowhere but at famous and immemorially holy places of worship. It is on this that the interest of such notifications depends; they are no mere antiquarian facts, but full of the most living significance for the present of the narrator. The altar built by Abraham at Shechem is the altar on which sacrifice still continues to be made, and bears "even unto this day" the name which the patriarch gave it. On the spot where at Hebron he first entertained Jehovah, there down to the present day the table has continued to be spread; even as Isaac himself did, so do his sons still swear Amosos viii.14; Hos. iv.15) by the sacred well of Beersheba, which he digged, and sacrifice there upon the altar which he built, under the tamarisk which he planted. The stone which Jacob consecrated at Bethel the generation of the living continues to anoint, paying the tithes which of old he vowed to the house of God there. This also is the reason why the sacred localities are so well known to the narrator, and are punctually and accurately recorded notwithstanding the four hundred years of the Egyptian sojourn, which otherwise would have made their identification a matter of some little difficulty. The altar which Abraham built at Bethel stands upon the hill to the east of the town, between Bethel on the west and Ai on the east; others are determined by means of a tree or a well, as that of Shechem or Beersheba. *1*

**************************** 1. The correct explanation of this is found in Ewald, Gesch. d. V. lsraels, i. 436 seq. (3d edit.). A. Bernstein (Ursprung der Sagen von Abrabam, *etc.*, Berlin, 1871) drags in politics in a repulsive way. "He does not indeed actually enter Shechem and Bethel— these are places hostile to Judah—but in a genuine spirit of Jewish demonstration he builds altars in their vicinity and calls on the name of Jehovah" (p. 22). Rather, he builds the altars precisely on the places where, as can be shown, they afterwards stood, and that was not inside the towns. In Gen. xviii. also the oak of Mamre is employed to fix not Abraham's residence, but the place of Jehovah's appearing. ***

44

But of course it was not intended to throw dishonour upon the cultus of the present when its institution was ascribed to the fathers of the nation. Rather, on the contrary, do these legends glorify the origin of the sanctuaries to which they are attached, and surround them with the nimbus of a venerable consecration. All the more as the altars, as a rule, are not built by the patriarchs according to their own private judgment wheresoever they please; on the contrary, a theophany calls attention to, or at least afterwards confirms, the holiness of the place. Jehovah appears at Shechem to Abraham, who thereupon builds the altar "to Jehovah who had appeared unto him;" he partakes of his hospitality under the oak of Mamre, which is the origin of the sacrificial service there; He shows him the place where he is to make an offering of his son, and here the sanctuary continues to exist. On the first night of Isaac's sleeping on the sacred soil of Beersheba (xxvi.24) he receives a visit from the Numen there residing, and in consequence rears his altar. Surprised by profane glances, Jehovah acts as a destroyer, but Himself spontaneously points out to His favoured ones the places where it is His pleasure to allow Himself to be seen; and where men have seen Him and yet lived, there a sanctuary marks the open way of access to Him. The substance of the revelation is in these cases comparatively indifferent: "I am God." What is of importance is the theophany in and for itself, its occurrence on that particular place. It must not be regarded as an isolated fact, but rather as the striking commencement of an intercourse [R)H PNY YHWH] between God and man which is destined to be continued at this spot, and also as the first and strongest expression of the sanctity of the soil. This way of looking at the thing appears most clearly and with incomparable charm in the story of the ladder which Jacob saw at Bethel. "He dreamed, and behold a ladder set up on the earth, and the top of it reached to heaven, and behold the angels of God ascending and descending on it. And he was afraid and said, How dreadful is this place! This is none other but the house of God, and this is the gate of heaven." The ladder stands at the place not at this moment merely, but continually, and, as it were, by nature. Bethel—so Jacob perceives from this—is a place where heaven and earth meet, where the angels ascend and descend, to carry on the communication between earth and heaven ordained by God at this gate.

All this is only to be understood as a glorification of the relations and arrangements of the cultus as we find them (say) in the first centuries of the divided kingdom. All that seems offensive and heathenish to a later age is here consecrated and countenanced by Jehovah Himself and His favoured ones,— the high places, the memorial stones (maccceboth), the trees, the wells. *1*

*************************** 1. But it is only the public cultus and that of certain leading sanctuaries that is thus glorified; on the other hand, the domestic worship of seraphim, to which the women are specially attached, is already discountenanced (in E) by Jacob. Asherim are not alluded to, molten images are rejected, particularly by E. Here perhaps a correction of the ancient legend has already taken place in *je*. ***********************************

An essential agreement prevails between the Jehovistic law which sanctions the existing seats of worship and the Jehovistic narrative; the latter is as regards its nucleus perhaps somewhat older. Both obviously belong to the pre-prophetic period; a later revision of the narrative in the prophetic sense has not altered the essential character of its fundamental elements. It is inconceivable that Amos or Hosea, or any like-minded person, could go with such sympathising love and believing reverence into narratives which only served to invest with a still brighter nimbus and higher respect the existing religious worship, carried on by the people on the high places of Isaac as their holiest occupation.

I.*Ii*.2. The Jehovistic Book of the Covenant lies indeed at the foundation of Deuteronomy, but in one point they differ materially, and that precisely the one which concerns us here. As there, so here also, the legislation properly so called begins (Deut. xii.) with an ordinance relating to the service of the altar; but now we have Moses addressing the Israeites in the following terms: "When ye come into the land of Canaan, ye shall utterly destroy all the places of worship which ye find there, and ye shall not worship Jehovah your God after the manner in which the heathen serve theirs. Nay, but only unto the place which the Lord your God shall choose out of all your tribes for His habitation shall ye seek, and thither shall ye bring your offerings and gifts, and there shall ye eat before Him and rejoice. Here at this day we do every man whatsoever is right in his own eyes, but when ye have found fixed abodes, and rest from your enemies round about, then shall the place which Jehovah shall choose for His habitation in one of your tribes be the one place to which ye shall bring your offerings and gifts. Take heed that ye offer not in every place that ye see; ye may not eat your holy gifts in every town, but only in the place which Jehovah shall choose."

The Law is never weary of again and again repeating its injunction of local unity of worship. In doing so, it is in conscious opposition to "the things that we do here this day," and throughout has a polemical and reforming attitude towards existing usage. It is rightly therefore assigned by historical criticism to the period of the attacks made on the Bamoth by the reforming party at Jerusalem. As the Book of the Covenant, and the whole Jehovistic writing in genera], reflects the first pre-prophetic period in the history of the cultus, so Deuteronomy is the legal expression of the second period of struggle and transition. The historical order is all the more certain because the literary dependence of Deuteronomy on the Jehovistic laws and narratives can be demonstrated independently, and is an admitted fact. From this the step is easy to the belief that the work whose discovery gave occasion to King Josiah to destroy the local sanctuaries was this very Book of Deuteronomy, which originally must have had an independent existence, and a shorter form than at present. This alone, at least, of all the books of the Pentateuch, gives so imperious an expression to the restriction of the sacrificial worship to the one chosen place; here only does the demand make itself so felt in its aggressive novelty and dominate the whole tendency of the law-maker. The old material which he makes use of is invariably shaped with a view to this, and on all hands he follows the rule out to its logical consequences. To make its fulfilment possible, he changes former arrangements, permitting what had been forbidden, and prohibiting what had been allowed; in almost every case this motive lies at the foundation of all his other innovations. This is seen, for example, when he permits slaying without sacrificing, and that too anywhere; when, in order not to abolish the right of asylum (Exodus xxi.13, 14; 1Kings ii. 28) along with the altars, he appoints special cities of refuge for the innocent who are pursued by the avenger of blood; when he provides for the priests of the suppressed sanctuaries, recommending the provincials to take them along with them on their sacrificial pilgrimages, and giving them the right to officiate in the temple at Jerusalem just like the hereditarily permanent clergy there. In other respects also the dominance of the same point of view is seen: for example, it is chiefly from regard to it that the old ordinances and customs relating to the religious dues and the festivals are set forth in the form which they must henceforth assume. A law so living, which stands at every point in immediate contact with reality, which is at war with traditional custom, and which proceeds with constant reference to the demands of practical life, is no mere velleity, no mere cobweb of an idle brain, but has as certainly arisen out of historical occasions as it is designed to operate powerfully on the course of the subsequent history. A judgment pronounced in accordance with the facts can therefore assign to it an historical place only within that movement of reformation which was brought to a victorious issue by King Josiah.

I.*Ii*.3. It is often supposed that the Priestly Code is somewhat indifferent to the question of the one sanctuary, neither permitting multiplicity of sacrificial centres nor laying stress upon the unity, and that on account of this attitude it must be assigned to an earlier date than Deuteronomy. *1*

************************************** 1. De Wette, in the fifth place of his Habilitationsschrift ueber das Deuteronomium (Jena, 1805): "De hoc unico cultus sacri loco... priores libri nihil omnino habent. De sacrificiis tantum unice ante tabernaculum conventus offerendis lex quaedam extat. Sed in legibus de diebus festis, de primitiis et decimis, tam saepe repetitis, nihil omnino monitum est de loco unico, ubi celebrari et offerri debeant " (Opusc. Theol, p. 163-165). *************************************

Such an idea is, to say the least, in the highest degree superficial. The assumption that worship is restricted to one single centre runs everywhere throughout the entire document. To appeal specially, in proof of the restriction, to Leviticus xvii. or Josh xxii., is to indicate a complete failure to apprehend the whole tenor of Exodus xxv.-Leviticus ix. Before so much as a single regulation having reference to the matter of worship can be given (such is the meaning of the large section referred to), the one rightful place wherein to engage in it must be specified. The tabernacle is not narrative merely, but, like all the narratives in that book, law as well; it expresses the legal unity of the worship as an historical fact, which, from the very beginning, ever since the exodus, has held good in Israel. One God one sanctuary, that is the idea. With the ordinances of the tabernacle, which form the sum of the divine revelation on Sinai, the theocracy was founded; where the one is, there is the other. The description of it, therefore, stands at the head of the Priestly Code, just as that of the temple stands at the head of the legislation in Ezekiel. It is the basis and indispensable foundation, without which all else would merely float in the air: first must the seat of the Divine Presence on earth be given before the sacred community can come into life and the cultus into force. Is it supposes that the tabernacle tolerates other sanctuaries besides itself? Why then the encampment of the twelve tribes around it, which has no military, but a purely religious significance, and derives its whole meaning from its sacred centre? Whence this concentration of all Israel into one great congregation [QHL, (DH], without its like anywhere else in the Old Testament? On the contrary, there is no other place besides this at which God dwells and suffers Himself to be seen; no place but this alone where man can draw near to Him and seek His face with offerings and gifts. This view is the axiom that underlies the whole ritual legislation of the middle part of the Pentateuch. It is indicated with special clearness by the LPNY (HL MW(D (before the tabernacle), introduced at every turn in the ordinances for sacrifice.

What then are we to infer from this as to the historical place of the Priestly Code, if it be judged necessary to assign it such a place at all? By all the laws of logic it can no more belong to the first period than Deuteronomy does. But is it older or younger than Deuteronomy? In that book the unity of the cultus is *commanded*, in the Priestly Code it is *presupposed*. Everywhere it is tacitly assumed as a fundamental postulate, but nowhere does it find actual expression; *1* it is nothing new, but quite a thing

*** 1. Except in Leviticus xvii.; but the small body of legislation contained in Leviticus xvii-xxvi is the transition from Deuteronomy to the Priestly Code. *******************************

of course. What follows from this for the question before us? To my thinking, this:—that the Priestly Code rests upon the result which is only the aim of Deuteronomy. The latter is in the midst of movement and conflict: it clearly speaks out its reforming intention, its opposition to the traditional "what we do here this day;" the former stands outside of and above the struggle,—the end has been reached and made a secure possession. On the basis of the Priestly Code no reformation would ever have taken place, no Josiah would ever have observed from it that the actual condition of affairs was perverse and required to be set right; it proceeds as if everything had been for long in the best of order. It is only in Deuteronomy, moreover, that one sees to the root of the matter, and recognises its connection with the anxiety for a strict monotheism and for the elimination from the worship of the popular heathenish elements, and thus with a deep and really worthy aim; in the Priestly Code the reason of the appointments, in themselves by no means rational, rests upon their own legitimacy, just as everything that is actual ordinarily seems natural and in no need of explanation. Nowhere does it become apparent that the abolition of the Bamoth and Asherim and memorial stones is the real object contemplated; these institutions are now almost unknown, and what is really only intelligible as a negative and polemical ordinance is regarded as full of meaning in itself.

The idea as idea is older than the idea as history. In Deuteronomy it appears in its native colours, comes forward with its aggressive challenge to do battle with the actual. One step indeed is taken towards investing it with an historical character, in so far as it is put into the mouth of Moses; but the beginning thus made keeps within modest limits. Moses only lays down the law; for its execution he makes no provision as regards his own time, nor does he demand it for the immediate future. Rather it is represented as not destined to come into force until the people shall have concluded the conquest of the country and secured a settled peace. We have already found reason to surmise that the reference to "menuha" is intended to defer the date when the Law shall come into force to the days of David and Solomon (1Kings viii.16). This is all the more probable inasmuch as there is required for its fulfilment "the place which Jehovah shall choose," by which only the capital of Judah can be meant. Deuteronomy, therefore, knows nothing of the principle that what ought to be must actually have been from the beginning. Until the building of Solomon's temple the unity of worship according to it had, properly speaking, never had any existence; and, moreover, it is easy to read between the lines that even after that date it was more a pious wish than a practical demand. The Priestly Code, on the other hand, is unable to think of religion without the one sanctuary, and cannot for a moment imagine Israel without it, carrying its actual existence back to the very beginning of the theocracy, and, in accordance with this, completely altering the ancient history. The temple, the focus to which the worship was concentrated, and which in reality was not built until Solomon's time, is by this document regarded as so indispensable, even for the troubled days of the wanderings before the settlement, that it is made portable, and in the form of a tabernacle set up in the very beginning of things. For the truth is, that the tabernacle is the copy, not the prototype, of the temple at Jerusalem. The resemblance of the two is indeed unmistakable, *1*

*************************** 1. In Wisdom of Solomon ix. 8 the temple is called MIMHMA SKHNHS HAGIAS. Josephus (Antiquities iii. 6,1) says of the tabernacle, (H D'OUDEN METAFEROMENOU NAOU DIEFERE. ******************************

but it is not said in 1Kings vi. that Solomon made use of the old pattern and ordered his Tyrian workmen to follow it. The posteriority of the Mosaic structure comes into clearer light from the two following considerations brought forward by Graf (p. 60 seq.). In the first place, in the description of the tabernacle mention is repeatedly made of its south, north, and west side, without any preceding rubric as to a definite and constantly uniform orientation; the latter is tacitly taken for granted, being borrowed from that of the temple, which was a fixed building, and did not change its site. In the second place, the brazen altar is, strictly speaking, described as an altar of wood merely plated with brass,—for a fireplace of very large size, upon which a strong fire continually burns, a perfectly absurd construction, which is only to be accounted for by the wish to make the brazen altar which Solomon cast (1Kings xvi. 14) transportable, by changing its interior into wood. The main point, however, is this, that the tabernacle of the Priestly Code in its essential meaning is not a mere provisional shelter for the ark on the march, but the sole legitimate sanctuary for the community of the twelve tribes prior to the days of Solomon, and so in fact a projection of the later temple. How modest, one might almost say how awkwardly bashful, is the Deuteronomic reference to the future place which Jehovah is to choose when compared with this calm matter-of-fact assumption that the necessary centre of unity of worship was given from the first! In the one case we have, so to speak, only the idea as it exists in the mind of the lawgiver, but making no claim to be realised till a much later date; in the other, the Mosaic idea has acquired also a Mosaic embodiment, with which it entered the world at the very first.

By the same simple historical method which carries the central sanctuary back into the period before Solomon does the Priestly author abolish the other places of worship. His forty-eight Levitical cities are for the most part demonstrably a metamorphosis of the old Bamoth to meet the exigencies of the time. The altar which the tribes eastward of Jordan build (Josh. xxii.) is erected with no intention that it should be used, but merely in commemoration of something. Even the pre-Mosaic period is rendered orthodox in the same fashion. The patriarchs, having no tabernacle, have no worship at all; according to the Priestly Code they build no altars, bring no offerings, and scrupulously abstain from everything by which they might in any way encroach on the privilege of the one true sanctuary. This manner of shaping the patriarchal history is only the extreme consequence of the effort to carry out with uniformity in history the semper ubique et ab omnibus of the legal unity of worship.

Thus in Deuteronomy the institution is only in its birth-throes, and has still to struggle for the victory against the praxis of the present, but in the Priestly Code claims immemorial legitimacy and strives to bring the past into conformity with itself, obviously because it already dominates the present; the carrying back of the new into the olden time always takes place at a later date than the ushering into existence of the new itself. Deuteronomy has its position in the very midst of the historical crisis, and still stands in a close relation with the older period of worship, the conditions of which it can contest, but is unable to ignore, and still less to deny. But, on the other hand, the Priestly Code is hindered by no survival to present times of the older usage from projecting an image of antiquity such as it must have been; unhampered by visible relics or living tradition of an older state, it can idealise the past to its heart's content. Its place, then, is after Deuteronomy, and in the third post-exilian period of the history of the cultus, in which, on the one hand, the unity of the sanctuary was an established fact, contested by no one and impugned by nothing, and in which, on the other hand, the natural connection between the present and the past had been so severed by the exile that there was no obstacle to prevent an artificial and ideal repristination of the latter.

I.III.

The reverse of this is what is usually held. In Deuteronomy, it is considered, there occur clear references to the period of the kings; but the Priestly Code, with its historical presuppositions, does not fit in with any situation belonging to that time, and is therefore older. When the cultus rests upon the temple of Solomon as its foundation, as in Ezekiel, then every one recognises the later date; but when it is based upon the tabernacle, the case is regarded as quite different. The great antiquity of the priestly legislation is proved by relegating it to an historical sphere, created by itself out of its own legal premises, but which is nowhere to be found within, and therefore must have preceded actual history. Thus (so to speak) it holds itself up in the air by its own waistband.

I.III.1. It may, however, seem as if hitherto it had only been asserted that the tabernacle rests on an historical fiction. In truth it is proved; but yet it may be well to add some things which have indeed been said long before now, but never as yet properly laid to heart. The subject of discussion, be it premised, is the tabernacle of the Priestly Code; for some kind of tent for the ark there may well have been: in fact, tents were in Palestine the earliest dwellings of idols (Hos. ix.6), and only afterwards gave place to fixed houses; and even the Jehovistic tradition (although not J) knows of a sacred tent *1*

************************************* 1. It is never, however, employed for legislative purposes, but is simply a shelter for the ark; it stands without the camp, as the oldest sanctuaries were wont to do outside the cities. It is kept by Joshua as aedituus, who sleeps in it, as did Samuel the aedituus for Eli. **

in connection with the Mosaic camp, and outside it, just as the older high places generally had open sites without the city. The question before us has reference exclusively to the particular tent which, according to Exodus xxv. seq., was erected at the command of God as the basis of the theocracy, the pre-Solomonic central sanctuary, which also in outward details was the prototype of the temple. At the outset its very possibility is doubtful. Very strange is the contrast between this splendid structure, on which the costliest material is lavished and wrought in the most advanced style of Oriental art, and the soil on which it rises, in the wilderness amongst the native Hebrew nomad tribes, who are represented as having got it ready offhand, and without external help. The incompatibility has long been noticed, and gave rise to doubts as early as the time of Voltaire. These may, however, be left to themselves; suffice it that Hebrew tradition, even from the time of the judges and the first kings, for which the Mosaic tabernacle was strictly speaking intended, knows nothing at all about it.

It appears a bold thing to say so when one sees how much many a modern author who knows how to make a skilful use of the Book of Chronicles has to tell about the tabernacle. For in 2 Chron. i.3 seq. we are told that Solomon celebrated his accession to the throne with a great sacrificial feast at Gibeon, because the tabernacle and the brazen altar of Moses were there. In like manner in 1Chron. xxi.29 it is said that David offered sacrifice indeed on the threshing-floor of Araunah, but that Jehovah's dwelling-place and the legitimate altar were at that time at Gibeon; and further (xvi. 39), that Zadok, the legitimate high priest, officiated there. From these data the Rabbins first, and in recent times Keil and Movers especially, have constructed a systematic history of the tabernacle down to the building of the temple. Under David and Solomon, as long as the ark was on Mount Zion, the tabernacle was at Gibeon, as is also shown by the fact that (2Samuel xxi.6, 9) offerings were sacrificed to Jehovah there. Before that it was at Nob, where ephod and shewbread (1Samuel xxi.) are mentioned, and still earlier, from Joshua's time onward, it was at Shiloh. But these were only its permanent sites, apart from which it was temporarily set up now here, now there, saving by its rapidity of movement— one might almost say ubiquity—the unity of the cultus, notwithstanding the variety and great distances of the places at which that cultus was celebrated. In every case in which a manifestation of Jehovah and an offering to Him are spoken of, the tabernacle must be tacitly understood. *1*

************************************** 1. Josh. xxiv. 24, 33 (LXX): after the death of Joshua and Eleazar, LABONTES (OI)UIOI)ISRAHL THN KIBWTON TOU QEOU PERIFEROSAN)EN)EAUTOIS. After J. Buxtorf and Sal. van Til (Ugol., Thes. viii.), this theory has been, worked out specially by Movers. See, on the other hand, De Wette, Beitraege, p. 108 seq., and Vatke, ut supra, p. 316, note.
****

The dogmatic character of this way of making history, and the absurd consequences to which it leads, need not in the meantime be insisted on; what is of greatest importance is that the point from which it starts is in the last degree insecure; for the statement of Chronicles that Solomon offered the offering of his accession upon the altar of the tabernacle at Gibeon is in contradiction with that of the older parallel narrative of 1Kings iii.1-4. The latter not only is silent about the Mosaic tabernacle, which is alleged to have stood at Gibeon, but expressly says that Solomon offered upon a high place (as such), and excuses him for this on the plea that at that time no house to the name of Jehovah had as yet been built. That the Chronicler draws from this narrative is certain on general grounds, and is shown particularly by this, that he designates the tabernacle at Gibeon by the name of Bamah—a contradictio in adjecto which is only to be explained by the desire to give an authentic interpretation of "the great Bamah at Gibeon" in 1Kings iii. Here, as elsewhere, he brings the history into agreement with the Law: the young and pious Solomon can have offered his sacrifice only at the legal place which therefore must be that high place at Gibeon. Along with 2 Chron. i.3 seq. also fall the two other statements (1Chron. xvi.39, xxi.29 both of which are dependent on that leading passage, as is clear revealed by the recurring phrase "the Bamah of Gibeon." The tabernacle does not elsewhere occur in Chronicles; it has not yet brought its consequences with it, and not yet permeated the historical view of the author. He would certainly have experienced some embarrassment at the question whether it had previously stood at Nob, for he lays stress upon the connection between the legitimate sanctuary and the legitimate Zadok-Eleazar priestly family, which it is indeed possible to assume for Shiloh, but not for Nob. *1*

The fact that Chronicles represents the Israelite history in accordance with the
Priestly Code has had the effect of causing its view of the history to be involuntarily
taken as fundamental, but ought much rather to have caused it to be left altogether
out of account where the object to ascertain what was the real and genuine tradition.
The Books of Judges and Samuel make mention indeed of many sanctuaries, but
never among them of the tabernacle, the most important of all. For the single
passage where the name Ohel Moed occurs (1Samuel ii.22 is badly attested, and
from its contents open to suspicion. 2

*************************************** 2. The passage does not occur in the
LXX, and everywhere else in 1Samueli-iii the sanctuary of Shiloh is called hekal,
that is to say, certainly not a tent. ***************************************

Of the existence of the ark of Jehovah there certainly are distinct traces towards the
end of the period of the judges (compare 1Samuel iv.-vi.) But is the ark a guarantee
of the existence of the tabernacle? On the contrary its whole history down to the
period of its being deposited in the temple of Solomon is a proof that it was regarded
as quite independent of any tent specially consecrated for its reception. But this
abolishes the notion of the Mosaic tabernacle; for according to the law, the two
things belong necessarily to each other; the one cannot exist without the other; both
are of equally great importance. The tabernacle must everywhere accompany the
symbol of its presence; the darkness of the holy of holies is at the same time the life-
element of the ark; only under compulsion of necessity, and even then not except
under the covering of the curtains, does it leave its lodging during a march, only to
return to it again as soon as the new halting-place is reached. But according to
1Samuel iv. seq., on the other hand, it is only the ark that goes to the campaign; it
alone falls into the hands of the Philistines. Even in chap. v., where the symbol of
Jehovah is placed in the temple of Dagon at Ashdod, not a word is said of the
tabernacle or of the altar which is necessarily connected with it; and chap. vi. is
equally silent, although here the enemy plainly gives back the whole of his sacred
spoil. It is assumed that the housing of the ark was left behind at Shiloh. Very
likely; but that was not the Mosaic tabernacle, the inseparable companion of the ark.
In fact, the narrator speaks of a permanent house at Shiloh with doors and doorposts;
that possibly may be an anachronism 1 (yet why ?) ;

*************************************** 1. Compare similar passages in
Josh. vi.19, 24, ix.27, where the very anachronism shows that the idea of the
tabernacle was unknown to the narrator. That, moreover. a permanent house did
actually exist then at Shiloh follows from the circumstance that Jeremiah (vii. 12)
speaks of its ruins. For he could not regard any other than a pre-Solomonic
sanctuary as preceding that of Jerusalem; and besides, there is not the faintest trace
of a more important temple having arisen at Shiloh within the period of the kings.
****

but so much at least may be inferred from it that he had not any idea of the tabernacle, which, however, would have had to go with the ark to the field. If on this one occasion only an illegal exception to the Law was made, why in that case was not the ark, at least after its surrender, again restored to the lodging from which, strictly speaking, it ought never to have been separated at all? Instead of this it is brought to Bethshemesh, where it causes disaster, because the people show curiosity about it. Thence it comes to Kirjathjearim, where it stays for many years in the house of a private person. From here David causes it to be brought to Jerusalem,— one naturally supposes, if one thinks in the lines of the view given in the Pentateuch and in Chronicles, in order that it may be at last restored to the tabernacle, to be simultaneously brought to Jerusalem. But no thought of this, however obvious it may seem, occurs to the king. In the first instance, his intention is to have the ark beside himself in the citadel; but he is terrified out of this, and, at a loss where else to put it, he at last places it in the house of one of his principal people, Obed-Edom of Gath. Had he known anything about the tabernacle, had he had any suspicion that it was standing empty at Gibeon, in the immediate neighbourhood, he would have been relieved of all difficulty. But inasmuch as the ark brings blessing to the house of Obed-Edom,—the ark, be it remembered, in the house of a soldier and a Philistine, yet bringing down, not wrath, but blessing,—*1*

*** 1. The Chronicle has good reason for making him a Levite. But Gath without any qualifying epithet, and particularly in connection with David, is the Philistine Gath, and Obed-Edom belongs to the bodyguard, which consisted chiefly of foreigners and Philistines. His name, moreover, is hardly Israelite.
****

the king is thereby encouraged to persevere after all with his original proposal, and establish it upon his citadel. And this he does in a tent he had caused to be made for it (2Samuel vi.17), which tent of David in Zion continued to be its lodging until the temple was built. Some mention of the tabernacle, had it existed, would have been inevitable when the temple took its place. That it did not serve as the model of the temple has already been said; but it might have been expected at least that in the account of the building of the new sanctuary some word might have escaped about the whereabouts of the old. And this expectation seems to be realised in 1Kings viii.4, which says that when the temple was finished there were brought into it, besides the ark, the Ohel Moed and all the sacred vessels that were therein. Interpreters hesitate as to whether they ought to understand by the Ohel Moed the tent of the ark upon Zion, to which alone reference has been made in the preceding narrative (1Kings i.39, ii.28-30), or whether it is the Mosaic tent, which, according to Chronicles, was standing at Gibeon, but of which the Book of Kings tells nothing, and also knows nothing (iii.2-4). It is probable that the author of viii.4 mixed up both together; but we have to face the following alternative. Either the statement belongs to the original context of the narrative in which it occurs, and in that case the Ohel Moed can only be the tent on Mount Zion, or the Ohel Moed of 1Kings viii.4 is the Mosaic tabernacle which was removed from Gibeon into Solomon's temple, and in that case the allegation has no connection with its context, and does not hang together with the premisses which that furnishes; in other words, it is the interpolation of a later hand. The former alternative, though possible, is improbable, for the name Ohel Moed occurs absolutely nowhere in the Books of Judges, Samuel, and Kings (apart from the interpolation in 1Samuel ii.22b), and particularly it is not used to denote David's tent upon Mount Zion; and, moreover, that tent had received too little of the consecration of antiquity, and according to 2Samuel vii. was too insignificant and provisional to be thought worthy of preservation in the temple. But if the Ohel Moed is here (what it everywhere else is) the tabernacle, as is indicated also by the sacred vessels, then the verse is, as has been said, an interpolation. The motive for such a thing is easily understood; the same difficulty as that with which we set out must have made it natural for any Jew who started from the ideas of the Pentateuch to look for the tabernacle here, and, if he did not find it, to introduce it. Yet even the interpolation does not remove the difficulties. Where is the Mosaic altar of burnt-offering? It was quite as important and holy as the tabernacle itself; even in Chronicles it is invariably mentioned expressly in connection with it, and did not deserve to be permitted to go to ruin at Gibeon, which, from another point of view, would also have been extremely dangerous to the unity of the sacrificial worship. Further, if the sacred vessels were transferred from the tabernacle to the temple, why then was it that Solomon, according to 1Kings vii., cast a completely new set? *1*

*************************************** 1. The brazen altar cast by Solomon (1Kings viii.64; 2Kings xvi.14, 15) is not now found in the inventory of the temple furniture in 1Kings vii.; but originally it cannot have been absent, for it is the most important article. It has therefore been struck out in order to avoid collision with the brazen altar of Moses. The deletion is the negative counterpart to the interpolation of the tabernacle in 1Kings viii.4. ***************************************

The old ones were costly enough, in part even costlier than the new, and, moreover, had been consecrated by long use. It is clear that in Solomon's time neither tabernacle, nor holy vessels, nor brazen altar of Moses had any existence.

But if there was no tabernacle in the time of the last judges and first kings, as little was it in existence during the whole of the previous period. This is seen from 2Samuel vii., a section with whose historicity we have here nothing to do, but which at all events reflects the view of a pre-exilic author. It is there told that David, after he had obtained rest from all his enemies, contemplated building a worthy home for the ark, and expressed his determination to the prophet Nathan in the words, "I dwell in a house of cedar, and the ark of God within curtains." According to vi.17, he can only mean the tent which he had set up, that is to say, not the Mosaic tabernacle, which, moreover, according to the description of Exodus xxv. seq., could not appropriately be contrasted with a timber erection, still less be regarded as a mean structure or unworthy of the Deity, for in point of magnificence it at least competed with the temple of Solomon. Nathan at first approves of the king's intention, but afterwards discountenances it, saying that at present God does not wish to have anything different from that which He has hitherto had. "I have dwelt in no house since the day that I brought the children of Israel out of Egypt, but have wandered about under tent and covering." Nathan also, of course, has not in his eye the Mosaic tabernacle as the present lodging of the ark, but David's tent upon Zion. Now he does not say that the ark has formerly been always in the tabernacle, and that its present harbourage is therefore in the highest degree unlawful, but, on the contrary, that the present state of matters is the right one,—that until now the ark has invariably been housed under an equally simple and unpretentious roof. As David's tent does not date back to the Exodus, Nathan is necessarily speaking of changing tents and dwellings; the reading of the parallel passage in 1Chron. xvii.5, therefore, correctly interprets the sense. There could be no more fundamental contradiction to the representation contained in the Pentateuch than that embodied in these words: the ark has not as its correlate a single definite sacred tent of state, but is quite indifferent to the shelter it enjoys—has frequently changed its abode, but never had any particularly fine one. Such has been the state of matters since the time of Moses.

Such is the position of affairs as regards the tabernacle; if it is determined that the age of the Priestly Code is to hang by these threads, I have no objection. The representation of the tabernacle arose out of the temple of Solomon as its root, in dependence on the sacred ark, for which there is early testimony, and which in the time of David, and also before it, was sheltered by a tent. From the temple it derives at once its inner character and its central importance for the cultus as well as its external form.

I.III.2. A peculiar point of view is taken up by Theodor Noldeke. He grants the premises that the tabernacle is a fiction, of which the object is to give pre-existence to the temple and to the unity of worship, but he denies the conclusion that in that case the Priestly Code presuppose; the unity of worship as already existing in its day, and therefore is late, than Deuteronomy. In his Untersuchungen zur Kritik des Alten Testaments (p. 127 seq.) he says:—

"A strong tendency towards unity of worship MUST have arisen as soon as Solomon's temple was built. Over against the splendid sanctuary with its imageless worship at the centre of the kingdom of Judah, the older holy places MUST ever have shrunk farther into the background, and that not merely in the eyes of the people, but quite specially also in those of the better classes and of those whose spiritual advancement was greatest (compare Amos iv. 4,viii.14). If even Hezekiah carried out the unification in Judah with tolerable thoroughness, the effort after it MUST surely have been of very early date; for the determination violently to suppress old sacred usages would not have been easily made, unless this had been long previously demanded by theory. The priests at Jerusalem MUST very specially at an early date have arrived at the conception that their temple with the sacred ark and the great altar was the one true place of worship, and an author has clothed this very laudable effort on behalf of the purity of religion in the form of a law, which certainly in its strictness was quite impracticable (ILeviticus xvii.4 seq.), and which, therefore, was modified later by the Deuteronomist with a view to practice."

What MUST have happened is of less consequence to know than what actually took place. Noldeke relies solely upon the statement of 2Kings xviii.4, 22, that Hezekiah abolished the high places and altars of Jehovah, and said to Judah and Jerusalem,

"Before this altar shall ye worship in Jerusalem." With reference to that statement doubts have already been raised above. How startling was the effect produced at a later date by the similar ordinance of Josiah! Is it likely then that the other, although the earlier, should have passed off so quietly and have left so little mark that the reinforcement of it, after an interval of seventy or eighty years, is not in the least brought into connection with it, but in every respect figures as a new first step upon a path until then absolutely untrodden? Note too how casual is the allusion to a matter which is elsewhere the chief and most favoured theme of the Book of Kings! And there is besides all this the serious difficulty, also already referred to above, that the man from whom Hezekiah must, from the nature of the case, have received the impulse to his reformatory movement, the prophet Isaiah, in one of his latest discourses expressly insists on a cleansing merely of the local sanctuaries from molten and graven images, that is to say, does not desire their complete removal. So much at least is certain that, if the alleged fact at present under discussion amounts to anything at all *1*

********************************* 1. Little importance is to be attached to 2Kings xviii.22. The narrative of the Assyrian siege of Jerusalem is not a contemporary one, as appears generally from the entirely indefinite character of the statements about the sudden withdrawal of the Assyrians and its causes, and particularly from xix.7, 36, 37. For in this passage the meaning certainly is that Sennacherib was assassinated soon after the unsuccessful expedition of 701, but in point of fact he actually reigned until 684 or 681 (Smith, Assyrian Eponym Canon, pp. 90, 170). Thus the narrator writes not twenty years merely after the event, but so long after it as to make possible the elision of those twenty years: probably he is already under the influence of Deuteronomy. 2Kings xviii.4 is certainly of greater weight than 2Kings xviii.22. But although highly authentic statements have been preserved to us in the epitome of the Book of Kings, they have all, nevertheless, been subjected not merely to the selection, but also to the revision of the Deuteronomic redactor, and it may very well be that the author thought himself justified in giving his subject a generalised treatment, according to which the cleansing (of the temple at Jerusalem in the first instance) from idols, urged by Isaiah and carried out by Hezekiah, was changed into an abolition of the Bamoth with their Macceboth and Asherim. It is well known how indifferent later writers are to distinctions of time and degree in the heresy of unlawful worship; they always go at once to the completed product. But in actual experience the reformation was doubtless accomplished step by step. At first we have in Hosea and Isaiah the polemic directed against molten and graven images, then in Jeremiah that against wood and stone, *i.e.*, against Macceboth and Asherim; the movement originated with the prophets, and the chief, or rather the only, weight is to be attached to their authentic testimony. *************************************

Hezekiah only made a feeble and wholly ineffectual attempt in this direction, and by no means "carried out the unification in Judah with tolerable thoroughness." At the same time, one might concede even this last point, and yet not give any ground for the theory at which Noldeke wishes to arrive.

For his assumption is that the effort after unity had its old and original seat precisely in the priestly circles of Jerusalem. If the Priestly Code is older than Deuteronomy, then of course the prophetic agitation for reform of worship in which Deuteronomy had its origin must have been only the repetition of an older priestly movement in the same direction. But of the latter we hear not a single word, while we can follow the course of the former fairly well from its beginnings in thought down to its issue in a practical result. It was Amos, Hosea, and Isaiah who introduced the movement against the old popular worship of the high places; in doing so they are not in the least actuated by a deep-rooted preference for the temple of Jerusalem, but by ethical motives, which manifest themselves in them for the first time in history, and which we can see springing up in them before our very eyes: their utterances, though historically occasioned by the sanctuaries of northern Israel, are quite general, and are directed against the cultus as a whole. Of the influence of a point of view even remotely akin to the priestly position that worship in this or that special place is of more value than anywhere else, and on that account alone deserves to be preserved, no trace is to be found in them; their polemic is a purely prophetic one, *i.e.*, individual, "theopneust" in the sense that it is independent of all traditional and preconceived human opinions. But the subsequent development is dependent upon this absolutely original commencement, and has its issue, not in the Priestly Code, but in Deuteronomy, a book that, with all reasonable regard for the priests (though not more for those of Jerusalem than for the others), still does not belie its prophetic origin, and above all things is absolutely free from all and every hierocratic tendency. And finally, it was Deuteronomy that brought about the historical result of Josiah's reformation. Thus the whole historical movement now under our consideration, so far as it was effective and thereby has come to our knowledge, is in its origin and essence prophetic, even if latterly it may have been aided by priestly influences; and it not merely can, but must be understood from itself. Any older or independent contemporary priestly movement in the same direction remained at least entirely without result, and so also has left no witnesses to itself. Perhaps it occurs to us that the priests of Jerusalem must after all have been the first to catch sight of the goal, the attainment of which afterwards brought so great advantage to themselves, but it does not appear that they were so clever beforehand as we are after the event. At least there are no other grounds for the hypothesis of a long previously latent tendency towards centralisation on the part of the Jerusalem priesthood beyond the presumption that the Priestly Code must chronologically precede, not Deuteronomy merely, but also the prophets. For the sake of this presumption there is constructed a purely abstract (and as such perfectly irrefragable) possibility that furnishes a door of escape from the historical probability, which nevertheless it is impossible to evade.

How absolutely unknown the Priestly Code continued to be even down to the middle of the exile can be seen from the Books of Kings, which cannot have received their present shape earlier than the death of Nebuchadnezzar. The redactor, who cites the Deuteronomic law and constantly forms his judgment in accordance with it, considered (as we have learned from 1Kings iii.2) that the Bamoth were permissible prior to the building of Solomon's temple; the tabernacle therefore did not exist for him. Jeremiah, who flourished about a generation earlier, is equally ignorant of it, but—on account of the ark, though not necessarily in agreement with traditional opinion—regards the house of God at Shiloh (whose ruins, it would seem, were at

58

that time still visible) as the forerunner of the temple of Jerusalem, and in this he is followed by the anonymous prophecy of 1Samuel ii.27-36, the comparatively recent date of which appears from the language (ii.33), and from the circumstance that it anticipates the following threatening in iii. In all these writers, and still more in the case of the Deuteronomist himself, who in xii. actually makes the unity of the cultus dependent on the previous choice of Jerusalem, it is an exceedingly remarkable thing that, if the Priestly Code had been then already a long time in existence, they should have been ignorant of a book so important and so profound in its practical bearings. In ancient Hebrew literature such an oversight could not be made so easily as, in similar circumstances, with the literature of the present day. And how comes it to pass that in the Book of Chronicles, dating from the third century, the Priestly Code suddenly ceases to be, to all outward seeming, dead, but asserts its influence everywhere over the narrative in only too active and unmistakable a way? To these difficulties Noldeke is unreasonably indifferent. He seems to be of the opinion that the post-exilian time would not have ventured to take in hand so thoroughgoing an alteration, or rather reconstruction, of tradition as is implied in antedating the temple of Solomon by means of the tabernacle. *1*

*** 1. Jahrb. fuer prot. Theol., i. p. 352: "And now let me ask whether a document of this kind presenting, as it does, a picture of the history, land distribution, and sacrificial rites of Israel, as a whole, which in so many particulars departs from the actual truth, can belong to a time in which Israel clung to what was traditional with such timid anxiety?" ***

But it is, on the contrary, precisely the mark which distinguished the post-exile writers that they treat in the freest possible manner, in accordance with their own ideas, the institutions of the bygone past, with which their time was no longer connected by any living bond. For what reason does Chronicles stand in the canon at all, if not in order to teach us this?

But when Noldeke excuses the ignorance with regard to the tabernacle on the plea that it is a mere creature of the brain, *2*

*********************************** 1. Unters., p. 130: "It must always be remembered that the author in his statements, as in his laws, does not depict actual relations, but in the first instance his own theories and ideals. Hence the glorification of the tabernacle," &c. &c. ***********************************

he for the moment forgets that there underlies this creation the very real idea of unity of worship, for the sake of which it would surely have been very welcome, to the Deuteronomist, for example, even as a mere idea. It is only the embodiment of the tabernacle that is fancy; the idea of it springs from the ground of history, and it is by its idea that it is to be apprehended. And when Noldeke finally urges in this connection as a plea for the priority of the Priestly Code that, in spite of the limitation of sacrifice to a single locality, it nevertheless maintains the old provision that every act of killing must be a sacrifice, while Deuteronomy, going a step farther, departs from this, here also his argument breaks down.

For we read in Leviticus xvii., "What man soever there be of the house of Israel that killeth an ox or sheep or goat in the camp, or out of the camp, and bringeth it not to the door of the tabernacle, to offer them as an offering unto the Lord before the tabernacle of the Lord, blood shall be imputed unto that man: he hath shed blood, and that man shall be cut off from among his people: to the end that the children of Israel may bring their sacrifices which they offer in the open field, even that they may bring them to the Lord, to the door of the tabernacle, to the priest, and offer them for peace-offerings unto the Lord....And they shall no more offer sacrifices unto devils, after whom they have gone a whoring." The intention of this prescription is simply and solely to secure the exclusive legitimation of the one lawful place of sacrifice; it is only for this, obviously, that the profane slaughtering outside of Jerusalem, which Deuteronomy had permitted, is forbidden. Plainly the common man did not quite understand the newly drawn and previously quite unknown distinction between the religious and the profane act, and when he slaughtered at home (as he was entitled to do), he in doing so still observed, half-unconsciously perhaps, the old sacred sacrificial ritual. From this arose the danger of a multiplicity of altars again furtively creeping in, and such a danger is met, in an utterly impracticable way indeed, in Leviticus xvii. And it is worth noticing how much this law, which, for the rest, is based upon the Book of Deuteronomy, has grown in the narrowness of its legitimistic mode of viewing things. Deuteronomy thoroughly recognises that offerings, even though offered outside of Jerusalem, are still offered to Jehovah; for the author of Leviticus xvii. this is an impossible Idea, and he regards such offerings simply as made to devils. *1*

*********************************** 1. With reference to these rural demons, compare my note in Vakidi's Maghazi (Berlin, 1882), p. 113. It is somewhat similar, though not quite the same thing, when the Moslems say that the old Arabs dedicated their worship to the Jinns; and other instances may be compared in which divinities have been degraded to demons. ***********************************

I refuse to believe that any such thing could have been possible for one who lived before the Deuteronomic reformation, or even under the old conditions that were in existence immediately before the exile.

Leviticus xvii., moreover, belongs confessedly to a peculiar little collection of laws, which has indeed been taken up into the Priestly Code, but which in many respects disagrees with it, and particularly in respect of this prohibition of profane slaughterings. With reference to the Priestly Code as a whole, Noldeke's assertion is quite off the mark. The code, on the contrary, already allows slaughter without sacrifice in the precepts of Noah, which are valid not merely for all the world, but also for the Jews. Farther on this permission is not expressly repeated indeed, but it is regarded as a thing of course. This alone can account for the fact that the thank-offering is treated so entirely as a subordinate affair and the sacrificial meal almost ignored, while in Leviticus vii.22-27 rules are even given for procedure in the slaughter of such animals as are not sacrificed. *2*

*********************************** 2. That Leviticus vii.22-27 is not a repetition of the old and fuller regulations about the thank-offering, but an appendix containing new ones relating to slaughtering, is clear from "the beast of which men offer an offering unto the Lord" (ver. 25), and "in all your dwellings" (ver. z6), as well as from the praxis of Judaism. ***********************************

Here accordingly is another instance of what we have already so often observed: what is brought forward in Deuteronomy as an innovation is assumed in the Priestly Code to be an ancient custom dating as far back as to Noah. And therefore the latter code is a growth of the soil that has been prepared by means of the former.

CHAPTER II. SACRIFICE.

With the Hebrews, as with the whole ancient world, sacrifice constituted the main part of worship. The question is whether their worship did not also in this most important respect pass through a history the stages of which are reflected in the Pentateuch. From the results already reached this must be regarded at the outset as probable, but the sources of information accessible to us seem hardly sufficient to enable us actually to follow the process, or even so much as definitely to fix its two termini.

II.I.1. The Priestly Code alone occupies itself much with the subject; it gives a minute classification of the various kinds of offerings, and a description of the procedure to be followed in the case of each. In this way it furnishes also the normative scheme for modern accounts of the matter, into which all the other casual notices of the Old Testament on the subject must be made to fit as best they can. This point accordingly presents us with an important feature by which the character of the book can be determined. In it the sacrificial ritual is a constituent, and indeed a very essential element, of the Mosaic legislation: that ritual is not represented as ancient use handed down to the Israelites by living practice from ancestral times: it was Moses who gave them the theory of it—a very elaborate one too—and he himself received his instruction from God (Exodus xxv. seq.; Leviticus i. seq.). An altogether disproportionate emphasis is accordingly laid upon the technique of sacrifice corresponding to the theory, alike upon the when, the where, and the by whom, and also in a very special manner upon the how. It is from these that the sacrifice obtains its specific value; one could almost suppose that even if it were offered to another God, it would by means of the legitimate rite alone be at once made essentially Jehovistic. The cultus of Israel is essentially distinguished from all others by its form, the distinctive and constitutive mark of the holy community. With it the theocracy begins and it with the theocracy; the latter is nothing more than the institution for the purpose of carrying on the cultus after the manner ordained by God. For this reason also the ritual, which appears to concern the priests only, finds its place in a law-book intended for the whole community; in order to participate in the life of the theocracy, all must of course, have clear knowledge of its essential nature, and in this the theory of sacrifice holds a first place.

The Jehovistic portion of the Pentateuch also knows of no other kind of divine worship besides the sacrificial, and does not attach to it less importance than the Priestly Code. But we do not find many traces of the view that the sacrificial system of Israel is distinguished from all others by a special form revealed to Moses, which makes it the [sic] alone legitimate. Sacrifice is sacrifice: when offered to Baal, it is heathenish; when offered to Jehovah, it is Israelite. In the Book of the Covenant and in both Decalogues it is enjoined before everything to serve no other God besides Jehovah, but also at the proper season to offer firstlings and gifts to Him. Negative determinations, for the most part directed against one heathenish peculiarity or another, occur but there are no positive ordinances relating to the ritual. How one is to set about offering sacrifice is taken for granted as already known, and nowhere figures as an affair for the legislation, which, on the contrary, occupies itself with quite other things. What the Book of the Covenant and the Decalogue leave still perhaps doubtful becomes abundantly clear from the Jehovistic narrative. The narrative has much more to say about sacrifice than the incorporated law books, and this may be regarded as characteristic; in the Priestly Code it is quite the other way. But what is specially important is that, according to the Jehovistic history, the praxis of sacrifice, and that too of the regular and God-pleasing sort, extends far beyond the Mosaic legislation, and, strictly speaking, is as old as the world itself. A sacrificial feast which the Hebrews wish to celebrate in the wilderness is the occasion of the Exodus; Moses already builds an altar at Rephidim (Exodus xvii.), and, still before the ratification of the covenant on Sinai, a solemn meal in the presence of Jehovah is set on foot on occasion of Jethro's visit (Exodus xviii.). But the custom is much older still; it was known and practiced by Abraham, Isaac, and Jacob. Noah, the father of all mankind, built the first altar after the Flood, and long before him Cain and Abel sacrificed in the same way as was usual in Palestine thousands of years afterwards. Balaam the Aramaean understands just as well as any Israelite how to offer sacrifices to Jehovah that do not fail of their effect. All this brings out, with as much clearness as could be desired, that sacrifice is a very ancient and quite universal mode of honouring the Deity, and that Israelite sacrifice is distinguished not by the manner in which, but by the being to whom, it is offered, in being offered to the God of Israel. According to this representation of the matter, Moses left the procedure in sacrifice, as he left the procedure in prayer, to be regulated by the traditional praxis; if there was any definite origination of the cultus of Israel, the patriarchs must be thought of, but even they were not the discoverers of the ritual; they were merely the founders of those holy places at which the Israelites dedicated gifts to Jehovah, a usage which was common to the whole world. The contrast with the Priestly Code is extremely striking, for it is well known that the latter work makes mention of no sacrificial act prior to the time of Moses, neither in Genesis nor in Exodus, although from the time of Noah slaughtering is permitted. The offering of a sacrifice of sheep and oxen as the occasion of the exodus is omitted, and in place of the sacrifice of the firstlings we have the paschal lamb, which is slaughtered and eaten without altar, without priest, and not in the presence of Jehovah. *1*

*** 1. With regard to sacrifice, Deuteronomy still occupies the same standpoint as JE. ***

The belief that the cultus goes back to pre-Mosaic usage is unquestionably more natural than the belief that it is the main element of the Sinaitic legislation; the thought would be a strange one that God should suddenly have revealed, or Moses discovered and introduced, the proper sacrificial ritual. At the same time this does not necessitate the conclusion that the Priestly Code is later than the Jehovist. Nor does this follow from the very elaborately-developed technique of the agenda, for elaborate ritual may have existed in the great sanctuaries at a very early period,—-though that, indeed, would not prove it to be genuinely Mosaic. On the other hand, it is certainly a consideration deserving of great weight that the representation of the exclusive legitimacy of so definite a sacrificial ritual, treated in the Priestly Code as the only possible one in Israel, is one which can have arisen only as a consequence of the centralisation of the cultus at Jerusalem. Yet by urging this the decision of the question at present before us would only be referred back to the result already arrived at in the preceding chapter, and it is much to be desired that it should be solved independently, so as not to throw too much weight upon a single support.

II.I.2. In this case also the elements of a decision can only be obtained from the historical documents dating from the pre-exilic time,—the Books of Judges, Samuel, and Kings on the one hand, and the writings of the prophets on the other. As regards those of the first class, they represent the cultus and sacrifice on all occasions as occupying a large place in the life of the nation and of the individual. But, although it would be wrong to say that absolutely no weight is attached to the RITE, it is certainly not the fact that the main stress is laid upon it; the antithesis is not between RITE and NON-RITE, but between sacrifice TO Jéhovah and sacrifice TO STRANGE GODS, the reverse of what we find in the Priestly Code. Alongside of splendid sacrifices, such as those of the kings, presumably offered in accordance with all the rules of priestly skill, there occur others also of the simplest and most primitive type, as, for example, those of Saul (1Samuel xiv.35) and Elisha (1Kings xix.2I); both kinds are proper if only they be dedicated to the proper deity. Apart from the exilian redaction of the Book of Kings, which reckons the cultus outside of Jerusalem as heretical, it is nowhere represented that a sacrifice could be dedicated to the God of Israel, and yet be illegitimate. Naaman (2Kings v. 17), it is to be supposed, followed his native Syrian ritual, but this does not in the least impair the acceptability of his offering. For reasons easily explained, it is seldom that an occasion arises to describe the ritual, but when such a description is given it is only with violence that it can be forced into accordance with the formula of the law. Most striking of all is the procedure of Gideon in Judges vi.19-21, in which it is manifest that the procedure still usual at Ophrah in the time of the narrator is also set forth. Gideon boils a he-goat and bakes in the ashes cakes of unleavened bread, places upon the bread the flesh in a basket and the broth in a pot, and then the meal thus prepared is burnt in the altar flame. It is possible that instances may have also occurred in which the rule of the Pentateuch is followed, but the important point is that the distinction between legitimate and heretical is altogether wanting. When the Book of Chronicles is compared the difference is at once perceived.

The impression derived from the historical books is confirmed by the prophets. It is true that in their polemic against confounding worship with religion they reveal the fact that in their day the cultus was carried on with the utmost zeal and splendour, and was held in the highest estimation. But this estimation does not rest upon the opinion that the cultus, as regards its matter, goes back to Moses or to Jehovah Himself, gives to the theocracy its distinctive character, and even constitutes the supernatural priesthood of Israel among the nations, but simply upon the belief that Jehovah must be honoured by His dependents, just as other gods are by their subjects, by means of offerings and gifts as being the natural and (like prayer) universally current expressions of religious homage. The larger the quantity, and the finer the quality, so much the better; but that the merit arising from the presentation depends upon strict observance of etiquette regarded as Jehovah's law is not suggested. Thus it is that the prophets are able to ask whether then Jehovah has commanded His people to tax their energies with such exertions? the fact presupposed being that no such command exists, and that no one knows anything at all about a ritual Torah. Amos, the leader of the chorus, says (iv.4 seq.), "Come to Bethel to sin, to Gilgal to sin yet more, and bring your sacrifices every morning, your tithes every three days, for so ye like, ye children of Israel." In passing sentence of rejection upon the value of the cultus he is in opposition to the faith of his time; but if the opinion had been a current one that precisely the cultus was what Jehovah had instituted in Israel, he would not have been able to say, "For so ye like." "Ye," not Jehovah; it is an idle and arbitrary worship. He expresses himself still more clearly in v.21 seq. "I hate, I despise your feasts, and I smell not on your holy days; though ye offer me burnt-offerings and your gifts, I will not accept them; neither do I regard your thank-offerings of fatted calves. Away from me with the noise of thy songs, the melody of thy viols I will not hear; but let judgment roll on like waters, and righteousness like a mighty stream. Did ye offer unto me sacrifices and gifts in the wilderness the forty years, O house of Israel?" In asking this last question Amos has not the slightest fear of raising any controversy; on the contrary, he is following the generally received belief. His polemic is directed against the praxis of his contemporaries, but here he rests it upon a theoretical foundation in which they are at one with him,—on this, namely, that the sacrificial worship is not of Mosaic origin. Lastly, if ii.4 be genuine, it teaches the same lesson. By the Law of Jehovah which the people of Judah have despised it is impossible that Amos can have understood anything in the remotest degree resembling a ritual legislation. Are we to take it then that he formed his own special private notion of the Torah? How in that case would it have been possible for him to make himself understood by the people, or to exercise influence over them? Of all unlikely suppositions, at all events it is the least likely that the herdsman of Tekoah, under the influence of prophetic tradition (which in fact he so earnestly disclaims), should have taken the Torah for something quite different from what it actually was.

Hosea, Isaiah, and Micah are in agreement with Amos. The first mentioned complains bitterly (iv.6 seq.) that the priests cultivate the system of sacrifices instead of the Torah. The Torah, committed by Jehovah to their order, lays it on them as their vocation to diffuse the knowledge of God in Israel,—the knowledge that He seeks truthfulness and love, justice and considerateness, and no gifts; but they, on the contrary, in a spirit of base self-seeking, foster the tendency of the nation towards cultus, in their superstitions over-estimate of which lies their sin and their ruin. "My people are destroyed for lack of knowledge; ye yourselves (ye priests!) reject knowledge, and I too will reject you that ye shall not be priests unto me; seeing ye have forgotten the law of your God, so will I also forget you. The more they are, the more they sin against me; their glory they barter for shame. They eat the sin of my people, and they set their heart on their iniquity." From this we see how idle it is to believe that the prophets opposed "the Law;" they defend the priestly Torah, which, however, has nothing to do with cultus, but only with justice and morality. In another passage (viii.11 seq.) we read, "Ephraim has built for himself many altars, to sin; the altars are there for him, to sin. How many soever my instructions (torothai) may be, they are counted those of a stranger." This text has had the unmerited misfortune of having been forced to do service as a proof that Hosea knew of copious writings similar in contents to our Pentateuch. All that can be drawn from the contrast "instead of following my instructions they offer sacrifice" (for that is the meaning of the passage) is that the prophet had never once dreamed of the possibility of cultus being made the subject of Jehovah's directions. In Isaiah's discourses the well-known passage of the first chapter belongs to this connection: "To what purpose is the multitude of your sacrifices unto me? saith the Lord. I am weary with the burnt-offerings of rams and the fat of fed beasts, and I delight not in the blood of bullocks and of lambs and of he-goats. When ye come to look upon my face, who hath required this at your hands?—to trample my courts!" This expression has long been a source of trouble, and certainly the prophet could not possibly have uttered it if the sacrificial worship had, according to any tradition whatever, passed for being specifically Mosaic. Isaiah uses the word Torah to denote not the priestly but the prophetical instruction (i.10, ii.3, v.24, viii.16, 20, xxx.9); as both have a common source and Jehovah is the proper instructor (xxx.20), this is easily explicable, and is moreover full of instruction as regards the idea involved; the contents of the Priestly Code fit badly in with the Torah of i.10. Lastly, Micah's answer to the people's question, how a return of the favour of an angry God is to be secured, is of conspicuous significance (vi.6 seq.): "Shall I come before Him with burnt-offerings with calves of a year old? Is the Lord pleased with thousands of rams, with ten thousands of rivers of oil? Shall I give my first-born for my transgression, the fruit of my body as atonement for my soul?—It hath been told thee, O man, what is good, and what Jehovah requireth of thee. Nay, it is to do justly, and to love mercy, and to walk humbly before thy God." Although the blunt statement of the contrast between cultus and religion is peculiarly prophetic, Micah can still take his stand upon this, "It hath been told thee, O man, what Jehovah requires." It is no new matter, but a thing well known, that sacrifices are not what the Torah of the Lord contains.

That we have not inferred too much from these utterances of the older prophets is clear from the way in which they are taken up and carried on by Jeremiah, who lived shortly before the Babylonian exile. Just as in vi.19 seq. he opposes the Torah to the cultus, so in vii.11 seq. he thus expresses himself: "Add your burnt-offerings to your sacrifices, and eat flesh! For I said nought unto your fathers, and commanded them nought, in the day that I brought them out of the land of Egypt, concerning burnt-offerings or sacrifices. But this thing commanded I them: hearken to my voice, and I will be your God, and ye shall be my people, and walk ye in the way that I shall always teach you, that it may be well with you." The view indeed, that the prophets (who, from the connection, are the ever-living voice to which Israel is to hearken) are the proper soul of the theocracy, the organ by which Jehovah influences and rules it, has no claim to immemorial antiquity. But no stress lies upon the positive element here; enough that at all events Jeremiah is unacquainted with the Mosaic legislation as it is contained in the Priestly Code. His ignoring of it is not intentional, for he is far from hating the cultus (xvii.26). But, as priest and prophet, staying continually in the temple at Jerusalem, he must have known it, if it had existed and actually been codified. The fact is one which it is difficult to get over.

Thus the historical witnesses, particularly the prophets, decide the matter in favour of the Jehovistic tradition. According to the universal opinion of the pre-exilic period, the cultus is indeed of very old and (to the people) very sacred usage, but not a Mosaic institution; the ritual is not the main thing in it, and is in no sense the subject with which the Torah deals. *1*

*********************************** 1. That the priests were not mere teachers of law and morals, but also gave ritual instruction (e.g, regarding cleanness and uncleanness), is of course not denied by this. All that is asserted is that in pre-exilian antiquity the priests' own praxis (at the altar) never constituted the contents of the Torah, but that their Torah always consisted of instructions to the laity. The distinction is easily intelligible to those who choose to understand it. **********************************

In other words, no trace can be found of acquaintance with the Priestly Code, but, on the other hand, very clear indications of ignorance of its contents.

II.I.3. In this matter the transition from the pre-exilic to the post-exilic period is effected, not by Deuteronomy, but by Ezekiel the priest in prophet's mantle, who was one of the first to be carried into exile. He stands in striking contrast with his elder contemporary Jeremiah. In the picture of Israel's future which he drew in B.C. 573 (chaps. xl.-xlviii.), in which fantastic hopes are indeed built upon Jehovah, but no impossible demand made of man, the temple and cultus hold a central place. Whence this sudden change? Perhaps because now the Priestly Code has suddenly awakened to life after its long trance, and become the inspiration of Ezekiel? The explanation is certainly not to be sought in any such occurrence, but simply in the historical circumstances. So long as the sacrificial worship remained in actual use, it was zealously carried on, but people did not concern themselves with it theoretically, and had not the least occasion for reducing it to a code. But once the temple was in ruins, the cultus at an end, its PERSONNEL out of employment, it is easy to understand how the sacred praxis should have become a matter of theory and writing, so that it might not altogether perish, and how an exiled priest should have begun to paint the picture of it as he carried it in his memory, and to publish it as a programme for the future restoration of the theocracy. Nor is there any difficulty if arrangements, which as long as they were actually in force were simply regarded as natural, were seen after their abolition in a transfiguring light, and from the study devoted to them gained artificially a still higher value. These historical conditions supplied by the exile sufffice to make clear the transition from Jeremiah to Ezekiel, and the genesis of Ezekiel xl.-xlviii. The co-operation of the Priestly Code is here not merely unnecessary, it would be absolutely disconcerting. Ezekiel's departure from the ritual of the Pentateuch cannot be explained as intentional alterations of the original; they are too casual and insignificant. The prophet, moreover, has the rights of authorship as regards the end of his book as well as for the rest of it; he has also his right to his picture of the future as the earlier prophets had to theirs. And finally, let its due weight be given to the simple fact that an exiled priest saw occasion to draft such a sketch of the temple worship. What need would there have been for it, if the realised picture, corresponding completely to his views, had actually existed, and, being already written in a book, wholly obviated any danger lest the cultus should become extinct through the mere fact of its temporary cessation?

Here again a way of escape is open by assuming a lifeless existence of the law down to Ezra's time. But if this is done it is unallowable to date that existence, not from Moses, but from some other intermediate point in the history of Israel. Moreover, the assumption of a codification either as preceding all praxis, or as alongside and independent of it, is precisely in the case of sacrificial ritual one of enormous difficulty, for it is obvious that such a codification can only be the final result of an old and highly developed use, and not the invention of an idle brain. This consideration also makes retreat into the theory of an illegal praxis impossible, and renders the legitimacy of the actually subsisting indisputable.

II.II.

At all times, then, the sacrificial worship of Israel existed, and had great importance attached to it, but in the earlier period it rested upon custom, inherited from the fathers, in the post-exilian on the law of Jehovah, given through Moses. At first it was naïve, and what was chiefly considered was the quantity and quality of the gifts; afterwards it became legal,—the scrupulous fulfilment of the law, that is, of the prescribed ritual, was what was looked to before everything. Was there then, apart from this, strictly speaking, no material difference? To answer this question our researches must be carried further afield, after some preliminary observations have been made in order to fix our position.

II.II.1. In the Pentateuch the sacrificial ritual is indeed copiously described, but nowhere in the Old Testament is its significance formally explained; this is treated as on the whole self-evident and familiar to every one. The general notion of a sacrifice is in the Priestly Code that of *qorban*, in the rest of the Old Testament that of *minha*, *1 ie.*, "gift;"

*** 1. Genesis iv. 3-5, Numbers xvi. 15; 1Samuel ii. 17, 29, xxvi. 19; Isaiah i. 13; Malachi i. 10-13, ii. 12, 13, iii. 3, 4. In the Priestly Code *minha* is exclusively a terminus technicus for the meal-offering. The general name in the LXX and in the New Testament is DWRON (Matthew v. 23-24, viii. 4, xv. 5, xxiii. 18, 19). Compare Spencer, "De ratione et origine sacrificiorum" (De Legibus Hebraeorum ritualibus, iii.2), by far the best thing that has ever been written on the subject. ***

the corresponding verbs are *haqrib* and *haggish*, *i.e.*, "to bring near." Both nouns and both verbs are used originally for the offering of a present to the king (or the nobles) to do him homage, to make him gracious, to support a petition (Judges iii. 17 seq.; 1Samuel x. 27; 1Kings v. 1 [A.V. iv.21]), and from this are employed with reference to the highest King (Malachi i.8).

DWRA QEOUS PEIQAI, DWR')AIDOIOUS BASILHAS

The gift must not be unseasonably or awkwardly thrust upon the recipient, not when the king's anger is at white heat, and not by one the sight of whom he hates.

With respect to the matter of it, the idea of a sacrifice is in itself indifferent, if the thing offered only have value of some sort, and is the property of the offerer. Under *qorban* and *minha* is included also that which the Greeks called *anathema*. The sacred dues which at a later date fall to the priest were without doubt originally ordinary offerings, and amongst these are found even wool and flax (Deut. xviii. 4; Hos. ii. 7, 11 [A.V. 5, 9]). But it is quite in harmony with the naïveté of antiquity that as to man so also to God that which is eatable is by preference offered; in this there was the additional advantage, that what God had caused to grow was thus rendered back to Him. In doing this, the regular form observed is that a meal is prepared in honour of the Deity, of which man partakes as God's guest. Offering without any qualifying expression always means a meat or drink offering. On this account the altar is called a table, on this account also salt goes along with flesh, oil with meal and bread, and wine with both; and thus also are we to explain why the flesh, according to rule, is put upon the altar in pieces and (in the earlier period) boiled, the corn ground or baked. Hence also the name "bread of Jehovah" for the offering (Leviticus xxi.22). It is of course true that "in his offering the enlightened Hebrew saw no banquet to Jehovah:" but we hardly think of taking the enlightened Protestant as a standard for the original character of Protestantism.

The manner in which the portions pertaining to God are conveyed to Him varies. The most primitive is the simple "setting in order" [(RK, struere] and "pouring out" [#pk, fundere) in the case of the shewbread and drink offerings; to this a simple eating and drinking would correspond. But the most usual is burning, or, as the Hebrews express it, "making a savour" (HQ+YR), to which corresponds the more delicate form of enjoyment, that of smelling. Originally, however, it is God Himself who consumes what the flame consumes. In any case the burning is a means of conveying the offering, not, as one might perhaps be disposed to infer from the "sweet savour" (RYX HNYXX Genesis viii.21), a means of preparing it. For in ancient times the Hebrews did not roast the flesh, but boiled it; in what is demonstrably the oldest ritual (Judges vi. 19), the sacrifice also is delivered to the altar flame boiled; and, moreover, not the flesh only but also the bread and the meal are burnt.

As regards the distinction between bloodless and bloody offerings, the latter, it is well known, are preferred in the Old Testament, but, strictly speaking, the former also have the same value and the same efficacy. The incense-offering is represented as a means of propitiation (Leviticus xvi., Numbers xvii. 12 [A.V. xvi. 47]), so also are the ten thousands of rivers of oil figuring between the thousands of rams and the human sacrifice in Micah vi. That the cereal offering is never anything but an accompaniment of the animal sacrifice is a rule which does not hold, either in the case of the shewbread or in that of the high priest's daily minxa (Leviticus vi. 13

70

[A.V. 20]; Nehemiahx.35). Only the drink-offering has no independent position, and was not in any way the importance it had among the Greeks.

When a sacrifice is killed, the offering consists not of the blood but of the eatable portions of the flesh. Only these can be designated as the "bread of Jehovah," and, moreover, only the eatable domestic animals can be presented. At the same time, however, it is true that in the case of the bloody offerings a new motive ultimately came to be associated with the original idea of the gift. The life of which the blood was regarded as the substance (2Samuel xxiii.17) had for the ancient Semites something mysterious and divine about it; they felt a certain religious scruple about destroying it. With them flesh was an uncommon luxury, and they ate it with quite different feelings from those with which they partook of fruits or of milk. Thus the act of killing was not so indifferent or merely preparatory a step as for example the cleansing and preparing of corn; on the contrary, the pouring out of blood was ventured upon only in such a way as to give it back to the Deity, the source of life. In this way, not by any means every meal indeed, but every slaughtering, came to be a sacrifice. What was primarily aimed at in it was a mere restoration of His own to the Deity, but there readily resulted a combination with the idea of sacrifice, whereby the latter was itself modified in a peculiar manner. The atoning efficacy of the gift began to be ascribed mainly to the blood and to the vicarious value of the life taken away. The outpouring and sprinkling of blood was in all sacrifices a rite of conspicuous importance, and even the act of slaughtering in the case of some, and these the most valued, a holy act.

II.II.2. The features presented by the various literary sources harmonise with the foregoing sketch. But the Priestly Code exhibits some peculiarities by which it is distinguished from the pre-exilian remains in matters sacrificial.

In the first place, it is characterised in the case of bloodless offerings by a certain refinement of the material. Thus in the meal-offerings it will have SLT (simila) not QMX (far). In the whole pre-exilian literature the former is mentioned only three times altogether, but never in connection with sacrifice, where, on the contrary, the ordinary meal is used (Judges vi. 19; 1Samuel i. 24). That this is no mere accident appears on the one hand from the fact that in the later literature, from Ezekiel onwards, QMX as sacrificial meal entirely disappears, and SLT invariably take its place; on the other hand, from this that the LXX (or the Hebrew text from which that version was taken) is offended by the illegality of the material in 1Samuel i. 24, and alters the reading so as to bring it to conformity with the Law. *1*

** 1. Ezekiel xvi. 13, 19, xlvi. 14; I Chronicles ix. 29, xxiii. 22; Ecclus. xxxv.2, xxxviii. 11, xxxix. 32; Isaiah i. 13 (LXX); lxvi. 3 (LXX). In the Priestly Code slt occurs more than forty times.
****

So also a striking preference is shown for incense. With every meal-offering incense is offered upon the altar; in the inner sanctuary a special mixture of spices is employed, the accurately given recipe for which is not to be followed for private purposes. The offering of incense is the privilege of the higher priesthood; in the ritual of the great Day of Atonement, the sole one in which Aaron must discharge the duties in person, it occupies a conspicuous place. It has an altogether dangerous sanctity; Aaron's own sons died for not having made use of the proper fire. It is the cause of death and destruction to the Levites of Korah's company who are not entitled to use it, while immediately afterwards, in the hands of the legitimate high priest, it becomes the means of appeasing the anger of Jehovah, and of staying the plague. Now of this offering, thus invested with such a halo of sanctity, the older literature of the Jewish Canon, down to Jeremiah and Zephaniah, knows absolutely nothing. The verb Q++R there used invariably and exclusively of the BURNING of fat or meal, and thereby making to God a sweet-smelling savour; it is never used to denote the OFFERING OF INCENSE, and the substantive Q+RT as a sacrificial term has the quite general signification of that which is burnt on the altar. 2

*** 2. The verb is used in *piel* by the older writers, in *hiphil* by the Priestly Code (Chronicles), and promiscuously in both forms during the transition period by the author of the Books of Kings. This is the case, at least, where the forms can with certainty be distinguished, namely, in the perfect, imperative, and infinitive; the distinction between YQ+R and YQ+YR, MQ+R and MQ+YR rests, as is well known, upon no secure tradition. Compare, for example, *qatter jaqtirun*, 1Samuel ii. 16; the transcribers and punctuators under the influence of the Pentateuch preferred the hiphil. In the Priestly Code (Chronicles) HQ+YR has both meanings alongside of each other, but when used without a qualifying phrase it generally means incensing, and when consuming a sacrifice is intended HMZBXH is usually added, "on the altar," that is, the place on which the incense-offering strictly so called was NOT offered. The substantive Q+RT in the sense of "an offering of incense" in which it occurs exclusively and very frequently in the Priestly Code, is first found in Ezekiel (viii. 11, xvi. 18, xxiii. 41) and often afterwards in Chronicles, but in the rest of the Old Testament only in Proverbs xxvii. 9, but there in a profane sense. Elsewhere never, not even in passages so late as 1Samuel ii.28; Psalms lxvi. 15, cxli. 2. In authors of a certainly pre-exilian date tbe word occurs only twice, both times in a perfectly general sense. Isaiah i. 13: "Bring me no more oblations; it is an abominable incense to me." Deuteronomy xxxiii. 10: "The Levites shall put incense (i.e.,the fat of thank-offerings) before thee, and whole burnt-offerings upon thine altar." The name LBNT (frankincense) first occurs in Jeremiah (vi. 20, xvii. 26, xli. 5); elsewhere only in the Priestly Code (nine times), in Isaiah xl.-lxvi. (three times), in Chronicles and Nehemiah (three times), and in Canticles (three times). Compare Zephaniah iii. 10; 1Kings ix. 25. ***

In enumerations where the prophets exhaust everything pertaining to sacred gifts and liturgic performances, in which, for the sake of lengthening the catalogue, they do not shrink from repetitions even, there is not any mention of incense-offerings, neither in Amos (iv. 4 seq., v. 21 seq.) nor in Isaiah (i. 11 seq.) nor in Micah (vi. 6 seq.). Shall we suppose that they all of them forget this subject by mere accident, or that they conspired to ignore it? If it had really existed, and been of so great consequence, surely one of them at least would not have failed to speak of it. The Jehovistic section of the Hexateuch is equally silent, so also the historical books, except Chronicles, and so the rest of the prophets, down to Jeremiah, who (vi.20) selects incense as the example of a rare and far-fetched offering: "To what purpose cometh there to me incense from Sheba, and the precious cane from a far country?" Thenceforward it is mentioned in Ezekiel, in Isaiah (xl.-lxvi.), in Nehemiah, and in Chronicles; the references are continuous. The introduction of incense is a natural result of increased luxury; one is tempted to conjecture that its use must have first crept into the Jehovah worship as an innovation from a more luxuriously-developed foreign cultus. But the importance which it has attained in the ritual legislation of the Pentateuch is manifest above all from this, that it has led to the invention of a peculiar new and highly sacred piece of furniture, namely, the golden altar in the inner tabernacle, which is unknown to history, and which is foreign even to the kernel of the Priestly Code itself.

We expect to find the altar of incense in Exodus xxv.-xxix., but find it instead as an appendix at the beginning of Exodus xxx. Why not until now? why thus separated from the other furnishings of the inner sanctuary? and not only so, but even after the ordinances relating to the adornment of the priests, and the inauguration of the divine service? The reason why the author of chaps. xxv.-xxix. is thus silent about the altar of incense in the passage in which the furniture of the tabernacle, consisting of ark, table, and candlestick, is described, is, that he does not know of it. There is no other possibility; for he cannot have forgotten it. *1*

*** 1. There is a peculiar perversity in meeting the objection by alleging other singularities in the ordinance as for example, that the vessels of the tabernacle are appointed (chap. xxv.) before the tabernacle itself (chap. xxvi.). This last is no eccentricity; the order in commanding is first the end, and then the means; but in obeying, the order is reversed. In like manner, it is not at all surprising if subsidiary implements, such as benches for slaughtering. or basins for washing, which have no importance for the cultus, properly so called, should be either passed over altogether, or merely brought in as an appendix. The case is not at all parallel with the omission of the most important utensil of the sanctuary from the very passage to which it necessarily belongs. ***

And the phenomenon is repeated; the altar of incense occurs only in certain portions of the Priestly Code, and is absent from others where it could not possibly have been omitted, had it been known. The rite of the most solemn atoning sacrifice takes place in Leviticus iv. indeed on the golden altar, but in Exodus xxix., Leviticus viii., ix., without its use. A still more striking circumstance is, that in passages where the holiest incense-offering itself is spoken of, no trace can be discovered of the corresponding altar. This is particularly the case in Leviticus xvi. To burn incense in the sanctuary, Aaron takes a censer, fills it with coals from the altar of burnt-offering (ver. 12, 18-20), and lays the incense upon them in the adytum. Similarly in Leviticus x., Numbers xvi., xvii., incense is offered on censers, of which each priest possesses one. The coals are taken from the altar of burnt-offering (Numbers xvii. 11; [A.V. xvi. 46]), which is plated with the censers of the Korahite Levites (xvii. 3, 4; [A.V. xvi. 38, 39]); whoever takes fire from any other source, incurs the penalty of death (Leviticus x. 1 seq.). The altar of incense is everywhere unknown here; the altar of burnt-offering is the only altar, and, moreover, is always called simply 'the altar', as for example, even in Exodus xxvii., where it would have been specially necessary to add the qualifying expression. Only in certain later portions of the Priestly Code does the name altar of burnt-offering occur, viz, in those passages which do recognise the altar of incense. In this connection the command of Exodus xxvii. as compared with the execution in Exodus xxxviii. is characteristic.

The golden altar in the sanctuary is originally simply the golden table; the variation of the expression has led to a doubling of the thing. Ezekiel does not distinguish between the table and the altar in the temple, but uses either expression indifferently. For he says (xii.21 seq.): "Before the adytum stood what looked like an altar of wood, three cubits in height, two cubits in length and breadth, and it had projecting corners, and its frame and its walls were of wood; this is the table which is before the Lord." In like manner he designates the service of the priests in the inner sanctuary as table-service (xliv.16); table is the name, altar the function. *1*

** 1. Malachi, on the other hand, designates the so-called altar of burnt-offering as a table. ***

In 1Kings vii. 48, it is true that the golden altar and the golden table are mentioned together. It seems strange, however, that in this case the concluding summary mentions one piece of furniture more— and that piece one of so great importance—- than the preceding detailed description; for in the latter only the preparation of the golden altar is spoken of, and nothing is said of the golden table (vi. 20-22). As matters stand, nothing is less improbable than that some later transcriber should have interpolated the golden table in vii. 48, regarding it, in accordance with the Pentateuch, as distinct from the golden altar, and therefore considering its absence as an omission. From other considerations also, it is clear that the text of the whole chapter is in many ways corrupt and interpolated.

It is not to be wondered at if in the post-exilian temple there existed both a golden altar and a golden table. We learn from 1Maccabees i. 21 seq., iv. 49, that both were carried off by Antiochus Epiphanes, and renewed at the Feast of the Dedication. But it causes no small surprise to find that at the destruction of Jerusalem the Romans found and carried off table and candlestick only. What can have become, in the meantime, of the golden altar of incense? And it is further worth remarking that in the LXX the passage Exodus xxxvii.25-29 is absent; that is to say, the altar of incense is indeed commanded, but there is no word of its execution. In these circumstances, finally, the vacillating statement as to its position in Exodus xxx. 6, and the supposed mistake of the author of the Epistle to the Hebrews, are important and intelligible. Compare also 2Maccabees ii.5, where only the table, but not the altar, is hidden by Jeremiah.

So much for the offering of incense and its altar. We may in like manner venture to regard it as a kind of refinement, though rather a refinement of idea, that the flesh of

74

the sacrifice in the Priestly Code is no longer boiled, but consigned to the altar flames in its raw condition. Such was not the ancient custom, as is seen, not only from the case of Gideon already cited (Judges vi.), but also from the procedure at Shiloh, described in 1Samuel ii., where the sons of Eli will not wait until the flesh of the sacrifice has been boiled, and the altar pieces burnt, but demand their share raw for roasting. The meal which the Deity shares with men is prepared in the same way as for men. This naïve conception gave way before advancing culture, and that at a comparatively early date. It is possible that another cause may also have co-operated towards this result. The old method of preparing flesh in general use among the people, at a later period also, was by boiling. The word B#L (to seethe in water) occurs with extreme frequency; CLH (to roast), on the other hand, only in Exodus xii. 8, and Isaiah xliv. 16, 19. All sacrificial flesh (B#LH) was boiled, and there was no other kind. *1*

** 1. Accordingly one must understand (#H also of boiling (Judges vi. 19). Compare the boiling-houses of the temple still found in Ezekiel xlvi. 20-24. In I Sam. i. 9 pronounce *beshela* instead of *beshilo*, and delete W)XRY #TH.
****

But among persons of the upper class roasting must also have come into use at an early period. "Give flesh to roast for the priest; for he will not take sodden flesh of thee, but raw," says the servant of the sons of Eli in 1Samuel ii. 15. The fact that in the interval the custom of boiling had gone generally somewhat out of fashion may accordingly have also contributed to bring about the abandonment of the old usage of offering the sacrificial portions boiled. In any case this is the explanation of the circumstance that the paschal lamb, which originally was boiled like all other offerings, could, according to the express appointment of the Priestly Code, be eaten roasted only. *2*

*********************************** 2. Compare the polemical ordinance of Exodus xii. 9 with Deuteronomy xvi. 7. **********************************

The phenomenon that in the Law meal is by preference offered raw, while in the earlier period, even as an adjunct of the burnt-offering, it was presented baked, belongs to the same category. The latter is the case in Judges vi. 19 at least, and the statement of 1Samuel i. 24 is also to be understood in the same sense; the sacrificer brings meal along with him in order to bake it into *maccah* on the spot (Ezekiel xlvi. 20). But he may bring along with him common, that is leavened, cakes also (1Samuel x. 3), which seem originally by no means to have been considered unfit to be offered as in Leviticus ii. 11. For under this law of Leviticus ii. even the presentation of the shewbread would be inexplicable, and moreover it is certain that at first the loaves of the feast of weeks were offerings, properly so called, and not merely dues to the priests. According, to Amos iv. 5, leavened bread was made use of precisely at a particularly solemn sacrifice, and a reminiscence of this usage has been preserved even in Leviticus vii. 13, although of course without any practical weight being attached to it. *1*

** 1. The loaves are passed over in silence in Leviticus vii. 29 seq., although it is in this very place that the matter of presenting on the part of the offerer is most fully described. And when it is said (vii. 12), "If he offer it for a thanksgiving (Todah), then he shall offer with it unleavened cakes mingled with oil, and unleavened wafers anointed with oil and fine flour (LXX), mingled with oil ;" vii. 13, "[With] leavened cakes shall he offer as a gift with the thank-offering of the Todah," the suspicion very readily occurs that verse 12 is an authentic interpretation prefixed, to obviate beforehand the difficulty presented by verse 13, and that similarly the first (1 in verse 13 is also a later correction, which does not harmonise well by any means with the second. Verse 13 connects itself better with verse 11 than with verse 12.—Exod xxxiv. 25. **

Moreover, massah also means, properly speaking, only the bread that is prepared in haste and in the most primitive manner for immediate use, and originally implies no contrast with leaven, but simply with the more artificial and tedious manners of producing ordinary bread 2

************************************** 2. Compare Genesis xviii. 6 with xix.3. ***************************************

In the Priestly Code the materials are finer, but they are as much as possible left in their raw condition; both are steps in advance.

II.II.3. There is another and much more important difference in the case of the animal sacrifice. Of this the older practice knows only two kinds apart from extraordinary varieties, which may be left out of account. These two are the burnt-offering (`Olah) and the thank-offering (Shelem, Zebah, Zebah Shelamim). In the case of the first the whole animal is offered on the altar; in the other God receives, besides the blood, only an honorary portion, while the rest of the flesh is eaten by the sacrificial guests. Now it is worth noticing how seldom the burnt-offering occurs alone. It is necessarily so in the case of human sacrifice (Genesis xxii. 2 seq.; Judges xi. 31; 1 2Kings iii. 27; Jeremiah xix.5);

******************************** 3. It is probable that Jephthah expected a human creature and not an animal to meet him from his house. ********************************

otherwise it is not usual (Genesis viii. 20; Numbers xxiii. 1 seq.; Judges vi. 20, 26, xiii. 16, 23; 1Samuel vii. 9 seq.; 1Kings iii. 4, xviii. 34,38); 1 moreover, all the examples

*** 1. In the above list of passages no notice is taken of the *sacrificium juge* of 2Kings xvi.15. The statement in 1Kings iii. 4 is perhaps to be taken along with iii. 15, but does not become at all more credible on that account. Of course it is understood that only those passages are cited here in which mention is made of offerings actually made, and not merely general statements about one or more kinds of offering. The latter could very well fix attention upon the `Olah alone without thereby throwing any light upon the question as to the actual practice. ***

just cited are extraordinary or mythical in their character, a circumstance that may not affect the evidence of the existence of the custom in itself, but is important as regards the statistics of its frequency. As a rule, the `Olah occurs only in conjunction with Zebahim, and when this is the case the latter are in the majority and are always in the plural, while on the other hand the first is frequently in the singular. 2

** 1. Exodus x. 25, xviii. 12, xxiv. 5, xxxii. 6; Joshua viii. 31; Judges xx. 26, xxi. 4; 1Samuel vi. 14 seq., x. 8, xiii. 9-12; 2Samuel vi. 17 seq., xxiv. 23-25, 1Kings iii. 15, viii. 63 seq.; 2Kings v. 17, x. 24, 25. The zeugma in Judges xx. 26, xxi.4 is inconsistent with the older *usus loquendi*. The proper name for the holocaust appears to be KLYL (Deuteronomy xxxiii. 10; 1Samuel vii.9) not (LH. It is impossible to decide whether the sacrificial due in all sorts of Zebah was the same, but most probably it was not. Probably the Shelamim are a more solemn kind of sacrifice than the simple Zebah. The word 'fat' is used in Genesis iv. 4; Exodus xxiii. 18 in a very general sense. It is not quite clear what is meant by the blessing of the Zebah in 1Samuel ix. 13; perhaps a kind of grace before meat. **

They supplement each other like two corresponding halves; the `Olah is, as the name implies, properly speaking, nothing more than the part of a great offering that reaches the altar. One might therefore designate as `Olah also that part of a single animal which is consecrated to the Deity; this, however, is never done; neither of the blood nor of the fat [Q+R] is the verb H(LH used, but only of the pieces of the flesh, of which in the case of the minor offering nothing was burnt. But the distinction is merely one of degree; there is none in kind; a small Zebah, enlarged and augmented, becomes an `Olah and Zebahim; out of a certain number of slaughtered animals which are eaten by the sacrificial company, one is devoted to God and wholly given to the flames. For the rest, it must be borne in mind that as a rule it is only great sacrificial feasts that the historical books take occasion to mention, and that consequently the burnt-offering, notwithstanding what has been said, comes before us with greater prominence than can have been the average case in ordinary life. Customarily, It is certain, none but thank-offerings were offered; necessarily so if slaughtering could only be done beside the altar. Where mention is made of a simple offering in the Books of Samuel and Kings, that it is a thank-offering is matter of course. 1Samuel ii. 12 seq. is in this connection also particularly instructive.

From what has been said it results that according to the praxis of the older period a meal was almost always connected with a sacrifice. It was the rule that only blood and fat were laid upon the altar, but the people ate the flesh; only in the case of very great sacrificial feasts was a large animal (one or more) given to Jehovah. Where a sacrifice took place, there was also eating and drinking (Exodus xxxii. 6; Judges ix. 27; 2Samuel xv. 11 seq.; Amos ii. 7); there was no offering without a meal, and no meal without an offering (1Kings i. 9); at no important Bamah was entertainment wholly wanting, such a LESXH as that in which Samuel feasted Saul, or Jeremiah the Rechabites (1Samuel ix. 22; Jeremiah xxxv. 2). To be merry, to eat and drink before Jehovah, is a usual form of speech down to the period of Deuteronomy; even Ezekiel calls the cultus on the high places an eating upon the mountains (1Samuel ix. 13,19 seq), and in Zechariah the pots in the temple have a special sanctity (Zech. xiv. 20). By means of the meal in presence of Jehovah is established a covenant fellowship on the one hand between Him and the guests, and on the other hand between the guests themselves reciprocally, which is essential for the idea of sacrifice and gives their name to the Shelamim (compare Exodus xviii. 12, xxiv. 11). In ordinary slaughterings this notion is not strongly present, but in solemn sacrifices it was in full vigour. It is God who invites, for the house is His; His also is the gift, which must be brought to Him entire by the offerer before the altar, and the greater portion of which He gives up to His guests only affer that. Thus in a certain sense they eat at God's table, and must accordingly propare or sanctify themselves for it. *1*

** 1. In order to appear before Jehovah the guest adorns himself with clothes and ornaments (Exodus iii. 22, xi. 2 seq.; Hosea ii. 15 [A.V. 13]; Ezekiel xvi. 13; compare Koran, Sur. xx. 61), sanctifies himself (Numbers xi. 18) and is sanctified (1Samuel xvi. 5; Exodus xix. 10, 14). The sacrificial meal is regarded as Kodesh (hallowed) for not only the priests, but all the sanctified persons eat Kodesh (1Samuel xxi. 5 seq. On what is meant by sanctification light is thrown by 1Samuel xxi. 5; 2Samuel xi. 2. Compare L) LPNW XNP YB) (Job xiii. 16; Leviticus vii. 20; Matthew xxii. 11-13). Jehovah invites the armies of the nations to His sacrifice, for which He delivers over to them some other nation, and calls the Medes, to whom He gives Babylon over, His sanctified ones, that is, His guests (Zephaniah i. 7 seq.; Jeremiah xlvi. 10; Ezekiel xxxix 17; Isaiah xiii. 3). **

Even on occasions that, to our way of thinking, seem highly unsuitable, the meal is nevertheless not wanting (Judges xx. 26, xxi. 4; 1Sam xiii. 9-12). That perfect propriety was not always observed might be taken for granted, and is proved by Isaiah xxviii. 8 even with regard to the temple of Jerusalem; "all tables are full of vomit, there is no room." Hence also Eli's suspicion regarding Hannah was a natural one, and by no means so startling as it appears.

How different from this picture is that suggested by the Priestly Code! Here one no longer remarks that a meal accompanies every sacrifice; eating before Jehovah, which even in Deuteronomy is just the expression for sacrificing, nowhere occurs, or at all events is no act of divine worship. Slaying and sacrificing are no longer coincident, the thank-offering of which the breast and right shoulder are to be consecrated is something different from the old simple Zebah. But, precisely for this reason, it has lost its former broad significance. The *mizbeah*, that is, the place where the *zebahim* are to be offered, has been transformed into a *mizbah ha-'olah*. The burnt-offering has become quite independent and comes everywhere into the foreground, the sacrifices which are unconnected with a meal altogether predominate,—so much that, as is well known, Theophrastus could declare there were no others among the Jews, who in this way were differentiated from all other nations. *1* Where formerly a

*** 1. Porphyry, De Abstin. ii.26. Compare Joseph., Contra Apion, ii. 13:)OUTOI)EUXONTAI <?> UEIN (EKATOMBAS TOIS QEOIS KAI XRWNTAI TOIS (IEREIOIS PROS)EUWXIAN. ***

thank-offering which was eaten before Jehovah, and which might with greater clearness be called a sacrificial meal, was prescribed, the Priestly Code, as we shall afterwards see, has made out of it simple dues to the priests, as, for example, in the case of the first-born and of firstlings. Only in this point it still bears involuntary testimony to the old custom by applying the names *Todah, Neder, and Nedabah*, of which the last two in particular must necessarily have a quite general meaning (Leviticus xxii. 18; Ezekiel xlvi. 12), exclusively to the thank-offering, while *Milluim* and paschal sacrifice are merely subordinate varieties of it.

II.II.4. What the thank-offering has lost, the sin and trespass offering have gained; the voluntary private offering which the sacrificer ate in a joyful company at the holy place has given way before the compulsory, of which he obtains no share, and from which the character of the sacred meal has been altogether taken away. The burnt-offering, it is true, still continues to be a meal, if only a one-sided one, of which God alone partakes; but in the case of the sin-offering everything is kept far out of sight which could recall a meal, as, for example, the accompaniments of meal and wine, oil and salt; of the flesh no portion reaches the altar, it all goes as a fine to the priest. Now, of this kind of sacrifice, which has an enormous importance in the Priestly Code, not a single trace occurs in the rest of the Old Testament before Ezekiel, neither in the Jehovist and Deuteronomist, nor in the historical and prophetical books. *1*

*** 1. How great is the difference in Deuteronomy xxi. 1-9; how very remote the sacrificial idea! ***

`Olah and Zebah comprehend all animal sacrifices, `Olah and Minhah, or Zebah and Minhah, all sacrifices whatsoever; nowhere is a special kind of sacrifice for atonement met with (1Samuel iii. 14). Hos. iv. 8 does indeed say: "They eat the sin of my people, and they are greedy for its guilts," but the interpretation which will have it that the priests are here reproached with in the first instance themselves inducing the people to falsification of the sacred dues, in order to make these up again with the produce of the sin and trespass offerings, is either too subtle or too dull. *2*

*** 2. The sin and guilt are the sacrificial worship generally as carried on by the people (viii. 11; Amos iv. 4); in the entire section the prophet is preparing the way for the here sharply accentuated reproach against the priests that they neglect the Torah and encourage the popular

propensity to superstitious and impure religious service. Besides, where is there any reproach at all, according to the Pentateuch, in the first section of iv. 8? And the second speaks of (WNM, not of)#MM.
****

It would be less unreasonable to co-ordinate with the similarly named sin and trespass offering of the Pentateuch the five golden mice, and the five golden emerods with which the Philistines send back the ark, and which in 1Samuel vi. 3, 4, 8 are designated *asham*, or, still better, the sin and trespass monies which, according to 2Kings xii. 17 [A.V. 16], fell to the share of the Jerusalem priests. Only the fact is that even in the second passage the *asham* and *hattath* are no sacrifices, but, more exactly to render the original meaning of the words, mere fines, and in fact money fines. On the other hand, the *hattath* referred to in Micah vi. 7 has nothing to do with a due of the priests, but simply denotes the guilt which eventually another takes upon himself. Even in Isaiah liii. 10, a passage which is certainly late, *asham* must not be taken in the technical sense of the ritual legislation, but simply (as in Micah) in the sense of guilt, borne by the innocent for the guilty. For the explanation of this prophetic passage Gramberg has rightly had recourse to the narrative of 2Samuel xi. 1-14. "Upon Saul and upon his house lies blood-guiltiness, for having slain the Gibeonites" is announced to David as the cause of a three years' famine. When asked how it can be taken away, the Gibeonites answer, "It is not a matter of silver and gold to us with respect to Saul and his house; let seven men of his family be delivered to us that we may hang them up unto the Lord in Gibeah of Saul upon the mountain of the Lord." This was done; all the seven were hanged.

A*sham and *hattath* as offerings occur for the first time in Ezekiel, and appear, not long before his day to have come into the place of the earlier pecuniary fines (2Kings xii. 17 [16]), which perhaps already also admitted of being paid in kind; probably in the seventh century, which seems to have been very open to the mystery of atonement and bloodshedding, and very fertile in the introduction of new religious usages. *1*

** 1. Consider for example the prevalence of child sacrifice precisely at this time, the introduction of incense, the new fashions which King Manasseh brought in, and of which certainly much survived that suited the temper of the period, and admitted of being conjoined with the worship of Jehovah, or even seemed to enhance its dignity and solemnity.
****

The sin and trespass offerings of the Pentateuch still bear traces of their origin in fines and penalties; they are not gifts to God, they are not even symbolical, they are simply mulcts payable to the priests, partly of fixed commutation value (Leviticus v. 15). Apart from the mechanical burning of the fat they have in common with the sacrifice only the shedding of blood, originally a secondary matter, which has here become the chief thing. This circumstance is an additional proof of our thesis. The ritual of the simple offering has three acts: (1.) the presentation of the living animal before Jehovah, and the laying on of hands as a token of manumission on the part of

80

the offerer; (2.) the slaughtering and the sprinkling of the blood on the altar; (3.) the real or seeming gift of the sacrificial portions to the Deity, and the meal of the human guests. In the case of the burnt-offering the meal in the third act disappears, and the slaughtering in the second comes into prominence as significant and sacred, inasmuch as (what is always expressly stated) it must take place in the presence of Jehovah, at the north side of the altar. In the case of the sin and trespass offering the third act is dropped entirely, and accordingly the whole significance of the rite attaches to the slaughtering, which of course also takes place before the altar, and to the sprinkling of the blood, which has become peculiarly developed here. It is obvious how the metamorphosis of the gift and the meal into a bloody atonement advances and reaches its acme in this last sacrificial act.

This ritual seems to betray its novelty even within the Priestly Code itself by a certain vacillation. In the older corpus of law (Leviticus xvii.-xxvi.) which has been taken into that document, all sacrifices are still embraced under one or other of the two heads ZBX and (LH (xvii. 8, xxii. 18, 21); there are no others. The *asham* indeed occurs in xix. 21 seq., but, as is recognised, only in a later addition; on the other hand,it is not demanded *1* in xxii.14,

*********************************** 1. Perhaps it would be more accurate to say that the *asham* here, in the case of property unlawfully held, is simply the impost of a fifth part of the value, and not the sacrifice of a ram, which in Leviticus v. is required in addition. In Numbers v. also, precisely this fifth part is called *asham.* ***************************************

where it must have been according to Leviticus v. and Numbers v. And even apart from Leviticus xvii.-xxvi there is on this point no sort of agreement between the kernel of the Priestly Code and the later additions, or "novels," so to speak. For one thing, there is a difference as to the ritual of the most solemn sin-offering between Exodus xxix., Leviticus ix. on the one hand, and Leviticus iv. on the other; and what is still more serious, the trespass-offering never occurs in the primary but only in the secondary passages, Leviticus iv.-vii., xiv.; Numbers v.7, 8, vi. 1, xviii. 9. In the latter, moreover, the distinction between *asham* and *hattath* is not very clear, but only the intention to make it, perhaps because in the old praxis there actually was a distinction between KSP XT)WT and KSP)#M, and in Ezekiel between X+)T and)#M. *2*

*************************************** 2. The three sections, Leviticus iv. 1-35 (hattath), v.1-13 (hattath-asham), and v. 14-26 (asham), are essentially not co-ordinate parts of one whole, but independent pieces proceeding from the same school. For v. 1-13 is no continuation of or appendix to iv. 27-35, but a quite independent treatment of the same material, with important differences of form. The place of the systematic generality of chap. iv. is here taken by the definite individual case, and what is analogous to it; the ritual is given with less minuteness, and the hierarchical subordination of ranks has no influence on the classification of offences. In this section also *asham* and *hattath* occur interchangeably as synonymous. In the third section a ram as an *asham* is prescribed (v. 17-19) for the very case in which in the first a he-goat or a she-goat is required as *hattath* (iv. 22, 27). The third section has indeed in form greater similarity to the second, but cannot be regarded as its true completion, for this simple reason, that the latter does not distiguish between *hattath* and *asham*. If Leviticus v. 13-16, 20-26 be followed simply without regard being had to vers. 17-19, the *asham* comes in only in the case of voluntary restitution of property illegally come by or detained, more particularly of the sacred dues. The goods must be restored to their owner augmented by a fifth part of their value; and as an *asham* there must be added a ram, which falls to the sanctuary. In Num v. 5-10 the state of the case is indeed the same, but the language employed is different, for in this passage it is the restored property that is called *asham*, and the ram is called)YL HKPRYM. Comp. Leviticus xxii. 14.

****

II.III.

The turning-point in the history of the sacrificial system was the reformation of Josiah; what we find in the Priestly Code is the matured result of that event. It is precisely in the distinctions that are characteristic of the sacrificial law as compared with the ancient sacrificial praxis that we have evidence of the fact that, if not all exactly occasioned by the centralisation of the worship, they were almost all somehow at least connected with that change.

In the early days, worship arose out of the midst of ordinary life, and was in most intimate and manifold connection with it. A sacrifice was a meal, a fact showing how remote was the idea of antithesis between spiritual earnestness and secular joyousness. A meal unites a definite circle of guests, and in this way the sacrifice brought into connection the members of the family, the associates of the corporation, the soldiers of the army, and, generally speaking, the constituents of any permanent or temporary society. It is earthly relationships that receive their consecration thereby, and in correspondence are the natural festal occasions presented by the vicissitudes of life. Year after year the return of vintage, corn-harvest, and sheep-shearing brought together the members of the household to eat and to drink in the presence of Jehovah; and besides these there were less regularly recurring events which were celebrated in one circle after another. There was no warlike expedition which was not inaugurated in this fashion, no agreement that was not thus ratified, no important undertaking of any kind was gone about without a sacrifice! *1*

*** 1. Sacrifice is used as a pretext in 1Samuel xvi. 1 seq.; 1Kings i. 9 seq. Compare Proverbs vii. 14. ***

When an honoured guest arrives, there is slaughtered for him a calf, not without an offering of the blood and fat to the Deity. The occasion arising out of daily life is thus inseparable from the holy action, and is what gives it meaning and character; an end corresponding to the situation always underlies it. Hence also prayer must not be wanting. The verb H(TYR, to "burn" (fat and *minha*), means simply to "pray," and conversely BQ#)T YHWH, "to seek Jehovah," in point of fact not unfrequently means to "sacrifice." The gift serves to reinforce the question or the request, and to express thankfulness; and the prayer is its interpretation. This of course is rather incidentally indicated than expressly said (Hos. v. 6; Isaiah i. 15; Jeremiah xiv. 12; 1Kings viii. 27 seq.; Proverbs xv. 8); we have a specimen of a grace for the offering of the festival gift only in Deuteronomy xxvi. 3 seq.; a blessing is pronounced when the slaughtering takes place (1Samuel ix. 13). The prayer of course is simply the expression of the feeling of the occasion, with which accordingly it varies in manifold ways. Arising out of the exigencies and directed to the objects of daily life, the sacrifices reflect in themselves a correspondingly rich variety. Our wedding, baptismal, and funeral feasts on the one hand, and our banquets for all sorts of occasions on the other, might still be adduced as the most obvious comparison, were it not that here too the divorce between sacred and secular destroys it. Religious

83

worship was a natural thing in Hebrew antiquity; it was the blossom of life, the heights and depths of which it was its business to transfigure and glorify.

The law which abolished all sacrificial seats, with a single exception, severed this connection. Deuteronomy indeed does not contemplate such a result. Here, in marked opposition to what we find in the Priestly Code, to eat and be merry before Jehovah is the standing phrase for sacrificing; the idea is that in concentrating all the worship towards Jerusalem, all that is effected is a mere change of place, the essence of the thing remaining unaltered. This, however, was a mistake. To celebrate the vintage festival among one's native hills, and to celebrate it at Jerusalem, were two very different things; it was not a matter of indifference whether one could seize on the spot any occasion that casually offered itself for a sacrificial meal, or whether it was necessary that one should first enter upon a journey. And it was not the same thing to appear by oneself at home before Jehovah and to lose oneself in a large congregation at the common seat of worship. Human life has its root in local environment, and so also had the ancient cultus; in being transplanted from its natural soil it was deprived of its natural nourishment. A separation between it and the daily life was inevitable, and Deuteronomy itself paved the way for this result by permitting profane slaughtering. A man lived in Hebron, but sacrificed in Jerusalem; life and worship fell apart. The consequences which lie dormant in the Deuteronomic law are fully developed in the Priestly Code.

This is the reason why the sacrifice combined with a meal, formerly by far the chief, now falls completely into the background. One could eat flesh at home, but in Jerusalem one's business was to do worship. Accordingly, those sacrifices were preferred in which the religious character came to the front with the utmost possible purity and without any admixture of natural elements, sacrifices of which God received everything and man nothing,—burnt-offerings, sin-offerings, and trespass-offerings.

If formerly the sacrifice had taken its complexion from the quality of the occasion which led to it, it now had essentially but one uniform purpose—to be a medium of worship. The warm pulse of life no longer throbbed in it to animate it; it was no longer the blossom and the fruit of every branch of life; it had its own meaning all to itself. It symbolised worship, and that was enough. The soul was fled; the shell remained, upon the shaping out of which every energy was now concentrated. A manifoldness of rites took the place of individualising occasions; technique was the main thing, and strict fidelity to rubric.

Once cultus was spontaneous, now it is a thing of statute. The satisfaction which it affords is, properly speaking, something which lies outside of itself and consists in the moral satisfaction arising out of the conscientiousness with which the ritual precepts, once for all enjoined by God on His people, are fulfilled. The freewill offering is not indeed forbidden, but value in the strict sense is attached only to those which have been prescribed, and which accordingly preponderate everywhere. And even in the case of the freewill offering, everything must strictly and accurately comply with the restrictions of the ordinance; if any one in the fulness of his heart had offered in a *zebah shelamim* more pieces of flesh than the ritual enjoined, it would have been the worse for him.

Of old the sacrifice combined with a meal had established a special relation between the Deity and a definite society of guests; the natural sacrificial society was the family or the clan (1Samuel i. 1seq., xvi. 1 seq., xx. 6). Now the smaller sacred fellowships get lost, the varied groups of social life disappear in the neutral shadow of the universal congregation or church [(DH, QHL]. The notion of this last is foreign to Hebrew antiquity, but runs through the Priestly Code from beginning to end. Like the worship itself, its subject also became abstract, a spiritual entity which could be kept together by no other means except worship. As now the participation of the "congregation of the children of Israel" in the sacrifice was of necessity always mainly ideal, the consequence was that the sacred action came to be regarded as essentially perfect by virtue of its own efficacy in being performed by the priest, even though no one was present. Hence later the necessity for a special sacrificial deputation, the *anshe ma'amad*. The connection of all this with the Judaising tendency to remove God to a distance from man, it may be added, is clear. *1*

*************************************** 1. It is not asserted that the cultus before the Iaw (of which the darker sides are known from Amos and Hosea) was better than the legal, but merely that it was more original; the standard of judgment being, not the moral element, but merely the idea, the primary meaning of worship. Nor is it disputed further that the belief in the dependence of sacrifices and other sacred acts upon a laboriously strict compliance with traditional and prescriptive rites occurs in the case of certain peoples, even in the remotest antiquity. But with the Israelites, judging by the testimony of the historical and prophetical books, this was not on the whole the case any more than with the ancient Greeks; there were no Brahmans or Magians in either case. Moreover, it must be carefully noted that not even in the Priestly Code do we yet find the same childish appreciation of the cultus as occurs in such a work as the Rigveda, and that the strict rules are not prescribed and maintained with any such notion in view as that by their observance alone can the taste of the Deity be pleased; the idea of God is here even strikingly remote from the anthropomorphic, and the whole cultus is nothing more than an exercise in piety which has simply been enjoined so once for all without any one being in any way the better for it. ***

Two details still deserve special prominence here. In the Priestly Code the most important sacrifice is the burnt-offering; that is to say, in point of fact, the *tamid*, the *holocaustum juge*, consisting of two yearling lambs which are daily consumed upon the "altar of burnt-offering," one in the morning, another in the evening. The custom of daily offering a fixed sacrifice at a definite time existed indeed, in a simpler form, *2*

************************************** 2. See Kuenen, Godsdietzst van Israel, ii. 271. According to 2Kings xvi. 15, an (LH in the morning and a MNXH in the evening were daily offered in the temple of Jerusalem, in the time of Ahaz. Ezekiel also (xlvi. 13-15) speaks only of the morning (LH. Compare also Ezra ix. 4;

Nehemiah x. 33. In the Priestly Code the evening *minhah* has risen to the dignity of a second _`olah_; but at the same time survives in the daily *minhah* of the high priest, and is now offered in the morning also (Leviticus vi. 12-16). The daily *minhah* appears to be older than the daily _`olah_. For while it was a natural thing to prepare a meal regularly for the Deity, the expense of a daily `olah was too great for an ordinary place of worship, and, besides, it was not in accordance with the custom of men to eat flesh every day. The offering of the daily *minhah* is already employed in 1Kings xviii. 29, 36, as a mark of time to denote the afternoon, and this use is continued down to the latest period, while the tamid, *ie.*, the `olah, is never so utilised. The oddest custom of all, however, was doubtless not the daily *minhah*, but the offering of the shewbread, which served the same purpose, but was not laid out fresh every day. **

even in the pre-exilian period, but alongside of it at that time, the freewill private offerings had a much more important place, and bulked much more largely. In the law the *tamid* is in point of fact the fundamental element of the worship, for even the sacrifices of Sabbaths and feast days consist only of its numerical increase (compare Numbers xxviii., xxix.). Still later, when it is said in the Book of Daniel that the *tamid* was done away, this is equivalent to saying that the worship was abolished (viii. 11-13, xi. 31, xii. 11). But now the dominant position of the daily, Sabbath day, and festival *tamid* means that the sacrificial worship had assumed a perfectly firm shape, which was independent of every special motive and of all spontaneity; and further (what is closely connected with this), that it took place for the sake of the congregation,—the "congregation" in the technical sense attached to that word in the Law. Hence the necessity for the general temple-tax, the prototype of which is found in the poll-tax of half a shekel for the service of the tabernacle in Exodus xxx. 11 seq. Prior to the exile, the regular sacrifice was paid for by the Kings of Judah, and in Ezekiel the monarch still continues to defray the expenses not only of the Sabbath day and festival sacrifices (xiv. 17 seq.), but also of the *tamid* (xlvi. 13-15). *1*

*************************************** 1. Compare LXX*. The Massoretic text has corrected the third person (referring to the princes) into the second, making it an address to the priests, which, however, is quite impossible in Ezekiel. ***********************************

It is also a mark of the date that, according to Exodus xxx., the expenses of the temple worship are met directly out of the poll-tax levied from the community, which can only be explained by the fact that at that time there had ceased to be any sovereign. So completely was the sacrifice the affair of the community in Judaism that the voluntary *qorban* of the individual became metamorphosed into a money payment as a contribution to the cost of the public worship (Mark vii., xii. 42 seq; Matthew xxvii. 6).

The second point is this: Just as the special purposes and occasions of sacrifice fall out of sight, there comes into increasing prominence the one uniform and universal occasion—that of sin; and one uniform and universal purpose—that of propitiation. In the Priestly Code the peculiar mystery in the case of all animal sacrifices is atonement by blood; this appears in its purest development in the case of the sin and trespass offerings, which are offered as well for individuals as for the congregation and for its head. In a certain sense the great day of atonement is the culmination of the whole religious and sacrificial service, to which, amid all diversities of ritual, continuously underlying reference to sin is common throughout. Of this feature the ancient sacrifices present few traces. It was indeed sought at a very early period to influence the doubtful or threatening mood of Deity, and make His countenance gracious by means of rich gifts, but the gift had, as was natural then, the character of a tentative effort only (Micah vi. 6). There was no such thought as that a definite guilt must and could be taken away by means of a prescribed offering. When the law discriminates between such sins as are covered by an offering and such sins as relentlessly are visited with wrath, it makes a distinction very remote from the antique; to Hebrew antiquity the wrath of God was something quite incalculable, its causes were never known, much less was it possible to enumerate beforehand those sins which kindled it and those which did not. *1*

********************************* 1. When the wrath is regulated by the conditions of the "covenant," the original notion (which scorns the thought of adjustment) is completely changed. What gave the thing its mysterious awfulness was precisely this: that in no way was it possible to guard against it, and that nothing could avail to counteract it. Under the pressure of Jehovah's wrath not only was sacrifice abandoned, but even the mention of His name was shunned so as to avoid attracting His attention (Hos iii. 4, ix. 4; Amos vi. 10). **********************************

An underlying reference of sacrifice to sin, speaking generally, was entirely absent. The ancient offerings were wholly of a joyous nature,—a merrymaking before Jehovah with music and song, timbrels, flutes, and stringed instruments (Hos. ix. 1 seq.; Amos v. 23, viii. 3; Isa xxx. 3). No greater contrast could be conceived than the monotonous seriousness of the so-called Mosaic worship.

NOMOS *de* PAREISHLQEN (INA PLEONASH| TO PARAPTWMA ["But law came in, with the result that the trespass multiplied". Romans 5:20 NRSV)]

In this way the spiritualisation of the worship is seen in the Priestly Code as advancing *pari passu* with its centralisation. It receives, so to speak, an abstract religious character; it separates itself in the first instance from daily life, and then absorbs the latter by becoming, strictly speaking, its proper business. The consequences for the future were momentous. The Mosaic "congregation" is the mother of the Christian church; the Jews were the creators of that idea.

We may compare the cultus in the olden time to the green tree which grows up out of the soil as it will and can; later it becomes the regularly shapen timber, ever more artificially shaped with square and compass. Obviously there is a close connection between the qualitative antithesis we have just been expounding and the formal one of law and custom from which we set out. Between "naturaliter ea quae legis sunt facere" ["do instinctively what the law requires" Romans 2:14 NRSV] and "secundum legem agere" there is indeed a more than external difference. If at the end of our first section we found improbable precisely in this region the independent co-existence of ancient praxis and Mosaic law, the improbability becomes still greater from the fact that the latter is filled with a quite different spirit, which can be apprehended only as Spirit of the age (Zeitgeist). It is not from the atmosphere of the old kingdom, but from that of the church of the second temple, that the Priestly Code draws its breath. It is in accordance with this that the sacrificial ordinances as regards their positive contents are no less completely ignored by antiquity than they are scrupulously followed by the post-exilian time.

CHAPTER III. THE SACRED FEASTS.

The feasts, strictly speaking, belong to the preceding chapter, for originally they were simply regularly recurring occasions for sacrifice. The results of the investigation there made accordingly repeat themselves here, but with such clearness and precision as make it worth while to give the subject a separate consideration. In the first place and chiefly, the history of the solar festivals, that of those festivals which follow the seasons of the year, claims our attention.

III.I.1 In the Jehovistic and Deuteronomistic parts of the Pentateuch there predominates a rotation of three great festivals, which alone receive the proper designation of *hag*: "Three times in the year shalt thou keep festival unto me, three times in the year shall all thy men appear before the Lord Jehovah, the God of Israel" (Exodus xxiii. 14, 17, xxxiv. 23; Deuteronomy xvi. 16). "The feast of unleavened bread (maccoth) shalt thou keep; seven days shalt thou eat *maccoth* as I commanded thee, in the time appointed of the month Abib, for in it thou camest out from Egypt; and none shall appear before me empty; and the feast of harvest (qasir), the first-fruits of thy labours, which thou hast sown in the field; and the feast of ingathering (asiph), in the end of the year, when thou gatherest in thy labours out of the field."
So runs the command in the Book of the Covenant (Exodus xxiii. 15, 16). The Law of the Two Tables (Exodus xxxiv. 18 seq.) is similar: "The feast of unleavened bread shalt thou keep. Seven days shalt thou eat unleavened bread, as I commanded thee, in the time of the month Abib: for in the month Abib thou camest out of Egypt. All that openeth the womb is mine; every firstling among thy cattle, whether ox or sheep, that is male. The firstling of an ass thou shalt redeem with a lamb: and if thou redeem him not, then shalt thou break his neck. All the firstborn of thy sons shalt thou redeem. And none shall appear before me empty. Six days shalt thou work; but on the seventh day shalt thou rest: even in ploughing time and in harvest shalt thou rest. And the feast of weeks (shabuoth) shalt thou observe, the feasts of the first-fruits of wheat harvest, and the feast of ingathering (asiph) at the change of the year." Minuter, on the other hand, and of a somewhat different character, are the precepts laid down in Deuteronomy xvi.: "Take heed to the month Abib, and keep the passover unto Jehovah thy God, for in the month Abib did Jehovah thy God bring thee forth out of Egypt by night. Thou shalt therefore sacrifice the passover unto Jehovah thy God, of the flock or of the herd, in the place which Jehovah shall choose for the habitation of His name. Thou shalt eat no leavened bread with it; seven days shalt thou eat unleavened bread (maccoth) therewith, the bread of affliction, for thou camest forth out of the land of Egypt in anxious haste, that all the days of thy life thou mayest remember the day when thou camest forth out of the land of Egypt. There shall no leavened bread be seen with thee in all thy border seven days, and of the flesh which thou didst sacrifice on the first day, in the evening, nothing shall remain all night until the morning. Thou mayest not sacrifice the passover within any of thy gates which the Lord thy God giveth thee, but at the place which Jehovah thy God shall choose for the habitation of His name, there shalt thou sacrifice the passover, in the evening, at the going down of the sun, at the time of thy coming forth out of Egypt. And thou shalt boil and eat it in the place which the Lord thy God shall choose, and in the morning shalt thou return to thy home. Six days shalt

thou eat *maccoth*, and on the seventh day shall be the closing feast to Jehovah thy God; thou shalt do no work therein" (ver. 1-8). "Seven weeks thenceforward shalt thou number unto thee; from such time as thou beginnest to put the sickle to the corn shalt thou begin to number seven weeks, and then thou shalt keep the feast of weeks (shabuoth) to Jehovah thy God, with a tribute of freewill offerings in thy hand, which thou shalt give, according as the Lord thy God hath blessed thee. And thou shalt rejoice before Jehovah thy God, thou, and thy son, and thy daughter, and thy man-servant, and thy maid-senant, and the Levite that is within thy gates, and the stranger, and the fatherless, and the widow that are among you in the place which Jehovah thy God shall choose for the habitation of His name. And thou shalt remember that thou wast a bondman in Egypt, and thou shalt observe and do these statutes" (ver. 9-12). "The feast of tabernacles (sukkoth) thou shalt observe seven days after thou hast gathered in thy corn and thy wine; and thou shalt rejoice in thy feast,—thou, and thy son, and thy daughter, and thy man-servant, and thy maid-servant, and the Levite, and the stranger, and the fatherless, and the widow that are within thy gates. Seven days shalt thou keep a solemn feast unto Jehovah thy God in the place which Jehovah shall choose, because Jehovah thy God cloth bless thee in all thine increase, and in all the works of thy hands, therefore thou shalt surely rejoice. Three times in a year shall all thy men appear before Jehovah thy God in the place which He shall choose: in the feast of unleavened bread, of weeks, and of tabernacles (hag ha-maccoth,— shabuoth,—sukkoth), and they shall not appear before me empty; every man shall give as he is able, according to the blessing of Jehovah thy God, which He hath given thee" (ver. 13-17). As regards the essential nature of the two last-named feasts, these passages are at one. The *sukkoth* of Deuteronomy and the *asiph* of the Jehovistic legislation do not coincide in time merely, but are in fact one and the same feast, the autumnal ingathering of the wine and of the oil from the vat and press, and of the corn from the threshing-floor. The name *asiph* refers immediately to the vintage and olive-gathering, to which the word *sukkoth* seems also to relate, being most easily explained from the custom of the whole household, old and young, going out to the vineyard in time of harvest, and there camping out in the open air under the improvised shelter of booths made with branches (Isaiah i. 8). *Qacir* and *shabuoth* in like manner are only different names for the same reality, namely, for the feast of the corn-reaping, or, more strictly, the wheat-reaping, which takes place in the beginning of summer. Thus both festivals have a purely natural occasion. On the other hand, the spring festival, which always opens the series, has a historical motive assigned to it, the exodus—most expressly in Deuteronomy—being given as the event on which it rests. The cycle nevertheless seems to presuppose and to require the original homogeneity of all its members. Now the twofold ritual of the *pesah* and the maccoth points to a twofold character of the feast. The *hag*, properly so named, is called not *hag ha-pesah*, 1 but hag ha-maccoth,

***************************** 1. The original form of the expression of Exodus xxxiv. 25 has been preserved in Exodus xxiii. 18 (XGGY not XG HPSX). In Deuteronomy, although PSX is more prominent, it is called XG HMCWT in xvi. 16.
****

and it is only the latter that is co-ordinated with the other two *haggim*; the name *pesah* indeed does not occur at all until Deuteronomy, although in the law of the two tables the sacrifice of the first-born seems to be brought into connection with the feast of unleavened bread. It follows that only the *maccoth* can be taken into account for purposes of comparison with *qasir* and *asiph*. As to the proper significance of *maccoth*, the Jehovistic legislation does not find it needful to instruct its contemporaries, but it is incidentally disclosed in Deuteronomy. There the festival of harvest is brought into a definite relation in point of time with that of *maccoth*; it is to be celebrated seven weeks later. This is no new ordinance, but one that rests upon old custom, for the name, "feast of weeks," occurs in a passage so early as Exodus xxxiv. (comp Jeremiah v. 24). Now "seven weeks after Easter " (Deuteronomy xvi. 9) is further explained with greater elaborateness as meaning seven weeks after the putting of the sickle to the corn. Thus the festival of *maccoth* is equivalent to that of the putting of the sickle to the corn, and thereby light is thrown on its fixed relation to Pentecost. Pentecost celebrates the close of the reaping, which commences with barley harvest, and ends with that of wheat; Easter its beginning in the "month of corn ears;" and between the two extends the duration of harvest time, computed at seven weeks. The whole of this *tempus classicum* is a great festal season rounded off by the two festivals. We gain further light from Leviticus xxiii. 9-22. *1*

*** 1. Against this there is of course possible the objection that the passage at present forms part of the Priestly Code. But the collection of laws embraced in Leviticus xvii.-xxvi, it is well known, has merely been redacted and incorporated by the author of the Priestly Code, and originally was an independent corpus marking the transition from Deuteronomy to the Priestly Code, sometimes approximating more to the one, and at other times to the other, and the use of Leviticus xxiii. 9-22 in this connection is completely justified by the consideration that only in this way do the rites it describes find meaning and vitality. ***

The Easter point is here, as in Deuteronomy, fixed as being the beginning of harvest, but is still more definitely determined as the day after the first Sabbath falling within harvest time, and Pentecost follows the same reckoning. And the special Easter ritual consists in the offering of a barley sheaf; before this it is not lawful to taste of the new crop; and the corresponding Pentecostal rite is the offering of ordinary wheaten loaves. The corn harvest begins with barley and ends with wheat; at the beginning the first-fruits are presented in their crude state as a sheaf, just as men in like manner partake of the new growth in the form of parched ears (Leviticus xxiii. 14; Josh. v. 11); at the end they are prepared in the form of common bread. Thus the *maccoth* now begin to be intelligible. As has been already said (see p. 69), they are not, strictly speaking, duly prepared loaves, but the bread that is hurriedly baked to meet a pressing emergency (1Sam. xxviii. 24); thus they are quite correctly associated with the haste of the exodus, and described as bread of affliction. At first people do not take time in a leisurely way to leaven, knead, and bake the year's new bread, but a hasty cake is prepared in the ashes; this is what is meant by maccoth. They are contrasted with the Pentecostal loaves precisely as are the sheaf and the parched ears, which last, according to Josh. v. 11, may be eaten in their stead, and without a doubt they were originally not the Easter food of men merely, but also of the Deity, so that the sheaf comes under the category of the later spiritual refinements of sacrificial material. Easter then is the opening, as Pentecost is the closing festivity, or (what means the same thing) `acereth, *1* of the seven

*** 1. Haneberg, Alterhuemer, 2d edit., p. 656. In Deuteronomy Pentecost as _`acereth_ lasts for only one day, while Easter and the feast of tabernacles each]ast a week.
****

weeks' "joy of harvest," and the spring festival no longer puzzles us by the place it holds in the cycle of the three yearly festivities. But what is the state of the case as regards the *pesah*? The meaning of the name is not clear; as we have seen, the word first occurs in Deuteronomy, and there also the time of the celebration is restricted to the evening and night of the first day of *maccoth*, from sunset until the following morning. In point of fact, the *pesah* points back to the sacrifice of the firstlings (Exodus xxxiv. 18 seq., xiii. 12 seq.; Deuteronomy xv. 19 seq., xvi. 1 seq.), and it is principally upon this that the historical character of the whole festivity hinges. It is because Jehovah smote the first-born of Egypt and spared those of Israel that the latter thenceforward are held sacred to Him. Such is the representation given not merely in the Priestly Code but also in Exodus xiii. 11 seq. But in neither of its sources does the Jehovistic tradition know anything of this. "Let my people go, that they may keep a feast unto me in the wilderness with sacrifices and cattle and sheep: "this from the first is the demand made upon Pharaoh, and it is in order to be suitably adorned for this purpose, contemplated by them from the first, that the departing Israelites borrow festal robes and ornaments from the Egyptians. Because Pharaoh refuses to allow the Hebrews to offer to their God the firstlings of cattle that are His due, Jehovah seizes from him the first-born of men. Thus the exodus is not the occasion of the festival, but the festival the occasion, if only a pretended one, of the exodus. If this relationship is inverted in Exodus xiii, it is because that passage is not one of the sources of the Jehovistic tradition, but is part of the redaction, and in fact (as is plain from other reasons with regard to the entire section xiii. 1-16) of a Deuteronomic redaction. From this it follows that the elaboration of the historical motive of the passover is not earlier than Deuteronomy, although perhaps a certain inclination to that way of explaining it appears before then, just as in the case of the *maccoth* (Exodus xii. 34). What has led to it is evidently the coincidence of the spring festival with the exodus, already accepted by the older tradition, the relation of cause and effect having become inverted in course of time. The only view sanctioned by the nature of the case is that the Israelite custom of offering the firstlings gave rise to the narrative of the slaying of the first-born of Egypt; unless the custom be pre-supposed the story is inexplicable, and the peculiar selection of its victims by the plague is left without a motive. The sacrifice of the first-born, of the male first-born, that is to say—for the females were reared as with us—does not require an historical explanation, but can be accounted for very simply: it is the expression of thankfulness to the Deity for fruitful flocks and herds. If claim is also laid to the human first-born, this is merely a later generalisation which after all resolves itself merely into a substitution of an animal offering and an extension of the original sacrifice. In Exodus xx. 28, 29 and xxxiv. 19 this consequence does not yet seem to be deduced or even to be suspected as possible; it first appears in xxxiv. 20 and presents itself most distinctly in the latest passage (xiii. 12), for there P+R

92

RXM is contrasted with P+R #GR, and for the first the expression H(BYR, a technical one in the time of Jeremiah and Ezekiel for child sacrifice, is used. The view of some scholars (most of them mere casual visitors in the field of Old Testament research) that the slaying of the first-born male children was originally precisely the main feature of the passover, hardly deserves refutation. Like the other festivals, this also, apart from the view taken of it in the Priestly Code, has a thoroughly joyous character (Exodus x. 9); Deuteronomy xvi. 7; comp. Isaiah xxx. 29). There are some historical instances indeed of the surrender of an only child or of the dearest one, but always as a voluntary and quite exceptional act; the contrary is not proved by Hosea xiii. 2. *1* The offering of

*** 1. "They make them molten images of their silver, idols according to their fancy. To them they speak, men doing sacrifice kiss calves!" The prophet would hardly blame human sacrifices only thus incidentally, more in ridicule than in high moral indignation; he would bring it to prominence the horrible and revolting character of the action much more than its absurdity. Thus ZBXY)DM means most probably, "offerers belonging to the human race." At the same time, even if the expression did mean "sacrificers of men," it would prove nothing regarding regular sacrifices of children. ***

human first-born was certainly no regular or commanded exaction in ancient times; there are no traces of so enormous a blood tax, but, on the contrary, many of a great preference for eldest sons. It was not until shortly before the exile that the burning of children was introduced on a grand scale along with many other innovations, and supported by a strict interpretation of the command regarding firstlings (Jeremiah vii. 31, xix. 5; Ezekiel xx. 26). In harmony with this is the fact that the law of Exodus xiii. 3-16 comes from the hand of the latest redactor of the Jehovistic history.

III.I.2. "Abel was a shepherd and Cain was a husbandman. And in process of time it came to pass that Cain brought of the fruit of the ground an offering unto the Lord; and Abel also brought an offering of the firstlings of his sheep." It is out of the simplest, most natural, and most wide-spread offerings, those of the first-fruits of the flock, herd, and field, the occasions for which recur regularly with the seasons of the year, that the annual festivals took their rise. The passover corresponds with the firstlings of Abel the shepherd, the other three with the fruits presented by Cain the husbandman; apart from this difference, in essence and foundation they are all precisely alike. Their connection with the *aparchai* of the

[first-fruits; firstlings for sacrifice or offering]

yearly seasons is indeed assumed rather than expressly stated in the Jehovistic and Deuteronomistic legislation. Yet in Exodus xxiii. 17-19, xxxiv. 23-26 we read: "Three times in the year shall all thy men appear before the Lord Jehovah; thou shalt not mingle the blood of my sacrifice with leaven, neither shall the fat of my sacrifice remain until the morning. The best of the first-fruits of thy land shalt thou bring into the house of Jehovah thy God; thou shalt not seethe the kid in the milk of its mother." It is forbidden to appear before Jehovah empty, hence the connection between the first general sentence and the details which follow it. Of these, the first seems to relate to the passover; doubtless indeed it holds good of all animal sacrifices, but in point of fact these are offered in preponderating numbers at the great festival after the herds and flocks have produced their young. The remaining sentences relate to the feasts of harvest and ingathering, whose connection with the fruits of the field is otherwise clear. As for Deuteronomy, there also it is required on the one hand that the dues from the flock and herd and field shall be personally offered at Jerusalem, and made the occasion of joyous sacrificial feasts; on the other hand, that three appearances in the year shall be made at Jerusalem, at Easter, at Pentecost, and at the feast of tabernacles, and not with empty hands. These requirements can only be explained on the assumption that the material of the feasts was that furnished by the dues. Clearly in Deuteronomy all three coincide; sacrifices, dues, feasts; other sacrifices than those occasioned by the dues can hardly be thought of for the purpose of holding a joyous festival before Jehovah; the dues are, properly speaking, simply those sacrifices prescribed by popular custom, and therefore fixed and festal, of which alone the law has occasion to treat. *1*

** 1. Deuteronomy xii. 6 seq., 11 seq., xiv. 23-26, xvi. 7, 11, 14. In the section xiv. 22-xvi. 17, dues and feasts are taken together. In the first half (xiv. 22-xv. 18) there is a progression from those acts which are repeated within the course of a year to those which occur every three years, and finally to those which occur every seven; in the second half (xv. 19-xvi. 17) recurrence is again made to the principal, that is, the seasonal dues, first to the firstlings and the passover feast, and afterwards to the two others, in connection with which the tithes of the fruits are offered.
****

It results from the very nature of the case that the people come together to offer thanks for Jehovah's blessing, but no special emphasis is laid upon this. In the Jehovistic legislation (Exodus xxiii., xxxiv.) the terms have not yet come to be fixed, so that it is hardly possible to speak of a "dies festus" in the strict sense; festal seasons rather than festal days are what we have. Easter is celebrated in the month Abib, when the corn is in the ear (Exodus ix. 31, 32), Pentecost when the wheat is cut, the autumn festival when the vintage has been completed,—rather vague and shifting determinations. Deuteronomy advances a step towards fixing the terms and intervals more accurately, a circumstance very intimately connected with the centralisation of the worship in Jerusalem. Even here, however, we do not meet with one general festive offering on the part of the community, but only with isolated private offerings by individuals.

In correspondence with this the amount of the gifts is left with considerable vagueness to the good-will of the offerers. Only the firstlings are definitely demanded. The redemption allowed in Deuteronomy by means of money which buys a substitute in Jerusalem has no proper meaning for the earlier time; yet even then the offerer may in individual instances have availed himself of liberty of exchange, all the more because even then his gift, as a sacrificial meal, was

94

essentially a benefit to himself (Exodus xxiii. 18; Genesis iv. 4, WMXBL<Y>HN). For the first-fruits of the field Exodus prescribes no measure at all, Deuteromony demands the tithe of corn, wine, and oil, which, however, is not to be understood with mathematical strictness, inasmuch as it is used at sacrificial meals, is not made over to a second party, and thus does not require to be accounted for. The tithe, as appears from Deuteronomy xxvi., is offered in autumn, that is, at the feast of tabernacles; this is the proper autumn festival of thanksgiving, not only for the wine harvest, but also for that of the threshing-floor (xvi. 13); it demands seven days, which must all be spent in Jerusalem, while in the case of maccoth only one need be spent there. It is self-evident that there is no restriction to the use of vegetable gifts merely, but sacrifices of flesh are also assumed—purchased perhaps with the proceeds of the sale of the tithe. In this way the special character of the feasts, and their connection with the first-fruits peculiar to them, could easily disappear, a thing which seems actually to have occurred in Deuteronomy, and perhaps even earlier. It is not to be wondered at that much should seem unclear to us which must have been obvious to contemporaries; in Deuteronomy, moreover, almost everything is left to standing custom, and only the one main point insisted on, that the religious worship, and thus also the festivals, must be celebrated only in Jerusalem. Leaving out of account the passover, which originally had an independent standing, and only afterwards through its connection with maccoth was taken into the regular cycle of the *haggim*, it cannot be doubted, generally speaking and on the whole, that not only in the Jehovistic but also in the Deuteronomic legislation the festivals rest upon agriculture, the basis at once of life and of religion. The soil, the fruitful soil, is the object of religion; it takes the place alike of heaven and of hell. Jehovah gives the land and its produce; He receives the best of what it yields as an expression of thankfulness, the tithes in recognition of His seigniorial right. The relation between Himself and His people first arose from His having given them the land in fee; it continues to be maintained, inasmuch as good weather and fertility come from Him.

It is in Deuteronomy that one detects the first very perceptible traces of a historical dress being given to the religion and the worship, but this process is still confined within modest limits. The historical event to which recurrence is always made is the bringing up of Israel out of Egypt, and this is significant in so far as the bringing up out of Egypt coincides with the leading into Canaan, that is, with the giving of the land, so that the historical motive again resolves itself into the natural. In this way it can be said that not merely the Easter festival but all festivals are dependent upon the introduction of Israel into Canaan, and this is what we actually find very clearly in the prayer (Deuteronomy xxvi.) with which at the feast of tabernacles the share of the festal gifts falling to the priest is offered to the Deity. A basket containing fruits is laid upon the altar, and the following words are spoken: "A wandering Aramaean was my father, and he went down into Egypt and sojourned there, a few men strong, and became there a nation, great, mighty, and populous. And the Egyptians evil-entreated them and oppressed them, and laid upon them hard bondage. Then called we upon]ehovah the God of our fathers, and He heard our voice and looked on our affliction and our labour and our oppression. And Jehovah brought us forth out of Egypt with a mighty hand, and with an outstretched arm, and with great terribleness, and with signs and with wonders, *and brought us unto this place, and gave us this land, a land where milk and honey flow!. And now, behold, I have brought the best of the fruits of the land, which thou, O Lord, hast given me."* Observe here how the act of salvation whereby Israel was founded issues in the gift of a fruitful land.

III.II. With this account of the Jehovistic-Deuteronomistic legislation harmonises the pre-exilic practice so far as that can be traced or is borne witness to in the historical and prophetical books. Ancient festivals in Israel must have had the pastoral life as their basis; only the passover therefore can be regarded as belonging, to the number of these. *1* It is

*** 1. The ancient Arabs also observed the sacrifice of the firstlings as a solemnity in the sacred month Rajab, which originally fell in spring (comp. Ewald, Ztschr. f.d. Kunde des Morgenlandes, 1840, p. 419; Robertson Smith, Prophets, p. 383 sq). A festivity mentioned among the earliest, and that for pastoral Judah, is the sheep-shearing (1Samuel xxv. 2 seq.; Genesis xxxviii. 12); but it does not appear to have ever developed into a regular and independent festival. *Aparchai* of wool and flax are mentioned in Hosea (ii. 7, 11 [A.V. 5, 9]) as of wool alone in Deuteronomy (xviii. 4). ***

with perfect accuracy accordingly that precisely the passover is postulated as having been the occasion of the exodus, as being a sacrificial feast that has to be celebrated in the wilderness and has nothing to do with agriculture or harvest. But it is curious to notice how little prominence is afterwards given to this festival, which from the nature of the case is the oldest of all. It cannot have been known at all to the Book of the Covenant, for there (Exodus xxii. 29, 30) the command is to leave the firstling seven days with its dam and on the eighth day to give it to Jehovah. Probably through the predominance gained by agriculture and the feasts founded on it the passover fell into disuse in many parts of Israel, and kept its ground only in districts where the pastoral and wilderness life still retained its importance. This would also explain why the passover first comes clearly into light when Judah alone survives after the fall of Samaria. In 2Kings xxiii. 21 seq. we are told that in the eighteenth year of King Josiah the passover was held according to the precept of the law (Deut xvi.), and that for the first time,—never until then from the days of the Judges had it been so observed. If in this passage the novelty of the institution is so strongly insisted on, the reference is less to the essence of the thing than to the manner of celebration as enjoined in Deuteronomy. Agriculture was learned by the Hebrews from the Canaanites in whose land they settled, and in commingling with whom they, during the period of the Judges, made the transition to a sedentary life. Before the metamorphosis of shepherds into peasants was effected, they could not possibly have had feasts which related to agriculture. It would have been very strange if they had not taken them also over from the Canaanites. The latter owed the land and its fruits to Baal, and for this they paid him the due tribute; the Israelites stood in the same relation to Jehovah. Materially and in itself, the act was neither heathenish nor Israelite; its character either way was determined by its destination. There was, therefore, nothing against a transference of the feasts from Baal to Jehovah; on the contrary, the transference was a profession of faith that the land and its produce, and thus all that lay at the foundations of the national existence, were due not to the heathen deity but to the God of Israel. The earliest testimony is that which we have to the existence of the vintage festival in autumn,—in the first instance as a custom of the Canaanite population of Shechem. In the old and instructive story of Abimelech the son of Jerubbaal we are told (Judges ix. 27) of the citizens of Shechem that "they went out into the fields, and gathered their vineyards, and trode the grapes, and celebrated *hillulim,* and went into the house of their god, and ate and drank, and cursed Abimelech." But this festival must also have taken root among the Israelites at a tolerably early period. According to Judges xxi. 19 seq. there was observed yearly at Shiloh in the vineyards a feast to Jehovah, at which the maidens went out to dance. Even if the narrative of Judges xix. seq. be as a whole untrustworthy as history, this does not apply to the casual trait just mentioned, especially as it is confirmed by 1Samuel i. In this last-cited passage a feast at Shiloh is also spoken of, as occurring at the end of the year, that is, in autumn at the time of the *asiph, 1* and as being an attraction to pilgrims

*** 1. LTQPT HYMYM (i.e., at the new year) 1Samuel i. 20; Exodus xxxiv. 22. In this sense is also to be understood MYMYM YMYMH Judges xxi. 19, 1Samuel i. 3. Comp. Zechariah xiv. 16. ***

from the neighbourhood. Obviously the feast does not occur in all places at once, but at certain definite places (in Ephraim) which then influence the surrounding district. The thing is connected with the origin of larger sanctuaries towards the end of the period of the Judges, or, more properly speaking, with their being taken over from the previous inhabitants; thus, for example, on Shechem becoming an Israelite town the *hillulim* were no more abolished than was the sanctuary itself. Over and above this the erection of great royal temples must have exerted an important influence. Alike at Jerusalem and at Bethel "the feast" was celebrated from the days of Solomon and Jeroboam just as previously at Shechem and Shiloh, in the former place in September, in the latter perhaps somewhat later. *2*

*** 2. 1Kings xii. 32 is, it must be owned, far from trustworthy. 1Kings viii. 2 is difficult to harmonise with vi. 38, if the interpretation of Bul and Ethanim is correct. **

This was at that period the sole actual *panegyris.* [national festivall The feasts at the beginning of summer may indeed also have been observed at this early period (Isa ix. 2), but in smaller local circles. This distinction is still discernible in Deuteronomy, for although in that book the feast of tabernacles is not theoretically higher than the others, in point of fact it alone is observed from beginning to end at the central sanctuary, while Easter, on the other hand, is for the most part kept at home, being only during the first day observed at Jerusalem; moreover, the smaller demand is much more emphatically insisted on than the larger, so that the first seems to have been an innovation, the latter to have had the sanction of older custom. Amos and Hosea, presupposing as they do a splendid cultus and great sanctuaries, doubtless also knew of a variety of festivals, but they have no occasion to mention any one by name. More definite notices occur in Isaiah. The threatening that within a year's time the Assyrians will be in the land is thus (xxix. 1) given: "Add ye year to year, let the feasts come round, yet I will distress Jerusalem," and at the close of the same discourse the prophet expresses himself as follows (xxxii. 9 seq.): "Rise up, ye women that are at ease; hear my voice, ye careless daughters; give ear unto my speech. Days upon a year shall ye be troubled, ye careless women; for the vintage shall fail, the ingathering shall not come. Ye shall smite upon the breasts, for the pleasant fields, for the fruitful vine." When the two passages are taken together we gather that Isaiah, following the universal custom of the prophets in coming forward at great popular gatherings, is here speaking at the time of the autumn festival, in which the women also took an active part (Judges xxi. 19 seq.). But this autumn festival, the joyous and natural character of which is unmistakably revealed, takes place with him at the change of the year, as may be inferred from a comparison between the YNQPW of xxix. I, and the TQPT of Exodus xxxiv. 22, 1Samuel i. 20, and closes a cycle of festivals here for the first time indicated.

2. The preceding survey, it must be admitted, scarcely seems fully to establish the alleged agreement between the Jehovistic law and the older praxis. Names are nowhere to be found, and in point of fact it is only the autumn festival that is well attested, and this, it would appear, as the only festival, as THE feast. And doubtless it was also the oldest and most important of the harvest festivals, as it never ceased to be the concluding solemnity of the year. What has been prosperously brought to close is what people celebrate most rightly; the conclusion of the ingathering, both of the threshing and of the vintage, is the most appropriate of all occasions for a great joint festival,—for this additional reason, that the term is fixed, not, as in the case of the joy of reaping, by nature alone, but is in man's hands and can be regulated by him. Yet even under the older monarchy the previous festivals must also have already existed as well (Isaiah xxix. 1). The peculiarity of the feast of tabernacles would then reduce itself to this, that it was the only general festival at Jerusalem and Bethel; local celebrations "at all threshing floors "—i.e., on all high places—are not thereby excluded (Host ix. 1). But the Jehovistic legislation makes no distinction of local and central, for it ignores the great temples throughout. *1* Possibly,

*************************************** 1. Exodus xx. 24-26 looks almost like a protest against the arrangements of the temple of Solomon,—especially ver. 26. *************************************

also, it to some extent systematises the hitherto somewhat vaguer custom; the transition from the *aparchai* to a feast was perhaps in practice still somewhat incomplete. In the paucity of positive data one is justified, however, in speaking of a substantial agreement, inasmuch as in the two cases the idea of the festivals is the same. Very instructive in this respect are two sections of Hosea (chaps. ii. and ix.), which on this account deserve to be fully gone into. In the first of these Israel is figured as a woman who receives her maintenance from her husband, that is, from the Deity; this is the basis of the covenant relationship. But she falls into error as to the giver of her meat and drink and clothing, supposing them to come from the idols, and not from Jehovah. "She hath said, I will go after my lovers, who give me my

98

bread and my water, my wool and my flax, mine oil and my drink. Doth she then not know that it is I (Jehovah) who have given her the corn and the wine and the oil, and silver in abundance, and gold—out of which she maketh false gods? Therefore will I take back again my corn in its time, and my wine in its season, and I will take away my wool and my flax that should cover her nakedness; and now will I discover her shame before the eyes of her lovers, and none shall deliver her out of my hand. And I will bring all her mirth to an end, her festival days, her new moons and her sabbaths, and all her solemn feasts. And I will destroy her vines and her fig-trees whereof she saith, 'They are my hire, that my lovers have given me,' and I will make them a wilderness, and the beasts of the field shall eat them. Thus will I visit upon her the days of the false gods, wherein she burnt fat offerings to them and decked herself with her rings and her jewels, and went after her lovers and forget me, saith the Lord. Therefore, behold, I will allure her and bring her into the wilderness, and there I will assign her her vineyards: then shall she be docile as in her youth, and as in the day when she came up out of the land of Egypt. Thereafter I betroth thee unto me anew for ever, in righteousness and in judgment, in loving kindness and in mercies. In that day, saith the Lord, will I answer the heavens, and they shall answer the earth, and the earth shall answer the corn and the wine and the oil, and these shall answer Jezreel" (ii. 7-24 [5-22]). The blessing of the land is here the end of religion, and that quite generally,—alike of the false heathenish and of the true Israelitish. *1*

*** 1. Comp. Zech. xiv. 16 seq. All that are left of the nations which came against Jerusalem shall go up from year to year to worship Jehovah of hosts and to keep the feast of tabernacles. And whoso of the families of the earth shall not come up unto Jerusalem to worship Jehovah of hosts, UPON THEM SHALL BE NO RAIN,. But for the Egyptians—- who on account of the Nile are independent of rain—another punishment is threatened if they do not come to keep the feast of tabernacles. ***

It has for its basis no historical acts of salvation, but nature simply, which, however, is regarded only as God's domain and as man's field of labour, and is in no manner itself deified. The land is Jehovah's house (viii. 1, ix. 15), wherein He lodges and entertains the nation; in the land and through the land it is that Israel first becomes the people of Jehovah, just as a marriage is constituted by the wife's reception into the house of the husband, and her maintenance there. And as divorce consists in the wife's dismissal from the house, so is Jehovah's relation to His people dissolved by His making the land into a wilderness, or as in the last resort by His actually driving them forth into the wilderness; He restores it again by "sowing the nation into the land" anew, causing the heavens to give rain and the earth to bear, and thereby bringing into honour the name of "God sown" for Israel (ii. 25 [23]). In accordance with this' worship consists simply of the thanksgiving due for the gifts of the soil, the vassalage payable to the superior who has given the land and its fruits. It *ipso facto* ceases when the corn and wine cease; in the wilderness it cannot be thought of, for if God bestows nothing then man cannot rejoice, and religious worship is simply rejoicing over blessings bestowed. It has, therefore, invariably and throughout the character given in the Jehovistic legislation to the feasts, in which also, according to Hosea's description, it culminates and is brought to a focus. For the days of the false gods, on which people adorned themselves and sacrificed, are just the feasts, and in fact the feasts of Jehovah, whom however the people worshipped by images, which the prophet regards as absolutely heathenish.

Equally instructive is the second passage (ix. 1-6). "Rejoice not too loudly, O Israel, like the heathen, that thou hast gone a whoring from thy God, and lovest the harlot's hire upon every threshing-floor. The floor and the wine-press shall not feed them, and the new wine shall fail them. They shall not dwell in Jehovah's land; Ephraim must return to Egypt, and eat what is unclean in Assyria. Then shall they no more pour out wine to Jehovah, or set in order sacrifices to Him; like bread of mourners is their bread, *1* all that eat thereof become unclean, for

************************************** 1. For Y(RBW (ix. 4) read Y(RKW, and LXMM for LXM. See Kuenen, National Religions and Universal Religions (1882), p. 312 seq. **************************************

their bread shall only be for their hunger, it shall not come into the house of the Lord. What will ye do in the day of festival and in the day of the feast of the Lord? For lo, after they have gone away from among the ruins, Egypt shall keep hold of them, Memphis shall bury them; their pleasant things of silver shall nettles possess, the thornbush shall be in their tents." It need not surprise us that here again the prophet places the worship which in intention is obviously meant for Jehovah on the same footing with the heathen worship which actually has little to distinguish it externally therefrom, being constrained to regard the "pleasant things of silver" in the tents in the high places not as symbols of Jehovah, but as idols, and their worship as whoredom. Enough that once more we have a clear view of the character of the popular worship in Israel at that period. Threshing-floor and wine-press, corn and wine, are its motives,—vociferous joy, merry shoutings, its expression. All the pleasure of life is concentrated in the house of Jehovah at the joyous banquets held to celebrate the coming of the gifts of His mild beneficence; no more dreadful thought than that a man must eat his bread like unclean food, like bread of mourners, without having offered the *aparchai* at the festival. *2* It is this

*** 2. Times of mourning are, so to speak, times of interdict, during which intercourse between God and man is suspended. Further, nothing at all was ever eaten except that of which God had in the first instance received His share;—not only no flesh but also no vegetable food, for the "first-fruits" of corn and wine represented the produce of the year and sanctified the whole. All else was unclean. Comp. Ezekiel iv. 13. **************************************

thought which gives its sting to the threatened exile; for sacrifice and feast are dependent upon the land, which is the nursing-mother and the settled home of the nation, the foundation of its existence and of its worship.

The complete harmony of this with the essential character of the worship and of the festivals in the Book of the Covenant, in the law of the Two Tables, and in

Deuteronomy, is clear in itself, but becomes still more evident by a comparison with the Priestly Code, to which we now proceed.

III.III.

In the Priestly Code the festal cycle is dealt with in two separate passages (Leviticus xxiii; Numbers xxviii., xxix.), of which the first contains a fragment (xxiii. 9-22, and partly also xxiii. 39-44) not quite homogeneous with the kernel of the document. In both these accounts also the three great feasts occur, but with considerable alteration of their essential character.

III.III.1. The festal celebration, properly so called, is exhausted by a prescribed joint offering. There are offered (I.) during Easter week and also on the day of Pentecost, besides the *tamid*, two bullocks, one ram, seven lambs as a burnt-offering, and one he-goat as a sin-offering daily; (2.) at the feast of tabernacles, from the first to the seventh day two rams, fourteen lambs, and, in descending series, from thirteen to seven bullocks; on the eighth day one bullock, one ram, seven lambs as a burnt offering, besides one he-goat daily as a sin-offering. Additional voluntary offerings on the part of individuals are not excluded, but are treated as of secondary importance. Elsewhere, alike in the older practice (1 Samuel i. 4 seq.) and in the law (Exodus xxiii. 18) it is precisely the festal offering that is a sacrificial meal, that is to say, a private sacrifice. In Deuteronomy it has been possible to find anything surprising in the joyous meals only because people are wont to know their Old Testament merely through the perspective of the Priestly Code; at most the only peculiar thing in that book is a certain humane application of the festal offering, the offerer being required to invite to it the poor and landless of his acquaintance. But this is a development which harmonises much more with the old idea of an offering as a communion between God and man than does the other self-sufficing general churchly sacrifice. The passover alone continues in the Priestly Code also to be a sacrificial meal, and participation therein to be restricted to the family or a limited society. But this last remnant of the old custom shows itself here as a peculiar exception; the festival in the house instead of "before Jehovah " has also something ambiguous about it, and turns the sacrifice into an entirely profane act of slaughtering almost—until we come to the rite of expiation, which is characteristically retained (Exodus xii. 7; comp. Ezekiel xiv. 19).

Of a piece with this is the circumstance that the "first-fruits" of the season have come to be separated from the festivals still more than had been previously the case. While in Deuteronomy they are still offered at the three great sacrificial meals in the presence of Jehovah, in the Priestly Code they have altogether ceased to be offerings at all, and thus also of course have ceased to be festal offerings, being merely dues payable to the priests (by whom they are in part collected) and not in any case brought before the altar. Thus the feasts entirely lose their peculiar characteristics, the occasions by which they are inspired and distinguished; by the monotonous sameness of the unvarying burnt-offering and sin-offering of the community as a whole they are all put on the same even level, deprived of their natural spontaneity, and degraded into mere "exercises of religion." Only some very slight traces continue to bear witness to, we might rather say, to betray, what was the point from which the development started, namely, the rites of the barley sheaf, the loaves of bread, and the booths (Leviticus xxiii.). But these are mere rites, petrified remains of the old custom; the actual first-fruits belonging to the owners of the soil are collected by the priests, the shadow of them is retained at the festival in the form of the sheaf offered by the whole community—a piece of symbolism which has now become quite separated from its connection and is no longer understood. And since the giving of thanks for the fruits of the field has ceased to have any substantial place in the feasts, the very shadow of connection between the two also begins to disappear, for the rites of Leviticus xxiii. are taken over from an older legislation, and for the most part are passed over in silence in Numbers xxviii., xxix. Here, again, the passover has followed a path of its own. Even at an earlier period, substitution of other cattle and sheep was permitted. But now in the Priestly Code the firstlings are strictly demanded indeed, but merely as dues, not as sacrifices; the passover, always a yearling lamb or kid, has neither in fact nor in time anything to do with them, but occupies a separate position alongside. But as it is represented to have been instituted in order that the Hebrew first born may be spared in the destruction of those of the Egyptians, this connection betrays the fact that the yearling lambs are after all only a substitute for the firstlings of all animals fit for sacrifice, but in comparison with the cattle and sheep of the Jehovistic tradition and Deuteronomy a secondary substitute, and one for the uniformity of which there is no motive; and we see further that if the firstlings are now over and above assigned to the priests this is equivalent to a reduplication, which has been made possible first by a complete obscuration, and afterwards by an artificial revival of the original custom.

A further symptom also proper to be mentioned here is the fixing of harvest festival terms by the days of the month, which is to be found exclusively in the Priestly Code. Easter falls upon the fifteenth, that is, at full moon, of the first, the feast of tabernacles upon the same day of the seventh month; Pentecost, which, strange to say, is left undetermined in Numbers xxviii., falls, according to Leviticus xxiii., seven weeks after Easter. This definite dating points not merely to a fixed and uniform regulation of the cultus, but also to a change in its contents. For it is not a matter of indifference that according to the Jehovistic-Deuteronomic legislation Easter is observed in "the month of corn ears" when the sickle is put to the corn, Pentecost at the end of the wheat harvest, and the feast of tabernacles after the ingathering; as harvest feasts they are from their very nature regulated by the condition of the fruits of the soil. When they cease to be so, when they are made to depend upon the phases of the moon, this means that their connection with their natural occasion is being lost sight of. Doubtless the accurate determination of dates is correlated with the other circumstance that the festivals are no longer kept in an isolated way by people at any place they may choose, but by the whole united nation at a single spot. It is therefore probable that the fixing of the date w as accomplished at first in the case of the autumn festival, which was the first to divest itself of its local character and most readily suffered a transposition of a week or two. It was hardest to change in the case of the *maccoth* festival; the putting of the sickle to the corn is very inconvenient to shift. But here the passover seems to have exerted an influence. For the passover is indeed an annual feast, but not by the nature of things connected with any particular season of the year; rather was it dependent originally on the phases of the moon. Its character as a *pannychis* [vigil] (Exodus xii. 42 [LYL #MWRYM]) points in this direction, as also does the analogy of the Arab feasts.

The verification of the alleged denaturalisation of the feasts in the Priestly Code lies in this, that their historical interpretation, for which the way is already paved by the Jehovistic tradition, here attains its full development. For after they have lost their original contents and degenerated into mere prescribed religious forms, there is nothing to prevent the refilling of the empty bottles in any way accordant with the tastes of the period. Now, accordingly, the feast of tabernacles also becomes historical (Leviticus xxiii.), instituted to commemorate the booths under which the people had to shelter themselves during the forty years of wandering in the wilderness. In the case of Easter a new step in advance is made beyond the assignation of its motive to the exodus, which is already found in Deuteronomy and in Exodus xiii. 3 seq. For in the Priestly Code this feast, which precisely on account of its eminently historical character is here regarded as by far the most important of all, is much more than the mere commemoration of a divine act of salvation, it is itself a saving deed. It is not because Jehovah smote the firstborn of Egypt that the passover is afterwards instituted on the contrary, it is instituted beforehand, at the moment of the exodus, in order that the firstborn of Israel may be spared. Thus not merely is a historical motive assigned for the custom; its beginning is itself raised to the dignity of a historical fact upon which the feast rests,—the shadow elsewhere thrown only by another historical event here becomes substantial and casts itself. The state of matters in the case of the unleavened cakes is very similar. Instead of having it as their occasion and object to keep in remembrance the hasty midnight departure in which the travellers were compelled to carry with them their dough unleavened as it was (Exodus xii. 34), in the Priestly Code they also are spoken of as having being enjoined beforehand (xii. 15 seq.), and thus the festival is celebrated in commemoration of itself; in other words, not merely is a historical motive assigned to it, it is itself made a historical fact. For this reason also, the law relating to Easter is removed from all connection with the tabernacle legislation (Exodus xii. 1 seq.), and the difficulty that now in the case of the passover the sanctuary which elsewhere in the Priestly Code is indispensable must be left out of sight is got over by divesting it as much as possible of its sacrificial character. *1*

** 1. The ignoring of the sanctuary has a reason only in the case of the first passover, and perhaps ought to be regarded as holding good for that only. The distinction between the PSX MCRYM and the PSX HDWRWT is necessary, if only for the reason that the former is a historical fact, the latter a commemorative observance. When it is argued for the originality of the passover ritual in the Priestly Code that it alone fits in with the conditions of the sojourn in Egypt, the position is not to be disputed.
****

In the case of Pentecost alone is there no tendency to historical explanation; that in this instance has been reserved for later Judaism, which from the chronology of the Book of Exodus discerned in the feast a commemoration of the giving of the law at Sinai. But one detects the drift of the later time.

It has been already pointed out, in what has just been said, that as regards this development the centralisation of the cultus was epochmaking. Centralisation is synonymous with generalisation and fixity, and these are the external features by which the festivals of the Priestly Code are distinguished from those which preceded them. In evidence I point to the prescribed sacrifice of the community instead of the spontaneous sacrifice of the individual, to the date fixed for the 15th of the month, to the complete separation between sacrifices and dues, to the reduction of the passover to uniformity; nothing is free or the spontaneous growth of nature, nothing is indefinite and still in process of becoming; all is statutory, sharply defined, distinct. But the centralisation of the cultus had also not a little to do with the inner change which the feasts underwent. At first the gifts of the various seasons of the year are offered by the individual houses as each one finds convenient; afterwards they are combined, and festivals come into existence; last of all, the united offerings of individuals fall into the back ground when compared with the single joint-offering on behalf of the entire community. According as stress is laid upon the common character of the festival and uniformity in its observance, in precisely the same degree does it become separated from the roots from which it sprang, and grow more and more abstract. That it is then very ready to assume a historical meaning may partly also be attributed to the circumstance that history is not, like harvest, a personal experience of individual households, but rather an experience of the nation as a whole. One does not fail to observe, of course, that the festivals—which always to a certain degree have a centralising tendency—have IN THEMSELVES a disposition to become removed from the particular motives of their institution, but in no part of the legislation has this gone so far as in the Priestly Code. While everywhere else they still continue to stand, as we have seen, in a clear relationship to the land and its increase, and are at one and the same time the great days of homage and tribute for the superior and grantor of the soil, here this connection falls entirely out of sight. As in opposition to the Book of the Covenant and Deuteronomy, nay, even to the corpus itself which forms the basis of Leviticus xvii.-xxvi., one can characterise the entire Priestly Code as the wilderness legislation, inasmuch as it abstracts from the natural conditions and motives of the actual life of the people in the land of Canaan and rears the hierocracy on the *tabula rasa* of the wilderness, the negation of nature, by means of the bald statutes of arbitrary absolutism, so also the festivals, in which the connection of the cultus with agriculture appears most strongly, have as much as possible been turned into wilderness festivals, but most of all the Easter festival, which at the same time has become the most important.

III.III.2. The centralisation of the cultus, the revolutionising influence of which is seen in the Priestly Code, is begun by Deuteronomy. The former rests upon the latter, and draws its as yet unsuspected consequences. This general relation is maintained also in details; in the first place, in the names of the feasts, which are the same in both,—*pesah, shabuoth, sukkoth.* This is not without its inner significance, for *asiph* (ingathering) would have placed much greater hindrances in the way of the introduction of a historical interpretation than does sukkoth (booths). So also with the prominence given to the passover, a festival mentioned nowhere previously—a prominence which is much more striking in the Priestly Code than in Deuteronomy. Next, this relation is observed in the duration of the feasts. While Deuteronomy certainly does not fix their date of commencement with the same definiteness, it nevertheless in this respect makes a great advance upon the Jehovistic legislation, inasmuch as it lays down the rule of a week for Easter and Tabernacles, and of a day for Pentecost. The Priestly Code is on the whole in agreement with this, and also with the time determination of the relation of Pentecost to Easter, but its provisions are more fully developed in details. The passover, in the first month, on the evening of the 14th, here also indeed begins the feast, but does not, as in Deuteronomy xvi. 4, 8, count as the first day of Easter week; on the contrary, the latter does not begin until the 15th and closes with the 21st (comp. Leviticus xxiii. 6; Numbers xxviii. 17; Exodus xii. 18). The beginning of the festival week being thus distinctly indicated, there arises in this way not merely an ordinary but also an extra-ordinary feast day more, the day after the passover, on which already, according to the injunctions of Deuteronomy, the pilgrims were required to set out early in the morning on the return journey to their homes. *1*

*** 1. It is impossible to explain away this discrepancy by the circumstance that in the Priestly Code the day is reckoned from the evening; for (1.) this fact has no practical bearing, as the dating reckons at any rate from the morning, and the evening preceding the 15th is always called the 14th of the month (Leviticus xiii. 27, 32); (2.) the first day of the feast in Deuteronomy is just the day on the evening of which the passover is held, and upon it there follow not seven but six days more, whereas in the Priestly Code the celebration extends from the 14th to the 21st of the month (Exodus xii. 18). When the MXRT H#BT: is made to refer, not as in Josh. v. 11 to the 14th, but as in Jewish tradition (LXX on Leviticus xxiii. 11) to the day following the 15th of Nisan, thee 16th of Nisan is added to the 14th and 15th as a special feast day. ***

Another advance consists in this, that not only the passover, as in Deuteronomy, or the additional first day of the feast besides, but also the seventh (which, according to Deuteronomy xvi. 8, is marked only by rest), must be observed as *miqra qodesh* in Jerusalem. In other words, such pilgrims as do not live in the immediate neighbourhood are compelled to pass the whole week there, an exaction which enables us to mark the progress made with centralisation, when the much more moderate demands of Deuteronomy are compared. The feast of tabernacles is in the latter law also observed from beginning to end at Jerusalem, but the Priestly Code has contrived to add to it an eighth day as an _`acereth_ to the principal feast, which indeed still appears to be wanting in the older portion of Leviticus xxiii. From all this it is indisputable that the Priestly Code has its nearest relations with Deuteronomy, but goes beyond it in the same direction as that in which Deuteronomy itself goes beyond the Jehovistic legislation. In any case the intermediate place in the series belongs to Deuteronomy, and if we begin that series with the Priestly Code, we must in consistency close it with the Sinaitic Book of the Covenant (Exodus xx. 23 seq.).

After King Josiah had published Deuteronomy and had made it the Book of the Covenant by a solemn engagement of the people (621 B.C.), he commanded them to "keep the passover to Jehovah your God as it is written in this Book;" such a passover had never been observed from the days of the judges, or throughout the entire period of the kings (2Kings xxiii. 21, 22). And when Ezra the scribe introduced the Pentateuch as we now have it as the fundamental law of the church of the second temple (444 B.C.), it was found written in the Torah which Jehovah had commanded by Moses, that the children of Israel were to live in booths during the feast in the seventh month, and further, to use branches of olive and myrtle and palm for this purpose, and that the people went and made to themselves booths accordingly; such a thing had not been done "since the days of Joshua the son of Nun even unto that day " (Nehemiah viii. 14 seq.). That Josiah's passover rests upon Deuteronomy xvi. and not upon Exodus xii. is sufficiently proved by the circumstance that the observance of the festival stands in connection with the new unity of the cultus, and is intended to be an exemplification of it, while the precept of Exodus xii., if literally followed, could only have served to destroy it. We thus find that the two promulgations of the law, so great in their importance and so like one another in their character, both take place at the time of a festival, the one in spring, the other in harvest; and we also discover that the festal observance of the Priestly Code first began to show life and to gain currency about two hundred years later than that of Deuteronomy. This can be proved in yet another way. The author of the Book of Kings knows only of a seven days' duration of the feast of tabernacles (1Kings viii. 66); Solomon dismisses the people on the eighth day. On the other hand, in the parallel passage in Chronicles (2Chronicles vii. 9) the king holds the _`acereth_ on the eighth, and does not dismiss the people until the following day, the twenty-third of the month; that is to say, the Deuteronomic use, which is followed by the older author and by Ezekiel (xiv. 25) who was, roughly speaking, his contemporary, is corrected by the later writer into conformity with that of the Priestly Code in force since the time of Ezra (Nehemiah viii. 18). In later Judaism the inclination to assert most strongly precisely that which is most open to dispute led to the well-known result that the eighth day of the feast was regarded as the most splendid of all (John vii. 37).

On this question also the Book of Ezekiel stands nearest the Priestly Code, ordaining as follows (xiv. 21-25):— "In the first month, on the fourteenth day of the month, ye shall keep the passover, ye shall eat maccoth seven days; on that day shall the prince offer for himself and for all the people of the land a bullock for a sin-offering, and during the seven days he shall offer a burnt-offering to the Lord, seven bullocks and seven rams daily for the seven days, and a he-goat daily for a sin offering; and he shall offer as a meal-offering an ephah for every bullock and every ram and a hin of oil for the ephah. In the seventh month, on the fifteenth day of the month, in the feast shall he do the like for seven days, according to the sin-offering, according to the burnt-offering, and according to the meal-offering, and according to the oil." Here indeed in details hardly any point is in agreement with the prescriptions of the ritual law of Leviticus xxiii., Numbers xxviii., xxix. Apart from the fact that the day of Pentecost is omitted (it is restored in the Massoretic text by an absurd correction in ver. 11), in the first place there is a discrepancy as to the DURATION of the feasts; both last seven and not eight days, and the passover is taken for the first day of Easter, as in Deuteronomy. Further, the offerings differ, alike by their never-varying number and by their quality; in particular, nothing is said of the passover lamb, but a bullock as a general sin-offering is mentioned instead. From the *minha* the wine is wanting, but this must be left out of the account, for Ezekiel banishes wine from the service on principle. Lastly, it is not the CONGREGATION that sacrifices, but the prince for himself and for the PEOPLE. But in spite of all differences the general similarity is apparent; one sees that here for the first time we have something which at all points admits of correlation with the Priestly Code, but is quite disparate with the Jehovistic legislation, and half so with that of Deuteronomy. On both hands we find the term fixed according to the day of the month, the strictly prescribed joint burnt-offering and sin-offering, the absence of relation first-fruits and agriculture, the obliteration of natural distinctions so as to make one general churchly festival. But Ezekiel surely could hardly have had any motive for reproducing Leviticus xxiii. and Numbers xxviii. seq., and still less for the introduction of a number of aimless variations as he did so. Let it be observed that in no one detail does he contradict Deuteronomy, while yet he stands so infinitely nearer to the Priestly Code; the relationship is not an arbitrary one, but arises from their place in time. Ezekiel is the forerunner of the priestly legislator in the Pentateuch; his pence and people, to some extent invested with the colouring of the bygone period of the monarchy, are the antecedents of the congregation of the tabernacle and the second temple. Against this supposition there is nothing to be alleged, and it is the rational one, for this reason, that it was not Ezekiel but the Priestly Code that furnished the norm for the praxis of the later period.

For, as the festival system of the Priestly Code absolutely refuses to accommodate itself to the manner of the older worship as we are made acquainted with it in Hos. ii., ix. and elsewhere, in the same degree does it furnish in every respect the standard for the praxis of post-exilian Judaism, and, therefore, also for our ideas thence derived. No one in reading the New Testament dreams of any other manner of keeping the passover than that of Exodus xii., or of any other offering than the paschal lamb there prescribed. One might perhaps hazard the conjecture that if in the wilderness legislation of the Code there is no trace of agriculture being regarded as the basis of life, which it still is in Deuteronomy and even in the kernel of Leviticus xvii.-xxvi., this also is a proof that the Code belongs to a very recent rather than to a very early period, when agriculture was no longer rather than not yet. With the Babylonian captivity the Jews lost their fixed seats, and so became a trading people.

III.III.3. No notice has as yet been taken of one phenomenon which distinguishes the Priestly Code, namely, that in it the tripartite cycle of the feasts is extended and interrupted. In the chronologically arranged enumeration of Leviticus xxiii. and Numbers xxviii., xxix., two other feast days are interpolated between Pentecost and Tabernacles: new year on the first, and the great day of atonement on the tenth of the seventh month. One perceives to what an extent the three originally connected harvest feasts have lost their distinctive character, when it is observed that these two heterogeneous days make their appearance in the midst of them;—the *yom kippur* in the same series with the old *haggim*, *i.e.*, dances, which were occasions of pure pleasure and joy, not to be named in the same day with fasts and mournings. The following points demand notice in detail.

In the period of the kings the change of the year occurred in autumn. The autumn festival marked the close of the year and of the festal cycle (Exodus xxiii. 16, xxxiv.

22; 1Samuel i. 21, 21; Isaiah xxix. 1, xxxii. 10). Deuteronomy was discovered in the eighteenth year of Josiah, and in the very same year Easter was observed in accordance with the prescriptions of that law—which could not have been unless the year had begun in autumn. Now the ECCLESIASTICAL festival of new year in the Priestly Code is also autumnal. *1* The *yom teruah* (Leviticus xxiii 24, 2;;

*** 1. In this way Tabernacles comes not before but after new year; this probably is connected with the more definite dating (on the fifteenth day of the month), but is quite contrary to the old custom and the meaning of the feast. **

Numbers xxix. 1 seq.) falls on the first new moon of autumn, and it follows from a tradition confirmed by Leviticus xxv. 9, 10, that this day was celebrated as new year [R)# H#NH). But it is always spoken of as the first of the seventh month. That is to say, the civil new year has been separated from the ecclesiastical and been transferred to spring; the ecclesiastical can only be regarded as a relic surviving from an earlier period, and betrays strikingly the priority of the division of the year that prevailed in the time of the older monarchy. It appears to have first begun to give way under the influence of the Babylonians, who observed the spring era. *1* For the designation of the

** 1. In Exodus xii. 2 this change of era is formally commanded by Moses: "This month (the passover month) shall be the beginning of months unto you, it shall be to you the first of the months of the year." According to George Smith, the Assyrian year commenced at the vernal equinox; the Assyrian use depends on the Babylonian (Assyrian Eponym Canon, p. 19). **

months by numbers instead of by the old Hebrew names, Abib, Zif, Bul, Ethanim and the like,—a style which arises together with the use of the spring era,—does not yet occur in Deuteronomy (xvi.1), but apart from the Priestly Code, and the last redactor of the Pentateuch (Deuteronomy i. 3) is found for the first time in writers of the period of the exile. It is first found in Jeremiah, but only in those portions of his book which were not committed to writing by him, or at least have been edited by a later hand; *2*

** 2. Kuenen, Hist.-Krit. Onderzoek (1863), ii. pp. 197, 214. **

then in Ezekiel and the author of the Book of Kings, who explains the names he found in his source by giving the numbers (1Kings vi. 37, 38, viii. 2); next in Haggai and Zechariah; and lastly in Chronicles, though here already the Babylonio-Syrian names of the months, which at first were not used in Hebrew, have begun to find their way in (Nehemiah i. 1, ii. 1; Zech. i. 7). The Syrian names are always given along with the numbers in the Book of Esther, and are used to the exclusion of all others in that of Maccabees. It would be absurd to attempt to explain this demonstrable change which took place in the calendar after the exile as a mere incidental effect of the Priestly Code, hitherto in a state of suspended animation, rather than by reference to general causes arising from the circumstances of the time, under whose influence the Priestly Code itself also stood, and which then had for their result a complete change in the greater accuracy and more general applicability of the methods by which time was reckoned. A similar phenomenon presents itself in connection with the metric system. The "shekel of the sanctuary," often mentioned in the Priestly Code, and there only, cannot possibly have borne this name until the most natural objects of the old Israelite *regime* had begun to appear surrounded by a legendary nimbus, because themselves no longer in actual existence. Over against it we have the "king's weight" mentioned in a gloss in 2Samuel xiv. 26, the king being none other than the great king of Babylon. It is an interesting circumstance that the "shekel of the sanctuary "spoken of in the Priestly Code is still the ordinary shekel in Ezekiel; compare Exodus xxx. 13 with Ezekiel xliv. 12.

During the exile the observance of the ecclesiastical new year seems to have taken place not on the first but on the tenth of the seventh month (Leviticus xxv. 9; Ezekiel xl. 1), and there is nothing to be wondered at in this, after once it had come to be separated from the actual beginning of the year. *1* This fact alone

*** 1. The tenth of the month is to be taken in Ezekiel as strictly new year's day; for the designation R)# H#NH occurs in no other meaning than this, and moreover it is by no mere accident that the prophet has his vision of the new Jerusalem precisely at the new year. But according to Leviticus xxv. 9 it is the seventh month that is meant, on the tenth day of which the trumpets are blown at the commencement of the year of jubilee.
****

would suffice to bring into a clear light the late origin of the great day of atonement in Leviticus xvi., which at a subsequent period was observed on this date; for although as a ceremonial of general purification that day occurs appropriately enough at the change of the year, the joyful sound of the new year trumpets ill befits its quiet solemnity, the YWM TRW(H in the Priestly Code being in fact fixed for the first of the seventh month. Notwithstanding its conspicuous importance, there is nothing known of the great day of atonement either in the Jehovistic and Deuteronomic portions of the Pentateuch or in the historical and prophetical books. It first begins to show itself in embryo during the exile. Ezekiel (xiv. 18-20) appoints two great expiations at the beginning of the two halves of the year; for in xiv. 20 the LXX must be accepted, which reads B#B(Y BXD#, "in the seventh month at new moon." The second of these, in autumn, is similar to that of the Priestly Code, only that it falls on the first and new year on the tenth, while in the latter, on the contrary, new year is observed on the first and the atonement on the tenth; the ritual is also much simpler. Zechariah towards the end of the sixth century looks back upon two regular fast days, in the fifth and the seventh month, as having been in observance for seventy years, that is, from the beginning of the exile (vii. 5), and to these he adds (viii. 19) two others in the fourth and in the tenth. They refer, according to the very probable explanation of C. B. Michaelis, to the historical days of calamity which preceded the exile. On the ninth day of the fourth month Jerusalem was taken (Jeremiah xxxix. 2); on the seventh of the fifth the city and the temple were burnt (2Kings xxv. 8); in the seventh month Gedaliah was murdered, and all that remained of the Jewish state annihilated (Jeremiah xli.); in the tenth the siege of the city by Nebuchadnezzar was begun (2Kings xxv. 1). Zechariah also still knows nothing of the great day of atonement in Leviticus xvi., but only mentions among others the fast of the seventh month as having subsisted for seventy years. Even in 444 B.C., the year of the publication of the Pentateuch by Ezra, the great day of atonement has not yet come into force. Ezra begins the reading of the law in the beginning of the seventh month, and afterwards the feast of tabernacles is observed on the fifteenth; of an atoning solemnity on the tenth of the month not a word is said in the circumstantial narrative, which, moreover, is one specially interested in the liturgical element, but it is made up for on the twenty-fourth (Nehemiah viii., ix.). This *testimonium e silentio* is enough; down to that date the great day of the Priestly Code (now introduced for the first time) had not existed. *1* The term is

*** 1. "If Leviticus xvi. belongs to the original of the Priestly Code, and the entire Pentateuch was published by Ezra in the year 444, and yet the day was not then celebrated, then it has *ipso facto* been conceded that it is possible that there can be laws which yet are not carried into effect." So writes Dillmann in his introduction to Leviticus xvi. (1880, p. 525); every one will grant him that the law, before it could attain public currency, must have been previously written and promulgated.
****

partly fixed, following Ezekiel, by reference to the old new year's day (Leviticus xxv. 9); partly, following Zechariah, by reference to the fast of Gedaliah, which indeed was still observed later as a separate solemnity.

Even before the exile general fast days doubtless occurred, but they were specially appointed, and always arose out of extraordinary occasions, when some sin was brought home to the public conscience, or when the divine anger threatened, especially in connection with calamities affecting the produce of the soil (1Kings xxi. 9, 12; Jeremiah xiv. 12, xxxvi. 6, 9; Joel i. 14, ii. 12, 15). In the exile they began to be a regular custom (Isaiah lviii.), doubtless in the first instance in remembrance of the *dies atri* that had been experienced, but also in a certain measure as a surrogate, suited to the circumstances, for the joyous popular gatherings of Easter, Pentecost, and Tabernacles which were possible only in the Holy Land. *l*

************************************** 1. After the second destruction of Jerusalem by Titus, the system of fasts received such an impulse that it was necessary to draw up a list of the days on which fasting was forbidden.
****

At last they came into a position of co-ordination with the feasts, and became a stated and very important element of the ordinary worship. In the Priestly Code, the great fast in the tenth of the seventh month is the holiest day of all the year. Nothing could illustrate more clearly the contrast between the new cultus and the old; fixing its regard at all points on sin and its atonement, it reaches its culmination in a great atoning solemnity. It is as if the temper of the exile had carried itself into the time of liberation also, at least during the opening centuries; as if men had felt themselves not as in an earlier age only momentarily and in special circumstances, but unceasingly, under the leaden pressure of sin and wrath. It is hardly necessary to add here expressly that also in regard to the day of atonement as a day sacred above all others the Priestly Code became authoritative for the post-exilian period. "Ritual and sacrifice have through the misfortunes of the times disappeared, but this has retained all its old sacredness; unless a man has wholly cut himself adrift from Judaism he keeps this day, however indifferent he may be to all its other usages and feasts."

III.IV. [.1?]

A word, lastly, on the lunar feasts, that is, new moon and Sabbath. That the two are connected cannot be gathered from the Pentateuch, but something of the sort is implied in Amos viii. 5, and 2Kings iv. 22, 23. In Amos the corn-dealers, impatient of every interruption of their trade, exclaim, "When will the new moon be gone, that we may sell corn; and the Sabbath, that we may set forth wheat?" In the other passage the husband of the woman of Shunem, when she begs him for an ass and a servant that she may go to the prophet Elisha, asks why it is that she proposes such a journey now, for "it is neither new moon nor Sabbath;" it is not Sunday, as we might say. Probably the Sabbath was originally regulated by the phases of the moon, and thus occurred on the seventh, fourteenth, twenty-first (and twenty-eighth) day of the month, the new moon being reckoned as the first; at least no other explanation can be discovered. 2 For that the week should

*********************************** 2 George Smith, Assyrian Eponymn Canon, pp. 19, 20. "Among the Assyrians the first twenty-eight days of every month were divided into four weeks of seven days each, the seventh, fourteenth, twenty-first, and twenty-eight days respectively being Sabbaths; and there was a general prohibition of work on these days." See further Hyde, Hist. Rel. Vet. Pers., p. 239. Among the Syrians $bbh means the week, just as among the Arabs *sanba* and *sanbata* (Pl. *sanabit*), dim. *suneibita*) mean a period of time (Lagarde, Ps. Hieronymi; p. 158), and in fact, according to the lexicographers, a comparatively long one. But in the sole case cited by the *Tag al 'Arus*, it means rather a short interval. "What is youth? It is the beginning of a *sanbata*," meaning something like the Sunday of a week. According to this it would appear as if the sabbath had been originally the week itself, and only afterwards became the weekly festival day. The identity of the Syriac word (ta sabbata) in the New Testament) with the Hebrew is guaranteed by the twofold Arabic form.
****

be conditioned by the seven planets seems very barely credible. It was not until after people had got their seven days that they began to call them after the seven planets; *1*

*** 1. The peculiar order in which the names of the planets are used to designate the days of the week makes this very clear; see Ideler, Handb. d. Chron. i. 178 seq., ii 77 seq.
****

the number seven is the only bond of connection between them. Doubtless the week is older than the names of its days.

Lunar feasts, we may safely say, are in every case older than annual or harvest feasts; and certainly they are so in the case of the Hebrews. In the pre-historic period the new moon must have been observed with such preference that an ancient name for it, which is no longer found in Biblical Hebrew, even furnished the root of the general word for a festive occasion, which is used for the vintage feast in a passage so early as Judges ix. 27. 2

*** 2. Sprenger (Leben Moh. iii. 527) and Lagarde have rightly correlated the Hebrew *hallel* with the Arabic *ahalla* (to call out, *labbaika*, see, for example Abulf. i. p. 180). But there is no uncertainty as to the derivation of *ahalla* from *hilal* (new moon) ***************************************

But it is established by historical testimonies besides that the new moon festival anciently stood, at least, on a level with that of the Sabbath. Compare 1Samuel xx. 5, 6; 2Kings iv. 23; Annos viii. 5; Isa i. 13; Hos. ii. 13 (A.V. 11). In the Jehovistic and Deuteronomic legislation, however, it is completely ignored, and if it comes into somewhat greater prominence in that of Ezekiel and the Priestly Code (but without being for a moment to be compared with the Sabbath), this perhaps has to do with the circumstance that in the latter the great festivals are regulated by the new moon, and that therefore it is important that this should be observed. It may have been with a deliberate intention that the new moon festival was thrust aside on account of all sorts of heathenish superstition which readily associated themselves with it; but, on the other hand, it is possible that the undersigned preponderance gained by the Sabbath may have ultimately given it independence, and led to the reckoning of time by regular intervals of seven days without regard to new moon, with which now it came into collision, instead of, as formerly, being supported by it.

As a lunar festival doubtless the Sabbath also went back to a very remote antiquity. But with the Israelites the day acquired an altogether peculiar significance whereby it was distinguished from all other feast days; it became the day of rest *par excellence*. Originally the rest is only a consequence of the feast, *e.g.* that of the harvest festival after the period of severe labour; the new moons also were marked in this way (Amos viii. 5; 2Kings iv. 23). In the case of the Sabbath also, rest is, properly speaking, only the consequence of the fact that the day is the festal and sacrificial day of the week (Isaiah i. 13; Ezekiel xlvi. 1 seq.), on which the shewbread was laid out; but here, doubtless on account of the regularity with which it every eighth day interrupted the round of everyday work, this gradually became the essential attribute. In the end even its name came to be interpreted as if derived from the verb "to rest." But as a day of rest it cannot be so very primitive in its origin; in this attribute it presupposes agriculture and a tolerably hard-pressed working-day life. With this it agrees that an intensification of the rest of the Sabbath among the Israelites admits of being traced in the course of the history. The highest development, amounting even to a change of quality, is seen in the Priestly Code.

According to 2Kings iv. 22, 23, one has on Sabbath time for occupations that are not of an everyday kind; servant and ass can be taken on a journey which is longer than that "of a Sabbath day." In Hos. ii. 13 (11) we read, "I make an end of all your joy, your feasts, your new moons and your Sabbaths," that is to say, the last-named share with the first the happy joyousness which is impossible in the exile which Jehovah threatens. With the Jehovist and the Deuteronomist the Sabbath, which, it is true, is

114

already extended in Amos viii. 5 to commerce, is an institution specially for agriculture; it is the day of refreshment for the people and the cattle, and is accordingly employed for social ends in the same way as the sacrificial meal is (Exodus xx. 10, xxiii. 12, xxxiv. 21; Deuteronomy v. 13, 14). Although the moral turn given to the observance is genuinely Israelitic and not original, yet the rest even here still continues to be a feast, a satisfaction for the labouring classes; for what is enjoined as a duty—upon the Israelite rulers, that is, to whom the legislation is directed—is less that they should rest than that they should give rest. In the Priestly Code, on the contrary, the rest of the Sabbath has nothing at all of the nature of the joyous breathing-time from the load of life which a festival affords, but is a thing for itself, which separates the Sabbath not only from the week days, but also from the festival days, and approaches an ascetic exercise much more nearly than a restful refreshment. It is taken in a perfectly abstract manner, not as rest from ordinary work, but as rest absolutely. On the holy day it is not lawful to leave the camp to gather sticks or manna (Exod. xvi.; Numbers xv.), not even to kindle a fire or cook a meal (Exodus xxxv. 3); this rest is in fact a sacrifice of abstinence from all occupation, for which preparation must already begin on the preceding day (Exodus xvi.). Of the Sabbath of the Priestly Code in fact it could not be said that it was made for man (Mark ii. 27); rather is it a statute that presents itself with all the rigour of a law of nature, having its reason with itself, and being observed even by the Creator. The original narrative of the Creation, according to which God finished His work on the seventh day, and therefore sanctified it, is amended so as to be made to say that He finished in six days and rested on the seventh. *1*

** 1 The contradiction is indubitable when in Genesis ii. 2 it is said in the first place that on the seventh day God ended the work which He had made; and then that He rested on the seventh day from His work. Obviously the second clause is an authentic interpretation added from very intelligible motives. **

Tendencies to such an exaggeration of the Sabbath rest as would make it absolute are found from the Chaldaean period. While Isaiah, regarding the Sabbath purely as a sacrificial day, says, "Bring no more vain oblations; it is an abominable incense unto me; new moon and Sabbath, the temple assembly—I cannot endure iniquity and solemn meeting," Jeremiah, on the other hand, is the first of the prophets who stands up for a stricter sanctification of the seventh day, treating it, however, merely as a day of rest: "Bear no burden on the Sabbath day, neither bring in by the gates of Jerusalem nor carry forth a burden out of your houses, neither do ye any work" (xvii. 21, 22). He adds that this precept had indeed been given to the fathers, but hitherto has not been kept; thus, what was traditional appears to have been only the abstinence from field work and perhaps also from professional pursuits. In this respect the attitude of Jeremiah is that which is taken also by his exilian followers, not merely by Ezekiel (xx. 16, xxii. 263 but also by the Great Unknown (Isaiah lvi. 2, lviii. 13), who does not otherwise manifest any express partiality for cultus. While according to Hos. ii. 13, and even Lam. ii. 6, the Sabbath, as well as the rest of the acts of divine worship, must cease outside of the Holy Land, it in fact gained in importance to an extraordinary degree during the exile, having severed itself completely, not merely from agriculture, but in particular also from the sacrificial system, and gained entire independence as a holy solemnity of rest. Accordingly, it became along with circumcision the symbol that bound together the Jewish diaspora; thus already in the Priestly Code the two institutions are the general distinguishing marks of religion [)WT Genesis xvii. 10, 11; Exodus xxxi. 13] which also continue to subsist under circumstances where as in the exile the conditions of the Mosaic worship are not present (Genesis ii. 3, xvii. 12, 13). The trouble which in the meantime the organisers of the church of the second temple had in forcing into effect the new and strict regulations is clear from Nehemiah xiii. 15 seq. But they were ultimately successful. The solemnisation of the Sabbath in Judaism continued to develop logically on the basis of the priestly legislation, but always approximating with increasing nearness to the idea; of absolute rest, so that for the straitest sect of the Pharisees the business of preparing for the sacred day absorbed the whole week, and half man's life, so to speak, existed for it alone. "From Sunday onwards think of the Sabbath," says Shammai. Two details are worthy of special prominence; the distinction between *yom tob* and *shabbath*, comparable to that drawn by the Puritans between Sundays and feast days, and the discussion as to whether the Sabbath was broken by divine worship; both bring into recognition that tendency of the Priestly Code in which the later custom separates itself from its original roots.

III.IV.2. Connected with the Sabbath is the sabbatical year. In the Book of the Covenant it is commanded that a Hebrew who has been bought as a slave must after six years of service be liberated on the seventh unless he himself wishes to remain (Exodus xxi. 2-6). By the same authority it is ordained in another passage that the land and fruit-gardens are to be wrought and their produce gathered for six years, but on the seventh the produce is to be surrendered (#M+), that the poor of the people may eat, and what they leave the beasts of the field may <e>at (xxiii. 10, 11). Here there is no word of a sabbatical year. The liberation of the Hebrew slave takes place six years after his purchase, that is, the term is a relative one. In like manner, in the other ordinance there is nothing to indicate an absolute seventh year; and besides, it is not a Sabbath or fallow time for the *land* that is contemplated, but a surrender of the *harvest*.

The first of these commands is repeated in Deuteronomy without material alteration, and to a certain extent word for word (xv. 12-18). The other has at least an analogue in Deuteronomy xv. 1-6: "At the end of every seven years thou shalt make a release (surrender, s*m+h), and this is the manner of it; no creditor that lendeth aught shall exact it of his neighbour or of his brother, because Jehovah's release has been proclaimed; of a foreigner thou mayst exact it again, but that which is of thine with thy brother, thy hand shall release." That this precept is parallel with Exodus xxiii. 10, 11, is shown by the word #m+h~; but this has a different meaning put upon it which plainly is introduced as new. Here it is not landed property that is being dealt with, but money, and what has to be surrendered is not the interest of the debt merely (comparable to the fruit of the soil), but the capital itself; the last clause admits of no other construction, however unsuitable the regulation may be. A step towards the sabbatical year is discernible in it, in so far as the seventh year term is not a different one for each individual debt according to the date when it was incurred (in which case it might have been simply a period of prescription), but is a uniform and common term publicly fixed: it is absolute, not relative. But it does not embrace the whole seventh year, it does not come in at the end of six years as in Exodus, but at the end of seven; the surrender of the harvest demands the whole year, the remission of debts, comparatively speaking, only a moment.

The sabbatical year is peculiar to the Priestly Code, or, to speak more correctly, to that collection of laws incorporated and edited by it, which lies at the basis of Leviticus xvii.-xxvi. In Leviticus xxv. 1-7 we read: "When ye come into the land which I give you, then shall the land keep a Sabbath to Jehovah. Six years shalt thou sow thy field and prune thy vineyard, and gather in the fruit thereof; but in the seventh year shall the land keep a Sabbath of rest unto Jehovah: thy field shalt thou not sow, thy vineyard shalt thou not prune; that which groweth of its own accord of thy harvest shalt thou not reap, neither shalt thou gather the grapes of thy vine undressed; the land shall have a year of rest, and the Sabbath of the land shall be food for you; for thee, and for thy servant, and for thy maid, and for thy hired servant, and for thy cattle, and for all the beasts that are in thy land, shall all the increase thereof be food." The expressions make it impossible to doubt that Exodus xxiii. 10, 11 lies at the foundation of this law; but out of this as a basis it is something different that has been framed. The seventh year, which is there a relative one, has here become fixed,—not varying for the various properties, but common for the whole land, a sabbatical year after the manner of the Sabbath day. This amounts to a serious increase in the difficulty of the matter, for it is not one and the same thing to have the abstinence from harvest spread over seven years and to have it concentrated into one out of every seven. In like manner a heightening of the demand is also seen in the circumstance that not merely harvesting but also sowing and dressing are forbidden. In the original commandment this was not the case; all that was provided for was that in the seventh year the harvest should not fall to the lot of the proprietor of the soil, but should be *publici juris,*—a relic perhaps of communistic agriculture. Through a mere misunderstanding of the verbal suffix in Exodus xxiii. 11, as has been conjectured by Hupfeld, a surrender of the *fruit* of the land has been construed into a surrender of tbe land itself—a general fallow year (Leviticus xxv. 4). The misunderstanding, however, is not accidental, but highly characteristic. In Exodus xxiii. the arrangement is made for man; it is a limitation, for the common good, of private rights of property in land,—in fact, for the benefit of the landless, who in the seventh year are to have the usufruct of the soil; in Leviticus xxv. the arrangement is for the sake of the land,—that it may rest, if not on the seventh day, at least on the seventh year, and for the sake of the Sabbath— that it may extend its supremacy over nature also. Of course this presupposes the extreme degree of Sabbath observance by absolute rest, and becomes comprehensible only when viewed as an outgrowth from that. For the rest, a universal fallow season is possible only under circumstances in which a people are to a considerable extent independent of the products of their own agriculture; prior to the exile even the idea of such a thing could hardly have occurred.

In the Priestly Code the year of jubilee is further added to supplement in turn the sabbatical year (Leviticus xxv. 8 seq.). As the latter is framed to correspond with the seventh day, so the former corresponds with the fiftieth, *i.e.,* with Pentecost, as is easily perceived from the parallelism of Leviticus xxv. 8 with Leviticus xxiii. 15. Asthe fiftieth day after the seven Sabbath days is celebrated as a closing festival of the forty-nine days' period, so is the fiftieth year after the seven sabbatic years as rounding off the larger interval; the seven Sabbaths falling on harvest time, which are usually reckoned specially (Luke vi. 1), have, in the circumstance of their interrupting harvest work, a particular resemblance to the sabbatic years which interrupt agriculture altogether. Jubilee is thus an artificial institution superimposed upon the years of fallow regarded as harvest Sabbaths after the analogy of Pentecost. Both its functions appear originally to have belonged also to the Sabbath year and to be deduced from the two corresponding regulations in Deuteronomy relating to the seventh year, so that thus Exod xxiii. would be the basis of Leviticus xxv. 1-7 and Deuteronomy xv. that of xxv. 8 seq. The emancipation of the Hebrew slave originally had to take place on the seventh year after the purchase, afterwards (it would seem) on the seventh vear absolutely; for practical reasons it was transferred from that to the fiftieth. Analogous also, doubtless, is the growth of the other element in the jubilee—the return of mortgaged property to its hereditary owner—- out of the remission of debts enjoined in Deuteronomy xv. for the end of the seventh year; for the two hang very closely together, as Leviticus xxv. 23 seq. shows.

As for the evidence for these various arrangements, those of the Book of the Covenant are presupposed alike by Deuteronomy and by the Priestly Code. It seems to have been due to the prompting of Deuteronomy that towards the end of the reign of Zedekiah the emancipation of the Hebrew slaves was seriously gone about; the expressions in Jeremiah xxxiv. 14 point to Deuteronomy xv. 12, and not to Exodus xxi. 2. The injunction not having had practical effect previously, it was in this instance carried through by all parties at the same date: this was of course inevitable when it was introduced as an extraordinary innovation; perhaps it is in connexion with this that a fixed seventh year grew out of a relative one. The sabbatical year, according to the legislator's own declaration, was never observed throughout the whole pre-exilic period; for, according to Leviticus xxvi. 34, 35, the desolation of the land during the exile is to be a compensation made for the previously neglected fallow years: "Then shall the land pay its Sabbaths as long as it lieth desolate; when ye are in your enemies' land then shall the land rest and pay its Sabbaths; all the days that it lieth desolate shall it rest, which it rested not in your Sabbaths when ye dwelt upon it." The verse is quoted in 2Chronicles xxxvi. 21 as the language of Jeremiah,— a correct and unprejudiced indication of its exilic origin. But as the author of Leviticus xxvi. was also the writer of Leviticus xxv. 1-7, that is to say, the framer of the law of the sabbatic year, the recent date of the latter regulation also follows at once. The year of jubilee, certainly derived from the Sabbath year, is of still later origin. Jeremiah (xxxiv. 14) has not the faintest idea that the emancipation of the slaves must according to "law" take place in the fiftieth year. The name drwr, borne by the jubilee in Leviticus xxv. 10, is applied by him to the seventh year; and this is decisive also for Ezekiel xlvi. 17: the gift of land bestowed by the prince on one of his servants remains in his possession only until the seventh year.

CHAPTER IV. THE PRIESTS AND THE LEVITES.

IV.I.

IV.I.1 The problem now to be dealt with is exhibited with peculiar distinctness in one pregnant case with which it will be well to set out. The Mosaic law, that is to say, the Priestly Code, distinguishes, as is well known, between the twelve secular tribes and Levi, and further within the spiritual tribe itself, between the sons of Aaron and the Levites, simply so called. The one distinction is made visible in the ordering of the camp in Numbers ii., where Levi forms around the sanctuary a cordon of protection against the immediate contact of the remaining tribes; on the whole, however, it is rather treated as a matter of course, and not brought into special prominence (Numbers xviii. 22). The other is accentuated with incomparably greater emphasis. Aaron and his sons alone are priests, qualified for sacrificing and burning incense; the Levites are hieroduli (3 Esdras i. 3), bestowed upon the Aaronidae for the discharge of the inferior services (Numbers iii. 9). They are indeed their tribe fellows, but it is not because he belongs to Levi that Aaron is chosen, and his priesthood cannot be said to be the acme and flower of the general vocation of his tribe. On the contrary, rather was he a priest long before the Levites were set apart; for a considerable time after the cultus has been established and set on foot these do not make any appearance,—not at all in the whole of the third book, which thus far does little honour to its name *Leviticus*. Strictly speaking, the Levites do not even belong to the clergy: they are not called by Jehovah, but consecrated by the children of Israel to the sanctuary,—consecrated in the place of the first-born, not however as priests (neither in Numbers iii., iv., viii., nor anywhere else in the Old Testament, is there a single trace of the priesthood of the first-born), but as a gift due to the priests, as such being even required to undergo the usual "waving" before the altar, to symbolise their being cast into the altar flame (Numbers viii.). The relationship between Aaron and Levi, and the circumstance that precisely this tribe is set apart for the sanctuary in compensation for the first-born, appears almost accidental, but at all events cannot be explained by the theory that Aaron rose on the shoulders of Levi; on the contrary, it rather means that Levi has mounted up by means of Aaron, whose priesthood everywhere is treated as having the priority. Equality between the two is not to be spoken of; their office and their blood relationship separates them more than it binds them together.

Now, the prophet Ezekiel, in the plan of the new Jerusalem which he sketched in the year 573, takes up among other things the reform of the relations of the *personnel* of the temple, and in this connection expresses himself as follows (xliv. 6-16):— "Thus saith the Lord Jehovah, Let it suffice you of all your abominations, O house of Israel! in that ye have brought in strangers, uncircumcised in heart and uncircumcised in flesh, to be in my sanctuary, to pollute it, even my house, when ye offer my bread, the fat and the blood, and have broken my covenant by all your abominations. And ye have not kept the charge of my holy things, inasmuch as ye have set these *I* to be keepers of my

*** In ver. 7 for WYPRW read WTPRW, in ver. 8 for WT#YMWN read WT#YMWM, and for LKM read LKN, in each case following the LXX. ***

charge in my sanctuary. Therefore, thus saith the Lord Jehovah, No stranger uncircumcised in heart and uncircumcised in flesh shall enter into my sanctuary; none, of all that are among the children of Israel. But the Levites who went away far from me when Israel went astray from me after their idols, they shall even bear their iniquity, and they shall be ministers in my sanctuary, officers at the gates of the house and ministers of the house; they shall slay for the people the burnt-offering and the thank-offering, and they shall stand before them to minister unto them. Because they ministered unto them before their idols, and caused the house of Israel to fall into iniquity, therefore have I lifted up my hand against them, saith the Lord Jehovah, and they shall bear their iniquity. They shall not come near unto me to do the office of a priest unto me, nor to come near to any of my holy things, but they shall bear their shame and their abominations which they have committed. And I will make them keepers of the charge of the house, for all its service, and for all that shall be done therein. But the priests, the Levites, sons of Zadok, that kept the charge of my sanctuary when the children of Israel went astray from me, they shall come near to me to minister unto me, and they shall stand before me to offer unto me the fat and the blood, saith the Lord Jehovah; they shall enter into my sanctuary, and come near to my table to minister unto me, and they shall keep my charge."

From this passage two things are to be learned. First, that the systematic separation of that which was holy from profane contact did not exist from the very beginning; that in the temple of Solomon even heathen (Zech. xiv. 21), probably captives, were employed to do hierodulic services which, according to the law, ought to have been rendered by Levites, and which afterwards actually were so rendered. Ezekiel, it is indeed true, holds this custom to be a frightful abuse, and one might therefore maintain it to have been a breach of the temple ordinances suffered by the Jerusalem priests against their better knowledge, and in this way escape accusing them of ignorance of their own law. But the second fact, made manifest by the above-quoted passage, quite excludes the existence of the Priestly Code so far as Ezekiel and his time are concerned. The place of the heathen temple-slaves is in future to be taken by the Levites. Hitherto the latter had held the priesthood, and that too not by arbitrary usurpation, but in virtue of their oun good right. For it is no mere relegation back to within the limits of their lawful position when they are made to be no longer priests but temple ministrants, it is no restoration of the *status quo ante*, the conditions of which they had illegally broken; it is expressly a degradation, a withdrawal of their right, which appears as a punishment and which must be justified as being deserved; "they shall bear their iniquity." They have forfeited their priesthood, by abusing it to preside over the cultus of the high places, which the prophet regards as idolatry and hates in his inmost soul. Naturally those Levites are exempted from the penalty who have discharged their functions at the legal place,—- the Levites the sons of Zadok,—namely, at Jerusalem, who now remain sole priests and receive a position of pre-eminence above those who hitherto have been their equals in office, and who are still associated with them by Ezekiel, under the same common name, but now are reduced to being their assistants and hieroduli.

It is an extraordinary sort of justice when the priests of the abolished Bamoth are punished simply for having been so, and conversely the priests of the temple at Jerusalem rewarded for this; the fault of the former and the merit of the latter consist simply in their existence. In other words, Ezekiel merely drapes the logic of facts with a mantle of morality. From the abolition of the popular sanctuaries in the provinces in favour of the royal one at Jerusalem, there necessarily followed the setting aside of the provincial priesthoods in favour of the sons of Zadok at the temple of Solomon. The original author of the centralisation, the Deuteronomic lawgiver, seeks indeed to prevent this consequence by giving to the extraneous Levites an equal right of sacrificing in Jerusalem with their brethren hereditarily settled there, but it was not possible to separate the fate of the priests from that of their altars in this manner. The sons of Zadok were well enough pleased that all sacrifices should be concentrated within their temple, but they did not see their way to sharing their inheritance with the priesthood of the high places, and the idea was not carried out (2Kings xxiii. 9). Ezekiel, a thorough Jerusalemite, finds a moral way of putting this departure from the law, a way of putting it which does not explain the fact, but is merely a periphrastic statement of it. With Deuteronomy as a basis it is quite easy to understand Ezekiel's ordinance, but it is absolutely impossible if one starts from the Priestly Code. What he regards as the original right of the Levites, the performance of priestly services, is treated in the latter document as an unfounded and highly wicked pretension which once in the olden times brought destruction upon Korah and his company; what he considers to be a subsequent withdrawal of their right, as a degradation in consequence of a fault, the other holds to have been their hereditary and natural destination. The distinction between priest and Levite which Ezekiel introduces and justifies as an innovation, according to the Priestly Code has always existed; what in the former appears as a beginning, in the latter has been in force ever since Moses,—an original datum, not a thing that has become or been made./1/ That the prophet should know

*** 1. "If by reason of their birth it was impossible for the Levites to become priests, then it would be more than strange to deprive them of the priesthood on account of their faults,—much as if one were to threaten the commons with the punishment of disqualification to sit or vote in a house of lords" (Kuenen, Theol. Tijdschr., iii. 465). ***

nothing about a priestly law with whose tendencies he is in thorough sympathy admits of only one explanation,—that it did not then exist. His own ordinances are only to be understood as preparatory steps towards its own exactment.

IV.I.2. Noldeke, however, interprets the parallelism between the sons of Aaron and the sons of Zadok in favour of the priority of the Priestly Code, which, after all, he points out, is not quite so exclusive as Ezekiel. / But, in the first place, this is a

** 1 Jahrb. f. prot. Theol., 1875, p. 351: "Its doctrine that the Aaronidae alone are true priests has its parallel in

Ezekiel, who *still more exclusively* recognises only the sons of Zadok as priests."
****

point of subordinate importance, the main thing being that Ezekiel has to make the distinction between priests and Levites, which is regarded in the Priestly Code as very ancient. In presence of the fact that the former introduces as a new thing the separation which the latter presupposes, the precise degree of the distinction drawn by the two is of no consequence whatever. In the next place, to bring the sons of Aaron into comparison with the sons of Zadok, as a proof of their higher antiquity, is just as reasonable as to bring the tabernacle into comparison with the temple of Jerusalem for a similar purpose. The former are priests of the tabernacle, the latter of the temple; but as in point of fact the only distinction to be drawn between the Mosaic and the actual central sanctuary is that between shadow and substance, so neither can any other be made between the Mosaic and the actual central priesthood. In the Priestly Code the ancient name is introduced instead of the historical one, simply in order to maintain the semblance of the Mosaic time; if the circumstance is to be taken as betokening the earlier origin of the work, then a similar inference must be drawn also from the fact that in it the origin and character of the Levites is quite obscure, while in Ezekiel it is palpably evident that they are the priests thrown out of employment by the abolition of the Bamoth, whom necessity has compelled to take a position of subordination under their haughty fellow-priests at Jerusalem. In truth it is, quite on the contrary, a proof of the post-exilian date of the Priestly Code that it makes sons of Aaron of the priests of the central sanctuary, who, even in the traditional understanding (2Chronicles xiii. 10), are in one way or other simply the priests of Jerusalem. By this means it carries their origin back to the foundation of the theocracy, and gives them out as from the first having been alone legitimate. But such an idea no one could have ventured to broach before the exile. At that time it was too well known that the priesthood of the Jerusalem sept could not be traced further back than David's time, but dated from Zadok, who in Solomon's reign ousted the hereditary house of Eli from the position it had long previously held, first at Shiloh and Nob, and afterwards at Jerusalem, at what had become the most prominent sanctuary of Israel.

In a passage of Deuteronomic complexion, which cannot have been written long before the exile, we read in a prediction made to Eli regarding the overthrow of his house by Zadok: "I said indeed, saith Jehovah the God of Israel, that thy house and the house of thy father shall walk before me for ever; but now I say, Be it far from me, for them that honour me I will honour, but they that despise me shall be lightly esteemed. Behold, the days come that I will cut off thine arm and the arm of thy father's house, ...and I will raise up for myself a faithful priest who shall do according to what is in my heart and in my mind; and I will build him a sure house, and he shall walk before mine anointed for ever" (1Samuel ii. 27-36). Here it is the house of Eli, and of Eli's father, that is the priestly family duly chosen in Egypt; *contrary* to hereditary title, and contrary to a promise of perpetual continuance, is it deposed at the higher claims of justice. The faithful priest who is to fill the vacant place is Zadok. This is expressly said in 1Kings 2:27; and no other than he ever had a "sure house" and walked uninterruptedly as its head and ruler before the kings of Judah. This Zadok, accordingly, belongs neither to Eli's house nor to that of Eli's father; his priesthood does not go back as far as the time of the founding of the theocracy, and is not in any proper sense "legitimate;" rather has he obtained it by the infringement of what might be called a constitutional privilege, to which there were no other heirs besides Eli and his family. Obviously he does not figure as an intermediate link in the line of Aaron, but as the beginner of an entirely new genealogy; the Jerusalem priests, whose ancestor he is, are interlopers dating from the beginning of the monarchical period, in whom the old Mosaic *sacerdotium* is not continued, but is broken off. If then they are called in the Priestly Code "sons of Aaron," or at least figure there among the sons of Aaron, with whom they can only in point of fact be contrasted, the circumstance is an unmistakable indication that at this point the threads of tradition from the pre-exilic period have been snapped completely, which was not yet the case in Ezekiel's time. *1*

*** 1. To satisfy the Pentateuch it is shown in the Book of Chronicles, by means of artificial genealogies, how the sons of Zadok derived their origin in an unbroken line from Aaron and Eleazar. Compare my Pharisaer u. Sadducaer, p. 48 seq. This point was first observed by Vatke (p. 344 seq.), then by Kuenen (Theol. Tijdschr., iii. p. 463-509) and lastly by me (Text der BB. Sam., p. 48-51). ***

The relation between the priestly legislation and the Book of Ezekiel, which has now been shown, gives direction and aim to the following sketch, in which it is sought to exhibit the individual phenomenon in its general connection.

IV.II.

IV.II.1. The setting apart from the rest of the people of an entire tribe as holy, and the strongly accentuated distinction of ranks within that tribe, presuppose a highly systematised separation between sacred and profane, and an elaborate machinery connected with cultus. In fact, according to the representation given in the Priestly Code, the Israelites from the beginning were organised as a hierocracy, the clergy being the skeleton, the high priest the head, and the tabernacle the heart. But the suddenness with which this full-grown hierocracy descended on the wilderness from the skies is only matched by the suddenness with which it afterwards disappeared in Canaan, leaving no trace behind it. In the time of the Judges, priests and Levites, and the congregation of the children of Israel assembled around them, have utterly vanished; there is hardly a *people* Israel,—only individual tribes which do not combine even under the most pressing necessities, far less support at a common expense a clerical *personnel* numbering thousands of men, besides their wives and families. Instead of the Ecclesiastical History of the Hexateuch, the Book of Judges forthwith enters upon a secular history completely devoid of all churchly character. The high priest, who according to the Priestly Code is the central authority by the grace of God, is here quite left out in the cold, for the really acting heads of the people are the Judges, people of an entirely different stamp, whose authority, resting on no official position, but on strength of personality and on the force of circumstances, seldom extends beyond the limits of their tribe. And it is plain that in this we behold not the sorry remains of an ecclesiastico-political system once flourishing under Moses and Joshua, now completely fallen into ruins, but the first natural beginnings of a civil authority which after a course of further development finally led to the monarchy.

In the kernel of the Book of Judges (chaps. iii.-xvi.) there nowhere occurs a single individual whose profession is to take charge of the cultus. Sacrifice is in two instances offered, by Gideon and Manoah; but in neither case is a priest held to be necessary. In a gloss upon 1Samuel vi. 13 seq. the divergence of later custom reveals itself. When the ark of Jehovah was brought back from exile in Philistia upon the new cart, it halted in the field of Bethshemesh beside the great stone, and the inhabitants of Bethshemesh, who were at the time busy with the wheat harvest, broke up the cart and made on the stone a burnt-offering of the kine by which it had been drawn. After they have finished, the Levites come up (ver. 15) (in the pluperfect tense) and proceed as if nothing had happened, lift the ark from the now no longer existent cart, and set it upon the stone on which the sacrifice is already burning;- of course only in order to fulfil the law, the demands of which have been completely ignored in the original narrative. Until the cultus has become in some measure centralised the priests have no *locus standi*; for when each man sacrifices for himself and his household, upon an altar which he improvises as best he can for the passing need, where is the occasion for people whose professional and essential function is that of sacrificing for others? The circumstance of their being thus inconspicuous in the earliest period of the history of Israel is connected with the fact that as yet there are few great sanctuaries. But as soon as these begin to occur, the priests immediately appear. Thus we find Eli and his sons at the old house of God belonging to the tribe of Ephraim at Shiloh. Eli holds a very exalted position, his sons are depicted as high and mighty men, who deal with the worshippers not directly but through a servant, and show arrogant disregard of their duties to Jehovah. The office is hereditary, and the priesthood already very numerous. At least in the time of Saul, after they had migrated from Shiloh to Nob, on account of the destruction by the Philistines of the temple at the former place, they numbered more than eighty-five men, who, however, are not necessarily proper blood-relations of Eli, although reckoning themselves as belonging to his clan (1Samuel xxii. 11). *1*

*** 1. In 1Samuel i. seq., indeed, we read only of Eli and his two sons and one servant, and even David and Solomon appear to have had only a priest or two at the chief temple. Are we to suppose that Doeg, single-handed, could have made away with eighty-five men ? ***

One sanctuary more is referred to towards the close of the period of the Judges,—that at Dan beside the source of the Jordan. A rich Ephraimite, Micah, had set up to Jehovah a silver-covered image, and lodged it in an appropriate house. At first he appointed one of his sons to be its priest, afterwards Jonathan ben Gershom ben Moses, a homeless Levite of Bethlehem-Judah, whom he counted himself happy in being able to retain for a yearly salary of ten pieces of silver, besides clothing and maintenance. When, however, the Danites, hard pressed by the Philistines, removed from their ancient settlements in order to establish a new home for themselves on the slopes of Hermon in the north, they in passing carried off both Micah's image and his priest; what led them to do so was the report of their spies who had formerly lodged with Micah and there obtained an oracle. It was in this way that Jonathan came to Dan and became the founder of the family which retained the priesthood at this afterwards so important sanctuary down to the period of the deportation of the Danites at the Assyrian captivity (Judges xvii., xviii.). His position seems very different from that of Eli. The only point of resemblance is that both are hereditary priests, Levites so called, and trace their descent from the family of Moses,— of which more anon. But while Eli is a man of distinction, perhaps the owner of the sanctuary, at all events in a position of thorough independence and the head of a great house, Jonathan is a solitary wandering Levite who enters the service of the proprietor of a sanctuary for pay and maintenance, and is indeed nourished as a son by his patron, but by no means treated with special respect by the Danites.

The latter case, it may well be conjectured, more nearly represents the normal state of matters than the former. An independent and influential priesthood could develop itself only at the larger and more public centres of worship, but that of Shiloh seems to have been the only one of this class. The remaining houses of God, of which we hear some word from the transition period which preceded the monarchy, are not of importance, and are in private hands, thus corresponding to that of Micah on Mount Ephraim. That of Ophra belongs to Gideon, and that of Kirjathjearim to Abinadab. In fact, it appears that Micah, in appointing one to minister at his sanctuary for hire, would seem to have followed a more general practice. For the expression ML(YDW, which still survived as a *terminus technicus* for the ordination of priests long after they had attained a perfectly independent position, can originally in this connection hardly have meant anything else than a filling of the hand with money or its equivalent; thus the priestly office would appear in the older time to have been a paid one, perhaps the only one that was paid. Whom he shall appoint is at the discretion of the proprietor: if no one else is available, he gives it to one of his sons (Judges xvii. 5; 1Samuel vii. 1),— of a "character indelibilis" there is of course in such a case no idea, as one can learn from the earliest example, in which Micah's son retires again from the service after a brief interval. David, when he removed the ark, intrusted it in the first instance to the house of Obededom, a captain of his, a Philistine of Gath, whom he made its keeper. A priest of regular calling, a Levite, is, according to Judges xvii. 13, a very unusual person to find at an ordinary sanctuary. Even at Shiloh, where, however, the conditions are extraordinary, the privilege of the sons of Eli is not an exclusive one; Samuel, who is not a member of the family, is nevertheless adopted as a priest. The service for which a stated minister was needed was not that of offering sacrifice; this was not so regular an occurrence as not to admit of being attended to by one's self. For a simple altar no priest was required, but only for a house which contained a sacred image; *1*

*** 1. BYT (LHYM, "house of God," is never anything but the house of an image. Outside of the Priestly Code, *ephod* is the image, *ephod bad* the priestly garment.
****

this demanded watching and attendance (1 Sam. vii. 1)—in fact, an ephod like that of Gideon or that of Micah (Judges viii. 26, 27, XVii. 4) was an article well worth stealing, and the houses of God ordinarily lay in an open place (Exodus xxxiii. 7). The expressions #MR and #RT to denote the sacred service were retained in use from this period to later times; and, while every one knows how to sacrifice, the art of dealing with the ephod and winning its oracle from it continues from time immemorial to be the exclusive secret of the priest. In exceptional cases, the attendant is occasionally not the priest himself, but his disciple. Thus Moses has Joshua with him as his *aedituus 2*

** 2 M#RT M#H, more precisely m'' (T YY PNY M#H HKHN, 1Samuel. ii. 11.
****

(Exodus xxxiii. 11), who does not quit the tent of Jehovah; so also Eli has Samuel, who sleeps at night in the inner portion of the temple beside the ark of the covenant; even if perhaps the narrative of Samuel's early years is not quite in accordance with the actual circumstances as they existed at Shiloh, it is still in any case a perfectly good witness to a custom of the existence of which we are apprised from other sources. Compare now with this simple state of affairs the fact that in the Priestly Code the sons of Aaron have something like the half of a total of 22,000 Levites to assist them as watchers and ministers of the sanctuary.

126

Any one may slaughter and offer sacrifice (1Samuel xiv. 34 seq.); and, even in cases where priests are present, there is not a single trace of a systematic setting apart of what is holy, or of shrinking from touching it. When David "entered into the house of God and did eat the shew-bread, which it is not lawful to eat save for the priests, and gave also to them that were with him" (Mark ii. 26), this is not represented in 1Sam. xxi. as illegitimate when those who eat are sanctified, that is, have abstained on the previous day from women. Hunted fugitives lay hold of the horns of the altar without being held guilty of profanation. A woman, such as Hannah, comes before Jehovah, that is, before the altar, to pray; the words WTTYCB LPNY YY (1Samuel i. 9) supplied by the LXX, are necessary for the connection, and have been omitted from the Massoretic text as offensive. In doing so she is observed by the priest, who sits quietly, as is his wont, on his seat at the temple door. The history of the ark particularly, as Vatke justly remarks (pp. 317, 332), affords more than one proof of the fact that the notion of the unapproachableness of the holy was quite unknown; I shall content myself with the most striking of these. Samuel the Ephraimite sleeps by virtue of his office every night beside the ark of Jehovah, a place whither, according to Leviticus xvi., the high priest may come only once in the year, and even he only after the strictest preparation and with the most elaborate atoning rites. The contrast in the TONE OF FEELING is so great that no one as yet has even ventured to realise it clearly to himself.

IV.II.2. With the commencement of the monarchical period the priests forthwith begin to come into greater prominence along with the kings; the advance in centralisation and in publicity of life makes itself noticeable also in the department of worship. At the beginning of Saul's reign we find the distinguished Ephraimitic priesthood, the house of Eli, no longer at Shiloh, but at Nob, in the vicinity of the king, and to a certain degree in league with him; for their head, Ahijah the priest, is in immediate attendance on him when arms are first raised against the Phiiistines, shares the danger with him, and consults the ephod on his behalf. Subsequently the *entente cordiale* was disturbed, Ahijah and his brethren fell a sacrifice to the king's jealousy, and thus the solitary instance of an independent and considerable priesthood to be met with in the old history of Israel came for ever to an end. Abiathar, who alone escaped the massacre of Nob (1Samuel xxii.), fled with the ephod to David, for which he was rewarded afterwards with high honours, but all that he became he became as servant of David. Under David the regius priesthood began to grow towards the importance which it from that time forward had. This king exercised unfettered control over the sanctuary of the ark which stood in his citadel, as also over the appointment of the priests, who were merely his officials. Alongside of Abiathar he placed Zadok (and subsequently Ira also), as well as some of his own sons. For when it is stated in 2Sam. viii. 18 that the sons of David were priests, the words must not out of regard to the Pentateuch be twisted so as to mean something different from what they say. We also (1Kings iv. 5) find the son of the prophet Nathan figuring as a priest, and on the other hand the son of Zadok holding a high secular office (ver. 2); even at this date the line of demarcation afterwards drawn between holy and non-holy persons has no existence. What under David was still wanting to the institution of the royal worship and the regius priests—a fixed centre—was added by the erection of the temple under his successor. At the beginning of Solomon's reign there was still no ISRAELITE place of sacrifice such as sufficed for the greater contingencies; he was compelled to celebrate his accession at the great Bamah at Gibeon, a town in the neighbourhood of Jerusalem, which, although it had been subjugated for a considerable time, was still entirely Canaanite. He now took care to make it possible that his colossal festivals should be celebrated at his own sanctuary. And next he made Zadok its priest after having previously deposed and relegated to his patrimonial property at Anathoth, a village adjoining Jerusalem, the aged Abiathar, a man of pure and honourable priestly descent, on account of the support he had given to the legitimate heir to the crown, thereby bringing to pass the fate with which the once so proud and powerful family of Eli had in 1Samuel ii. been threatened. Doubtless other priests also by degrees attached themselves to the family of Zadok, and ultimately came even to call themselves his sons, just as the Rechabites regarded Jonathan ben Rechab, or the "children of the prophets" one or other of the great prophets, as their father.

Regarding their sanctuaries as their own private property, precisely as Micah does in the classical instance recorded in Judges xvii., xviii., and proceeding quite untrammelled in the appointment and removal of the officials employed, neither do these early kings hesitate in the least to exercise personally the rights which had emanated from themselves, and been delegated to others. Of Saul, who indeed was in the habit of delegating but seldom, and of doing with his own hand all that required to be done, it is several times mentioned that he sacrificed in person; and it is clear that this is not brought as a charge against him in 1Samuel xiv. and xv. David sacrificed on the occasion of his having successfully brought the ark to Jerusalem; that it was he himself who officiated appears from the fact that he wore the priestly ephod—*the ephod bad*—and at the close of the offering pronounced the benediction (2Samuel vi. 14, 18). In the same way was the consecration of the temple conducted by Solomon; it was he who went before the altar, and after praying there upon his knees with outstretched arms, rose and blessed the people (1Kings viii. 22, 54, 53),—doubtless also it was he who with his own hands offered the first sacrifice. The priests' technical skill is necessary only for inquiring of the oracle before the ephod (1Samuel xiv. 18).

IV.II.3. These beginnings are continued in the history of the priesthood after the division of the kingdom. Jeroboam I., the founder of the kingdom of Israel, is treated by the historian as the founder also of Israel's worship in so far as the latter differed from the Judaean ideal: "he made the two calves of gold, and set them up at Bethel and at Dan; he made the Bamoth-houses and made priests from the mass of the people, who were not of the sons of Levi, and ordained a feast in the eighth month and ascended to the altar to burn incense" (1Kings xii. 28 seq., xiii. 33). Here indeed after the well-known manner of pious pragmatism retrospective validity is given to the Deuteronomic law which did not come into force until three centuries afterwards, and judgment is thus passed in accordance with a historically inadmissable standard; moreover, the facts on which the judgment is based are on the one hand too much generalised, and on the other hand laid too exclusively to the charge of Jeroboam. The first king bears the weight of all the sins in worship of all his successors and of the whole body of the people. But the recognition of the sovereign priesthood of the ruler, of the formative influence which he exercised over the worship, is just. The most important temples were royal ones, and the priests who attended at them were the king's priests (Amos vii. 10 seq.). When therefore Jehu overthrew the house of Ahab, he did not extirpate all its members merely, and its officials and courtiers, but also its priests as well; they too were servants of the crown and in positions of trust (2Kings x. 11I; comp. 1Kings iv. 5). The statement that they were chosen at the pleasure of the king is therefore to be taken as implying that, as in David's and Solomon's time, so also later they could and might be chosen at pleasure; on the other hand, in point of fact the sacred office, in Dan at least, continued from the period of the Judges down to the Assyrian deportation hereditary in the family of Jonathan. One must, moreover, avoid imagining that all the "houses of the high places" and all the priestly posts *1* belonged to the king; it was impossible that the

** 1. The parallelism between "Bamoth-houses" and a priestly appointment in 1Kings xii. 31 seems not to be casual merely. Whilst a Bamah may be a simple altar, a "Bamoth-house" presupposes a divine   image,   and   renders   an   *aedituus*   necessary.
****

government should be so all-pervading in such matters. At this period most of the sanctuaries were public, but not therefore as yet on that account royal, and so also doubtless there were numerous priests who were not servants of the king. The preponderance of official cultus and of an official personnel to carry it on was counteracted in the northern kingdom by the frequent dynastic changes and the unattached particularism of the separate tribes; the conditions may be presumed to have developed themselves with great variety and freedom, hereditary and unhereditary priests, priests with independent benefices and others in complete poverty, subsisting side by side; the variety and the equality of rights enjoyed by all is the distinguishing mark of the time.

Speaking generally, however, the priesthood has distinctly consolidated itself as compared with its former condition, and gained not a little alike in number and in influence; it has become an important power in public life, without which the nation cannot be imagined. It would perhaps be somewhat bold to assert this on the strength merely of the brief and inadequate indications in the Book of Kings, which is chiefly interested in the extraordinary interventions of the prophets in the course of Israel's history, but other and more authentic testimonies justify us in doing so. First of these is the Blessing of Moses, an independent document of northern Israel which speaks for itself. Here we read: "Thy Thummim and thy Urim belong to the man of thy friendship, whom thou didst prove at Massah, for whom thou didst strive at the waters of Meribah; who saith of father and mother, I have never seen them, and acknowledgeth not his brethren nor knoweth his own children— for they observe thy word and keep thy covenant, they teach Jacob thy judgments and Israel thy law; they bring savour of fat before thee and whole burnt sacrifice upon thine altar; bless, O Lord, his strength, and accept the work of his hands; smite through the loins of them that rise up against him, and of them that hate him that they rise not again" (Deuteronomy xxxiii. 8-11). In this passage the priests appear as a strictly close corporation, so close that they are mentioned only exceptionally in the plural number, and for the most part are spoken of collectively in the singular, as an organic unity which embraces not merely the contemporary members, but also their ancestors, and which begins its life with Moses, the friend of Jehovah who as its beginning is identified with the continuation just as the man is identified with the child out of which he has grown. The history of Moses is at the same time the history of the priests, the Urim and Thummim belong—one is not quite sure to which, but it comes to the same thing; every priest to whom the care of an ephod has been intrusted interrogates before it the sacred oracle. The first relative clause relating to Moses passes over without change of subject into one that refers to the priests, so that the singular immediately falls into plural and the plural back to the singular. Yet this so strongly marked solidarity of the priesthood as a profession rests by no means upon the natural basis of family or clan unity; it is not blood, but on the contrary the abnegation of blood that constitutes the priest, as is brought out with great emphasis. He must act for Jehovah's sake as if he had neither father nor mother, neither brethren nor children. Blind prepossession in people's conceptions of Judaism has hitherto prevented the understanding of these words, but they are thoroughly unambiguous. What they say is, that in consecrating himself to the service of Jehovah a man abandons his natural relationships, and severs himself from family ties; thus, with the brotherhood of the priests in northern Israel the case is precisely similar as with that of the religious guilds of the sons of the prophets—the Rechabites, and doubtless too the Nazarites (Amos ii. 11 seq.)—also native there. Whosoever chose (or, whomsoever he chose) was made priest by Jeroboam—such is the expression of the Deuteronomic redactor of the Book of Kings (1Kings xiii. 33). A historical example of what has been said is afforded by the young Samuel, as he figures in the narrative of his early years contained in 1Samuel i.-iii.—a narrative which certainly reflects the condition of things in Ephraim at the period of the monarchy. The child of a well-to-do middle class family at Ramah, in the district of Zuph Ephraim, he is even before his birth vowed to Jehovah by his mother, and as soon as possible afterwards is handed over to the sanctuary at Shiloh,—not to become a Nazarite or one of the Nethinim in the sense of the Pentateuch, but to be a priest,—for in his ministry he wears the linen ephod, the *ephod bad*, and even the pallium (1Samuel ii. 18) *1* And it is made very plain that

*** 1. Comp. Koran, iii. 31: "I vow to thee that which is in my womb as a devotee of the mosque, to serve it." [pallium. "1.Antiq. A large rectangular cloak or mantle worn by men' chiefly among the Greeks; esp. by philosophers and by early Christian ascetics...Himation...2.Eccl. A vestment of wool worn by patriarchs and metropolitans... SOED. Heb. m(yl q+n ii.19?] ***

the mother's act, in thus giving up her son, who is properly hers, or (as she expresses it) lending him to Jehovah for ever (1Samuel i. 28: #MW)L=MW#)L), is regarded as a renunciation of family rights. The circumstance that it is by the parents and not by Samuel himself that the consecration is made makes no material difference; the one thing is on the same plane with the other, and doubtless occurred as well as the other, although seldomer. But, on the other hand, it can hardly have been the rule that any one should abandon not parents and brethren merely, but also wife and children as well in order to enter the priesthood; in Deuteronomy xxxiii. 9 this is

130

adduced only as an extreme instance of the spirit of self-sacrifice. In any case it is not to be inferred that celibacy was demanded, but only that the priestly office was often barely sufficient to support the man, not to speak of a family.

So fixed and influential, so independent and exclusive had the priesthood become at the date of the composition of the Blessing of Moses, that it takes a place of its own alongside of the tribes of the nation, is itself a tribe, constituted, however, not by blood, but by community of spiritual interests. Its importance is brought into clearness even by the opposition which it encounters, and which occasions so vigorous a denunciation of its enemies that one might well believe the person who committed it to writing to have been himself a priest. The cause of the hostility is not stated, but it seems to be directed simply against the very existence of a professional and firmly organised clergy, and to proceed from laymen who hold fast by the rights of the old priestless days.

Next to the Blessing of Moses the discourses of Hosea contain our most important materials for an estimate of the priesthood of Northern Israel. How important that institution was for public life is clear from his expressions also. The priests are the spiritual leaders of the people; the reproach that they do not fulfil their high vocation proves in the first place that they have it. Degenerate they are, to be sure; in Hosea's representation they are seen in the same light as that in which the sons of Eli appear as described in 1Samuel ii. 22 seq., from which description one conjectures the author to have derived his colours from a state of matters nearer his own day than the period of the judges. The priests of Shechem are even taxed by the prophet with open highway robbery (vi. 9), and in one charge after another he accuses them of taking advantage of their office for base gain, of neglecting its most sacred duties, and in this way having the principal blame for the ruin of the people. "Hear the word of Jehovah, ye children of Israel, for the Lord hath a controversy with the inhabitants of the land, because there is no truth, nor mercy, nor knowledge of God in the land. (2.) There is swearing, and lying, and killing, and stealing, and committing adultery; they use violence and add murder to murder. (3.) Therefore the land mourneth, and every creature that dwelleth therein languisheth, even to the wild beasts of the field and the fowls of heaven; and even the fishes of the sea are taken away. (4.) Yet let no man strive and no man reprove; for the people do just as their priests. (5.) Therefore shall ye (priests) stumble on that day, and also the prophets with you on that night; and I will destroy your kin. (6.) My people are destroyed for lack of knowledge, because ye yourselves reject knowledge; I will therefore reject you that ye shall be no longer priests unto me; ye have forgotten the doctrine of your God, so will I forget your children. (7.) The more they are, the more they sin against me; their glory they turn into shame. (8.) They eat up the sin of my people, and they set their heart on their iniquity. (9.) And it shall be as with the people so with the priest; I will punish them for their ways and requite them for their doings. (10.) They shall eat and not have enough, they shall commit whoredom and shall not increase, because they have ceased to take heed to the Lord" (Hosea iv. 1-10). *1*

** 1. In the introductory words the people are invited to hear what it is that Jehovah complains of them for;

sin prevails to such an extent that the complete ruin of the country is inevitable (vers. 1-3). With the word "yet" at the beginning of the following verse the prophet changes the course of his thought; from the people he passes to the priests; the root of the general corruption is the want of divine knowledge (the knowledge, namely, that "I will have mercy and not sacrifice; "compare Jeremiah xxii. 16), and for this the priests are to blame, whose task it was to diffuse "knowledge," but who, instead of this for their own selfish interests fostered the tendency of the people to seek Jehovah's grace by sacrifice rather than by righteousness. For if it be conceded that it is the priests who are addressed from ver. 6 onwards, then it is not easy to see why a change in the address should take place between ver. 5 and ver. 6, especially as the co-ordination of priests with prophets seems more reasonable in ver. 5 than that of prophets and people. As ver. 4 in this way occupies an intermediate position between the complaint made against the people in vers. 1-3, and that against the priests in vers. 5-10, the transition from the one to the other, indicated by the "yet," must occur in it. Hosea abruptly breaks off from reproaching the people, "Yet let no man strive and no man reprove"—why not, the words that follow must explain. In verse 4b some circumstance must be mentioned which excuses the people, and at the same time draws down indignation upon the priests who are the subjects of the following. These considerations necessarily determine the thought which we are to expect, namely, this—"for the people do just as their priests." . This meaning is obtained by the conjectural reading W(MY KKMRYW instead of W(MKKMRYB. Comp. ver. 9. The remaining YKH must be deleted. The ordinary view of ver. 4 is hardly worth refuting. The)L YWKH, it is said, is spoken from the people's point of view. The people repel the prophet's reproach and rebuke, because (such is the interpretation of ver. 4b) they themselves have no scruples in striving EVEN with the priest. "Even," for want of subjection to the priests is held to be specially wicked. But the prophet Hosea would hardly have considered it a capital offence if the people had withheld from the priests the respect of which, according to his own language, they were so utterly unworthy. Moreover, every exegesis which finds in ver. 4 a reproach brought against the people, leaves in obscurity the point at which the transition is made from reproach of the people to reproach of the priests.
****

In the northern kingdom, according to this, the spiritual ascendancy of the priests over the people seems hardly to have been less than that of the prophets, and if in the history we hear less about it, *1* the explanation is to be sought in the

** 1. According to 2Kings xvii. 27, 28, the foreign colonies introduced by the Assyrians into Samaria after it had been depopulated, were at first devoured by lions because they were ignorant of the right way of honouring the deity of the land. Esarhaddon therefore sent one of the exiled Samaritan priests, who fixed his abode at Bethel, the ancient chief sanctuary, and instructed (MWRH) the settlers in the religion of the god of the country. This presupposes a definite priesthood, which maintained itself even in exile for a considerable time. **

fact that they laboured quietly and regularly in limited circles, taking no part in politics, and fully submissive to the established order, and that for this reason they attracted less notice and were less talked about than the prophets who, like Elijah and Elisha, stirred up Israel by their extraordinary and oppositional action.

IV.II.4. In Judah the nucleus of the development was the same as in Israel. The idea that in Judah the genuine Mosaic priesthood had by the grace of God been maintained, while in Israel, on the other hand, a schismatic priesthood had intruded itself by the favour of the king and man's device, is that of the later Judaeans who had the last word, and were therefore of course in the right. The B'ne Zadok of Jerusalem as contrasted with the B'ne Eli whom they superseded were originally illegitimate (if one may venture to apply a conception which at that time was quite unknown), and did not inherit their right from the fathers, but had it from David and Solomon. They always remained in this dependent condition, they at all times walked, as 1Samuel ii. 35 has it, "before Jehovah's anointed," as his servants and officers. To the kings the temple was a part of their palace which, as is shown by 1Kings vii. and 2Kings xi., stood upon the same hill and was contiguous with it; they placed their threshold alongside of that of Jehovah, and made their door-posts adjoin to His, so that only the wall intervened between Jehovah and them (Ezekiel xliii. 8). They shaped the official cultus entirely as they chose, and regarded the management of it, at least so far as one gathers from the epitome of the "Book of the Kings," as the main business of their government. They introduced new usages and abolished old ones; and as they did so the priests always bent to their will and were merely their executive organs. *1* That they were at

*** 1. Compare for example 2Kings xii. 5 seq. (Joash and Jehoiada), xvi. 10 seq. Ahaz and Urijah), and, finally, chap.   xxii.   (Josiah   and   Hilkiah).
****

liberty to offer sacrifice also is a thing of course; they did it, however, only on exceptional occasions, such as, perhaps, at the dedication of a new altar (2Kings xvi. 12, 13). Even with Jeremiah, who as a rule does not consider sacrifice and drawing near to Jehovah (Numbers xvi 5) as every man's business, the king as such is held to be also the supreme priest; for at the beginning of the exile and the foreign domination his hope for the future is: "Their potentate shall be of themselves, and their governor shall proceed from the midst of them, and I will cause him to draw near, and he shall approach unto me; for who else should have the courage to approach unto me? saith the Lord" (xxx. 21). Ezekiel is the first to protest against dealing with the temple as a royal dependency; for him the prerogative of the prince is reduced to this, that it is his duty to support the public cultus at his own expense.

The distinction between the Judaean and the Israelite priesthood did not exist at first, but arose out of the course of events. The sheltered and quiet life of the little state in the south presents a marked contrast with the external and internal conflicts, the easily raised turmoil, of the northern kingdom. In the latter, the continual agitation brought extraordinary personalities up to the surface; in the former, institutions based upon the permanent order of things and supported by permanent powers were consolidated./1/

*** 1. The Rechabites, who arose in the northern kingdom, continued to subsist in Judah, and Jeremiah prophesied to them that there should never fail them a priestly head of the family of their founder (xxxv. 19). ***

Naturally the monarchy itself benefited most by this stability. The king's cultus, which in the kingdom of Samaria was in no position to supersede the popular and independent worship, easily obtained a perceptible preponderance in the smaller Judah; the king's priesthood, which in the former was incidentally involved in disaster by the overthrow of the dynasty, in the latter gained in strength side by side with the house of David—even Aaron and Amminadab were according to the Priestly Code related to the royal family, as Jehoiada and Ahaziah were in actual fact. Thus at an early period was the way paved for the Act of Uniformity by which Josiah made the king's cultus the official and the only one. One effect which accompanied the measures he took was naturally the exclusive legitimation of the king's priesthood at Jerusalem. But the principle of heredity had already pervaded the other priestly families so thoroughly that to enter any secular calling was nowhere expected of them. The Deuteronomic legislator had conferred upon them the right of carrying on their office at Jerusalem, and of executing it there on behalf of any one who requested their services; but this regulation, from the opposition of the B'ne Zadok, was found on the whole impracticable (2Kings xxiii. 9), although doubtless some extraneous elements may at that time have succeeded in making their way into the temple nobility. The bulk of the priests of the high places who had been superseded had to content themselves (since they could not now get rid of their spiritual character) with being degraded among their brethren at Jerusalem, and with admission to a subordinate share in the service of the sanctuary (comp. 1Samuel ii. 36). It was thus, at the close of the pre-exilic history, that the distinction between priests and Levites arose to which Ezekiel is at pains to give the sanction of law.

IV.III.

IV.III.1. On the whole it is easy here to bring the successive strata of the Pentateuch into co-ordination with the recognisable steps of the historical development. In the Jehovistic legislation there is no word of priests (Exodus xx.-xxiii., xxxiv.), and even such precepts as "Thou shalt not go up by steps unto mine altar, that thy nakedness be not discovered thereon " (Exodus xx. 26) are directed to the general "thou," that is, to the people. With this corresponds the fact that in the solemn ratification of the covenant of Sinai (Exodus xxiv. 3-8), it is young men of the children of Israel who officiate as sacrificers. Elsewhere in the Jehovist Aaron (Exodus iv. 14, xxxii. 1 seq.) and Moses (xxxiii. 7-lI; Deuteronomy xxxiii. 8) figure as the founders of the clerical order. Twice (in Exodus xix. 22 and xxxii 29) mention is made of other priests besides; but Exodus xxxii. 29 rests upon Deuteronomy, and even Exodus xix. 22 can hardly have been an original constituent of one of the Jehovistic sources.

IV.III.2. In Deuteronomy the priests, as compared with the judges and the prophets, take a very prominent position (xvi. 18-xviii. 22) and constitute a clerical order, hereditary in numerous families, whose privilege is uncontested and therefore also does not require protection. Here now for the first time begins the regular use of the name of Levites for the priests,—a name of which the consideration has been postponed until now.

In the pre-exilic literature apart from the Pentateuch it occurs very seldom. First in the prophets, once in the Book of Jeremiah (xxxiii. 17-22), in a passage which in any case is later than the capture of Jerusalem by the Chaldaeans, and certainly was not written by Jeremiah. *1* The use of the name is an

*** 1. In the LXX, chap. xxxiii. 14-26 is wanting. The parallelism between vers. 17-22 and 23-26 is striking. It looks as if David and Levi arose out of a misunderstanding of the families mentioned in ver. 24, namely, Judah and Ephraim. In any case wdwd in ver. 26 is an interpolation. ***

established thing in Ezekiel (573 B.C.), and henceforward occurs without interruption in the writings of the later prophets, a sign that its earlier absence is not to be explained as accidental, not even in Jeremiah, who speaks so frequently of the priests. *2*

*** 1. Ezekiel xl. 46, xliii. 19, xliv. 10, 15, xlv. 5, xlviii. 11-13, 22, 31; Isaiah lxvi. 21; Zechariah xii. 13; Malachi ii. 4, 8, iii. 3. ***

In the historical books the Levites (leaving out of account 1Samuel vi. 15, 2Samuel xv. 24, and 1Kings viii. 4, xii. 31) *1*

all that is necessary has been said at IV.II.1; on 1Kings viii. 4 see. I.III.1. That
1Kings xii. 31 proceeds from the Deuteronomic redactor, the date of whose writing
is not earlier than the second half of the exile, needs no proof. The hopeless
corruptness of 2Samuel xv. 24 I have shown in Text. d. BB. Sam. (Goettingen,
1871). ***

occur only in the two appendices to the Book of Judges (chaps. xvii., xviii., and xix.,
xx.), of which, however, the second is unhistorical and late, and only the first is
certainly pre-exilic. But in this case it is not the Levites who are spoken of, as
elsewhere, but A LEVITE, who passes for a great rarity, and who is forcibly carried
off by the tribe of Dan, which has none.

Now this Jonathan, the ancestor of the priests of Dan, notwithstanding that he
belongs to the tribe of Judah, is represented as a descendant of Gershom the son of
Moses (Judges xviii. 30). The other ancient priestly family that goes back to the
period of the Judges, the Ephraimitic, of Shiloh, appears also to be brought into
connection with Moses; at least in 1Samuel ii. 27 (a passage, however, which is
certainly post-Deuteronomic), where Jehovah is spoken of as having made himself
known to the ancestors of Eli in Egypt, and as thereby having laid the foundation for
the bestowal of the priesthood, it is clearly Moses who is thought of as the recipient
of the revelation. Historical probability admits of the family being traced back to
Phinehas, who during the early period of the judges was priest of the ark, and from
whom the inheritance on Mount Ephraim and also the second son of Eli were named;
it is not to be supposed that he is the mere shadow of his younger namesake, as the
latter predeceased his father and was of quite secondary importance beside him. But
Phinehas is both in the Priestly Code and in Josh. xxiv. 33 (E) the son of Eleazar, and
Eleazar is, according to normal tradition, indeed a son of Aaron, but according to the
sound of his name (Eliezer) a son of Moses along with Gershom. Between Aaron
and Moses in the Jehovistic portion of the Pentateuch no great distinction is made; if
Aaron, in contradistinction from his brother, is characterised as THE LEVITE
(Exodus iv. 14), Moses on the other hand bears the priestly staff, is over the
sanctuary, and has Joshua to assist him as Eli had Samuel (Exodus xxxiii. 7-11).
Plainly the older claims are his; in the main Jehovistic source, in J, Aaron originally
does not occur at all, *2* neither

present in J, but owed his introduction to tile redactor who combined J nnd E
together into JE, can be shown best from Exod vii. x. For Jehovah's COMMAND to
appear before Pharaoh is in J given to Moses alone (vii. 14, 26 [viii. 1], viii. 16 [20],
ix. 1, 13, x. 1); it is only in the sequel that Aaron appears along with him four times,
always when Pharaoh in distress summons Moses and Aaron in order to ask their
intercession. But strangely enough Aaron is afterwards completely ignored again;
Moses alone makes answer, speaking solely in his own name and not in Aaron's also
(viii. 5, 22, 25 [9, 26, 29]; ix. 29), and although he has not come alone ; he goes so
and makes his prayer in the singular (viii. 8, 26 [12, 30], ix. 33, x. 18), the change of
the number in x. 17 is under these circumstances suspicious enough. It appears as if

the Jehovistic editor had held Aaron's presence to be appropriate precisely at the intercession. *********************************

is he mentioned in Deuteronomy xxxiii. 8. In the genealogies of the Priestly Code one main branch of the tribe of Levi is still called, like the eldest son of Moses, Gershom, and another important member is actually called Mushi, 2:e., the Mosaite.

It is not impossible that the holy office may have continued in the family of Moses, and it is very likely that the two oldest houses in which it was hereditary, those at Dan and at Shiloh, may have claimed in all seriousness to have been descended from him. Afterwards, as Deuteronomy xxxiii. 8 seq. informs us, all priests honoured Moses as their father, not as being the head of their clan but as being the founder of their order. The same took place in Judah, but there the clerical guild ultimately acquired a hereditary character, and the order became a sort of clan. *Levite*, previously an official name, now became a patronymic at the same time, and all the Levites together formed a blood-kinship, *1*

** 1. The instance of the Rechabites shows how easily the transition could made.
****

a race which had not received any land of its own indeed, but in compensation had obtained the priesthood for its heritage. This hereditary clergy was alleged to have existed from the very beginning of the history of Israel, and even then as a numerous body, consisting of many others besides Moses and Aaron. Such is the representation made by Deuteronomist and subsequent writers, but in Deuteronomy we read chiefly of the *Levites* in the provincial towns of Judah and of the *priests*, the *Levites* in Jerusalem, seldom of Levi as a whole (x. 8 seq., xviii. 1) *2*

** 2. On Deut xxvii. compare Kuenen, Theol. Tidjdschr., 1878, p. 297.
****

That the hereditary character of the priesthood is here antedated and really first arose in the later period of the Kings, has already been shown in the particular instance of the sons of Zadok of Jerusalem, who were at first parvenus and afterwards became the most legitimate of the legitimate. But it is very remarkable how this artificial construction of a priestly family,—a construction which has absolutely nothing perplexing in itself— was suggested and favoured by the circumstance that in remote antiquity there once actually did exist a veritable tribe of Levi which had already disappeared before the period of the rise of the monarchy. This tribe belonged to the group of the four oldest sons of Leah,—Reuben, Simeon, Levi, Judah,—who are always enumerated together in this order, and who settled on both sides of the Dead Sea, towards the wilderness. Singularly no one of them succeeded in holding its own except Judah; all the others became absorbed among the inhabitants of the wilderness or in other branches of their kindred. The earliest to find this destiny were the two tribes of Simeon and Levi (in Genesis xlix. regarded as one), in consequence of a catastrophe which must have befallen them at some time during the period of the judges. "Simeon and Levi are brethren, their shepherds' staves are weapons of slaughter; O my soul, come not thou into their assembly! mine honour, be thou far from their band! for they slew men in their anger, and in their self-will they houghed oxen; cursed be their anger—so fierce! and their wrath—so cruel! I will divide them in Jacob and scatter them over Israel!" (Genesis xlix.5-7). The offence of Simeon and Levi here rebuked cannot have been committed against Israelites, for in such a case the thought could not have occurred, which is here emphatically repelled, that Jacob, that is to say, Israel as a whole, could have made common cause with them. What is here spoken of must be some crime against the Canaanites, very probably the identical crime which is charged upon the two brothers in Genesis xxxiv., and which there also Jacob (ver. 30) repudiates,—the treacherous attack upon Shechem and massacre of its inhabitants, in disregard of the treaty which had been made. In Judges ix. it is related that Shechem, until then a flourishing town of the Canaanites, with whom moreover Israelite elements were already beginning to blend, was conquered and destroyed by Abimelech, but it is quite impossible to bring into any connection with this the violent deed of Simeon and Levi, which must have taken place earlier, although also within the period of the judges. The consequences of their act, the vengeance of the Canaanites, the two tribes had to bear alone; Israel, according to the indication given in Genesis xlix. 6, xxxiv. 30, did not feel any call to interfere on their behalf or make common cause with them. Thus they fell to pieces and passed out of sight,—in the opinion of their own nation a just fate. In the historical books they are never again mentioned.

It is quite impossible to regard this Levi of the Book of Genesis as a mere shadow of the caste which towards the end of the monarchy arose out of the separate priestly families of Judah. The utterance given in Genesis xlix. 5-7 puts the brothers on an exact equality, and assigns to them an extremely secular and blood-thirsty character. There is not the faintest idea of Levi's sacred calling or of his dispersion as being conditioned thereby; the dispersion is a curse and no blessing, an annihilation and no establishment of his special character. But it is equally an impossibility to derive the caste from the tribe; there is no real connection between the two, all the intermediate links are wanting; the tribe succumbed at an early date, and the rise of the caste was very late, and demonstrably from unconnected beginnings. But in these circumstances the coincidence of name is also very puzzling: Levi the third son of Jacob, perhaps a mere patronymic derived form his mother Leah, and levi the official priest. If it were practicable to find a convincing derivation of levi in its later use from the appellative meaning of the root, then one might believe the coincidence to be merley fortuitous, but it is impossible to do so. the solution therefore has been suggested that the violent dissolution of the tribe in the period of the judges led the individual Levites, who now were landless, to seek their maintenance by the exercise of sacrificial functions; this lay to their hand and was successful because Moses them an of God had belonged to their number and had transmitted to them by hereditary succession a certain preferential claim to the sacred office. But at that time priestly posts were not numerous, and such an entrance of the levites *en masse* into the service of Jehovah in that early time is in view of the infrequency of the larger sanctuaries a very difficult assumption. It is perhaps correct to say that Moses actually was descended from Levi, and that the later significance of the name Levite is to be explained by reference to him. In point of fact, the name does appear to have been given in the first instance only to the descendants of Moses, and not to have been transferred until a later period to those priests as a body, who were quite unconnected with him by blood, but who all desired to stand related to him as their head. Here it will never be possible to get beyond conjecture.

IV.III.3 While the clerical *tribe of the Levites* is still brought forward only modestly in Deuteronomy (x. 8 seq. xviii. 1; Joshua xiii. 14, 33), it is dealt with in very real earnest in the Priestly Code. The *tribe of Levi* (Numbers i. 47, 49, iii. 6, xvii. 3, xviii. 2) is given over by the remaining tribes to the sanctuary, is catalogued according to the genealogical system of its families, reckons 22,000 male members, and even receives a sort of tribal territory, the forty-eight Levitical cities (Josh. xxi.). At the beginning of this chapter we have already spoken of a forward step made in the Priestly Code, connected with this enlargement of the clergy, but of much greater importance; hitherto the distinction has been between clergy and laity, while here there is introduced the great division of the order itself into sons of Aaron and Levites. Not in Deuteronomy only, but everywhere in the Old Testament, apart from Ezra, Nehemiah, and Chronicles, Levite is the priest's title of honour. *1* Aaron himself is so styled in the

** 1. Exodus iv. 14; Deuteronomy xxxiii. 8; Judges xvii. seq.; Exodus xxxii. 26-28; Deuteronomy x. 8 seq., xii. 12, 18 seq. xiv. 27, 29, xvi. 11, 14, xvii. 9, 18, xviii. 1-8, xxiv. 8, xxvii. 9, 14, xxxi. 9, 25; Joshua iii. 3,xiii. 14, 33, xiv. 3 seq., xviii. 7; Judges xix. seq., 1Samuel vl. 15; 1Kings xii. 31, Jeremiah xxxiii 17-22; Ezekiel xliv. 8 seq.; Isaiah lxvi. 2, Zechariah xii. 13, Malachi Ii. 4, 8, iii. 3. Only the glosses 2Samuel xv. 24, and 1Kings viii. 4 (compare, however, 2Chronicles v. 5) can rest upon the Priestly Code. **

often-quoted passage, Exodus iv. 14, and that too to denote his calling, not his family, for the latter he has in common with Moses, from whom, nevertheless, it is intended to distinguish him by the style, "thy brother the Levite." In Deuteronomy we are struck by the deliberate emphasis laid on the equal right of all the Levites to sacrificial service in Jerusalem— "The priests, the Levites, the whole tribe of Levi, shall have no portion or inheritance with Israel; they shall eat the offerings of Jehovah and his inheritance....And if a Levite come from any of thy cities out of all Israel, where he sojourned, and come to the place which Jehovah shall choose, then he shall minister in the name of Jehovah his God as all his brethren the Levites do who stand there before Jehovah" (Deuteronomy xviii. 1, 6, 7). Here the legislator has in view his main enactment, *viz.*, the abolition of all places of worship except the temple of Solomon; those who had hitherto been the priests of these could not be allowed to starve. Therefore it is that he impresses it so often and so earnestly on the people of the provinces that in their sacrificial pilgrimages to Jerusalem they ought not to forget the Levite of their native place, but should carry him with them. For an understanding of the subsequent development this is very important, in so far as it shows how the position of the Levites outside of Jerusalem was threatened by the centralisation of the worship. In point of fact, the good intention of the

Deuteronomist proved impossible of realisation; with the high places fell also the priests of the high places. In so far as they continued to have any part at all in the sacred service, they had to accept a position of subordination under the sons of Zadok (2Kings xxiii. 9). Perhaps Graf was correct in referring to this the prophecy of 1Samuel ii. 36 according to which the descendants of the fallen house of Eli are to come to the firmly established regius priest, to beg for an alms, or to say, "Put me, I pray thee, into one of the priests' offices, that I may eat a piece of bread:" that historically the deposed Levites had no very intimate connection with those ancient companions in misfortune is no serious objection to such an interpretation in the case of a post-Deuteronomic writer. In this way arose as an illegal consequence of Josiah's reformation, the distinction between priests and Levites. With Ezekiel this distinction is still an innovation requiring justification and sanction; with the Priestly Code it is a "statute for ever," although even yet not absolutely undisputed, as appears from the Priestly version of the story of Korah's company. *1* For all Judaism subsequent to Ezra, and so for

** 1. Distorted references to the historical truth are round also in Numbers xvii. 25 and xviii. 23, passages which are unintelligible apart from Ezekiel xliv. Compare Kuenen, Theol. Tijdschr., 1878, p. 138 seq. **

Christian tradition, the Priestly Code in this matter also has been authoritative. Instead of the Deuteronomic formula "the priests the Levites," we henceforward have "the priests and the Levites," particularly in Chronicles, *2* and in the

** 2. Except in 2 Chrom v. 5, xxx. 27. **

ancient versions the old *usus* loquendi is frequently corrected. *3*

** 3. *E.g.*, Josh. iii. 3 and Isaiah lxvi. 21 in the LXX, Deuteronomy xviii. 1 and Judges xvii. 13 in "Jerome; and many passages in the Syriac. On the carrying out of the new organisation of the temple *personnel* after the exile, see Vatke, p. 568, Graf (in Merx's Archiv, i., p. 225 seq.), and Kuenen (Godsdienst, ii. p. 104 seq). With Zerubbabel and Joshua, four priestly families, 4289 persons in all, returned from Babylon in 538 (Ezra iv. 36-39); with Ezra in 458 came two families in addition, but the number of persons is not stated (viii. 2). Of Levites there came on the first occasion 74 (ii. 40); on the second, of the 1500 men who met at the rendezvous appointed by Ezra to make the journey through the wilderness, not one was a Levite, and it was only on the urgent representations of the scribe that some thirty were at last induced to join the company (viii. 15-20). How can we explain this preponderance of priests over Levites, which is still surprising even if the individual figures are not to be taken as exact? Certainly it cannot be accounted for if the state of matters for a thousand years had been that represented in the Priestly Code and in Chronicles. On the other hand, all perplexity vanishes if the Levites were the degraded priests of the high places of Judah. These were certainly not on the whole more numerous than the

Jerusalem college, and the prospect of thenceforward not being permitted to sacrifice in their native land, but of having slaughtering and washing for sole duties, cannot have been in any way very attractive to them; one can hardly blame them if they were disinclined voluntarily to lower themselves to the position of mere laborers under the sons of Zadok. Besides, it may be taken for granted that many (and more particularly Levitical) elements not originally belonging to it had managed to make way into the ranks of the Solomonic priesthood; that all were not successful (Ezra ii. 61) shows that many made the attempt, and considering the ease with which genealogies hoary with age were then manufactured and accepted, every such attempt cannot have failed.

How then came it to pass that afterwards, as one must conclude from the statements in Chronicles, the Levites stood to the priests in a proportion so much more nearly, if even then not quite fully corresponding to the law? Simply by the "Levitising" of alien families. At first in the community of the second temple the Levites continued to be distinguished from the singers, porters, and Nethinim (Ezra ii. 41-58), guilds which from the outset were much more numerous and which rapidly grew (Nehemiah xi. 17, 19, 36, xii. 28 seq.; 1Chronicles ix. 16, 22, 25). But the distinction had in fact no longer any actual basis, once the Levites had been degraded to the rank of temple-servitors and become Nethinim to the priests (Numbers iii. 9). Hence, where the Chronicler, who is at the same time the author of the Books of Ezra and Nehemiah, is not reproducing old sources but is writing freely, he regards the singers also and the porters as Levites. By artificial genealogies of rather a rough and ready kind the three families of singers, Heman, Asaph, and Ethan are traced up (1Chronicles vl.. 1 seq.) to the old Levitical families of Kohath, Gershon, and Merari (see Graf, as above, p. 231; and Ewald, iii. p. 380 seq.). How far the distinction between the Nethinim and the Levites was afterwards maintained (Josh. ix. 21 seq., I Esdras i. 3; Ezra viii. 20) is not clear. It would not be amiss if Ezekiel's intention of banishing foreigners from the temple found its fulfilment only through these heathen hieroduli, the Mehunim, the Nephisim, the sons of Shalmai, and the others whose foreign-sounding names are given in Ezra ii. 43 seq., obtaining admission into the tribe of Levi by artificial genealogies. A peculiar side light is thrown upon the course of development by the fact that the singers who in Ezra's time were not yet even Levites, afterwards felt shame in being so, and desired at least externally to be placed on all equality with priests. They begged of King Agrippa II. to obtain for them the permission of the synedrium to wear the white priestly dress.
****

The copestone of the sacred structure reared by the legislation of the middle books of the Pentateuch is the high priest. As the Aaronites are above the Levites so is Aaron himself above his sons; in his person culminates the development of the unity of worship inaugurated by Deuteronomy and the agency of Josiah. No figure of such incomparable importance occurs anywhere else in the Old Testament; a high priest of pre-eminent sanctity is still unknown to Ezekiel even. Even before the exile, it is true, the temple worship at Jerusalem had become so magnificent and its personnel so numerous as to render necessary an orderly division of offices and a gradation of ranks. In Jeremiah's time the priests constituted a guild divided into classes or families with elders at their head; the principal priest had a potent voice in the appointment of his inferior colleagues (1Samuel ii. 36); alongside of him stood the second priest, the keepers of the threshold, the captain of the watch as holders of prominent charges. *I* But in the Law the position of Aaron is not merely

*** I The Kohen ha-rosh first occurs in 2Samuel xv. 27, but here HR)# (so read, instead of HRW)H) comes from the interpolator of ver. 24. So again 2Kings xii. 11, HKHN HGDWL, but 2Kings xii. is from the same hand as 2Kings xvi. 10 seq. Elsewhere we have simply "the priest," compare besides 2Kings xix. 2; Jeremiah xix. 1; 2Kings xxiii. 4; xxv. 18; Jeremiah xx. 1; xxix. 25, 26; In 1Samuel ii. 36 SPXNY "incorporate me" shows that KHNH must mean "priestly guild" or "order." In connection with the name LWY it is   noteworthy   that   SPX   is   parallel   with   LWH   in   Isaiah   xiv.   1.
****

superior but unique, like that of the Pope in relation to the episcopate; his sons act under his oversight (Numbers iii. 4); he alone is the one fully qualified priest, the embodiment of all that is holy in Israel He alone bears the Urim and Thummim and the Ephod; the Priestly Code indeed no longer knows what those articles are for, and it confounds the ephod of gold with the ephod of linen, the plated image with the priestly robe; but the dim recollections of these serve to enhance the magical charm of Aaron's majestic adornment. He alone may enter into the holy of holies and there offer incense; the way at other times inaccessible (Nehemiah vi. 10, 11) is open to him on the great day of atonement. Only in him, at a single point and in a single moment, has Israel immediate contact with Jehovah. The apex of the pyramid touches heaven.

The high priest stands forth as absolutely sovereign in his own domain. Down to the exile, as we have seen, the sanctuary was the property of the king, and the priest was his servant; even in Ezekiel who on the whole is labouring towards emancipation, the prince has nevertheless a very great importance in the temple still; to him the dues of the people are paid, and the sacrificial expenses are in return defrayed by him. In the Priestly Code, on the other hand, the dues are paid direct into the sanctuary, the worship is perfectly autonomous, and has its own head, holding not from man but from the grace of God. Nor is it merely the autonomy of religion that is represented by the high priest; he exhibits also its supremacy over Israel. He does not carry sceptre and sword; nowhere, as Vatke (p. 539) well remarks, is any attempt made to claim for him secular power. But just in virtue of his spiritual dignity, as the head of the priesthood, he is head of the theocracy, and so much so that there is no room for any other alongside of him; a theocratic king beside him cannot be thought of (Numbers xxvii. 21). He alone is the responsible representative of the collective nation, the names of the twelve tribes are written on his breast and shoulders; his transgression involves the whole people in guilt, and is atoned for as that of the whole people, while the princes, when their sin-offerings are compared with his, appear as mere private persons (Leviticus iv. 3, 13, 22, ix. 7, xvi. 6). His death makes an epoch; it is when the high priest—not the king—dies that the fugitive slayer obtains his amnesty (Numbers xxxv. 28). At his investiture he receives the chrism like a king, and is called accordingly the anointed priest; he is adorned with the diadem and tiara (Ezekiel xxi. 31, A.V. 26) like a king, and like a king too he wears the purple, that most unpriestly of all raiment, of which he therefore must divest himself when he goes into the holy of holies (Lev. xvi. 4). What now can be the meaning of this fact,—that he who is at the head of the worship, in this quality alone, and without any political attributes besides, or any share in the government, is at the same time at the head of the nation? What but that civil power has been withdrawn from the nation and is in the hands of foreigners; that Israel has now merely a spiritual and ecclesiastical existence? In the eyes of the Priestly Code Israel in point of fact is not a people, but a church; worldly affairs are far removed from it and are never touched by its laws; its life is spent in religious services. Here we are face to face with the church of the second temple, the Jewish hierocracy, in a form possible only under foreign domination. It is customary indeed to designate in the Law by the ideal, or in other words blind, name of theocracy that which in historical reality is usually called hierarchy; but to imagine that with the two names one has gained a real distinction is merely to deceive oneself. But, this self-deception accomplished, it is easy further to carry back the hierocratic churchly constitution to the time of Moses, because it excludes the kingship, and then either to assert that it was kept secret throughout the entire period of the judges and the monarchy, or to use the fiction as a lever by which to dislocate the whole of the traditional history.

To any one who knows anything about history it is not necessary to prove that the so-called Mosaic theocracy, which nowhere suits the circumstances of the earlier periods, and of which the prophets, even in their most ideal delineations of the Israelite state as it ought to be, have not the faintest shadow of an idea, is, so to speak, a perfect fit for post-exilian Judaism, and had its actuality only there. Foreign rulers had then relieved the Jews of all concern about secular affairs; they had it in their power, and were indeed compelled to give themselves wholly up to sacred things, in which they were left completely unhampered. Thus the temple became the sole centre of life, and the prince of the temple the head of the spiritual commonwealth, to which also the control of political affairs, so far as these were still left to the nation, naturally fell there being no other head! *1*

*** 1. Very interesting and instructive is Ewald's proof of the way in which Zech. vi. 9-15 has been tampered with, so as to eliminate Zerubbabel and leave the high priest alone. Just so in dealing with Caliphs and Sultans, the Patriarchs were and are the natural heads of the Greek and   Oriental   Christians   even   in   secular   matters. ***

The Chronicler gave a corresponding number of high priests to the twice twelve generations of forty years each which were usually assumed to have elapsed between the exodus and the building of Solomon's temple, and again between that and the close of the captivity; the official terms of office of these high priests, of whom history knows nothing, have taken the place of the reigns of judges and kings, according to which reckoning was previously made (1Chronicles v. 29, seq.). One sees clearly from Sirach l., and from more than one statement of Josephus (e.g., Ant., xviii. 4, 3, xx. 1, 11), how in the decorations of Aaron (where, however, the Urim and Thummim were wanting; Nehemiah vii. 65) people reverenced a transcendent majesty which had been left to the people of God as in some sense a compensation for the earthly dignity which had been lost. Under the rule of the Greeks the high priest became ethnarch and president of the synedrium; only through the pontificate was it possible for the Hasmonaeans to attain to power, but when they conjoined it with full-blown secular sovereignty, they created a dilemma to the consequences of which they succumbed.

CHAPTER V. THE ENDOWMENT OF THE CLERGY.

The power and independence of the clergy run parallel with its material endowment, which accordingly passes through the same course of development. Its successive steps are reflected even in the language that is employed, in the gradual loss of point sustained by the phrase "to fill the hand," at all times used to denote ordination. Originally it cannot have had any other meaning than that of filling the hand with money or its equivalent; we have seen that at one time the priest was appointed by the owner of a sanctuary for a salary, and that, without being thus dependent upon a particular employer, he could not then live on the income derived from those who might employ him sacrificially. But when the Levitical hereditary priesthood arose in the later kingdom of Judah the hands of the priests were no longer filled by another who had the right to appoint and to dismiss, but they themselves at God's command "filled their own hand," or rather they had done so in the days of Moses once for all, as is said in Exodus xxxii. 26-29, an insertion corresponding with the position of Deuteronomy. It is obvious that such a statement, when carefully looked at, is absurd, but is to be explained by the desire to protest against outside interference. Even here the etymological sense is still sufficiently felt to create an involuntary jar and leads to a change of the construction; but finally all sense of it is lost, and the expression becomes quite colourless: "to fill the hand " means simply "to consecrate." In Ezekiel not only the priest but also the altar has its "hand filled" (xliii. 26); in the Priestly Code the abstract *milluim* ["consecrations"] is chiefly used, with subject and object left out, as the name of a mere inaugural ceremony which lasts for several days (Leviticus viii. 33; Exodus xxix. 34), essentially consists in the bringing of an offering on the part of the person to be consecrated, and has no longer even the remotest connection with actual filling of the hand (2Chronicles xiii. 7; comp. xxix. 31). The verb, therefore, now means simply the performance of this ceremony, and the subject is quite indifferent (Leviticus xvi. 32, xxi. 10; Numbers iii. 3); the installation does not depend upon the person who performs the rite, but upon the rite itself, upon the unction, investiture, and other formalities (Exodus xxix. 29).

This variation in the *usus loquendi* is the echo of real changes in the outuard condition of the clergy, which we must now proceed to consider more in detail.

V.I.

V.I.1. Of the offerings, it was the custom in the earlier time to dedicate a portion to the deity but to use the greater part in sacred feasts, at which a priest, if present, was of course allowed also in one way or another to participate. But he does not appear to have had a legal claim to any definite dues of flesh. "Eli's sons were worthless persons, and cared not about Jehovah, or about the priests' right and duty with the people. When any man offered a sacrifice the servant of the priest came (that is all we have here to represent the 22,000 Levites) while the flesh was in seething, with a three-pronged flesh-hook in his hand, and stuck it into the pan, or kettle, or caldron, or pot; and all that the flesh-hook brought up the priest took. So they did in Shiloh unto all the Israelites that came thither. Even before the fat was burnt, the servant of the priest came and said to the man that sacrificed: "Give flesh to roast for the priest; he will not take sodden flesh of thee, but raw. And if the other said to him: Let the fat first be burnt, and then take according to thy soul's desire; then he would answer: Nay, but thou shalt give it now; and if not, I will take it by force" (1Samuel ii. 12-16). The tribute of raw portions of flesh before the burning of the fat is here treated as a shameless demand which is fitted to bring Jehovah's offering into contempt (ver. 17), and which has the ruin of the sons of Eli as its merited reward. More tolerable is it, though even that is an abuse, when the priests cause boiled flesh to be brought them from the pot, though not seeking out the best for themselves, but leaving the selection to chance; they ought to wait and see what is given to them, or be contented with an invitation to the banquet. On the other hand we have it in Deuteronomy as "the priest's due from the people" (xviii. 3 = 1Samuel ii. 12) that he receives the shoulder and the two cheeks and the maw of the slaughtered animal; and yet this is a modest claim compared with what the sons of Aaron have in the Priestly Code (Leviticus vii. 34),—the right leg and the breast. The course of the development is plain; the Priestly Code became law for Judaism. In sacrifice, ITS demands were those which were regarded; but in order to fulfil all righteousness the precept of Deuteronomy was also maintained, this being applied—against the obvious meaning and certainly only as a result of later scrupulosity of the scribes—not to sacrifices but to ordinary secular slaughterings, from which also accordingly the priests received a portion, the cheeks (according to Jerome on Malachi ii. 3), including the tongue, the precept being thus harmonistically doubled. *1* At an earlier

*** 1. Philo, De praem. sacerd., sec. 3. Josephus, Ant., iii. 9. 2; iv. 4, 4.
****

date the priests at Jerusalem received money from those who employed them (Deuteronomy xviii. 8), but for this had the obligation of maintaining the temple; from this one can discern that the money was properly speaking paid to the sanctuary, and was only conditionally delivered to its servitors. When they failed to observe the condition, King Jehoash took the money also from them (2Kings xii. 7 seq.).

The meal-offerings are in the Priestly Code a subordinate matter, and the share that falls to the priests is here trifling compared with what they receive of the other sacrifices. The meal, of which only a handful is sprinkled upon the altar, the baked bread, and the minha altogether are theirs entirely, so also the sin and trespass offerings so frequently demanded, of which God receives only the blood and the fat and the offerer nothing at all (Ezekiel xliv. 29); of the burnt-offering at least the skin falls to their lot, These perquisites, however, none of them in their definite form demonstrably old, and some of them demonstrably the reverse, may be presumed to have had their analogues in the earlier period, so that they cannot be regarded absolutely as augmentation of the priestly income. In Josiah's time the mac,c,oth were among the principal means of support of the priests (2Kings xxiii. 9); doubtless they came for the most part from the minha. Instead of sin and trespass offerings, which are still unknown to Deuteronomy, there were formerly sin and trespass dues

146

in the form of money payments to the priests,—payments which cannot, however, have been so regular (2Kings xii. 17). It is as if money payments were in the eye of the law too profane; for atonement there must be shedding of blood. That the skin of the holocaust, which cannot well be consumed on the altar, should fall to the priest is so natural an arrangement, that one will hardly be disposed to regard it as new, although Ezekiel is silent about a due which was not quite worthless (xliv. 28-31).

So far then as departures from earlier custom can be shown in the sacrificial dues enjoined by the Priestly Code, they must not indeed be treated as purely local differences, but neither are they to be regarded as on the whole showing a serious raising of the tariff. But in the Code the sacrificial dues are only a subordinate part of the income of the priests. In Deuteronomy the priests are entirely thrown upon the sacrifices; they live upon them (xviii. 1) and upon invitations to the sacred banquets (xii. I2, 18 seq.); if they are not exercising the priestly function they must starve (1Samuel ii. 36). On the other hand, the Aaronidae of the Priestly Code do not need to sacrifice at all, and yet have means of support, for their chief revenue consists of the rich dues which must be paid them from the products of the soil.

V.I.2. The dues falling to the priests according to the law were all originally offerings—the regular offerings which had to be brought on the festivals; and these all originally were for sacred banquets, of which the priests received nothing more than the share which was generally customary. This is true in the first instance of the male firstlings of cattle. As we have seen in the chapter on the sacred feasts, these are sacrifices and sacrificial meals, alike in the Jehovistic legislation and in the Jehovistic narrative of the exodus and of Abel, as were all the offerings brought by private individuals in the olden time. When in Exodus xxii. 29 it is said that they must be given to Jéhovah, this does not mean that they must be given to THE PRIESTS; no such thing is anywhere said in the Book of the Covenant. Matters still stand on essentially the same footing in Deuteronomy also: "THOU SHALT SANCTIFY THEM UNTO Jéhovah; thou shalt not plough with the firstling of the bullock, nor shear the firstling of thy sheep; THOU SHALT EAT IT BEFORE Jéhovah year by year in the place which He shall choose; and if there be any blemish therein, thou shalt not OFFER IT TO Jéhovah THY GOD" (Deuteronomy xv. 19, 20). To sanctify to Jehovah, to eat before Jehovah, to offer to Jehovah, are here three equivalent ideas. If now, in Numbers xviii. 15 seq., every first birth is assigned without circumlocution to the priest, and a special paschal offering is appointed in addition, this can only be understood as the last phase in the development, partly because the idea of dues altogether is secondary to that of offerings, and partly because the immense augmentation in the income of the priests points to an increase of the hierocratic power. Ezekiel does not yet reckon the firstlings among the revenues of the clergy (xliv. 28-3I); the praxis of Judaism, on the other hand, since Nehemiah x. 37, is regulated, as usual, in accordance with the norm of the Priestly Code.

The tithe also is originally given to God, and treated just as the other offerings are; that is to say, it is not appropriated by the priests, but eaten by those who bring it in sacred banquets. It does not occur in the Jehovistic legislation, but Jacob dedicates it

(Genesis xxviii. 22) to the God of Bethel, a place where, although the whole story is a projection out of a later time, it would hardly be in harmony with the conceptions of the narrator to think of the presence of priests. The prophet Amos, who probably represents much the same stage of the cultus as the Jehovist does, says: "Come to Bethel to transgress, to Gilgal to sin still more; and bring every morning your sacrifices, every three days your tithes, and offer with bread pieces of flesh to the flames, and proclaim free offerings aloud, for so ye like, ye children of Israel" (Amos iv. 4 seq.). He ironically recommends them to persevere in the efforts they have hitherto made in honour of God, and to double them; to offer daily, instead of, as was usual (1Samuel i.), yearly at the chief festival; to pay tithes every three days, instead of, as was the custom, every three years. It is clear that the tithe here holds rank with Zebah, Toda, and Nedaba; it is a sacrifice of joy, and a splendid element of the public cultus, no mere due to the priests. Now, in this point also Deuteronomy has left the old custom, on the whole, unchanged. According to xiv. 22 seq. the tithe of the produce of the soil, or its equivalent in money, must be brought year by year to the sanctuary, and there consumed before Jehovah that is, as a sacrificial meal; only every third year it is not to be offered in Jerusalem, but is to be given as alms to the people of the locality who have no land, to which category the Levites in particular belong. This last application is an innovation, connected on the one hand with the abolition of the sanctuaries, and on the other with the tendency of the Deuteronomist to utilise festal mirth for humane ends. *1*

** 1. Connection is, however, possible with some older custom, such as must certainly be assumed for Amos iv. 4. Comp. Deuteronomy xxvi. 12, "the year of tithing." **

But this is a mere trifle compared with what we find in the Priestly Code, where the whole tithe has become a mere due to be collected by the Levites (Nehemiah x. 38 [37]) on behalf of the clergy, whose endowment thereby is again very largely increased. Ezekiel is silent on this point also (xliv. 18-31), but as the tithe is demanded in Numbers (xviii. 21 seq.), so was it paid from the days of Nehemiah (x. 38 [37] seq.) by the church of the second temple. Later there was added over and above, so as to meet the divergent requirement of Deuteronomy, the so-called second tithe, which usually was consumed at Jerusalem, but in every third year was given to the poor (so Deuteronomy xxvi. 12, LXX), and in the end the tithe for the poor was paid separately over and above the first and second (Tobit i. 7, 8; Jos., Ant., iv. 8, 22).

It is absolutely astounding that the tithe which in its proper nature should apply only to products of definite measure, such as corn and wine and oil (Deuteronomy xiv. 23), comes to be extended in the Priestly Code to cattle also, so that besides the male firstlings every tenth head of cattle and of sheep must also be paid to the priests. This demand, however, is not yet met with in Numbers xviii., nor even in Nehemiah x. 38, 39, but first occurs as a novel in Lev. xxvii. 32 (1Samuel viii. 17). Whether it ever came into the actual practice of Judaism seems doubtful; in 2Chronicles xxxi. 6 the tithe of cattle is indeed mentioned, but on the other hand the firstlings are not; in

148

the pre-rabbinical literature no traces of it are discoverable,—especially not in Philo, who knows only of the ordinary tithes due to the Levites, and not of the tithes of cattle due to the priests (De praem. sacerd. 6).

With the tithe of the fruit of the soil the first fruits are at bottom identical; the latter were reduced to definite measure later and through the influence of the former. This is no doubt the reason why in the Jehovistic legislation tithe and first fruits are not both demanded, but only a gift of the first and best of corn, wine, and oil, left to the free discretion of the offerer, which is conjoined with the firstling of cattle and sheep (Exodus xxii. 28 [29]. xxiii. 19, xxxiv. 26). In a precisely similar way the TITHE of the field stands conjoined with the firstlings of cattle in Deuteronomy (xiv. 22, 23, xv. 19 seq.). But also the *reshith*, usually translated first-fruits, occurs in Deuteronomy,—as a payment of corn, wine, oil, and wool to the priests (xviii. 4); a small portion, a basketful, thereof is brought before the altar and dedicated with a significant liturgy (xxvi. 1 seq.). It appears that it is taken from the tithe, as might be inferred from xxvi. 12 seq. taken as the continuation of vers. 1-11; in one passage, xxvi. 2, the more general *usus loquendi* reappears, according to which the *reshith* means the entire consecrated fruit, which as a whole is consumed by the offerers before Jehovah, and of which the priests receive only a portion. But in the Priestly Code not only is the entire tithe demanded as a due of the clergy, the *reshith* also is demanded in addition (Numbers xviii. 12), and it is further multiplied, inasmuch as it is demanded from the kneading-trough as well as from the threshing-floor: in every leavening the *halla* belongs to Jehovah (xv. 20). Nor is this all; to the *reshith* (xviii. 12) are added the *bikkurim* also (xviii. 13), as something distinct. The distinction does not occur elsewhere (Exodus xxxiv. 26); prepared fruits alone are invariably spoken of, the yield of the threshing-floor and the wine-press, of which first produce—"the fulness and the overflow "—was to be consecrated. The FAT of oil, wine, and corn is the main thing in Numbers xviii. also, and is called *reshith* (ver 12) or *terumah* (ver. 27); but the *bikkurim* (ver. 13) seem to be a separate thing, and, if this be really the case, must mean those raw fruits which have ripened earliest. Judaism, here once more moulding itself essentially in accordance with the tenor of the Priestly Code, actually drew this distinction; from the publication of the Law through Ezra the community pledged itself to bring up yearly the *bikkurim* to the house of Jehovah, and to deliver the *reshith* into the temple cells (Nehemiah x. 36 [35]). The former was a religious solemnity, associated with processions, and the use of the ritual in Deuteronomy xxvi.; the latter was rather a simple tax paid from natural products,—a distinction which perhaps is connected with the different expressions *they shall bring* (Numbers xviii. 13) and *they shall give* (xviii. 12). The LXX keeps)APARXH and PRWTOGENNHMATA strictly apart, as also do Philo (De praem. sacerd. 1, 2) and Josephus (Ant., iv. 4, 8, 22).

V.I.3. The amount which at last is required to be given is enormous. What originally were alternatives are thrown together, what originally was left free and undetermined becomes precisely measured and prescribed. The priests receive all the sin and trespass offerings, the greater share of the vegetable offerings, the hides of the burnt offerings, the shoulder and breast of meat offerings. Over and above are the firstlings, to which are added the tithes and first-fruits in a duplicate form, in short, all *kodashim*, which originally were demanded merely as ordinary meat offerings (Deuteronomy xii. 26 = ver. 6, 7, and so on), and were consumed at holy places and by consecrated guests indeed, but not by the priest. And, notwithstanding all this, the clergy are not even asked (as in Ezekiel is the prince, who there receives the dues, xlv. 13 seq.) to defray the cost of public worship; for this there is a poll-tax, which is not indeed enjoined in the body of the Priestly Code, but which from the time of Nehemiah x. 33 [32] was paid at the rate of a third of a shekel, till a novel of the law (Exodus xxx. 15) raised it to half a shekel.

V.II.

V.II.1. To the endowment of the clergy in the Priestly Code belong finally the forty-eight cities assigned by Joshua in accordance with the appointment of Moses (Numbers xxxv.; Josh. xxi.). The tribes gave them up freely; the smaller giving few and the larger more (Numbers xxxv. 8). The Aaronidae and the three families of the Levites cast lots about them in four divisions; the sons of Aaron get thirteen cities in Judah, the Levites ten in Ephraim-Manasseh, thirteen in Galilee, and twelve in the territory eastward of Jordan. It is not merely the right to inhabit, but, in spite of all apologetic rationalism, the right of absolute possession that they receive (Josh. xxi. 12), inclusive of a portion of land two thousand ells square (square in the strictly literal sense; Numbers xxxv. 5), which serves as public common.

The physical impracticability of such an arrangement has been conclusively shown, after Gramberg, by Graf (Merx, Archiv, i. p. 83). The 4 x 12 or the substituted 13+10+13+12 cities, of which in spite of Numbers xxxv. 8 for the most part four belong to each of the twelve tribes, are already sufficient to suggest a suspicion of artificial construction; but the regulation that a rectangular territory of two thousand ells square should be measured off as pasture for the Levites around each city (which at the same time is itself regarded only as a point; Numbers xxxv. 4) might, to speak with Graf, be very well carried out perhaps in a South Russian steppe or in newly founded townships in the western States of America, but not in a mountainous country like Palestine, where territory that can be thus geometrically portioned off does not exist, and where it is by no means left to arbitrary legal enactments to determine what pieces of ground are adapted for pasturage and what for tillage and gardening; there, too, the cities were already in existence, the land was already under cultivation, as the Israelites slowly conquered it in the course of centuries. Besides, from the time of Joshua there is not a historical trace of the existence of the Levitical cities. Quite a number of them were in the days of the judges and down to the early monarchy still in the hands of the Canaanites,— Gibeon, Shechem, Gezer, Taanach; some perhaps may even have so continued permanently. Those on the other hand which passed into the possession of the Israelites at no time belonged to the Levites. Shechem, Hebron, Ramoth, were the capital cities of Ephraim, Judah, and Gilead; and Gibeon, Gezer, Heshbon were in like manner important but by no means ecclesiastical towns. In the Deuteronomic period the Levites were scattered throughout Judah in such a manner that each locality had its own Levites or Levite; nowhere did they live separated from the rest of the world in compact masses together, for they made their living by sacrificing for others, and without a community they could not exercise their calling. Some indeed possessed land and heritage; such were at an earlier period the Silonic family at Gibeath-Phineas, Amaziah at Bethel, and Abiathar at Anathoth, and at a later period Jeremiah, also at Anathoth. But Anathoth (for example) was not on that account a priestly city in the sense of Joshua xxi.; Jeremiah had his holding there as a citizen and not as a priest, and he shared not with the priests but with the people (xxxvii. 12). As a tribe Levi was distinguished from the other tribes precisely by holding no land, and its members joined themselves to the settled citizens and peasants, for the most part as dependent inmates (Deuteronomy x. 9, xviii. 1).

Even after the exile, indeed, matters were not different in this respect. "Ab excidio templi prioris sublatum est Levitis jus suburbiorum," says R. Nachman (B. Sotah, 48b), and he is borne out by the silence of Nehemiah x. The execution of the law was probably postponed to the days of the Messiah; it was not in truth within the power of man, and cannot be seriously demanded in the Priestiy Code itself, which contemplates a purely ideal Israel, with ideal boundaries, and leaves the sober reality so far out of sight that on archaeological grounds it never once so much as mentions Jerusalem, the historical capital of the priests.

The circumstance that these towns lay *in partibus infiidelium* seems to make them unavailable as a means of fixing the antiquity of the Priestly Code. It is possible with Bleek to explain the transcendence of history as Mosaicity; such a view is not to be argued against. But it is also possible with Noldeke to insist that an invention so bold cannot possibly be imputed to the spirit of the exilic and post-exilic time, which in everything is only anxiously concerned to cleave to what is old and to restore it; and such a contention deserves and admits of refutation. It is not the case that the Jews had any profound respect for their ancient history; rather they condemned the whole earlier development, and allowed only the Mosaic time along with its Davidic reflex to stand; in other words, not history but the ideal. The theocratic ideal was from the exile onwards the centre of all thought and effort, and it annihilated the sense for objective truth, all regard and interest for the actual facts as they had been handed down. It is well known that there never have been more audacious history-makers than the Rabbins. But Chronicles affords evidence sufficient that this evil propensity goes back to a very early time, its root the dominating influence of the Law, being the root of Judaism itself. Judaism is just the right soil for such an artificial growth as the forty-eight priestly and Levitical cities. It would hardly have occurred to an author living in the monarchical period, when the continuity of the older history was still unbroken, to look so completely away from all the conditions of the then existing reality; had he done so, he would have produced upon his contemporaries the impression merely that he had scarcely all his wits about him. But after the exile had annihilated the ancient Israel, and violently and completely broken the old connection with the ancient conditions, there was nothing to hinder from planting and partitioning the *tabula rasa* in thought at pleasure, just as geographers are wont to do with their map as long as the countries are unknown.

But, of course, no fancy is pure fancy; every imagination has underlying it some elements of reality by which it can be laid hold of, even should these only be certain prevailing notions of a particular period. It is clear, if a proper territory is assigned

151

to the clergy, that the notion of the clerical tribe which already had begun to strike root in Deuteronomy has here grown and gathered strength to such a degree that even the last and differentiating distinction is abolished which separates the actual tribes from the Levites, *viz.* communal independence and the degree of concentration which expresses itself in separate settlements. For when we read, notwithstanding, in the Priestly Code that Aaron and Levi are to have no lot nor inheritance in Israel (Numbers xviii. 20, 23), this is merely a form of speech taken over from Deuteronomy and at the same time an involuntary concession to fact; what would the forty-eight cities have been, had they actually existed, if not a lot, a territorial possession, and that too a comparatively large one? The general basis which serves as starting-point for the historical fiction being thus far recognisable, we are able also to gain a closer view of its concrete material. The priestly and Levitical cities stand in close connection with the so-called cities of refuge. These are also appointed in Deuteronomy (xix.), although not enumerated by name (for Deuteronomy iv. 41-43 cannot be regarded as genuine). Originally the altars were asylums (Exodus xxi. 14; 1Kings ii. 28), some in a higher degree than others (Exodus xxi. 13). In order not to abolish the asylums also along with the altars, the Deuteronomic legislator desired that certain holy places should continue as places of refuge, primarily three for Judah, to which, when the territory of the kingdom extended, three others were to be afterwards added. The Priestly Code adopts the arrangement, and specifies three definite cities on this side and three on the other side of Jordan (Numbers xxxv.; Joshua xx.), four of which are demonstrably famous old seats of worship,—all the three western ones, and Ramoth, that is, Mizpah, of the eastern ones (Genesis xxxi.; Judges xi. 11). But as all these asylums are at the same time priestly and Levitical cities, it is an obvious conjecture that these also in like manner arose out of old sanctuaries. We need not suppose that there is more in this than an echo of the general recollection that there were once in Israel many holy places and residences of priesthoods; it is by no means necessary to assert that each of the towns enumerated in Joshua xxi. had actually been an ancient sanctuary. In many cases, however, this also admits of being shown, *1* although some of the

*** 1. In the cases of Hebron, Gibeon, Shechem, Ramoth, Mahanaim and Tabor (Host v. 1) by historical data; in those of Bethshemesh, Ashtaroth, Kadesh,, perhaps also Rimmon, by the names. Not even here can one venture to credit the Priestly Code with consistent fidelity to history. As for Hosea v. 1, 2, the original meaning seems to be: "A snare have ye become for Mizpah, and an outspread net upon Tabor, and the pit-fall of Shittim (#XT H#+YM) have they made deep." Shittim as a camping-place under Moses and Joshua must certainly have been a sanctuary, just like Kadesh, Gilgal, and Shiloh; the prophet names these seats at which in his opinion the worship was especially seductive and soul-destroying; his reproach is levelled at the priests most famous (or according to the later view, infamous) high places, such as Bethel, Dan, Gilgal, and Beersheba are omitted, probably of set purpose.

The immediate starting-point, however, for this territorial donation to the Levites is perhaps to be sought in Ezekiel, in the picture of the future Israel which he draws at the close of his book. He concerns himself there in a thorough-going manner about the demarcation of the national and tribal boundaries, and in doing so sets quite freely to work, taking, so to speak, the yard measure in his hand. Leaving the land eastward of Jordan wholly to the Saracens, he divides the western portion into thirteen parallel transverse sections; in the middle of the thirteenth (the rest of which is assigned to the prince), lying between Judah and Benjamin, the twelve tribes give up a square with a base line of 25,000 ells as a sacred offering to Jehovah. This square is divided into three parallelograms, 25,000 ells long, running east and west; the southernmost of these, 5000 ells broad, includes the capital with its territory; the middle one, 10,000 ells broad, contains the temple and the priestly territory; the northernmost, also 10,000 ells broad, has the inheritance and the cities of the Levites. *1*

*** 1. For (S#RYM L#KT (xlv. 5), read, with the LXX, #(RYM L#BT "to dwell within the gates." Compare a similar transposition of letters in xiii. 3, LXX. The expression "gates" for "cities" has its origin in Deuteronomy. ***

Thus we have here also a surrender of land to the clergy on the part of the tribes; the comparison with Josh. xxi. is not to be put aside,—all the less, because nowhere else in the Old Testament is anything similar met with. Now Ezekiel is quite transparent, and requires no interpreter but himself. In order that the temple may be protected in its sanctity in the best possible manner, it is placed in the centre of the priestly territory, which in its turn is covered by the city on the south, and by the Levites on the north. At the same time the *personnel* connected with the function of worship is to dwell as much as possible apart on its own soil and territory, which *shall serve them for separate houses to sanctify them*, as is expressly remarked for the priests (xiv. 4), and in an inferior degree holds good also, of course, for the Levites beside them. Here everything starts from, and has its explanation in, the temple. Its original is unmistakably the temple of Solomon; its site is beside the capital, in the heart of the sacred centre of the land between Judah and Benjamin; there the sons of Zadok have their abode, and beside them are the Levites whom Josiah had brought up from all the country to Jerusalem. Obviously the motives are not here far to seek. In the Priestly Code, on the other hand, which was not in a position to shape the future freely out of the present, but was compelled to accept archaeological restrictions, the motives are historically concealed and almost paralysed. The result has remained, namely, the holding of separate territory by the clergy, but the cause or the purpose of it can no longer be recognised on account of the sanctuary being now an abstract idea. Jerusalem and the temple, which, properly speaking, occasioned the whole arrangement, are buried in silence with a diligence which is in the highest degree surprising; and on the other hand, in remembrance of the priesthoods scattered everywhere among the high places of Israel in earlier days, forty-eight fresh Levitical cities are created, from which, however, their proper focus, a temple to wit, is withheld only in the circumstance that precisely the thirteen cities of Judah and Benjamin happen to fall to the lot of the sons of Aaron, does the influence of Jerusalem unconsciously betray itself.

V.II.2. Apart from this historical fiction, the other claims that are made for the endowment of the clergy are, however exorbitant, nevertheless practicable and seriously meant. So far as the circumstances of their origin are concerned, two possibilities present themselves. Either the priests demanded what they could hope to obtain, in which case they were actually supreme over the nation, or they set up claims which at the time were neither justified nor even possible; in which case they were not indeed quite sober, yet at the same time so sane prophetically, that centuries afterwards the revenues they dreamed of became in actuality theirs. Is it to be supposed that it was (say) Moses, who encouraged his people as they were struggling for bare life in the wilderness to concern themselves about a superabundantly rich endowment of their clergy? Or is it believed that it was in the period of the judges, when the individual tribes and families of Israel, after having forced their way among the Canaanites, had a hard fight to maintain their position, get somehow settled in their new dwelling-places and surroundings, that the thought first arose of exacting such taxes from a people that was only beginning to grow into a national unity, for an end that was altogether remote from its interest? What power could then have been able in those days, when every man did what was right in his own eyes, to compel the individual to pay? But even when actually, under the pressure of circumstances, a political organisation had arisen which embraced all the tribes, it could hardly have occurred to the priests to utilise the secular arm as a means for giving to themselves a place of sovereignty; and still less could they have succeeded WITHOUT the king on whom they were so completely dependent. In short, the claims they make in the Law would in the pre-exilic period have been regarded as utopian in the strict sense of that word; they allow of explanation only by the circumstances which from the beginning of the Chaldaean rule, and still more that of the Persians, lent themselves to the formation of a hierocracy, to which, as to the truly national and moreover divine authority, the people gave voluntary obedience, and to which the Persians also conceded rights they could not have granted to the family of David. At the very beginning of the exile, Ezekiel begins to augment the revenues of the priests (xliv. 28-30), yet he still confines himself on the whole to the lines of Deuteronomy, and makes no mention of tithes and firstlings. Of the demands of the Priestly Code in their full extent we hear historically in Nehemiah x. for the first time; there it is stated that they were carried through by men who had the authority of Artaxerxes behind them. This was the most difficult and at the same time the most important part of the work Ezra and Nehemiah had to do in introducing the Pentateuch as the law of the Jewish Church; and that is the reason why it is so specially and minutely spoken of. Here plainly lies the material basis of the hierocracy from which the royal throne was ultimately reached.

For all these dues, apart from sacrificial perquisites, flowed into a common coffer, and benefited those who had the control of this, *viz.*, the priestly aristocracy of Jerusalem, whom it helped to rise to a truly princely position. The ordinary priests, and especially the Levites, did not gain by all this wealth. The latter indeed ought, according to law, to have had the tithes, and to have handed over the tithes of these again to the sons of Aaron, but as the general tendency of the time was to depress the Levites, this legal revenue was also gradually withdrawn from them and appropriated by the priests. Afterwards the chief priests claimed the tithes for themselves alone,

154

while their inferior brethren had to suffer severe privation and even hunger itself (Josephus, Ant., xx. 8, 8; 9, 2).

Upon the difference just stated between the later practice and the Law, one argument more has recently been founded against assigning the latter to the Babylonio-Persian period. "Another testimony borne by tradition completely excludes the idea of the Elohistic torah (i.e., the Priestly Code) having been composed by Ezra. As is well known, it is the Elohistic torah that carefully regulates the mutual relations of priests and Levites, while Deuteronomy groups the two together without bringing forward the distinction. It is the former that assigns the tithes to the Levites, while requiring these in their turn to hand over the tithe of their tithes as a due to the priests. Such was also the practice (Nehemiah x. 38 seq.) soon after the exile [i.e., a hundred years later; Nehemiah vii. 5]. But subsequently the payment of the tithes to the Levites fell entirely into disuse; these were rendered immediately and exclusively to the priests, so that Jose ben Hanina actually confesses: "We do not pay the tithes according to the command of God" (Sota, 47b). But everywhere the Talmud refers this practice back to Ezra. Ezra it was who punished the Levites by withdrawal of the tithes, and that because they had not come out from Babylon (Jebam. 386b; Chullin 11b). The point to be noted is that Ezra, according to the testimony of tradition, superseded a precept of the Elohistic torah, supporting himself in this perhaps by reference to the Deuteronomic torah." So Delitzsch in the Zeitschr. fuer luth. Theol., 1877, p. 448 seq. That Ezra is not the author of the Priestly Code may readily be granted—only not on such an argument as this. If the genuine historical tradition expressly names Ezra as the man who introduced the Levites' tithe just as prescribed by law (Nehemiah x. 38 seq.), what conscientious man can attach any weight to the opposite assertion of the Talmud ?

But, even assuming that the divergence of practice from the legal statute actually does go back to the time of Ezra, what would follow from that against the post-exilic origin of the Priestly Code? For this is what the question comes to, not to Ezra's authorship, which is made the main point by a mere piece of transparent controversial tactics. The demands of the Priestly Code, which demonstrably were neither laid down, nor in any sense acted on before the exile, attained the force of law one hundred years after the return from Babylon (Nehemiah x.); the whole taxation system of Judaism ever afterwards rested upon it;- — shall this be held to have no meaning as against the trifling circumstance that the tithe also was indeed paid to the clergy, in full accordance with the Priestly Code, and inconsistently with ancient custom, but paid to the higher, and not to the lower order?

In point of fact any other difference whatever between Jewish practice and the Law might better have been adduced against the thesis of Graf,—for example, the absence of Urim and Thummim (Nehemiah vii. 65), or of the forty-eight Levitical cities, the church of the returned exiles instead of that of the twelve tribes of Israel, the second temple instead of the tabernacle, Ezra instead of Moses, the sons of Zadok instead of the sons of Aaron, the absence of the other marks of Mosaicity. For the position of the Levites is the Achilles heel of the Priestly Code. If the Levites at a later date were still further lowered beneath the priests, and put into a worse position in favour of these, this nevertheless presupposes the distinction between the two; let it first then be shown that the distinction is known to the genuine Old Testament, and that, in particular, it is introduced by Ezekiel not as a new thing, but as of immemorial antiquity. Or is the primary fact that the separation between priests and Levites was set up only in the Priestly Code and in Judaism, and that its genesis can be traced with confidence from the time of Josiah downwards, a fact of less importance than the secondary one that the distinction extended itself somewhat further still in the subsequent development of Judaism ?

B.   HISTORY OF TRADITION.

PLEON (HMISU PANTOS— Hesiod *Op. 40*

156

CHAPTER VI. CHRONICLES

Under the influence of the spirit of each successive age, traditions originally derived from one source were very variously apprehended and shaped; one way in the ninth and eighth centuries, another way in the seventh and sixth, and yet another in the fifth and fourth. Now, the strata of the tradition show the same arrangement as do those of the legislation. And here it makes no difference whether the tradition be legendary or historical, whether it relates to pre-historic or to historic times; the change in the prevailing ideas shows itself equally in either case. To show the truth of this in the case of the Hexateuch is of course our primary object, but we make our commencement rather with the properly historical books. For on various grounds we are here able with greater certainty to assert: Such was the aspect of history at this period and such at that; such were the influences that had the ascendancy at one time, and such those which prevailed at another.

We begin the inquiry where the matter is clearest—namely, with the Book of Chronicles. Chronicles, which properly speaking forms but a single book along with Ezra and Nehemiah, is a second history running parallel with the Books of Samuel and Kings, and we are here in the favourable position of starting with the objects of comparison distinctly defined, instead of having as usual to begin by a critical separation of sources of various age combined in one document. And, what is more, we can also date the rival histories with tolerable certainty. The Books of Samuel and of Kings were edited in the Babylonian exile; Chronicles, on the other hand, was composed fully three hundred years later, after the downfall of the Persian empire, out of the very midst of fully developed Judaism. We shall now proceed to show that the mere difference of date fully accounts for the varying ways in which the two histories represent the same facts and events, and the difference of spirit arises from the influence of the Priestly Code which came into existence in the interval. De Wette's "Critical Essay on the Credibility of the Books of Chronicles" (Beitraege, i.; 1806), is throughout taken as the basis of the discussion: that essay has not been improved on by Graf (Gesch. Bucher d. A. T. p. 114 seq.), for here the difficulty, better grappled with by the former, is not to collect the details of evidence, but so to shape the superabundant material as to convey a right total impression.

VI.I.

VI.I.1. After Jehovah had slain Saul (so begins the narrative of Chronicles), He turned the kingdom unto David the son of Jesse. All Israel gathered themselves unto David to Hebron and anointed him king over Israel, according to the word of Jehovah by Samuel (I Chronicles x. 1.-xi. 3). How simply and smoothly and wholly without human intervention according to this version did the thing come to pass! Quite otherwise is it in the narrative of the Book of Samuel. This also indeed has the statement of Chronicles word for word, but it has something over and above which gives a quite different aspect to the matter. Here David, on the lowest step to the throne, is the guerilla leader in the wilderness of Judah who finally is compelled by Saul's persecutions to pass over to Philistine territory, there under the protection of the enemies of his nation, carrying on his freebooter life. After the battle of Gilboa he avails himself of the dissolution of the kingdom to set up a separate principality in the south as a vassal of the Philistines; he is not chosen, but comes with a following six hundred strong, and offers himself to the elders of Judah, whom he has already at an earlier period laid under obligations to him by various favours and gifts. In the meantime Saul's cousin Abner takes over what of the kingdom there is, not for himself but for the legitimate heir Ishbaal; from Gilead, whither the government had been transferred after the great catastrophe, he gradually reconquers the territory west of Jordan, and is scheming how to recover also the lost Judah. Thus it comes to protracted struggles between Abner and David, in which fortune is most on the side of the latter; yet he does not leave the defensive or gain the sovereignty over Israel. That falls into his hands rather by treachery. Abner himself, indignant at the ingratitude of his royal nephew, offers the crown to his rival, and enters into negotiations with him about it; but as he immediately afterwards falls a victim to blood revenge, nothing comes of the matter until Ishbaal is privily murdered in his sleep by two of his captains; then at last the elders of Israel come to Hebron, and David becomes king in succession to Saul. What a length of time these affairs demand, how natural is their development, how many human elements mingle in their course,—cunning, and treachery, and battle, and murder! Chronicles indeed knows them all well enough, as is clear from incidental expressions in chaps. xi. and xii., but they are passed over in silence. Immediately after his predecessor's death the son of Jesse is freely chosen by all Israel to be king, according to the word of Jehovah by Samuel. The sequence of x. 13, 14, xi. 1 does not admit of being understood in any other way, nor is it in point of fact otherwise understood, for it has actually been successful, at least to this extent, that the kingship of Ishbaal has virtually dropped out of traditional Bible history; after Saul came David is what is said. We have before us a deliberate and in its motives a very transparent mutilation of the original narrative as preserved for us in the Book of Samuel.

As all Israel has made David the successor of Saul, and all Israel gone out with him to the conquest of Jerusalem (xi. 4),—in 2Samuel v. 6 we hear only of David's following,—so now immediately afterwards, the noblest representatives of all the tribes of Israel, who even before he had attained the throne were in sympathy and indeed already on his side, are enumerated by name and numbers in three lists (xi. 10-xii. 40), which are introduced between what is said in 2Samuel v. 1-1110 and in 2Samuel v. 11 seq. The first (xi. 10-47: "these are the mighty men who took part with him with all Israel to make him king") is the list of 2Samuel xxiii., which the Chronicler, as he betrays in chaps. xx., xxi., was acquainted with as it stood in that place, and here gives much too early, for it is for the most part warriors of David's later campaigns who are enumerated. *1* The second list (xii.

*************************************** 1. The division into a group of three and another of thirty heroes, obscured in 2Samuel xxiii. by corruption of the text (Text der BB. Sam. p. 213-216), has not been understood by the Chronicler, and thus been made quite unrecognisable. In this way he has been able to bring in at the end (xi. 42-47) a string of additional names exceeding the number of thirty. In ver. 42 his style unmistakably betrays itself, wherever it may be that he met with the elements. **

1-22: "these are they that came to David to Ziklag, while he yet kept himself close because of Saul") is not taken from the Book of Samuel, but one also observes this difference: along with old and genuine there are extremely common names, and hardly one that occurs here only; the notes of ancestry carefully given in chap. xi. are almost always wanting; and instead of performing before our eyes such deeds as the rescue of a field of barley from the enemy, the purchase of a draught of water with blood, the slaying of a lion in a pit, the heroes receive all sorts of *epitheta ornantia* (xii. 1-3) and titles of honour (xii. 14, 20), and ordinarily talk a highly spiritual language (xii. 17, 18). And as for the historical situation, how impossible that a great Israelite army should have been gathered around David as the feudatory of the Philistines in Ziklag (xii. 2 2), with a crowd of captains of hundreds and thousands! Plainly the banished fugitive is according to this representation the splendid king and illustrious ancestor of the established dynasty; hence also the naïve remark of ver. 29. No better is it with the third list (xii. 23-40: "these are the numbers of the bands, ready armed for the war, who came to David to Hebron"). Observe the regular enumeration of the twelve tribes, which nowhere occurs in the older historical books, and is quite artificial; then the vast numbers, which are not matters of indifference here, but the principal thing and make up the entire contents; finally, the 4600 Levites and 3700 priests, who also take their place in the martial train, and constitute the proper guard of the king; to Chronicles the distinction between secular and spiritual soldiers is not altogether clear. There are but a few details of a special kind; the remark in xii. 32 is perhaps connected with 2Samuel xx. 18; Jehoiada the prince of the house of Aaron, *i.e.*, the high priest, alongside of the historically certain series,—Eli, Phinehas, Ahitub, Ahiah (Ahimelech), Abiathar,—an utterly impossible person, is a reflection of the Jehoiada of 2Kings xi., xii., and the allegation that Zadok at that time joined David at the head of twenty-two chief priests is a hardly credible substitute for what is stated in Samuel, according to which Abiathar, whose older claims were disagreeable to the B'ne Zadok and those who came later, was the priest who from the beginning held with David; the twenty-two chief priests appear to correspond to the heads of the twenty-two post-exilian priestly families (Nehemiah xii. 1-7, 12-21, x. 3-9; 1Chronicles xxiv. 7-18). Yet it is hardly necessary to go so minutely into the contents of the above lists, for the purpose with which they are given is stated without circumlocution at the close (2Chronicles xii. 38, 39): "All these men of war, in order of battle, came with a perfect heart to Hebron to make David king over all Israel, and all the rest of Israel also were of one heart to make David king. And they were there with David three days, eating and drinking, for there was joy in Israel."

After the explication of the idea "all Israel" thus inappropriately interpolated, the narrative proceeds to reproduce the contents of 2 Samuel v.-vii. David's first deed, after the conquest of the stronghold of Jebus, is in Chronicles to make it the holy city by transferring the ark of Jehovah thither (xiii. 1 seq.). It seems as if the building of a palace and the Philistine war (2Samuel v. 11-25) were to be omitted; but after the narrative in 2Samuel vi. 1 seq. has been given down to the place "and the ark of Jehovah abode in the house of Obed-edom three months " (1Chronicles xiii. 14 = 2Samuel vi. 11), the pause of a quarter of a year is utilised for the purpose of overtaking what had been left out (xiv. 1-17 = 2Samuel v. 11-25), and then the history of the ark is completed. This indeed is to separate things mutually connected, but at the same time the secular business which, according to the older narrative, is the nearest and most pressing, is reduced to the level of a mere episode in the midst of the sacred. That there is no room for the building of a house and a Philistine war within the three months which offer themselves so conveniently for the interpolation is a subordinate affair.

As regards the sacred business, the transference of the ark to Zion, almost everything that is said in 2Samuel vi. is repeated word for word in Chronicles also (xiii., xv., xvi., xvii. 1). Two traits only are absent in Chronicles, and in neither case is the omission helpful to the connection David's wife Michal, it is said in 2Samuel vi. 16, 20-23, when she saw the king dancing and leaping in the procession, despised him in her heart; afterwards when he came home she told him what she thought of his unworthy conduct. The first of these two statements is found in Chronicles also (xv. 29), but the second is (all but the introductory notice, xvi. 43 = 2Samuel vi. 20, here torn from its connection) omitted, although it contains the principal fact, for the historical event was the expression of her contempt, not its psychological origin; a woman—such is the idea—must not say a thing like that to David. The other case is quite similar. On account of the calamity by which those who were bringing up the ark were overtaken, David does not at first venture to receive it into his citadel, but deposits it in the house of Obed-edom, one of his captains; but when Jehovah blesses the house of Obed-edom, he takes courage to bring the ark to his own home (2Samuel vi. 10-12). Chronicles also tells that Jehovah blessed the house of Obed-edom (xiii. 14), but mentions no consequent result; again the cause is given without the effect. Another explanation is substituted; David perceived that the disaster connected with the removal of the ark was due to the fact of its not having been carried by the Levites in accordance with the Law; the Levites accordingly were made to bear it and no harm ensued (xv. 2, 13-15). This is in complete and manifest contradiction to the older narrative, and as Chronicles (chapter xiii.) copies that narrative, it also contradicts itself (xiii. 10), and that all the more strikingly as by the addition in xiii. 2 it represents the accompanying clergy as tacitly approving the carrying of the ark on the ox-cart. Then due participation in the sacred procession having been thus once secured them, 1Chronicles xv. positively revels in priests and Levites, of whom not a single word is to be found in 2 Samuel vi., and moreover a sort of musical service is instituted by David himself before the ark, and a festal cantata made up by him out of post-exilian psalms is quoted (chapter xvi.). In this way, out of the original narrative, the scattered fragments of which now show themselves very strangely in the new connection, something quite different has grown. "In the former everything is free, simply the affair of king and people, here all is priestly ceremonial; there the people with their king shout and dance with joy before the ark,, here the levites are the musicians and singers in formal order. To seek to combine the two versions is wholly against the laws of historical interpretation. If the first were curt and condensed the unification of the two might perhaps be possible, but no story could be more particular or graphic, and could it have been that the Levites alone should be passed over in silence if they had played so very important a part? The author of Chronicles was able to introduce them only by distorting and mutilating his original and landing himself in contradiction after all. He cannot allow anything to happen without Levites; and was the ark of the covenant to be fetched to Jerusalem without them? was the Law to be even a second time broken under the pious king David? This seemed to him impossible. That Uzzah perished in the first attempt to fetch the ark, and that on the second occasion—when only a quite short journey is spoken of—the ark was carried, *2Samuel vi. 13, may have been the suggestions by which he was led. Fertile in combinations, he profited by the hint." So, justly, De Wette (Beitraege, i. 88-91).*

The narrative of 2Samuel vi. having been broken off at the first half of ver. 19 (1Chronicles xvi. 3), the second half of the verse and the beginning of the next are reproduced (xvi. 43) after the interpolation of xvi. 4-42, and then 2Samuel vii. is appended word for word (1Chronicles xvii.),—the resolution of David to build a house for the ark, and what Jehovah said to him about the subject through Nathan. The point of the prophet's address turns on the antithesis (2Samuel vii.). "Thou wilt build a house FOR ME? rather will I build a house FOR THEE;" the house of David is of course the Davidic dynasty. But an interpolation has already crept into the text of Samuel (vii. 13), which apprehends the antithesis thus: "THOU wilt build a house for me? Nay, THY SON shall build a house for me." Now Chronicles, for which David comes into consideration merely as the proper founder of the Solomonic temple, takes up the narrative of 2 Samuel vii. precisely on account of this interpolation, as is clear from xxii. 9, 10— increases the misunderstanding by going back to it in an addition (xvii. 14)—and at the outset destroys the original antithesis by the innocent alteration, "Thou shalt not build THE HOUSE for me" instead of "Wilt thou build A house for me? "The house can here mean only that imperatively needed one, long kept in view alike by God and men, which must by all means he built, only not by David but by Solomon; it is without any ambiguity the temple, and does not, like a house, contain that possibility of a double meaning on which the original point depends. It is interesting also to compare 2Samuel vii. 14 with 1Chronicles xvii. 13: "I will be to thy seed a father, and he shall be to me a son. *If he commit iniquity, then I will chasten him with the rod of men, and with the stripes of the sons of men; but* my mercy shall not depart from him." The words in italics are wanting in Chronicles; the meaning, that Jehovah will not withdraw His grace from the dynasty of Judah altogether, even though some of its members should deserve punishment, is thereby destroyed and volatilised into an abstract idealism, which shows that to the writer the Davidic kingly family is known only as a dissolving view, and not by historical experience as it is to the author of 2Samuel vii.

In chaps xviii.-xx., Chronicles seems to refresh itself with a little variety, relating as it does the foreign wars of David after the order of 2Samuel, viii., x., xi. 1, xii. 30, 30, xxi. 18-22. But in this it still keeps in view its purpose, which is directed towards David as founder of the Jerusalem worship; those wars brought him the wealth that was required for the building of the temple. On the other hand, everything so fully and beautifully told in the Book of Samuel about the home occurrences of that period is omitted, for after all it does not contribute much to the glorification of the king. So the story of Meribaal and Ziba (chap. ix.), of Bathsheba and Uriah (xi., xii.), of Tamar and Amnon (xiii., xiv.), of Absalom's rebellion (xv.-xx.), and of the delivering-up of the sons of Saul (xxi. 1-14). The rude and mechanical manner in which statements about foreign wars are torn from the connection with domestic events in which they stand in the older narrative is shown in 1Chronicles xx. 1, 2, as compared with 2Samuel xi. 1, xii. 30. In 2Samuel xi. the mention of the fact that

David remained in Jerusalem when the army set out against Rabbah, prepares for the story of his adultery with the wife of a captain engaged in active service in the field; but 1Chronicles xx. 1 is meaningless, and involves a contradiction with ver. 2. according to which David appears after all in the camp at Rabbah, although the connection,—namely, that he followed the army—and all the intermediate occurrences relating to Bathsheba and Uriah, are left out (De Wette, pp. 19, 20, 60). To what extent the veil is drawn over the scandalous falls of saints may be judged also from the fact that from the list of David's foreign encounters also, which are otherwise fully given, a single one is omitted which he is supposed not to have come through with absolute honour, that with the giant Ishbi-benob (2Samuel xxi. 15-17). Lastly, the alteration made in 1Chronicles xx. 5 is remarkable. Elhanan the son of Jair of Bethlehem, we read in 2Samuel xxi. 19, was he who slew Goliath of Gath, the shaft of whose spear was as thick as a weaver's beam. But on the other hand, had not David of Bethlehem according to 1Samuel xvii. vanquished Goliath the giant, the shaft of whose spear was as thick as a weaver's beam? In Chronicles accordingly Elhanan smites the brother of the veritable Goliath.

2. The closing chapters of 2Samuel (xxi.-xxiv.) are, admittedly, an appendix of very peculiar structure. The thread of xxi. 1-14 is continued in xxiv. 1-25, but in the interval between the two passages occurs xxi. 15-xxiii. 39, in a very irrational manner, perhaps wholly due to chance. In this interposed passage itself, again, the quite similar lists xxi. 15-22 and xxiii. 8-39 are very closely connected; and the two songs, xxii. 1-51, xxiii. 1-7, are thus an interpolation within an interpolation. This want of order is imitated by the author of Chronicles also, who takes 2Samuel xxiii. 8-39 as separated from xxi. 15-22, and gives 2Samuel xxiv. last, a position which does not belong to it from any material considerations, but merely because it had originally been tagged on as an appendix, and besides had been separated from its connection with xxi. 1-14 by a large interpolation.

1Chronicles xxi. (the pestilence as punishment of David's sin in numbering the people, and the theophany as occasioning the building of an altar on the threshing-floor of Araunah) is on the whole a copy of 2Samuel xxiv., but with omission of the precise and interesting geographical details of ver. 5 seq, and with introduction of a variety of improving touches. Thus (xxi. 1): "And Satan stood up against Israel and moved David;" instead of: "And the anger of Jehovah was kindled against Israel, and he moved David." Similarly (xxi. 6): "Levi and Benjamin Joab counted not among them; for the king's word was abominable to him,"— an addition which finds its explanation on the one hand in Numbers i. 49, and on the other in the circumstance that the holy city lay within the territory of Benjamin. Again (xxi. 16, 27): "David saw the angel of Jehovah standing between heaven and earth, and his sword drawn in his hand and stretched out towards Jerusalem;" compare this with Sam xxiv. 16 (1Chronicles xxi. t5): "The angel stretched out his hand to Jerusalem to destroy it, and he was by the threshing floor of Araunah;" according to the older view, angels have no wings (Genesis xxviii.). Further (xxi. 25): "David gave to Araunah for his threshing-floor 600 shekels of gold ;" compare with 2Samuel xxiv. 24, 50 shekels of silver; to make the king pay right royally costs the Chronicler nothing. But lastly, his most significant addition is the fire from heaven which consumes the burnt-offering (xxi. 26); by this means the altar on the threshing-floor of Araunah, in other words, that of the sanctuary of Jerusalem, is intended to be put on a level with that of the tabernacle, its predecessor, the fire on which was also kindled from heaven (Leviticus ix. 24). Whoever has understood the narratives of altar-buildings by the Patriarchs, by Joshua, Gideon, and Manoah, will grant that the author of Chronicles has quite correctly understood the intention of 2Samuel xxiv., in accordance with which he here proposes to relate the divine inauguration of the place of worship at Jerusalem; but what in that passage, as in similar older legends about the indication of consecrated places by means of a theophany, is only hinted at for contemporaries who understood the idea conveyed, he requires to retouch strongly in order that a later generation may notice it; and yet he has half spoiled the point by making the angel not stand by the threshing-floor of Araunah on the sacred spot, but hover aloft in the air.

2Samuel xxiv. = 1Chronicles xxi. serves further as a starting point for the free construction of 1Chronicles xxii.-xxix. The circumstance that in the last chapter of the Book of Samuel David builds the altar at Jerusalem is expanded into the statement that in the last year of his reign he prepared beforehand the building of the temple of Solomon in all its parts down to the minutest detail. Unhampered by historical tradition, the author here expatiates with absolute freedom in his proper element. All that has hitherto been said about the king on the basis of the older source is by means of additions and omissions fashioned into what shall serve as a mere prologue to the proper work of his life, which is now described thoroughly *con amore*. He himself unfortunately has not been allowed to build the house, having shed much blood and carried on great wars (xxii. 8, xxviii. 3), but he yet in the last year of his reign forestalls from his successor the whole merit of the business (xxiii. 1, xxviii. 1). My son Solomon, he says, is young and tender, but the house to be built for Jehovah must be great and glorious; I will therefore prepare it for him (xxii. 5). Accordingly he gets ready beforehand the workmen and artificers, in particular bringing into requisition the non-Israelitic population; he provides the material, stone and wood and brass and iron, and gold and silver and jewels without number; he also gives the plan or rather receives it direct from Jehovah, and that in black and white (xxviii. 19), while Moses built the tabernacle only according to his recollection of the heavenly pattern which had been shown to him on Sinai. But before all he appoints the *personnel* for the temple service,—priests, Levites, porters, singers,-divides their thousands into classes, and assigns to them their functions by lot. In doing so he interests himself, naturally, with special preference, in the music, being the designer of the instruments (xxiii. 5), and himself acting as principal conductor (xxv. 2, 6). And as he is still king after all, he at the close takes an inventory also of his secular state, after having duly ordered the spiritual. All this he does for the future, for his son and successor; not in reality, but only in plan, are the door-keepers, for example, assigned to their posts (xxvi. 12 seq.), but none the less with strictest specification and designation of the localities of the temple,—and that too the second temple! His preparations concluded, David calls a great assembly of prelates and notables (xxiii. 1, xxviii. 1), has Solomon anointed as king, and Zadok as priest (xxix. 22), and in a long discourse hands over to the former along with the kingdom the task of his reign, namely, the execution of what he himself has prepared and appointed; on this occasion yet more precious stones and noble metals—among them gold of Ophir and Persian darics—are presented by David and the princes for the sacred building. The whole section 1Chronicles xxii.-xxix. is a startling instance of that statistical phantasy of the Jews which revels in vast sums of money on paper (xxii. 14), in artificial marshallings of names and numbers (xxiii.-xxvii.), in the enumeration of mere subjects without predicates, which simply stand on parade and neither signify nor do anything. The monotony is occasionally broken only by unctuous phrases, but without refreshing the reader. Let the experiment of reading the chapters through be tried.

According to 1Kings i., ii., King David in his closing days was sick and feeble in body and mind, and very far from being in a condition thus to make preparations on behalf of his successor shortly before his own death, or to prepare his bread for him so far that nothing remained but to put it into the oven. His purpose of building a house to Jehovah is indeed spoken of in 2 Samuel vii. in connection with vi. 17, but it is definitively abandoned in consequence of Jehovah's refusal, on the ground that it is not man's part to build a house for God, but God's to build a house for man. In strange contrast with this explanation is that of Chronicles that David is a man of war and has shed much blood, and therefore dare not set up the temple; that he had waged the wars of Jehovah, that Jehovah had given victory by his hand, would in the older warlike time have seemed no reason against but rather an argument establishing his fitness for such a work. But the worst discrepancy is that between the solemn installation of Solomon as king and of Zadok as priest with all the forms of law and publicity as related in 1Chronicles xxviii., xxix. (comp. xxii., xxiii. 1) and the older narrative of 1Kings i., ii. According to the latter it was much more an ordinary palace intrigue, by means of which one party at court succeeded in obtaining from the old king, enfeebled with age, his sanction for Solomon's succession. Until then Adonijah had been regarded as heir-apparent to the throne, by David himself, by all Israel, and the great officers of the kingdom, Joab and Abiathar; what above all things turned the scale in favour of Solomon was the weight of Benaiah's six hundred praetorians, a formidable force in the circumstances of the period. The author of Chronicles naively supposes he has successfully evaded all difficulties by giving out the coronation of Solomon related by himself to be the second (xxix. 22),—an advertence to 1Kings i., ii. which does not remove but only betrays the contradiction.

Yet this is as nothing over against the disharmony of the total impression. See what Chronicles has made out of David! The founder of the kingdom has become the founder of the temple and the public worship, the king and hero at the head of his companions in arms has become the singer and master of ceremonies at the head of a swarm of priests and Levites; his clearly cut figure has become a feeble holy picture, seen through a cloud of incense. It is obviously vain to try to combine the fundamentally different portraits into one stereoscopic image; it is only the tradition of the older source that possesses historical value. In Chronicles this is clericalised in the taste of the post-exilian time, which had no feeling longer for anything but cultus and torah, which accordingly treated as alien the old history (which, nevertheless, was bound to be a sacred history), if it did not conform with its ideas and metamorphose itself into church history. Just as the law framed by Ezra as the foundation of Judaism was regarded as having been the work of Moses, so what upon this basis had been developed after Moses—particularly the music of the

164

sanctuary and the ordering of the temple *personnel*—was carried back to King David, the sweet singer of Israel, who had now to place his music at the service of the cultus, and write psalms along with Asaph, Heman, and Jeduthun, the Levitical singing families.

VI.I.3. With regard to Solomon, Chronicles (2Chronicles i.-ix.) nowhere departs very far from the lines of the Book of Kings. As the story of 1Kings i., ii., which is not an edifying one, and mercilessly assails that of 1Chronicles xxii.-xxix., required to be omitted, the narrative accordingly begins with 1Kings iii., with Solomon's accession, sacrifices on the great altar at Gibeon, and the revelation of Jehovah, which was thereupon communicated to him in a dream. This last is transcribed with slight alterations, but at the outset a characteristic divergence is found. "Solomon loved Jehovah, walking in the statutes of David his father, only he sacrificed and burnt incense on the high places (because there was no house built unto the name of Jehovah until those days). And the king went to Gibeon to sacrifice there; for that was the great high place; a thousand burnt-offerings did Solomon offer upon that altar, and Jehovah appeared unto him in a dream: Ask what I shall give thee." So 1Kings iii. 2 seq. Chronicles, after its manner, first surrounds the king with a great assemblage of captains of hundreds and thousands, of judges and princes and heads of houses, and purely Pentateuchal dignities, and then proceeds: "And Solomon and all the congregation with him went to the high place in Gibeon, for there was God's tent of meeting, which Moses, the servant of God, had made in the wilderness. But the ark of God had David brought up from Kirjath-jearim, where he had prepared for it; for he had pitched a tent for it at Jerusalem. But the brazen altar that Bezaleel, the son of Uri, the son of Hur, had made, stood there, before the tabernacle of Jehovah, and Solomon and the congregation sought unto it. And Solomon offered there, upon the brazen altar, before Jehovah, by the tent of meeting, he offered a thousand burnt-offerings, and God appeared to him in a dream, saying, Ask what I shall give thee" (2Chronicles i. 3 seq.). In the older narrative there is nothing about the tabernacle, it being assumed that no apology would be either necessary or possible for Solomon having sacrificed on a high place. Chronicles, dominated in its views of antiquity by the Priestly Code, has missed the presence of the tabernacle and supplied the want in accordance with that norm; the young and pious king could not possibly have made his solemn inaugural sacrifice, for which he had expressly left Jerusalem, anywhere else than at the legally prescribed place; and still less could Jehovah otherwise have bestowed on him His blessing. It betokens the narrowness, and at the same time the boldness of the author, that he retains the expression *high place* used in 1Kings iii. 3, and co-ordinates it with *tabernacle*, although the one means precisely the opposite of the other. But it is instructive to notice how, on other occasions, he is hampered by his Mosaic central sanctuary, which he has introduced *ad hoc* into the history. According to 1Chronicles xvi. David is in the best position to institute also a sacrificial service beside the ark of Jehovah, which he has transferred to Zion; but he dare not, for the Mosaic altar stands at Gibeon, and he must content himself with a musical surrogate (vers. 37-42). The narrative of 1Chronicles xxi., that David was led by the theophany at the threshing-floor of Araunah to build an altar there, and present upon it an offering that was accepted by heaven, is at its close maimed and spoiled in a similar way by the remark, with anticipatory reference to 2Chronicles i., that the Mosaic tabernacle and altar of burnt offering were indeed at that time in the high place at Gibeon, but that the king had not the strength to go before it to inquire of Jehovah, being so smitten with fear of the angel with the drawn sword. So also must the sacrifice which Solomon should have offered on his return from Gibeon before the ark at Jerusalem be similarly ignored (2Chronicles i. 13), because it uould destroy the force of the previous explanation of the high place at Gibeon. Thus the shadow takes the air from the body. In other places the tabernacle is significantly confounded with the temple of Jerusalem (Graf, p. 56), but on the whole it remains a tolerably inert conception, only made use of in the passage before us (2Chronicles i.) in an *ex machina* manner in order to clear Solomon of a heavy reproach.

Upon the last solemn act of worship at the Mosaic sanctuary immediately follows the building of the temple (i. 18 [ii.1]-vii. 11), 1Kings iii. 10-v. 14 [AV. 34] being passed over. A few little touches are however brought in to show the wealth of Solomon (i. 14-17); they do not occur in Kings until chap. x. (vers. 26-29), and are also repeated in Chronicles (ix. 25 seq.) in this much more appropriate connection (comp. 1Kings iii., LXX). Strictly speaking indeed, David has taken the preparations for the sacred building out of the hands of his successor, but the latter appears not to be satisfied with these (ii. 16 [17]) and looks after them once more (i. 18-ii. 17 [ii. 1-18]). A comparison with Ezra iii. (preparation of the second temple) shows that the story is an elaboration of the author, although suggested by 1Kings v. 16 [2] seq., and with preservation of many verbal reminiscences. While Hiram and Solomon according to the older record are on a footing of equality and make a contract based on reciprocity of service, the Tyrian king is here the vassal of the Israelite, and renders to him what he requires as tribute; instead of as there explaining himself by word of mouth, he here writes a letter in which he not only openly avows his faith in Jehovah the God of Israel, the maker of heaven and earth, but also betrays an extraordinary acquaintance with the Pentateuchal Priestly Code. The brassfounder whom Solomon brings from Tyre (1Kings vii. 13, 14) is (ii. 13) described as a very Daedalus and prodigy of artistic skill, like Bezaleel (Exodus xxxi. 2 seq.); his being made the son of a woman of Dan and not of a widow of Naphtali supplies interpreters with the materials for the construction of a little family romance, *1*

** 1. She was by birth a woman of Dan, married into the tribe of Napthali, lost her husband, and as widow out of the tribe of Naphtali became the wife of the Tyrian. So Bertheau *in loc.* **************************************

but has no more real value than the idea that sandalwood is obtained from Lebanon. The statement of 1Kings v. 27 [13] (xi. 28, xii. 4) that Israel was requisitioned in large numbers to render forced service to the king has substituted for it by the Chronicler that which occurs in another place (1Kings ix. 2I), that only the Canaanite serfs were employed for this purpose; at the same time, he reckons their number from the figures supplied in 1Kings v. 29 [15] seq. Lastly, the manner in which Solomon (ii. 2 [3]) assures Hiram that he will arrange the divine service in the new house in a thoroughly correct manner according to the ordinance of the Priestly Code, is also characteristic; similar remarks, from which the uninterrupted practice of the Mosaic cultus according to the rules of the Law is made to appear, are afterwards repeated from time to time (viii. 12-16, xiii. 11).

In chaps. iii., iv. the author repeats the description of the temple in 1Kings vi., vii., with the omission of what relates to profane buildings. Perhaps in one passage (1Kings vii. 23) he found the now very corrupt text in a better state; otherwise he has excerpted from it in a wretchedly careless style or word for word transcribed it, adding merely a few extravagances or appointments of later date (e.g., the specification of the gold in iii. 4 seq. 8, 9, of the ten golden tables and hundred golden basins in iv. 8, of the brass-covered doors of the outer gateway in iv. 9, of the court of the priests in iv. 9, of the curtain between the holy place and the holy of holies in iii. 14; compare Vatke, pp. 332, 333, 340, 341). To deny that the original (to which reference must in many places be made in order that the meaning may be understood) exists in 1Kings vi., vii., requires an exercise of courage which might be much better employed, all the more because in 2Chronicles iv. 11-v. 1, the summary list follows the description of details precisely as in 1Kings vii. 40 — 51.

While the concrete and material details of 1Kings vi., vii. are reproduced only in an imperfect and cursory manner, the act of consecration on the other hand, and the discourse delivered by Solomon on the occasion, is accurately and fully given (v. 2-vii. 10) in accordance with 1Kings viii.; such additions and omissions as occur are all deliberate. In 1Kings viii. the priests and Levites on an occasion which so closely concerned their interests do not play any adequate part, and in particular give none of the music which nevertheless is quite indispensable at any such solemnity. Accordingly, the Chronicler at the word "priests" inserts between the violently separated clauses of 1Kings viii. 10, 11, the following: "For all the priests present had sanctified themselves without distinction of classes, and the Levites, the singers, all stood in white linen with cymbals and psalteries and harps at the east end of the altar, and with them an hundred and twenty priests sounding with trumpets. And it came to pass when the trumpeters and singers were as one to make one sound to be heard in praising and thanking the Lord, and when the music began with trumpets, and cymbals, and instruments, and the song of praise, Praise ye Jehovah, for He is good; for His mercy endureth for ever, then the house was filled with a cloud" (v. 11-13). Proceeding, the narrative of 1Kings viii. 22 that Solomon came in front of the altar and there prayed is indeed in the first instance copied (vi. 12), but forthwith authoritatively interpreted in the sense that the king did not really and actually stand before the altar (which was lawful for the priests alone), but upon an improvised pulpit in the inner court upon a propped-up caldron of brass (vi. 13), an excellent idea, which has met with the due commendation of expositors. The close of Solomon's prayer (1Kings viii. 49-53) is abridged (vi. 39, 40)—perhaps in order to get rid of viii. 50—and there is substituted for it an original epilogue (vi. 41, 42) recalling post-exilian psalms. Then comes a larger omission, that of 1Kings viii. 54-61, explained by the difficulty involved in the king's here kneeling, not upon the caldron, but before the altar, then standing up and blessing like a priest; in place of this it is told (vii. 1-3) how the altar was consecrated by fire from heaven, which indeed had already descended upon it (1Chronicles xxi.26), but as it appears had unaccountably gone out. In vii. 4 the author again returns to his original at 1Kings viii. 62 seq., but tricks it out, wherever it appears to him too bare, with trumpeting priests and singing Levites (vii. 6), and finally dismisses the people, not on the eighth day of the feast of tabernacles (1Kings viii. 66), but on the ninth (vii. to), in accordance with the enactment in Numbers xxix. 35.

The rest of Solomon's history (vii. 11-ix. 28) is taken over from 1Kings ix., x. In doing so what is said in 1Kings ix. 10-IO, to the effect that Solomon handed over to Hiram twenty Galilaean cities, is changed into the opposite—that Hiram ceded the cities to Solomon, who settled them with Israelites (viii. 1, 2); and similarly the already observed statement of 1Kings ix. 24 about the removal of Solomon's Egyptian wife out of the city of David into his new palace *1* is altered and put in quite a

*** 1. Even in the text of Kings this statement has been obscured; Comp. 1Kings iii. 1. In ix. 24 we must at least say *betho   asher   bana   lo*,   but   this   perhaps   is   not   enough. ***

false light: "Solomon brought up the daughter of Pharaoh out of the city of David unto the house that he had built for her; for he said, No woman shall dwell in the house of David, for the place is holy whereunto the ark of Jehovah hath come" (viii. 11). There is no further need to speak of viii. 12-16 (1Kings ix. 25); more indifferent in their character are the addition in vii. 12-15, a mere compilation of reminiscences, the embellishment in viii. 3-6, derived from 1Kings ix. 17-19, and the variations in viii. 17 seq., ix. 2I, misunderstood from 1Kings ix. 26 seq., x. 22. The concluding chapter on Solomon's reign (1Kings xi.), in which the king does not appear in his most glorious aspect, is passed over in silence, for the same motives as those which dictated the omission of the two chapters at the beginning.

The history of the son is treated after the same plan and by the same means as that of the father, only the subject accommodates itself more readily to the purpose of the change. The old picture is retouched in such wise that all dark and repulsive features are removed, and their place taken by new and brilliant bits of colour not in the style of the original but in the taste of the author's period,—priests and Levites and fire from heaven, and the fulfilment of all righteousness of the law, and much music, and all sorts of harmless legendary anachronisms and exaggerations besides. The material of tradition seems broken up in an extraneous medium, the spirit of post-exilian Judaism.

VI.II.

VI.II.1. After Solomon's death the history of Israel in Chronicles is traced only through Jehovah's kingdom in the hand of the sons of David, and all that relates to the ten tribes is put aside. For according to the notions of the Judaistic period Israel is the congregation of true worship, and this last is connected with the temple at Jerusalem, in which of course the Samaritans have no part. Abijah of Judah makes this point of view clear to Jeroboam I. and his army in a speech delivered from Mount Zemaraim before the battle. "Think ye to withstand the kingdom of Jehovah in the hand of the sons of David, because ye are a great multitude, and with you are the golden calves which Jeroboam made you for gods ? Have ye not cast out the priests of Jehovah, the sons of Aaron and the Levites, and made for yourselves priests after the manner of the Gentiles? so that whosoever cometh to fill his hands with a young bullock and seven rams, even he may become a priest for the false gods? But as for us, we have not forsaken Jehovah our God, and our priests minister to Jehovah, the sons of Aaron and the Levites in the service; and they burn unto Jehovah every morning and every evening burnt sacrifices and sweet incense; the shewbread also is upon the pure table; for we have maintained the service of Jehovah our God, but ye have forsaken Him. And behold, God Himself is with us at our head, and His priests, and the loud-sounding trumpets to cry an alarm against you. O children of Israel, fight ye not against Jehovah the God of your fathers, for ye shall not prosper" (2Chronicles xiii. 8-12; comp. xi. 13-17).

The kingdom which bore the name of Israel was actually in point of fact in the olden time the proper Israel, and Judah was merely a kind of appendage to it. When Amaziah of Judah after the conquest of the Edomites challenged to battle King Jehoash of Samaria, whose territory had at that time suffered to the utmost under the continual wars with the Syrians, the latter bid say to him: "The thistle that was in Lebanon sent to the cedar that was in Lebanon, saying, Give thy daughter to my son to wife;—then passed by a wild beast that was in Lebanon and trode down the thistle. Thou hast indeed smitten Edom, and thy heart hath lifted thee up. Enjoy thy glory, but tarry at home." (2Kings xiv. 9, 10). And as the other would not listen, he punished him as if he had been a naughty boy and then let him go. Religiously the relative importance of the two corresponded pretty nearly to what it was politically and historically. Israel was the cradle of prophecy; Samuel, Elijah, and Elisha exercised their activity there; what contemporary figure from Judah is there to place alongside of these? Assuredly the author of the Book of Kings would not have forgotten them had any such there been, for he is a Judaean with all his heart, yet is compelled purely by the nature of the case to interest himself chiefly about the northern kingdom. And yet again at the very close it was the impending fall of Samaria that called into life a new phase of prophecy; he who inaugurated it, the Judaean Amos of Tekoah, was sent not to Judah but to Israel, the history of which had the first and fullest sympathy of his inmost soul as that of the people of Jehovah. Isaiah was the first who placed Jerusalem in the centre of his field of vision and turned away from Israel; for at the time of his first public appearance war was raging between the sister nations, and when his activity was at its acme all was over with the northern kingdom and all hope had to cling to the remnant,— the fallen

169

tabernacle of David. As regards the cultus, certainly, matters may have been somewhat less satisfactory in Israel than in Judah, at least in the last century before the Assyrian captivity, but at the outset there was no essential difference. On all hands Jehovah was worshipped as the peculiar divinity of the nation at numerous fanes, in the service at the high places there were wanting neither in the one nor in the other sacred trees, posts, and stones, images of silver and gold (Isaiah ii. 8 seq., xvii. 8, xxxi. 22; Micah v. 12). It is a question whether in the time before Hezekiah the cultus of the kingdom at Jerusalem had so much to distinguish it above that at Bethel or at Dan; against Jeroboam's golden calves must be set the brazen serpent of Moses, and the ark of Jehovah itself—which in ancient times was an idol (1Samuel iv.-vi.) and did not become idealised into an ark of the covenant, *ie.*, of the law, until probably it had actually disappeared. As for the prophetic reaction against the popular cultus, the instance of Hosea shows that it came into activity as early and as powerfully in Israel as in Judah. Even after Josiah's reformation Jeremiah complains that the sister who hitherto had been spared is in no respect better than the other who a hundred years before had fallen a victim to the Assyrians (iii. 6-1O); and though in principle the author of the Book of Kings, taking his stand upon Deuteronomy, prefers Judah and Jerusalem, yet he does not out of deference to this judgment alter the facts which show that old Israel was not further than old Judah from compliance with the Deuteronomic precepts. Chronicles, on the other hand, not only takes the Law—the Penta<teu>chal Law as a whole, but more particularly the Priestly Code therein preponderating—as its rule of judgment on the past; but also idealises the facts in accordance with that norm, and figures to itself the old Hebrew people as in exact conformity with the pattern of the later Jewish community,—as a monarchically graded hierocracy with a strictly centralised cultus of rigidly prescribed form at the holy place of Jerusalem. When, accordingly, the ten tribes fail to exhibit all the marks of the kingdom of God, this is taken to mean their falling away from the true Israel; they have made goats and calves their gods, driven away the priests and Levites, and in a word broken quite away from the institutions which shaped themselves in Judah during the period subsequent to Josiah and received their finishing-touches from Ezra. *1*

*************************************** 1. The Chronicler indeed is unable, even in the case of these schismatics, to divest himself of his legal notions, as appears almost comically in the circumstance that the priests of Jeroboam set about their heretical practices quite in accordance with the prescriptions of the Priestly Code, and procure their consecration by means of a great sacrifice (2 Chron xiii. 9).
****

Like other heathen, therefore, they are taken account of by the sacred history only in so far as they stood in relations of friendship or hostility with the people of Jehovah properly so called, the Israel in the land of Judah (2Chronicles xxiii. 2), and in all references to them the most sedulous and undisguised partisanship on behalf of Judah is manifested, even by the inhabitants of the northern kingdom itself. *2* If one seriously takes the Pentateuch as Mosaic law, this exclusion of the ten tribes is, in point of fact, an inevitable consequence, for the mere fact of their belonging to the people of Jehovah destroys the fundamental pre-supposition of that document, the unity and legitimacy of the worship as basis of the theocracy, the priests and Levites as its most important organs, "the sinews and muscles of the body politic, which keep the organism together as a living and moving whole."

VI.II.2. The reverse side is, of course, the idealisation of Judah from the point of view of the legitimate worship,—a process which the reader can imagine from the specimens already given with reference to David and Solomon. The priests and Levites who migrated from Israel are represented as having strengthened the southern kingdom (xi. 17), and here constitute the truly dominant element in the history. It is for their sake that kings exist as protectors and guardians of the cultus, with the internal arrangements of which, however, they dare not intermeddle (xxvi. 16 seq.); to deliver discourses and ordain spiritual solemnities (which figure as the culminating points in the narrative) are among the leading duties of their reign. *1*

Those among them who are good apprehend their task and are inseparable from the holy servants of Jehovah,—so, in particular, Jehoshaphat, Hezekiah, and Josiah. Of the first mentioned we are told that in the third year of his reign he appointed a royal commission of notables, priests, and Levites, to go about with the Book of the Law, and teach in the cities of Judah (xvii. 7-9); in the larger places, in the strongholds, he further instituted colleges of justice, and over them a supreme tribunal at Jerusalem, also consisting of priests, Levites, and notables, under the presidency of the high priest for spiritual, and of the Prince of the house of Judah for secular affairs (xix. 5-11). There is nothing about this in the Book of Kings, although what is of less importance is noticed (1Kings xxii. 47); the Chronicler makes the statement in his own language, which is unmistakable, especially in the pious speeches. Probably it is the organisation of justice as existing in his own day that he here carries back to Jehoshaphat, so that here most likely we have the oldest testimony to the synedrium of Jerusalem as a court of highest instance over the provincial synedria, as also to its composition and presidency. The impossibility of such a judiciary system in antiquity is clear from its presupposing the Book of the Law as its basis, from its co-ordination of priests and Levites, and also from its actual inconsistency with incidental notices, particularly in Isaiah and the older prophets (down to Jeremiah xxvi.), in which it everywhere is taken for granted as a thing of course that the rulers are also at the same time the natural judges. Moreover, Chronicles already tells us about David something similar to what it says about Jehoshaphat (1Chronicles xxiii. 4, xxvi. 29-32); the reason why the latter is selected by preference for this work lies simply in his name " Jehovah is Judge," as he himself is made to indicate in various ways (xix. 5-11; compare Joel iv. 12). But the king of Judah is strengthened by the

171

priests and Levites, not only in these domestic affairs, but also for war. As the trumpets of the priests give to Abijah courage and the victory against Jeroboam of Israel, so do the Levites also to Jehoshaphat against Moab and Ammon. Having fasted, and received, while praying, the comfortable assurance of the singer Jahaziel ("See God"), he advances next morning, with his army, against the enemy, having in the van the Levites, who march in sacred attire in front of the armed men and sing: "Praise ye the Lord, for His mercy endureth for ever." He then finds that the fighting has already been done by the enemy themselves, who, at the sound of that song of praise, have fallen upon and annihilated one another. Three days are spent in dividing the spoil, and then he returns as he came, the Levitical music leading the van, with psalteries, and harps, and trumpets to the house of Jehovah (2Chronicles xx. 1-28). Hezekiah is glorified in a similar manner. Of the Assyrian siege of Jerusalem and the memorable relief, comparatively little is made (xxxii. 1 seq.; comp. De Wette, i. 75); according to Chronicles, his master-work is that, as soon as he has mounted the throne, in the first month of the year, and of his reign (Exodus xl. 2; Leviticus ix. 1). he institutes by means of the priests and Levites, whom he addresses quite paternally as his children (xxix. 11), a great feast of consecration of the temple, alleged to have been closed and wasted by Ahaz; thereupon in the second month to celebrate the passover in the most sumptuous manner; and finally, from the third to the seventh month to concern himself about the accurate rendering of their dues to the clergy. All is described in the accustomed style, in the course of three long chapters, which tell us nothing indeed about the time of Hezekiah, but are full of information for the period in which the writer lived, particularly with reference to the method then followed in offering the sacred dues (xxix. 1-xxxi. 21). In the case of Josiah also the account of his epoch-making reformation of the worship is, on the whole, reproduced in Chronicles only in a mutilated manner, but the short notice of 2Kings xxiii. 21-23 is amplified into a very minute description of a splendid passover feast, in which, as always, the priests and above all the Levites figure as the leading personalities. In this last connection one little trait worth noticing remains, namely, that the great assembly in which the king causes the Book of the Law to be sworn to, is, in every other respect, made up in 2Chronicles xxxiv. 29 seq. exactly as it is in 2Kings xxiii. 1, , except that instead of "the priests and *prophets*" we find "the priests and *Levites*." The significance of this is best seen from the Targum, where "the priests and prophets" are translated into "the priests and scribes."

By this projection of the legitimate cultus prescribed in the Law and realised in Judaism, the Chronicler is brought however into a peculiar conflict with the statements of his authority, which show that the said cultus was not a mature thing which preceded all history, but came gradually into being in the course of history; he makes his escape as well as he can, but yet not without a strange vacillation between the timeless manner of looking at things which is natural to him, and the historical tradition which he uses and appropriates. The verses in 1Kings (xiv. 22, 23): Judah (not Rehoboam merely) did that which was evil in the sight of Jehovah and provoked Him to jealousy by their sins which they sinned, above all that their fathers had done; and they set up for themselves high places, macceboth and asherim, &c., which in the passage where they occur are, like the parallel statement regarding Israel (xii. 25 seq.), of primary importance, and cancel by one bold stroke the alleged difference of worship between the Levitical and non-Levitical kingdom, are omitted as quite too

172

impossible, although the whole remaining context is preserved (2Chronicles xii. 1-16). In the same way the unfavourable judgment upon Rehoboam's successor Abijah (1Kings xv. 3-5) is dropped, because the first kings of Judah, inasmuch as they maintain the true religion against those of Israel who have fallen away from it, must of necessity have been good. But though the Chronicler is silent about what is bad, for the sake of Judah's honour, he cannot venture to pass over the improvement which, according to 1Kings xv. 12 seq., was introduced in Asa's day, although one does not in the least know what need there was for it, everything already having been in the best possible state. Nay, he even exaggerates this improvement, and makes of Asa another Josiah (2Chronicles xv. 1-15), represents him also (xiv. 3) as abolishing the high places, and yet after all (xv. 1 7) repeats the statement of 1Kings xv. 14 that the high places were not removed. So also of Jehoshaphat, we are told in the first place that he walked in the first ways of his father Asa and abolished the high places in Judah (2Chronicles xvii. 3, 6, xix. 3), a false generalisation from 1Kings (xxii. 43, 47); and then afterwards we learn (xx. 32, 33) that the high places still remained, word for word according to 1Kings xxii. 43, 44. To the author it seems on the one hand an impossibility that the worship of the high places, which in spite of xxxiii.17 is to him fundamentally idolatry, should not have been repressed even by pious, *i.e.*, law-observing kings, and yet on the other hand he mechanically transcribes his copy.

In the case of the notoriously wicked rulers his resort is to make them simply heathen and persecutors of the covenant religion, for to him they are inconceivable within the limits of Jehovism, which always in his view has had the Law for its norm, and is one and the same with the exclusive Mosaism cf Judaism. So first, in the case of Joram: he makes high places on the hills of Judah and seduces the inhabitants of Jerusalem to commit fornication, and Judah to apostatise (xxi. 11), and moreover slays all his brethren with the sword (ver. 4)—the one follows from the other. His widow Athaliah breaks up the house of Jehovah by the hand of her sons (who had been murdered, but for this purpose are revived), and makes images of Baal out of the dedicated things (xxiv. 7); none the less on that account does the public worship of Jehovah go on uninterrupted under Jehoiada the priest. Most unsparing is the treatment that Ahaz receives. According to 2Kings xvi. 10 seq., be saw at Damascus an altar which took his fancy, and he caused a similar one to be set up at Jerusalem after its pattern, while Solomon's brazen altar was probably sent to the melting-pot; it was Urijah the priest who carried out the orders of the king. One observes no sign of autonomy, or of the inviolable divine right of the sanctuary; the king commands and the priest obeys. To the Chronicler the story so told is quite incomprehensible; what does he make of it? Ahaz introduced the idolatrous worship of Damascus, abolished the worship of Jehovah, and shut up the temple (2Chronicles xxviii. 23 seq.). He regards not the person of a man, the inflexible unity of the Mosaic cultus is everything to the Chronicler, and its historical identity would be destroyed if an orthodox priest, a friend of the prophet Isaiah, had lent a helping hand to set up a foreign altar. To make idolaters pure and simple of Manasseh and Amon any heightening of what is said in 2Kings xxi. was hardly necessary; and besides, there were here special reasons against drawing the picture in too dark colours. It is wonderful also to see how the people, which is always animated with alacrity and zeal for the Law, and rewards its pious rulers for their fidelity to the covenant (xv. 15, xvii. 5, xxiv. 10, xxxi. 10), marks its censure of these wicked kings by withholding from them, or impairing, the honour of royal burial (xxi. 19, 20, xxviii. 27, xxxiii. 10),—in spite of 2Kings ix. 28, xvi. 20, xxi. 1 8.

The periodically recurring invasions of heathenism help, at the same time, to an understanding of the consequent reforms, which otherwise surpass the comprehension of the Jewish scribe. According to the Books of Kings, Joash, Hezekiah, and Josiah hit upon praiseworthy innovations in the temple cultus, set aside deeply rooted and immemorial customs, and reformed the public worship of Jehovah. These advances WITHIN Jehovism, which, of course, are quite incompatible with its Mosaic fixity, are made by the Chronicler to be simple restorations of the pure religion following upon its temporary violent suspension. It is in Hezekiah's case that this is done in the most thoroughgoing manner. After his predecessor has shut the doors of the house of Jehovah, put out the lights, and brought the service to an end, he sets all in operation again by means of the resuscitated priests and Levites; the first and most important act of his reign is the consecration of the temple (2Chronicles xxix.), with which is connected (xxx., xxx.) the restoration of the passover and the restitution of the temporalia to the clergy, who, as it seems, have hitherto been deprived of them. That 2Kings xviii. 1-7, although very different, has supplied the basis for all these extravagances, is seen by comparing 2Chronicles xxix. 1, 2, xxxi. 1, 20, 21, xxxii. 22 only, that the king destroyed the brazen serpent Nehushtan (2Kings xviii. 4) is passed over in silence, as if it were incredible that such an image should have been worshipped down to that date in the belief that it had come down from the time of Moses; the not less offensive statement, on the other hand, that he took away *the Asherah* (by which only that of the temple altar can be understood; comp. Deuteronomy xvi. 21) is got over by charging the singular into the plural; he took away *the Asherahs* (xxx). 1), which occurred here and there throughout Judah, of course at heathen altars.

In the cases of Joash and Josiah the free flight of the Chronicler's law-crazed fancy is hampered by the copy to which he is tied, and which gives not the results merely, but the details of the proceedings themselves (2Chronicles xxii., xxiii.; 2Kings xi., xii.). It is precisely such histories as these, almost the only circumstantially told ones relating to Judah in the Book of Kings, which though in their nature most akin to our author's preference for cultus, bring him into the greatest embarrassment, by introducing details which to his notions are wholly against the Law, and yet must not be represented otherwise than in the most favourable light.

It cannot be doubted that the sections about Joash in 2Kings (xi. 1-xii. 17 [16]), having their scene end subject laid in the temple, are at bottom identical with 2Chronicles xxii. 10-xxiv. 14. In the case of 2Kings xi., to begin with, the beginning and the close, vers. 1-3, vers. 13-20, recur verbatim in 2Chronicles xxii. 10-12, xxiii. 12-21, if trifling alterations be left out of account. But in the central portion also there occur passages which are taken over into 2Chronicles without any change. Only here they are inappropriate, while in the original connection they are intelligible. For the meaning and colour of the whole is entirely altered in Chronicles, as the following comparison in the main passage will show; to understand it one must bear in mind that the regent Athaliah has put to death all the members of the house of David who had escaped the massacre of Jehu, with the exception of the child Joash, who, with the knowledge of Jehoiada, the priest, has found hiding and protection in the temple.

2 KINGS xi 2CHRONICLES xxiii.

4. In the seventh year Jehoiada 1. *In the seventh year Jehoiada*
sent and took the captains of sent and took the captains of
the Carians and runners, strengthened himself and *took the*
captains, Azariah the son of Jeroham,
and Ishmael the son of Jehohanan,
and Azariah the son of Obed,
and Maaseiah the son of Adaiah,
and Elishaphat the son of Zichri,
into covenant with him.

2. And they went about in Judah and gathered the Levites out of all the cities in Judah, and the chiefs of the fathers of Israel, and they came to Jerusalem.

and brought them to him into   3. And the whole
congregation
the house of Jehovah, and made a   made *a covenant in*
the house of
covenant with them, and took   God with the king.
And he said
an oath of them in the house of   unto them, *Behold,*
the king's
Jehovah, and showed them the   son shall reign, as
Jehovah said
king's son;   concerning the sons
of David.

5. And commanded them, saying, 4. *This is the thing that ye shall This is the thing that ye shall do: the third part of you, which do; the third part of you which enter on the Sabbath*, of the enter on the Sabbath and keep the priests and of the Levites, watch of the king's house, shall keep the doors.

[6. And the third part in the   5. And the third
part of you shall
gate of Jesod, and the third   be *in the house of*
the king, and
part in the gate behind the   the third part in the
gate Jesod; and
runners, and ye shall keep   all the people shall
be in the courts
the watch in the house...]:   of the house of
Jehovah.

175

7. And the two other third parts of you, those who go 6. And no one shall come into the forth on the Sabbath and house of Jehovah save the priests keep the watch in the house and they of the Levites that minister; of Jehovah about the king. but all the people shall keep the

ordinance of Jehovah.

8. Ye shall encompass the king 7. And the Levites shall *compass round about, every man with the king round about, every man his weapons in his hand, with his weapons in his hands, and and whosoever cometh within whosoever cometh* into the house, the ranks, shall be put to *shall be put to death; and they shall death, and ye shall be with be with the king whithersoever he the king whithersoever he goeth.* goeth.

9. And the captains did according 8. And the Levites and all Judah to all that Jehoiada the priest *did according to all that Jehoiada had commanded, and took each his the priest had commanded, and took men, those that were to come in each his men, those that were to come on the Sabbath with those that in on the Sabbath with those that were to go out on the Sabbath, were to go out on the Sabbath,* for and came to Jehoiada the priest. Jehoiada the priest dismissed not

the divisions.

10. And to the captains the 9. And Jehoiada the priest delivered priest gave King David's to the captains of hundreds the spears spears and shields that were and the bucklers and the shields that in the house of Jehovah. King David had, which were in the

house of God.

11. And the runners stood, every 10. And he set all the people, *every man with his weapons in his hand, man having his weapon in his hand, from the south side of the house from the south side of the house to to the north side, along by the north side, along by the altar the altar and the house, and the house, round about the king.* round about the king.

12. And he brought forth the 11. *And they brought out the king's king's son and put upon him son and put upon him the crown and the crown and the bracelet, the bracelet and they made him king,* and they made him king and and Jehoiada and his sons *anointed anointed him, and they clapped him and said: their hands and said: Long live the king.* Long live the king.

Can the enthronement of Joash, as on a former occasion that of Solomon, possibly have been accomplished by the agency of the bodyguard of the kings of Judah? Is it possible that the high priest should have made a covenant with the captains within the house of Jehovah, and himself have held out the inducement to those half-pagan mercenaries to penetrate into the temple precincts? That were indeed an outrage upon the Law not lightly to be imputed to so holy a man! Why then did not Jehoiada make use of his own guard, the myriads of Levites who were at his command? Such a course was the only right one, and therefore that which was followed. "No one

176

shall come into the house of Jehovah save the priests and they of the Levites that minister:" in accordance with this fundamental principle stated by himself (xxiii. 6; comp ver. 7 INTO THE HOUSE instead of WITHIN THE RANKS), our pious historian substitutes his priests and Levites for the Carians and runners. Hereby also Jehoiada comes into the place that belongs to him as sovereign of the sanctuary and of the congregation. He therefore needs no longer to set on foot in secret a conspiracy with the chiefs of the body-guard, but through his own spiritual officers calls together the Levites and heads of houses from all the cities of Judah into the temple, and causes the whole assemblage there to enter into a covenant with the young king. The glaring inconsistencies inevitably produced by the new colouring thus given to individual parts of the old picture must simply be taken as part of the bargain. If Jehoiada has unrestricted sway over such a force and sets about his revolution with the utmost publicity, then it is he and not Athaliah who has the substance of power; why then all this trouble about the deposition of the tyrant? Out of mere delight in Levitical pomp and high solemnities? What moreover is to be done with the captains who are retained in xxiii. 1, 9, and in ver. 14 are even called officers of the host as in 2Kings xi 15, after their soldiers have been taken from them or metamorphosed? Had the Levites a military organisation, and, divided into three companies, did they change places every week in the temple service? The commentators are inclined to call in to their aid such inventive assumptions, with which, however, they may go on for ever without attaining their end, for the error multiplies itself. As a specially striking instance of the manner in which the procedure of Chronicles avenges itself may be mentioned chapter xxiii. 8: "and they took each his men," &c. The words are taken from 2Kings xi. 9, but there refer to the captains, while here the antecedents are the Levites and all the men of Judah—as if each one of these last had a company of his own which entered upon service, or left it, every Sabbath day.

The comparison of 2Chronicles xxiv. 4-14 with 2Kings xii. 5-17 [4-16] is not much less instructive. According to 2Kings xii. Joash enjoined that all the money dues payable to the temple should in future fall to the priests, who in turn were to be under obligation to maintain the building in good repair. But they took the money and neglected the other side of the bargain, and when they and Jehoiada in particular were blamed by the king on that account, they gave up the dues so as not to be liable to the burden. Thereupon the king set up a kind of sacred treasury, a chest with a hole in the lid, near the altar, "on the right hand as one goes into the temple," into which the priests were to cast the money which came in, with the exception of the sin and trespass moneys, which still belonged to them. And as often as the chest became full, the king's scribes and the chief priest removed the money, weighed it, and handed it over to the contractors for payment of the workmen; that none of it was to be employed for sacred vessels is expressly said (ver. 14). This arrangement by King Joash was a lasting one, and still subsisted in Josiah's time (2Kings . . xxii. 3 seq.).

The arbitrary proceeding of Joash did not well suit the ideas of an autonomous hierocracy. According to the Law the current money dues fell to the priests; no king had the right to take them away and dispose of them at his pleasure. How was it possible that Jehoiada should waive his divine right and suffer such a sacrilegious invasion of sacred privileges? how was it possible that he should be blamed for his (at first) passive resistance of the illegal invasion; how was it possible at all that the priest in his own proper department should be called to account by the king? Chronicles knows better than that. The wicked Athaliah had wasted and plundered the temple; Joash determined to restore it, and for this purpose to cause money to be collected throughout all Israel by the agency of the Levites. But as these last were in no hurry, he made a chest and set it outside in the doorway of the sanctuary; there the people streamed past, and gentle and simple with joyful heart cast in their gifts until the chest was full. This being announced by the keepers of the door, the king's scribe and the delegate of the high priest came to remove the money; with it the king and the high priest paid the workmen, and what remained over was made into costly vessels (2Chronicles xxiv. 5-14). According to this account Joash makes no arrangement whatever about the sacred dues, but sets on foot an extraordinary collection, as had once been done by Moses for the building of the tabernacle (xxiv. 6, 9); following upon this, everything else also which in 2Kings xii. is a permanent arrangement, here figures as an isolated occurrence; instead of necessary repairs of the temple constantly recurring, only one extraordinary restoration of it is mentioned, and for this occasional purpose only is the treasure chest set up,— not, however, beside the altar, but only at the doorway (xxiv. 8; comp. 2Kings xii. 10). The clergy, the Levites, are charged only with making the collection, not with maintaining the building out of the sacred revenues; consequently they are not reproached with keeping the money to themselves, but only with not being heartily enough disposed towards the collection. It appears, however, that they were perfectly justified in this backwardness, for the king has only to set up the "treasury of God," when forthwith it overflows with the voluntary offerings of the people who flock to it, so that out of the proceeds something remains over (ver. 14) for certain other purposes—which according to 2Kings xii. 14 [13] were expressly excluded. Joash imposes no demands at all upon the priests, and Jehoiada in particular stands over against him as invested with perfectly equal rights; if the king sends his scribe, the high priest also does not appear personally, but causes himself to be represented by a delegate (xxiv. 11; comp. 2Kings xii. 11 [10]). Here also many a new piece does not come well into the old garment, as De Wette (i. 10O) shows. Chronicles itself tacitly gives the honour to the older narrative by making Joash at last apostatise from Mosaism and refuse the grateful deference which he owed to the high priest; this is the consequence of the unpleasant impression, derived not from its own story, but from that of the Book of Kings, with regard to the undue interference of the otherwise pious king in the affairs of the sanctuary and of the priests.

Chronicles reaps the fruits of its perversion of 2Kings xii. in its reproduction of the nearly related and closely connected section 2Kings xxii. 3-IO. It is worth while once more to bring the passages together.

2Kings xxii. 2Chronicles xxxiv.

3. And in the eighteenth year 8. And in the eighteenth year of king Josiah the king sent of his reign, to cleanse the Shaphan the son of Azaliah, land and the house, he sent the son of Meshullam, the scribe, Shaphan the son of Azaliah, to the house of

178

Jehovah, saying, and Maaseiah the governor of
the city, and Joah the son of
4. Go up to Hilkiah the high Joahaz the recorder, to repair priest, that he may empty
the the house of Jehovah his God. money which hath been brought into the house of
Jehovah 9. And they came to Hilkiah which the keepers of the the high priest, and
they threshold have gathered of delivered the money that had the people. been
brought into the house
of God which the Levites that
5. And let them deliver it into kept the threshold had gathered the hand of the doers
of the from Ephraim and Manasseh and work that have the oversight all the remnant
of Israel and of the house of Jehovah, and from all Judah and Benjamin, let them
give it to the doers and had returned therewith of the work who are in the to
Jerusalem. house of Jehovah to repair the breaches of the house. 10. And they gave
it into the
hand of the workmen that had the
6. Unto carpenters, and builders, oversight of the house of Jehovah, and masons, and
to buy timber and of the workmen that wrought in and hewn stones to repair the the
house of Jehovah to repair house. and amend the house.

7. But let no reckoning be 11. They gave it to the artificers
made with them as to the money and to the builders to buy that is
delivered into their hewn stone and timber for roofs hand, because they
deal faithfully. and beams of the houses which
the kings of Judah had destroyed.
12. And the men did the work faithfully. And the overseers of them
were Jahath and Obadiah, the Levites, of the sons of Merari; and
Zechariah and Meshullam, of the Kohathites, to preside; and all the
Levites that had skill in instruments of music
13. Were over the bearers of burdens and overseers of all that wrought
the work in any manner of service; and others of the Levites were
scribes and officers and porters.
14. And when they brought out the money that had been brought into
the house of Jehovah, Hilkiah the priest found the book of the law of
Jehovah by the hand of Moses.

8. And Hilkiah the high priest answered and	15. And Hilkiah
said unto Shaphan the scribe:	said to Shaphan the scribe:
I have found the book of the book of the law	I have found the
law in the house of Jehovah. Jehovah. And	in the house of
And Hilkiah gave the book to the book	Hilkiah delivered
Shaphan, and he read it.	to Shaphan.

179

9. And Shaphan the scribe came 16. And Shaphan carried the book to the king and
brought the king to the king, and besides brought word again, and said: Thy word
back to the king, saying: servants have emptied out the All that was committed to
thy money that was found in the servants they are doing. house and have delivered it
into the hand of them that 17. And they have emptied out do the work, that have the
the money that was found in the oversight of the house of house of Jehovah, and
have Jehovah. delivered it into the hand

of the overseers and into

10. And Shaphan the scribe the hand of the workmen. told the king, saying: Hilkiah
the priest hath delivered 18. And Shaphan the scribe to me a book. And Shaphan
told the king, saying: Hilkiah read it before the king. the priest hath given me a
book.

And Shaphan read out of it
before the king.

The occasion on which the priest introduces the Book of the Law to the notice of Shaphan has presuppositions in the arrangement made by Joash which Chronicles has destroyed, substituting others in its place,—that the temple had been destroyed under the predecessors of Josiah, but that under the latter money was raised by the agency of peripatetic Levites throughout all Israel for the restoration, and in the first instance deposited in the treasure-chest. At the emptying of this chest the priest is then alleged to have found the book (ver. 14, after Deuteronomy xxxi. 26), notwithstanding that on this occasion Shaphan also and the two accountants added in ver. 8 were present, and ought therefore to have had a share in the discovery which, however, is excluded by ver. 15 (= 2Kings xxii. 8). There are other misunderstandings besides; in particular, the superintendents of the works (*muphkadim*), to whom, according to the original narrative, the money is handed over for payment, are degraded to the rank of simple workmen, from whom, nevertheless, they are again afterwards distinguished; and while in 2Kings xxii. 7 they are represented as dealing faithfully *in paying out the money*, in 2Chronicles xxxiv. 12 they deal faithfully in their work. Perhaps, however, this is no mere misunderstanding, but is connected with the endeavour to keep profane hands as far off as possible from that which is holy, and, in particular, to give the management of the work to the Levites (vers. 12,13). To what length the anxiety of later ages went in this matter is seen in the statement of Josephus (Ant., xv. 11, 2), that Herod caused one thousand priests to be trained as masons and carpenters for the building of his temple. The two most interesting alterations in Chronicles are easily overlooked. In ver. 1 8 the words: "He read the book to the king," are changed into "He read out of the book to the king;" and after "Hilkiah gave the book to Shaphan" (ver. 15) the words "and he read it" are omitted. In 2Kings the book appears as of very moderate size, but the author of Chronicles figures to himself the whole Pentateuch under that name.

In the sequel 2Kings xxii. 11-xxiii.3 is indeed repeated verbatim in 2Chronicles xxxiv. 19-32, but the incomparably more important section connected with it (xxiii. 4-10), giving a detailed account of Josiah's vigorous reformation, is omitted, and its place taken by the meagre remark that the king removed all abominations out of Israel (xxxiv. 33); in compensation his passover feast is described all the more fully

180

(chap. xxxv.). In recording also the finding and publication of the Law, Chronicles fails to realise that this document begins now for the first time to be historically operative, and acquires its great importance quite suddenly. On the contrary, it had been from the days of Moses the basis on which the community rested, and had been in force and validity at all normal times; only temporarily could this life-principle of the theocracy be repressed by wicked kings, forthwith to become vigorous and active again as soon as the pressure was removed. As soon as Ahaz has closed his eyes, Hezekiah, in the first month of his first year, again restores the Mosaic cultus; and as soon as Josiah reaches years of discretion he makes good the sins of his fathers. Being at his accession still too young, the eighth year of his reign is, as a tribute to propriety, selected instead of the eighth year of his life, and the great reformation assigned to that period which in point of fact he undertook at a much later date (xxxiv. 3-7 = 2Kings xxiii. 4-20> Thus the movement happily becomes separated from its historical occasion, and in character the innovation appears rather as a simple recovery of the spring after the pressure on it has been removed. The mist disappears before the sun of the Law, which appears in its old strength; its light passes through no phases, but shines from the beginning with uniform brightness. What Josiah did had also been done before him already by Asa, then by Jehoshaphat, then by Hezekiah; the reforms are not steps in a progressive development, but have all the same unchanging contents. Such is the influence upon historical vision of that transcendental Mosaism raised far above all growth and process of becoming, which can be traced even in the Book of Kings, but is so much more palpable in the Book of Chronicles.

VI.II.3. Apart from the fact that it represents the abiding tradition of the legitimate cultus at Jerusalem, the history of Judah in the Book of Chronicles has yet another instructive purpose. In the kingdom of Judah it is not a natural and human, but a divine pragmatism that is operative. To give expression to this is what the prophets exist for in unbroken succession side by side with high priests and kings; they connect the deeds of men with the events of the course of the world, and utilise the sacred history as a theme for their preaching, as a collection of examples illustrative of the promptest operation of the righteousness of Jehovah. In doing so they do not preach what is new or free, but have at their command, like Jehovah Himself, only the Law of Moses, setting before their hearers prosperity and adversity in conformity with the stencil pattern, just as the law is faithfully fulfilled or neglected. Of course their prophecies always come exactly true, and in this way is seen an astonishing harmony between inward worth and outward circumstance. Never does sin miss its punishment, and never where misfortune occurs is guilt wanting.

In the fifth year of Rehoboam Judah and Jerusalem were ravaged by Pharaoh Shishak (1Kings xiv. 25). The explanation is that three years they walked in the ways of David and Solomon, because for three years they were strengthened and reinforced by the priests and Levites and other pious persons who had immigrated from the northern kingdom (2Chronicles xi. 17); but thereafter in the fourth year, after the kingdom of Rehoboam had been strengthened and confirmed, he forsook the Law and all Israel with him (xii. 1)— and in the fifth year followed the invasion of Shishak. A prophet announces this, and in consequence the king humbles himself along with his people and escapes with comparatively trifling punishment, being thought worthy to reign yet other twelve years.

Asa in his old age was diseased in his feet (1Kings xv. 23). According to 2Chronicles xvi. 12, he died of this illness, which is described as extremely dangerous, in the forty-first year of his reign, after having already been otherwise unfortunate in his later years. And why? He had invoked foreign aid, instead of the divine, against Baasha of Israel. Now, as Baasha survived only to the twenty-sixth year of Asa, the wickedness must have been perpetrated before that date. But in that case its connection with the punishment which overtook the king only towards the close of his life would not be clear. Baasha's expedition against Jerusalem, accordingly, and the Syrian invasion of Israel occasioned by Asa on that account are brought down in Chronicles to the thirty-sixth year of the latter (xvi. 1). It has been properly observed that Baasha was at that date long dead, and the proposal has accordingly been made to change the number thirty-six into sixteen,—without considering that the first half of the reign of Asa is expressly characterised as having been prosperous, that the thirty-fifth year is already reached in chap. xv. 19, and that the correction destroys the connection of the passage with what follows (xvi. 7 seq.). For it is in connection with that flagitious appeal for aid to the Syrians that the usual prophet makes his appearance (xvi. 7), and makes the usual announcement of impending punishment. It is Hanani, a man of Northern Israel (1Kings xvi. 7), but Asa treats him as if he were one of his own subjects, handles him severely, and shuts him in prison. By this he hastens and increases his punishment, under which he falls in the forty-first year of his reign.

Jehoshaphat, the pious king, according to 1Kings xxii., took part in the expedition of the godless Ahab of Israel against the Damascenes. Chronicles cannot allow this to pass unrebuked, and accordingly when the king returns in peace, the same Hanani announces his punishment, albeit a gracious one (2Chronicles xix. I-3). And gracious indeed it is; the Moabites and Ammonites invade the land, but Jehoshaphat without any effort on his part wins a glorious victory, and inexhaustible plunder (xx. 1 seq.). One cannot blame him, therefore, for once more entering into an alliance with Ahab's successor for a naval expedition to be undertaken in common, which is to sail from a port of the Red Sea, probably round Africa, to Tarshish (Spain, 2Chronicles ix. 21). But this time he is punished more seriously as Eliezer the son of Dodavah had prophesied, the ships are wrecked. Compare on the other hand 1Kings xxii. 48, 49: "Jehoshaphat made ships of Tarshish to go to Ophir for gold, but they went not, for the ships were wrecked in the harbour on the Red Sea. At that time Ahaziah the son of Ahab had said to Jehoshaphat: Let my servants go with thy servants in the ships; but Jehoshaphat would not." So the original statement. But in Chronicles a moral ground must be found for the misfortune, and Jehoshaphat therefore makes with the king of Samaria a sinful alliance, which in point of fact he had declined, not indeed from religious motives.

Joram, the son of Jehoshaphat, conducted himself very ill, it is said in 2Kings viii. 18; Chronicles enhances his offence, and above all adds the merited reward (xxi. 4, seq.). Elijah, although he had quitted this earth long before (2Kings iii. 11 seq.),

182

must write to the offender a letter, the threats of which are duly put into execution by Jehovah. The Philistines and Arabians having previously pressed him hard, he falls into an incurable sickness of the bowels, which afflicts him for years, and finally brings him to his end in a most frightful manner (xxi. 12, seq.). In concurrence with the judgment of God, the people withhold from the dead king the honours of royalty, and he is not buried beside his fathers, notwithstanding 2Kings viii. 24.

Joash, according to 2Kings xii., was a pious ruler, but met with misfortune; he was compelled to buy off Hazael, who had laid siege to Jerusalem, at a heavy price, and finally he died by the assassin's hand. Chronicles is able to tell how he deserved this fate. In the sentence: "He did what was right in the sight of the Lord all his days, because Jehoiada the high priest had instructed him " (2Kings xii. 3 [2]), it alters the last expression into "all the days of Jehoiada the priest," (xxiv. 2). After the death of his benefactor he fell away, and showed his family the basest ingratitude; at the end of that very year the Syrians invade him; after their departure his misfortunes are increased by a dreadful illness, under which he is murdered (xxiv. 17 seq.).

Amaziah was defeated, made prisoner, and severely punished by Jehoash, king of Samaria, whom he had audaciously challenged (2Kings xiv. 8 seq.). Why? because he had set up in Jerusalem idols which had been carried off from Edom, and served them (2Chronicles xxv. 1 4). He prefers the plundered gods of a vanquished people to Jehovah at the very moment when the latter has proved victorious over them! From the time of this apostasy— a crime for which no punishment could be too great—his own servants are also stated to have conspired against him and put him to death (xxv. 27), and yet we are assured in ver. 25 (after 2Kings xiv. I;) that Amaziah survived his adversary by fifteen years.

Uzziah, one of the best kings of Judah, became a leper, and was compelled to hand over the regency to his son Jotham (2Kings xv. 5); for, adds Chronicles, "when he had become strong, his heart was lifted up, even to ruin, so that he transgressed against Jehovah his God, and went into the temple of Jehovah, to burn incense upon the altar of incense. And Azariah the priest went in after him, and with him fourscore priests of Jehovah, and withstood him and said: It is not for thee to burn incense, but only for the sons of Aaron who are consecrated thereto. Then Uzziah was wroth and laid not the censer aside, and the leprosy rose up in his forehead, and the priests thrust him out from thence" (xxvi. 16-20). The matter is now no longer a mystery.

Ahaz was a king of little worth, and yet he got fairly well out of the difficulty into which the invasion of the allied Syrians and Israelites had brought him by making his kingdom tributary to the Assyrian Tiglath-Pileser (2Kings xvi. 1 seq.). But Chronicles could not possibly let him off so cheaply. By it he is delivered into the hand of the enemy: the Israelites alone slaughter 120,000 men of Judah, including the king's son and his most prominent servants, and carry off to Samaria 200,000 women and children, along with a large quantity of other booty. The Edomites and Philistines also fall upon Ahaz, while the Assyrians whom he has summoned to his aid misunderstand him, and come up against Jerusalem with hostile intent; they do not, indeed, carry the city, but yet become possessors, without trouble, of its treasures, which the king himself hands over to them (xxviii. 1-21).

The Book of Kings knows no worse ruler than Manasseh was; yet he reigned undisturbed for fifty-five years—a longer period than was enjoyed by any other king (2Kings xxi.1-18). This is a stone of stumbling that Chronicles must remove. It tells that Manasseh was carried in chains by the Assyrians to Babylon, but there prayed to Jehovah, who restored him to his kingdom; he then abolished idolatry in Judah (xxxiii. 11-20). Thus on the one hand he does not escape punishment, while on the other hand the length of his reign is nevertheless explained. Recently indeed it has been sought to support the credibility of these statements by means of an Assyrian inscription, from which it appears that Manasseh did pay tribute to Esarhaddon. That is to say, he had been overpowered by the Assyrians; that is again to say, that he had been thrown into chains and carried off by them. Not so rapid, but perhaps quite as accurate, would be the inference that as a tributary prince he must have kept his seat on the throne of Judah, and not have exchanged it for the prison of Babylon. In truth, Manasseh's temporary deposition is entirely on the same plane with Nebuchadnezzar's temporary grass-eating. The unhistorical character of the intermezzo (the motives of which are perfectly transparent) follows not only from the silence of the Book of Kings (a circumstance of no small importance indeed), but also, for example, from Jeremiah xv. 4; for when it is there said that all Judah and Jerusalem are to be given up to destruction because of Manasseh, it is not presupposed that his guilt has been already borne and atoned for by himself.

To justify the fact of Josiah's defeat and death at Megiddo, there is attached to him the blame of not having given heed to the words of Necho from the mouth of God warning him against the struggle (xxxv. 21, 22). Contrariwise, the punishment of the godless Jehoiakim is magnified; he is stated to have been put in irons by the Chaldaeans and carried to Babylon (xxxvi. 6)—an impossibility of course before the capture of Jerusalem, which did not take place until the third month of his successor. The last prince of David's house, Zedekiah, having suffered more severely than all his predecessors, must therefore have been stiff-necked and rebellious (xxxvi.12, 13),—characteristics to which, according to the authentic evidence of the prophet Jeremiah, he had in reality the least possible claim.

It is thus apparent how inventions of the most circumstantial kind have arisen out of this plan of writing history, as it is euphemistically called. One is hardly warranted, therefore, in taking the definiteness of statements vouched for by Chronicles alone as proof of their accuracy. The story about Zerah the Ethiopian (2Chronicles xiv. 9 seq.) is just as apocryphal as that of Chushan-Rishathaim (Judges iii 10). Des Vignoles has indeed identified the first-named with the Osorthon of Manetho, who again occurs in the Egyptian monuments as Osorkon, son of Shishak, though not as renewing the war against Palestine; but Osorkon was an Egyptian, Zerah an Ethiopian, and the resemblance of the names is after all not too obvious. But, even if Zerah were really a historical personage, of what avail would this be for the unhistorical connection? With a million of men the king of the Libyans and Moors, stepping over Egypt, comes against Judah. Asa, ruler of a land of about sixty

184

German square miles, goes to meet the enemy with 580,000, and defeats him on the plain to the north of Mareshah so effectually that not a single soul survives. Shall it be said that this story, on account of the accurate statement of locality (although Mareshah instead of Gath is not after all suggestive of an old source), is credible-at all events after deduction of the incredibilities? If the incredibilities are deducted, nothing at all is left. The invasion of Judah by Baasha of Israel, and Asa's deportment towards him (1Kings xv. 17 seq.), are quite enough fully to dispose of the great previous victory over the Ethiopians claimed for Asa. The case is no better with the victory of Jehoshaphat over the Ammonites and Moabites (2Chronicles xx.); here we have probably an echo of 2Kings iii., where we read of Jehoshaphat's taking part in a campaign against Moab, and where also recurs that characteristic feature of the self-destruction of the enemy, so that for the opposing force nothing remains but the work of collecting the booty (iii. 23; compare 2Chronicles xx. 23). The Chronicler has enemies always at his command when needed,—Arabians, Ethiopians (xvii. 11, xxi. 16, xxii. 1, xxvi. 7), Mehunims (xx. 1, xxvi. 1), Philistines (xvii. 11, xxi. 16, xxvi. 6 seq., xxviii. 18), Ammonites (xx. 1, xxvi. 8, xxvii. 5), whose very names in some cases put them out of the question for the older time. Such statements as that the Ammonites became subject to Kings Uzziah and Jotham, are, in the perfect silence of the credible sources, condemned by their inherent impossibility; for at that period the highway to Ammon was Moab, and this country was by no means then in the possession of Judah, nor is it anywhere said that it was. The Philistines as vindictive enemies are rendered necessary by the plan of the history (xxi. 16, xxviii. 18), and this of itself throws suspicion upon the previous statements (xvii. 11, xxvi. 6 seq.) that they were laid under tribute by Jehoshaphat, and subjugated by Uzziah; it is utterly impossible to believe that the latter should have broken down the walls of Ashdod (Amos i. 7), or have established fortresses in Philistia. According to the Book of Kings, he did indeed conquer Edom anew; Edom is according to this authority the one land to which the descendants of David lay claim and against which they wage war, while Moab and Philistia (the most important towns being excepted, however, in the case of the latter) virtually belong to the territory of Ephraim.

The triumphs given by the Chronicler to his favourites have none of them any historical effect, but merely serve to add a momentary splendour to their reigns. Merit is always the obverse of success. Joram, Joash, Ahaz, who are all depicted as reprobates, build no fortresses, command no great armies, have no wealth of wives and children; it is only in the case of the pious kings (to the number of whom even Rehoboam and Abijah also belong) that the blessing of God manifests itself by such tokens. Power is the index of piety, with which accordingly It rises and fall. Apart from this it is of no consequence if, for example, Jehoshaphat possesses more than 1,100.000 soldiers (xvii, 14 seq.), for they are not used for purposes of war; the victory comes from God and from the music of the Levites (chap. xx.). In the statements about fortress-building which regularly recur in connection with the names of good rulers, *1*

*** 1 viii. 3-6, xi. 5-12, xiii. 19, xiv. 5, 6 [6, 7], xvii. 12, xix. 5, xxvi. 9, 10, xxvii. 4, xxxii. 5,, xxxiii. 14.
****

general statements, such as those of Hosea viii. 14, 2Kings xviii. 13, are illustrated by concrete examples, a few elements of tradition being also employed (Lachish). It is not possible, but, indeed, neither is it necessary, to demonstrate in every case the imaginary character of the statements; according to xix. 5 it would appear as if simply every city of any kind of consequence was regarded as a fortress and in the list given in chap. xi. 6 seq., we chiefly meet with names which were also familiar in the post-exile period. That Abijah deprived Jeroboam of Bethel amongst others, and that Jehoshaphat set governors over the Ephraimite cities which had been taken by Asa his father (xiii. 19, xvii. 2), would excite surprise if it stood anywhere else than in Chronicles. In forming a judgment on its family history of the descendants of David, the statement contained in xiii. 21 is specially helpful both in manner and substance: "And Abijah waxed mighty, and he married fourteen wives, and begat twenty and two sons, and sixteen daughters." This can only be taken as referring to the reign of Abijah, and that too after the alleged victory over Jeroboam; but he reigned altogether for only three years, and is it to be supposed that within this interval one of his sons should even have attained to man's estate? In reality, however, Abijah had no son at all, but was succeeded by his brother, for the definite and doubtless authentic statement that Maachah, the wife of Rehoboam, was the mother both of Abijah and of Asa, and that the latter removed her from her position at court (1Kings xv. 2, 10, 13), must override the allegation of ver. 8, that the successor of Abijah was his son. After Jehoshaphat's death it is said in the first place that Jehoram slew all his brethren (2 Chr. xxi. 4), and afterwards that the Arabians slew all Jehoram's children with the exception of one (xxii. 1); how many of the Davidic house in that case survive for Jehu, who nevertheless slew forty-two of them (2Kings x. 14)? In short, the family history of the house of David is of equal historical value with all the other matters on which the Chronicler is more widely and better informed than all the older canonical books. The remark applies to names and numbers as well; about such trifles, which produce an appearance of accuracy, the author is never in any embarrassment.

VI.II.4. The Book of Kings then everywhere crops up as the real foundation of the portion of Chronicles relating to Judah after the period of Solomon. Where the narrative of the former is detailed and minute, our author also has fuller and more interesting material at his command; so, for example, in the history relating to the temple and to the common and mutual relations of Judah and Israel (2 Chr. x., xviii., xxiii., seq., xxv. 17-24, xxxiii. seq.). Elsewhere he is restricted to the epitome that constitutes the framework of the Book of Kings; by it he is guided in his verdicts as to the general character of the successive sovereigns as well as in his chronological statements, although, in accordance with his plan, he as a rule omits the synchronisms (xiii. 1, xxv. 25). The positive data also, given by the epitome with reference to the legislation in matters of worship by the various kings, are for the most part reproduced word for word, and float in a fragmentary and readily distinguishable way in the mixture of festivals, sermons, choruses, law, and prophets. For this is an important verification of all the results already obtained; all in Chronicles that is not derived from Samuel and Kings, has a uniform character not only in its substance, but also in its awkward and frequently unintelligible language—plainly belonging to a time in which Hebrew was approaching extinction—in its artificiality of style, deriving its vitality exclusively from Biblical

186

reminiscences. This is not the place for the proof of these points, but the reader may compare Staehelin's Einleitung (1862), p. 139 seq.; Bertheau, p. xiv. seq., and Graf, p. 116.

VI.III.

VI.III.1. When the narrative of Chronicles runs parallel with the older historical books of the canon, it makes no real additions, but the tradition is merely differently coloured, under the influence of contemporary motives. In the picture it gives the writer's own present is reflected, not antiquity. But neither is the case very different with the genealogical lists prefixed by way of introduction in 1Chronicles i.-ix.; they also are in the main valid only for the period at which they were drawn up—whether for its actual condition or for its conceptions of the past.

The penchant for pedigrees and genealogical registers, made up from a mixture of genealogico-historical and ethnologico-statistical elements, is a characteristic feature of Judaism; along with the thing the word YX# also first came into use during the later times. Compendious histories are written in the form of TLDWT and YWX#YN. The thread is thin and inconspicuous, and yet apparently strong and coherent; one does not commit oneself to much, and yet has opportunity to introduce all kinds of interesting matter. Material comes to one's hand, given a beginning and an end, the bridge is soon completed. Another expression of the same tendency is the inclination to give a genealogical expression to all connections and associations of human society whatsoever, to create artificial families on all hands and bring them into blood relationship, as if the whole of public life resolved itself into a matter of cousinship,—an inclination indicative of the times of political stagnation then prevalent. We hear of the families of the scribes at Jabesh, of the potters and gardeners and byssus-workers, of the sons of the goldsmiths, apothecaries, and fullers, these corporations being placed on the same plane with actual families. The division into classes of the persons engaged in religious service is merely the most logical development of this artificial system which is applied to all other social relations as well.

Proceeding now to a fuller examination of the contents of 1 Chron i.-ix. and other texts connected with that, we have here, apart from the first chapter, which does not demand further attention, an ethno-genealogical survey of the twelve tribes of Israel, which is based mostly on the data of the Priestly Code (Genesis xlvi.; um. <?> xxvi.), expanded now more now less. But while the statements of the Priestly Code have to hold good for the Mosaic period only, those of Chronicles have also to apply to the succeeding ages,—those, for example, of Saul and David, of Tiglath-Pileser and Hezekiah. As early as the time of the judges, however, very important changes had taken place in the conditions. While Dan continued to subsist with difficulty, Simeon and Levi had been completely broken up (Genesis xlix. 7); in the Blessing of Moses the latter name denotes something quite different from a tribe, and the former is not even so much as named, although the enumeration is supposed to be complete; in David's time it had already been absorbed by families of mingled Judaic and Edomitic descent in the district where it had once had independent footing. Eastward of Jordan Leah's first-born had a similar fate, although somewhat later. After it has been deposed from its primacy in Genesis xlix. and twitted in Judges v. with its brave words unaccompanied by corresponding deeds, the faint and desponding wish is expressed in Deuteronomy xxxiii. 6 that "Reuben may live and not die," and King Mesha is unaware that any other than the Gadite had ever dwelt in the land which, properly speaking, was the heritage of Reuben. But in Chronicles these extinct tribes again come to life—and not Levi alone, which is a special case, but also Simeon and Reuben, with which alone we are here to deal—and they exist as independent integral twelfths of Israel, precisely like Ephraim and Manasseh, throughout the whole period of the monarchy down to the destruction of the kingdom by the Assyrians. *1* This is

*** 1. For Reuben see (in addition to 1Chronicles v. 1-10) v. 18, xi. 42, xii. 37. xxvi. 32, xxvii. 16, for Simeon, 1Chronicles iv. 24-43, with xii. 25, and 2Chronicles xv. 9, xxxiv. 6, observing that in the last two passages Simeon is reckoned as belonging to the northern kingdom, so as   to   complete   the   number   of   the   ten   tribes.
****

diametrically opposed to all authentic tradition; for to maintain that nothing else is intended than a continued subsistence of individual Simeonite and Reubenite families within other tribes is merely a desperate resort of the harmonists, and every attempt to tone down the fact that those extinct and half-mythical tribes are in Chronicles placed side by side with the rest without any distinction is equally illegitimate. The historical value thus lost by the narrative as a whole cannot be restored by the seeming truthfulness of certain details. Or is more significance really to be attached to the wars of the Simeonites and Reubenites against the Arabians than to the rest of the extemporised wars of the kings of Judah against these children of the wilderness? If only at least the names had not been "sons of Ham, and Mehunim and Hagarenes " (iv. 40 seq. [Heb.], v. 10)! As for the pedigrees and genealogical lists, are they to be accepted as historical merely because their construction is not apparent to us, and they evade our criticism? The language affords no room for the conjecture that we here possess extracts from documents of high antiquity (iv. 33, 38, 4I, v. 1 seq., 7, 9 seq.), and proper names such as Elioenai and the like (iv. 35 seq.) are not striking for their antique originality.

Of the remaining tribes, so far as they belong to Israel and not to Judah, the next in the series after Reuben are the trans-Jordanic (v. 11-26). They are said to have been numbered in the days of Jotham of Judah and Jeroboam of Israel, on which occasion 44,760 warriors were returned; they took the field against the Hagarenes, Ituraeans, Nephishites, and Nabataeans, gaining the victory and carrying off much booty, "for they cried to God in the battle, and He was entreated of them because they put their trust in Him." But afterwards they fell away from the God of their fathers, and as a punishment were carried off by Pul and Tiglath-Pileser to Armenia by the Chaboras and the river of Gozan. Apart from the language, which in its edifying tone is that of late Judaism, and leaving out of account the enumeration "the sons of Reuben and the Gadites and half of the tribe of Manasseh," the astonishing and highly doubtful combinations are eloquent: Pul and Tiglath-Pileser, the Chaboras and the river of Gozan, are hardly distinguished from each other; Jotham and Jeroboam, on the other hand, make so impossible a synchronism that the partisans of Chronicles will have it that none is intended,—forgetful, to be sure, of Hosea i. 2, and omitting to say what in that case Jotham of Judah has to do here at all in this connection. The Hagarenes and Ituraeans too, instead of (say) the Moabites and Ammonites, furnish food for reflection, as also do the geographical statements that Gad had his seat in Bashan and Manasseh in and near Lebanon. As for the proper names of families and their heads, they are certainly beyond our means of judging; the phrases however of the scheme they fill (anshe shemoth rashe l'beth abotham, migrash, jahes) are peculiar to the Priestly Code and Chronicles, and alongside of elements which are old and attested from other quarters, occur others that look very recent, as for example (v. 24) Eliel, Azriel, Jeremiah, Hodaviah, Jahdiel.

In the introduction the Galilaean tribes have no prominent place, but in the rest of the book they make a favourable appearance (see especially 1Chronicles xii. 32-34, 40, and 2Chronicles xxx. 10, 11, 18); it readily occurs to one, especially in the last-cited passage, to think of the later Judaising process in Galilee. In Issachar there are stated to have been 87,000 fighting men in David's time (misparam l'toledotham l'beth abotham, vii. 1-5); out of Zebulun and Naphtali, again, exactly 87,000 men came to David at Hebron, to anoint him and be feasted three days,—it is carefully mentioned, however (xii. 40), that they took their provisions up with them. The proper kernel of Israel, Ephraim and Manasseh, is, in comparison with Simeon, Reuben, Gad, Issachar, treated with very scant kindness (vii. 14-29),—a suspicious sign. The list of the families of Manasseh is an artificial *rechauffe* of elements gleaned anywhere; Maachah passes for the wife as well as the sister of Machir, but being a Gileaditess (Beth-Maachah), ought not to have been mentioned at all in this place where the cis-Jordanic Manasseh is being spoken of; to fill up blanks every contribution is thankfully received. *1* In the case of Ephraim a long and meagre genealogy

** 1 Kuenen, Th. Tijdschr., 1877, pp.   484,   488;   Godsdienst   v.   Isr.,   i.   165.
****

only is given, which, begun in vers. 20, 21, and continued in ver. 25, constantly repeats the same names (Tahath, Tahan, 1Samuel i. 1; Eladah, Laadan, Shuthelah, Telah), and finally reaches its end and goal in Joshua, whose father Nun alone is known to the older sources! Into the genealogy a wonderful account of the slaying of the children of Ephraim by the men of Gath (1Samuel iv.?) has found its way, and (like viii. 6, 7) according to the prevailing view must be of venerable antiquity. But in that case the statement of iv. 9 must also be very ancient, which yet obviously is connected with the rise of the schools of the scribes stated in ii. 55 to have existed in Jabez.

Everywhere it is presupposed that Israel throughout the entire period of the monarchy was organised on the basis of the twelve tribes (ii.-ix.; xii.; xxvii.), but the assumption is certainly utterly false, as can be seen for example from 1Kings iv. Further, the *penchant* of later Judaism for statistics is carried back to the earlier time, to which surveys and censuses were repugnant in the extreme. In spite of 2Samuel xxiv., we are told that under David enumerations both of the spiritual and of the secular tribes were made again and again; so also under his successors, as may be inferred partly from express statements and partly from the precise statistics given as to the number of men capable of bearing arms: in these cases the most astounding figures are set down,—always, however, as resting on original documents and accurate enumeration. In the statistical information of Chronicles, then, so far as it relates to pre-exilic antiquity, we have to do with artificial compositions. It is possible, and occasionally demonstrable, that in these some elements derived from tradition have been used. But it is certain that quite as many have been simply invented; and the combination of the elements—the point of chief importance— dates, as both form and matter show, from the very latest period. One might as well try to hear the grass growing as attempt to derive from such a source as this a historical knowledge of the conditions of ancient Israel.

VI.III.2. As regards Judah and Benjamin, and to a certain extent Levi also, the case of course is somewhat different from that of the ten extinct tribes. It is conceivable that here a living ethno-genealogical tradition may have kept the present connected with the past. Nevertheless, on closer examination, it comes out that most of what the Chronicler here relates has reference to the post-exilic time, and that the few fragments which go up to a higher antiquity are wrought into a connection which on the whole is of a very recent date. Most obtrusively striking is it that the list of the heads of the people dwelling in Jerusalem given in ix. 4—17 is simply identical with Nehemiah xi. 3-19. In this passage, introducing as it does the history of the kings (x. seq.), one is by no means prepared to hear statements about the community of the second temple; but our author is under the impression that in going there he is letting us know about the old Jerusalem; from David to Nehemiah is no leap for him, the times are not distinct from one another to his mind. For chap. viii. also, containing a full enumeration of the Benjamite families, with special reference to those which had their seat in the capital, Bertheau has proved the post-exilic reference; it is interesting that in the later Jerusalem there existed a widespread family which wished to deduce its origin from Saul and rested its claims to this descent on a long genealogy (viii. 33-40). *1*

** 1. Equivalent to ix. 35-44, which perhaps   proves   the   later   interpolation   of   ix.   1-34.
****

It cannot be said that this produces a very favourable impression for the high antiquity of the other list of the Benjamites in vii. 6-11; to see how little value is to be attached to the pretensions of the latter to be derived from original documents of hoary antiquity, it is only necessary to notice the genuinely Jewish phraseology of vers. 7, 9, 11, such proper names as Elioenai, and the numbers given (22,034 + 20,200 + 17,200, making in all 59,434 fighting men).

The registers of greatest historical value are those relating to the tribe of Judah (ii. 1- iv. 23). But in this statement the genealogy of the descendants of David must be excepted (chapter iii.), the interest of which begins only with Zerubbabel, the rest being merely an exceedingly poor compilation of materials still accessible to us in the older historical books of the canon, and in Jeremiah. According to iii. 5, the first four of David's sons, born in Jerusalem, were all children of Bathsheba; the remaining seven are increased to nine by a textual error which occurs also in the LXX version of 2Samuel v. 16. Among the sons of Josiah (iii. 15 seq.), Johanan, *i.e.* Jehoahaz, is distinguished from Shallum (Jeremiah xxii. 11), and because he immediately succeeded his father, is represented as the first-born, though in truth Jehoiakim was older (2Kings xxiii. 3I, 36); Zedekiah, Jehoiakim's brother, is given out to be the son of Jeconiah, the son of Jehoiakim, because he was the successor of Jeconiah, who succeeded Jehoiakim. Similar things occur also in the Book of Daniel, but are usually overlooked, with a mistaken piety. Whoever has eyes to see cannot assign any high value except to the two great Jewish genealogies in chaps. ii. and iv. Yet even here the most heterogeneous elements are tossed together, and chaff is found mingled with wheat. *1*

*************************************** 1. For further details the reader is referred to the author's dissertation De gentibus et familiis Judaeis, Gottingen, 1870.
****

Apart from the introduction, vers.1-8, chap. ii. is a genealogy of the children of Hezron, a tribe which in David's time had not yet been wholly amalgamated with Judah, but which even then constituted the real strength of that tribe and afterwards became completely one with it. The following scheme discloses itself amid the accompanying matters: "The sons of Hezron are Jerahmeel and Celubai" (Caleb) (ver. 9). "and the sons of Jerahmeel, the first-born of Hezron, were..." (ver. 25). "These were the sons of Jerahmeel. And the sons of Caleb the brother of Jerahmeel were..." (ver. 42). "These were the sons of Caleb " (ver. 50 a). That which is thus formally defined and kept by itself apart (compare in this connection "Jerahmeel the first-born of Hezron," "Caleb the brother of Jerahmeel") is materially also distinguished from all else. It is the kernel of the whole, and refers to the pre-exilian time. Even the unusual *et fuerunt* (vers. 25, 33, 50) points to this conclusion, as well as, in the case of Caleb, the positive fact that the towns named in ver. 42-49 are all situated near Hebron and in the Negeb of Judah, where after the exile the Idumaeans were settled, and, in the case of Jerahmeel, the negative circumstance that here no towns at all are mentioned among the families, Molid, ver. 29, being perhaps a single exception, and thus the extreme south is indicated. But this kernel is amplified by a number of post-exilian additions. In the first place, in connection with Jerahmeel, an appendix (vers. 34-41) is given which is not ethnological but purely genealogical, and brings a pedigree of fifteen members manifestly down to near the age of the Chronicler, and which moreover is only in apparent connection with what precedes it (comp. ver. 34 with ver. 31), and invariably uses the hiphil form *holid*, a form which occurs in vers. 25-33 never, and in vers. 42-50 only sporadically in three places open to the suspicion of later redaction (comp. especially ver. 47). Much more important, however, are the additions under Caleb; of these the one is prefixed (vers. 18-24), the other, more appropriately, brought in at the close (vers. 50-55, beginning with "and the sons of Hur, the firstborn of Ephrath," Caleb's second wife, ver. 19). Here Caleb no longer presents himself in the extreme south of Judah and the vicinity of Jerahmeel (1Samuel xxv. 3, xxvii. 10, xxx. 14, 29), where he had his settlement prior to the exile, but his families, which are all of them descended from his son Hur, inhabit Bethlehem, Kirjath-jearim, Zorah, Esthaol, and other towns in the north, frequently mentioned in Ezra and Nehemiah. Thus the Calebites in consequence of the exile have forsaken their old seats and have taken up new ones on their return; this fact is expressed in ver. 18 to the effect that Caleb's first wife Azubah bath Jerioth (Deserta filia Nomadum) had died, and that he had then married a second, Ephrath, by whom he became the father of Hur: Ephrath is the name of the district in which Bethlehem and Kirjath-jearim are situated, and properly speaking is merely another form of Ephraim, as is shown by the word Ephrathite. In addition to these appendices to Jerahmeel and Caleb, we have also the genealogy of David (vers. 10-17). The Book of Samuel knows only of his father Jesse; on the other hand, Saul's genealogy is carried further back, and there was no reason for not doing so in David's case also if the materials had existed. But here, as in Ruth, the pedigree is traced backwards through Jesse, Obed, Boaz, up to Salma. Salma is the father of Bethlehem (ii. 54), and hence the father of David. But Salma is the father of Bethlehem and the neighbouring towns or fractions of towns AFTER THE EXILE; he belongs to Kaleb Abi Hur. *1*

*** I In the Targum, Caleb's kindred the Kenites are designated as Salmaeans; the name also occurs in Canticles (i. 5, the tents of Kedar, the curtains of Salmah), and also as the name of a Nabataean tribe in Pliny. Among the families of the Nethinim enumerated in Nehemiah vii. 46-60 the B'ne Salmah also occur, along with several other names which enable us distinctly to recognise (Ezekiel xliv.) the non-Israelite and foreign origin of these temple slaves; see, for example, vers. 48, 52, 55, 57. ***

But if anything at all is certain, it is this, that in ancient times the Calebites lived in the south and not in the north of Judah, and in particular that David by his nativity belonged not to them but rather to the older portion of Judah which gravitated towards Israel properly so called, and stood in most intimate relations with Benjamin. Of the first three members of the genealogy, Nahshon and Amminadab occur as princes of Judah in the Priestly Code, and are fitly regarded as the ancestors of those who come after them; Ram is the first-born of Hezron's first-born (ver. 25), and by the meaning of his name also (Ram = the high one), is, like Abram, qualified to stand at the head of the princely line.

While in chap ii. we thus in point of fact fall in with an old kernel, and one that necessarily goes back to sound tradition (apparently preserved indeed, however, merely for the sake of the later additions), the quite independent and parallel list, on the other hand, contained in iv. 1-23 is shown by many unmistakable indications to be a later composition having its reference only to post-exilian conditions, perhaps incorporating a few older elements, which, however, it is impossible with any certainty to detect. *2*

*** I Pharez, Hezron, Carmi, Hur, Shobal (iv. 1), is a genealogically descending series; Chelubai must therefore of necessity be read instead of Carmi, all the more because Chelub and not Carmi appears in the third place in the subsequent expansion; for this, ascending from

193

below, begins with Shobal (ver. 2), then goes on to Hur (vers. 5-10), who stands in the same relation to Ash-hur as Tob to Ish-tob, and finally deals with Chelub or Caleb (vers. 11-15). ***

Levi of course receives the fullest treatment (1Chronicles v. 27 [vi. 1]-vi. 66 [81], ix. 10 seq., xv., xvi., xxiii.-xxvii., &c.). We know that this clerical tribe is an artificial production, and that its hierarchical subdivision, as worked out in the Priestly Code, was the result of the centralisation of the cultus in Jerusalem. Further, it has been already shown that in the history as recorded in Chronicles the effort is most conspicuous to represent the sons of Aaron and the Levites, in all cases where they are absent from the older historical books of the canon, as playing the part to which they are entitled according to the Priestly Code. How immediate is the connection with the last-named document, how in a certain sense that code is even carried further by Chronicles, can be seen for example from this circumstance, that in the former Moses in a novel reduces the period of beginning public service in the case of a Levite from thirty years of age to twenty-five (Numbers iv. 3 seq., viii. 23 seq.), while in the latter David (1Chronicles xxiii. 3, 24 seq.) brings it down still further to the age of twenty; matters are still to some extent in a state of flux, and the ordering of the temple worship is a continuation of the beginning made with the tabernacle service by Moses. Now, in so far as the statistics of the clergy have a real basis at all, that basis is post-exilian. It has long ago been remarked how many of the individuals figuring under David and his successors (e.g., Asaph, Heman, Jeduthun) bear names identical with families or guilds of a later time, how the two indeed are constantly becoming confluent, and difficulty is felt in determining whether by the expression "head" a person or a family ought to be understood. But, inasmuch as the Chronicler nevertheless desires to depict the older time and not his own, he by no means adheres closely to contemporary statistics, but gives free play at the same time to his idealising imagination; whence it comes that in spite of the numerous and apparently precise data afforded, the reader still finds himself unable to form any clear picture of the organisation of the clergy,—the ordering of the families and tribes, the distribution of the offices,—nay, rather, is involved in a maze of contradictions. Obededom, Jeduthun, Shelomith, Korah, occur in the most different connections, belong now to one, now to another section of the Levites, and discharge at one time this function, at another, that. Naturally the commentators are prompt with their help by distinguishing names that are alike, and identifying names that are different.

Some characteristic details may still be mentioned here. The names of the six Levitical classes according to 1Chronicles xxv. 4, Giddalti, V'romamti-Ezer, Joshbekashah, Mallothi, Hothir, Mahazioth, are simply the fragments of a consecutive sentence which runs: I have magnified | and exalted the help | of him who sat in need: | I have spoken | abundance of | prophecies. The watchman or singer Obededom who is alleged to have discharged his functions in the days of David and Amaziah, is no other than the captain to whom David intrusted for three months the custody of the ark, a Philistine of Gath. The composition of the singers' pedigrees is very transparent, especially in the case of Heman (1Chronicles vi. 7-12 [22-27] = ver 18-23, [33-37]). Apart from Exodus vi. 16-19, use is chiefly made of what is said about the family of Samuel (1Samuel i. 1, viii. 2), who must of course

194

have been of Levitical descent, because his mother consecrated him to the service of the sanctuary. Heman is the son of Joel b. Samuel b. Elkanah b. Jeroham b. Eliab b. Tahath b. Zuph, only the line does not terminate with Ephraim as in 1Samuel i. 1 (LXX) because it is Levi who is the goal; Zuph. *sic* however, is an Ephraitic district, and Tahath (Tohu, Toah, Tahan, Nahath) is an Ephraimite family (vii. 20). Further back the same elements are individually repeated more than once, Elkanah four times in all; he occurs once as early as in Exodus vi. 24, where also he is doubtless borrowed from 1Samuel i. The best of it is that, contrary to the scope of the genealogies recorded in1 Chronicles vi., which is to provide a Levitical origin for the guilds of singers, there is found in close contiguity the statement (ii. 6) that Heman and Ethan were descendants of Zerah b. Pharez, b. JUDAH. The commentators are indeed assisted in their efforts to differentiate the homonyms by their ignorance of the fact that even as late as Nehemiah's time the singers did not yet pass for Levites, but their endeavours are wrecked by the circumstance that the names of fathers as well as of sons are identical (Psalm lxxxviii. 1, lxxxix. 1; Ewald, iii. 380 seq.). In point of history these musicians of the second temple are descended of course neither from Levi nor from the sons of Mahol (1Kings v. 11 [iv. 31), but they have at least derived their names from the latter. On all hands we meet with such artificial names in the case of Levites. One is called Issachar; it would not be surprising to meet with a Naphtali Cebi, or Judah b. Jacob. Jeduthun is, properly speaking, the name of a tune or musical mode (Psalm xxxix. 1, lxii. 1, [xxvii. 1), whence also of a choir trained in that. Particularly interesting are a few pagan names, as for example Henadad, Bakbuk, and some others, which, originally borne by the temple servitors (Nehemiah vii. 46 seq.), were doubtless transferred along with these to the Levites.

With the priests, of whom so many are named at all periods of the history of Israel, matters are no better than with the inferior Levites, so far as the Books of Samuel and Kings are not drawn upon. In particular, the twenty-four priestly courses or orders are an institution, not of King David, but of the post-exilic period. When Hitzig, annotating Ezekiel viii. 16, remarks that the five-and-twenty men standing between the temple and the altar worshipping the sun toward the east are the heads of the twenty-four priestly courses with the high priest at their head (because no one else had the right to stand in the inner court between temple and altar), he reveals a trait that is characteristic, not only of himself, but also of the entire so-called historico-critical school, who exert their whole subtlety on case after case, but never give themselves time to think matters over in their connection with each other; nay, rather simply retain the traditional view as a whole, only allowing themselves by way of gratification a number of heresies. It is almost impossible to believe that Hitzig, when he annotated Ezekiel viii., could have read those passages Ezekiel xliii. 7 seq., xliv. 6 seq, from which it is most unambiguously clear that the later exclusion of the laity from the sanctuary was quite unknown in the pre-exilic period. The extent of the Chronicler's knowledge about the pre-exilic priesthood is revealed most clearly in the list of the twenty-two high priests in 1Chronicles v. 29-41 (vi. 3-15). From the ninth to the eighteenth the series runs—Amariah, Ahitub, Zadok, Ahimaaz, Azariah, Johanan, Azariah, Amariah, Ahitub, Zadok. As for the first five, Azariah was not the son, but the brother of Ahimaaz, and the latter apparently not a priest (1Kings iv. 2); but Ahitub, the alleged father of Zadok, was, on the contrary, the grandfather of Zadok's rival, Abiathar, of the family of Eli (1Samuel xiv. 3, xxii.

20); the whole of the old and famous line—Eli, Phinehas, Ahitub; Ahimelech, Abiathar—which held the priesthood of the ark from the time of the judges down into the days of David, is passed over in absolute silence, and the line of Zadok, by which it was not superseded until Solomon (1Kings ii. 35), is represented as having held the leadership of the priesthood since Moses. As for the last four in the above-cited list, they simply repeat the earlier. In the Book of Kings, Azariah II., Amariah, Ahitub, Zadok, do not occur, but, on the contrary, other contemporary high priests, Jehoiada and Urijah, omitted from the enumeration in Chronicles. At the same time this enumeration cannot be asserted to be defective; for, according to Jewish chronology, the ancient history is divided into two periods, each of 480 years, the one extending from the exodus to the building of the temple, the other from that epoch down to the establishment of the second theocracy. Now, 480 years are twelve generations of forty years, and in 1Chronicles v. there are twelve high priests reckoned to the period during which there was no temple (ver. 36b to come after ver. 35a), and thence eleven down to the exile; that is to say, twelve generations, when the exile is included. The historical value of the genealogy in 1Chronicles v. 26-41 is thus inevitably condemned. But if Chronicles knew nothing about the priestly princes of the olden time, its statements about ordinary priests are obviously little to be relied on.

VI.III.3. To speak of a tradition handed down from pre-exilic times as being found in Chronicles, either in 1Chronicles i.-ix. or in 1Chronicles x.-2Chronicles xxxvi., is thus manifestly out of the question. As early as 1806 this had been conclusively shown by the youthful De Wette (then twenty-six years of age). But since that date many a theological Sisyphus has toiled to roll the stone again wholly or half-way up the hill—Movers especially, in genius it might seem the superior of the sober Protestant critic—with peculiar results. This scholar mixed up the inquiry into the historical value of those statements in Chronicles which we are able to control, with the other question as to the probable sources of its variations from the older historical books of the canon. In vain had De Wette, at the outset, protested against such a procedure, contending that it was not only possible, but conceded that Chronicles, where at variance or in contradiction, was following older authority, but that the problem still really was, as before, how to explain the complete difference of general conception and the multitude of discrepancies in details; that the hypothesis of "sources," as held before Movers by Eichhorn, was of no service in dealing with this question, and that in the critical comparison of the two narratives, and in testing their historical character, it was after all incumbent to stick to what lay before one (Beitr., i. pp. 24, 29, 38). For so ingenious an age such principles were too obvious; Movers produced a great impression, especially as he was not so simple as to treat the letters of Hiram and Elijah as authentic documents, but was by way of being very critical. At present even Dillmann also unfortunately perceives "that the Chronicler everywhere has worked according to sources, and that in his case deliberate invention or distortion of the history are not for a moment to be spoken of" (Herzog, Realencyk., ii. p. 693, 1st edit.; iii. 223, 2d edit.). And from the lofty heights of science the author of Part V. of the Biblical Commentary on the Old Testament looks compassionately down upon K. H. Graf, "who has loitered so far behind the march of Old Testament research, as to have thought of resuscitating the views of De Wette;" in fact, that Chronicles may be established on an independent footing and placed on a level with the Books of Samuel and Kings, he utterly denies any indebtedness at all, on its part, to these, and in cases where the transcription is word for word, maintains that separate independent sources were made use of,—a needless exaggeration of the scientific spirit, for the author of the Book of Kings himself wrote the prayer of Solomon and the epitome, at least, without borrowing from another source; the Chronicler therefore can have derived it, directly or indirectly, only from him.

In reply to all this, one can only repeat what has already been said by De Wette. It may be that the Chronicler has produced this picture of old Israel, so different in outline and colour from the genuine tradition, not of his own suggestion and on his own responsibility, but on the ground of documents that lay before him. But the historical character of the work is not hereby altered in the smallest degree, it is merely shared by the so-called "sources." 2Maccabees and a multitude of other compositions have also made use of "sources," but how does this enhance the value of their statements? That value must in the long run be estimated according to their contents, which, again, must be judged, not by means of the primary sources which have been lost, but by means of the secondary literary products which have survived. The whole question ultimately resolves itself into that of historical credibility; and to what conclusions this leads we have already seen. The alterations and additions of Chronicles are all traceable to the same fountain-head—the Judaising of the past, in which otherwise the people of that day would have been unable to recognise their ideal. It was not because tradition gave the Law and the hierocracy and the *Deus ex Machina* as sole efficient factor in the sacred narrative, but because these elements were felt to be missing, that they were thus introduced. If we are to explain the *omissions* by reference to the "author's plan," why may we not apply the same principle to the *additions*? The passion displayed by Ewald (Jahrbb. x. 261) when, in speaking of the view that Manasseh's captivity has its basis in Jewish dogmatic, he calls it "an absurdly infelicitous idea, and a gross injustice besides to the Book of Chronicles," recalls B. Schaefer's suggestive remark about the Preacher of Solomon, that God would not use a liar to write a canonical book. What then does Ewald say to the narratives of Daniel or Jonah? Why must the new turn given to history in the case of Manasseh be judged by a different standard than in the equally gross case of Ahaz, and in the numerous analogous instances enumerated in preceding pages (p. 203 seq.). With what show of justice can the Chronicler, after his statements have over and over again been shown to be incredible, be held at discretion to pass for an unimpeachable narrator? In those cases at least where its connection with his "plan" is obvious, one ought surely to exercise some scepticism in regard to his testimony; but it ought at the same time to be considered that such connections may occur much oftener than is discernible by us, or at least by the less sharp-sighted of us. It is indeed possible that occasionally a grain of good corn may occur among the chaff, but to be conscientious one must neglect this possibility of exceptions, and give due honour to the probability of the rule. For it is only too easy to deceive oneself in thinking that one has come upon some sound particular in a tainted whole. To what is said in 2Samuel v. 9, "So David dwelt in the stronghold (Jebus), and he called it the city of David, and he built round about from the rampart and inward," there is added in 1Chronicles xi. 8, the statement that "Joab restored the rest of the city (Jerusalem)." This looks innocent enough, and is generally accepted as a fact. But the word XYH for BNH shows the comparatively modern date of the statement, and on closer consideration one remembers also that the town of Jebus at the time of its conquest by David consisted only of the citadel, and the new town did not come into existence at all until later, and therefore could not have been repaired by Joab; in what interest the statement was made can be gathered from Nehemiah vii. 11. In many cases it is usual to regard such additions as having had their origin in a better text of Samuel and Kings which lay before the Chronicler; and this certainly is the most likely way in which good additions could have got in. But the textual critics of the *Exegetical Handbook* are only too like-minded with the Chronicler, and are always eagerly seizing with both hands his paste pearls and the similar gifts of the Septuagint.

It must be allowed that Chronicles owes its origin, not to the arbitrary caprice of an individual, but to a general tendency of its period. It is the inevitable product of the conviction that the Mosaic law is the starting-point of Israel's history, and that in it these is operative a play of sacred forces such as finds no other analogy; this conviction could not but lead to a complete transformation of the ancient tradition. Starting from a similar assumption, such an author as C. F. Keil could even at the present day write a book of Chronicles, if this were not already in existence. Now, in this aspect, for the purpose of appraising Chronicles as the type of that conception of history which the scribes cherished, the inquiry into its "sources" is really important and interesting. References to other writings, from which further particulars can be learned, are appended as a rule, to the account of each sovereign's reign, the exceptions being in the cases of Joram, Ahaziah, Athaliah, Amon, Jehoahaz, Jehoiakim, Zedekiah. The titles referred to in this way may be classed under two groups: (1.) The Book of the Kings of Israel and Judah, or of Judah and Israel (in the cases of Asa, Amaziah, Jotham; Ahaz, Josiah, and Jehoiakim), with which the Book of the Kings of Israel (in the cases of Jehoshaphat and Manasseh; comp. 1Chronicles ix. 1) is identical, for the kingdom of the ten tribes is not reckoned by the Chronicler. (2.) The Words of Samuel the Seer, Nathan the Prophet, and Gad the Seer (for David; 1Chronicles xxix. 29; comp. xxvii. 24; Ecclus. xlvi. 13, xlvii. 1); the Words of Nathan the Prophet, the Prophecy of Ahijah of Shiloh and the Vision of Iddo the Seer concerning Jeroboam ben Nebat (for Solomon; 2Chronicles ix. 29); the Words of Shemaiah the Prophet and Iddo the Seer (for Rehoboam; xii. 15); the words of Jehu ben Hanani, which are taken over into the Book of the Kings of Israel (Jehoshaphat; xx. 34); a writing of Isaiah the prophet (Uzziah; xxvi. 22), more precisely cited as the Vision of Isaiah the Prophet, the son of Amoz, in the Book of the Kings of Judah and Israel (Hezekiah; xxxii. 32); the Words of the Seer in the Book of the Kings of Israel (Manasseh; xxxiii. 18; comp. also ver. 19). Following in the footsteps of Movers, Bertheau and others have shown that under these different citations it is always one and the same book that is intended, whether by its collective title, or by the conventional sub-titles of its separate sections. *1* Bertheau calls

*** 1. In Ezra and Nehemiah also the Chronicler has not used so many sources as are usually supposed. There is no reason for refusing to identify the "lamentations" of 2Chronicles xxxv. 25, with our Lamentations of Jeremiah: at least the reference to the death of Josiah (Jos., Ant. x.

5, 1), erroneously attributed to them, ought not in candour to be regarded as such.
****

attention to the fact that ordinarily it is either the one or the other title that is given, and when, as is less usual, there are two, then for the most part the prophetic writing is designated as a portion of the Book of the Kings of Israel (xx. 34, xxxii. 32; and, quite vaguely, xxxiii. 18). The peculiar mode of naming the individual section-1-at a time when chapters and verses were

** 1 Romans xi. 2:)EN (HLLLA| TI LEGEI)H GRAFH *i.e.*, How stands it written in the section relating to Elijah?
****

unknown—has its origin in the idea that each period of the sacred history has its leading prophet [)AXRIBHS TWN PROFHTWN DIADOXH; Jos., c. Ap. i. 8), but also at the same time involves (according to xxvi. 22, in spite of ix. 29, xii. 15, xiii. 22; 1Chronicles xxix. 29) the notion that each prophet has himself written the history of his own period. Obviously, this is the explanation of the title *prophetae priores* borne by the Books of Joshua, Judges, Samuel, and Kings in the Jewish canon, and of the view which led to the introduction of 2Kings xviii. 18 seq. into the Book of Isaiah. The claims of history being slight, it was easy to find the needful *propheta eponymus* for each section. Jehu ben Hanani, a northern Israelite of Baasha's time, has to do duty for Asa, and also for Jehoshaphat as well. Iddo the seer, who prophesied against Jeroboam ben Nebat, is the anonymous prophet of 1Kings xiii. (Jos., Ant. viii. 8, 5; Jer. on Zechariah i. 1); by this time it was possible, also, to give the names of the wives of Cain, and of the patriarchs.

As regards a more definite determination of the date of the "Book of Kings" which lies at the foundation of Chronicles, a co-ordination of the two series of the Kings of Israel and Judah can only have been made after both had been brought to a close; in other words, not before the Babylonian exile. And in the Babylonian exile it was that the canonical Book of Kings actually came into existence, and the "Chronicles" of Israel and those of Judah were for the first time worked together by its author; at least he refers only to the separate works and knows of no previous combination of them. It would seem, therefore, very natural to identify the work alluded to in Chronicles with our present canonical book, which is similar in title and has corresponding contents. But this we cannot do, for in the former there were matters of which there are in the latter no trace; for example, according to 1Chronicles ix. 1, it contained family and numerical statistics for the whole of Israel after the manner of 1Chronicles i.-ix. (chapters for the most part borrowed from it) and according to 1Chronicles xxxiii 19, the Prayer of Manasseh. From these two data, as well as from the character of the items of information which may have been conjectured to have been derived from this source, the conclusion is forced upon us that the Book of Kings cited by the Chronicler is a late compilation far removed from actual tradition, and in relation to the canonical Book of Kings it can only be explained as an apocryphal amplification after the manner in which the scribes treated the sacred history. This conclusion, derived from the contents themselves, is supported by an important positive datum, namely, the citation in 2Chronicles xxiv. 27 of the Midrash [A.V. "Story"] of the Book of Kings, and in xiii. 22 of the Midrash of the prophet Iddo. Ewald is undoubtedly right when he recognises here the true title of the writing elsewhere named simply the Book of Kings. Of course the commentators assert that the word Midrash, which occurs in the Bible only in these two passages, there means something quite different from what it means everywhere else; but the natural sense suits admirably well and in Chronicles we find ourselves fully within the period of the scribes. Midrash is the consequence of the conservation of all the relics of antiquity, a wholly peculiar artificial reawakening of dry bones, especially by literary means, as is shown by the preference for lists of names and numbers. Like ivy it overspreads the dead trunk with extraneous life, blending old and new in a strange combination. It is a high estimate of tradition that leads to its being thus modernised; but in the process it is twisted and perverted, and set off with foreign accretions in the most arbitrary way. Jonah as well as Daniel and a multitude of apocryphal writings (2Maccabees ii. 13) are connected with this tendency to cast the reflection of the present back into the past; the Prayer of Manasseh, which now survives only in Greek, appears, as Ewald has conjectured, actually to have been taken direct from the book quoted in 2Chronicles xxxiii. 19. Within this sphere, wherein all Judaism moves, Chronicles also has had its rise. Thus whether one says Chromcles or Midrash of the Book of Kings is on the whole a matter of perfect indifference; they are children of the same mother, and indistinguishable in spirit and language, while on the other hand the portions which have been retained verbatim from the canonical Book of Kings at once betray themselves in both respects.

CHAPTER VII. JUDGES, SAMUEL, AND KINGS.

In the history of Hebrew literature, so full as it is of unfortunate accidents, one lucky circumstance at least requires to be specially mentioned. Chronicles did not succeed in superseding the historical books upon which it was founded; the older and the newer version have been preserved together. But in Judges, Samuel, and Kings even, we are not presented with tradition purely in its original condition; already it is overgrown with later accretions. Alongside of an older narrative a new one has sprung up, formerly independent, and intelligible in itself, though in many instances of course adapting itself to the former. More frequently the new forces have not caused the old root to send forth a new stock, or even so much as a complete branch; they have only nourished parasitic growths; the earlier narrative has become clothed with minor and dependent additions. To vary the metaphor, the whole area of tradition has finally been uniformly covered with an alluvial deposit by which the configuration of the surface has been determined. It is with this last that we have to deal in the first instance; to ascertain its character, to find out what the active forces were by which it was produced. Only afterwards are we in a position to attempt to discern in the earlier underlying formation the changing spirit of each successive period.

VII.I.

VII.I.1. The following prologue supplies us with the point of view from which the period of the judges is estimated. "After the death of Joshua, the children of Israel did evil in the sight of the Lord and forsook the Lord God of their fathers, who brought them out of the land of Egypt, and followed other gods, of the gods of the people that were round about them, the Baals and Astartes. And the anger of the Lord was hot against Israel, and He delivered them into the hands of spoilers, that spoiled them and sold them into the hand of their enemies round about; whithersoever they went out the hand of the Lord was against them for evil, as the Lord had said, and as the Lord had sworn unto them; and they were greatly distressed. Nevertheless the Lord raised up unto them judges, and was with the judge, and delivered them out of the hand of their enemies all the days of the judge, for it repented the Lord because of their groanings, by reason of them that oppressed them and vexed them. And it came to pass when the judge was dead that they returned and corrupted themselves more than their fathers, in following other gods to serve them; they ceased not from their own doings, nor from their stubborn way. And the anger of the Lord was hot against Israel," &c. &c. (Judges ii.).

Such is the text, afterwards come the examples. "And the children of Israel did evil in the sight of the Lord, and forget the Lord their God, and served the Baals and Astartes. Therefore the anger of the Lord was hot against Israel, and He sold them into the hand of Chushan-Rishathaim, king of Mesopotamia, and they served him eight years. And when the children of Israel cried unto the Lord, the Lord raised up to them a helper, Othniel b. Kenaz, and delivered the king of Mesopotamia into his hand, and the land had rest forty years. And Othniel b. Kenaz died." The same points of view and also for the most part the same expressions as those which in the case of Othniel fill up the entire cadre, recur in the cases of Ehud, Deborah, Gideon, Jephthah, and Samson, but there form only at the beginning and at the end of the narratives a frame which encloses more copious and richer contents, occasionally they expand into more exhaustive disquisitions, as in vi. 7, x. 6. It is in this way that Judges ii.-xvi. has been constructed with the workman-like regularity it displays. Only the six great judges, however are included within the scheme; the six small ones stand in an external relation to it, and have a special scheme to themselves, doubtless having been first added by way of appendix to complete the number twelve.

The features which characterise this method of historical work are few and strongly distinctive. A continuous chronology connects the times of rest and their separating intervals, and thereby the continuity of the periods is secured. In order justly to estimate this chronology, it is necessary to travel somewhat beyond the limits of Judges. The key to it is to be found in 1Kings vi. 1. "In the four hundred and eightieth year after the children of Israel were come out of the land of Egypt, in the fourth year of the reign of Solomon, he began to build the house of the Lord." As observed by Bertheau, and afterwards by Noldeke, who has still farther pursued the subject, these 480 years correspond to 12 generations of 40 years each. Analogously in 1Chronicles v. 29-34 [vi. 2-8], 12 high priests from Aaron to Ahimaaz are assumed for the same period of time, and the attempt was made to make their successions determine those of the generations (Numbers xxxv. 28). Now it is certainly by no means at once clear how this total is to be brought into accord with the individual entries. Yet even these make it abundantly plain that 40 is the fundamental number of the reckoning. The wandering in the wilderness, during which the generation born in Egypt dies out, lasts for 40 years; the land has 40 years of rest under Othniel, Deborah, and again under Gideon; it has 80 under Ehud; the domination of the Philistines lasts for 40 years, the duration also of David's reign. On the necessary assumption that the period of the Philistines (Judges xiii. 1), which far exceeds the ordinary duration of the foreign dominations, coincides with that of Eli (1Samuel iv. 18), and at the same time includes the 20 years of Samson (Judges xvi. 31), and the 20 of the interregnum before Samuel (1Samuel vii. 2), we have already 8 x 40 accounted for, while 4 x 40 still remain. For these we must take into account first the years of the two generations for which no numbers are given, namely, the generation of Joshua and his surviving contemporaries (Judges ii. 7), and that of Samuel to Saul, each, it may be conjectured, having the normal 40, and the two together certainly reckoning 80 years. For the remaining 80 the most disputable elements are the 71 years of interregna or of foreign dominations, and the 70 of the minor judges. One perceives that these two figures cannot both be counted in,—they are mutually exclusive equivalents. For my own part, I prefer to retain the interregna; they alone, so far as we can see at present, being appropriate to the peculiar scheme of the Book of Judges. The balance of 9 or IO years still remaining to be applied are distributed between Jephthah (6 years), and Solomon (down to the building of the temple), who claims 3 or 4 years, or, if these are left out of account, 3 years may be given to Abimelech.

The main thing, however, is not the chronology, but the religious connection of the events. The two are intimately associated, not only formally, as can be gathered from the scheme, but also by a real inner connection. For what is aimed at in both alike is a connected view of large periods of time, a continuous survey of the connection and succession of race after race, the detailed particulars of the occurrences being disregarded; the historical factors with which the religious pragmatism here has to do are so uniform that the individual periods in reality need only to be filled up with the numbers of the years. One is reminded of the "Satz," `"Gegensatz," and "Vermittelung" of the Hegelian philosophy when one's ear has once been caught by the monotonous beat with which the history here advances, or rather moves in a circle. Rebellion, affliction, conversion, peace; rebellion, affliction, conversion, peace. The sole subjects of all that is said are Jehovah and Israel; their mutual relation alone it is that keeps the course of things in motion, and that too in opposite directions, so that in the end matters always return to their original position.

"They did what was evil in the sight of Jehovah, they went a-whoring after strange gods,"-such is the uninterrupted key-note. Although Jehovistic monolatry is so potently recommended from without, it yet takes no firm root, never becomes natural to the people, always remains a precept above and beyond their powers. For decennia on end indeed they hold fast to it, but soon their idolatrous tendency, which has only been repressed by fear of the judge during his lifetime, again finds expression; they must have a change. Now this rebellion is indeed quite indispensable for the pragmatism, because otherwise there would be nothing at all to tell; it is on the unrest in the clock that the whole movement depends. But at the same time this is of course no extenuation; the conduct of the people is manifestly totally inexcusable, the main actions, the deeds of the judges, are for this manner of historical treatment always only proofs of Israel's sin and of the unmerited grace of Jehovah that puts them to shame.

That all this is no part of the original contents of the tradition, but merely a uniform in which it is clothed, is admitted. *Numero Deus impare gaudet.* It is usual to call this later revision Deuteronomistic. The law which Jehovah has enjoined upon the fathers, and the breach of which He has threatened severely to punish (ii. 15, 21), is not indeed more definitely characterised, but it is impossible to doubt that its quintessence is the injunction to worship Jehovah alone and no other God. Now in this connection it is impossible to think of the Priestly Code, for in that document such a command is nowhere expressly enjoined, but, on the contrary, is assumed as a matter of course. Deuteronomy, on the other hand, has in fact no precept on which it lays greater emphasis than the "Hear, O Israel-"-that Jehovah is the only God, and the worship of strange gods the sin of sins. This precept was apprehended much more clearly by contemporaries than the moral demands in the interest of humanity and kindness which are also insisted on in Deuteronomy, but are not new, being derived from older collections; on this side alone, in so far as it follows up the monotheism of the prophets into its practical consequences within the sphere of worship, has Josiah's law-book had historical importance, on this side alone has it continued to act upon Ezekiel and those who came after him. If, then, the norm of the theocratic relationship assumed in the redaction of the Book of Judges is to be sought in a written Torah, this can indubitably only be that of Deuteronomy. The decisive settlement of the question depends in a comparison with the Book of Kings, and must accordingly be postponed until then.

VII.I.2. As for the relation between this superstructure and that on which it rests, there is a striking difference between the two styles. The revised form in which the Book of Judges found its way into the canon is unquestionably of Judaean origin, but the histories themselves are not such,—nay, in the song of Deborah, Judah is not reckoned at all as belonging to Israel. The one judge who belongs to the tribe of Judah is Othniel, who however is not a person, but only a clan. What is said of him is quite void of contents, and is made up merely of the schematic devices of the redactor, who has set himself to work here, so as to make the series open with a man of Judah; the selection of Othniel was readily suggested by Judges i. 12-15. Here again we have an exception which proves the rule. More important are the inner differences which reveal themselves. To begin with the most general,—the historical continuity on which so much stress is laid by the scheme, is in no way shown in the individual narratives of the Book of Judges. These stand beside one another unconnectedly and without any regard to order or sequence, like isolated points of light which emerge here and there out of the darkness of forgetfulness. They make no presence of actually filling up any considerable space of time; they afford no points of attachment whereon to fasten a chronology. In truth, it is hardly the dim semblance of a continuity that is imparted to the tradition by the empty framework of the scheme. The conception of a period of the judges between Joshua and Saul, during which judges ruled over Israel and succeeded one another almost as regularly as did the kings at a later period, is quite foreign to that tradition. It is impossible to doubt that Judges i., xvii., xviii. have the best right to be reckoned as belonging to the original stock; but these portions are excluded from reception within the scheme, because they have nothing to say about any judges, and give a picture of the general state of affairs which accords but ill with that plan. *1*

** 1. The redaction, as is well knows, extends only from ii. 6 xvi. 31, thus excluding both i. 1-ii. 5, and xvii. 1-xxi. 24. But it is easy to perceive how excellently the first portion fits into its place as a general introduction to the period between Moses and the monarchy, and how much more informing and instructive it is in this respect than the section which follows. There exists besides a formal connection between i. 16 and iv. 11. As regards chaps. xvii., xviii., this story relating to the migration of Dan northwards is plainly connected with that immediately preceding where the tribe still finds itself "in tbe camp of Dan," but is hard pressed and obtains no relief even with the aid of Samson. In the case of chaps. xix.-xxi., indeed, it admits of doubt whether they were excluded from the redaction, or whether they were not extant as yet; but it is worth noticing that here also chaps. xvii., xviii. are assumed as having gone before. The Levite of Bethlehem-Judah testifies to this, and especially the reminiscence contained in xix. 1, which, as we shall see, has nothing to rest on in chaps. xix.-xxi. Compare further xx. 19 with i. 1 seq.
****

At the bottom of the spurious continuity lies an erroneous widening of the areas in which the judges exerted their influence. Out of local contiguity has arisen succession in time, what was true of the part having been transferred to the whole; it is always the children of Israel in a body who come upon the scene, are oppressed by the enemy, and ruled by the judges. In reality it is only the individual tribes that come into the action; the judges are tribal heroes,—Ehud of Benjamin, Barak and Deborah of Issachar, Gideon of Joseph, Jephthah of Gilead, Samson of Dan. It was only for the struggle against Sisera that a number of tribes were united, receiving on that account extraordinary praise in the song of Deborah. It is nowhere said "at the time when the judges ruled," but "at the time when there was yet no king over Israel, and every man did what was right in his own eyes; " the regular constitution of the period is the patriarchal anarchy of the system of families and septs. And in chap. i, division and isolation are made to appear not unclearly as the reason why the Canaanites were so long of being driven out from the greater cities; matters did not change until Israel became strong, that is to say, until his forces were welded into one by means of the monarchy.

But the unity of Israel is the presupposition upon which rests the theocratic relation, the reciprocal attitude between Israel and Jehovah, whereby according to the scheme the course of the history is solely conditioned. In the genuine tradition the presupposition disappears, and in connection with this the whole historical process assumes an essentially different, not to say a more natural aspect. The people are no longer as a body driven hither and thither by the same internal and external impulses, and everything that happens is no longer made to depend on the attraction and repulsion exercised by Jehovah. Instead of the alternating see-saw of absolute peace and absolute affliction, there prevails throughout the whole period a relative unrest; here peace, there struggle and conflict. Failure and success alternate, but not as the uniform consequences of loyalty or disobedience to the covenant. When the anonymous prophet who, in the insertion in the last redaction (chap. vi. 7-10), makes his appearance as suddenly as his withdrawal is abrupt, improves the visitation of the Midianites as the text for a penitential discourse, the matter is nevertheless looked at immediately thereafter with quite different eyes. For to the greeting of the angel, "Jehovah is with thee, thou mighty man of velour," Gideon answers, "If Jehovah be with us, why then is all this befallen us? and where be all His miracles, of which our fathers told us ? "He knows nothing about any guilt on the part of Israel. Similarly the heroic figures of the judges refuse to fit in with the story of sin and rebellion: they are the pride of their countrymen, and not humiliating reminders that Jehovah had undeservedly again and again made good that which men had destroyed. Finally, with what artificiality the sins which appear to be called for are produced, is incidentally made very clear. After the death of Gideon we read in chap. viii. 33, "the children of Israel went a-whoring after the Baals, and made Baal Berith their god." But from the following chapter it appears that Baal or El Berith was only the patron god of Shechem and some other cities belonging to the Canaanites; the redactor transforms the local worship of the Canaanites into an idolatrous worship on the part of all Israel. In other cases his procedure is still more simple,—for example, in x. 6 seq., where the number seven in the case of the deities corresponds with the number seven of the nations mentioned in that connection. Ordinarily he is content with "Baals " or "Astartes " or "Asheras," where the plural number is enough to show how little of what is individual or positive underlies the idea, not to mention that Asheras are no divinities at all, but only sacred trees or poles.

In short, what is usually given out as the peculiar theocratic element in the history of Israel is the element which has been introduced by the redaction. There sin and grace are introduced as forces into the order of events in the most mechanical way, the course of events is systematically withdrawn from all analogy, miracles are nothing extraordinary, but are the regular form in which things occur, are matters of course, and produce absolutely no impression. This pedantic supra-naturalism, "sacred history" according to the approved recipe, is not to be found in the original accounts. In these Israel is a people just like other people, nor is even his relationship to Jehovah otherwise conceived of than is for example that of Moab to Chemosh (chap. xi. 24). Of theophanies and manifestations of the Godhead there is no lack, but the wonders are such as to make one really wonder. Once and again they interrupt the earthly nexus, but at the same time they form no connected system; they are poetry, not prose and dogma. But on the whole the process of history, although to appearance rougher and more perplexed, is nevertheless in reality much more intelligible, and though seemingly more broken up, actually advances more continuously. There is an ascent upward to the monarchy, not a descent from the splendid times of Moses and Joshua (Judges i. 28-35, xiii. 5, xviii. 1).

One narrative, it is true, apart from that relating to Othniel, which is not to be reckoned here, is exactly what sacred history ought to be in order to fit into the theoretical scheme,—I mean Judges xix.-xxi. To appreciate it rightly it will be well first of all to cast a glance upon the preceding narrative relating to the migration of the tribe of Dan to the north. The Danites, 600 strong, fall upon the Canaanite town of Laish not because it lies within the limits assigned to the people of God, and because its conquest is a duty—though they inquire of the oracle, they are nevertheless far from relying on the divine right so plainly made known in the Book of Joshua—but because it is inhabited by a peaceable and unsuspecting people, which is quite defenceless against such a band of desperadoes; and they have as little scruple in practicing the same treachery to Israelites such as Micah. They take it that might is right, and recognise no restraining consideration; their conduct is natural to the verge of absolute shamelessness. And yet they are pious in their way; how highly they value Jehovah they show by this, that they steal His image out of the house of God, and the priest who keeps it into the bargain. As for the religious usages mentioned in the two chapters, hardly an abomination forbidden by the Law is wanting: the private sanctuary in the possession of the Ephraimite Micah, the grandson of Moses as priest in his service and pay, ephod and teraphim as the requisite necessaries in the worship of Jehovah; and yet all this is so recounted by the narrator as if it were all quite regular and void of offence, although his purpose in doing so is not to narrate temporary departures from rule, but the origin of permanent institutions at a chief sanctuary of ancient Israel. One is translated into another world on passing from this to the narrative immediately following, about the shameful deed of the Benjamites and their exemplary punishment; a greater or more instructive contrast as regards religious history is hardly to be found in all the Old Testament. In Judges xx.-xxi. it is not as invariably elsewhere the individual tribes which act, not even the people Israel, but the congregation of the covenant, which has its basis in the unity of worship. The occasion of their action is a sin committed in their midst which must be done away; it is the sanctity of the theocracy which brings these 400,000 men to arms and fills them at once with unction and with sanguinary zeal. The clerical instincts have entirely taken possession of this uniform mass, have passed into their flesh and blood, and moulded them into a single automaton, so that all that takes place is invariably done by all at once. No individuals come to the front, not even by name, still less by deeds of velour; the moral tone is anything but heroic. When the godless reprobates of Gibeah seek to assail the person of the Levite who is passing the night there, he hands over to them his wife in order to save himself, and all Israel finds nothing objectionable in this revolting act of cowardice, the opinion probably being that by his conduct the holy man had kept the sinners from still graver guilt. "Of the Mosaic law not a word is said in these chapters, but who could fail to perceive that the spirit which finds its expression in the law pervaded the community which acted thus? Had we more narratives of similar contents we should be able to solve many a riddle of the Pentateuch. Where under the monarchy could we find an Israel so united, vigorous, earnest, so willing to enter upon the severest conflict for the sake of the highest ends? "Thus Bertheau, rightly feeling that this story has a quite exceptional position, and contradicts all that we learn from other quarters of the period of the judges or even the kings. Only we cannot reckon it a proof of the historic value of the story, that it gives the lie to the rest of the tradition in the Books of Judges, Samuel, and Kings, and is homogeneous not with these books but with the Law. On the other hand, the writer betrays himself with a self-contradiction, when, unconsciously remembering the preceding chapters, he laments the disorganisation of the time he is dealing with (xix. 1, xxi. 25), and yet describes Israel to us as existing in a religious centralisation, such as demonstrably was never attained in the earlier life of the nation, but only came about as a consequence of the exile, and is the distinctive mark of Judaism.

As this narrative is not one of those included in the Deuteronomistic scheme of the Book of Judges, there may be a question whether it presupposes the Deuteronomic law only, or the priestly law as well. Its language has most points of contact with Deuteronomy; but one extremely important expression and notion, that of "the congregation of the children of Israel," points rather to the Priestly Code. The same may be said of Phinehas ben Eleazar ben Aaron (xx. 28). The latter, however, occurs but once, and that in a gloss which forms a very awkward interruption between "and the children of Israel inquired of Jehovah," and the word "saying" which belongs to that phrase. We have also to remark that there is no mention of the tabernacle, for which there is no room in addition to Mizpeh (p. 256), so that the principal mark of the Priestly Code is wanting. It is only in preparation, it has not yet appeared: we are still standing on the ground of Deuteronomy, but the way is being prepared for the transition.

VII.I.3. Going a step further back from the last revision we meet with an earlier effort in the same direction, which, however, is less systematically worked out, in certain supplements and emendations, which have here and there been patched on to the original narratives. These may be due in part to the mere love of amplification or of talking for talking's sake, and in so far we have no further business with them here. But they originated partly in the difficulty felt by a later age in sympathising with the religious usages and ideas of older times. Two instances of this kind occur in the history of Gideon. We read (vi. 25-32), that in the night after his call Gideon destroyed, at the commandment of Jehovah, the altar of Baal in Ophra, his native town, as well as the Ashera which stood beside it; and that in place of it he built an altar to Jehovah, and burned on it a yearling bullock, with the wood of the Ashera for fuel. The next morning the people of Ophra were full of indignation, and demanded that the author of the outrage should be given up to them to be put to death; his father, however, withstood them, saying, "Will ye contend for Baal? Will ye save him? If he be a god, let Baal contend (Heb. Jareb Baal) for himself." In consequence of this speech Gideon received his second name of Jerubbaal. This conflicts with what is said in an earlier part of the chapter. There Gideon has already made an altar of the great stone under the oak of Ophra, where he saw Jehovah sitting, and has offered upon it the first sacrifice, which was devoured by flames breaking out of themselves, the Deity Himself ascending in the flames to heaven. Why the two altars and the two stories of their inauguration, both tracing their origin to the patron of Ophra? They do not agree together, and the reason is plain why the second was added. The altar of a single stone, the flames bursting out of it, the evergreen tree, the very name of which, Ela, seems to indicate a natural connection with El, *1*—all this was in the eyes of a later

*************************************** 1.)LH,)LWN, in Aramaic simply tree, in Hebrew the evergreen, and in general the holy tree (Isaiah i. 29 seq.) mostly without distinguishing the species. Not only are oaks and terebinths included, but also palms. For the)LWN DBWRH at Bethel is elsewhere called TMR; Elim derives its names from the 70 palms, and the same may be the case with Elath on the Red sea. ***************************************

generation far from correct, indeed it was Baal-work. A desire that the piety of Gideon should be above suspicion gave rise to the second story, in which he erects an altar of Jehovah in place of the former altar of Baal. How far this desire attained its end we may best judge from the kindred effort to remove another ground of offence, which lies in the name Jerubbaal. In accordance with the occasion out of which the name is said to have arisen it is said to mean, "Let Baal contend." Etymologically this derivation is extremely far-fetched, and from every point of view impossible: the name of a god is only assumed by those who are his worshippers. In Hebrew antiquity Baal and El are interchangeable and used indifferently; Jehovah Himself is spoken of up to the times of the prophet Hosea as the Baal, *i.e.*, the lord. This is distinctly proved by a series of proper names in the families of Saul and David, Ishbaal, Meribaal, Baaljada, to which we may now add the name Jerubbaal given to the conqueror of Midian. If then even in the time of the kings Baal was by no means simply the antipode of Jehovah, whence the hostile relation of the two deities, which Jerubbaal displays by the acts he does, although he praises the great Baal by wearing his name? The view, also, that the Ashera was incompatible with the worship of Jehovah, does not agree with the belief of the earlier age; according to Deuteronomy xvi. 21, these artificial trees must have stood often enough beside the altars of Jehovah. The inserted passage itself betrays in a remarkable manner that its writer felt this sort of zeal for the legitimate worship to be above the level of the age in question. We receive the impression that the inhabitants of Ophra do not know their worship of Baal to be illegitimate, that Gideon also had taken part in it in good faith, and that there had never been an altar of Jehovah in the place before.

Of a somewhat different form is a correction which is to be found at the close of the history of Gideon (viii. 22 seq.). After the victory over the Midianites the Israelites are said to have asked Gideon to be king over them. This he declined out of regard to Jehovah the sole ruler of Israel, but he asked for the gold nose-rings which had been taken from the enemy, and made of them an image of Jehovah, an ephod, which he set up in Ophra to be worshipped. "And all Israel went thither a-whoring after it, and it became a snare to Gideon and to his house." Now the way in which such a man acts in such a moment is good authority for the state of the worship of Israel at the time, and not only so, but we cannot impute it to the original narrator that he chose to represent his hero as showing his thankfulness to the Deity by the most gratuitous declension from His worship, as in fact crowning His victory with an act of idolatry. This is seen to be the more impossible when we consider that according to the testimony of Hosea, Isaiah, and Micah, such images were even in the Assyrian period a regular part of the belongings of the "houses of God" not only in Samaria but in Judah as well. We have also to remember that the contradiction between a human kingship and the kingship of Jehovah, such as is spoken of in these verses, rests upon theories which arose later, and of which we shall have more to say. *1* Studer will thus be correct in his assertion that the

*** 1. "The words of Gideon are only intelligible on the presupposition that the rule of Jehovah had a visible representative prophet or priest. But this was not the case in the period of the judges, as Gideon's own history shows us." Vatke, p. 263. We see besides from ix. 1 seq. that Gideon really was the ruler of Ephraim and Manasseh. ***

old tradition could not see anything in Gideon's refusing the gold for himself and dedicating it to God but a fine proof of his unselfishness and piety, and that in viii. 22-27 we have a secondary product, in which the original features of the story are distorted so as to make them suit later tastes. The second hand has unfortunately supplanted in this instance the work of the first. The older narrative breaks off (viii. 21) with the words: "Gideon took away the ornaments that were on the necks of the camels of the kings." What he did with them we do not learn, but naturally we must suppose that it was of them that he made the ephod. According to the secondary passage, which begins immediately after viii. 21, he used for this purpose the nose-rings which the whole of Israel had taken from all the Midianites, amounting in weight to 1700 shekels, besides the ornaments of the kings and of their camels. The proportion is similar to that between the 600 Danites in chap. xviii. and the 25,700 Benjamites in chap. xx., or between the 40,000 men of Israel in v. 8, and the 400,000 in xx. 2.

VII.I.4. In the last place it is possible to trace even in the original narratives themselves certain differences of religious attitude which indicate to us unobtrusively and yet clearly that tendency in the development of the tradition which reached its end in the revision and ornamentation of which we have hitherto been speaking. This is especially the case with regard to those narratives which are preserved to us in a double form. These are not frequent in Judges, but they do occur. A very simple case of the kind is seen on comparing chap. iv. with chap. v.

The Canaanites again lift their heads under their great king Sisera, and from their towns in the plains harass the hill villages of the new settlers. Deborah unites the Hebrew tribes for the contest. From the North and from the South the hosts of Jehovah descend before our eyes towards Jezreel, the prophetess Deborah at their head, the warrior Barak at her side. The conflict takes place at the brook Kishon, and ends with the defeat of the kings of Canaan. Sisera himself is killed in the flight by Jael, the wife of a nomad Kenite. Such are the contents of the song in chap. v. In the preceding narrative (chap. iv.) we should expect to find a historical commentary on the song, but we find a mere reproduction in which the special features of the story are blurred and falsified. Instead of the kings of Canaan we have the king of Canaan, as if Canaan had been a kingdom. Sisera, the head of the Canaanite kings, is transformed into a mere general; the oppression of the Hebrews is made general and indefinite. Jael murders Sisera when he is lying in a deep sleep by driving a tent-peg into the ground through his temples. There is nothing of this in the song: there he is drinking when she strikes the blow, and is conceived as standing at the time, else he could not bow down at her feet and fall, and lie struck dead where he fell (ver. 27).

In the song the campaign is prepared with human means. Negotiations are carried on among the tribes, and in the course of these differences crop up. The lukewarmness or the swelling words of some tribes are reproved, the energetic public spirit and warlike courage of others praised. In the narrative, on the contrary, the deliverance is the work of Jehovah alone; the men of Israel are mere dummies, who show no merit and deserve no praise. To make up for this, interest is concentrated on the act of Jael, which instead of being an episode becomes the central point of the whole narrative. Indeed it is announced as being so, for Deborah prophesies to Barak that the glory of the conflict will not be his but a woman's, into whose hand the enemy is to be sold; it is not the hero, not human strength, that accomplishes what is done: Jehovah shows His strength in man's weakness. And Barak's part in the work is depreciated in yet another way. Deborah summons him to go not to the battle, but to the holy hill of Tabor, where Jehovah will bring about what is further to happen; he, however, objects to this, and insists that the prophetess herself shall go with him. This is regarded as a caprice of unbelief, because the prophetess is thought to have exhausted her mission when she transmitted the command of the Deity to His instrument: she has appeared for no end but to make it known through her prophecy that Jehovah alone brings everything to pass. In the song this is different. There Barak is not summoned against his will; on the contrary, he has a personal motive for taking up arms: "Arise, Barak; take captive thy captors, thou son of Ahinoam." And the prophetess has not only to prophesy; she works in a more psychological manner; she is part of the battle, and inflames with her song the courage of the fighting battalions: "Awake, Deborah, awake, sing the song!" *1* Throughout these variations of

1. Ver. 12 is a summons
to begin the battle, and Deborah cannot here be singing the song of triumph which
celebrates its happy issue. For a similar reason the translation given above, "take
captive   thy   captors,"   is   the   more   natural   and   correct.
****

the prose reproduction we feel that the rich colour of the events as they occurred is
bleached out of them by the one universal first cause, Jehovah. The presence and
energy of Jehovah are not wanting in the song; they are felt in the enthusiasm which
fills the Hebrew warriors, and in the terror and panic which confound the prancing
vigour of the foe. But in the prose narrative, the Divine action is stripped of all
mystery, and mechanic prophecy finds no difficulty in showing distinctly and with
sober accuracy what the part of the Deity in the history has been. But the more
special the intervention of Deity, the further is it from us; the more precise the
statements about it, the less do we feel it to be there.

There is another instance in the Book of Judges of the occurrence of the same
historical material in two different forms; it is the story of Gideon of the Manassite
house of Abiezer. Studer saw that there is a break between viii. 3 and viii. 4, and
that the two stories, from the one of which we pass to the other at that point, have to
be understood separately; viii. 1-3 is the conclusion of the first story. We have been
told how, after the success of the first attack on the Midianites, Gideon raised the
levy of all Israel for the pursuit, and how then the Ephraimites seized the fords of the
Jordan before the arrival of the flying nomads and got the two leaders of the
Midianites into their hands. Now we hear in conclusion that the Ephraimites, elated
by their success began to find fault with Gideon, but that he pacified their wrath by
saying, "What have I done now in comparison of you? Is not the gleaning of the
grapes of Ephraim better than the vintage of Abiezer? God hath delivered into your
hand the princes of Midian, and what was I able to do in comparison of you?" A
domestic contention like this about the respective shares in the victory could only
arise when the victory had been gained, when the strife with the enemy was fought
out; the metaphor of harvest and gleaning shows that the victory was complete and
all the fruits of it gathered in. Chapter viii. 1-3 concludes the business, and the
following narrative is not a continuation of what has gone before, but a second
version of the story in which many of the circumstances are quite different.
According to vii. 23 seq. there was a great army on foot, but in viii. 4 seq. Gideon
has only his own three hundred men with him. In viii. 1-3 the vintage and the
gleaning are over and the object of the fighting is attained; but in viii. 4 seq. Gideon
pursues the enemy without any interruption, and when he asks the men of Succoth
and Penuel for bread for his wearied and hungry troops, they inquire sarcastically
whether he is already certain of success, so that it should be necessary for them to
espouse his cause. The two chiefs who in the former account are called the princes
Oreb and Zeeb, and are already taken, are here called the kings Zebah and Zalmunna,
and are not taken yet. Unfortunately the beginning of viii. 4 seq. is not preserved,
and we cannot make out whether the pursuit in which we find Gideon here engaged
was preceded by an action. Such a supposition is not exactly impossible, yet the
distance to which the nomads had carried their booty, and their carelessness in camp,
make it more likely that the occurrence was like that in 1Samuel xxx. This,

however, makes no difference as to the particulars with regard to which the two narratives conflict with each other.

But how did the difference arise? This we shall best learn by comparing the beginnings of the two stories. We remarked that the second, as it stands, wanted a beginning, but what is wanting may be to some extent supplied from what follows. According to viii. 4 seq., Gideon's aim is to get hold of the two kings of the Midianites: these appear all through as the particular enemies whom he is pursuing: as to the rest of the Midianites he is more or less indifferent. And the reason, as we learn from viii. 18 seq., is that the two kings had slain his brothers at Tabor; it is to take vengeance for them that he sets out to pursue the slayers, and does not rest till they are in his hand. It is the duty of blood-revenge which causes him to take the war-path with his household, unconcerned by the disproportion in numbers between his followers and theirs: it is the powerful sentiment of family which sets him in motion and causes him to become, as it were incidentally, the liberator of Israel from the spoilers. In the first account (vi. 11-viii. 3) these natural motives have completely disappeared, and others have taken their place which are almost of an opposite character. Before anything has happened, before the Midianites have made their yearly incursion, Gideon, who expects nothing of the kind, is summoned by a theophany to battle against them. When they arrive he is seized by the Spirit and sets out against them. What is human in him has no part in the act he is called to do; flesh and blood set themselves against it. He is impelled by the direct impulse of Jehovah, and here, of course, he goes forth in behalf of the public interests of Israel, against the Midianites, not against their princes personally. And accordingly everything possible is done to cast the man into the shade behind the Deity. Gideon, according to the second account a distinguished and royal man, is in the first of a poor house and family; in the second story he is remarkable for irrepressible energy, but here he is timid and shrinking up to the last moment, and new miracles have constantly to be wrought to encourage and strengthen him. The 32,000 men with whom he takes the field he is ordered by Jehovah to send away all but 1,000 and again all but 300, "lest Israel vaunt themselves against Me, and say, Mine own hand hath saved me." The weapons with which the nocturnal attack of the 300 is made are torches, pitchers, and trumpets; the men have not a hand left to hold swords (vii. 20); and the hostile army has accordingly to do itself the work of its own destruction (vii. 22).

Few of the deviations of the religious version from the natural one are not transparent; one of these few is the removal of the scene to this side of the Jordan. Most of them are at once recognisable as due to the process of glorification, illumination, and religious inflation, by which the body of the tradition is etherealised and the story lifted up into the region of the air. For example, the company of Gideon at the main action, the attack on the hostile camp, consists of 300 men in chap. vii. as well as in chap viii.; but in chap. vii., to draw out the significance of the small number, they are treated as the last residuum of what was at first quite a considerable army; and this gives rise to a long story. We may also remark that chap. vi. begins with the relation in which the judge stood to the sanctuary of his native town, while chap. viii. closes with this. In the one case he discovers by a theophany, like the patriarchs in Genesis, the sacredness of the altar-stone under the oak; in the other he sets up, in far more realistic fashion, the plated image (ephod) he has made of the golden ornaments of the Midianite kings. History has to take account principally, if not exclusively, of the natural version, which is dry in tone and lets things speak for themselves, not overlaying the simple story with the significance of its consequences. The relation, however, is somewhat different from that which we found existing between Judges iv. and v. Chapter vi. seq. is not based directly on chap. viii., but was probably formed from independent oral material Though the local colour is lively, the historical reminiscences are extremely vague, and there has been a much freer growth of legend than in Jud. iv., producing pictures of greater art and more naïveté. But in the field of miracle poetry is manifestly earlier than prose.

In the case of those narratives which have come down to us in double form, the difference of standpoint is unmistakable; but it may also be perceived in cases where we have no direct parallels to compare. How noticeably does the story of Abimelech differ, say from that of Jephthah which follows it, in the rich detail of its facts, and in the spontaneous interest it shows in the secondary and subordinate links in the chain of events! There is no gilding with a supernatural nimbus; facts are simply and plainly set down such as they are; the moral is left to speak for itself as the story goes on. In the Samson legends again we find two souls united, as it were, in one body. Traits belonging to the rough life and spirit of the people are wrought, especially at the beginning and end of the narrative, into a religious national form; yet the two stand in an inner contrast to each other, and it is scarcely probable that the exploits of this grotesque religious hero were at first conceived in the Spirit of Jehovah, of which, in the story as we have it, they are the product. More probably the religious way of telling the story was preceded by a way considerably more profane; but we cannot now separate the older stage from that which is more recent. We may also remark that the contrast of historical and unhistorical is obviously inapplicable to this case, and, moreover, is unessential for the end we have in view. Only it may stand as a general principle, that the nearer history is to its origin the more profane it is. In the pre-Deuteronomic narratives, the difference is to be recognised less in the *kind* of piety than in the *degree* of it.

VII.II.

VII.II.1. The comprehensive revision which we noticed in the Book of Judges has left its mark on the Books of Samuel too. As, however, in this case the period is short, and extremely rich in incident, and really forms a connected whole, the artificial frame- and net-work does not make itself so much felt. Yet it is by no means wanting, as the dates of themselves indicate, whose place in the chronological system was shown above. It is worthy of notice how very loosely these are fitted into their context. In 1Samuel iv. 18 seq. we read: "And when the messenger made mention of the ark of God, Eli fell backwards off his seat, and his neck brake, and he died, for he was an old man and heavy, and *he judged Israel forty years*; and when his daughter-in-law, the wife of Phinehas, who was with child, heard the tidings," *etc*. The statement of the date is not altogether inappropriately dragged in, indeed, yet it is easy to see that it is dragged in. In 2Samuel ii. 8-13 we read: "Abner, the captain of Saul's host, took Ishbaal the son of Saul, and brought him over the Jordan to Mahanaim, and made him king over Gilead and Geshur, and Jezreel, and Ephraim, and Benjamin, and all Israel. *Ishbaal was forty years old when he began to reign over Israel, and he reigned two years.* But the house of Judah followed David. And the time that David was king in Hebron was seven years and six months. And Abner and the servants of Ishbaal went out from Mahanaim to Gibeon, and Joab with the servants of David went out to meet him." The words in italics <_...._> manifestly interrupt the connection; and with regard to Ishbaal's dates we have also to remark that from what we learn of him elsewhere he was, in the first place, still in the years of pupilage, and in the next must have reigned as long in Mahanaim as Oavid in Hebron. The number two connected with his reign is to be explained as in the case of Saul (1Samuel xiii. 1): *Saul was...years old when he began to reign, and he reigned two years over Israel.* In this verse, which is not found in the LXX, the number for the years of his life is wanting; and originally the number for the years of his reign was left out too: the *two* is quite absurd, and has grown out of the following word for year, which in Hebrew has a somewhat similar appearance.

In company with the chronological formulas, we find also the religious (1Samuel vii. 2-4). "While the ark abode in Kirjath-jearim, it was twenty years; and all the house of Israel came together after Jehovah. And Samuel spake unto the whole house of Israel, saying: 'If ye do return to Jehovah with all your hearts, then put away the strange gods and the Astartes from among you, and prepare your hearts unto Jehovah, and serve Him only; and He will deliver you out of the hand of the Philistines.' And the children of Israel did put away the Baals and Astartes, and served Jehovah only." We are not told, in what precedes this passage, of any act of declension from Jehovah, and according to chap. iv. the Israelites showed no want of faith in Jehovah in the unfortunate battle with the Philistines. This taking for granted that the yoke of a foreign rule was laid on them as a punishment for their sins is characteristic. A further example occurs in the speech of Samuel (1Samuel. xii.), which, as the introduction to the time of the kings, may be compared with Judges ii., the introduction to the time of the judges. "Stand still that I may reason with you before Jehovah of all the righteous acts of Jehovah with which He did right to you and to your fathers! When Jacob was come into Egypt, your fathers cried to

214

Jehovah, and He sent Moses and Aaron and brought your fathers out of Egypt and made them dwell in this land. And when they forget Jehovah their God, He sold them into the hand of Sisera, captain of the host of Hazor, and into the hand of the Philistines, and the Moabites, and they fought against them. And they cried unto Jehovah, and said, We have sinned, because we have forsaken Jehovah and have served Baal and Astarte, but now deliver us out of the hand of our enemies and we will serve Thee. And Jehovah sent Jerubbaal, and Barak, and Jephthah, and Samuel, and delivered you out of the hand of your enemies on every side, and ye dwelled safe. And when ye saw that Nahash the king of the children of Ammon came against you, ye said unto me, Nay, but a king shall reign over us, when Jehovah your God is your king. Now therefore behold the king whom ye have desired; behold, Jehovah has set a king over you. If ye will hear Jehovah and serve Him and obey His voice, and not rebel against the commandment of Jehovah, good: but if ye rebel against the commandment of Jehovah, then shall the hand of Jehovah be against you as it was against your fathers." It is the familiar strain: rebellion, affliction, conversion, peace, Jehovah the keynote, and the first word and the last. The eye does not dwell on the details of the story; the gaps in the tradition are turned to account as well as its contents, which are concentrated at so few points. Details are regarded only as they bear on the whole; the periods are passed in review in a broad and general style, and the law enunciated which connects them with one another. In doing this Samuel seems to presuppose in his hearers a knowledge of the biblical history in a distinct form; and he even speaks without hesitation of his own historical significance. The hearers are bidden to look back upon a period in the living movement of which they themselves are standing, as if it were a dead past. As they are thus lifted up to the height of an objective contemplation of themselves and their fathers, in the end the result which was to be expected takes place: they become conscious of their grievous sin. Confronted with the Deity they have always an uneasy feeling that they deserve to be punished.

VII.II.2. The Deuteronomist revision asserts itself, it is true, only in these two places, or rather this one place; but this is the principal epoch in the book—the transition to the monarchy which is associated with the name of Samuel. And on this account the revision here acts the more trenchantly; it is not only an addition to give a new flavour to the older tradition; it changes the nature of the tradition entirely. For the passages we have just quoted from it are merely fragments of a considerable connected historical scheme. The first piece of this scheme, vii. 2-17, first claims our attention. After summoning the children of Israel to repentance (vii. 2-4), Samuel convokes an assembly of them at Mizpeh, near Jerusalem, in order to entreat for them that the Philistine affliction may be turned away. This measure is of course closely connected with the previously-mentioned abolition of idolatry: for, after the guilt has ceased, the punishment also must be removed. They assemble, draw water to pour it out before Jehovah, fast, and confess their sins, at Mizpeh. When the Philistines hear this, they are on the spot the very same day and fall upon the assembly at its prayers. Samuel, however, sacrifices a sucking lamb and cries for help to Jehovah, and the engagement takes place while he is so occupied. Jehovah thunders terribly against the Philistines and throws them into disorder, so that they are forced to yield, and are pursued to a great distance. And the Philistines, this is the end of the narrative, were humbled and came no more into the coasts of Israel;

and the hand of Jehovah was against the Philistines all the days of Samuel, and the cities which the Philistines had taken from Israel were recovered; Ekron and Gath and their coasts did Israel take from the Philistines, and there was peace between Israel and the Amorites.

The mere recapitulation of the contents of this narrative makes us feel at once what a pious make-up it is and how full of inherent impossibilities: to think of all that is compressed into the space of this one day! But we have also to remark the utter contradiction of the whole of the rest of the tradition. In the history which follows we find the domination of the Philistines by no means at an end; not only do they invade the Israelite territory several times in Samuel's lifetime, they are in possession of the land of Israel, and one of their governors lives at Gibeah in the midst of Benjamin. The struggle with them is the true and real origin and task of the monarchy. The writer had no idea that Samuel had discharged this labour and won this victory already, and had even "restored " Ekron and Gath. On the contrary, the yoke of the Philistines lay most heavily on Israel just in his days. There cannot be a word of truth in the whole narrative. Its motives, however, are easily seen. Samuel is a saint of the first degree (Jeremiah xv. 1), and in the theocracy, *i.e.*, in the religious community such as ancient Israel is represented to have been, cut to the pattern of Judaism, such a man must take his place at the head of the whole. His influence must have prevailed to exclude idolatry and unfaithfulness to Jehovah on the part of the people; and the general character of the time must on the whole have answered to the type he set before it. But here a very unpleasant difficulty suggests itself. If the fact of Samuel being at the head is sufficient guarantee that all was as it should be within the state, how can there have been such great pressure externally, so as to endanger the very existence of the people? If men do their part, how can Jehovah fail to do His? On the contrary, it must be believed that the righteousness which prevailed within had its counterpart in the external vindication of His people by Jehovah. Even under Samuel the Philistines were with God's help driven across the border, and as long as he lived they were not seen within it again. The piety of a praying assembly was suitably acknowledged by Jehovah, who dropped into its lap a success such as in after times the sword of warlike kings sought long and in vain to achieve.

But this example of history corrected does not stand alone, and becomes completely intelligible only when taken in connection with the similar pieces which belong to it. 1Samuel vii. is continued in chap. viii., and chap. viii. again in x. 17-xii. 25. Samuel, after setting the land free from foreign tyranny, conducts a quiet and successful reign till old age comes upon him. His sons, however, whom he has made his assessors, do not walk in his steps; and the elders of Israel make this the occasion to ask him to give them a king. But this is a mere pretext for their sinful desire to shake off the divine rule and to be like the heathen round about them. Samuel is extremely indignant at their ingratitude, but is directed by Jehovah to comply with their request. "They have not rejected thee, but they have rejected Me, that I should not reign over them; according to all the works that they have done since the day that I brought them up out of Egypt, wherewith they have forsaken Me and served other gods. so do they also unto thee." It is in vain that Samuel exhibits to them an alarming catalogue of the rights of the king: they are not to be moved from their

216

determination, and he accordingly summons a general convention of the people at Mizpeh (viii. 22, x. 17). There, after the opening lecture, lots are drawn for the king, and Saul is chosen, whereupon Samuel has still to write down the law of the kingdom and lay it up before Jehovah. The people are then dismissed; "and Saul also went home to Gibeah, and with him the warriors whose heart God had touched, but the children of Belial despised him, and said 'How shall this man save us!'"

But Saul is at this point only king *de jure*; he does not become king *de facto* until after he has proved himself, chap. xi. After an interval of a month (x. 27 LXX) the men of Jabesh, besieged by the Ammonites and in great straits, send messengers throughout Israel to implore speedy assistance, since in seven days they have to surrender to their enemies and each of them to lose his right eye. The messengers come to the town of Saul, Gibeah in Benjamin, and tell their message before the people; the people lift up their voices and weep. Saul meanwhile comes from the field with a yoke of oxen, and, observing the general weeping, asks what has happened. The story is told him, and at once the Spirit of God comes upon him and his anger is kindled greatly; he hews in pieces his oxen and sends the pieces throughout Israel with the summons: Whoever does not come forth to the battle, so shall it be done to his oxen! And the fear of Jehovah falls on the people, and they go out as one man and relieve the besieged town. Hereupon "the kingdom is renewed" for Saul at Gilgal, and only now does Samuel abdicate his government, in the long speech (chap. xii.) a considerable portion of which was given above.

That chap. xi. is now an integral part of this version of the history is clear from xii. 12, and also from xi. 12-14. But it was not originally designed for this connection. For we hear nothing of the warriors who according to x. 26 were in company with Saul; it is not on his account that the messengers of Jabesh came to Gibeah. When the supposed king comes home from ploughing, nothing is done to indicate that the news concerns him specially: no one tells him what has happened, he has to ask the reason of the general weeping. He summons the levy of Israel not in virtue of his office as king, but in the authority of the Spirit, and it is owing to the Spirit acting on the people that he is obeyed. Only after he has showed his power and defeated the Ammonites do the people make him king (xi. 15); the "renewal" of the kingdom (xi. 14), after a month's interval, is a transparent artifice of the author of viii. 10, 1) seq. to incorporate in his own narrative the piece which he had borrowed from some other quarter: the verses xi. 12-14 are due to him.

Chapter xi. stood originally in connection with the other narrative of the elevation of Saul (ix. 1-X. 16). Hero Saul first appears engaged in searching for strayed she-asses. After a vain search of several days he arrives in the neighbourhood of Ramah, and at the suggestion of his servant applies for information as to the asses to a seer there, to Samuel. His approach has been announced to the seer by Jehovah the day before: "To-morrow I will send to thee a man out of the land of Benjamin, and thou shalt anoint him to be ruler over My people Israel; he shall save them from the Philistines." He was accordingly expecting him, and had instituted a sacrificial feast on the bamah for him even before he arrived. At this moment Samuel has gone down to the town between the sacrificial act and the meal which followed it, and just as he is going back to his guests he meets in the gate Saul, who is asking for him, and at a whisper from Jehovah he recognises in him his man. He takes him up with him to the bamah, reassures him about the asses, and then at once tells him to what high things he is called, and gives him convincing proofs that he had reckoned on his presence at the feast as the guest of the occasion. He then gives him lodgings for the night, and accompanies him on his way next morning. The servant is sent on a little way before, Samuel stands still and anoints Saul, for a sign that he is chosen by Jehovah to be the king and deliverer of Israel, and in conclusion instructs him that, when the opportunity for action comes, he is to use it, in the consciousness that God is with him. On his way home three signs come to pass which the seer had announced to him. He is thus assured that all that was said to him was true; his heart is changed by degrees till he cannot contain himself; on his arrival at Gibeah his acquaintances are struck with his strange demeanour, but he does not disclose even to his most intimate friend at home what Samuel had said to him, but waits for the things that shall come to pass.

This is the point arrived at in x. 16. It is clear that thus far no conclusion has yet been reached: the seed that is sown must spring up, the changed spirit must produce its effects. And this requirement is abundantly satisfied if chap. xi. is regarded as immediately continuing the story from x. 16. After about a month, the opportunity presents itself for Saul to act, which Samuel had bidden him to look for. While others are weeping at the disgrace which threatens an Israelite town at the hands of the Ammonites, he is filled with the Spirit and with rage, the arrow is still in his heart from that conversation, and he now does "what his hand finds to do." The result is a great success; the word of the seer finds its fulfilment in the most natural way in the world.

If chap. xi. belongs originally to the narrative of ix. 1.-x. 16, it follows at once that the other sections are dependent and later. But what is the inner relation of the one version to the other? They coincide in their ideas here and there. In the one story Saul seeks the asses and finds the crown, in the other he hides himself among the stuff and is drawn forth king. In the one he is called by the seer, in the other he is chosen by lot—the divine causality operative in both cases. But how the idea is exaggerated at the later stage, and how nakedly it is put forward! And if there is this similarity of view, yet the deviation of the secondary version from the original is much more striking than the resemblance. For its tendency we are prepared by chapter vii. Samuel has set his countrymen free from their enemies, and ruled over them afterwards in righteousness and prosperity; why then should they desire a change in the form of government? They have just as much and as little reason for desiring this as for the falling away from Jehovah, which also is a periodical craving on their part, whenever they have had some years' rest: it is the expression of the deep-seated heathenism of their nature. That is the account of chapter viii. with what belongs to it. Chapter ix. seq., however, gives quite a different account. Here, at the end of the period of the judges, Israel is not at the summit of power and prosperity, but in a state of the deepest humiliation and the means of saving the people from this state is seen in the monarchy alone. And this difference is closely connected with another as to the view taken of the authority of Samuel. In chap. viii. as in chap. vii. he is the vicegerent of Jehovah, with unlimited authority. He feels the institution of the monarchy to be his own deposition, yet the children of Israel by no means rebel against him; they come to him to ask him for a king. He might have refused the request; he might also have given them a ruler according to his own good pleasure, but as a correct theocrat he leaves the decision to Jehovah. At the end he solemnly lays down the government he has hitherto carried on, and hands it over to his successor. The latter is superior to him in point of title, but not in point of power: indeed in the latter respect he is rather inferior to Samuel, being a mere earthly prince (xii. 23 seq.). But how do matters stand in chap. ix. seq.? Here Samuel is quite a stranger to Saul, who knows neither his name nor his residence. Only his servant has heard of Samuel, who enjoys a high reputation as a seer in his own neighbourhood. What we are to think of when we read of a seer of that period, we are clearly and circumstantially informed: for Samuel is consulted as to the whereabouts of strayed she-asses, and a fee of a quarter of a silver shekel is tendered to him for his advice. This seer stands, it is clear, above the average of those who practiced the same calling; yet his action on the history is quite within the limits of what was possible, say to Calchas: it exhibits not a trace of the legislative and executive power of a regent of the theocracy. He does not bring help; he only descries help and the helper. The very event which, according to chap. viii. seq., involved the removal of Samuel from his place and his withdrawal to the background of the history, is here the sole basis of his reputation: the monarchy of Saul, if not his work, is his idea. He announces to the Benjamite his high calling, interpreting in this the thoughts of the man's own heart (ix. 19). With this his work is done; he has no commission and no power to nominate his successor in the government. Everything else he leaves to the course of events and to the Spirit of Jehovah which will place Saul on his own feet.

In the great difference which separates these two narratives we recognise the mental interval between two different ages. In the eyes of Israel before the exile the monarchy is the culminating point of the history, and the greatest blessing of Jehovah. It was preceded by a period of unrest and affliction, when every man did what was right in his own eyes, and the enemies of Israel accordingly got everything their own way. Under it the people dwell securely and respected by those round about; guarded by the shelter of civil order, the citizen can sit under his own vine and his own fig-tree. That is the work of the first two kings, who saved Israel from his spoilers, and gave him power and rest. No difference is made between them in this respect: the one commenced the work which the other completed (1Samuel ix. 16, xiv. 48; 2Samuel iii. 18, xix. 9). Before them there was no breathing space left in the hard work of fighting, but now there is time to think of other things. Even Deuteronomy, which was written not long before the exile, regards the period before the monarchy as a time of preparation and transition, not to be counted complete in itself: Israel must first acquire fixed seats and a settled way of living, and then Jehovah also will choose a seat for Himself and make known His desires with regard to the cultus. David brought things so far that the people had room and struck firm roots into the ground, and ceased to tremble before their enemies, who had kept them on the strain from the beginning, and all the days of the judges; and under his successor the time came when the temple could be built and higher interests receive attention. That Hebrew antiquity knew nothing of any hostility or incompatibility between the heavenly and the earthly ruler is plain from the title Anointed of

Jehovah, and from the hope of the prophets, whose ideal future would be incomplete without a human king. The ancient Israelites were as fully conscious as any other people of the gratitude they owed to the men and to the institutions by whose aid they had been lifted out of anarchy and oppression, and formed into an orderly community, capable of self-defence. Of this the Books of Samuel afford the most eloquent testimony. *1*

*** 1 In Balaam's view of the happy future of Israel (Numbers xxiii. seq.), the monarchy is spoken of as one of Israel's chief blessings. Generally (xxiii. 21): "Jehovah his God is with him, and the shout of a king is among them." With reference to Saul (xxiv. 7): "And his king triumphs over Agag. and his kingdom shall be exalted." To David (xxiv. 17): "I see him, though not now; I behold him, though not nigh: there rises (ZRX) a star out of Jacob and a rod out of Israel, and smites in pieces the temples of Moab and the skull of all the sons of Seth: and Edom also becomes a conquest." According to Deuteronomy xxxiii. 4, 5, the monarchy and the Torah are the two great gifts of God's grace to Israel. **

The position taken up in the version of 1 Samuel vii. viii. x. 17 seq. xii., presents the greatest possible contrast to this way of thinking. There, the erection of the monarchy only forms a worse stage of backsliding from Jehovah. There can be no progress beyond the Mosaic ideal; the greater the departure from it the greater the declension. The capital sin of placing a human ruler on the throne of Jehovah makes even the period of the judges appear not quite black. Dark as the colours are with which that period is generally painted, it held fast to the original form of the theocracy, and so appears somewhat brighter: at last indeed, to heighten the contrast, it is represented as a splendid age. Under the rule of Samuel, everything was as it should be. Should we ask, *how* were things then? what was exactly the nature of the theocratic constitution? we receive, it is true, no satisfactory answer to the question. We might draw conclusions with regard to the body from the head: but what sort of an idea can we form of the position of Samuel? As he appears in these chapters, we entirely fail to dispose of him in any of the categories applicable to the subject; he is not a judge, not a priest, not a prophet,—if at least we use these words with their true historical meaning. He is a second Moses? Yes, but that does not tell us much. So much only is clear, that the theocracy is arranged on quite a different footing from the kingdoms of this world, and that it amounts to a falling away into heathenism when the Israelites place a king at their head like other nations, and he keeps courtiers and ministers, officers and soldiers, horses and chariots. It is accordingly a spiritual community: the spiritual character of the regent places this beyond doubt. Samuel admonishes the people to give up idolatry; he presides at the great day of repentance at Mizpeh, which forms an epoch in the sacred history; and Jehovah can refuse nothing to his prayers and cries (xii. 1 7). "God forbid," he says in taking leave of them (xii. 23), "that I should cease to pray for you and teach you the good way." Such is his position: and the citizens of the theocracy have the corresponding duty of cultivating the worship of Jehovah, and not withdrawing themselves from the guidance of the representative of Deity. They do not need to trouble themselves about means for warding off the attacks of their enemies; if they fast and pray, and give up their sins, Jehovah hurls back the foe with His thunder and lightning, and so long as they are pious He will not allow their land to be invaded. All the expenses are then naturally superfluous by which a people usually safeguards it own existence. That this view is unhistorical is self-evident; and that it contradicts the genuine tradition we have seen. The ancient Israelites did not build a church first of all: what they built first was a house to live in, and they rejoiced not a little when they got it happily roofed over (xi. 15). But we have still to add, in conclusion, that the idea here before us can only have arisen in an age which had no knowledge of Israel as a people and a state, and which had no experience of the real conditions of existence in these forms; in other words. It is the offspring of exilic or post-exilic Judaism. At that time the nation was transformed into a religious community, whose members were at liberty to concentrate themselves on what they held to be the great business of life, worship and religiousness, because the Chaldeans or the Persians had relieved them of all care for worldly concerns. At that time, accordingly, the theocracy *existed*, and it is from that time that it is transported in an idealised form to early times. The material basis on which the theocracy rested in fact, namely, the foreign domination, is put out of sight, and it is counted heathenism in the old Israelites that they cared for the external conditions of their national existence, that they are a people in the full sense of the word, and seek to maintain themselves as such with the weapons which are found necessary in the work-a-day world. It naturally never came into the heads of these epigoni to conceive that the political organisation and centralisation which the monarchy called into being provided the basis for the organisation and centralisation of the worship, and that their church was merely a spiritualised survival of the nation. What is added to Moses is taken away from the monarchy.

One more point has to be noticed. The chapters vii. viii. x. 17 seq. xii. betray a close relationship with Judges xix.-xxi., not only by their general tendency, but by a geographical detail in which the two passages agree. It is only here that Mizpeh, near Jerusalem, occurs as the place of meeting of all Israel; we find no further mention of the place in the whole period of the judges and the kings. Only after the destruction of Jerusalem is it mentioned, and there as the centre of the new Jewish community instituted by the Chaldeans (Jeremiah xl. seq.) as the substitute of the old capital. It appears once more, and in a similar character, in I Maccabees iii. 46 seq. at a time when the temple of Jerusalem was in the hands of the Syrians, and the Jews could not get to it. The Mizpeh of Judges xx., 1Samuel vii. 10, is probably the same as that of Jeremiah xl. seq., and intended to be, like these, in place of Jerusalem, the only legitimate sanctuary, which, however, did not exist at that early time. This is a further proof of the post-Deuteronomic and Jewish origin of these narratives, but at the same time an indication that, with every inclination to the views of the Priestly Code, the writer yet had not that code before him. For in that work the projection of Jerusalem into the period before Solomon is carried out in quite a different way: the tabernacle renders Mizpeh superfluous. It has also to be remarked that the rite of pouring out water (1Samuel vii.) is foreign to the Priestly Code.

VII.II.3. The relation of Saul to Samuel is a subject which lends itself readily to general views, and the development of the tradition is visible in it in other particulars besides those we have mentioned. Taking the view of 1Samuel vii. viii. xii. as the lower limit, the narrative nearest in character is the story about Samuel contained in an insertion in chap. xiii. After Saul is made king at Gilgal by the levy with which he relieved Jabesh, he selects from it a body of men who camp with him and Jonathan at Gibeah and the neighbouring Michmash: and Jonathan, by killing the officer at Gibeah, gives the signal for battle with the old enemy of his race. The Philistines advance, and take up a position to the north of Gibeah, with only a deep valley between them and the Israelites. But Saul, we hear all at once, xiii. 7 (cf. ver. 4) was yet in Gilgal, and waited seven days for Samuel, according to the set time the latter had appointed; but Samuel did not come, and the warriors began to scatter. As he was himself offering the sacrifice without which no campaign could be commenced, Samuel arrived, and at once opened upon him. Saul defended his act with great force: the people were scattering, and Samuel had not come at the appointed time, and as the Philistines had advanced close up to Gibeah, he had found it impossible to delay longer, and had offered the sacrifice in order to advance against them. To all this Samuel's only answer was: "Thou hast done foolishly; if thou hadst kept the commandment of Jehovah, He would have established thy kingdom for ever, but now thy kingdom shall not continue; Jehovah has sought Him a man after His own heart, and appointed him to be ruler over His people, because thou hast not kept that which Jehovah commanded thee." So he said, and walked off; but Saul went with the army from Gilgal to Gibeah. At Gibeah, the following verse (xiii. 16) goes on, abode Saul and Jonathan, and their men, when the Philistines encamped in Michmash.

The change of place distinctly shows the whole passage about the meeting of the king with the prophet at Gilgal (xiii. 7-15) to be an insertion by a later hand. At the beginning of the narrative Saul is at Gibeah (ver. 2, 3), and the Philistines seek him there, and halt before the place because they meet with resistance. All at once, at ver. 7, it is assumed without being stated, that Saul had stayed at Gilgal since he was chosen king till now, and had only now advanced from there against the Philistines who were waiting for him before Gibeah. Verse 16, however, gives us the impression that Saul had been posted at Gibeah with his men for some time, when the Philistines took up their camp over against them. Only in this way is justice done to the contrasted participle of state (*sedentes*) and inchoative perfect (*castrametati sunt*). And in the sequel the triumphant continuation of the story, especially in chap. xiv., shows no indication that the ominous scene in Gilgal weighed on the mind of Saul, or of the people, or of the historian.

According to xiii. 7-15, Saul is to wait seven days for Samuel at Gilgal. Here there is a reference to x. 8, where the seer says to the future king, "Thou shalt go down before me to Gilgal, and I will come after thee there to offer sacrifices; seven days shalt thou tarry till I come and show thee what thou shalt do." This verse is condemned by other arguments than its connection with xii. 7-15. Samuel's object at this point, according to x. I-7, is to overcome the reluctance of the Benjamite who had gone forth to seek his asses, to undertake the high calling announced to him, and to inspire him with faith and confidence,—not to give him unintelligible directions as to what he is to do first when he has actually become king, and how long he has to wait for the seer at Gilgal. The schoolmaster tone of x. 8 is particularly out of place after the preceding words of ver. 7, that, when the three signs have come to pass, Saul is to do what his hand finds, because God is with him. This is surely giving him perfect freedom of action, and for the reason that God's Spirit is working in him, which "bloweth where it listeth," and suffers no interference from any authority. *1* *************************************** 1. It is also clear that the writer of x. 8, xiii. 7-15 cannot possibly have found Samuel in Gilgal in chap. xi. before making him go there in chap. xiii. We have already seen xi. 12-14 to be a later addition; the name of Samuel must be interpolated in xi.7, too. In fact in xi. 15 the people, *i.e.*, the army, acts quite of itself even in our present text. Hence it follows also, that x. 8, xiii. 7-15 are older than vii. viii. x. 17 seq. xii. ***************************************

This insertion is based on an older account of the breach between Samuel and Saul in 1Samuel xv. Here also the matter of dispute is a sacrifice, and Gilgal is the scene; and this alone serves to explain how Gilgal is adhered to in xiii. 7-15 in spite of all impossibility, as being the right and necessary place for the occurrence. Jehovah, by the mouth of Samuel, commands the king to devote the Amalekites to destruction because of an act of treachery they had committed against Israel in ancient times, and to spare no living thing. Saul accordingly makes war on the Amalekites and defeats them; but he does not carry out the proscription entirely, as he spares the best of their cattle and their king Agag, whom he takes prisoner. At Gilgal, where the victory is celebrated before Jehovah, he is called to account for this by Samuel, and states that he intended the booty for a sacrifice to Jehovah. His statement, however, makes no impression. "Behold, to obey is better than sacrifice, and to hearken than the fat of rams: behold, rebellion is as the sin of witchcraft, and stubbornness is as idolatry and teraphim. Because thou hast rejected the word of Jehovah, He also hath rejected thee." The king acknowledges his guilt, and tries to pacify Samuel; but the latter turns from him in anger, and when Saul lays hold of him, his mantle tears. "Jehovah hath torn the kingdom of Israel from thee this day, and given it to one better than thee; and the Truthful One of Israel will not lie nor repent; for He is not a man, that He should repent." Yet at Saul's entreaty that he would at least not refuse to honour him before the people, Samuel takes part in the sacrifice, and even begins it by hewing Agag in pieces before Jehovah. Then they part, never to see each other again; but Samuel mourns for Saul, that Jehovah had repented of having made him king over Israel. There is another narrative intimately connected with this one in subject and treatment, thought and expression, namely, that of the witch of Endor. When Saul, shortly before the battle in which he fell, surveyed the hostile army, he was seized with anxiety and terror. He inquired of Jehovah, but received no answer, neither by dreams, nor by the ephod, nor by prophets. In his extremity he was driven into the arms of a black art which he had formerly persecuted and sought to extirpate. By night and in disguise, with two companions, he sought out a woman at Endor who practiced the raising of the dead, and after reassuring her with regard to the mortal danger connected with the practice of her art, he bade her call up Samuel. She, on seeing the spirit ascending, at once perceives that the man he had come up to converse with is the king himself; she cries out loud, but allows herself to be reassured, and describes the appearance of the dead person. Saul does not see him, only hears him speak. "Why hast thou disquieted me, to bring me up? Jehovah doeth to thee as He spake by me: He rends the kingdom out of thy hand, and gives it to another, because thou obeyedst not the voice of Jehovah, nor executedst His fierce wrath upon Amalek; to-morrow shalt thou and thy sons be with me, and Jehovah also shall deliver the host of Israel into the hands of the Philistines." At these words Saul falls all his length on the ground. He had eaten nothing all the day before and all night; he is with difficulty induced to take some food: then he rises up with his men to go and meet his fate (1 Samuel xxviii. 3-25).

Comparing with this original the copy in xiii. 7-15, we are struck, in the first place, with the placing of the rupture so much earlier. Scarcely is Saul made king when he is deposed, on the spot, at Gilgal. And for what reason? Samuel has fixed, in a purely arbitrary fashion, the time he is to wait, and Saul waits, and makes arrangements for departure only when the time has run out, although the need is pressing; and for this he is rejected! It is clear that Samuel has from the first felt towards him as a legitimate prince feels to a usurper; he has arranged so as to find an occasion to show unmistakably where they both stand. Strictly speaking he did not find the occasion, Saul having observed the appointed time; but the opinion is present, though unexpressed, that the king was not entitled to sacrifice, either before the expiry of the seven days or at any time: his sacrificing is regarded as sacrilege. And thus the autonomous theocracy stands all at once before our eyes, which no one thought of before Ezekiel. We are reminded of the stories of Joash and Uzziah in the Chronicles. The incidents in 1Samuel xv. xxviii. are similar, but the spirit of the narrative is different and more antique. The rejection does not come here with such mad haste, and we do not get the impression that Samuel is glad of the opportunity to wash his hands of the king. On the contrary, he honours him before the people, he mourns that Jehovah has rejected him; and Saul, who never again sees him alive, turns to him dead in the hour of his extremity, and does not regard him as his implacable enemy. Again, in the former case the king's offence is that he has too low an estimate of the sacredness of sacrifice, and fails to regard the altar as unapproachable to the laity: while in the latter case he is reproached with attaching to sacrifice far too high a value. In the former case, in fine, the Deity and the representative of the Deity act with absolute caprice, confront men stiffly with commands of incredible smallness, and challenge them to opposition; in the latter, the conduct of Samuel is not (supposing it to have been the custom to devote enemies to destruction) unintelligible, nor his demeanour devoid of natural spirit; he appeals not to an irresponsible position, but to the manifest truth that obedience is better than the fat of rams.

Not that chapters xv. and xxviii. belong to the original growth of the tradition. In the case of xxviii. 3-25 it is easy to show the insertion: the thread of xxviii. 1, 2, coming from chapter xxvii. is continued at xxix. 1. According to xxviii. 4 the Philistines have advanced as far as Shunem in Jezreel; in xxix. 1 they are only at Aphek in Sharon, and they do not go on to Jezreel till xxix. 11. To prove an insertion in the case of chap. xv. we might point to the fact that there is a direct connection between xiv. 52 and xvi. 14; but this must be proved somewhat circumstantially. Let it suffice, then, to say that in the preceding narrative of Saul's history, the war with the Amalekites appears in quite a different light (ix. 1-X. 16, xi. xiii. xiv.; cf. also Numbers xxiv. 7). The occasion of it, according to xiv. 48, lay in the needs of the time, and the object was the very practical one of "saving Israel out of the hands of them that spoiled them." There is nothing here to suggest that the campaign was undertaken in consequence of a religious command, to punish the Amalekites for an offence over which long ages had passed, and information about which could only be gathered from historical books dealing with the age of Moses. Both the narratives, chap. xv. as well as chap. xxviii, are preludes of events afterwards to happen. At chap. xvi. David appears upon the scene; he is thenceforth the principal person of the story, and thrusts Saul on one side. Chapter xv. is the prophetic introduction to this change. The fact had been handed down that Saul was chosen by Jehovah to be king. How was it possible that in spite of this his rule had no continuance? Jehovah, who as a rule does not change His mind, was mistaken in him; and Samuel, who called the king, had now to his great sorrow to pronounce the sentence of rejection against him. The occasion on which he does this is evidently historical, namely, the festival of victory at Gilgal, at which the captured leader of the Amalekites was offered up as the principal victim. The sacrifice of Agag being quite repugnant to later custom, it was sought to account for it by saying that Saul spared the king, but Jehovah required his death, and caused him to be hewn in pieces at the altar by Samuel. The rest could easily be spun out of this; it is superfluous to discuss how. Chapter xxviii., again, is related to chap. xv. as the second step to the first. No proof is wanted to show that this is the prophetic shadow cast before the fall of Saul in his last fight with the Philistines. His turning to the witch to call up to him the departed Samuel suggests in the most powerful way his condition of God-forsakenness since Samuel turned away from him. And, to conclude-the general colouring of the hostile relation between Saul and Samuel is borrowed from the actual relations which must have come to subsist between the prophets and the kings, particularly in the kingdom of Samaria (I Kings xiv. 7). In their treatment of this relation our narratives manifestly take up the prophetic position; and the doctrinal ideas of which they are made the vehicles clearly show them to be prophetic conceptions.

VII.II.4. David is the first hero of Judah whom we meet with; and he at once throws all others into the shade. His acts are narrated to us in two detailed and connected works which are mutually complementary. The first of these is contained in 1Samuel xiv. 52-2 Sam viii 18, and in it we are circumstantially informed how David rose to the throne. There follows his principal achievement as king, the humiliation of the Philistines and the foundation of Jerusalem, the work concluding with a short notice of other remarkable circumstances. This narrative is preserved to us complete, only not in the earliest form, but with many interruptions and alterations. The second work, 2Samuel ix.-2Kings ii. is mutilated at its commencement, but otherwise almost completely intact, if 2Samuel xxi.-xxiv. be removed. It tells chiefly of the occurrences at the court of Jerusalem in the later years of the king, and carefully traces the steps by which Solomon, whose birth, with its attendant circumstances, is narrated at the outset, reached the throne over the heads of his brothers Amnon, Absalom, and Adonijah, who stood before him. Both works are marked by an essentially historical character. The treatment is much more detailed, while not nearly so poetical as in the history of Saul (1Samuel ix. seq.). There are no exaggerations, such as xiv. 46 seq. The second is the better work of the two, and frequently affords us a glance into the very heart of events, showing us the natural occasions and human motives which gave rise to the different actions. The point of view is, however, the narrow one of Jerusalem; for example, the real reasons of the revolt of the men of Judah under Absalom are scarcely even hinted at. The leading sentiment of the writer, there can be no doubt, is enthusiasm for David, but his weaknesses are not concealed; the relations prevailing at his court, far from edifying as they are, are faithfully reported, and the palace intrigue which placed Solomon upon the throne is narrated with a naïveté which is almost malicious. The first work (1Samuel xvi.- 2Samuel viii.) gives a less circumstantial narrative, but follows the thread of events not less conscientiously, and is based on information little inferior to that of the second. The author's partisanship is more noticeable, as he follows the style of a biographer, and makes David the hero of the history from his very first appearance, although king Saul is the ruling and motive power in it. But Judaistic leanings were unavoidable, and they have not gone so far as to transform the facts, nor indeed operated in a different way or to a greater degree here than local interest in the tribal hero, which is always the earliest motive for narration, has done in other cases. This praise applies to 1Samuel xvi. seq., however, only so far as its original form goes. It is different with the insertions, here very numerous, which have crept into the older connection, or replaced a genuine piece of the old story with a newer edition of it. In these the tendency to idealise the founder of the dynasty of Judah has worked creatively, and here we find rich materials for the history of the tradition, in the rude style in which alone it is possible as yet to construct that history. The beginning of the first work especially is overgrown with later legendary formations.

David, known as a man of courage and prudence, and of a skilful tongue, and recommended, moreover, by his skill on the harp, came to the king's court and became his armour-bearer (xvi. 14-23). He so approved himself in the war with the Philistines that Saul advanced him step after step, and gave him his daughter in marriage (xviii. 6 seq.). But the success and fame of the man of Judah filled Saul with jealousy, and in one of his fits of frenzy (to which x. 10 also shows him to have been subject) he threw his javelin at David, who was seeking to drive away the evil spirit by his playing (xix. 8-10). David agreed with Jonathan that it was advisable for him to absent himself, but this only confirmed the king's suspicions, which prompted him to destroy the priests of Nob, because their head had provided David with food and consulted the oracle for him (xxi 2-7, xxii. 6-23). The fugitive himself Saul failed to lay hands on; he gathered round him his own family and other desperate men, and became their leader in the wilderness of Judah (xxii. 1-5, xxiii. 1-13, xxv. 2 seq.). To escape the repeated persecutions of Saul, he at length passed over to the country of the Philistines, and received the town of Ziklag in Judah as a fief from the hands of the prince Achish (xxvii. 1 seq.).

Such is the beginning of the history of David according to the simple thread of the old narrative. The first accretion we notice is the legend of the encounter of the shepherd boy with Goliath (xvii. 1-xviii. 5), which is involved in contradiction both with what goes before and with what follows it. According to xvi. 14-23, David, when he first came in contact with Saul, was no raw lad, ignorant of the arts of war, but "a mighty valiant man, skilful in speech, and of a goodly presence;" and according to xviii. 6 the women sang at the victorious return of the army, "Saul has slain his thousands of the Philistines, and David his tens of thousands," so that the latter was the leader of Israel beside the king, and a proved and well-known man. Evidently something of a different nature must originally have stood between xvi. 23 and xviii. 6. Now the fate of the story of Goliath (xvii. 1-xviii. 5) involves that of the story of the anointing of David (xvi. 1-13), which is dependent on it (xvi. 12, xvii.

42); and, as we have already decided that chapter xv. is a secondary production, xiv. 52 joins on at once to xvi. 14. In xviii. 6 seq., where we are told of the origin of Saul's jealousy, several of the worst additions and interruptions are wanting in the LXX, especially the first throwing of the javelin (xviii. 9-11) and the betrothal to Merab (xviii. 17-19). The insertions are most varied and confusing in the account of the outbreak of the hostility of Saul and of David's flight (chapters xix. xx). Chapter xix. 1-7, a pointless and artificial passage, betrays its later origin by its acquaintance with chapter xvii.; xviii. 29a (LXX) is continued at xix. 8. After Saul's spear-cast David takes flight for the first time, but at verse 11 he is still at home, and makes his escape the second time with the aid of feminine artifice, going to Samuel at Ramah, but to appear in chap. xx. at Gibeah as before. The king remarks his absence from table; Jonathan assures him of his father's favour, which, however, David doubts, though he has no distinct evidence to the contrary. When quite certain of the deadly hatred of the king, David takes flight in earnest; in chapter xxi. seq. we find him at Nob on his way to Judah, but at xxi. 10 he goes away afresh from the face of Saul. It is evident that in reality and in the original narrative the flight took place only once, and that it must from the first have been directed to the place of refuge, *i.e.*, to Judah. This is enough to dispose of xix. 11-24: the twentieth chapter is impossible in the connection, at least in its present form, and in chapter xxi. verses 8-10 and 11-16 must be left out. In the section which deals with the freebooter life of David, chaps. xxiii xxvii., considerable pieces have been added; xxvii. 7-12 of course is one; but also the encounters of David with his pursuers. There are two versions: the one, xxvi. 1-25, is placed before chapter xxvii. on account of verse 19; the other, xxiii. 14-xxiv. 22, is placed before chapter xxv. to avoid too near a contact. There is a good deal of verbal coincidence between the two, and we are entitled to regard the shorter and more pointed version (chapter xxvi.) as the basis. But the sequence (xxvi. 25, xxvii. 1) shows beyond a doubt that chapter xxvi. does not belong to the original tradition. The process of inserting the additions naturally was not completed without all sorts of editorial changes in the older materials, *e.g.*, xvi. 14.

Though proceeding from the same root, these offshoots are by no means of the same nature, nor do they all belong to the same stage of the process. Some of them are popular legends and unconscious fictions. Of this nature is the story of Michal, who takes the part of her husband against her father, lets him down in the evening with a rope through the window, detains the spies for a time by saying that David is sick, and then shows them the household god which she has arranged on the bed and covered with the counterpane (xix. 11-17). The scenes in which Saul and David meet are of a somewhat different colour, yet we notice that the conviction that the latter is the king of the future does not interfere with the recognition of the former as the king *de facto* and the anointed of Jehovah; Saul too appears not wicked, but blinded. The secondary version (xxiii. 14 seq.) contains (not to speak of the distinctly later insertion between verse 15 and 19), in addition to the touching features of the story, a good-natured jest, telling how the two played hide-and-seek round a hill, which took its name from the circumstance. These stories present certain marks which serve to fix their date in the history of the religion: one is, that the image in David's house is spoken of quite simply; another, the expression in xxvi. 19, "If Jehovah have stirred thee up against me, let Him accept an offering, but if it be men, cursed be they before Jehovah, because they have driven me out this day from the fellowship in the land of Jehovah, and obliged me to serve other gods." It is perhaps not by mere chance that this speech is wanting in the parallel version, and that there is added in place of it a formal act of recognition which Saul pays at the end to his destined successor. As for the story of Goliath, it is also quite artless, but its religious colouring is much more marked. The speech with which David goes to meet the giant is characteristic on this side (xvii. 4 seq.): "Thou comest to me with a sword and with a spear, but I come unto thee in the name of Jehovah of hosts, whom thou hast defied. This day will He deliver thee into mine hand, that all the earth may know that there is a God in Israel, and that this assembly (hqhl = Israel) may know that Jehovah saveth not with sword and spear, for the battle is His." This approaches to the religious language of the post-Deuteronomic time. According to 2Samuel xxi. 19, Goliath of Gath, whose spear-shaft was as thick as a weaver's beam, *1* fought in the

*** 1. This expression occurs in I Samuel xvii., and shows this legend to be dependent on 2Samuel xxi. xxiii., a collection of anecdotes about heroes from the Philistine wars of David in the genuine short popular style. Cf., on 1Chronicles xii., supra, p. 173. ***

wars, not in Saul's time, but in that of his successor, and was killed, not by a shepherd boy but by a warrior of Bethlehem named Elhanan.

The theme of David and Jonathan has no doubt a historical basis, but for us it is found only in second-hand versions. The story of the farewell (chapter xx.) must be placed in this category. Yet it appears to point back to an earlier basis, and the earlier story may very possibly have belonged to the connection of the original work. For the shooting of the arrow could only have a meaning if it was impossible for the two friends to have an interview. But as the story goes, they come together and speak out freely what they have in their hearts, and so the dumb signal is not only superfluous, but unintelligible and meaningless. But if the most characteristic trait of the whole story does not fit into it as it now stands, that is just saying that the story has not come down to us in its true form. Originally Jonathan only discharged the arrow, and called to his boy where it lay; and David, hid in the neighbourhood of the shooting range, heard in the call to the boy the preconcerted signal. In calling that the arrow was nearer him or beyond him, Jonathan was apparently telling the boy, but in reality telling his friend, to come towards him or go farther away from him. The latter was the case, and if so, the friends could not enter into conversation; the tearful farewell then disappears, and the sentimental speeches spoken before it in the same style, in which Jonathan virtually admits that his father is right, and yet decidedly espouses David's cause, disregarding the fact that David will deprive him of his inheritance. *2*

*** 2. Only in one direction does he set limits to his self-denial: he makes the future king solemnly promise to spare his family. Here manifests itself an interest belonging to the time of the narrator. The oriental custom according to which the new ruler extirpates the

preceding dynasty, was not systematically carried out by David, and a special exception was made in favour of a son left by Jonathan. "All my father's house," says Meribaal (2Samuel xix. 28), "were dead men before my lord the king yet thou didst set me at thy table: what right have I therefore yet to complain unto the king (even about injustice)?" Now this son of Jonathan was the ancestor of a Jerusalem family which flourished till after the exile. Older traits in 1Samuel xx. are the importance attached to the new moon, the family sacrifice at Bethlehem, perhaps the stone)BN)CL which appears to have implied something inconsistent with later orthodoxy, the name being in two passages so singularly corrupted.
****

Chapter xviii. 6 seq. manifests tendency in a bad sense, even apart from the additions of the Masoretic text. Here Saul's enmity against David is carried back to the very beginning of their relations together, and even his friendship is represented as dissembled hatred. All the honours with which the king covers his armour-bearer are interpreted as practices to get rid of him. He makes him his son-in-law in order to expose him to deadly danger in his efforts to procure the hundred foreskins of the Philistines which were the price of the daughter. The connection cannot dispense with xviii. 6 seq, but at the same time it is beyond doubt that the venomous way of interpreting the facts is a mark of later revision. For Saul here practices his perfidies with the cognisance of his servants, who must therefore have been well aware of his disposition towards David; but the old narrator proceeds on the opposite assumption, that his hatred appeared all at once, and that David had been held by all up to that time to be one of the king's favourite servants: cf. xxi. 2-xxii. 14 seq., not to speak of chapter xx. And this alone agrees with the nature of Saul as it is everywhere described to us.

It is a characteristic circumstance that the corruption of the tradition is greatest in those narratives in which Samuel enters into the history of David. There are two insertions of this kind. According to xix. 18-24 David flees to the old man at Ramah, where the school of the prophets is; Saul sends messengers to take him, but these, when they come near Samuel and see him in command of a troop of ecstatic enthusiasts, are seized by the frenzy like the rest. The second set of messengers whom Saul sends, and the third, fare no better; and Saul has at last to come himself. But he also is drawn into the vortex, tears off his clothes and dances before Samuel and David, the only self-possessed spectators of the bacchantic company, till he falls down; and he lies naked as he is a whole day and a whole night upon the ground——whence the proverb, "Is Saul also among the prophets?" But that David when he fled, fled in earnest and went in the direction of Judah, instead of amusing himself by going first towards the north, is perfectly evident, as much so as that it is a serious abuse of the spirit of prophecy to make it serve ends which are foreign to its nature, and turn it into a mere instrument for the personal safety of David, who had no need whatever to wait for Saul at Ramah to play him a trick there. The narrative, which is unknown to the author of xv. 35, arose out of the proverb which is quoted in it, but this receives elsewhere (x. 12) a much more worthy interpretation. We can scarcely avoid the suspicion that what we have before us here is a pious caricature; the point can be nothing but Samuel's and David's enjoyment of the disgrace of the naked king. For the general history of the tradition the most interesting circumstance is that

Samuel has here become the head of a school of prophets and the leader of their exercises. In the original view of the matter (chaps. ix. x.) he appears alone and independent, and has nothing to do with the companies of the ecstatics, the Nebiim. He is a *Roeh* or seer, not a *Nabi* or prophet. True, it is asserted in the gloss, ix. 9, that the two words mean the same thing, that what is now called *Nabi* was formerly called *Roeh*. But that is scarcely quite correct. The author of ix. x. knows the name *Nabi* very well too, but he never applies it to Samuel; he only uses it, in the plural, of the troops of Jehovah—intoxicated dervishes. He gives it quite a different meaning from *Roeh*, and also quite a different meaning from that in which Isaiah and Jeremiah use the word *Nabi. 1*

*** 1 As the words are used in 1Samuel i.Y., Isaiah and Jeremiah would rather be called Roeh; and this is the justification of the gloss, ix. 9. *** We cannot doubt that these distinctions rest on a historical basis, and only gradually melted away in later times: so that Samuel the seer need not be degraded into one of the flagellants.

David's flight to Samuel presupposes some previous relation to him, and xix. 18 seq. seems to point back to xvi. 1-13. In this piece David's career begins with his being anointed king in Saul's place at Jehovah's command, when a mere shepherd boy, who was not even counted in the family he belonged to. But in the sequel no one knows anything about this. Even in the story of Goliath (which in other respects harmonizes better with xvi. 1-13 than any other piece) the older brothers, here three, not seven, know nothing of the anointing of the youngest, although they were present and heard their own claims discussed (xvii. 28). In the stories of David's persecution also, chapter xxiv. xxvi., Saul alone is the sacred person, the anointed of Jehovah, not David. A belief that David is chosen for high things by God is quite a different matter from an anointing which has already taken place in fact. And if consequent and antecedent be inseparable, we must remember how, according to xv. 35, Samuel not only withdraws himself from Saul till his death, but also feels grieved for him till his death. It is a harsh transition from xv. 35: "Samuel came no more to see Saul till the day of his death, because he mourned over him," to xvi. 1: "and Jehovah spake to him, How long wilt thou mourn for Saul, seeing I have rejected him?" But it appears clearly that the appointment of the successor was connected with, and a consequence of, the deposition of the predecessor.

The anointing of David by Samuel is at the same time the set-off to the anointing of Saul by Samuel. This is clearly seen on comparing x. 6, xi. 6, "and the Spirit of God leapt upon Saul," with xvi. 13, 14, "and the Spirit of Jehovah leapt upon David, and it departed from Saul." In the former case the inspiration is a momentary foaming over, in the latter (the leaping notwithstanding) it is a permanent property; and this difference alone leaves no doubt as to where the original is to be looked for, and where the imitation. Saul alone, according to the old tradition, was made king in a divine, *i.e.* an overpowering and ideal manner: David was made king in a tedious human way, and after many intermediate stages. Of Saul alone was it originally told that the sudden outbreak of the spirit with which he, unelected as he was, summoned the levy of Israel, placed himself at its head, defeated the Ammonites, and became king, was quietly prepared by an old seer, who pointed out to him his great calling, and filled him with confidence in himself by secretly anointing him in the name of Jehovah. All that was known of David was how by his own energy he raised himself from a soldier to be the leader of a band, from that to be the vassal prince, under the Philistines, of Ziklag and Judah, and from a vassal prince to be the independent and powerful king of Israel. He also was anointed, not, however, beforehand by God, but after his elevation, by the elders of Judah and Israel. But this human origin and this inferiority in point of divine consecration to a predecessor whose kingdom, as it turned out, Jehovah had not made to stand, was found by a later age to be unworthy of him: he must at least have received his anointing from Samuel as well as Saul. And this was accordingly made good by the legend (xvi. 1-13). It is a step further on this downward path that in the Judaistic version (x. 17 seq.) all mention is omitted of the anointing of Saul.

We return to Samuel. The Books of Samuel take their name from him, and he is a figure of great importance, if not for the history itself, yet for the history of the tradition, the progress of which may be measured by the change of view about his person. In the views taken about him we may distinguish four stages. Originally (ix. 1-x. 16) he is simply a seer, but at the same time a patriotic Israelite, who feels deeply the need of his country, and uses his authority as seer to suggest to the ear and to the mind of one whom he recognises as fit for the purpose, his destination to be Israel's deliverer and leader. This relation between seer and warrior must be held fast and regarded as historical if Samuel is to mean anything at all. Similar instances are those of Deborah and Barak in earlier times, and later, that of Elisha and Hazael, and still more, that of Elisha and Jehu. Samuel's greatness consists in this, that he rouses to activity the man who comes after him, and is greater than he: after kindling the light which now burns in its full brightness, he himself disappears. But his meteoric appearance and disappearance excited wonder, and this in early times produced a story of his youth, in which, while still a boy, he predicts the ruin of pre-monarchical Israel (1Samuel i.-iii.). After he has done this, darkness closes completely around him. Even in chapter iv. he has completely disappeared, and when we meet him again he is an old man. On the other side the circumstance that we hear nothing more of the seer after his meeting with Saul, caused it to be believed that a rupture very soon took place between the two.

This belief we meet with at the second stage of the tradition which is represented by the prophetical narratives recorded in chaps. xvi. and xxviii. It arose out of the inconsistency involved in the fact that Jehovah did not afterwards confirm in his reign the man whom He had chosen to be king, but overthrew his dynasty. Thus it becomes necessary that Samuel, who anointed Saul, should afterwards sorrowfully reject him. Even here he appears no longer as the simple seer, but as a prophet in the style of Elijah and Elisha who regards the Lord's anointed as his own handiwork, and lays on him despotic commands (xv. 1), though according to x. 7 he had expressly left him to be guided by his own inspiration.

The transition from the second to the third stage is easy. Here Samuel, after withdrawing the unction from Saul, at once transfers it to David, and sets him up against his rejected predecessor as being now de jure king by the grace of God. The respect with v.hich he is regarded has meanwhile increased still further; when he comes to Bethlehem the elders tremble at his approach (xvi. 4 seq.); and in xix. 18 seq. he has a magical power over men. Up to this stage, however, he has always been regarded as intellectually the author of the monarchy. It is reserved for the last (exilian or post-exilian) stage of the development of the tradition to place him in the opposite position of one who resists to the uttermost the desire of the people to have a king. Here pre-monarchical Israel is advanced to a theocracy, and Samuel is the head of the theocracy, which accounts for the feelings aroused in him by their demand.

The modern judgment has been prejudiced in Saul's favour by Samuel's curse, and to David's disadvantage by Samuel's blessing; the picture of the one has not suffered from the blackening so much as that of the other from the glorification. *1*

************************************** 1. The efforts of later writers to glorify David are at their worst in their account of his last testament (1Kings ii. 1-12). Even the language betrays this piece as a post-Deuteronomic insertion (v. 2-4); the contents are borrowed from the succeeding narrative. But in the narrative Solomon's conduct towards Adonijah, Abiathar, Joab, and Shimei is not dictated by any means by the testament, but by other considerations; and it is the declared object of the narrator to show how Solomon's throne was established by the removal of the elements of danger. Nor do the acute calculations of the weak old king agree very well with the general impression given of him at this time by 1Kings i. ii.
****

Some critics, who are unencumbered either by prejudice or by knowledge of the subject, regard Saul as the antagonist and David as the creature of the clerical lust of rule, of which they see the embodiment in Samuel. But this view gives Samuel a powerful position over against the king such as he cannot have possessed unless he had broad ground under his feet and an influence well and extensively organised. Did he find support in the Nebiim? These were only then rising into view out of an irregular enthusiasm which was not yet confined to any definite circle or school; and besides, the old tradition speaks of a close connection between them and the king, but not between them and the seer. The belief that the latter was the founder and president of their guild is based on the worthless anachronistic anecdote, 1Samuel xix. 18 seq. Or was Samuel in conspiracy with the priests against Saul? This is inferred from 1Samuel xxi.-xxii. where Abimelech of Nob provides David with bread on his wanderings, and expiates this offence with his own death and that of the whole race of Eli. But in the first place these priests have no connection with Samuel. In the second place there is nothing to make it probable that they had an understanding with David, or were acquainted with his ambitious plans if he had then begun to cherish them. In the third place, it is positively certain that they represented no distinct power in the state as against the king, but on the contrary were entirely the creatures of his smile or frown; on the occurrence of a faint

232

suspicion they were put to death to a man without a dog barking to remonstrate. The liberal view we are discussing of Samuel's relation to Saul and David is based on the erroneous assumption that Samuel had the hierocracy to rest on in his acts of opposition to the monarchy. But the student who carries back the hierocracy to these early times has still to learn the very elements of what is necessary to a true historical appreciation of Hebrew antiquity.

VI.III.

It is in the Book of Kings that the last revision works most unrestrictedly. Here also chronological and religious elements combine to the building up of the framework, and we begin with examining the chronological system.

From the exodus from Egypt to the beginning of the building of the temple was a period of 430 years; and from the latter to the destruction of Jerusalem, a period, according to the numbers of the kings of Judah, of 430 years, or reckoning the exile, of 480 years, as before. In Chronicles, the succession from Azariah ben Ahimaaz, who was, according to the correct reading, the first to officiate in the temple of Solomon, to Jozadak, who was carried away in the captivity, consists of eleven high priests; thus, reckoning the exile, we have again twelve generations of 40 years each. The detailed figures which compose the total are here more complicated, which is no doubt partly due to the fact that some of them are dates which the reviser found given. Yet in this instance also the number 40 is the basis of calculation, as we see in the reigns of the kings of Judah. From the division of the kingdom to the destruction of Samaria in the 6th year of Hezekiah, the numbers are as follows: Rehoboam and Abijam, 20; Asa, 41; Jehoshaphat, Joram, Ahaziah, Athaliah, 40; Joash, 40; Amaziah and Uzziah, 81; Jotham, Ahaz, Hezekiah, 38. From the destruction of Samaria to the last date in Kings (2Kings xxv. 27), Hezekiah, Manasseh, Amon, have 80; Josiah, Jehoahaz, Jehoiakim, Jehoiachin, 79 1/4. Let him believe who can that it is a mere chance that the figures 41 + 81 + 38 make up exactly 40 + 80 + 40.

The series of the kings of Israel is in point of chronology dependent on the series of Judah. According to the numbers of the latter, 393 years elapsed from the division of the kingdom to the Babylonian captivity; and if we assume with Ezekiel (iv. 4) that Samaria fell 150 years earlier than Judah, 243 years remain for the duration of the northern kingdom. The figures given amount in fact to 242 years. These 150 Israelite years, from the destruction of Samaria to the destruction of Jerusalem, exceed, it is true, by 17 the sum of the parallel years of Judah; and the Israelite years from 1 Jeroboam to 9 Hosea fall short of the years in Judah from 1 Rehoboam to 6 Hezekiah by about the same number. This shows that no effort was made at first to synchronise the individual reigns in the two series. The 242 years of the northern kingdom are divided, by the epoch of 1 Jehu, into 98 and 144. If we take them at 240, the half of 480, the 98 must be changed into 96, which then agree with the contemporary 96 Jewish years. The deduction must be made at the reign of Baasha. Then we get the following play of figures: Jeroboam 22, Nadab 2, Baasha 22, Elah 2, Omri 12, Ahab 22, Ahaziah 2, Joram 12. That is to say, the eight kings have together 96 years, the first four and the last four 48 each. Two have the average number 12; the other 6 consists of three pairs of father and son; and the twice 12 years belonging to each pair are divided so that the father gets 12 + 10, and the son 12 — 10, obviously because the father was considered much more important than the son. *1*

** 1. Numbers of the kings of Judah from Solomon : 37+ 17+ 3 + 41 + 25 + 8 + 1 + 6 + 40 + 29 + 52 + 16 + 29 + 55 + 2 + 31 + 11 + 11=430 years. Jehoahaz and Jechoiachin are not counted; if they are included and a year allowed for them, we must say 36 for Solomon. Numbers of the kings of Israel from 1 Jeroboam: 22 + 2 + 24 +2+ 12 + 22 + 2+ 12 + 28 + 17 + 16 + 41 + 1 + 10 + 2 + 20 + 9. The artificial relations of the numbers, as explained above, were communicated to me by Ernst Krey. On the point that the synchronisms do not belong to the original arrangement, see Jahrb. fur Deutsche Theol., 1875, p. 607 seq. The correct view of Ezekiel iv. was first published by Bernhard Duhm (Theol. dir Proph., p. 253). The number 390, given in the Massoretic text in verse 5 for the duration of the captivity of the northern Israelites, is impossible. For Ezekiel cannot mean that they have been 350 years in exile already, and on the other hand he cannot reckon the remaining period of their punishment at more than 40 years, because 40 years is his calculation of the period of exile of Judah, and the restitution of Israel and that of Judah are in his view to take place at the same time; and indeed that of Egypt as well, obviously because brought about by the same cause (xxix. 1 1-16), the fall of the Chaldeans, which may be expected to take place in 40 years. The number 390 has got into verse 5 by mistake from verse 9, where it is used of a quite different subject, not the years of the exile, but the days of the last siege of Jerusalem. The gloss verse 13 rests on a similar confusion. The Septuagint correctly gives for the Israelite exile the number of 150 years, or 190, according as the last 40 years in which their punishment continued, along with that of Judah, were included or omitted. It may be remarked that 390 = 240 + 150. Compare further Robertson Smith, in the Journal of Philologie, vol x., p. 209-213. ***

The great period thus marked off and artificially divided into subperiods, is surveyed and appraised at every important epoch in sermon-like discourses. These are much more frequent in Kings than in Judges and Samuel. It makes no difference whether the writer speaks in his own person, or by the mouth of another; in reviews of the past he speaks himself, 2Kings xvii.; in anticipations of the future he makes another speak (1Kings viii. ix.). A few examples must be cited to show what we mean.

The great epoch of the work is the building of the temple. On this occasion Solomon makes a great dedicatory oration, in which he entreats Jehovah to hear from heaven the prayer of those who shall seek Him in this place. He concludes as follows: "If they sin against Thee (for there is no man that sinneth not) and Thou be angry with them and deliver them to be carried away captive into the land of the enemy, far or near, if they then bethink themselves and make supplication to Thee, saying, We have sinned and have done perversely and are guilty, and so return unto Thee with all their heart and all their soul in the land of the enemies which led them away captive, and pray unto Thee toward their land which Thou gavest unto their fathers, the city which Thou hast chosen, and the house which Thou hast built for Thy name, then hear Thou in heaven their prayer and their supplication, and maintain their cause, and forgive thy people their unfaithfulness, and give them compassion before them that carried them away captive, that they may have compassion upon them. For they be Thy people and Thine inheritance, which Thou broughtest forth out of Egypt from the midst of the furnace of iron, and didst separate them to Thyself from among all the people of the earth, as Thou spakest by Moses thy servant." What Jehovah answered to this we learn in chapter ix. "I have heard thy prayer and thy supplication which thou hast made before me; I have hallowed this house, to put my name there for ever, and mine eyes and my heart shall be there perpetually. If thou wilt walk before me, as did David thy father, in integrity of heart and in uprightness, to do all that I have commanded thee, and wilt keep my statutes and my judgments, I will establish the throne of thy kingdom upon Israel for ever, as I promised to David thy father, saying, There shall not fail thee a man upon the throne of Israel. But if YE or YOUR CHILDREN turn away from me, and will not keep my statutes and my judgments which I have set before you, but worship other gods, then will I cut off Israel out of the land which I have given them, and this house which I have hallowed for my name I will cast out of my sight, and Israel shall be a proverb and a byword among all people, and this house a ruin. And when they ask: Why hath Jehovah done thus to this land and to this house? the answer shall be: Because they forsook Jehovah their God, who brought forth their fathers out of the land of Egypt, and have taken hold upon other gods, and have worshipped them and served them."

The division of the kingdom is also a very marked era in the history. It is introduced by a prophecy of Abijah to the first Jeroboam. "Behold, I rend the kingdom out of the hand of Solomon, and will give ten tribes to thee; but he shall have one tribe for my servant David's sake, and for Jerusalem's sake, the city which I have chosen; because he has forsaken me, and worshipped Astarte of Sidon, and Chemosh of Moab, and Milcom of Ammon, and has not walked in my ways to do that which is right in my eyes, my statutes, and my judgments, like David his father. And it shall be, if thou wilt hearken unto all that I command thee, and wilt walk in my ways, and do what is right in my sight, to keep my statutes and my commandments as David my servant did, that I will be with thee and build thee a sure house as I built for David, and will give Israel unto thee. And I will for this afflict the seed of David, but not for ever."

We pass over a series of prophecies in a similar strain which occur regularly at the changes of dynasty in the northern kingdom, and cite only the concluding words which accompany the fall of the kingdom of the ten tribes (2Kings xvii.). This fall came about "because the children of Israel sinned against Jehovah their God, which brought them up out of the land of Egypt, and feared other gods, and walked in the statutes of the heathen whom they had driven out, and in the innovations of the kings of Israel; and because the children of Israel imputed to Jehovah their God things which are not so, and built them high places in all their cities, from the tower of the watchman to the fenced city; and they set up pillars and Asheras on every high hill and under every green tree, and there they sacrificed in all the high places, as did the people whom Jehovah had driven out before them: and wrought wicked things to provoke Jehovah to anger, and served the abominations which Jehovah had forbidden. Yet Jehovah testified to them by all the prophets and seers, saying, Turn ye from your evil ways, and keep my commandments and my statutes according to all the torah which I commanded your fathers, and which I sent unto you by my servants the prophets; but they would not hear, but hardened their necks like their fathers, that they did not believe in Jehovah their God; and they rejected His statutes and His covenant that He made with their fathers, and His testimonies with which He warned them, and they followed vanity and became vain, and went after the heathen that were round about them, concerning whom Jehovah had charged them that they should not do like them. And they left all the commandments of Jehovah their God, and made them molten images and an Asherah, and worshipped the whole host of heaven, and served Baal; and they caused their children to pass through the fire, and used divination and enchantments, and sold themselves to do evil in the sight of Jehovah, to provoke Him to anger. And Jehovah was very wroth with Israel, and removed them out of His sight; there was none left but the men of Judah only. But they of Judah also kept not the commandment of their God, but walked in the manner of Israel: and Jehovah rejected the whole race of Israel, and humbled them, and delivered them unto the hand of spoilers, until He had cast them out of His sight." No special concluding discourse is given for Judah, but that for Israel applies to Judah as well. This we see both directly from the last words of the passage cited, and from the circumstance that two very characteristic abominations in the foregoing catalogue, the worship of the host of heaven and the sacrifice of children, were introduced, according to the testimony of the prophets, which alone can determine the point, not in the eighth but only in the seventh century, under Manasseh, and accordingly are not chargeable on Israel, but only on Judah.

The water accumulates, so to speak, at these gathering places of the more important historical epochs: but from these reservoirs it finds its way in smaller channels on all sides. *1* The first

*********************************** 1. Such additions as MCWT YHWH, 1Kings xviii. 18 [LXX has correctly YHWH, without MCWT] (ZBW BRYTK [LXX correctly (ZBW without BRYTK] and more extensive ones, as 1Kings xviii. 31, 32a; 2Samuel vii. 2b [)#R NQR) WGW''] *error! read vi. 2b*) I do not reckon because they proceed from various periods, and are mostly younger than the Deuteronomic revision, and belong rather to textual than to literary criticism. It is certainly in itself very important to detect and remove these re-touchings. The whole old tradition is covered with them. ***

question asked with regard to each ruler is, what position he took up to the pure religion—whether he did what was right or what was evil in the sight of Jehovah. Even in the case of those who only reigned a week, this question receives an answer. In general it has to be stated that they did evil. All except David and Hezekiah and Josiah, were defective, says Jesus Sirach (xlix. 4),—not quite accurately perhaps, but yet truly in so far as there is always some objection even to the good kings. But the sin here reproved is no longer, at least not principally, the worship of strange gods; it is the perverted worship of Jehovah. A more special standard, and therefore a

236

stricter one, is now employed, and we know the reason of this: the temple having once been built in the place which Jehovah has chosen for Himself, the kindly naturalness hitherto belonging to His worship comes to an end (Deuteronomy xii. 8): and in particular the prohibition of the bamoth comes into force (1Kings iii. 2). That these continued to exist is the special sin of the period, a sin widespread and persistent. It is aggravated by the fact, that with the bamoth all kinds of unlawful abuses crept into the worship of Jehovah, Maccebas and Asheras, evergreen trees, and prostitutes of both sexes. Israel, continually compared with Judah in the matter, is further charged with a second great sin, the sin of Jeroboam, *i.e.*, the golden calves at Bethel and at Dan. The religious estimate combines with the chronological facts to form that scheme in which every single reign of the kings of Israel and Judah is uniformly framed. Sometimes the frame is well filled in with interesting matter, but in not a few cases historical matter is almost entirely absent. The scheme appears most nakedly in such chapters as 1Kings xv. xvi., 2Kings xiii. xiv. xv.

That this redaction of our book is essentially uniform with that of the two historical books which precede it, requires no proof. Only it has here a warmer and more lively tone, and a much closer relation to the facts. In consequence of this we find it much easier to determine the point of view from which it proceeds. The mere fact that the narrative extends to the destruction of Jerusalem, nay, to the death of the captive king Jehoiachin, shows that we must place the date of the work not earlier than the Babylonian exile, and, indeed, the second part of the exile. The chronology reckons the exile in the period of 480 years, giving 50 years to it; and this would bring us still lower down; but it is open to us to assume that this is a later modification, which has not further affected the general character of the work. *1*

** 1. Krey surmises that the last date mentioned, the liberation from prison of, Jehoiachin in the 37th year after his accession to the throne, was originally intended to form the lower limit of the chronology, especially as the periods of 40 years under which, as we have seen, the Jewish figures naturally fall, come exactly to this date. But if this be the case, we cannot regard the 4th or 5th year of Solomon as the era started from, for then there is no room for the 36 or 37 remaining years of Solomon's reign. But such a starting-point is entirely unnatural; Solomon's 40 years cannot be torn up in this way: if we are to make a division at all in that period, it must be at the disruption of the monarchy, the natural point of departure for the series of kings of Israel and of Judah. It deserves remark, that the 37 years of Jehoiachin, at the close of the older mode of calculation, which perhaps only tried to bring out generations of 40 years, but also perhaps a period of 500 years from David (40+40+20+ 41+40+40+81 + 38+ 80 + 79 1/4), answer to the 37 years of Solomon at the beginning of the method now carried through. That a process of alteration and improvement of the chronology was busily carried on in later times, we see from the added synchronisms of the kings of Israel and Judah, from the uncertain statements in the Book of Judges, some of them parallel with each other (e.g., the interregna and minor judges, and the threefold counting of the time of the Philistines) and even from the variants of the LXX. **

The writer looks back on the time of the kings as a period past and closed, on which judgment has already been declared. Even at the consecration of the temple the thought of its destruction is not to be restrained; and throughout the book the ruin of the nation and its two kingdoms is present to the writer's mind. This is the light in which the work is to be read; it shows why the catastrophe was unavoidable. It was so because of unfaithfulness to Jehovah, because of the utterly perverted tendency obstinately followed by the people in spite of the Torah of Jehovah and His prophets. The narrative becomes, as it were, a great confession—of sins of the exiled nation looking back on its history. Not only the existing generation, but the whole previous historical development is condemned—a fashion which we meet with first in Jeremiah (ii. 1 seq., iv. 3), who was actually confronted with the question as to the cause of the calamity. 2

*************************************** 1. The fall of Samaria suggested similar reflections to the earlier prophets with reference to the northern kingdom, but their views are, as a rule (Amos v., Isaiah ix.), not nearly so radical nor so far-fetched. Hosea does certainly trace the guilt of the present up to the commencement, but he exemplifies the principle (like Micah, chapter vi.) chiefly from the early history of Jacob and Moses: as for the really historical period he belongs to it too much himself to survey it from so high a point of view. In this also he is a precursor of later writers, that he regards the human monarchy as one of the great evils of Israel: he certainly had very great occasion for this in the circumstances of the time he lived in. **

Ezekiel carried out this negative criticism of the past to greater lengths, with particular reference to the abominations of the older worship (chapter xvi., xx., xxiii.); and it is also to be found in Isaiah xl.-xlvi. (xlii. 24, xliii. 27), though here it is supplemented by a positive and greatly more suggestive view; we find it also in Deuteronomy xxviii.-xxx., and in Leviticus xxvi. The whole of the past is regarded as one enormous sin, which is to be expiated in the exile (Jeremiah xxxii. 30; Ezekiel xviii. 2, xxxiii. 10; Isaiah xl. 1); the duration of the punishment is even calculated from that of the sin (Leviticus xxvi. 34). The same attitude towards old times is continued after the return (Zechariah viii. 13 seq., ix. 7 seq.; Nehemiah ix. 7 seq.).

The treatment is naturally from a Judaean point of view. Outside of Jerusalem the worship of Jehovah is heretical, so that the political revolt of the Northern Israelites was at the same time an ecclesiastical schism. Yet they are not excluded in consequence from community with the people of God, as in the Chronicles: the old traditions are not thrown so completely overboard as yet: only after the destruction of Samaria by the Assyrians does Judah continue the history alone. Almost the same reverence is paid to David and his house as to the city and the temple. His house has the promise of eternal continuance, with regard to which the writer likes to make use of the words of Jeremiah xxxiii. 17. The book closes, doubtless not by chance, with the liberation from prison of the Davidide Jehoiachin; this is the earnest of greater things yet in store. In the words of Abijah to Jeroboam, also, when he says that the humiliation of the house of David and the revolt from it of the ten tribes will not last for ever, we see the Messianic hope appear, which, as we learn from Haggai and Zechariah, largely occupied the minds of the Jews at the time of the exile and after it.

In the case of the books of Judges and Samuel it is not perhaps possible to decide with perfect certainty what was the norm applied by the last reviser in forming his estimates of the past. In the Books of Kings there can be no doubt on this point. The writer deals not only in indefinite references to the will of Jehovah, which Israel ought to obey, but resists; he speaks now and again (1Kings ii. 3, 2Kings xiv. 6, xvii. 37) of the written Torah in which the judgments and statutes of Jehovah are contained, a difference which indicates, one must allow, a historical feeling. Now the code which is implicitly regarded as the standard is that the discovery of which under Josiah is circumstantially narrated in 2Kings xxii. xxiii., *viz.*, Deuteronomy. We are led to this conclusion, it is allowed on all hands, both by the phraseology of the reviser and by the spirit of his judgments. He condemns those sins specially against which Deuteronomy and the reformation of King Josiah were directed. And the one verbal quotation made from the book of the Torah is from Deuteronomy (2Kings xiv. 6; Deuteronomy xxiv. 16). On the other hand, there are clear signs that the author of the revision was not acquainted with the Priestly Code. Nowhere is any distinction drawn between priests and Levites; the sons of Aaron are never mentioned. The idea of a central sanctuary before Solomon is contradicted by 1Kings iii. 2. In one section only, a section which has been greatly exposed to corrections and interpolations of all kinds, namely, the description of the temple and its consecration, 1Kings vi.-viii., do we meet with signs of the influence of the Priestly Code, especially in the Massoretic text; in the Septuagint this is not so much the case. The most important example of this has already been investigated, p. 43, 44.

If, accordingly, we are fully justified in calling the revision Deuteronomistic, this means no more than that it came into existence under the influence of Deuteronomy, which pervaded the whole century of the exile. The difference between Deuteronomistic and Deuteronomic is one not of time only but of matter as well: *1* Deuteronomy itself has not yet come to regard

** 1. Post-deuteronomic, but still from the time of the kings, are 1Samuel ii. 27 seq.; 2Samuel vii, 1 seq.; 2Kings xviii. 13, 17 seq., xix. 1 seq.; chaps. xi. xii. xxi. xxiii. **

the cultus in this way as the chief end of Israel, and is much closer to the realism of the actual life of the people. A difference in detail which allows of easy demonstration is connected with the mode of dating. The last reviser distinguishes the months not by their old Hebrew names, Zif, Bul, Ethanim, but by numbers, commencing with spring as the beginning of the year. In this he differs not only from his older sources (1Kings vi. 37, 38, viii. 2), but also from Deuteronomy.

VII.III.2. This revision is, as we expect to find, alien to the materials it found to work on, so that it does violence to them. They have been altered in particular by a very one-sided selection, which is determined by certain religious views. In these views an interest in the prophets mingles with the interest in worship. It is not meant that the selection is due entirely to the last reviser, though it is thoroughly according to his taste; others had probably worked before him in this direction. But for us it is neither possible nor important to distinguish the different steps in the process of sifting through which the traditions of the time of the kings had to pass.

The culminating point of the whole book is the building of the temple; almost all that is told about Solomon has reference to it. This at once indicates to us the point of view; it is one which dominates all Judaistic history: the history is that of the temple rather than of the kingdom. The fortunes of the sanctuary and its treasures, the institution and arrangements of the kings with reference to worship—we are kept *au courant* about these, but about hardly anything else. The few detailed narratives given (2Kings xi seq. xvi. xxii. seq.) have the temple for their scene, and turn on the temple. Only in *2Kings?* xviii. seq. does the prophetical interest predominate.

As for the kingdom of Israel, the statements about the cultus of that state are very scanty and for the most part rather vague. Here the prophetical narratives come to the front, generally such as are told from the prophetic point of view, or at least tell of the public appearances and acts of the prophets. Here and there we are told of occasions on which the Northern kingdom came in contact with Judah; here the Jewish feeling appears which dictated the selection. What is merely historical, purely secular, is communicated only in the scantiest measure: often there is nothing but the names and succession of the kings. We learn hardly anything about King Omri, the founder of the town of Samaria and re-founder of the kingdom, who seems to have reduced Judah also to the position of a dependent ally, nor do we learn more about Jeroboam II., the last great ruler of Israel; while the conflict with the Assyrians and the fall of Samaria are despatched in a couple of verses which tell us scarcely anything at all. Sometimes a brilliant breaks in on the surrounding night (2Kings ix. x.), but after it we grope in the dark again. Only so much of the old tradition has been preserved as those of a later age held to be of religious value: it has lost its original centre of gravity, and assumed an attitude which it certainly had not at first. It may have been the case in Judah that the temple was of more importance than the kingdom, but there can be no doubt that the history of Israel was not entirely, not even principally, the history of prophecy. The losses we have to deplore must have affected the Israelitish tradition most seriously.

The damage done by the revision by its *positive* meddling with the materials as found in the sources, is not so irreparable; yet it is considerable enough. The change of colour which was effected may be best seen and characterised in the far-reaching observations which introduce the Israelite series of kings; "Jeroboam said in his heart, Now shall the kingdom return to the house of David; if this people go up to do sacrifice in the house of Jehovah at Jerusalem, then shall the heart of this people turn again to their rightful lord, and they will kill me, and become subject again to Rehoboam king of Judah. Whereupon the king took counsel and made two calves of gold, and said unto them, Cease to go up to Jerusalem; behold thy gods, O Israel, which brought thee up out of the land of Egypt. And he set the one in Bethel and the other in Dan. And this thing became a sin; for the people went as one man, even unto Dan. And he made temples of high places, and took priests from the midst of the people which were not of the house of Levi; whomsoever he would he installed as priest of the high places " (1Kings xii. 26-30, xiii. 33). The perversion is scarcely so great as in Chronicles, but the anachronism is sufficiently glaring in the mode of view discernible in these reflections of Jeroboam, who appears to feel that the Ephraimite kingdom was illegitimate in its origin and could only be kept separate from the south by artificial means. The blessing of Jacob and the blessing of Moses show us what the sentiment of Northern Israel actually was. In the former Joseph is called the crowned of his brethren, in the second we read "His first-born bullock, full of majesty (the king), has the horns of a buffalo, with which he thrusts down the peoples; these are the ten thousands of Ephraim and the thousands of Manasseh." Whence came the charm of the name of Ephraim but from its being the royal tribe, and the most distinguished representative of the proud name of Israel? Of Judah we read in the same chapter, "Hear, Jehovah, the voice of Judah, and bring him back to his people." There can be no doubt what the people is to which Judah belongs: we cannot but agree with Graf, that this tribe is here regarded as the alienated member, and its reunion with the greater kingdom spoken of as the desire of Judah itself, and this is not so remarkable when we reflect that the part belongs to the whole and not the whole to the part. Only by long experience did Judah learn the blessing of a settled dynasty, and Ephraim the curse of perpetual changes on the throne.

Judah's power of attraction for the inhabitants of the Northern Kingdom is thought to lie in the cultus of the Solomonic temple; and Jeroboam is said to have tried to meet this by creating new sanctuaries, a new form of the worship of Jehovah, and a new order of priesthood. The features in which the Samaritan worship differed from the Jewish pattern are represented as intentional innovations of the first king, in whose sin posterity persisted. But in making Bethel and Dan temples of the kingdom—that he set up high places, is a statement which need not be considered—Jeroboam did nothing more than Solomon had done before him; only he had firmer ground under his feet than Solomon, Bethel and Dan being old sanctuaries, which Jerusalem was not. The golden calves, again, which he set up, differed in their gold but not in their object from the ephods and idols of other kinds which were everywhere to be found in the older "houses of God"; *e.g.* from the brazen serpent at Jerusalem. *l*

*** 1. "Although Jeroboam had lived in Egypt, it would he wrong to say that he brought animal worship with him from that country, as wrong as to regard Aaron's golden calf as a copy of Apis. The peculiarity of the animal-worship of Egypt, and of its bull-worship in particular, was that sanctity was attributed to *living* animals." Vatke, p. 398. Egyptian gods cannot help against Egypt, Exodus xxxii. 4; 1Kings xii. 28. **

Even Eichhorn remarked with force and point, that though Elijah and Elisha protested against the imported worship of Baal of Tyre, they were the actual champions of the Jehovah of Bethel and Dan, and did not think of protesting against His pictorial representation; even Amos makes no such protest, Hosea is the first who does so. As for the non-Levitical priests whom the king is said to have installed, all that is necessary has been said on this subject above (p. 138 seq.).

A remarkable criticism on this estimate of the Samaritan worship follows immediately afterwards in the avowal that that of Judah was not different at the time, at any rate not better. In the report of Rehoboam's reign we read (1Kings xiv. 22 seq.): "They of Judah also set up high places and pillars on every high hill, and under every green tree, and whoredom at sacred places was practiced in the land." This state of things continued to exist, with some fluctuations, till near the time of the exile. If then the standard according to which Samaria is judged never attained to reality in Judah either, it never existed in ancient Israel at all. We know the standard is the book of the law of Josiah: but we see how the facts were not merely judged, but also framed, in accordance with it.

One more instance is worthy of mention in this connection. King Solomon, we are told, had, besides the daughter of Pharaoh, many foreign wives, from Moab, Ammon, and other peoples, intermarriage with whom Jehovah had forbidden (Deuteronomy xvii 17). And when he was old, they seduced him to the worship of their gods, and he erected on the Mount of Olives at Jerusalem high places for Chemosh of Moab, and for Milcom of Ammon, and for the gods of his other wives. As a punishment for this Jehovah announced to him that his kingdom should be torn from him after his death and given to his servant, and also raised up adversaries to him, in Hadad the Edomite, who freed Edom, and in the Syrian Rezon teen Eliadah, who made Damascus independent. And by the prophet Abijah of Shiloh, he caused the Ephraimite Jeroboam, who then had the supervision of the forced labour of the house of Joseph in the fortification of the city of David, to be nominated as the future king of the ten tribes. So we read in 1Kings xi. But Edom, and, as it appears, Damascus as well, broke away from the kingdom of David immediately after his death (xi. 2I seq., 25); and the fortification of the citadel, in which Jeroboam was employed when incited to revolt by Abijah, though it falls somewhat later, yet belongs to the first half of Solomon's reign, since it is connected with the rest of his buildings (ix. 15, 24). Now Solomon cannot have been punished by anticipation, in his youth, for an offence which he only committed in his old age, and the moral connected with these events is contradicted by chronology and cannot possibly be ascribed to the original narrator. The Deuteronomistic revision betrays itself, in fact, in every word of xi. 1-13. To the original tradition belongs only the mention of the many wives—without the reprobation attached to it,—and the statement about the building of the altars of Chemosh and Milcom and perhaps Astarte, on the Mount of Olives, where they stood till the time of Josiah (2Kings xxiii. 13). The connection of the two events, in the relation of cause and effect, belongs to the last editor, as well as the general statement that the king erected altars of the gods of all the nationalities represented by his wives.

In the Books of Kings, it is true, the tradition is not systematically translated into the mode of view of the Law, as is the case in Chronicles. What reminds us most strongly of Chronicles is the introduction from time to time of a prophet who

242

expresses himself in the spirit of Deuteronomy and in the language of Jeremiah and Ezekiel, and then disappears. *l*

*** 1. Cf. Kuenen, Profeten onder Israel (1875), ii. p. 143; English translation (1877), p 398. One of these Deuteronomistic prophecies is cited above, p. 275. They are in part anonymous, e.g, 2Kings x. 30, xxi. 10 seq, in part connected with old names, e.g 1Kings xvi. 1 seq. In many instances no doubt the reviser found flints in his sources and worked them out in his own style; thus, 1Kings xiv. 7 seq., xxi 21 seq. 2Kings ix. 7 seq. In these passages the Deuteronomistic ideas and the phraseology of Jeremiah and Ezekiel are distinctly present [HNNY MBY) R(h], but detached expressions of an original type also occur,—which, it is true, are then constantly repeated, *e.g.* (CWN W(ZWB. Names, too, like Jehu ben Hanani, are certainly not fictitious: we are not so far advanced as in Chronicles. Cf. 1Samuel ii. 27 seq.; 2Samuel vii. 1 seq. **

In this way the Law is introduced into the history in a living way; the prophets keep it effective and see it applied, according to the principle stated, 2Kings xvii. 13, which is founded on Jeremiah vii. 25; Deuteronomy xviii. 18: "Jehovah testified to them by all the prophets and seers saying, Turn ye from your evil ways and keep my commandments and statutes, according to all the Torah which I commanded your fathers and which I sent unto you by my servants the prophets." The most unblushing example of this kind, a piece which, for historical worthlessness may compare with Judges xix.-xxi. or 1Samuel vii. seq., or even stands a step lower, is 1Kings xiii. A man of God from Judah here denounces the altar of Bethel, at which King Jeroboam is in the act of offering sacrifice, in these terms: "O altar, altar, behold a son shall be born to the house of David, Josiah by name; and upon thee shall he offer the priests of the high places, that burn incense upon thee, and men's bones shall be burned upon thee." And to guarantee the truth of this prophecy, to be fulfilled three hundred years afterwards, he gives the sign that the altar shall burst asunder, and the ashes of the sacrifice upon it be poured out—which at once takes place. This legend, however, does not really belong to the Deuteronomist, but is a still later addition, as is easily to be seen from the fact that the sentence xii. 31 is only completed at xiii. 34. It deserves remark that in the two verses which introduce the thirteenth chapter, xii. 32 seq., the feast of tabernacles is fixed, in accordance with the Priestly Code, as the 15th of the 7th month.

VII.III.3. In this case also we are able to discern considerable shades and gradations in the sources the reviser had at command. In the Books of Kings for the first time we meet with a series of short notices which arrest attention, in the surroundings they are in, by their brevity and directness of statement and the terseness of their form, and have the semblance of contemporary records. In spite of their looseness of arrangement these form the real basis of our connected knowledge of the period; and the religious chronological framework is regularly filled in with them (e.g. 1Kings xiv.-xvi.); their loose connection and neutral tone made it specially easy for later editors to interweave with them additions of their own, as has actually been done to no small extent. *l*

*************************************** 1. The passage discussed above, 1Kings xi. 1 seq., gives a good example of this; we at once pick out the terse)z ybnh wgw'' from the barren diffuseness surrounding it.
****

These valuable notes commence even with Solomon, though here they are largely mixed with anecdotic chaff. They are afterwards found principally, almost exclusively, in the series of Judah. Several precise dates point to something of the nature of annals, 2

*************************************** 2. 5th of Rehoboam (1Kings xiv. 25); 23rd of Jehoash (2Kings xii, 6); 14th of Hezekiah (2Kings xviii. 13); 18th of Josiah (2Kings xxii. 3); 4th and 5th of Solomon (1Kings vi. 37, 38). These dates occur, it is true, partly in circumstantial Jewish narratives, but these are intimately related to the brief notices spoken of above, and appear to be based on them. It may be surmised that such definite numbers, existing at one time in much greater abundance, afforded the data for an approximate calculation of the figures on which the systematic chronology is built up. These single dates at any rate are not themselves parts of the system. The same is true of the statements of the age of the Jewish kings when they ascended the throne. These also perhaps go back to the "Annals." The)Z is found 1Kings iii. 16, viii. 1, 12, ix. 11, xi. 7, xvi. 21, xxii. 50; 2Kings viii. 22, xii. 18, xiv. 8, xv. 16, xvi. 5.
****

and with these the characteristic then might be thought to be connected, which frequently introduces the short sentences, and as it now stands is generally meaningless. In what circles these records were made, we can scarcely even surmise. Could we be certain that the reference to the royal temple of Judah, which is a prevailing feature of them, is due not to selection at a later time but to the interest of the first hands, we should be led to think of the priesthood at Jerusalem. The loyalist, perfectly official tone would agree very well with this theory, for the sons of Zadok were, down to Josiah's time, nothing else than the obedient servants of the successors of David, and regarded the unconditional authority claimed by these kings over their sanctuary as a matter of course (2Kings xvi. TO seq., xii. 18). These notices, however, as we have them, are not drawn from the documents themselves, but from a secondary compilation, perhaps from the two sets of chronicles cited at the end of each reign of the kings of Israel and those of Judah, from which at all events the succession of the rulers appears to the drawn. These chronicles are not to be identified, it is clear, with the original annals. The *book* of the annals must be distinguished from the Dibre-hajamim themselves. Whether the chronicle of Israel_- hardly anything out of which is communicated to us—was composed much earlier than the chronicle of Judah (which seems to close with Jehoiachim), and whether it and the chronicle of Solomon (1Kings xi. 41) are a quite independent work, I am inclined to consider doubtful.

The excerpts from the annals are interrupted by more extensive episodes which are interwoven with them, and are also embraced in the Deuteronomistic scheme. Of

244

these the Jewish ones are the minority, the greater part are Samaritan, but they all belong to a very limited period of time. I select the miraculous history of Elijah as an example of these, to show the sentiment and the change of sentiment in this instance also.

The prophet Elijah, from Tishbeh in Gilead, appears before King Ahab of Samaria, and says, "By the life of Jehovah the God of Israel, whom I serve, there shall not be dew nor rain these years but according to my word." The story begins abruptly; we require to know that Ahab, stirred up by Jezebel, has been propagating in Israel the worship of the Tyrian Baal, and has killed the prophets of Jehovah by hundreds: this is the reason of the punishment which comes on him and his land (xviii. 13, 22). Elijah vanishes as suddenly as he appeared. We find him again at the brook Cherith, which flows into the Jordan; then in the land of Baal with a widow at Zarepta; while following his fortunes we are made to feel in a simple and beautiful way the severity of the famine. Ahab in the meantime had sent out messengers to take him, and had required of every state to which the vain search had extended, an oath that he was not to be found there. Now, however, necessity obliged him to think of other things; he had to go out himself with his minister Obadiah to seek fodder for the still remaining war-horses (Amos vii. 1). In this humiliating situation he all at once met the banished man. He did not believe his eyes. "Is it thou, O troubler of Israel?" "I have not troubled Israel, but thou and thy father's house!" After this greeting Elijah challenged the king to institute a contest between the 450 prophets of Baal, and him, the only prophet of Jehovah left remaining. A trial by sacrifice took place on Mount Carmel before the whole people. Each party was to prepare a bullock and lay it on the altar without setting fire to the wood; and the divinity who should answer by fire was the true God. The prophets of Baal came first and sought after their own manner to influence their deity. They shouted and leapt wildly, wounded themselves with swords and lances till they were covered with blood, and kept up their raving ecstasy from morning till mid-day, and from mid-day till evening. During this time Elijah looked at them and mocked them, saying, "Cry louder, for he is a god; either he is talking, or he is somehow engaged, or he is asleep and must be awaked." At last his turn came; he repaired the altar of Jehovah, which was broken down, spread the pieces of the sacrifice upon it, and, to make the miracle still more miraculous, caused them to be flooded two or three times with water. Then he prayed to Jehovah, and fire fell from heaven, and consumed the sacrifice. The people, up to this point divided in their mind, now took the side of the zealot for Jehovah, laid hold of the prophets of Baal, and slaughtered them down below at the brook. A great storm of rain at once came to refresh the land.

This triumph of Elijah was only a prelude. When Jezebel heard what had happened she swore vengeance against him, and he fled for his life to Beersheba in Judah, the sanctuary of Isaac. Wearied to death he lay down under a juniper-bush in the wilderness, and with the prayer, It is enough: now, O Jehovah, take away my life, he fell asleep. Then he was strengthened with miraculous food by a heavenly messenger, and bidden to go to Horeb, the mount of God. He arrived there after a long journey, and withdrew into a cave; a rushing wind sweeps past; the wind and the earthquake and the lightning are the forerunners of Jehovah; and after them He comes Himself in the low whispering that follows the storm. His head covered,

Elijah steps out of the cave and hears a voice ask what ails him. Having poured out his heart, he receives the divine consolation that his cause is by no means lost; that the direst vengeance, the instruments of which he is himself to summon to their task, is to go forth on all the worshippers of Baal, and that those 7000 who have not bowed their knee to Baal shall gain the day—"Thou shalt anoint Hazael to be King over Damascus, and Jehu ben Nimshi shalt thou anoint to be iiing over Israel, and Elisha ben Shaphat to be prophet in thy room; and him that escapeth the sword of Hazael shall Jehu slay, and him that escapeth the sword of Jehu shall Elisha slay." The account of the execution of these commands by Elijah is at present wanting; we shall soon see why it was omitted. The conclusion of chapter xix. only tells us that he called Elisha from the plough to follow him. Of the account of the judgment which overtook the worshippers of Baal, this group of narratives contains only the beginning, in chapter xxi. Ahab wanted to have a vineyard which was situated beside his palace in Jezreel, his favourite residence: but Naboth, the owner, was unwilling to enter on a sale or an exchange. The king was angry, yet thought he could do no more in the matter; but Jezebel of Tyre had other notions of might and right and said to him, "Dost thou now govern the kingdom of Israel? be of good courage; I will get thee the vineyard." She wrote a letter to the authorities of the town, and got Naboth put out of the way by means of corrupt judges. As Ahab was just going to take possession of the vineyard which had fallen into his hands, his enemy came upon him. The prophet Elijah, always on the spot at the right moment, hurled the word at him, "Hast thou killed and also taken possession? Behold, in the place where dogs licked the blood of Naboth, shall dogs lick thy blood also." Here this story breaks off. What follows is not the true continuation.

The thread of the narrative xvii.-xix. xxi. is also broken off here, without reaching its proper conclusion. The victory of Jehovah over Baal, of the prophet over the king, is wanting; the story of Naboth is, as we said, only the introduction to it. We are sufficiently informed about the facts, but in form the narratives do not answer to the announcement in chapter xix. and xxi.; they are drawn from other sources. According to xix. 1 7 the Syrian wars ought to result in vengeance on the worshippers of Baal, and specially on the idolatrous royal house; but in the narrative of the wars (1Kings xx. xxii. 2Kings vii. ix.) this point of view does not prevail. On the contrary, Ahab and Joram there maintain themselves in a manly and honourable way against the superior power of Damascus it is ONLY AFTER the extirpation of Baal worship under Jehu that affairs took an unfortunate turn, and Hazael, who brought about this change, was not anointed by Elijah but by Elisha (2Kings viii. 7 seq.) /.l/

*********************************** 1. The same applies to Jehu (2Kings ix. 1 seq.). This is the reason of the above remarked omission after 1Kings xix. 21: cf. Thenius's commentary. ***

The massacre at Jezreel, too, which is predicted in the threat of 1Kings xxi. 19, would need to be told otherwise than in 2Kings ix. x., to form a proper literary sequel to the story of Naboth. According to 1Kings xxi. 19 the blood of Ahab is to be shed at Jezreel; according to 2Kings ix. 25 his son's blood was shed there, to avenge

Naboth. It is true, the explanation is appended in xxi. 27-29, that, as the king took to heart the threats of Elijah, Jehovah made a supplementary communication to the prophet that the threat against Ahab's house would only be fulfilled in the days of his son; but who does not see in this an attempt to harmonise conflicting narratives? 2 A whole series of

*************************************** 2 In spite of xxi. 27-29, an attempt is made at xxii. 38 to show that the threat was fulfilled in Ahab himself. We are told that Ahab was shot in his chariot and that his servants brought his body from Ramoth-Gilead to bury it there. Then we read xxii. 38 "and they washed the chariot in the pool of Samaria, and the dogs licked up his blood, and the harlots bathed in it, according to the word of Jehovah." Thus it is explained how the dogs were able to lick his blood in Samaria, though it had had plenty of time to dry up after the battle! The fact was unfortunately over-looked that according to xxi. 19 the dogs were to lick the blood of Ahab not at Samaria but at Jezreel, the place of Naboth. The verse xxii. 38 is an interpolation which does credit to Jewish acuteness. ***

subordinate discrepancies might be mentioned, which prove that 2Kings ix. x. does not look back to the story of the murder of Naboth as told in 1Kings xxi. According to ix. 25, 26, the dispute was not about the vineyard, but about the field of Naboth, which lay some distance from the town. His family was put to death along with him, and on the following day, when Ahab rode out IN COMPANY WITH JEHU and Ben Deker to take possession of the field, the word of the prophet (not framed so specially against him personally) met him: "Surely I have seen yesterday the blood of Naboth and of his sons, and I will requite it in this plat."

With the help of these other accounts, among which there is a considerable group of uniform character (1Kings xx. xxii. 2Kings iii. vi. 24-xii. 20. ix. 1-x. 27) favourably distinguished from the rest, we are placed in a position to criticise the history of Elijah, and to reach a result which is very instructive for the history of the tradition, namely that the influence of the mighty prophet on his age has after all been appraised much too highly. His reputation could not be what it is but for the wide diffusion of Baal worship in Israel: and this is not a little exaggerated. Anything like a suppression of the national religion at the time of Elijah is quite out of the question, and there is no truth in the statement that the prophets of Jehovah were entirely extirpated at the time and Elijah alone left surviving. The prophetic guilds at Bethel, Jericho, and Gilgal continued without any interruption. In the Syrian wars prophets of Jehovah stand by the side of Ahab; before his last campaign there are four hundred of them collected in his capital, one of them at least long known to the king as a prophet of evil, but left alive before and left alive now, though he persisted in his disagreeable practices. Of the sons whom Jezebel bore him, Ahab called one Ahaziah, *i.e.* Jehovah holds, and another Jehoram, *i.e.* Jehovah is exalted: he adhered to Jehovah as the god of Israel, though to please his wife he founded at Samaria a temple and a cultus of the Syrian goddess. This being so, Elijah's contest with Baal cannot have possessed the importance attributed to it from the point of view of a later time. In the group of popular narratives above referred to, there is no trace of a religious commotion that tore Israel asunder: the whole strength of the people is absorbed in the Syrian wars. The kings are the prominent figures, and do well and according to their office in battle: Elijah stands in the background. From several indications, though from no direct statements, we learn of the high esteem which Ahab enjoyed from friend and foe alike (xx. 3I, xxii. 32-34 seq.). Joram also, and even Jezebel, are drawn not without sympathy (2Kings vi. 30, ix. 31). We can scarcely say the same of Jehu, the murderer, instigated by the prophets, of the house of Ahab (2Kings ix. 10).

It is the fact, certainly, that the prophets' hatred of Baal succeeded at last in overturning the dynasty of Omri. But in what manner was this done? At a time when King Joram was prevented by a wound he had received from being with his army in the field, a messenger of Elisha went to the camp, called the captain apart from a banquet at which he found him, to a secret interview, and anointed him king. When Jehu returned to his comrades at their wine, they asked him what that mad fellow had wanted, and, his evasive answers failing to satisfy them, he told them the truth. They at once raised him on an improvised throne, and caused the trumpets to proclaim him king: they were quite ready for such an exploit, not that they cared in the least for "that mad fellow." Jehu justified their confidence by his astounding mastery in treachery and bloodshed, but he placed his reliance entirely on the resources of his own talent for murder. He was not borne along by any general movement against the dynasty; the people, which he despised (x. 9), stood motionless and horrified at the sight of the crimes which came so quickly one after another; even a hundred years afterwards the horror at the massacre of Jezreel still lived (Hosea i. 4). The crown once gained, the reckless player showed his gratitude to the fanatics, and sent the priests and worshippers of Baal after the priests of Jehovah whom he had slaughtered along with all belonging to the royal house (x. 11). The manner in which he led them into the snare (x. 18 seq.) shows that no one had thought before this of regarding him as the champion of Jehovah; and even at this time his zeal was manifestly only ostensible: he was not fighting for an idea (x. 15. seq.). Thus we see that Baal did not bring about the fall of the house of Ahab, but common treason; the zealots employed for their purposes a most unholy instrument, which employed them in turn as a holy instrument for its purposes; they did not succeed in rousing the people to a storm against Baal, far from it. The execution of Naboth seems to have excited greater indignation: it was a crime against morals, not against religion. Even in the history of Elijah the admission is made that this struggle against Baal, in spite of his sacrificial victory on Carmel, was in the end without result, and that only the judicial murder of Naboth brought about a change in the popular sentiment. But according to 2Kings ix. 25, this murder proved a momentous event, not because it led, as we should expect, to a popular agitation, but from the fortuitous circumstance that Jehu was a witness of the never-to-be-forgotten scene between Ahab and Elijah, and seemed therefore to the prophets to be a fit person to carry out his threatenings.

It is certainly the case that the grand figure of Elijah could not have been drawn as we have it except from the impression produced by a real character. *1* But it is too much torn away from the

248

historical position it belongs to, and is thereby magnified to colossal proportions. It may be said of this class of narratives generally, that the prophets are brought too much into the foreground in them, as if they had been even in their lifetime the principal force of Israelite history, and as if the influence which moved them had ruled and pervaded their age as well. That was not the case; in the eyes of their contemporaries they were completely overshadowed by the kings; only to later generations did they become the principal personages. They were important ideally, and influenced the future rather than the present; but this was not enough, a real tangible importance is attributed to them. In the time of Ahab and Jehu the Nebiim were a widespread body, and organised in orders of their own, but were not highly respected; the average of them were miserable fellows, who ate out of the king's hand and were treated with disdain by members of the leading classes. Amos of Tekoa, who, it is true, belonged to a younger generation, felt it an insult to be counted one of them. Elijah and Elisha rose certainly above the level of their order; but the first, whose hands remained pure, while he no doubt produced a great impression at the time by his fearless words, effected nothing against the king, and quite failed to draw the people over to his side: while Elisha, who did effect something, made use of means which could not bear the light, and which attest rather the weakness than the strength of prophecy in Israel.

VII.III.4. Let us conclude by summing up the results to which we have been led by our eclectic pilgrimage through the historical books. What in the common view appears to be the specific character of Israelite history, and has chiefly led to its being called sacred history, rests for the most part on a later re-painting of the original picture. The discolouring influences begin early. I do not reckon among these the entrance of mythical elements, such as are not wanting even in the first beginnings to which we can trace the course of the tradition, nor the inevitable local colour, which is quite a different thing from tendency. I think only of that uniform stamp impressed on the tradition by men who regarded history exclusively from the point of view of their own principles. Here we observe first a religious influence, which in the Books of Samuel and Kings turns out to be the prophetical one. The view appears to me erroneous that it is to the prophets that the Hebrew people owe their history as a whole. The song, Judges v., though perhaps the oldest historical monument in the Old Testament, cannot be cited in support of that view, for even if it were actually composed by Deborah, the seer stands in no connection with the prophets. Least of all can the colleges of the B'ne Nebiim at Gilgal and other places be regarded as nurseries of historic tradition: the products which are to be traced to these circles betray a somewhat narrow field of vision (2Kings ii., iv. 1-6, 23). The prophets did not form the tradition at first, but came after, shedding upon it their peculiar light. Their interest in history was not so great that they felt it necessary to write it down; they only infused their own spirit into it subsequently.

But the systematic recoining of the tradition was only effected when a firmer stamp had become available than the free ideas of the prophets, the will of God having been formulated in writing. When this point was reached, no one could fail to see the discrepancy between the ideal commencement, which was now sought to be restored as it stood in the book, and the succeeding development. The old books of the people, which spoke in the most innocent way of the most objectionable practices and institutions, had to be thoroughly remodelled according to the Mosaic form, in order to make them valuable, digestible, and edifying, for the new generation. A continuous revision of them was made, not only in the Chronicles, at the beginning of the Greek domination, but, as we have seen in this chapter, even in the Babylonian exile. The style of the latter revision differed from that of the former. In Chronicles the past is remodelled on the basis of the law: transgressions take place now and then, but as exceptions from the rule. In the Books of Judges, Samuel, and Kings, the fact of the radical difference of the old practice from the law is not disputed. In these works also the past is in some cases remodelled on the basis of the ideal, but as a rule it is simply condemned. That is one difference; another has to be added which is of far greater importance. In the Chronicles the pattern according to which the history of ancient Israel is represented is the Pentateuch, *i.e.* the Priestly Code. In the source of Chronicles, in the older historical books, the revision does not proceed upon the basis of the Priestly Code, which indeed is completely unknown to them, but on the basis of Deuteronomy. Thus in the question of the order of sequence of the two great bodies of laws, the history of the tradition leads us to the same conclusion as the history of the cultus.

CHAPTER VIII. THE NARRATIVE OF THE HEXATEUCH.

In the historical books the tradition is developed by means of supplement and revision; double narratives occur here and there, but not great parallel pieces of connected matter side by side. In the Hexateuch additions and supplements have certainly taken place on the most extensive scale, but the significant feature is here that continuous narratives which can and must be understood each by itself are woven together in a double or threefold cord. Critics have shown a disposition, if not in principle yet in fact, to take the independence of these so-called sources of the Hexateuch as if it implied that in point of matter also each is a distinct and independent source. But this is, even *a priori*, very improbable. Even in the case of the prophets who received their word from the Lord the later writer knows and founds upon the earlier one. How much more must this be the case with narrators whose express business is with the tradition? Criticism has not done its work when it has completed the mechanical distribution; it must aim further at bringing the different writings when thus arranged into relation with each other, must seek to render them intelligible as phases of a living process, and thus to make it possible to trace a graduated development of the tradition.

The striking agreement of the different works, not only in matter, but in their arrangement of the narratives, makes the office of criticism as now described not less but more necessary. There is no primitive legend, it is well known, so well knit as the biblical one, and thus it is no wonder that it became the frame for many others and infused into them some of its own colour. This connection is common in its main features to all the sources alike. The Priestly Code runs, as to its historical thread, quite parallel to the Jehovist history. This alone made it possible to interfuse the two writings as we now have them in the Pentateuch. That this was not done altogether without violence is less to be wondered at than that the violence which was done is so small, and particularly that the structure of each writing is left almost unimpaired. This can only be explained from the intimate agreement of the two works in point of plan. When the subject treated is not history but legends about pre-historic times, the arrangement of the materials does not come with the materials themselves, but must arise out of the plan of a narrator: even the architecture of the generations, which forms the scaffolding of Genesis, is not inseparably bound up with the matters to be disposed of in it. From the mouth of the people there comes nothing but the detached narratives, which may or may not happen to have some bearing on each other: to weave them together in a connected whole is the work of the poetical or literary artist. Thus the agreement of the sources in the plan of the narrative is not a matter of course, but a matter requiring explanation, and only to be explained on the ground of the literary dependence of one source on the other. The question how this relation of dependence is to be defined is thus a much more pressing one than is commonly assumed. *1*

** 1. The agreement extends not only to the thread of the narrative, but also to particulars, and even to expressions. I do not speak of *mabbul* (flood), or *tebah* (ark), but the following examples have struck me:-In Q Genesis vi. 9, Noah is said to be *righteous in his generations*, in J E

vii. 1 he is *righteous in his generation*— an unusual form of speech, which gave a vast amount of trouble to the Rabbins and to Jerome. Similarly Q Genesis xvii. 21, *the son whom Sarah shall bear at this set time next year*, and JE xviii. 14: *at the same time I will come to thee again next year, and then Sarah shall have a son.* In the same way Q Exodus vi. 12 vii. 1. (Moses) *I am of uncircumcised lips.* (Jehovah) *See, I make thee a god to Pharaoh, and Aaron thy brother shall be thy prophet*; compared with JE iv. 10, 16. (Moses) *I am slow of speech, and of a slow tongue*; (Jehovah) *Aaron shall be to thee instead of a mouth, and thou shalt be to him instead of God.* Comp. Genesis xxvii. 46, with xxv: 22. ***************************************

This, however, is not the place to attempt a history of the development of the Israelite legend. We are only to lay the foundation for such a work, by comparing the narrative of the Priestly Code with the Jehovistic one. In doing so we shall see that Buttmann (Mythologus, i. p. 122 seq.) is right in asserting against de Wette (Beitraege, ii.), that, the Jehovistic form of the legend is the earlier of the two . 2

*** 2. The line indicated by Buttmann was first taken up again by Th. Noldeke in his Essay on the main-stock of the Pentateuch, which opened the way to a proper estimate of the narrative part of the work. ***

VIII.I.

VIII.I.1 The Bible begins with the account of the Priestly Code of the creation of the world. In the beginning is chaos; darkness, water, brooding spirit, which engenders life, and fertilises the dead mass. The primal stuff contains in itself all beings, as yet undistinguished: from it proceeds step by step the ordered world; by a process of unmixing, first of all by separating out the great elements. The chaotic primal gloom yields to the contrast of light and darkness; the primal water is separated by the vault of heaven into the heavenly water, out of which there grows the world above the firmament which is withdrawn from our gaze, and the water of the earth: the latter, a slimy mixture, is divided into land and sea, whereupon the land at once puts on its green attire. The elements thus brought into existence, light, heaven, water, land, are then enlivened, pretty much in the order in which they were created, with individual beings; to the light correspond the lamps of the stars, fishes to the water, to the heaven the birds of heaven, and the other creatures to the land. The last act of creation is markedly emphasised. "And God said: Let us make man after our likeness; and let them have dominion over the fish of the sea, and over the fowl of the air, and over the cattle, and over all the living creatures of the earth, and over every creeping thing that creepeth upon the earth. So God created man after His own image, in the image of God created He him, and He created them male and female. And God blessed them, and said: Be fruitful and multiply, and replenish the earth, and subdue it: and have dominion over the fish of the sea, and over the fowl of the air, and over every living thing that moveth upon the face of the earth. And God said, Behold, I have given unto you every herb bearing seed, which is upon the face of all the earth, and every tree with seed-fruits: to you it shall be for food: and to every beast of the earth and to every fowl of the air, and to everything that creepeth upon the earth, wherein there is life, I have given the green herb for meat. Thus the heavens and the earth were made and all the host of them, and on the seventh day God ended His work, and blessed the seventh day, and hallowed it." (Genesis i. 1-ii. 4a).

It is commonly said that the aim of this narrative is a purely religious one. The Israelite certainly does not deny himself in it: the religious spirit with which it is penetrated even comes at some points into conflict with the nature of its materials. The notion of chaos is that of uncreated matter; here we find the remarkable idea that it is created in the beginning by God. Brooded over by the Spirit, it is further of a nature for development to take place out of it, and the trait that the creation is represented throughout as a separation of elements which in chaos were mixed together, betrays even now the original design: but in the Hebrew narrative the immanent Spirit has yielded to the transcendent God, and the principle of evolution is put aside in favour of the fiat of creation. Yet for all this the aim of the narrator is not mainly a religious one. Had he only meant to say that God made the world out of nothing, and made it good, he could have said so in simpler words, and at the same time more distinctly. There is no doubt that he means to describe the actual course of the genesis of the world, and to be true to nature in doing so; he means to give a cosmogonic theory. Whoever denies this confounds two different things—the value of history for us, and the aim of the writer. While our religious views are or seem to be in conformity with his, we have other ideas about the beginning of the world, because we have other ideas about the world itself, and see in the heavens no vault, in the stars no lamps, nor in the earth the foundation of the universe. But this must not prevent us from recognising what the theoretical aim of the writer of Genesis i. really was. He seeks to deduce things as they are from each other: he asks how they are likely to have issued at first from the primal matter, and the world he has before his eyes in doing this is not a mythical world but the present and ordinary one.

The pale colour which generally marks the productions of the earliest reflection about nature, when they are not mythical theories, is characteristic of Genesis i. also. We are indeed accustomed to regard this first leaf of the Bible as surrounded with all the charm that can be derived from the combination of high antiquity and childlike form. It would be vain to deny the exalted ease and the uniform greatness that give the narrative its character. The beginning especially is incomparable: "The earth was without form and void, and darkness lay upon the deep, and the Spirit of God moved upon the water. Then God said: Let there be light, and there was light." But chaos being given, all the rest is spun out of it: all that follows is reflection, systematic construction; we can easily follow the calculation from point to point. The considerations are very simple which lead the writer to make first what is great appear, and then what is small; first the foundation and then that which exists upon it, the water before the fishes, heaven before the birds of heaven, land and plants before the animals. The arrangement of the things to be explained stands here for the explanation; there is nothing more than a succession which proceeds from the simple to the complicated; there is no effort of fancy to describe the process more closely; everywhere cautious consideration which shrinks from going beyond generalities. Only the framework of creation, in fact, is given; it is not filled up. Hence also the form of the whole, the effect of which cannot be reproduced in an epitome; the formula gets the better of the contents, and instead of descriptions our ears are filled with logical definitions. The graduated arrangement in separating particular things out of chaos indicates the awakening of a "natural" way of looking at nature, and of a reasoned reflection about natural objects, just as this is manifest in the attempts of Thales and his successors, which are also remarkable as beginnings of the theory of nature and of an objective interest in the things of the outer world, but further than this do not exactly rouse us to enthusiasm. *1*

*** 1. "There is nothing whatever in the piece that merits the name of invention but the chronological order of the various creations." Buttmann, p. 133. ***

The first sentence of the Jehovistic account of the beginning of the world's history has been cut off by the reviser. [It was all a dry waste] when Jehovah formed the earth, and nowhere did the green herb spring up, for Jehovah had not yet caused it to rain upon the earth, and there was not a man to till the ground. But a mist (?) went up out of the earth, and watered the face of the ground. And Jehovah formed man of the dust of the ground, and breathed into his nostrils the breath of life. Then he planted a garden far to the eastward in Eden, in the place where the four chief rivers of the earth part asunder from their common source; there grow among other fine trees the tree of life and the tree of knowledge. In this garden Jehovah placed the man, to dress it and keep it and to eat of all the trees, forbidding him to eat of the fruit of the tree of knowledge only. But the man is utterly alone in his garden: he must have company that is suitable for him. So Jehovah first forms the beasts, if perchance the man will associate with them and make friends with them. He brings them to him one after another to see what impression they make on him, and what the man will call them. He calls them by their right names, ox, ass, bear, thus expressing his feeling that he finds in them nothing relate to himself, and Jehovah has to seek other counsel. Then he forms the woman out of a rib of the sleeping man, and causes him to awake. Wearied as it were by all the fruitless experiments with the beasts, the man cries out delighted when he looks at the woman: This surely is flesh of my flesh and bone of my bone; she may be called wo-man.

Thus the scene is drawn, the persons introduced, and an action secretly prepared: now the tragedy begins, which ends with the expulsion of man from the garden. Seduced by the serpent, man stretches out his hand after the food which is forbidden him, in order to become like God, and eats of the tree of knowledge. The first consequence of this is the beginning of dress, the first step in civilisation; other and sadder consequences soon follow. In the evening the man and his wife hear Jehovah walking in the garden; they hide before Him, and by doing so betray themselves. It is useless to think of denying what has taken place, and as each of them puts the blame on the other, they show themselves one after the other to be guilty. The sentence of the judge concludes the investigation. The serpent is to creep on its belly, to eat dust, and to perish in the unequal contest with man. The woman is to bear many children with sorrow, and to long for the man, who yet will be her tyrant.

The principal curse is directed against the man. "Cursed be the ground for thy sake: in sorrow shalt thou eat of it all the days of thy life. Thorns also and thistles shall it bring forth to, thee, and thou shalt eat the herb of the field, till thou return unto the ground, for out of it wast thou taken: for dust thou art, and unto dust shalt thou return." Sentence being thus spoken, Jehovah prepares the man and woman for their future life by making coats of skins to dress them with. Then turning to His celestial company, "Behold," He says, "the man is become like one of us to know good and evil; and now lest he put forth his hand, and take also of the tree of life, and eat, and live for ever." With these words he drives man out of Paradise, and places before it the cherubs, and the flaming sword, which turns every way, to keep the way of the tree of Life (Genesis i. 4b-iii. 24).

The gloomiest view of life as it now is, lies at the root of this story. Man's days are mere hardship and labour and task-work, a task-work with no prospect of relief, for the only reward of it is that he returns to the earth from which he was taken. No thought appears of any life AFTER death, and life WITHOUT death might have been, but has been forfeited, now the cherub guards the approach to the tree of life, of which man might have eaten when in Paradise but did not. This actual, cheerless lot of man upon the earth is the real problem of the story. It is felt to be the very opposite of our true destiny; at first, things must have been otherwise. Man's lot now is a perversion of what it was at first, it is the punishment of primeval guilt now resting on us all. At first man lived in Paradise; he had a happy existence, and one worthy of his nature, and held familiar intercourse with Jehovah; it was his forbidden striving after the knowledge of good and evil that drove him out of Paradise and brought all his miseries upon him.

What is the knowledge of good and evil? The commentators say it is the faculty of moral distinction,—conscience, in fact. They assume accordingly that man was in Paradise morally indifferent, in a state which allowed of no self-conscious action and could not be called either good or evil. A state like this not being an ideal one, some of them consider that man gained more than he lost by the fall, while others admit that it could not be the divine intention to keep him always at this stage of childish irresponsibility, and that this cannot be the view of the narrator either.

But it is plain that the narrator is not speaking of a relative prohibition of knowledge, but an absolute one: he means that it is only for God, and that when man stretches out his hand towards it he is transcending his limits and seeking to be as God. On the other side he cannot of course mean to say that conscience is a doubtful blessing, and its possession to be deplored, or that it is a thing that God in fact refuses to men and reserves to Himself alone. The knowledge spoken of cannot be moral knowledge. What could the assertion mean that God would have no one but Himself know the difference between good and evil, and would deny to man this knowledge? One would think that conscience is a thing belonging specifically to man and not to God.

And what could be the sense of representing Adam and Eve as so intent to know what was sin and what was virtue? No one is curious about that, and sin never came into existence in the way of ethical experiment, by men's desiring to know what it is. And it is manifestly assumed that men knew in paradise that obedience to Jehovah was good and disobedience evil. And finally, it conflicts with the common tradition of all peoples to represent the first man as a sort of beast; he is regarded as undeveloped only in point of outward culture. The knowledge which is here forbidden is rather knowledge as such, general knowledge, or getting the eyes opened, as it is afterwards called. This is what transcends, in the writer's view, the limits of our nature; prying out the secret of things, the secret of the world, and overlooking, as it were, God's hand to see how He goes to work in His living activity, so as, perhaps, to learn His secret and imitate Him. For knowledge is to the ancient world also power, and no mere metaphysic. This knowing in the highest sense is the attribute of God alone, who stands in the creative centre of things and penetrates and surveys the whole; it is sealed to man, who has to labour and weary himself at little things. And yet the forbidden good has the most powerful attraction for him; he burns to possess it, and instead of resigning himself in trust and reverence he seeks to steal the jewel which is jealously guarded from him, and so to become like God—to his own sorrow.

This explanation is not new; it is the old and popular one, for which reason also Goethe adopted it in Faust. One objection certainly may be taken to it; the words are not merely *knowledge*, but *knowledge of good and evil*. But good and evil in Hebrew mean primarily nothing more than salutary and hurtful; the application of the words to virtue and sin is a secondary one, these being regarded as serviceable or hurtful in their effects. Good and evil as spoken of in Genesis ii. iii. point to no contrast of some actions with others according to their moral distinctions: the phrase is only a comprehensive one for things generally, according to the contradictory attributes which constitute their interest to man, as they help or injure him: for, as said, he desires to know not what things are metaphysically, but what is the use of them. *1* Besides the

*************************************** I Sur. 20, 91. Hudh. 22, 10 (Agh. xv. 105, 12). Hamasa, 292, 8 seq. Tabari i. 847, 18 ***************************************

lengthier expression we have the shorter one, knowledge, simply (iii. 6); and it must also be remarked that the phrase is not: know the good and the evil, but know good and evil.

But more, we must regard this knowledge not as it affects the individual, but in the light of history; what is meant is what we call civilisation. As the human race goes forward in civilisation, it goes backward in the fear of God. The first step in civilisation is clothing; and here this is the first result of the fall. The story is continued in chapter iv. Adam's sons begin to found cities, Jubal is the first musician, Cain discovers the oldest and the most important of the arts, that of the smith— hence the sword and bloody vengeance. Of the same tendency is the connected story of the city and the tower of Babel, in which is represented the foundation of the great empires and cities of the world, which concentrate human strength and seek to use it to press into heaven itself. In all this we have the steps of man's emancipation; with his growing civilisation grows also his alienation from the highest good; and—this is evidently the idea, though it is not stated—the restless advance never reaches its goal after all; it is a Sisyphus-labour; the tower of Babel, which is incomplete to all eternity, is the proper symbol for it. The strain is that strain of unsatisfied longing which is to be heard among all peoples. On attaining to civilisation they become aware of the value of those blessings which they have sacrificed for it. *1*

*********************************** 1. Dillmann thinks this idea insipid: Genesis (1882), p. 44 ***************************************

It was necessary to discuss the notion of knowledge at some length, because the misunderstanding of this point on the part of philosophers and theologians has cast over our story an appearance of modernness, which has, in its turn, done something to influence general opinion as to the age of this story compared with the other. Having got rid of this impression we turn to those features of Genesis ii. iii. which help to determine positively its relation to chapter i.

What has been untruly asserted of Genesis i. is true of Genesis ii. iii. The Jehovist narrative does shine by the absence of all efforts after rationalistic explanation, by its contempt for every kind of cosmological speculation. The earth is regarded as being at first not moist and plastic but (as in Job xxxviii. 38) hard and dry: it must rain first in order that the desert may be turned into a green meadow, as is the case still every year when the showers of spring come. The ground further requires cultivation by man that the seed may spring forth. No regard is paid to any natural sequence of the acts of creation: man, the most helpless of all beings, appears first, and finds himself placed on a world entirely bare, without tree or bush, without the animals, without woman. Man is confessedly the exclusive object of interest, the other creatures are accounted for by their importance to him, as if this only conferred on them a right to exist. The idea explains matter: mechanical possibility is never consulted, and we do not think of asking about it. Want of taste could find no lower deeps than when this or that scholar goes from Genesis ii. 21 to count his ribs, or comes to the conclusion that the first man was hermaphrodite.

In the first account we stand before the first beginnings of sober reflection about nature, in the second we are on the ground of marvel and myth. Where reflection found its materials we do not think of asking; ordinary contemplation of things could furnish it. But the materials for myth could not be derived from contemplation, at least so far as regards the view of nature which is chiefly before us here; they came from the many-coloured traditions of the old world of Western Asia. Here we are in the enchanted garden of the ideas of genuine antiquity; the fresh early smell of earth meets us on the breeze. The Hebrews breathed the air which surrounded them; the stories they told on the Jordan, of the land of Eden and the fall, were told in the same way on the Euphrates and the Tigris, on the Oxus and the Arius. The true land of the world, where dwells the Deity, is Eden. It was not removed from the earth after the fall; it is there still, else whence the need of cherubs to guard the access to it? The

257

rivers that proceed from it are real rivers, all well known to the narrator, they and the countries they flow through and the products that come from these countries. Three of them, the Nile, the Euphrates, and the Tigris, are well known to us also; and if we only knew how the narrator conceived their courses to lie, it would be easy to determine the position of their common source and the situation of Paradise. Other peoples of antiquity define the situation of their holy land in a similar manner; the streams have different names, but the thing is the same. The wonderful trees also in the garden of Eden have many analogies even in the Germanic mythology. The belief in the cherubs which guard Paradise is also widely diffused. *Krub* is perhaps the same name, and certainly represents the same idea, as *Gryp* in Greek, and *Greif* in German. We find everywhere these beings wonderfully compounded out of lion, eagle, and man. They are everywhere guardians of the divine and sacred, and then also of gold and of treasures. The ingredients of the story seem certainly to have parted with some of their original colour under the influence of monotheism. The Hebrew people no doubt had something more to tell about the tree of life than now appears. It is said to have been in the midst of the garden, and so it seems to have stood at the point whence the four streams issued, at the fountain of life, which was so important to the faith of the East, and which Alexander marched out to discover. Paradise, moreover, was certainly not planted originally for man, it was the dwelling of the Deity Himself. Traces of this may still be recognised. Jehovah does not descend to it from heaven, but goes out walking in the garden in the evening as if He were at home. The garden of Deity is, however, on the whole somewhat naturalised. A similar weakening down of the mythic element is apparent in the matter of the serpent; it is not seen at once that the serpent is a demon. Yet parting with these foreign elements has made the story no poorer, and it has gained in noble simplicity. The mythic background gives it a tremulous brightness: we feel that we are in the golden age when heaven was still on earth; and yet unintelligible enchantment is avoided, and the limit of a sober chiaroscuro is not transgressed.

The story of the creation in six days played, we know, a great part in the earlier stages of cosmological and geological science. It is not by chance that natural science has kept off Genesis ii. iii. There is scarcely any nature there. But poetry has at all times inclined to the story of Paradise. Now we do not require to ask at this time of day, nor to argue the question, whether mythic poetry or sober prose is the earlier stage in the contemplation of the world.

Intimately connected with the advanced views of nature, which we find in Genesis i., is the "purified" notion of God found there. The most important point is that a special word is employed, which stands for nothing else than the creative agency of God, and so dissociates it from all analogy with human making and shaping— a word of such exclusive significance that it cannot be reproduced either in Latin, or in Greek, or in German. In a youthful people such a theological abstraction is unheard of; and so with the Hebrews we find both the word and the notion only coming into use after the Babylonian exile; they appear along with the emphatic statement of the creative omnipotence of Jehovah with reference to nature, which makes its appearance, we may say suddenly, in the literature of the exile, plays a great part in the Book of Job, and frequently presents itself in Isaiah xl.-lxvi. In Genesis ii. iii., not nature but man is the beginning of the world and of history; whether a creation

258

out of nothing is assumed there at all, is a question which only the mutilation of the commencement (before ii. 4b) makes it not quite impossible to answer in the affirmative. At any rate it is not the case here that the command of the Creator sets things in motion at the first so that they develop themselves to separate species out of the universal chaos; Jehovah Himself puts His hand to the work, and this supposes that the world in its main features was already in existence. He plants and waters the garden, He forms man and breathes life into his nostrils, He builds the woman out of the man's rib, having made a previous attempt, which was unsuccessful, to provide him with company; the beasts are living witnesses of the failure of His experiments. In other respects, too, He proceeds like a man. In the evening when it grows cool He goes to walk in the garden, and when there discovers by chance the transgression which has taken place, and holds an investigation in which He makes not the least use of His omniscience. And when He says: "Behold, the man is become like one of us to know good and evil: and now lest he stretch forth his hand, and take of the tree of life, and eat and live for ever," that is not said in irony, any more than when He expresses Himself on the occasion of the building of Babel; "Behold, the people is one, and they have all one language, and this is only the beginning of their doings, and now nothing will be too difficult for them that they have imagined to do; go to, let us go down and confound their language." That at the same time the majesty of Jehovah is in no way compromised is the mystery of poetic genius. How would the colourless God of abstraction fare in such a situation ?

The treatment, finally, of the microcosm in the two accounts, reflects the difference between them. In chapter i. man is directed at the very outset to the ground on which he moves to this day: "Replenish the earth, and subdue it," he is told; a perfectly natural task. In chaps. ii. iii. he is placed in Paradise, and his sphere of activity there, nestled, as he may be said still to be, in the lap of the Deity, is very limited. The circumstances of his life as it now is, the man's toil in the fields, the woman's toil in bearing children, do not answer to his original destiny; they are not a blessing, but a curse. In the Jehovistic narrative man is as wonderful to himself as the external world; in the other he is as much a matter of course as it is. In the one he sees astonishing mysteries in the difference of the sexes, in marriage, in child-birth (iv. 1); in the other these are physiological facts which raise no questions or reflections: "He made them male and female, and said, Be fruitful and multiply." There his attitude towards the beasts is one of mixed familiarity and bewilderment; he does not know exactly what to make of them; they are allied to him and yet not quite suitable society for him; here they are beings not related to him, over which he rules.

The chief point in which the difference between the two accounts comes to a head is this. In Genesis ii. iii., man is virtually forbidden to lift the veil of things, and to know the world, represented in the tree of knowledge. In Genesis i. this is the task set him from the beginning; he is to rule over the whole earth, and rule and knowledge come to the same thing—they mean civilisation. There nature is to him a sacred mystery: here it is a mere fact, an object; he is no longer bewildered over against nature, but free and superior. There it is a robbery for man to seek to be equal with God: here God makes him at first in His own image and after His own likeness, and appoints him His representative in the realm of nature. We cannot regard it as fortuitous that in this point Genesis i. asserts the opposite of Genesis ii.

259

iii.; the words spoken with such emphasis, and repeated i. 27, v. 1, ix. 6, sound exactly like a protest against the view underlying Genesis ii. iii., a protest to be explained partly by the growth of moral and religious cultivation, but partly also no doubt due to the convulsive efforts of later Judaism to deny that most firmly established of all the lessons of history, that the sons suffer for the sins of the fathers. *1*

*** 1. A coarser counterpart to Genesis ii. iii, is Genesis vi. 1-4. Here also there is a kind of fall of man in an attempt to overpass the boundary between the human race and the divine. In the priestly narrative (Q) the gulf between spirit, which is divine substance, and flesh, which is human substance, is bridged over by the doctrine of man's creation in the image of God. ***

What are generally cited as points of superiority in Genesis i. over Genesis ii. iii. are beyond doubt signs of progress in outward culture. The mental individuality of the two writers, the systematiser and the genius, cannot be compared, and the difference in this respect tells nothing of their respective dates; but in its general views of God, nature, and man, Genesis i. stands on a higher, certainly on a later, level. To our way of thinking its views are more intelligible, simpler, more natural, and on this account they have been held to be also older. But this is on the one hand to identify naturalness with originality, two things which every one knows not to be the same, and on the other hand it is applying a standard to prehistoric tradition which applies to historical tradition only: freedom from miracle and myth count in favour of the latter, but not of the former. But the secret root of the manifest preference long shown by historic-critical theology for Genesis i. appears to lie in this, that scholars felt themselves responsible for what the Bible says, and therefore liked it to come as little as possible in conflict with general culture. *1*

*** 1. I merely assert that Genesis ii. iii. is prior to Genesis i.; I do not believe the story of Paradise and of the Fall to be very old with the Israelites. We are led to think so by the fact that the man and the woman stand at the head of the genealogy of the human race; a place we should rather expect to be assigned to the serpent (according to primitive Semitic belief the serpent was by no means opposed to God). This is the case in the Chronicon Edessenum and in Abyssinian legend, and a trace of this is perhaps preserved in the name of Eve, as Noldeke thinks. The name certainly receives this interpretation in Philo (de agric. Noe, # 21) and in the Midrash Rabba on Genesis iii. 20 (D. M. Z. 1877, p. 239, 326). Moreover, the true seat of God to the Hebrews was Mount Sinai, and the original Hebrew life was the nomadic life of the patriarchs, not gardening or agriculture. And finally we cannot believe barbarians to have indulged in reflections on the advantages and disadvantages of civilisation. The materials of Genesis ii. iii. can hardly have been imported before the time of Solomon. Where they came from we can scarcely guess; it would be most natural to think of the Phoenicians or the Canaanites generally, and this theory is favoured by Genesis iv. But in JE Babel is regarded as the last home of the primitive human race, Eden and Nod having preceded it; and the Hebrews probably derived the legend in the last

instance from Babylon. But this does not prove that this or that parallel brought forward by Assyriologists is necessarily of value.
****

VIII.I.2. After the beginning of the world we have in Genesis i.-xi., both in the Priestly Code and in the Jehovist, the transition from Adam to Noah (chapters iv. v.), then the flood (vi.-ix.), then the transition from Noah to Abraham (chapters x. xi.).

In the dry names, which are enumerated in Genesis v. and Genesis iv. Buttmann recognised the remains of an historical connection once woven together out of primitive stories. These narratives were evidently mythological: their original contents are destroyed both in Genesis v. (Q) and in Genesis iv. (JE), but only the list of the Jehovist now bears the appearance of a ruin. In the other the fragments have been used for a careful new building in which they no longer look like fragments. Here they are made to serve as the pillars of a chronology which descends from Adam to Moses, computing the period from the one to the other as 2666 years. These 2666 years represent 26 2/3 generations of a hundred years each: namely, 1-20 Adam to Abraham, 21 Isaac, 22 Jacob, 23 Levi, 24 Kohath, 25 Amram, 26 Aaron; the last 2/3 of a generation is Eleazar, who was a man of mature years at the time of the Exodus. *2*

************************************* 2. So Noldeke in the Jahrbb. fuer protest. Theol., 1875, p. 344. Genesis xv. 13-16 expressly states that the generation is reckoned as 100 years in this period.
****

Such a chronology is totally at variance with the simplicity of the legend. *1* It is also evident, that if even in the case of the

************************************ 1. "Exact chronological dates are a sure sign of later working up of old poetical legends." Buttmann, I. p. 181.
****

historical books the systematic chronology is no older than the period of the exile, that of the Pentateuch must be of still later origin. For the historical period there were certain fixed points for chronology to lay hold of; it cannot have begun with the patriarchs and gone on to the kings, it must have begun with the kings and then gone higher up to the patriarchs; it must have begun at the lower end, where alone it had any firm ground to stand on. The belief that the men of the early world lived to a great age is no doubt old, but the settled chronology, based on the years in which each patriarch begat his son, is an artifice in which we manifestly see the doctrinaire treatment of history which was coming into vogue for later periods, attempting to lay hold of the earliest legends as well. Only when the living contents of the legend had completely disappeared could its skeleton be used as a framework of chronology.

Buttmann has also shown that the elements of the ten-membered genealogy of Q (Genesis v.) and of the seven-membered of JE (Genesis iv.) are identical. In Q,

Noah comes after Lamech at the end, and at the beginning Adam Cain is doubled and becomes Adam Seth Enos Cainan. Adam and Enos being synonymous, this amounts to Adam Seth Adam Cainan: that is to say Adam Seth are prefixed, and the series begins anew with Enos Cainan, just as in JE. The Priestly Code itself offers a remarkable testimony to the superior originality of the Jehovist genealogy, by ascribing to Lamech, here the ninth in order, the age of 777 years. This can only be explained from JE, where Lamech is seventh in order, and moreover specially connects himself with the number seven by his speech. Cain is avenged seven times, and Lamech seventy times seven. Another circumstance shows Q to be posterior to E. The first man is called here not Ha Adam as in JE, but always Adam, without the article (v. 1-5), a difference which Kuenen pertinently compares with that between ho Xristos and Xristos. But in Q itself (Genesis i.) the first man is only the generic man; if in spite of this he is called simply Adam (Genesis v.), as if that were his proper name, the only way to account for this is to suppose a reminiscence of Genesis ii. iii., though here the personification does not as yet extend to the name.

We come to the story of the flood, Genesis vi.-ix. In JE the flood is well led up to: in Q we should be inclined to ask in surprise how the earth has come all at once to be so corrupted, after being so far in the best of order, did we not know from JE. In omitting the fall, the fratricide of Cain, the sword-song of Lamech, the intercourse of the sons of God with the daughters of men, and parting with the distinctive gloomy colouring which is unmistakably spread over the whole early history of man in JE, the Priestly Code has entirely lost the preparation for the flood, which now appears in the most abrupt and unaccountable way. As to the contents of the story, the priestly version here agrees to an unusual extent with the Jehovistic one; differing from it chiefly in the artificial, mathematical marking out of the framework. The flood lasts twelve months and ten days, *i.e.*, exactly a solar year. It begins in the six hundredth year of Noah, on the seventeenth of the second month, rises for one hundred and fifty days, and begins to fall on the seventeenth of the seventh month. On the first month the tops of the mountains become visible; in the six hundred and first year, on the first of the first month, the water has abated; on the twenty-seventh of the second month the earth is dry. God Himself gives instructions and measurements for the building of the ark, as for the tabernacle: it is to be three stories high, and divided throughout into small compartments; three hundred cubits long, fifty cubits broad, thirty cubits high; and Noah is to make it accurately according to the cubit. When the water is at its height, on the seventeenth of the second month, the flood is fifteen cubits above the highest mountains—Noah having apparently not forgotten, in spite of his anxiety, to heave the lead and to mark the date in his log-book. This prematurely modern measuring and counting cannot be thought by any one to make the narrative more lifelike; it simply destroys the illusion. All that is idyllic and naïve is consistently stripped off the legend as far as possible. As the duration of the flood is advanced from forty days (JE) to a whole year, its area also is immeasurably increased. The Priestly Code states with particular emphasis that it was quite universal, and went over the tops of the highest mountains; indeed it is compelled to take this view by its assumption that the human race was diffused from the first over the whole earth. Such traits as the missions of the birds and the broken-off olive-leaf are passed over: poetic legend is smoothed down into historic prose. But the value and the charm of the story depend on such little traits as these; they are not mere incidents, to poetry they are the most important thing of all. These are the features which are found just in the same way in the Babylonian story of the flood; and if the Jehovist has a much greater affinity with the Babylonian story than the Priestly Code, that shows it to have preserved more faithfully the international character of those early legends. This appears most plainly in his accounting for the flood by the confounding of the boundaries between spirit and flesh, and the intercourse of the sons of God and the daughters of men: the Jehovist here gives us a piece, but little adulterated, of mythical heathenism—a thing quite inconceivable in Q.

The Priestly Code has the rainbow, which the Jehovist, as we now have him, wants. But we have to remember that in Genesis vi.-ix. the Jehovist account is mutilated, but the priestly one preserved entire. If the rainbow occurred both in JE and in Q, one of the accounts of it had to be omitted, and according to the editor's usual procedure the omission had to be from JE. It is accordingly very possible that it was not at first wanting in JE; it agrees better, indeed, with the simple rain, which here brings about the flood, than with the opening of the sluices of heaven and the fountains of the deep, which produce it in Q, and it would stand much better after viii. 21, 22 than after ix. 1-7. In the Priestly Code, moreover, the meaning of the rainbow is half obliterated. On the one hand, the story is clumsily turned into history, and we receive the impression either that the rainbow only appeared in the heavens at this one time after the flood, or that it had been there ever since; on the other hand, it is made the token of the covenant between Elohim and Noah, and the use of language in other passages, with the analogy of Genesis xvii., would point to the covenant described in ix. 1-7: the rainbow would then be the counterpart of circumcision. *1* The covenant,

********************************** 1. The celestial bow is originally the instrument of the arrow-darting God, and therefore a symbol of His hostility; but He lays it out of His hand to signify that He has laid aside His wrath, and it is a token of His reconciliation and favour. When there has been such a storm that one might dread a repetition of the flood, the rainbow appears in heaven, the sun, and grace, breaking forth again. In the 0. T. Q#T has not the meaning of a mere arc, it always means the war-bow. And what is most important of all, the Arabs also always take the iris to be the war-bow of God; Kuzah shoots arrows from his bow, and then hangs it up in the clouds (D. M. Z. 1849, p. 200 seq.). With the Jews and their kin, the rainbow has retained far into Christian times a remarkably near relation to the Deity. It is singular that the Edomites have a God named Kaus, as well as Kuzah. **********************************

i.e., the law of ch. ix. 1-7, a modification of the first ordinance given to Adam (i.229, 30) for the world after the flood which still subsists, is for the Priestly Code the crown, the end, the substance, of the whole narrative. Its interest in the law always completely absorbs the simple interest of its story.

We have also to remark that in this source vengeance for the spilling of blood is not the affair of the relatives but the affair of God; and that it is demanded for man as man, whether master or slave, and no money compensation allowed. The words sound simple and solemn: "Whoso sheddeth man's blood, by man shall his blood be shed: for in the image of God made He man." Yet the religious notion of HUMANITY underlying this sentence is not ancient with the Hebrews any more than with other nations; cf. Genesis iv. 15, 24, and Exodus xxi. 20 seq. *1*

*** 1. De Wette, Beitrage, p. 57. The   religious   notion   of   the   people   is   old. ***

The ark lands, according to Q, on Mount Ararat. In JE, as we have it, no landing-place is named. But this is not original, as mythic geography belongs to the Jehovist in all other passages where it occurs. In Q the primitive history is never localised, the whole earth is given to man for a dwelling from the first. In JE, on the contrary, they live first in the land of Eden far to the East, and presumably high up in the North; expelled from Eden they come to the land of Nod, where Cain builds the town of Enoch, and departing from this district, which is still far to the East, they settle in the land of Shinar, at the mouths of the Euphrates and Tigris, where they build the town of Babel. Shinar is the point of departure of that history of the world which is no longer merely mythical, it is the home of the present human race. In this point the contrast is very noticeable between the local definiteness of the Jehovist legend, which lends it the character of the idyllic, and the vague generalness of the other. In Shinar, according to JE, Genesis xi. 1-9, men are still all together, and they desire to remain together there. Not to be scattered, they build a great city, which is to hold them all; and to make themselves a name, they add to it a high tower which is to reach heaven. Jehovah, perceiving in these attempts the danger of further progress in the same direction, comes down to confound their language, and by such violent means brings about the dispersion of the human race by the unity of which He feels himself threatened. In Q it is understood that men are scattered over the whole earth; they are never represented as all living at one point, and pains are accordingly taken to describe the flood as quite universal. The division of the people comes about quite simply in the way of genealogy, and the division of the languages is not the cause but the result of it. Accompanying this we find once more a notable difference in point of mental attitude; what JE regards as unnatural, and only to be understood as a violent perversion of the original order, is in Q the most natural thing in the world.

The period between the flood and Abraham is filled up in Q by another ten-membered genealogy, which, to judge from the analogy of Genesis iv., had probably only seven members in JE. It cannot have been wanting there, and may have passed straight from Shem to Heber, and left out the grandfather Nahor (x. 21, 24, xxiv. 15, xxix. 5), who is even less to be distinguished from his grandson of the same name than Adam from Enos. The original dwelling-place of the Terahites is, according to Q, not the Mesopotamian Haran (Carrhae), as in JE (xii. 1, xxiv. 4), but Ur Casdim, which can only mean Ur of the Chaldees. From there Terah, the father of Abraham, Nahor, and Haran, is said to have emigrated with Abraham and Lot, the son of Haran, who was already dead. If this was so, Nahor must have stayed at Ur Casdim, and Haran must have died there. But neither of these assumptions is consistent with the indications of the narrative. The different aspirates notwithstanding, it is scarcely allowable to separate the man Haran from the town Haran and to make him die elsewhere. It is equally impossible to regard Ur in Chaldaea as the residence of Nahor, whether the grandfather or the grandson of the same name matters nothing; for it is obviously not without relation to real facts that the place, which in any case must be in Syria, where the Nahorides Laban and Rebecca dwell, is called in J the town of Nahor, and in E Haran. Even in Q though Nahor stays in Ur, Laban and Rebecca do not live in Chaldaea, but in Padan Aram, ie., in Mesopotamian Syria. What helps to show that Ur Casdim does not belong to the original form of the tradition, is that even in Serug the father of Nahor, we are far away from Babylon towards the West. Serug is the name of a district which borders Haran on the North; how can the son of Serug all at once leap back to Ur Casdim? What the reasons were for making Babylon Abraham's point of departure, we need not now consider; but after having left Ur Casdim with Terah, it is curious how he only gets as far as Haran, and stays there till his father's death. In Q also it is from Haran that he enters Palestine. Here, if anywhere, we have in the doubling of the point of departure an attempt to harmonise and to gain a connection with JE.

VII.I.3. The view is happily gaining ground that, in the mythical universal history of mankind in Genesis i.-xi., the Jehovist version is more primitive than the priestly one. And we are, in fact, compelled to adopt this view when we observe that the materials of the narratives in question have not an Israelite, but a universal ethnic origin. The traces of this origin are much more distinctly preserved in the Jehovist, whence it comes that comparative mythology occupies itself chiefly with his narratives, though without knowing that it is doing so. The primitive legend has certainly undergone alterations in his hands too; its mythic character is much obliterated, and all sorts of Israelite elements have crept in. Even the fratricide of Cain, with the contrast in the background between the peaceful life of the Hebrews in the land of Canaan and the restless wanderings of the Cainites (Kenites) in the neighbouring desert, quite falls out of the universal historical and geographical framework. Still more does the curse of Canaan do so; here the trait is evidently old, that Noah was the first to make wine, but this has been made a merely subordinate feature of a pronouncedly national Israelite narrative. But in the Jehovist the process of emptying the primitive legend of its true meaning and contents has not gone nearly so far as in the Priestly Code, where it actually creates surprise when some mythic element shines through, as in the cases of Enoch, and of the rainbow.

The mythic materials of the primitive world-history are suffused in the Jehovist with a peculiar sombre earnestness, a kind of antique philosophy of history, almost bordering on pessimism: as if mankind were groaning under some dreadful weight, the pressure not so much of sin as of creaturehood (vi. 1-4). We notice a shy, timid spirit, which belongs more to heathenism. The rattling of the chains at intervals only aggravates the feeling of confinement that belongs to human nature; the gulf of alienation between man and God is not to be bridged over. Jehovah does not stand high enough, does not feel Himself secure enough, to allow the earth-dwellers to come very near Him; there is almost a suggestion of the notion of the jealousy of the gods. This mood, though in many ways softened, is yet recognisable enough in

265

Genesis ii. iii., in vi. 1-4, and xi. 1-9. In the Priestly Code it has entirely disappeared; here man no longer feels himself under a secret curse, but allied to God and free, as lord of nature. True, the Priestly Code also recognises in its own fashion the power of sin—this we saw in the chapter on sacrifice; but sin as the root of ruin, explaining it and capable of being got rid of, is the very opposite of blind, not-to-be-averted fate. The slavery of sin and the freedom of the children of God are in the Gospel correlated. The mythical mode of view is destroyed by the autonomy of morality; and closely connected with this is the rational way of looking at nature, of which we find the beginnings in the Priestly Code. This view of nature presupposes that man places himself as a person over and outside of nature, which he regards as simply a thing. We may perhaps assert that were it not for this dualism of Judaism, mechanical natural science would not exist.

The removal of colour from the myths is the same thing as the process of Hebraising them. The Priestly Code appears to Hebraise less than the Jehovist; it refrains on principle from confounding different times and customs. But in fact it Hebraises much more: it cuts and shapes the whole of the materials so that they may serve as an introduction to the Mosaic legislation. It is true that the Jehovist also placed these ethnic legends at the entrance to his sacred legend, and perhaps selected them with a view to their forming an introduction to it; for they are all ethical and historical in their nature, and bear on the problems of the world of man, and not the world of nature. *1*

*********************************** 1 Yet it is possible the selection presented him with no difficulty, since cosmological myths were not popular tales, but priestly speculations, with which he was quite unacquainted. **********************************

But with the Jehovist justice was yet done to some extent to the individuality of the different narratives: in the Priestly Code their individuality is not only modified to suit the purpose of the whole, but completely destroyed. The connection leading up to the Torah of Moses is everything, the individual pieces have no significance but this. It follows of course from this mode of treatment that the connection itself loses all living reality; it consists, apart from the successive covenants, in mere genealogy and chronology. De Wette thinks all this beautiful because it is symmetrical and intelligible, and leads well up to a conclusion. But this will not be every one's taste; there is such a thing as poetical material without manufacture.

How loosely the narratives of the primitive history are connected with each other in the Jehovist we see very clearly in the section dealing with the flood. It disagrees both with what goes before and with what follows it. The genealogy Genesis iv. 16-24 issues not in Noah but in Lamech; instead of Shem, Ham, and Japhet, the sons of Noah, we have Jabal, Jubal, Tubal, the sons of Lamech, as the inaugurators of the second period. We have also the characteristic difference, that Shem, Ham, and Japhet give us a division of mankind according to nations, while Jabal, Jubal, Tubal give a division according to guilds, which are necessarily those of the same people, as no people consists entirely of musicians or entirely of smiths. And it is

266

undoubtedly the aim of chapter iv. 16 seq. to describe the origin of the present civilisation, not of that which is extinct, having been destroyed by the flood. Tubal-Cain is the father of the smiths of the present, not of those before the flood; Jubal the father of the musicians, Jabal of the shepherds of the narrator's own period; hence they stand at the end of the genealogy and open the second period. But as Genesis iv. 16-24 does not look forward to the flood, so neither does Genesis xi. 1-9 (the building of the tower of Babel) look back to it. This piece is obviously not the continuation of chapter x. That chapter brought us to a point at which the earth was occupied by different peoples and different tongues; and here (xi. 1) we are suddenly carried back to a time when the whole earth was of one language and one speech. Can this have been the time when Noah's family made up the whole population of the earth? or in other words, does xi. 1-9 go back before chap x. and join on to vi.-ix.? Manifestly not: "the whole earth" (xi. 1) is not merely Shem and Ham and Japhet; the multitude of men who seek by artificial means to concentrate themselves, and are then split up into different peoples, cannot consist of only one family. The point of view is quite different from what it would be if chaps. vi.-ix. were taken into account; the narrator knows nothing of the flood, which left Noah's family alone surviving out of the whole world. Nor would it avail to place xi. 1 at a period so long subsequent to the flood that the family might have increased again to a great people; even this would not give the requisite connection with the idea of Noah and his three sons. If the latter united themselves afterwards in one family, and one coherent people thus grew out of them, which was then split up by a higher power into different languages, then Shem, Ham, and Japhet entirely lose their significance as the great heads of the nations.

The fact is simply this, that the whole section of the flood (Genesis vi.-ix.) is an isolated piece without any connection with the rest of the narrative of the Jehovist. Another strange erratic boulder is the intercourse of the sons of God with the daughters of men (Genesis vi. 1-4). *l* The connection between

this piece and the story of the flood which follows it, is of the loosest; and it is in entire disagreement with the preceding part of the Jehovist narrative, as it tells of a second fall of man, with a point of view morally and mentally so different from that of the first, that this story can in no wise be regarded as supplementing or continuing that one. In Genesis vi. 1-4 morality has nothing to do with the guilt that is incurred. We have further examples which illustrate the fragmentary character of the Jehovist primitive history as we have it, in the story of the fratricide of Cain, and the curse of Canaan, which indeed ought not to be here at all, but belong by rights to the history of the patriarchs.

We may close this section by reproducing the words in which Buttmann (i. 208 seq.) indicates his disagreement with De Wette in regard to the treatment of the early legends of the Bible: they are well worth noting. "Thoroughly familiar with the antiquities of the race in whose sacred writings these monuments have been preserved to us, De Wette recognises and follows the national spirit of that race in their most ancient records. In this way he discovers amidst these ruins the thread of an old connection, a kind of epos, the theme of which was the glorification of the people of Israel, a theme which finds a prelude even in the primitive history of the human race. This view is of the first importance for the object he has before him, which is the true criticism of these books; and for the moment other considerations must necessarily yield to it. My object in this whole investigation is only to find the universal element in the legends of different nations, and especially to discover what is common property in the myths of the different branches of the great family of nations to which the Hebrews and the Greeks and we ourselves alike belong. Thus each myth reveals itself to me as existing for itself, having a basis and completeness of its own, and even when I find it in other nations I at once assert for it its character as already known to me. Thus De Wette and I come to differ in the view we take of individual myths. To him they commonly appear as spontaneous free inventions of individual men for their own purposes; not in the ignoble sense in which the vulgar view speaks of the religious narratives of ancient peoples, but free inventions in which there is no intention to deceive. I, on the contrary, can allow no invention in these oldest portions of mythology. A true myth is never invented; it is handed down. It is not true, but it is honest. From small elements which fancy offered as true, these myths arose and grew, without any contributor to their growth feeling that he had of himself added to them. Those only had any conscious intention in the matter, who touched up the oldest pure myths, and drew them into the great circle of their national history; and their intention, though conscious, was quite innocent and harmless, as De Wette describes it. Now De Wette sees the chief traces of that unity, or of that national epos which winds its way through the Mosaic history, in the Elohim document. For his critical purpose, therefore, this document is the most important, and it he for the most part follows. My aim forbids me to attend to anything but the inner completeness of the stories taken one by one, and this I see most clearly in the Jehovah fragments; whence I have had to yield the preference to them in the foregoing discussions. Should each of us attain his end, our views will excellently supplement each other."

We may add that just that linked unity of its narrative, which has procured for the Priestly Code the title of the "mainstock," shows that it presents us with a more developed form of the myths; while the Jehovist, just because of the defective connection (in form) of his "fragments," which long caused him to be regarded as a mere filler-up of the fundamental work, must be judged to stand nearer to the fountain.

VIII.II.

VIII.II.1. In the history of the patriarchs also, the outlines of the narrative are the same in Q and in JE. We find in both Abraham's immigration into Canaan with Sarah and Lot, his separation from Lot, the birth of Ishmael by Hagar, the appearance of God for the promise of Isaac, Isaac's birth, the death of Sarah and Abraham, Ishmael, Isaac's marriage with Rebecca, Jacob and Esau, Jacob's journey to Mesopotamia and the foundation of his family there, his return, Esau, Joseph in

268

Egypt, Jacob in Egypt, Jacob's blessing on Joseph and his other sons, his death and burial. The materials here are not mythical but national, and therefore more transparent, and in a certain sense more historical. It is true, we attain to no historical knowledge of the patriarchs, but only of the time when the stories about them arose in the Israelite people; this later age is here unconsciously projected, in its inner and its outward features, into hoar antiquity, and is reflected there like a glorified mirage. The skeleton of the patriarchal history consists, it is well known, of ethnographic genealogy. The Leah-tribes are connected with the Rachel-tribes under the common father Jacob-Israel: then entire Israel is connected with the people of Edom under the old name of Isaac (Amos vii 9, 16). Isaac again is connected under Abraham with Lot, the father of Moab and Ammon. All these nearly related and once closely allied Hebrew tribes are shown to be intimately connected with the inhabitants of the Mesopotamian desert, and sharply marked off from the Canaanites, in whose land they dwelt. The narrative speaks of its characters as succeeding each other in time or contemporary; in this form it indicates logical or statistical subordination and co-ordination. As a fact the elements are generally older than the groups and the smaller groups than the greater. The migrations which are mentioned of peoples and tribes are necessary consequences of the assumed relationship. It would be quite possible to present the composition and relative position of any given people at a given time in a similar way in the form of a genealogical early history. True genealogy can scarcely represent precisely the existing relations. It cannot always be determined as a matter of fact whether a tribe is the cousin or the brother or the twin-brother of another tribe, or whether there is any affinity at all between the two; the affinity can be understood and interpreted in different ways, the grouping always depends to some extent on the point of view of the genealogist, or even on his likings and antipathies. The reason why the Arameans are made so nearly related to the Israelites is probably that the patriarchal legend arose in Middle and North Israel; as indeed the pronounced preference shown for Rachel and Joseph clearly proves to have been the case. Did the legend belong originally to Judah, it is likely that more prominence would be given to the Cainite (Kenite) tribes of the peninsula of Sinai, which, as it is, are too much thrust into the background; for there can be no doubt that in the earliest history of Israel these tribes were of no small importance. Nor are apparent contradictions wanting in the ethnographic genealogy. Ishmael, Edom, and the Cainite tribes first mentioned, come into mutual contact in different ways, which may be quite naturally explained from different views and arrangements of their mutual relationships. And lastly we may add that the genealogical form lends itself to the reception of every sort of materials. In the patriarchal legend, however, the ethnographic element is always predominant. Abraham alone is certainly not the name of a people like Isaac and Lot: he is somewhat difficult to interpret. That is not to say that in such a connection as this we may regard him as a historical person; he might with more likelihood be regarded as a free creation of unconscious art. He is perhaps the youngest figure in the company, and it was probably at a comparatively late period that he was put before his son Isaac. *1*

** 1. The stories about Abraham and those about Isaac are so similar, that they cannot possibly be held to be independent of each other. The stories about Isaac, however, are more original, as may be seen in a striking way on comparing Genesis xx. 2-16 with xxvi 6-12. The short nnd profane version, of which Isaac is the hero, is more lively and pointed; the long and edifying version in which Abraham replaces Isaac, makes the danger not possible but actual, thus necessitating the intervention of the Deity and so bringing about a glorification of the patriarch, which he little deserved. All the commentators on Genesis indeed, regard chapter xx. as the original of xxvi.; they do not base their judgment, however, on a comparison of the parallel passages, but merely consider that as the father is older than the son, the story about the father is older than the corresponding story about the son; and they regard Isaac generally as a mere echo of Abraham. The obviousness of this principle is too great, and against it we have to consider that the later development of the legend shows a manifest tendency to make Abraham the patriarch par excellence and cast the others into the shade. In the earlier literature, on the other hand, Isaac is mentioned even by Amos, Abraham first appears in Isaiah xl.-lxvii. Micah vii 20 belongs to the exile, and the words "who redeemed Abraham" in Isaiah xxix. 22 are not genuine; they have no possible position in the sentence, and the idea of the salvation of Abraham (from the fire of the Chaldaeans) is of late occurrence. I certainly do not mean to maintain that Abraham was not yet known when Amos wrote; but he scarcely stood by this time at the same stage as Isaac and Jacob. As a saint of Hebron he might he of Calibite ordain, and have something to do with Ram (1Chronicles ii.). Abram may stand for Abiram, as Abner for Abiner and Ahab for Ahiab. The name Abu Ruham occurs in the Hadith as *nomen proprium viri.* **

In the Jehovist this skeleton of ethnographic genealogy is found covered throughout with flesh and blood. The patriarchs, Abraham, Isaac, and Jacob, are not mere names, but living forms, ideal prototypes of the true Israelite. They are all peace-loving shepherds, inclined to live quietly beside their tents, anxious to steer clear of strife and clamour, in no circumstances prepared to meet force with force and oppose injustice with the sword. Brave and manly they are not, but they are good fathers of families, a little under the dominion of their wives, who are endowed with more temper. They serve Jehovah in essentially the same way as their descendants in historical times; religion with them does not consist of sacrifice alone, but also of an upright conversation and trustful resignation to God's providence. Jacob is sketched with a more realistic touch than the other two; he has a strong dash of artifice and desire of gain, qualities which do not fail to secure the ends he aims at. He escapes from every difficulty and danger, not only safely but with profit: Jehovah helps him, but above all he helps himself, without showing, as we should judge, any great scruple in his choice of means. The stories about him do not pretend to be moral, the feeling they betray is in fact that of undissembled joy in all the successful artifices and tricks of the patriarchal rogue. Of the subordinate figures Esau is drawn with some liking for him, then Laban, and the weak-kneed saint, Lot. Ishmael is drawn as the prototype of the Bedouin, as a wild ass of a man, whose hand is against every man, and every man's hand against him.

It is remarkable that the heroes of Israelite legend show so little taste for war, and in this point they seem to be scarcely a true reflection of the character of the Israelites as known from their history. Yet it is not difficult to understand that a people which found itself incessantly driven into war, not only dreamed of an eternal peace in the future, but also embodied the wishes of its heart in these peaceful forms of the golden age in the past. We have also to consider that the peaceful shepherd life of the patriarchs is necessary to the idyllic form in which the early history of the people is cast; only peoples or tribes can make war, not single men. / This also must serve to explain why

*** 1. This consideration is certainly less decisive than the foregoing one. Jacob is a peaceful shepherd, not only because of the idyllic form of the narrative, but in his own being and character. He forms the strongest contrast to his brother Esau, who in spite of the idyllic form is a man of war. Such exceptions as Genesis xiv. and xlviii.'22 (chapter xxxiv.) only prove the rule. ***

the historical self-consciousness of the nation finds so little expression in the personal character of the patriarchs. It makes vent for itself only in the inserted prophecies of the future; in these we trace that national pride which was the fruit of the exploits of David, yet always in a glorified form, rising to religious exaltation.

In the traits of personal character ascribed to the patriarchs they represent substantially the nature and the aspirations of the individual Israelite. The historic-political relations of Israel are reflected with more life in the relations borne by the patriarchs to their brothers; cousins, and other relatives. The background is never long concealed here, the temper of the period of the kings is everywhere discernible. This is the case most clearly perhaps in the story about Jacob and Esau. The twins are at variance, even in the womb; even in the matter of his birth the younger refuses precedence to the elder, and tries to hold him back by the heel. This is interpreted to the anxious mother by the oracle at Beersheba as follows: "Two nations are in thy womb, and two peoples are separated from thy bowels, and the one people shall be stronger than the other, and the elder shall serve the younger." The boys grow up very different. Esau is a rough and sunburnt hunter, ranges about in the desert, and lives from day to day without care: Jacob, a pious, smooth man, stays at home beside the tents, and understands the value of things which his unsophisticated brother disregards. The former is the favourite of his father, the autochthonous Isaac, the latter is preferred by the mother, the Aramaean Rebecca; the former stays in his own land and takes his wives from the original population of south Canaan and the Sinaitic peninsula, the latter emigrates, and brings his wives from Mesopotamia. Thus the contrast is distinctly prefigured, which at a later time appeared, between the rough Edom, sprung from the soil and having his roots in it, and smoother, more civilised Israel, which had more affinity with the great powers of the world. By means of deceit and trickery the younger brother succeeds in depriving the elder of the paternal blessing and of the right of the first-born; the elder, in consequence of this, determines to kill him, and the situation becomes strained. Edom was a people and a kingdom before Israel, but was then overshadowed by Israel, and even subjugated at last by David: hence the fierce hatred between the brother nations, of which Amos speaks. The words of the blessing of Jacob show this quite distinctly to be the historical basis of the legend, a basis of which the Jews were perfectly conscious: we hear in the blessing of repeated attempts of the Edomites to cast off the yoke of Israel, and it is predicted that these efforts will be at last successful.

Thus the stories about Jacob and Esau cannot have taken form even in outline, before the time of David; in their present form (Genesis xxvii. 40) their outlook extends to times still later. The roots of the legend being thus traceable in later history, a circumstance which the Jehovist does not attempt to conceal, it is no more than an apparent anachronism when he takes occasion to give a complete list of the Edomite kings down to David, interspersing it with historical notes, as, for example, that Hadad ben Bedad (possibly a contemporary of Gideon) defeated the Midianites on the plains of Moab. In the story of Jacob and Laban, again, the contemporary background shines through the patriarchal history very distinctly. The Hebrew, on his half-migration, half-flight from Mesopotamia to the land of Jordan, is hotly pursued by his Aramean father-in-law, who overtakes him at Gilead. There they treat with each other and pile up a heap of stones, which is to be the boundary between them, and which they mutually pledge themselves not to overstep with hostile intentions. This answers to the actual state of the facts. The Hebrew migration into Canaan was followed by the Aramaean, which threatened to overwhelm it. Gilead was the boundary between the two peoples, and the arena, during a long period, of fierce conflicts which they waged with each other. The blessing of Jacob, in the oracle on Joseph, also mentions the Syrian wars: the archers who press Joseph hard, but are not able to overcome him, can be no other than the Arameans of Damascus, to whose attacks he was exposed for a whole century. Joseph here appears always as the pillar of the North-Israelite monarchy, the wearer of the crown among his brethren, a position for which he was marked out by his early dreams. The story of Joseph, however, in so far as historical elements can be traced in it at all, and not merely the free work of poetry, is based on much earlier events, from a time when the union was just being accomplished of the two sections which together became the people of Israel. The trait of his brother's jealousy of him points perhaps to later events. *1*

** 1. It deserves to be considered that at first Joseph is in Egypt alone, and that his brothers came after, at his request. When the notion of united Israel was transferred to the distant past, one consequence was that the fortunes of the part could not be separated from those of the whole. In the same way, Rachel being an Aramaean, Leah must be one too. Perhaps the combination of Rachel and Leah in a national unity was only accomplished by Moses. Moses came from the peninsula of Sinai (Leah) to lead the Israelites there from Goshen (Joseph). The designation of Levite he could not receive in Joseph, only in Leah. ***

The historical associations which form the groundwork of the stories of the other sons of Jacob are also comparatively old. They afford us almost the only information we possess about the great change which must have taken place in the league of the tribes soon after Moses. This change principally affected the group of the four old Leah tribes which were closely connected with each other. Reuben assumes the rights of his father prematurely and loses the leadership. Simeon and Levi make, apart from the others, a faithless attack on the Canaanites, and collective Israel lets them suffer the consequences alone, so that they succumb to the vengeance of their enemies and cease to be tribes. Hence the primogeniture is transferred to Judah. Judah also suffers great losses, no doubt in the conflict which accompanied the settlement in the land of Canaan, and is reduced to a fraction of his former importance. But this breach is made good by fresh accessions from the mother-stock of the Leah tribes, by the union of Pharez and Zarah, *i.e.* of Caleb, Kenaz, Cain (Ken), Jerahmeel, with the remnant of ancient Judah. The Jehovist narratives about Reuben, Simeon, Levi, and Judah, are undoubtedly based on occurrences connected with the period of the conquest of the holy land; but this is not the place to trace the historical interpretation of the stories further. *1*

*** 1. See "Israel," sec. 2, infra. Genesis iv. 1-15 is a similar tribal history. The old tribe of Cain, the name of which is indicative of settlement and culture, appears to have been broken up and scattered to the four winds in very early times (Judges v. 24) in the same way as Levi, with which it appears to have divided the priesthood. We have already said that Genesis iv. 1-15 can only have found its way into the primitive legend by interpolation. ***

It may, however, be remarked, and it is important to do so, that even where true historic motives are indisputably present in the patriarchal legend, it is not exactly a reproduction of the facts as they occurred. In reality Edom always kept up his hatred against Israel and suppressed his feeling of relationship (Amos i. 11); in Genesis he meets his brother returning from Mesopotamia, and trembling with anxiety at the encounter, in a conciliatory temper which is quite affecting. The touch is one to reflect no small honour on the ancient Israelite. To set against this we have the touch, manifestly inspired by hatred, of Genesis xix. 30-38. No one can fail to wonder why the daughters of Lot are nameless, but this shows that they are inserted between Lot and his sons Moab and Ammon purely for the sake of the incest. Sympathies and antipathies are everywhere at work, and the standpoint is throughout that of Northern Israel, as appears most evidently from the circumstance that Rachel is the fair and the beloved wife of Jacob, whom alone in fact he wished to marry, and Leah the ugly and despised one who was imposed on him by a trick. *2. On the whole, the rivalries*

*** 2 This, however, only warrants us to conclude that these legends first arose in Ephraim, not that they were written down there in the form in which we have them. ***

which really existed are rather softened than exaggerated in this poetical illustration of them; what tends to unity is more prominent and is more carefully treated than what tends to separation. There is no trace of any side glances at persons and events of the day, as, *e.g.*, at the unseemly occurrences at the court of David, and as little of any twisting or otherwise doctoring the materials to make them advance this or that tendency.

But these stories would be without point were it not for other elements which enter into them and attach them to this and that particular locality. In this aspect we have first of all to consider that the patriarchs are regarded as the founders of the popular worship at Shechem, Bethel, Beersheba, and Hebron, as we saw above, *I.II.1.* *"In perfect correspondence..."*. A whole series of stories about them are cultus-myths; in these they discover by means of a theophany that a certain spot of earth is holy ground; there they erect an altar, and give it the name of the place. They dwell exclusively at places which were afterwards regarded as primeval sanctuaries and inaugurate the sacrifices which are offered there. The significance of these stories is entirely bound up with the locality; they possess an interest only for those who still sacrifice to Jehovah on the same altar as Abraham once did, under the same sacred oak of Moreh or Mamre. In the same way the patriarchs discover or excavate the caves, or springs, or wells, and plant the trees, which their posterity still count sacred or at least honourable, after the lapse of thousands of years. In some cases also striking or significant formations of the earth's surface receive a legendary explanation from the patriarchal age. Were the Dead Sea not there, Sodom and Gomorrha would not have perished; were there not a small flat tongue of land projecting into the marsh from the south-east, Lot would have directed his flight straight to the mountains of his sons Moab and Ammon, and would not have made the detour by Zoar, which only serves to explain why this corner was not included in the ruin to the area of which it properly belongs. The pillar of salt into which Lot's wife was turned was still pointed out in the days of Josephus; perhaps the smoke of the furnace which Abraham saw from the Jewish shore the morning after the catastrophe has some connection with the town of the same name which was situated there. *1*

** 1 Joshua HNB#N xv. 62 is no doubt more correctly HKB#N: the name, having the article prefixed to it, must be susceptible of a clear meaning. **

The origin of Mount Gilead is explained from its historical significance: it is an immense mound which was once heaped up by Laban and Jacob in order to serve as a boundary between Aram and Israel. In many instances the names of places gave rise to a legend which does not always hit upon the true reason of the name. The spring of Lahai Roi, for example, is an instance of this. The discovery of this spring saved Hagar and Ishmael from dying of thirst. Hagar called the name of Jehovah who spoke with her, El Roi (God of Seeing), for she said, "Have I seen God, and am I kept in life after my seeing?" Wherefore the well is called Beer Lahai Roi (he lives who sees me); it is between Kadesh and Berdan. According to Judges xv. 18-20, 2Samuel xxiii. 11, a more correct interpretation of Lahai Roi would be " jawbone of the antelope "—this being the appearance presented by a series of rocky teeth standing close together there. *1*

********************************** 1 Compare Onugnathos and the camel's jawbone in Vakidi, op. cit. p. 298, note 2: Jakut iv. 353, 9 seq. R)Y is an obsolete name of an animal. For HLM, Genesis xvi. 15, we should read)LHYM (cf. 1Samuel iii. 13), and before)XRY we should probably insert W)XY. **********************************

The original motive of the legend, however, as we have now indicated it, appears in the Jehovist always and everywhere covered over with the many-coloured robe of fancy. The longer a story was spread by oral tradition among the people, the more was its root concealed by the shoots springing from it. For example, we may assume with regard to the story of Joseph that, just because it has almost grown into a romance, its origin stretches back to a remote antiquity. The popular fancy plays as it will; yet it does not make such leaps as to make it impossible to trace its course. Miracles, angels, theophanies, dreams, are never absent from the palette. When Rachel eats the mandrakes which Reuben had found, and which Leah had given up to her, and they remove her barrenness so that she becomes the mother of Joseph, we have a story based on a vulgar superstition. Purely mythical elements are found isolated in the story of Jacob's wrestling with the Deity at the ford of the Jabbok. Etymology and proverbs are a favourite motive, and often give rise to lively and diversified tales. Even in pieces which we should be inclined to attribute to the art of individuals, old and characteristic themes may be involved. The story of Jacob and Laban, for example, is entirely composed of such materials. The courtship at the well is twice repeated with no great variation. The trait of the father-in-law's wish to get his oldest daughter first off his hands and craftily bringing her to the son-in-law after the wedding-feast, is scarcely due to the invention of an individual. The shepherd's tricks, by which Jacob colours the sheep as he likes, have quite the flavour of a popular jest. The observance of hospitality or transgressions against it, occupy a prominent place in the Genesis of the Jehovist; Lot's entertainment, and the Sodomites' insulting maltreatment, of the Deity who comes among them in disguise, is an incident that appears in the legends of many races. There is little psychological embellishment, little actual making-up; for the most part we have the product of a countless number of narrators, unconsciously modifying each other's work. How plastic and living the materials must have been even in the ninth and eighth century, we see from the manifold variants and repetitions of the same stories, which, however, scarcely change the essential character of the themes.

One more trait must be added to the character of the Jehovist. Each of his narratives may be understood by itself apart from the rest; the genealogy serves merely to string them together; their interest and significance is not derived from the connection in which they stand. Many of them have a local colour which bespeaks a local origin; and how many of them are in substance inconsistent with each other, and stand side by side only by compulsion! The whole literary character and loose connection of the Jehovist story of the patriarchs reveals how gradually its different elements were brought together, and how little they have coalesced to a unity. In this point the patriarchal history of the Jehovist, stands quite on the same footing with his legend of the origins of the human race, the nature of which we have already demonstrated.

VIII.II.2. It is from the Jehovistic form of the legends that we derive our picture of the patriarchs, that picture which children learn at school and which they find it easy to retain. To compare the parallel of the Priestly Code it is necessary to restore it as a whole, for few are aware of the impression it produces.

"And Abram was seventy-five years old when he departed out of Haran. And Abram took Sarai his wife, and Lot his brother's son, and all their substance that they had gathered, and the souls that they had gotten in Haran, and they went forth to go into the land of Canaan, and into the land of Canaan they came (xii. 4b, 5). And the land was not able to bear them that they might dwell together, for their substance was great so that they could not dwell together. And they separated themselves the one from the other; Abram dwelled in the land of Canaan, and Lot dwelled in the cities of the Kikkar. *1*

** 1. Where the Dead Sea was afterwards. **

And it came to pass when God destroyed the cities of the Kikkar, that God remembered Abram, and sent Lot out of the midst of the overthrow-, when he overthrew the cities in which Lot dwelt... (xiii. 6, 11b, 12ab, xix. 29). And Sarai was barren: she had no child. And Sarai, Abram's wife, took Hagar the Egyptian, her maid, after Abram had dwelt ten years in the land of Canaan, and gave her to her husband Abram to be his wife. And Hagar bare Abram a son; and Abram called his son's name which Hagar bare, Ishmael. And Abram was eighty-six years old when Hagar bare Ishmael to Abram" (xi. 30, xvi. 3, 15, 16) Then follows the covenant of God with Abram, whose name he now changes to Abraham, and the institution of circumcision as the mark of those who belong to the covenant; then the announcement of the birth of Isaac by Sarai, now ninety years old, who is henceforth to be called Sarah, and Isaac's nomination as heir of the covenant in place of Ishmael (chapter xvii.). "And Sarah bore Abraham a son at the set time of which God had spoken to him. And Abraham called the name of his son that was born unto him, whom Sarah bare to him, Isaac. And Abraham circumcised his son Isaac, after eight days, as God had commanded him. And Abraham was an hundred years old when Isaac his son was born unto him (xxi. 2-5). And the life of Sarah was an hundred and twenty seven years; these were the years of the life of Sarah. And Sarah died in Kirjath-Arba, the same is Hebron in the land of Canaan" (xxiii. 1, 2). Then comes the treaty of Abraham, reported with all due legal accuracy, with Ephron the Hittite, from whom he purchases the cave of Machpelah, which is over against Mamre, for a family burying-place (xxiii.). "And these are the days of the years of Abraham's life which he lived, a hundred and seventy five years. And Abraham gave up the ghost, and died in a good old age, an old man and full of years; and was gathered to his fellow tribesmen. And his sons Isaac and Ishmael buried him in the cave of Machpelah, in the field of Ephron ben Zohar the Hittite, which is before Mamre; the field which Abraham purchased of the sons of Heth; there was Abraham buried and Sarah his wife. And after Abraham was dead, God blessed his son Isaac" (xxv. 7-11a). Next come the Toledoth (generations) of Ishmael according to the regular practice of first exhausting the collaterals (xxv. 12-17). "These are the Toledoth of Isaac the son of Abraham. Abraham begat Isaac...and Isaac was 40 years old when he took Rebecca to wife, the daughter of Bethuel the Syrian of Padan Aram, the sister to Laban the Syrian....And Isaac was 60 years old when Esau and Jacob were born (xxv. 19, 20, 26c). And Esau was 40 years old when he took to wife Judith the daughter of Beeri the Hittite, and Bashemath, the daughter of Elon the Hittite, and they were a grief of mind unto Isaac and to Rebekah. And Rebekah said to Isaac, I am weary of my life because of the daughters of Heth; if Jacob also take such wives of the daughters of Heth, of the daughters of the land, what good shall my life do to me? Then Isaac called Jacob and blessed him and charged him, saying, Thou shalt not take a wife of the daughters of Canaan; arise, go to Padan-Aram to the house of Bethuel thy mother's father, and take thee a wife from thence of the daughters of Laban thy mother's brother. And El Shaddai will bless thee, and make thee fruitful and multiply thee, and give thee the blessing of Abraham, to thee and to thy seed with thee, that thou mayest inherit the land wherein thou art a stranger, which God gave unto Abraham. And Isaac sent away Jacob, and he went to Padan-Aram unto Laban ben Bethuel, the Syrian, the brother of Rebecca, Jacob and Esau's mother. And Esau saw that Isaac blessed Jacob, and sent him to Padan-Aram to take him a wife from thence, and that as he blessed him, he gave him a charge, saying, Thou shalt not take a wife of the daughters of Canaan. Now Jacob hearkened to his father, and went to Padan-Aram. But Esau saw that the daughters of Canaan pleased not Isaac his father; then went Esau unto Ishmael, and took unto the wives which he had Mahalath the sister of Nebaioth to be his wife (xxvi. 34 seq., xxvii. 46, xxviii. 1-9). And Laban gave unto his daughter Leah Zilpah his maid for her handmaid. And he gave him Rachel his daughter to wife. And Laban gave to Rachel his daughter Bilhah his handmaid to be her maid (xxix.24, 28b, 29). And the sons of Jacob were twelve. The sons of Leah: Reuben, Jacob's firstborn, Simeon, Judah, Issachar, Zebulun. The sons of Rachel: Joseph and Benjamin. The sons of Bilhah, Rachel's handmaid: Dan and Naphtali. The sons of Zilpah, Leah's handmaid: Gad and Asher; these are the sons of Jacob, which were born to him in Padan-Aram (xxxv. 23-26)....[and Jacob took] all his goods which he had gotten, the gear of his property which he had gotten in Padan-Aram, to go home to Isaac his father in the land of Canaan (xxx). 18). And God appeared unto Jacob when he was coming home from Padan-Aram, and blessed him; and God said unto him, Thy name is Jacob; thy name shall not be called any more Jacob, but Israel shall be thy name. And God said unto him; I am El Shaddai; be fruitful and multiply; a nation and a company of nations shall be of thee, and kings shall come out of thy loins; and the land which I gave Abraham and Isaac, to thee will I give it, and to thy seed after thee will I give the land. And God went up from him in the place where He talked with him. And Jacob called the name of the place where God spake with him Bethel (xxxv. 9-13, 15). And they departed from Bethel; and when there was but a little way to come unto Ephrath, Rachel died, and was buried there in the way to Ephrath; the same is Bethlehem (xxxv. 16a, 19, cf. xlviii. 7, xlix. 3I). And Jacob came unto Isaac his father unto Mamre, unto Kirjath-Arba, which is Hebron, where Abraham and Isaac dwelt as strangers. And the days of Isaac were a hundred and eighty years. And Isaac gave up the ghost, and died, and was gathered unto his people, being old and full of days; and his sons Esau and Jacob buried him" (xxxv. 27-29.) Then follow the generations of Esau in chapter xxxvi. *1*

************************************ 1. Only part of this chapter, however, belongs to the Priestly Code. ************************************

"And Esau took his wives, and his sons, and his daughters, and all the souls of his house, and his cattle, and all his beasts, and all his substance, which he had got in the land of Canaan, and went into the land of Seir from the face of his brother Jacob.

For their riches were more than that they might dwell together, and the land of their sojourn could not bear them because of their cattle. And Esau dwelt in Mount Seir; Esau is Edom. And Jacob dwelt in the land of the sojourn of his father, in the land of Canaan (xxxvi. 6-8, xxxvii. 1). These are the Toledoth of Jacob...(xxxxvii. 2). And they took their cattle, and their goods, which they had gotten in the land of Canaan, and came into Egypt, Jacob and all his seed with him, his sons, and his sons' sons, and all his seed, brought he with him into Egypt" (xlvi. 6, 7). Then follows the enumeration of the seventy souls of which his seed was then composed. "And Jacob and his sons came to Egypt to Joseph; and Pharaoh the king of Egypt heard it. And Pharaoh said to Jacob, How many are the days of the years of thy life? And Jacob said to Pharaoh, The days of the years of my sojourning are a hundred and thirty years; few and evil have the days of the years of my life been, and have not attained unto the days of the years of the life of my fathers, in the days of their sojourning. And Joseph placed his father and his brethren, and gave them a possession in the land of Egypt, in the best part of the land, in the land of Rameses, as Pharaoh had commanded (xlvii. 5b, 6, LXX, xlvii. 7-11). And they settled there, and grew and multiplied exceedingly. And Jacob lived in the land of Egypt seventeen years, and the whole age of Jacob was 7 years and 140 years (xlvii. 27b, 28)....And Jacob said unto Joseph, El Shaddai appeared unto me at Luz, in the land of Canaan, and blessed me, and said unto me, Behold, I will make thee fruitful and multiply thee, and I will make of thee a multitude of peoples; and will give this land to thy seed after thee for an everlasting possession. And now thy two sons which were born unto thee in Egypt, before I came unto thee in Egypt, are mine; Ephraim and Manasseh shall be mine, as Reuben and Simeon. And the issue which thou begettest after them shall be thine, and shall be called after the name of their brethren in their inheritance. And when I came from Padan, Rachel died to me in the land of Canaan, in the way, when there was but a little way to come into Ephrath, and I buried her there, in the way to Ephrath; the same is Bethlehem (xlviii. 3-7, and v. 7, cf. xlix. 31)...[and his other sons also] he blessed; and he charged them, and said unto them, I am to be gathered unto my people, bury me with my fathers in the cave of the field of Machpelah, which is before Mamre, in the land of Canaan, which field Abraham bought from Ephron the Hittite, for a hereditary burying-place-there they buried Abraham and Sarah his wife, there they buried Isaac and Rebekah his wife, and there I buried Leah—the possession of the field and of the cave that is therein from the children of Heth. And Jacob made an end of commanding his sons, and he gathered up his feet into the bed, and yielded up the ghost, and was gathered unto his fellow-tribesmen (xlix. 28b-33). And his sons carried him into the land of Canaan, and buried him in the cave of the field of Machpelah, which Abraham had bought for a hereditary burying-place from Ephron the Hittite, over against Mamre (l. 12, 13). And these are the names of the children of Israel which came into Egypt, with Jacob they came, every one with his house; Reuben, Simeon, Levi, Judah, Issachar, Zebulon, Benjamin, Dan, Naphtali, Gad, Asher. And all the souls that came out of Jacob's loins were seventy souls; and Joseph was in Egypt. And the children of Israel were fruitful and increased abundantly, and the land was filled with them, and the Egyptians made the children of Israel their servants with rigour, in all their work which they wrought by them with rigour, and they made their lives bitter with hard bondage (Exodus i. 1-7, 13, 14). And the children of Israel sighed by reason of the bondage; and they cried, and their cry because of the bondage came up unto God,

278

and God heard their groaning, and God remembered His covenant with Abraham, with Isaac, and with Jacob, and God took notice (ii. 23-25). And God spake unto Moses, and said unto him, I am Jehovah. I appeared unto Abraham, unto Isaac, and unto Jacob by the name of El Shaddai; but by my name Jehovah was I not known unto them; and I made a covenant with them to give them the land of Canaan, the land of their pilgrimage, wherein they were strangers. And I have heard the groaning of the children of Israel, that the Egyptians keep them in bondage, and I have remembered my covenant" (vi. 2 seq.).

That is the whole of it. As a rule nothing more is aimed at than to give the mere links and articulations of the narrative. It is as if Q were the scarlet thread on which the pearls of JE are hung. In place of the somewhat loose connections of the Jehovist, the narrative of the Priestly Code shows a firmly jointed literary form; one remarkable feature of which is to be seen in the regular titles which stand at the head of the various sections. Each section begins with the words)LH TWLDWT (*hae sunt generationes*), from which Genesis derives its name. *l*

*** 1 *)AUTH (H BIBLOS GENESEWS ii. 4 LXX. Hence Ewald's name for the Priestly Code, which is very appropriate for Genesis, or perhaps generally for the book of the four covenants—the Book of Origins. ***************************************

In the rest of the historical literature of the Old Testament nothing like this as yet appears. It is also characteristic that whenever the title occurs, introducing a new, section, the contents of the preceding section are first of all briefly recapitulated so as to show the place of the link upon the chain.

The Priestly Code enters as little as possible on the contents of the various narratives. The predicates are stripped off, so far as they admit of such treatment, and the subjects duly entered in a catalogue with connecting text. In this way the history almost shrinks to the compass of a genealogy with explanations— the genealogy at least forms the principal contents of the history, and here appears in such proportions and such systematic fashion as nowhere else. This has been regarded as a proof that Q belongs to an older stage of development of Hebrew historiography than JE. There can be no doubt, it is said, *l* that the oldest Hebrew,

*** I Riehm, "die s.g. Grundschrift des Pentateuchs" in Studien und Kritiken, 1872, p. 296. ***

or indeed Oriental, history began with the historical notices and traditions inserted in the tribal or family catalogues. Yet we know positively that in the Books of Judges, Samuel, and Kings, there are no genealogical statistics at all, while Chronicles, and what belongs to Chronicles, is full of them. We know also that songs such as those in Josh. x. 12, 13; Jud. v.; 2Samuel i. 19 seq., iii. 33 seq. are the oldest historical monuments, and that a number of them are found in JE and not a single one in Q.

Herder's theory of the development of history out of genealogy will not apply here, 2 but indeed what we have

********************************* 2 Nor in the case of the Arabs, as has been well shown by Sprenger against Caussin de Perceval (Essai, preface, p. ix.). *********************************

to do with here is not history proper at all, but folklore.

It is true that with the Jehovist also the genealogy underlies the narrative as its skeleton. It is the natural chain to link the different stories together, and even at a time when the latter were still separate and only circulated orally, the genealogy was not unknown to the people. When stories were told of Isaac and Ishmael, and Lot and Esau, every one knew at once who these personages were, and how they were related to Israel and to one another. But this was merely the presupposition of the narratives, known as a matter of course to the hearers; the interesting element in them consisted in those traits which the Priestly Code omits. Stories of this kind compel attention because they set forth the peculiarities of different peoples as historically and really related to each other, not according to an empty embryological relation. It is the temper displayed by different races, not the stem of their relationship, that makes the point of the stories; their charm and their very life depend on their being transparent and reflecting the historic attitude of the time which gave them birth. The clearer the traces they display of love and hatred, jealousy of rivals and joy in their fall, the nearer are we to the forces which originated the tradition about early times. In the Priestly Code all those stories are absent in which there is anything morally objectionable,— those for example in which the cowardice of the patriarchs endangers the honour of their wives, those of Sarah's cruel jealousy of Hagar, and of the unlovely contention of Leah and Rachel for husband and children, of the incest of Lot's daughters, of the violation of Dinah. All hatred, and strife, and deceit in the patriarchal family disappear: Lot and Abraham, Isaac and Ishmael, Jacob and Esau, agree to separate: of the tricks of Laban and Jacob to each other, of the treachery of Simeon and Levi to Shechem, of the enmity Joseph's brethren bore to him, there is not a word in the Priestly Code. It is not merely that "psychological decorations," as they have been called, are left out; the very heart of the business has been cut out. That Moab and Ammon, Ishmael and Edom, were Hebrew peoples, all more nearly or more distantly related to the Israelites, that the Aramaeans too were closely connected with the Hebrews by blood and by marriage, that this tribe lives in one district contiguous to Palestine, that in another—this is what the Priestly Code has to tell. Dry ethnographical and geographical facts like these are presented in a genealogical form; all we learn of the patriarchs is their marriages and births and how they separated to the various dwelling-places of their descendants. And folklore could not possibly be directed to such facts as these at a period when these relations were all matters of fact and familiar to every child. The Priestly Code, moreover, strips the legends of the patriarchs of their local as well as their historical colour; they are kept at a distance from all the places of the sacredness of which the Jehovist makes them the founders.

1

1. Hupteld gives a curious turn to this, saying that in the Priestly Code Abraham, Isaac, and Jacob have much more permanent settlements. But it is this work that insists so often on the fact that the patriarchs were pilgrims and had nowhere a fixed residence: it only says that Abraham dwelt in the land of Canaan, and names no particular place even as the scene of the theophany in chapter xvii. It is only when the question of burying Sarah and Abraham arises that there is a change. Something must be done, and the field of Machpelah near Hebron is acquired (no doubt JE reported this, but the account of it in that source is lost) as a possession of the patriarchal family, where it now settles more permanently. That Isaac and Jacob continue to dwell at the grave of Abraham is a statement of which the significance is negative rather than positive, and on the other hand the patriarchal journeys up and down in JE are not designed to represent them as wandering nomads, but serve to bring them in contact with all the sacred places   with   which   they   had   special   associations,

No historical geography is needed in order to understand the narrative of the Priestly Code in Genesis: but that is only to say that it stands quite away from the soil out of which oral tradition arises. It deals in no etymology, no proverbs nor songs, no miracles, theophanies nor dreams, and is destitute of all that many-coloured poetic charm which adorns the Jehovistic narratives. But this proves not its original simplicity but its neglect of the springs from which legend arises, and of its most essential elements. *1* What remains is anything but historical objectivity: it is the formula and nothing more.

1. Riehm (op. cit. p. 302 seq.) thinks it is made out that the religious tradition of remote antiquity is distinguished by its "modest simplicity", and by a "style suited to its exalted subject." Only in the course of time was it adorned with all sorts of miraculous and mysterious elements, and that by the "fancy of the people," which, however, does not so easily gain entrance into serious literature(!) He appeals to the fact that the conception of angels, though certainly long developed with the people, occurs in the earlier prophets only in isolated instances, and in the later prophets, as Ezekiel, Zechariah, Daniel, more frequently. It is difficult to sift out what is true and what is false in this confused argument. In the Priestly Code there are, it is true, no angels, but on the other hand we have Azazel and Seirim (2Chronicles xi. 15; Isaiah xiii. 21, xxxiv. 14, comp. supra), for where the gods are not, the ghosts have sway. In one of the two main sources of the Jehovist (J), we find chiefly the Mal'ak Jahve (message of Jehovah); that is Jehovah Himself in so far as He appears and manifests Himself, whether in a natural phenomenon or in human form. Different are the B'ne Elohim, beings of divine substance: they perhaps are indicated in the 1st plural in the mouth of Jehovah (Genesis iii. 22, xi. 7). Both of these are doubtless very old. In the other principal source (E) a mixture appears to have taken place: the heavenly hosts are not only the children and companions of Deity, but also its messengers, conductors of the communication between heaven and earth (:xviii. 12); here we have the Mal'akim beside God and in the plural. This view also is not exactly a late one, as we see from the vision of Micaiah (t Kings xxii. 19). What does Riehm mean by high antiquity? A period from which no monuments are preserved to us? Why does

he limit his attention to the prophetic literature? He concedes that the idea of angels was early present "in the fancy of the people," and he should have been equal to the further concession that those who wrote down the FOLKLORE occupied a somewhat different position to POPULAR BELIEF from that of the prophetic preachers of repentance. Not even the historical books admit of being measured by the same standard in this matter as the pre-historic tradition. And which is the more original—that the angels use a ladder as in Genesis, or that they have wings as in Isaiah? And finally as for the reference to Ezekiel (?), Zechariah, and Daniel, the difference appears to me to be tolerably plain between a systematic angelology which operates always with numbers and names and the childlike belief in angels. The former removes God to a distance, the latter brings Him near.
****

As with the legend of the beginnings of things, so with the legend of the patriarchs: what is essential and original is the individual element in the several stories; the connection is a secondary matter, and only introduced on the stories being collected and reduced to writing. But in the Priestly Code the individuality of the several stories is simply destroyed: to such an extent is the connection dwelt on. What meaning is there in the statement that Jacob was all at once called Israel, i.e., Fight-God (xxxv. 10), if no mention is made of his wrestling with El, which was the occasion of his change of name? Have we anything like the true history of Joseph in the Priestly Code? Can we regard it as the original history, when the destruction of Sodom and Gomorrah is dismissed in a subordinate clause, as is done in xix. 29 ? The remarkable admission has been made, *1* that it is plain from the summary

** 1.   Riehm, op.. cit. p. 292.
****

manner of reporting of the Priestly Code, that the author could have told his story at much greater length, had it been consistent with the plan of his work to do so, and that this certainly points to sources where greater detail was used. The more detailed source, however, which is thus taken for granted, need by no means, it is said, have been a written one, and least of all the Jehovistic narrative before us; on the contrary, we are told, the state of the case is best satisfied by the assumption that the author held a more detailed narrative to be unnecessary, because the oral tradition, living in the mouth of the people, was quite able to fill in the colours in his outlines and to convert his chronistic notices into living pictures. But this is merely an attempt to elude the necessity for exactly comparing the Priestly Code and the Jehovist. The question is, which of the two writings stands nearest to the starting-point? Is it the one which attaches most importance to elements which are foreign to the nature of oral tradition altogether and only added in literary composition? It would be a curious thing if the writing down of the tradition began with writing down what the legend did not contain. What is set before us in the Priestly Code is the quintessence not of the oral tradition, but of the tradition when already written down. And the written account of the primitive history which it employs is the Jehovistic narrative. The order in which the popular legends are there placed here becomes the very kernel of the narrative. There the plan was hidden behind the execution, but here it

282

comes forward not indeed essentially changed, but sharp and accentuated, as the principal feature of the whole.

VIII.II.3. The Jehovist still lives in the spirit of the legend, but the Priestly Code is strange to that spirit, and does violence to the legend, by treating it from its own point of view, which is quite different from the old one. Moral and religious culture is further advanced; and hence the removal of real or apparent offences against morality and of notions which are too childish, or superstitious, or even mythical. If the Godhead appears, it must not be patent to the senses, at least it must not be seen in visible form. Jehovah speaks with Jacob, but not in a dream from the heavenly ladder; He reveals Himself to Moses, but not in the burning bush; the notion of revelation is retained, but the subsidiary incidents which must be added to make a concrete of the abstract, are stripped off. It is a matter of indifference under what forms or through what media a man receives revelation, if only the fact stands sure; in other words, revelation is no longer a living reality of the present, but a dead dogma for the past. The progress of culture in the Priestly Code is most of all evident in the learned historical treatment with which the legend is overlaid. First of all there is the chronology, which we encountered even in the legend of the origins of mankind, and which is naturally continued in the patriarchal legend. Here indeed we see with special plainness how foreign learned calculation is to the poetical materials; in some instances the facts lead to quite a different view from that of the numbers. Following the numbers of the Priestly Code we may, with the Rabbis, regard Shem and Eber as the venerable heads of the Jewish school in which the child Jacob learned his letters and the Torah. Then Jacob's sojourn in Mesopotamia lasts about eighty years, and all this time Isaac is lying on his death-bed; after being long dead for us, he suddenly appears again, but only to die. And hand in hand with the chronology there goes the general predilection of the Priestly Code for numbers and names, which displays itself even in Genesis, though not nearly so marked there as in the later books of the Pentateuch. Oral folklore can very well contain round numbers, such as the twelve sons and the seventy souls of the family of Jacob, the twelve wells and the seventy palm trees at Elim, the seventy elders and the twelve spies; but a chronological system, whole lists of exact and considerable numbers, bare catalogues of personal names, none of them having any significance, dates and measurements such as those in the account of the flood in the Priestly Code, require writing even to originate, not to speak of transmitting them. These art-products of pedantry toke the place of the living poetic detail of the Jehovist narrative; the element of episode has to give way to the seriousness of dry history.

It is also a mark of historical pedantry that the mixing up of the period of the patriarchs with a later period is avoided as anachronistic. In the Jehovist the present everywhere shines through, he in no way conceals his own age; we are told that Babylon is the great world-city, that the Assyrian Empire is in existence, with the cities of Niniveh and Calah and Resen; that the Canaanites had once dwelt in Palestine, but had long been absorbed in the Israelites. The writer of the Priestly Code is very careful not to do anything like this. / He brushes up the legend and makes history of it according to the rules of art; he kills it as legend, and deprives it of all real value, such as it possesses, not indeed for the history of primitive times, but for that of the age of the kings.

The history of the first men and of the patriarchs is divided by the Priestly Code into three periods, each of them opened by a covenant. The covenant with Adam (Genesis i. 28-ii. 4) is the simplest; it is not called a covenant, but it is the basis of the second covenant with Noah (ix. 1-17), which modifies it in important particulars, and brings it nearer to the present age. The covenant with Abraham (Genesis xvii.), which alone is ratified with the succeeding patriarchs, does not apply to the whole of mankind, but only to Abraham's seed, and especially to Israel. The first sign of the covenant is the Sabbath (Genesis ii. 3; comp. Exodus xxxi. 12 seq.; Ezekiel xx. 12, 20), the second the rainbow (Genesis ix. 12), the third circumcision (xvii. 10). The first parent of mankind is enjoined to use a purely vegetable diet, the father of mankind after the, flood receives permission to slaughter animals; but he is expressly ordered not to eat flesh in the blood, and besides, to shed the blood of no man. What is said to Noah remains good for Abraham; but to the latter God promises that his posterity by Sarah shall possess the land of Canaan, and this is further assured by the purchase of the cave of Machpelah for a family burying-place, the purchase being executed according to all the forms of law, with prolonged negotiations. Further, God reveals Himself to Abraham as El Shaddai, and under this name He also manifests Himself to Isaac (xxviii. 3) and Jacob (xxxv. 11), repeating to them the promise of the possession of the land. It is pointed out with emphasis that God was not known to the pre-Mosaic time under His Israelite name, that He revealed Himself to the patriarchs only as El Shaddai, and as Jehovah first to Moses (Exod. vi. 2, 3). With a similar intention, which is not far to seek, the time of the patriarchs is kept free of the other Mosaic forms of worship; hence we have here no sacrifices nor altars, no distinction of clean and unclean beasts, nor anything of the kind. Now till within a short time ago, there was a great inclination (no one will be found at this date to acknowledge that he felt it) to admire the sobriety and faithfulness of the Priestly Code, as shown in this observance of the different religious stages. But in fact we can only admire these advantages in it, if we believe that the religion was at first naturalistic, that then all at once it became a good deal more positive, and then quite positive in the year 1500 B.C. How can we regard it as showing historical faithfulness, that the patriarchs were allowed to slaughter, but not to sacrifice, and that first the Sabbath was introduced, then the rainbow, then circumcision, and at last sacrifice, under Moses? It is natural that Jacob at Bethel should give tithes of all that he possesses, unnatural that the eponymous hero should not in worship above all things have left a good example to his posterity. What is it but a theory, that the name Jehovah was first revealed to Moses, and through him to the Israelites, and that it was quite unknown before?—a theory which certainly cannot be upheld, for Moses could have done nothing more irrational than to introduce a new name for the God of their fathers, to whom he directed his people,—and yet a theory which, from the correlation between Jehovah the God of Israel and Israel the people of Jehovah, readily suggests itself, and is not altogether peculiar to the author of the Priestly Code. *1*. He had a pattern which suggested

************************************** 1. Exodus vi. 2, 3 (Q) = iii. 13, 14 (JE). The burning bush shows the theophany in the Jehovist to be the earlier. In the Priestly Code it almost loses the character of a theophany entirely. But this is also quite clear on a comparison of Exodus vii. 1 (Q) and iv. 16 (JE). The phrase vii. 1, " Behold, I make thee a god to Pharaoh, and Aaron thy brother shall be thy prophet," is a degradation of the corresponding passage, iv. 16 "Aaron shall be to thee for a mouth, and thou shalt be to him for a god." For if Aaron is the prophet or the mouth of Moses, then in the original and only appropriate way of thinking of the matter, Moses is a god for Aaron, not for Pharaoh. By the way is there anything in the similarity between Sene and Sinai?
****

certain lines, and these he traces strongly and with a system; and he even goes so far as to avoid the name of Jehovah even in his own narrative of the pre-Mosaic period. Even when speaking in his own person, he says Elohim, not Jehovah, down to Exodus vi.

The three periods and the three corresponding covenants of the early age are preliminaries to the fourth period and the fourth covenant. The narrator everywhere has an eye to the Mosaic law, and the thought of it determined the plan which comes so prominently into view in his representation of the origins of human history. The great features of this plan are the great official transactions of Jehovah with the patriarchs. In these we have not a narrative but only speeches and negotiations; the preliminary laws are given in them, which, as they advance step by step, prepare the way for the great Law, namely, the Mosaic. The law of worship has taken the place of the legend of worship. In the legend the sacred usages and customs arise, as it were, spontaneously, in connection with any occasion, placed in the early sacred time, which may serve to account for them. Jehovah does not make it statutory that the sinew of the thigh may not be eaten; but He wrestles with Israel, and injures the sinew of his thigh during the wrestling, and for this reason the children of Israel do not eat thereof. In the following story it is explained how it came about that the Israelites circumcise young boys (Exodus iv. 25 seq.). As Moses was returning from Midian to Goshen, he spent a night on the road, and Jehovah fell upon him with the intention of killing him. His wife, Zipporah, however, took a flint and cut off the foreskin of her son, and touched Moses L:RAGLFYW with it, saying, Thou art a blood-bridegroom to me. Then Jehovah let him go. Thus Zipporah circumcises her son instead of her husband, makes the latter symbolically a blood-bridegroom, and thereby delivers him from the wrath of Jehovah to which he is exposed, because he is not a blood-bridegroom, *ie.*, because he has not submitted to circumcision before his marriage. In other words, the circumcision of male infants is here explained as a milder substitute for the original circumcision of young men before marriage. *1* Compare with this the style in which in Genesis xvii

** 1. That this is in fact the
original custom is clear from the word XTN, which signifies both circumcision and
bridegroom (or in Arabic, son-in-law). This explains the meaning of XTN DMYM
in Exodus iv. 25. The original usage is still in force with some Arab tribes. In
Genesis xxxiv. Shechem has to submit to circumcision before marriage.
****

the Priestly Code institutes the circumcision of male children on the eighth day after
birth. This institution completely throws into the shade and spoils the story out of
which it arose, namely, the promise of the birth of Isaac as a reward to Abraham of
the hospitality he showed Jehovah at Hebron. But there is more than a difference in
form, there is a material contradiction between the Jehovistic legend and the priestly
law. The law purifies the legend, that is to say, denies all its main features and
motives. As we saw in the first chapter there is a conscious polemic at work in the
representation in the Priestly Code that Abraham, Isaac, and Jacob erect no altars,
and practice no religious rites, and that they have no connection with the sacred
places with which in JE they are inseparably associated. The popular religious book
preserved to us in the Jehovistic Genesis, not corrected to any great extent, though
certainly to some extent, tells how the ancestors and representatives of Israel founded
the old popular worship at the principal sites at which it was kept up. The law of the
legitimate cultus of Jerusalem, as it lies before us in the Priestly Code, reforms and
destroys the old popular worship on the basis of Mosaic, *i.e.*, prophetical ideas. The
tabernacle does not harmonize with the sanctuaries of Hebron, Beersheba, Shechem,
Kadesh, Mahanaim, Lahai-Roi, Bethel; the patriarchs live at Hebron only because
they are to be buried there, not to entertain the Deity under the oak of Mamre and to
build an altar there. The heretical mac,c,ebas, trees and wells, disappear, and with
them the objectionable customs: that God should have summoned Abraham to offer
up to Him his only son is an idea the Priestly Code could not possibly entertain. The
whole material of the legend is subordinated to legislative designs: the modifying
influence of the law on the narrative is everywhere apparent.

The attitude of Judaism to the old legend is on the whole negative, but it added some
new elements. While the patriarchs are not allowed to sacrifice, only to slaughter,
they have, on the other hand, the Sabbath *l* and circumcision. In this they are like

** I The Sabbath is not a Mosaic
institution according to the Priestly Code. But it is presupposed in Exodus xvi., and
according to Genesis ii. 3, it was in force from the beginning of the world. With the
old Israelites the Sabbath was much less important in relation to worship than the
festivals: in Judaism the opposite was the case.
****

the Jews in Babylon, who were deprived of the national cultus, and replaced it with
these two symbols of religious membership and union, which were independent of
the temple of Jerusalem. In the exile, after the cessation of the service of the altar,
the Sabbath and circumcision attained that significance as symbols—in the genuine
old meaning of the Greek word—as practical symbols of Judaism, which they retain

to the present day. The emphasis is noteworthy with which the Priestly Code always insists on the fact that the patriarchs sojourned in a strange land, that they were *Gerim*. If we also consider that Abraham is said to have migrated into Palestine from Ur, from Chaldaea, it is hardly possible to reject the idea that the circumstances of the exile had some influence in moulding the priestly form of the patriarchal legend. In spite of all the efforts of the historian, and all the archaic appearance of his work, it may in that case still be the fact that the surroundings of the narrator found positive expression in his description of the patriarchal times.

VIII.III.

VIII.III.1. In the Jehovistic history-book Genesis is a most important part, and occupies at least a half of the whole work: in the Priestly Code, Genesis quite disappears in comparison with the later books. Only with the Mosaic legislation does this work arrive at its own ground, and it at once stifles the narrative under a mass of legislative matter. Here also there is a thin historical thread running parallel to the Jehovist, but we constantly lose sight of it from the repeated interruptions made by extensive ritual laws and statistical statements.

"These last four books of Moses have been made quite unreadable by a most melancholy, most incomprehensible, revision. The course of the history is everywhere interrupted by the insertion of innumerable laws, with regard to the greater part of which it is impossible to see any reason for their being inserted where they are." The dislocation of the narrative by these monstrous growths of legislative matter is not, as Goethe thinks, to be imputed to the editor; it is the work of the unedited Priestly Code itself, and is certainly intolerable; nor can it be original; the literary form of the work at once shows this. It is still possible to trace how the legal matter forces its way into the narrative, and once there spreads itself and takes up more and more room. In the Jehovist, one form of the tradition may still be discerned, according to which the Israelites on crossing the Red Sea at once proceeded towards Kadesh, without making the detour to Sinai. We only get to Sinai in Exodus xix., but in Exodus xvii. we are already at Massah and Meribah, *ie.*, on the ground of Kadesh. That is the scene of the story of Moses striking water out of the rock with his staff: there the fight with the Amalekites took place—they lived there and not at Sinai—there also the visit of Jethro, which requires a locality at some distance from his home (at Sinai), a place where the people had not merely a temporary encampment, but their permanent seat of justice. *1*

** 1. Kadesh is also called Meribah, the seat of justice, or Meribath Kadesh, the seat of justice at the holy spring. Meribah is in its meaning the same as Midian. **

Hence the narratives which are told before the arrival at Sinai are repeated after the departure from it, because the locality is the same before and after, namely, the wilderness of Kadesh, the true scene of the Mosaic history. The institution of judges and elders concludes the narrative before the great Sinai section, and begins the narrative after it (Ex. xviii., Numbers xi). The story of the manna and the quails occurs not only in Exodus xvi., but also in Numbers xi; and the rocky spring called forth by Moses at Massah and Meribah is both in Exodus xvii. and Numbers xx. In other words, the Israelites arrived at Kadesh, the original object of their wanderings, not after the digression to Sinai but immediately after the Exodus, and they spent there the forty years of their residence in the wilderness. Kadesh is also the original scene of the legislation. "There He made them statute and judgment, and there He proved them," we read in a poetical fragment, before the Sinai section (Exodus xv. 25), which is now placed in the narrative of the healing of the waters at Marah, but stands there quite isolated and without bearing on its context. The curious conjunction of judgment and trial points unmistakably to Massah and Meribah (ie., judgment and trial-place), that is, to Kadesh, as the place spoken of. But the legislation at the seat of judgment at Kadesh is not represented as a single act in which Moses promulgates to the Israelites once for all a complete and comprehensive body of laws; it goes on for forty years, and consists in the dispensation of justice at the sanctuary, which he begins and the priests and judges carry on after him according to the pattern he set. This is the idea in the extremely instructive narrative in Exodus xviii., of which Kadesh is the scene. And in this way the Torah has its place in the historical narrative, not in virtue of its matter as the contents of a code, but from its form as constituting the professional activity of Moses. It is in the history not as a result, as the sum of the laws and usages binding on Israel, but as a process; it is shown how it originated, how the foundation was laid for the living institution of that Torah which still exists and is in force in Israel.

The true and original significance of Sinai is quite independent of the legislation. It was the seat of the Deity, the sacred mountain, doubtless not only for the Israelites, but generally for all the Hebrew and Cainite (Kenite) tribes of the surrounding region. The priesthood of Moses and his successors was derived from the priesthood there: there Jehovah appeared to him in the burning bush when he was keeping the sheep of the priest of Midian, from there He sent him to Egypt. There, to the Israelites, Jehovah still dwelt long after they had settled in Palestine; in the song of Deborah He is summoned to come from Sinai to succour His oppressed people and to place Himself at the head of His warriors. According to the view of the poet of Deuteronomy xxxiii. the Israelites did not go to Jehovah to Sinai, but the converse; He came to them from Sinai to Kadesh: "Jehovah came from Sinai and shone from Seir unto them; He lightened from Mount Paran and came to Meribath Kadesh." *1*

*** 1. We do not know where Sinai was situated, and the Bible is scarcely at one on the subject. Only dilettanti care much for controversy on the matter. The Midian of Exodus ii. tells us most: it is probably Madian on the Arabic shore of the Ked sea. In our passage Sinai seems to be S.E. of Edom; the way from Sinai to Kadesh is by Seir and Paran. ***

But it is not difficult to see how it came to be thought more seemly that the Israelites should undertake the journey to Jehovah. This was at first put in the form that they appeared there before the face of Jehovah to worship Him and offer Him a sacrifice (Exodus iii. 12), and at their departure they received the ark instead of Jehovah Himself, who continued to dwell on Sinai (Exodus xxxiii.); for the ark represents Jehovah, that constitutes its significance, and not the tables of the law, which were not in it at first. It was a further step to make Sinai the scene of the solemn inauguration of the historical relation between Jehovah and Israel. This was done under the poetic impulse to represent the constituting of the people of Jehovah as a dramatic act on an exalted stage. What in the older tradition was a process which went on quietly and slowly, occupied completely the whole period of Moses, and was at the beginning just such as it still continued to be, was now, for the sake of solemnity and vividness, compressed into a striking scene of inauguration. If this were done, the covenant between Jehovah and Israel must receive a positive (as well as a negative) character, that is to say, Jehovah Himself must announce to the people the basis and the conditions of it. Thus the necessity arose to communicate in this place the contents of the fundamental laws, and so the matter of the legislation made its way into the historical narrative. But that it did not belong originally to this place we see from the confusion which obtains even in the Jehovistic Sinai section (Exodus xix.-xxiv., xxxii.-xxxiv.). The small bodies of laws which are here communicated may in themselves be old enough, but they are forced into the narrative. It is only of what is relatively the most recent corpus, the Decalogue (in E), that this cannot be asserted.

As the Jehovistic work was originally a pure history-book, so Deuteronomy, when it was first discovered, was a pure law-book. *1*

** 1. Chapters xii.-xxvii. The two historical introductions, chapter i.-iv. and chapter v.-xi. were added later, as well as the appendices, chapter xxviii. seq. **

These two works, the historical and legal, were at first quite independent of each other; only afterwards were they conjoined, perhaps that the new law might share in the popularity of the old people's book, and at the same time infuse into it its own spirit. It made it the easier to do this, that, as we have just seen, a piece of law had already been taken up into the Jehovistic history-book. To the Decalogue, at the beginning of the period of the forty years, was now added Deuteronomy at the close of that period. The situation—of which the law itself knows nothing—is very well chosen, not only because Moses is entitled when making his testament to anticipate the future and make a law for the time to come, but also because, the law being placed at the close of his life, the thread of the narrative is not further interrupted, the law being simply inserted between the Pentateuch and the Book of Joshua. This combination of Deuteronomy with the Jehovist was the beginning of the combination of narrative and law; and the fact that this precedent was before the author of the Priestly Code explains how, though his concern was with the Torah alone, he yet went to work from the very outset and comprised in his work the history of the creation, as if it also belonged to the Torah. This manner of setting forth the Torah in the form of a history book is not in the least involved in the nature of the case; on the contrary, it introduces the greatest amount of awkwardness. How it came about can only be explained in the way above described; an antecedent process of the same nature in literary history led the way and made the suggestion. *2*

*** 2. That the author of the Priestly Code had before him the combination of the Sinai legislation of the Jehovist and Deuteronomy is shown further by the circumstance that he has both a legislation at Mount Sinai and a legislation in the Arboth Moah, and in addition to these one in the wilderness of Sinai. ***

As from the literary point of view, so also from the historical, the Moses of the Jehovist appears more original than the Moses of the Priestly Code. To prove this is, it is true, the aim of the entire present work: yet it will not on that account be thought out of place if we take advantage of this convenient opportunity for a brief sketch and criticism of the conflicting historical views of Moses and his work in the two main sources of the Pentateuch. According to the Priestly Code Moses is a religious founder and legislator, as we are accustomed to think of him. He receives and promulgates the Torah, *1* perhaps not as a book—though, when we

** 1. The law might accordingly be
called   Moses,   as   with   the   Ethiopians   the   Psalter   is   called   David,
****

come to think of it, we can hardly represent the transaction to ourselves in any other way—but certainly fixed and finished as an elaborate and minutely organised system, which comprises the sacred constitution of the congregation for all time to come. The whole significance of Moses consists in the office of messenger which he holds as mediator of the law; what else he does is of no importance. That the law is given once for all is the great event of the time, not that the people of Israel begins to appear on the stage of the world. The people is there for the sake of the law, not the law for the sake of the people. With the Jehovist, on the contrary, Moses' work consists in this, that he delivers his people from the Egyptians and cares for it in every way in the wilderness. In the prelude scene from his youth, when he smites the Egyptian and seeks to adjust the dispute of his brethren (Exodus ii. 11 seq.), his whole history is prefigured. His care for the Israelites embraces both catering for their sustenance, and making and preserving peace and order among them (Numbers xi.). The Torah is but a part of his activity, and proceeds from his more general office as the guardian of the young people, who has, as it were, to teach the fledgling to fly (Numbers xi. xii.). According to Exodus xviii. his Torah is nothing but a giving of counsel, a finding the way out of complications and difficulties which had actually arisen. Individuals bring their different cases before him; he pronounces judgment or gives advice, and in so doing teaches the people the way they should go. Thus he is the beginner of the teaching of Jehovah which lives on after him in priest and prophet. Here all is life and movement: as Jehovah Himself, so the man of God, is working in a medium which is alive; is working practically, by no means theoretically, in history, not in literature. His work and activity may be told in a narrative, but the contents of it are more than a system, and are not to be reduced to a compendium; it is not done and finished off, it is the beginning of a series of infinite activities. In the Priestly Code the work of Moses lies before us clearly defined and rounded off; one living a thousand years after knows it as well as one who saw it with his eyes. It is detached from its originator and from his age: lifeless itself, it has driven the life out of Moses and out of the people, nay, out of the very Deity. This precipitate of history, appearing as law at the beginning of the history, stifles and kills the history itself. Which of the two views is the more historical, we can accordingly be at no loss to decide. It may be added that in the older Hebrew literature the founding of the nation and not the giving of the law is regarded as the theocratic creative act of Jehovah. The very notion of the law is absent: only covenants are spoken of, in which the representatives of the people undertake solemn obligations to do or leave undone something which is described in general terms.

Another point of difference must be mentioned here, though indeed it is a matter which has been before us more than once already. That which is in the Priestly Code the subject-matter of the Torah of Moses, namely, the institution of the cultus, the Jehovist traces to the practice of the patriarchs—one more result of the difference between law and legend. The Moses of the Priestly Code conflicts not only with the future, but with the past; he comes into collision with history on every side. That view is manifestly the only natural one according to which the worship is not specifically Israelite, not a thing instituted by Moses in obedience to a sudden command of the Deity, but an ancestral tradition. But at the time when the Priestly Code was drawn up the worship was certainly the one thing that made Israel Israel. In it the church, the one congregation of worship, takes the place of the people even in the Mosaic age—sorely against history, but characteristically for the author's point of view.

Now even such authorities as Bleek, Hupfeld, and Knobel have been misled by the appearance of historical reality which the Priestly Code creates by its learned art here as well as in the history of the patriarchs. They have regarded the multiplicity of numbers and names, the minute technical descriptions, the strict keeping up of the scenery of camp-life, as so many signs of authentic objectivity. Noldeke made an end of this critical position once for all, but Colenso is properly entitled to the credit of having first torn the web asunder. *1*

*** 1. See Kuenen in the Theol. Tijdschrift, 1870, p. 393-401. **

The boldness with which numbers and names are stated, and the preciseness of the details about indifferent matters of furniture, do not prove them to be reliable: they are not drawn from contemporary records, but are the fruit solely of late Jewish fancy, a fancy which, it is well known, does not design nor sketch, but counts and constructs, and produces nothing more than barren plans. Without repeating the description of the tabernacle in Exodus xxv. word for word, it is difficult to give an idea how circumstantial it is; we must go to the source to satisfy ourselves what the narrator can do in this line. One would imagine that he was giving specifications to measurers for estimates, or that he was writing for carpet-makers and upholsterers; but they could not proceed upon his information, for the incredibly matter-of-fact statements are fancy all the same, as was shown in chapter i. The description of the tabernacle is supplemented in the Book of Numbers by that of the camp; the former being the centre, this is the circle drawn about it, and consists of an outer ring, the twelve secular tribes, a middle ring, the Levites, and an innermost one, the sons of Aaron: a mathematical demonstration of the theocracy in the wilderness. The two first chapters contain the census of the twelve tribes, and their allocation in four quarters, nothing but names and numbers. To this first census chapter xxxiv. adds another at the close of the forty years, in which the various detailed figures are different, but the total is about the same. This total, 600,000 warriors, comes from the older tradition, but is proved to be quite worthless by the fact that in a really authentic document the levy of Israel in the time of Deborah is stated to be 40,000 strong. Still, the Priestly Code is entitled to the credit of having made the total a little less round, and of having broken it up into artificial component parts. The muster of the people is followed in Numbers iii. iv. by the dedication of the tribe of Levi to the sanctuary, in compensation for the firstborn males of the Israelites who up to that time had not been sacrificed nor yet redeemed. There are 22,273 firstborn males to be provided for, and there are 22,000 male Levites above a month old. The 273 extra firstborn males are specially redeemed at five shekels a head. What accuracy! But what of the fact that a people of at least two millions has only 22,273 firstborn males, or say 50,000 firstborn of both sexes? This gives an average of forty children to every woman, for the firstborn in the sense of the law is that which first opens the womb. The continuation of Numbers iii. iv. is in chapter viii. As the Levites are an offering of firstlings to the sanctuary on the part of the people, which, however, is not to be sacrificed but made over to the priests, the characteristic rite of this sort of sacred due has to be gone through with them, namely, an act imitating that of throwing into the flame of the altar (Aristeas 31,1. 5). To think of Moses and Aaron heaving the 22,000 men! Not less striking as an example of this kind of fiction is the story of Numbers xxxi. Twelve thousand Israelites, a thousand from each tribe, take the field against Midian, extirpate without any fighting—at least nothing is anywhere said of this important point—the whole people, slay all the men and a part of the women, take captive the unmarried girls, and suffer themselves no loss whatever. The latter point is asserted very definitely. "The captains of thousands and the captains of hundreds came to Moses, and said to him, Thy servants have taken the sum of the men of war which are under our charge, and there lacketh not one of us." Of the immeasurable booty of men and cattle Jehovah assigns half to those who took the field and took part in the battle, the other half to the congregation; and the former are to give the 500th part to the priests, the latter the 50th part to the Levites. The execution of this order is especially reported as follows: "The booty which the men of war had taken was 675,000 sheep, 72,000 beeves, 61,000 asses, and 32,000 women that had not lain by man. And the half which was the portion of them that went out to war was 337,500 sheep, and Jehovah's tribute of the sheep was 675; 36,000 beeves, tribute to Jehovah 72; 30,500 asses, tribute to Jehovah 61; 16,000 persons, tribute to Jehovah 32. And Moses gave the tribute to Jehovah to Eleazar the priest. But the other half, which Moses divided to the children of Israel, the half due to the congregation, was 337,500 sheep, 36,000 beeves, 30,500 asses, 16,000 persons, and of the children of Israel's half Moses took one of fifty and gave them to the Levites." The calculation of the contribution to Jehovah was quite easy for Moses, as the 500th part of the half is equivalent to the 1000th part of the whole; he had only to leave off the thousands from the first totals. In conclusion, the captains brought offerings to Jehovah of golden dishes, chains, bracelets, rings, and earrings, altogether 16,750 shekels weight, as atonement for their souls "But that was only the gold which the captains had taken as booty, for the men of war had taken spoil, every man for himself." We may perhaps be allowed to speculate as to the relation between these 16,750 shekels which in this passage the captains alone offer to the tabernacle OF THE GOLD ORNAMENTS OF THE MIDIANITES, and the 1700 shekels which in Judges viii. the whole people dedicate

293

OF THE GOLD ORNAMENTS OF THE MIDIANITES to set up an image in Ophra.

It is less easy to account on the theory of pure fiction for the numerous names sometimes arranged together like a catalogue than for reported circumstances and numbers. There can certainly be no doubt that the forty places which are mentioned in the list of encampments in the wanderings, really existed in the region the Israelites are reported to have traversed. But he who is satisfied with this as evidence that we have before us here a historical document of primitive antiquity, will never be disturbed by criticism. Was it such a difficult matter to find out forty definite stations in the wilderness for the forty years of the wanderings? Even if the elements of the composition are not fictitious, that is far from proving the composition itself to be authentic. And in the case of lists of the names of persons, the elements are often of an extremely doubtful nature; and here it is well to keep in view the principle of Vatke (op. cit. p. 675) that no confidence is to be placed in subjects devoid of predicates, and that persons are not to be taken for real who have nothing to do. The dozens of names in Numbers i. vii. x. are almost all made to the same pattern, and have no similarity whatever to the names genuinely old. The fact that the name of Jehovah does not enter into their composition only shows that the composer was not forgetful of his religio-historical theory.

By its taste for barren names and numbers and technical descriptions, the Priestly Code comes to stand on the same line with the Chronicles and the other literature of Judaism which labours at an artificial revival of the old tradition [VI.I.2 VI.III.2., VI.III.3. ad fin.]. Of a piece with this tendency is an indescribable pedantry, belonging to the very being of the author of the Priestly Code. He has a very passion for classifying and drawing plans; if he has once dissected a genus into different species, we get all the species named to us one by one every time he has occasion to mention the genus. The subsuming use of the prepositions Lamed and Beth is characteristic of him. He selects a long-drawn expression wherever he can; he does not weary of repeating for the hundredth time what is a matter of course (Numbers viii.), he hates pronouns and all abbreviating substitutes. What is interesting is passed over, what is of no importance is described with minuteness, his exhaustive clearness is such as with its numerous details to confuse our apprehension of what is in itself perfectly clear. This is what used to be described in the phraseology of historical criticism as epic breadth. *1*

************************************** 1. Riehm, p. 292. "The style is quiet, simple, free from all rhetorical and poetical ornament, and the expression in speaking of similar objects has an epic uniformity. Impressive as many pieces are, just from their unassuming simplicity and objectivity, there is nowhere any apparent effort to produce effect or to raise the interest of the reader by the resources of literary art." For an opposite opinion compare Lichtenberg, Werke, ii. 162. **************************************

VIII.III.2. Having thus attempted to describe the general contrast of the Priestly Code and the Jehovist in the Mosaic period, it remains for us to compare the several stories in the two works. The Exodus from Egypt is everywhere regarded as the commencement of Israelite history. In the Priestly Code it is made the epoch of an era (Exodus xii. 2), which is afterwards dated from, not only in years but even in months and days. It is unquestionable that this precise style of dating only came into use among the Hebrews at a very late period. *We find in the historical books only one statement of the month in which an event took place (1Kings vi. 38), and in that case the day is not given. To the prophetic writers dates were of some importance, and the growth of the practice may to some extent be traced with them. Amos first came forward "two years before the earthquake." /2/*

*** 2. Agh. xv. 11, 17: when al-Walid b. al-Mughira was dead, the Arabs dated after his death to the year of the elephant, which thereafter was made an epoch. According to others they reckoned nine years after the death of Hisham b. al-Mughira, to the time when they built the Caaba, and then they dated from the building of the Caaba. Comp. the 'Am al Ramada and the 'Am al Ru'af. ***

The most precise date in Isaiah is "the year in which king Uzziah died." Numbers of years are first found in Jeremiah, "the thirteenth year of king Josiah," and a few more instances. All at once there was a change: Haggai and Zechariah, prophets who grew up in the Babylonian exile, always give dates, not only the year and month, but the day of the month as well. In the Priestly Code this precise reckoning, which the Jews obviously learned from the Chaldeans, is in use from the age of Moses onwards.

In the Jehovist the ostensible occasion of the Exodus is a festival which the children of Israel desire to hold in honour of their God in the wilderness. In the Priestly Code this occasion disappears; there can be no pre-Mosaic festivals. But with this the reason falls away for which Jehovah kills the firstborn of the Egyptians, He does it because the king of Egypt is keeping from Him the firstborn of the Israelites, which ought to be offered to Him at the festival; for the celebration in question is the sacrificial festival of the first-fruits of cattle in spring. In the older tradition the festival is the first thing; it explains the circumstances of the Exodus and the time of year at which it took place: in the later one the relation is reversed—the killing of the firstborn of the Egyptians leads to the sacrifice of the firstborn of Israel, the Exodus in spring is followed by the festival in spring as its consequence. The Priestly Code follows this younger tradition, and deviates from the original account still more widely in the view it gives of the passover. It obliterates completely the connection between the passover and the sacrifice of the firstborn, and represents it not as a giving of thanks to Jehovah for having slain the firstborn of Egypt, but as instituted at the moment of the Exodus to induce Jehovah to spare the firstborn of Israel. How all this is to be understood and judged of we have discussed more at large in the chapter on the festivals (III.I.1., III.III.1.).

As to the accounts given in the two sources of the crossing of the Red Sea, all we can say is that that of the Jehovist (J) is the more complicated. According to him the sea is dried up by a strong wind, and the Egyptians succeed at first in crossing it, and encounter the Hebrews on the eastern shore during he night. "But in the morning watch Jehovah turned, in the pillar of fire and of the cloud, against the host of the Egyptian, and overthrew the host of the Egyptian, and hindered the wheels of his chariot and caused him to drive heavily. Then the Egyptian said: I will flee before Israel, for Jehovah fighteth for them against Egypt. But the sea turned back towards morning to its ordinary level, and the Egyptians fled against it, and Jehovah shook them into the midst of the sea" (Exodus xiv. 24, 25, 27). According to the Priestly Code *1* the waves meet over the pursuers,

*************************************** 1. And the younger tradition generally: also according to the song Exodus xv., which apart from the beginning, which is old, is a psalm in the manner of the Psalms and has no similarity with the historical songs, Judges v., 2Samuel i., Numbers xxi. **************************************

before they reach the further shore; the idea is much simpler, but poorer in incidental features.

The miracle of the manna (Exodus xvi.) is taken advantage of in the Priestly Code as a very suitable occasion for urging on the people a strict sanctification of the Sabbath: none falls on the seventh day, but what is gathered on the sixth keeps two days, while at other times it requires to be eaten quite fresh. This pursuit of a legal object destroys the story and obscures its original meaning, as no one can help seeing. Nor is it any sign of originality, rather of senility, that in the Priestly Code the manna is not eaten raw, but boiled and baked.

At Mount Sinai Moses receives, according to the Priestly Code, the revelation of—— the model of the tabernacle, and he follows the pattern thus presented to him in the construction, down below, of the real tabernacle. All further revelation takes place, even in Moses' time, as far as possible in the tabernacle (Exodus xxv. 22). Even Sinai must not stand any longer than necessary by the side of the one legitimate seat of Deity. *1*

** 1. Compare, however, Jahrbb.fur Deutsche Theologie, 1877, p. 453, note 1. **

The tables of the law, it appears, are silently presupposed without being mentioned beforehand, it being of course assumed that the readers would know all about them from the old tradition. The outside of the ark, however, is furnished in the most extravagant style, and with a splendour which other descriptions of the chest of acacia-wood are far from suggesting. The ark in the Priestly Code differs indeed in every way from the appearance of it in 1Kings vii. 23 seq. We are reminded of the Haggada by the covering which Moses has to put before his face, which is shining with the reflection of the glory of Jehovah (Exodus xxxiv. 29-35), and by the making of the brazen laver of the looking-glasses of the women who serve the temple

(Exodus xxxviii. 8, cf. Numbers xvii. 1, 9); these traits do not, it is true, belong to the original contents of the Priestly Code, but they belong to its circle.

From Sinai the old tradition takes us by this and that station, mentioned by name, without delay to Kadesh. Here the chief part of the forty years' sojourn in the wilderness is spent; this, as we said before, is the true scene of all the stories that are told about Moses. The Priestly Code takes us in this period, as in the legend of the patriarchs, not to definite places, but up and down in the wilderness of Sinai, in the wilderness of Paran, in the wilderness of Sin. Kadesh is with evident intention thrust as far as possible into the background—no doubt on account of the high sanctity the place originally had as the encampment for many years of the Israelites under Moses.

The spies are sent out according to the Jehovist from Kadesh, according to the Priestly Code from the wilderness of Paran. In the former authority they penetrate to Hebron, whence they bring back with them fine grapes, but they find that the land where these grow is not to be conquered. In the latter they proceed without any difficulty throughout the whole of Palestine to Lebanon, but have nothing to bring back with them, and advise against attacking the land because they have not found it particularly desirable, as if its advantages had been accessible to faith alone and not to be discovered by unbelieving eyes, as was actually the case in the time of Haggai and Zechariah, and at the time of Ezra and Nehemiah. To the genuine Israelite of old, however, the goodness of his beloved land was not a mere point of faith which he could ever have doubted. In the former source, as we judge from Deuteronomy i. 23, only the number of the spies was given; in the latter all the twelve are named. In the former Caleb is the only good spy, in the latter Caleb and Joshua. At first probably neither the one nor the other belonged to this story; but Caleb easily came to be named as an exception, because he actually conquered the district from Kadesh to Hebron, which the spies had declared it impossible to take, and which the Israelites, alarmed by their account, had not ventured to attack. Joshua, again, was added from the consideration that, according to the principle enunciated by the Jehovist in Numbers xiv. 23, 24, he must have shared the merit of Caleb, because he partook of the same exceptional reward with him.

In the Jehovist Moses alone instructs the spies and receives their report on their return; in the Priestly Code Moses and Aaron do so. In the oldest source of the Jehovist (J) Aaron has not yet made his appearance; in the Priestly Code Moses must not do any public act without him. *1*

*** 1. In the same way, in the former source Joshua always acts alone; in the latter, he always has the priest Eleazar at his side. Compare notes [in IV.III.2.]
****

Moses is still the moving spirit here as well as there, but Aaron is the representative of the theocracy, and pains are taken to secure that he shall never be absent where the representatives of the theocracy are brought face to face with the community. The desire to introduce the leader of the hierocracy, and with its leader the hierocracy itself, into the Mosaic history, has borne the most remarkable fruits in the so-called story of the rebellion of the company of Korah. According to the Jehovistic tradition the rebellion proceeds from the Reubenites, Dathan, and Abiram, prominent members of the firstborn tribe of Israel, and is directed against MOSES AS LEADER AND JUDGE OF THE PEOPLE. According to the version of the main-stock of the Priestly Code (Q), the author of the agitation is Korah, a prince of the tribe of Judah, and he rebels not only against Moses, but against MOSES AND AARON AS REPRESENTING THE PRIESTHOOD. In a later addition, which, to judge from its style, belongs likewise to the Priestly Code, but not to its original contents, the Levite Korah appears at the head of a revolt of the Levites against AARON AS HIGH PRIEST, and demands the equalisation of the lower with the higher clergy. Starting from the Jehovistic version, the historical basis of which is dimly discerned to be the fall of Reuben from its old place at the head of the brother-tribes, we have no difficulty in seeing how the second version arose out of it. The people of the congregation, *i.e.*, of the church, having once come on the scene, the spiritual heads, Moses and Aaron, take the place of the popular leader Moses, and the jealousy of the secular grandees is now directed against the class of hereditary priests, instead of against the extraordinary influence on the community of a heaven-sent hero. All these changes are the natural outcome of the importation of the hierocracy into Mosaic times. From the second version we can go further and understand the origin of the third. In the earlier version the princes of the tribe of Reuben were forced to give way to a prince of the tribe of Judah. In the progress of time Korah the prince of the tribe of Judah is replaced by the eponymous head of a post-exilic Levitical family, of the same name. The contest between clergy and aristocracy is here transformed into a domestic strife between the higher and the inferior clergy, which was no doubt raging in the time of the narrator. Thus the three versions are developed, the origin and collocation of which appears from every other point of view to be an insoluble enigma. The one arises out of the other in the direct line of descent: the metamorphoses took place under the influence of great historical changes which are well known to us; and in the light of Jewish history from Josiah downwards they are by no means unintelligible. *1*

** 1 The details of the demonstration will be found in the Jahrbb. fuer Deutsche Theologie, 1776, p. 572 seq., 1877, p. 454, note, and in the Leyden Theol. Tijdschrift, 1878, p. 139 seq. ***

We come to the migration of the Israelites to the land east of the Jordan. According to the Jehovist the neighbouring tribes place obstacles in their way, and the land in which they desire to settle has to be conquered with the sword. The Priestly Code tells us as little of all this as in an earlier instance of the war with Amalek; from all it says we should imagine that the Israelites went straight to their mark and met with no difficulty in the region in question; the land is ownerless, and the possession of it is granted by Moses and Eleazar to the two tribes Reuben and Gad (Numbers xxxii.). But that war may not be completely wanting under Moses, we have afterwards the war with the Midianites, on which we have already commented (Numbers xxxi.). There is not much story about it, only numbers and directions; and in verse 27 there is a suspicion of 1Samuel xxx. 24, as if that passage were the groundwork of the whole. The passage is extremely interesting as showing us the views taken of war by the Jews of the later time who had grown quite unaccustomed to it. The occasion of the war also is noticeable; it is undertaken not for the acquisition of territory, nor with any other practical object, but only to take vengeance on the Midianites for having seduced some of the Israelites to uncleanness.

The elders of Midian, so the story goes, went to the soothsayer Balaam to ask his advice as to what should be done against the Israelite invaders. He suggested a means by which the edge of the invasion might be broken; the Midianites should give their daughters to the Israelites for wives, and so deprive the holy people of their strength, the secret of which lay in their isolation from other peoples. The Midianites took Balaam's advice and succeeded in entangling many of the Israelites with the charms of their women; in consequence of which Jehovah visited the faithless people with a severe plague. The narrative of the Priestly Code up to this point has to be pieced together from Numbers xxxi. 8, 16 and Joshua xiii. 22, and from what is implied in the sequel of it; at this point the portion of it begins which is preserved to us (Numbers xxv. 6 seq.), and we are told how the plague was ultimately stayed. A certain man coolly brings a Midianitish woman into the camp before the very eyes of Moses and the weeping children of Israel: then the young hereditary priest Phinehas takes a spear, transfixes the godless pair, and by this zeal averts the anger of Jehovah. This narrative is based on the Jehovistic one, which is also preserved to us only in part (Numbers xxv. 1-5), about the backsliding of Israel in the camp of Shittim to the service of Baal-Peor, to which they were seduced by the daughters of Moab. In the Priestly Code the idolatry has quite disappeared, all but some unconscious reminiscences, and no sin is alleged but that of whoredom, which in the original story merely led up to the main offence. This is done manifestly with the idea that marriage with foreign women is in itself a falling away from Jehovah, a breach of the covenant. This change was extremely suitable to the circumstances of exilic and post-exilic Judaism, for in these later days there was no immediate danger of gross idolatry, but it took a good deal of trouble to prevent heathenism from making its way into the midst of the people under the friendly form of mixed marriages. The version of the Priestly Code, however, mixes up with the Baal-Peor story of the Jehovist the figure of Balaam, which is also borrowed from the Jehovist but entirely transformed in the process. In the form under which he appears in the early history he transgresses all the ideas of the Priestly Code. An Aramaean seer, who is hired for money and makes all sorts of heathen preparations to prophesy, but who yet is not an impostor, but a true prophet as much as any in Israel, who even stands in the most intimate relations with Jehovah, though cherishing the intention of cursing Jehovah's people—that is too much for exclusive Judaism. The correction is effected by the simple device of connecting Balaam with the following section, and making him the intellectual instigator of the devilry of the Midianitish women; and in this new form which he assumes in the Priestly Code he lives on in the Haggada. The reason for changing the Moabites into Midianites is not made clear; but the fact is undoubted that the Midianites never lived in that part of the world.

In the Book of Numbers the narrative sections, which are in the style and colour of the Priestly Code, have more and more the character of mere additions and editorial supplements to a connection which was already there and had a different origin. The independent main stock of the Priestly Code, the Book of the Four Covenants, or the Book of Origins (Q), more and more gives way to later additions, and ceases altogether, it appears, at the death of Moses. It is at least nowhere to be traced in the first half of the Book of Joshua, and so we cannot reckon as part of it those extensive sections of the second half, belonging to the Priestly Code, which treat of the division of the land. Without a preceding history of the conquest these sections are quite in the air; they cannot be taken as telling a continuous story of their own, but presuppose the Jehovistic-Deuteronomic work. In spite of distaste to war and to records of war (1Chronicles xxii. 8, xxviii. 3), an independent work like the Book of the Four Covenants could not possibly have passed over the wars of Joshua in silence.

A comparison of the different accounts of the entry of the Israelite tribes into the occupation of the conquered land may close this discussion. The Priestly Code, agreeing in this with the Deuteronomistic revision, represents the whole of Canaan as having been made a *tabula rasa*, and then, masterless and denuded of population, submitted to the lot. First the tribe of Judah receives its lot, then Manasseh and Ephraim, then the two tribes which attached themselves to Ephraim and Judah, Benjamin and Simeon, and lastly the five northern tribes, Zebulon, Issachar, Asher, Naphtali, Dan. "These are the inheritances which Eleazar the priest, and Joshua ben Nun, and the heads of the tribes of the children of Israel divided for an inheritance by lot in Shiloh before Jehovah at the door of the tabernacle."

According to the Jehovist, Judah and Joseph appear to have had their territory allocated to them at Gilgal (xiv. 6), and not by lot, and to have entered into occupation of it from there. A good while afterwards the land remaining over is divided by lot among the seven small tribes still unprovided for, from Shiloh, or perhaps originally from Shechem (xviii. 2-10). Joshua alone casts the lot and gives instructions; Eleazar the priest does not act with him. Even here the general principle of the Priestly Code, which knows no differences among the tribes, is somewhat limited; but it is much more decidedly contradicted by the important chapter, Judges i.

The chapter is, in fact, not a continuation of the Book of Joshua at all, but a parallel to it, which, while it presupposes the conquest of the east-Jordan lands, does not speak of the west-Jordan lands as conquered, but tells the story of the conquest, and that in a manner somewhat differing from the other source. From Gilgal, where the "Angel of Jehovah" first set up his tent, the tribes march out one by one to conquer their "lot" by fighting; first Judah, then Joseph. We hear only of these two, and with regard to Joseph we only hear of the very beginning of the conquest of his land. There is no mention of Joshua; nor would his figure as commander-general of Israel suit the view here given of the situation; though it would very well admit of him as leader of his tribe. The incompleteness of the conquest is acknowledged unreservedly; the Canaanites lived on quietly in the cities of the plain, and not till the period of the monarchy, when Israel had grown strong, were they subdued and made tributary. This chapter, as well as the main stem of the Book of Judges, corresponds to the Jehovistic stratum of the tradition, to which also passages in Joshua, of an identical or similar import, may be added without hesitation. The Angel of Jehovah is enough to tell us this. The difference which exists between it and the Jehovistic main version in the Book of Joshua is to be explained for the most part by the fact that the latter is of Ephraimite origin, and in consequence ascribes the conquest of the whole land to the hero of Ephraim or of Joseph, while Judges i. leans more to the tribe of Judah. Moreover, we find in the Book of Joshua itself the remnant of a version (ix. 4-7, 12-14) in which, just as in Judges i., the actors are the "men of Israel," who "ask counsel of the mouth of Jehovah," while elsewhere Joshua alone has anything to say, being the successor of Moses, and drawing his decisions from no source but the authority of his own spirit. And finally, we have to consider Exodus xxiii., 20 seq., where also there is a correspondence with Judges i., in the fact that not Joshua but the Angel of Jehovah (Judges v. 23) is the leader of Israel, and that the promised land is not conquered all at once but gradually, in the process of time.

Judges i. presents certain anachronisms, and is partly made up of anecdotes, but these should not prevent us from acknowledging that the general view given in this chapter of the process of the conquest, is, when judged by what we know of the subsequent period of Israel, incomparably more historical than that in the Book of Joshua, where the whole thing is done at once with systematic thoroughness, the whole land being first denuded of its inhabitants, and then divided by lot among the different tribes. The latter view may have come about partly from a literal interpretation of "lot" (Judges xviii. 1), an expression which properly applies to the farm of a family but is here used for the territory of a tribe. It was also favoured no doubt by the tendency to compress a long development into its first great act; and as this tendency is carried out with the greatest thoroughness in the Priestly Code, that document stands furthest from the origin of the tradition. *1* The same conclusion is led up

** 1. In the Deuteronomistic revision (Joshua xxi, 43-45) there is still a trace of hesitation, a certain difficulty in parting with the old view altogether (Deuteronomy vii. 22; Judg. iii. 1, 2); and besides the motives for the change are much plainer here: the Canaanites are extirpated to guard against the infection of the new settlers with their idolatary. ***

to by the circumstance that the tribe of Joseph is never mentioned, one of the two tribes, Ephraim and Manasseh, being always spoken of instead, and that these two tribes are almost put out of sight by Judah. And yet Joshua, the leader of Ephraim, is leader here also of all Israel, having been preserved from the old original tradition, which was Ephraimitic.

It involves no contradiction that, in comparing the versions of the tradition, we should decline the historical standard in the case of the legend of the origins of mankind and of the legend of the patriarchs, while we employ it to a certain extent for the epic period of Moses and Joshua. The epic tradition certainly contains elements which cannot be explained on any other hypothesis than that there are historical facts underlying them; its source is in the period it deals with, while the patriarchal legend has no connection whatever with the times of the patriarchs. *1* This justifies the difference of treatment.

** 1. Some isolated statements there are here also to which the historical standard may be applied. We may call it a more accurate representation that Hebron was inhabited in the time of Abraham by the, Canaanites and Perizzites, than that the Hittites dwelt there at that time. The latter, according to 2Samuel xxiv. 6 (Bleek, Einleitung, 4th edition, pp. 228, 597), dwelt in Coele-Syria, and according to 2Kings vii. 6, in the neihbourhood of the Aramaeans of Damascus. The statement that the Israelites received from Pharaoh because they were shepherds the pasture-land of Goshen on the north-east frontier of Egypt and there dwelt by themselves, is to be preferred to the statement that they were settled among the Egyptians in the best part of the land, **

Our last result is still the same: whether tried by the standard of poetry or by that of history, the Priestly Code stands both in value and in time far below the Jehovist.

VIII.III.3. In rough strokes I have sought to place before the reader's view the contrast between the beginning and the end of the tradition of the Hexateuch. It would not be impossible to trace the inner development of the tradition in the intermediate stages between the two extremities. To do this we should have to make use of the more delicate results of the process of source-sifting, and to call to our aid the hints, not numerous indeed, but important, which are to be found in Deuteronomy and in the historical and prophetical books, especially Hosea. It would appear that legend from its very nature causes those who deal with it to strike out variations, that it cannot be represented objectively at all. Even at the first act of reducing it to writing the discolouring influences are at work, without any violence being done to the meaning which dwells in the matter. We can trace first of all the influence on the tradition of that specific prophetism which we are able to follow from Amos onwards. This is least traceable in the old main source of the Jehovist, in J; and yet it is remarkable that the Asheras never occur in the worship of the patriarchs. The second Jehovistic source, E, breathes the air of the prophets much more markedly, and shows a more advanced and thorough-going religiosity. Significant in this view are the introduction of Abraham as a Nabi, Jacob's burying the teraphim, the view taken of the macceba at Shechem (Jos. xxiv. 27), and above all the story of the golden calf. The Deity appears less primitive than in J, and does not approach men in bodily form, but calls to them from heaven, or appears to them in dreams. The religious element has become more refined, but at the same time more energetic, and has laid hold even of elements heterogeneous to itself, producing on occasion such strange mixtures as that in Genesis xxxi. 10-13. Then the law comes in and leavens the Jehovistic narrative, first the Deuteronomic (in Genesis even, and then quite strongly in Exodus and Joshua), while last of all, in the Priestly Code, under the influence of the legislation of the post-exile restoration, there is brought about a complete metamorphosis of the old tradition. The law is the key to the understanding even of the narrative of the Priestly Code. All the distinctive peculiarities of the work are connected with the influence of the law: everywhere we hear the voice of theory, rule, judgment. What was said above of the cultus may be repeated word for word of the legend: in the early time it may be likened to the green tree which grows out of the ground as it will and can; at a later time it is dry wood that is cut and made to a pattern with compass and square. It is an extraordinary objection to this when it is said that the post-exile period had no genius for productions such as the tabernacle or the chronology. It certainly was not an original age, but the matter was all there in writing, and did not require to be invented. What great genius was needed to transform the temple into a portable tent? What sort of creative power is that which brings forth nothing but numbers and names? In connection with such an age there can be no question at least of youthful freshness. With infinitely greater justice may it be maintained that such theoretical modelling and adaptation of the legend as is practiced in the Priestly Code, could only gain an entrance when the legend had died away from the memory and the heart of the people, and was dead at the root.

The history of the pre-historic and the epic tradition thus passed through the same stages as that of the historic; and in this parallel the Priestly Code answers both as a whole, and in every detail, to the Chronicles. The connecting link between old and new, between Israel and Judaism, is everywhere Deuteronomy.

The Antar-romance says of itself, that it had attained an age of 670 years, 400 years of which it had spent in the age of ignorance (i.e. old Arabic heathenism), and the other 270 in Islam. The historical books of the Bible might say something similar, if they were personified, and their life considered to begin with the reduction to writing of the oldest kernel of the tradition and to close with the last great revision. The time of ignorance would extend to the appearance of "the book," which, it is true, did not in the Old Testament come down from heaven all at once like the Koran, but came into existence during a longer period, and passed through various phases.

C. ISRAEL AND JUDAISM.

"The Law came in between."—VATKE, p. 183.

CHAPTER IX. CONCLUSION OF THE CRITICISM OF THE LAW.

Objections have been made to the general style of the proof on which Graf's hypothesis is based. It is said to be an illicit argument *ex silentio* to conclude from the fact that the priestly legislation is latent in Ezekiel, where it should be in operation, unknown where it should be known, that in his time it had not yet come into existence. But what would the objectors have? Do they expect to find positive statements of the non-existence of what had not yet come into being? Is it more rational, to deduce *ex silentio*, as they do, a positive proof that it did exist?-*to say, that as there are no traces of the hierocracy in the times of the judges and the kings it must have originated in the most remote antiquity, with Moses? The problem would in this case still be the same, namely, to explain how it is that with and after the exile the hierocracy begins to come into practical activity. What the opponents of Graf's hypothesis call its argument* ex silentio_, is nothing more or less than the universally valid method of historical investigation.

The protest against the argument *ex silentio* takes another form. It is pointed out that laws are in many cases theories, and that it is no disproof of the existence of a theory that it has not got itself carried out into practice. Deuteronomy was really nothing more than a theory during the pre-exile period, but who would argue from this that it was not there at all? Though laws are not kept, this does not prove they are not there,—provided, that is to say, that there is sufficient proof of their existence on other grounds. But these other proofs of the existence of the Priestly Code are not to be found—not a trace of them. It is, moreover, rarely the case with laws that they are theory and nothing more: the possibility that a thing may be mere theory is not to be asserted generally, but only in particular cases. And even where law is undoubtedly theory, the fact does not prevent us from fixing its position in history. Even legislative fancy always proceeds upon some definite presupposition or other; and these presuppositions, rather than the laws themselves, must guide the steps of historical criticism. *1*

*** 1. Cf. *I.III.2. ad fin., IV.III.3., V.II.1., VII.II.2..* This is the reason why the strata of the tradition require to be compared   as   carefully   as   those   of   the   law. ***

An argument which is the very opposite of this is also urged. The fact is insisted on that the laws of the Priestly Code are actually attested everywhere in the practice of the historical period; that there were always sacrifices and festivals, priests and purifications, and everything of the kind in early Israel. These statements must, though this seems scarcely possible, proceed on the assumption that on Graf's hypothesis the whole cultus was invented all at once by the Priestly Code, and only introduced after the exile. But the defenders of Graf's hypothesis do not go so far as to believe that the Israelite cultus entered the world of a sudden,—as little by Ezekiel or by Ezra as by Moses,—else why should they be accused of Darwinism by Zoeckler and Delitzsch? They merely consider that the works of the law were done before the law, that there is a difference between traditional usage and formulated law, and that even where this difference appears to be only in form it yet has a material basis, being connected with the centralisation of the worship and the hierocracy which that centralisation called into existence. Here also the important point is not the matter, but the spirit which is behind it, and may everywhere be recognised as the spirit of the age at one period or another. *2*

** 2. Comp. *II.III., III.III.1.*
****

All these objections, meanwhile, labour under the same defect, namely, that they leave out of view that which is the real point at issue. The point is not to prove that the Mosaic law was not in force in the period before the exile. There are in the Pentateuch three strata of law and three strata of tradition, and the problem is to place them in their true historical order. So far as the Jehovist and Deuteronomy are concerned, the problem has found a solution which may be said to be accepted universally, and all that remains is to apply to the Priestly Code also the procedure by which the succession and the date of these two works has been determined—that procedure consisting in the comparison of them with the ascertained facts of Israelite history. *3*

************************************* 3. The method is stated in the introduction: and special pains are taken to bring it out distinctly in the first chapter, that about the place of worship. **

One would imagine that this could not be objected to. But objections have been raised; the procedure which, when applied to Deuteronomy, is called historico-critical method, is called, when applied to the Priestly Code, construction of history. But history, it is well known, has always to be constructed: the order, Priestly Code, Jehovist, Deuteronomy, is not a thing handed down by tradition or prescribed by the nature of the case, but a hypothesis as yet only a score of years old or thereby, the reasons for which were somewhat incomprehensible, so that people have forgotten them and begun to regard the hypothesis as something objective, partaking of the character of dogma. The question is whether one constructs well or ill. Count Baudissin thinks a grave warning necessary of a certain danger, that, namely, of an exaggerated application of logic: that the laws follow each other in a certain order logically, he says, does not prove that they appeared in the same order in history. But it is not for the sake of logical sequence that we consider the development which began with the prophets to have issued finally in the laws of cultus; and those who set out from "sound human reason" have generally forced the reverse process of this on the history, in spite of the traces which have come down to us, and which point the other way. *1*

************************************** 1. And it would not be surprising when we consider the whole character of the polemic against Graf's hypothesis, if the next objection should be the very opposite of the above, *viz.* that it is not able to construct the history. ************************************

306

After laboriously collecting the data offered by the historical and prophetical books, we constructed a sketch of the Israelite history of worship; we then compared the Pentateuch with this sketch, and recognised that one element of the Pentateuch bore a definite relation to this phase of the history of worship, and another element of the Pentateuch to that phase of it. This is not putting logic in the place of historical investigation. The new doctrine of the irrationality of what exists is surely not to be pushed so far, as that we should regard the correspondence between an element of the law and a particular phase of the history as a reason for placing the two as far as possible asunder. At least this principle would have to be applied to the Jehovist and Deuteronomy too, and not to the Priestly Code only. What is right in the one case is fair in the other too; a little logic unfortunately is almost unavoidable.

Not everything that I have brought forward in the history of the cultus and the tradition, is a proof of the hypothesis; there is much that serves merely to explain phenomena at the basis of the hypothesis, and cannot be used as proving it. This is a matter of course. My procedure has intentionally differed from that of Graf in this respect. He brought forward his arguments somewhat unconnectedly, not seeking to change the general view which prevailed of the history of Israel. For this reason he made no impression on the majority of those who study these subjects; they did not see into the root of the matter, they could still regard the system as unshaken, and the numerous attacks on details of it as unimportant. I differ from Graf chiefly in this, that I always go back to the centralisation of the cultus, and deduce from it the particular divergences. My whole position is contained in my first chapter: there I have placed in a clear light that which is of such importance for Israelite history, namely, the part taken by the prophetical party in the great metamorphosis of the worship, which by no means came about of itself. Again I attach much more weight than Graf did to the change of ruling ideas which runs parallel with the change in the institutions and usages of worship; this has been shown mostly in the second part of the present work. Almost more important to me than the phenomena themselves, are the presuppositions which lie behind them.

Not everything that we have hitherto discussed proves, or is meant to prove, Graf's hypothesis. On the other hand, however, there is abundance of evidence, which has not yet been noticed. To discuss it all in detail, would take another book: in this work only a selection can be with all brevity indicated, if the limits are not to be transgressed which are imposed by the essentially historical character of these prolegomena. In these discussions the Pro will as a rule naturally suggest itself in the refutation of the Contra.

IX.I.

IX.I.1. Eberhard Schrader mentions, in his Introduction to the Old Testament, that Graf assigns the legislation of the middle books of the Pentateuch to the period after the exile; but he does not give the least idea of the arguments on which that position is built up, simply dismissing it with the remark, that "even critical analysis enters its veto" against it. Even critical analysis? How does it manage that? How can it prove that the one and sole cultus, worked out on every side to a great system, the denaturalising of the sacrifices and festivals, the distinction between the priests and Levites, and the autonomous hierarchy, are older than the Deuteronomic reform? Schrader's meaning is perhaps, that while the signs collected by a comparison of the sources as bearing on the history of worship show the order of succession to be Jehovist, Deuteronomy, Priestly Code, other signs of a more formal and literary nature would show the Priestly Code to be entitled to the first place, or at any rate not the last, and that the latter kind of evidence is of as much force as the former. Were this so, the scales would be equally balanced, and the question would not admit of a decision. But this awkward situation would only occur if the arguments of a literary nature to be urged on that side really balanced those belonging to the substance of the case which plead for Graf's hypothesis. In discussing the composition of the Hexateuch, *1*

** 1. Jahrb. Deutsche Theol., 1876, p. 392 seq, 531 seq; 1877, p. 407 seq. **

I have shown, following in the steps of other scholars, that this is by no means the case; and for the sake of completeness I will here repeat the principal points of that discussion.

IX.I.2. It is asserted that the historical situation of Deuteronomy is based not only on the Jehovistic, but also on the Priestly narrative. Deuteronomy proper (chaps. xii.-xxvi.) contains scarcely any historical matter, but before Moses comes to the business in hand, we have two introductions, chapter v.-xi. and chapter i.-iv., to explain the situation in which he promulgates "this Torah" shortly before his death. We are in the Amorite kingdom, east of the Jordan, which has already been conquered. The forty years' wanderings are about to close: the passage to the land of Canaan, for which this legislation is intended, is just approaching. Till this time, we hear in chapter v. 9, 10, the only law was that which is binding in all circumstances, and was therefore promulgated by God Himself from Horeb, the Law of the Ten Words on that occasion. The people deprecated any further direct revelation by Jehovah, and commissioned Moses to be their representative; and he accordingly betook himself to the sacred mount, stayed there forty days and forty nights, and received the two tables of the decalogue, and besides them the statutes and laws which now, forty years after, he is on the point of publishing, as they will come into force at the settlement. In the meantime the golden calf had been made down below; and when Moses descended from the mount, in his anger he broke the tables and destroyed the idol. Then he betook himself for a second period of forty days and nights to the mount, pleaded for mercy for the people and for Aaron; and after he had made, according to divine command, two new tables and a wooden chest for them, Jehovah once more wrote down exactly what stood on the tables which were broken. On this occasion, it is remarked in x. 8 seq., the Levites received their appointment as priests.

This is evidently a reproduction of the Jehovistic narrative, Exodus xix. xx. xxiv. xxxii-xxxiv. The Priestly Code, on the contrary, is entirely ignored. Deuteronomy

knows only two laws, the decalogue, which the people received, and the statutes and judgments which Moses received, at Mount Horeb. They were both given at the same time, one directly after the other: but only the decalogue had till now been made public. Where is the whole wilderness-legislation as given from the tabernacle? Is it not denying the very notion of its existence, that Moses only publishes the Torah at the passage into the Holy Land, because it has application and force for that land, and not for the wilderness? Apart from the fact that the Deuteronomist, according to chapter xii., knew nothing of a Mosaic central sanctuary, can he have read what we now read between Exodus xxiv. and xxxii.? He passes over all that is there inserted from the Priestly Code. Noldeke finds, it is true,
1

*** 1. Jahrbb. fuer prot. Theologie, 1875, p. 350. ***

a reminiscence of that code in the ark of acacia wood, Deuteronomy x. 1. But the ark is here spoken of in a connection which answers exactly to that of the Jehovist (Exod xxxii. xxxiii.), and is quite inconsistent with that, of the Priestly Code (Exodus xxv. seq.). It is only instituted after the erection of the golden calf, not at the very beginning of the divine revelation, as the foundation-stone of the theocracy. True, the ark is not mentioned in JE, Exodus xxxiii., as we now have it, but in the next Jehovistic piece (Numbers x. 33) it suddenly appears, and there must have been some statement in the work as to how it came there. The tabernacle also appears ready set up in xxxiii. 7, without any foregoing account of its erection. The institution of the ark as well as the erection of the tabernacle must have been narrated between xxxiii. 6 and 7, and then omitted by the present editor of the Pentateuch from the necessity of paying some regard to Q, Exodus xxv.; that this is the case many other considerations also tend to prove. *2*

** 2. Without the ark there is no use of the tabernacle, and the distinction in Exodus xxxiii. which is treated as one of importance, between the representation (Mal'ak) of Jehovah and Jehovah Himself, has no meaning. By making an image the Israelites showed that they could not do without a sensible representation of the Deity, and Jehovah therefore gave them the ark instead of the calf. **

That the Deuteronomist found JE in a more complete form, before it was worked up with Q, than that in which we have it after the working up, is not such a difficult assumption that one should be driven into utter impossibilities in order to avoid it. For according to Noldeke either the author of Deuteronomy v.-xi. had before him the Pentateuch as it now is, and was enabled, very curiously, to sift out JE from it, or he used JE as an independent work, but read Q as well, only in such a way that his general view was in no way influenced by that of the priestly work, but on the contrary contradicts it entirely and yet unconsciously—since his work leaves no opening for a ritual legislation given side by side with the Decalogue, and that ritual legislation is the whole sum and substance of the Priestly Code. To such a dilemma are we to make up our minds, because one trait or another of the Deuteronomic narrative cannot be traced in JE as we now have it, and is preserved in Q? Does this amount, in the circumstances, to a proof that such traits were derived from that source? Must not some regard in fairness be paid to the ensemble of the question ?

We may, further, remember in this connection Vatke's remark, that the wooden ark in Deuteronomy x. 1, is by no means very similar to that of Exodus xxv., which, to judge by the analogy of the golden table and altar, must rather have been called a golden ark. It takes even more good will to regard the statement about Aaron's death and burial in Mosera and the induction of Eleazar in his place (Deuteronomy x. 6, 7) as a reminiscence of Q (Numbers xx. 22 seq.), where Aaron dies and is buried on Mount Hor. In JE also the priests Aaron and Eleazar stand by the side of Moses and Joshua (cf. Joshua xxiv. 33). The death and burial of Aaron are certainly no longer preserved in JE; but we cannot require of the editor of the Pentateuch that he should make a man die twice, once according to Q and once according to JE. And it must further be said that Deuteronomy x. 6, 7 is an interpolation; for the following verses x. 8 seq., in which not only Aaron and Eleazar, but all the Levites are in possession of the priesthood, are the continuation of x. 5, and rest on Exodus xxxii. Here we are still in Horeb, not in Mosera.

The historical thread which runs through Deuteronomy v. ix. x. may be traced further in chaps. i.-iv. After their departure from Horeb the Israelites come straight to Kadesh Barnea, and from this point, being commanded to invade the hill-land of Judaea, they first send twelve spies to reconnoitre the country, guided thereto by their own prudence, but also with the approval of Moses. Caleb is one of the spies, but not Joshua. After penetrating as far as the brook Eshcol they return; and though they praise the goodness of the land, yet the people are so discouraged by their report, that they murmur and do not venture to advance. Jehovah is angry at this, and orders them to turn back to the wilderness, where they are to wander up and down till the old generation is extinct and a new one grown up. Seized with shame they advance after all, but are beaten and driven back. Now they retreat to the wilderness, where for many years they march up and down in the neighbourhood of Mount Seir, till at length, 38 years after the departure from Kadesh, they are commanded to advance towards the north, but to spare the brother-peoples of Moab and Ammon. They conquer the territory of the Amorite kings, Sihon of Heshbon and Og of Bashan. Moses assigns it to the tribes of Reuben and Gad and the half-tribe of Manasseh, on condition that their army is to yield assistance in the remaining war. The continuous report comes to an end with the nomination of Joshua as future leader of the people.

This same narrative, with the addition of some scattered particulars in the Book of Deuteronomy, *1* will serve perfectly

************************************** 1. Appointment of judges and wardens (#W+RYM = peace-officials, who, according to xx. 9, are in war replaced by the captains), i. 9-18, Taberah, Massah, Kibroth Taavah (ix. 22), Dathan and Abiram (xi. 6), Balaam (xxiii. 5), Baal-peor (iv. 3). Only the Jehovist narrative of

Numbers xii. seems to be nowhere referred to. In Deuteronomy i. 9-18 the scene is still at Horeb, but this passage shows acquaintance with Numbers xi. and uses both versions   for   a   new   and   somewhat   different   one.
****

well as a thread to understand JE. What, on the contrary, is peculiar to the Priestly Code is passed over in deep silence, and from Exodus xxxiv. Deuteronomy takes us at once to Numbers x. While not a few of the narratives which Deuteronomy repeats or alludes to, occur only in JE and not in Q, the converse does not occur at all. And in those narratives which are found both in JE and in Q, Deuteronomy follows, in every case in which there is a distinct divergence, the version of JE. The spies are sent out from Kadesh, not from the wilderness of Paran; they only reach Hebron, not the neighbourhood of Hamath; Caleb is one of them, and not Joshua. The rebels of Numbers xvi. are the Reubenites Dathan and Abiram, not Korah and the Levites. After the settlement in the land east of Jordan the people have to do with Moab and Ammon, not with Midian: Balaam is connected with the former, not with the latter. The same of Baal-peor: Deuteronomy iv. 3 agrees with JE (Numbers xxv. 1-5), not with Q (Numbers xxv. 6 seq.). Things being so, we cannot, with Noldeke, see in the number of the spies (Deuteronomy i. 23) an unmistakable sign of the influence of Q (Numbers xiii. 2). Had the author read the narrative as it is now before us in Numbers xiii. xiv., it would be impossible to understand how, as we have seen, the Jehovist version alone made any impression on him. He must, accordingly, have known Q as a separate work, but it is a bold step to argue from such a small particular to the use of a source which everywhere else is entirely without influence and unknown, especially as the priority of this source is by no means established on independent grounds, but is to be proved by this alleged use of it. If there were a palpable difference between JE and Q in this point, if we could say that in Q there were twelve spies sent out, and in JE; three, the case would be different; but in Numbers xiii. the beginning of the narrative of JE has been removed and that of Q put in place of it, so that we do not know how the narrative of JE began, and what number, if any, was given in it. In such a state of matters the only reasonable course is to supply what is lacking in JE from Deuteronomy, which generally follows the Jehovist alone, and to conclude that the spies were twelve in number in this source also.

The instance in which the proof would be strongest that Deuteronomy was acquainted with the narrative of the Priestly Code, is x. 22. For the seventy souls which make up the whole of Israel at the immigration into Egypt, are not mentioned in JE, and there is no gap that we are aware of in the Jehovist tradition at this point. But they are by no means in conflict with that tradition, and even should we not take Deuteronomy x. 22 for a proof that the seventy souls found a place in it also, yet it must at least be acknowledged, that that passage is by no means sufficient to break down the evidence that the priestly legislation has the legislation of Deuteronomy for its starting-point. *1*

*** 1. Noldeke frequently argues from such numbers as 12 and 70, as if they only occurred in Q. But that is not the

case. As Q in the beginning of Genesis has groups of 10, JE has groups of 7; 12 and 40 occur in JE as frequently as in Q, and 70 not less frequently. It is therefore surprising to find the story of the 12 springs of water and the 70 palm-trees of Elim ascribed to Q for no other reason than because of the 12 and the 70. Not even the statements of the age of the patriarchs—except so far as they serve the chronological system—are a certain mark of Q: compare Genesis xxxi. 18, xxxvii. 2, xli. 26, l. 26; Deuteronomy xxxiv. 7; Joshua xxiv. 29. Only the names of the 12 spies and the 70 souls are incontestably the property of the Priestly Code, but it is by no means difticult to show (especially in Genesis xlvi. 8-27) that they are far less original than the figures. The numbers are round numbers, and in fact do not admit of such a recital of the items of which they are made up.
****

VIII.I.3. As a further objection to Graf's hypothesis, the Deuteronomistic revision of the Hexateuch is brought into the field. That revision appears most clearly, it is said, in those parts which follow the Deuteronomic Torah and point back to it. It used to be taken for granted that it extends over the Priestly portions as well as the Jehovistic; but since the occasion arose to look into this point, it is found that it is not so. The traces which Noldeke brings together on the point are trifling, and besides this do not stand the test. He says that the Deuteronomistic account of the death of Moses (Deuteronomy xxxii. 48 seq., xxxiv. 1 seq.) cannot be regarded as anything else than an amplification of the account of the main stem (Q), which is preserved almost in the same words. But Deuteronomy xxxiv. 1b-7 contains nothing of Q and xxxii. 48-52 has not undergone Deuteronomistic revision. He also refers to Josh. ix. 27: "Joshua made the Gibeonites at that day hewers of wood and drawers of water for the congregation and for the altar of Jehovah even unto this day, in the place which He should choose." The second part of this sentence, he says, is a Deuteronomistic addition to the first, which belongs to the Priestly narrative. But Noldeke himself acknowledges that the Deuteronomistically-revised verses ix. 22 seq. are not the continuation of the priestly version 15c, 17-21, but of the Jehovistic version 15ab, 16; and between verse 16 and verse 22 there is nothing wanting but the circumstance referred to in verse 26. The phrase *hewer of wood and drawer of water* is not enough to warrant us to separate verse 27 from 22-26; the phrase occurs not only in verse 21 but also in JE verse 23. The words FOR THE CONGREGATION do certainly point to the Priestly Code, but are balanced by the words which follow, FOR THE ALTAR OF Jéhovah, which is according to the Jehovistic view. The original statement is undoubtedly that the Gibeonites are assigned to the altar or the house of Jehovah. But according to Ezekiel xliv. the hierodulic services in the temple were not to be undertaken by foreigners, but by Levites; hence in the Priestly Code the servants of the altar appear as servants of the congregation. From this it results that LMZBX is to be preferred in verse 27 to L(DH W, the latter being a later correction. As such it affords a proof that the last revision of the Hexateuch proceeded from the Priestly Code, and not from Deuteronomy. As for Joshua xviii. 3-10, where Noldeke sees in the account of the division of the land another instance of Deuteronomistic addition, I have already indicated my opinion, *VIII.III.2.*. The piece is Jehovistic, and if the view were to be found in the Priestly Code at all, that Joshua first allotted their territory to Judah and Ephraim, and then, a good while after, to the other seven tribes, that source must have derived such a view from JE, where alone it has its roots. *1*

** 1. Jahrbb. fur Deutsche Theol., 1876, p. 596 seq. **

And lastly, Noldeke considers Josh. xxii. to speak quite decidedly for his view; but in the narrative of the Priestly Code, xxii. 9-34, to which the verses 1-8 do not belong, there is no sign of Deuteronomistic revision to be found. *2*

** 2. Joh. Hollenberg in Stud. und Krit., 1874, p. 462 seq. **

There is a more serious difficulty only in the case of the short chapter, Josh. xx., of which the kernel belongs to the Priestly Code, though it contains all sorts of additions which savour strongly of the Deuteronomistic revision. Kayser declares these awkward accretions to be glosses of quite a late period. This may seem to be pure tendency-criticism; but it is reinforced by the confirmation of the Septuagint, which did not find any of those alleged Deuteronomistic additions where they now are. *3*

** 3. Aug. Kayser, Das vorexilische Buch der Urgeschichte Israels (Strassburg, 1874), p. 147, seq.; Joh. Hollenberg, der Character der Alex. Uebersetzung des B. Josua (Programm des Gymn. zu Moers, 1876), p. 15. **

But were it the case that some probable traces of Deuteronomistic revision were actually to be found in the Priestly Code, we must still ask for an explanation of the disproportionately greater frequency of such traces in JE. Why, for example, are there none of them in the mass of laws of the middle books of the Hexateuch? This is undoubtedly and everywhere the fact, and this must dispose us a priori to attach less weight to isolated instances to the contrary: the more so, as Joshua xx. shows that the later retouchings of the canonical text often imitate the tone of the Deuteronomist.

IX.II.

IX.II.1. I have said that in the L)DH W of Josh. ix. 27, we have the addition of a final priestly revision. Such a revision must be assumed to have taken place, if the Priestly Code is younger than Deuteronomy. But the assumption of its existence does not depend on deduction merely: Kuenen argued for it inductively, even before he became a supporter of Graf's hypothesis. *1*

*** 1. Historisch-Kritisch Onderzoek I. (Leyden, 1861), p. 165; the reviser of the Pentateuch must be sought in the same circles in which the Book of Origins (Q) arose and was gradually extended and modified, *i.e.*, among the priests of Jerusalem, p. 194; it is generally thought that the Deuteronomist is the reviser of the whole Book of Joshua, but his hand is not to be traced everywhere,—not, for example, in the priestly sections; the last reviser is to be distinguished from the Deuteronomist. In certain narratives of Numbers and Joshua, Kuenen detected very considerable additions by the last reviser, and the results of his investigation have now been published in the first part of the second edition of his great isagogic work (Leyden, 1885). **

This may be best demonstrated by examining the chapters Leviticus xvii.-xxvi. At present they are incorporated in the Priestly Code, having undergone a revision with that view, which in some places adds little, in others a good deal. Viewed, however, as they originally were, they form a work of a peculiar character by themselves, a work pervaded by a somewhat affected religious hortatory tone, which harmonises but little with the Priestly Code. The author worked largely from earlier authorities, which explains, for example, how chapter xviii. and chapter xx. both find a place in his production. Leviticus xvii.-xxvi is incomparably instructive for the knowledge it affords of literary relationships: it is a perfect compendium of the literary history of the Pentateuch. *2*

*** 2. Compare Jahrbb. fur Deutsche Theol., 1877, p. 422-444, especially on the elimination of the additions of the reviser. In the present discussion I shall not take these into account. In chapter xxiii., for example, I only take account of verses 9-22, 39-44, in chapter xxiv. only of vers. 15-22 ***

As with Deuteronomy, so with this legislation; it is clear that it goes back to the Jehovistic legislation of Sinai (Exodus xx.-xxiii.) as its source. It also bears to have been given on Mount Sinai (xxv. 1, xxvi. 46). It is addressed to the people, and is popular in its contents, which are chiefly of a civic and moral character. It is meant only for the promised land and for settled life, not for the wilderness as well. The festivals are three in number, and have not quite parted with their character as feasts of harvest. Among the sacrifices the sin-offering and the trespass-offering are wanting. The legislation does deal with the cultus to a disproportionate extent, but the directions about it do not go into technical details, and are always addressed to the people. Even in those directions which concern the priests the people are addressed, and the priests are spoken of in the third person. Nor are palpable points of contact wanting. Leviticus xix. 2-8, 9-18, may be regarded as counterparts of the first and second tables of the decalogue. The precept, "Thou shalt not respect the person of the poor, nor honour the person of the mighty," xix. 15, is a development of that in Exodus xxiii. 3, and a number of other precepts in Leviticus xix. could stand with equal appropriateness in Exodus xxii. 17 seq. The directions in Leviticus xxii. 27-29 are similar to those of Exodus xxii. 29, xxiii. 18, 19. In the same way those of Leviticus xxiv. 15-22 are based both in contents and form on Exodus xxi. 12. *1*

** 1. Compare xxiv. 15 seq. with Exodus xxii. 27 (xxi. 17); xxiv. 18 with Exodus xxi. 28 seq.; xxiv. 19, 20 with Exodus xxi. 33, 34; xxiv. 21 with Exodus xxi. 28 seq. **

In xxiv. 22 we notice a polemical reference to Exodus xxi. 20 seq., 26 seq. In xxv. 1-7 the whole of the expressions of Exodus xxiii. 10, 11 are repeated. In xx. 24, we have the Jehovistic phrase, "a land flowing with milk and honey."

Yet Leviticus xvii.-xxvi. only takes its starting-point from the Jehovistic legislation, and modifies it very considerably, somewhat in the manner of Deuteronomy. There is a demonstrable affinity with Deuteronomy both in the ideas and in the expressions. Common to both is the care for the poor and the undefended: to both humanity is a main object of legislation. "If a stranger sojourn with thee in your land, ye shall not vex him; he shall be unto you as one born among you, and thou shalt love him as thyself; for ye were strangers in the land of Egypt" (xix. 34).

Leviticus xvii. seq. attaches great importance to unity of worship. It is still a demand, not a presupposition (xvii. 8 seq., xix. 30, xxvi. 2); the motive of it is to guard against heathen influences and to secure the establishment of a monotheism without images. *2*

** 2. xvii. 7 (cf. 2Chronicles xi. 15), xviii. 21, xix. 4, 19, 26, 29, 31, xx. 2 seq. 6, xxvi. 1, 30. With regard to the date we have to note the stern prohibition of the service of Moloch. On Lev, xvii. see above, p. 376. **

This is quite recognisable, and forms an important point of contact with Deuteronomy. The same contact may be observed in the prohibition of certain observances of mourning (xix. 27 seq.), the calculation of Pentecost from the beginning of barley harvest (xxiii. 15), the seven days' duration of the feast of tabernacles, and the cheerful sacrificial feasts which are to accompany its observance. Add to this a similarity by no means slight in the colour of the language, *e.g.*, in xviii. 1-5, 24-30, xix. 33-37, xx. 22 seq., xxv. 35 seq. Some of the phrases may be mentioned. "When ye are come into the land that I shall give you." "Ye shall rejoice before Jehovah." "I am Jehovah that brought you up out of the land of Egypt." "Ye shall keep my commandments and statutes and laws, to do them."

But the legislation we have here is further advanced than Deuteronomy. In the festivals the joint sacrifice of the congregation is already prominent (xxiii. 9-22). The priests are not the Levites, but the sons and brothers of Aaron, their income has grown materially, their separate holiness has reached a higher point. Stricter demands are also made on the laity for personal holiness, especially as regards continence from the sins of the flesh, and the marriage of relatives (Leviticus xviii. xx.). Marriage with an uncle's wife is forbidden (xviii. 14, xx. 20), whereas in Deuteronomy it is still legal. The work dates from a time when exile was a familiar idea: xviii. 26 seq.: "Ye shall keep my statutes and my judgments, and shall not commit any of those abominations; for the men that were in the land before you did these things, and the land vomited them out. Take care that the land spue not you out also as it spued out the nations that were before you." Similarly xx. 23 seq.: and in a legislative work such utterances prove more than they would in a prophecy. Now as our section departs from Deuteronomy, it approaches to Ezekiel. This is its closest relationship, and that to which attention has been most drawn. It appears in the peculiar fusion of cultus and morality, in the notion of holiness, in a somewhat materialistic sense, as the great requirement of religion, and in the fact that the demand of holiness is made to rest on the residence of the people near the sanctuary and in the holy land. *1*

** 1. On Leviticus xxii. 24, 25, compare Kuenen's Hibbert Lectures. **

But the affinity is still more striking in the language: many unusual phrases, and even whole sentences, from Ezekiel, are repeated in Leviticus xvii. seq. *2*

** 2. Compare Colenso, Pentateuch and Joshua, vi. p. 3-23. Kayser, op. cit. p. 177- 179. Smend on Ezekiel, p. xxv. **

The 10th of the 7th month is in Leviticus xxv. 9 as in Ezekiel, new-year's day, not, as in the Priestly Code, the great day of atonement. This led Graf to regard Ezekiel himself as the author of this collection of laws in Leviticus; and Colenso and Kayser followed him. But this is out of the question; notwithstanding the numerous points of contact both in linguistic and material respects, the agreement is by no means complete. Ezekiel knows no seed of Aaron, and no wine at the sacrifices (Leviticus xxiii. 13); his festival legislation shows considerable differences, and in spirit is more akin to the Priestly Code. And if he were the author he would have said something about the proper place in the cultus of the Levites and of the prince.

The corpus in question, which Klostermann called, not inappropriately, the Law of Holiness, inclines from Ezekiel towards the Priestly Code: in such pieces as xvii. xxi. xxii. it takes some closeness of attention to see the differences from the latter, though in fact they are not inconsiderable. It stands between the two, somewhat nearer, no doubt, to Ezekiel. How are we to regard this fact? Jehovist, Deuteronomy, Ezekiel, are a historical series; Ezekiel, Law of Holiness, Priestly

Code, must also be taken as historical steps, and this in such a way as to explain at the same time the dependence of the Law of Holiness on the Jehovist and on Deuteronomy. To assume that Ezekiel, having the Pentateuch in all other respects as we have it, had a great liking for this piece of it, and made it his model in the foundation of his style of thought and expression—such an assumption does not free us from the necessity of seeking the historical order, and of assigning his natural place in that order to Ezekiel; we cannot argue on such a mere chance. Now the question is not a complicated one, whether in the Law of Holiness we are passing from the Priestly Code to Ezekiel or from Ezekiel to the Priestly Code. The Law of Holiness underwent a last revision, which represents, not the views of Ezekiel, but those of the Priestly Code, and by means of which it is incorporated in that code. This revision has not been equally incisive in all parts. Some of its corrections and supplements are very considerable, *e.g.*, xxiii. 1-8, 23-38; xxiv. 1-14, 23. Some of them are quite unimportant, *e.g.*, the importation of the Ohel Moed (instead of the Mikdash or the Mishkan), xvii. 4, 6, 9, xix. 21 seq.; the trespass-offering, xix. 21 seq.; the Kodesh Kodashim, xxi. 22. Only in xxv. 8 seq. is the elimination of the additions difficult. But the fact that the last edition of the Law of Holiness proceeds from the Priestly Code, is universally acknowledged. Its importance for the literary history of Israel cannot be over-estimated. *1*

*** 1. L. Horst, in his discussion on Leviticus XVii,-XXYi, and Ezekiel (Colmar, 1881), has strikingly shown that the mechanical style of criticism in which Dillmann even surpasses his predecessor Knobel, is not equal to the problem presented by the Law of Holiness. He goes on, however, to an attempt to save, by modifying it, the old Strassburg view of Ezekiel's authorship; and as Kuenen justly remarks, he makes ship-wreck on Leviticus xxvi. (Theol. Tijdschr. 1882, p. 646). Cf. *next note, beginning "Horst...".*
****

IX.II.2. The concluding oration, Leviticus xxvi. 3-46, calls for special consideration. Earlier scholars silently assumed that this piece belonged to Leviticus xvii. 1-XXVI. 2; but many critics, Noldeke for example, now regard it as an interpolation in Leviticus of a piece which from its character should be elsewhere. At any rate the oration is composed with special reference to what precedes it. If it is not taken as a peroration, such as Exodus xxiii. 30-33, Deuteronomy xxviii., its position in such a part of the Priestly Code is quite incomprehensible. It has, moreover, a palpable connection with the laws in xvii.-xxv. The *land*, and *agriculture*, have here the same significance for religion as in chaps. xix. xxiii. xxv.; the threat of vomiting out (xviii. 25 seq., xx. 22) is repeated here more circumstantially; the only statute actually named is that of the fallow of the seventh year (xxvi. 34, xxv. 1-7). The piece begins with the expression, which is so characteristic of the author of chapter xvii. seq. "If ye walk in my statutes, and keep my commandments, and do them," and the same phrase recurs, with slight alteration, in vers. 15 and 43. The conclusion, verse 46, is, "These are the statutes and judgments and laws which Jehovah gave, to regulate the relation between Him and Israel on Mount Sinai, by Moses." This is obviously the subscription of a preceding corpus of statutes and judgments, such as we have in, xvii. 1-xxvi. 2. Mount Sinai is mentioned also in xxv. 1 as the place of revelation.

If Leviticus xxvi. is incontestably intended to form the conclusion of chaps. xvii.-xxv., it would be natural to suppose that the author of that collection was also the author of the oration. Noldeke thinks, however, that the language differs too much from that of xvii.-xxv. Yet he is obliged to acknowledge several resemblances, and these not unimportant; while some of the differences which he adduces (Bamoth, Gillulim, Hammanim, xxvi. 30) are really examples of similarity. Rare and original words may be found in the preceding chapters also. It may be that in chapter xxvi they are more frequent in proportion: yet this does not entitle us to say that the language generally is very original. On the contrary, it is everywhere characterised by borrowed expressions. So much of linguistic difference as actually remains is sufficiently accounted for by the difference of subject: first come laws in a dry matter-of-fact style, then prophecy in a poetical pathetic style. The idiosyncrasy of the writer has no scope in the former case, from the nature of the materials, some of which had already assumed their form before he made use of them. In the latter case he can express himself freely; and it is fair that this should not be overlooked.

The arguments brought forward by Noldeke against the probability that Leviticus xxvi. belongs to chaps. xvii.-xxv. and is not merely tacked on to them, disappear completely on a closer comparison of the literary character of the two pieces. Chapter xxvi. reminds us most strongly of Ezekiel's style, both in thought and language. The most significant passage is Leviticus xxvi. 39. The threat has been uttered that Israel is to be destroyed as a people, and that the remnant which escapes the destroying sword of the enemy is to be carried into exile, to sink under the weight of past calamity and present affliction. Then the speech goes on: "And they that are left of you shall *pine away* in their iniquity in your enemies' land; and also in the iniquities of their fathers shall they *pine away*. Then they will confess their own sin and the sin of their fathers." In Ezekiel, this confession actually occurs in the mouth of one of his fellow-exiles: they say (xxxiii. 10), "Our transgressions and our sins are heavy upon us, and we *pine away* in them, and cannot live." In the same strain the prophet says (xxiv. 23) that in his dull sorrow for the death of his wife he will be an emblem of the people: "ye shall not mourn nor weep, but ye shall *pine away* in your iniquities."

Nor are the other traits wanting in the oration which, as we say, accompanied the Ezekielic colouring of the preceding chapters. We do not expect to find traces of the influence of the Jehovist legislation (further than that Exodus xxiii. 20 seq. formed the model both for Deuteronomy xxviii. and Leviticus xxvi.); but to make up for this we find very distinct marks of the influence of the prophets, the older prophets too, as Amos (verse 31). We can as little conceive the existence of the Book of Ezekiel as of this chapter without the prophetic literature having preceded it and laid the foundation for it.

As for the relation to Deuteronomy, the resemblance of Leviticus xxvi. to Deuteronomy xxviii. is very great, in the arrangement as well as in the ideas. True, there are not many verbal coincidences, but the few which do occur are important. The expressions of xxvi. 16 occur nowhere in the Old Testament but in Deuteronomy xxviii. 22, 65: similarly R)#YM with the meaning it has in verse 45 only occurs in Deuteronomy xix. 14 and in the later literature (Isaiah lxi. 6). The metaphor of the uncircumcised heart (verse 41) only occurs in one other passage in the law, in Deuteronomy; the other instances of it are in prophecy, of contemporary or later date (Jeremiah iv. 4, ix. 24, 25, Ezekiel xliv. 7, 9). There are several more reminiscences of Jeremiah, most of them, however, not very distinct. We may remark on the relation between Jeremiah xvi. 18 in one respect to verse 30, and in another to verse 18 of our chapter. Here the sin is punished sevenfold, in Jeremiah double. The same is said in Isaiah xl. 2, lx. 7; and our chapter has also in common with this prophet the remarkable use of rtc,h (with sin or trespass as object). Did not the chapter stand in Leviticus, it would, doubtless, be held to be a reproduction, some small part of it of the older prophecies, the most of it of those of Jeremiah and Ezekiel: Leviticus xxvi. 34 is actually quoted in 2Chronicles xxxvi 22 as a word of the prophet Jeremiah.

Leviticus xxvi. has points of contact, finally, with the Priestly Code, in PRH WRBH, HQYM BRYT, HTWDH,)NY, (never)NKY), in the excessive use of the accusative participle and avoidance of verbal suffixes, and in its preferring the colourless NTN to verbs of more special meaning.

The only reason for the attempt to separate Leviticus xxvi. from xvii.-xxv. lies in the fact, that the exilic or post-exilic origin of this hortatory and denunciatory oration is too plain to be mistaken. To us, this circumstance can only prove that it belongs to xvii.-xxv., providing a weighty confirmation of the opinion we have already formed on other grounds as to the period which produced these laws. "If ye will not for all this hearken unto me, but walk contrary to me, then I will also walk contrary to you in fury; and I will chastise you seven times for your sins. Ye shall eat the flesh of your sons and daughters, and I will destroy your high places, and cast down your sun-pillars' and cast your carcasses upon the carcasses of your idols, and my soul shall abhor you. And I will make your cities waste, and bring your sanctuaries into desolation, and I will not smell the savour of your sweet odours. And I will bring the land into desolation, and your enemies who settle therein shall be astonished at it; and I will scatter you among the peoples, and will draw out the sword after you, and your land shall be desolate and your cities ruins. Then shall the land pay her sabbaths all the years of the desolation when you are in your enemies' land: even then shall the land rest and pay her sabbaths. As long as it lieth desolate it shall make up the celebration of the sabbaths which it did not celebrate as long as you dwelt in it. And upon them that are left alive of you I will send a faintness into their hearts in the land of their enemies, and the sound of a shaken leaf shall chase them, and they shall flee as fleeing from a sword, and they shall fall when none pursueth. And they shall fall one upon another as it were before a sword when none pursueth, and there shall be no stopping in the flight before your enemies. And ye shall lose yourselves among the peoples, and the land of your enemies shall eat you up. And they that are left of you shall pine away in their iniquity in your enemies' lands, and also in the iniquities of their fathers shall they pine away. And they shall confess their iniquity and the iniquity of their fathers in regard to their unfaithfulness which they committed against me, and that because they have walked contrary to me, I also walk contrary to them, and bring them into the land of their enemies. Then their uncircumcised heart is humbled, and then they pay their penalty, and I remember my covenant with Jacob, and also my covenant with Isaac, and also my covenant with Abraham, and I remember the land. The land also, left by them, pays its sabbaths, while she lieth without inhabitant and waste, and they themselves pay the penalty of their iniquity because, even because, they despised my judgments, and their soul abhorred my statutes. And yet for all that, when they be in the land of their enemies, I have not rejected them, neither have I abhorred them to destroy them utterly, and to break my covenant with them: for I am Jehovah their God. And I will for their sakes remember the covenant of their ancestors whom I brought forth out of the land of Egypt in the sight of the peoples, that I might be their God: I am Jehovah" (xxvi. 27-45).

These words undoubtedly cannot have been written before the Babylonian exile. It is said that the Assyrian exile will explain the passage: but where is there any similarity between the oration before us and the old genuine Isaiah? In Ezekiel's day such thoughts, feelings, and expressions as we have here can be shown to have prevailed: but it would be difficult to show that the fall of Samaria gave rise to such depression at Jerusalem: and Leviticus xxvi. was not written outside Jerusalem, for it presupposes unity of worship. The *Jews* are addressed here, as in Deuteronomy xxix., xxx., and they had no such lively feeling of solidarity with the deported Israelites as to think of them in connection with such threats. I even think it certain that the writer lived either towards the end of the Babylonian exile or after it, since at the close of the oration he turns his eyes to the restoration. In such prophets as Jeremiah and Ezekiel there is a meaning in such forecasting of the joyful future but here it contradicts both the historical position and the object of the threats, and appears to be explained most naturally as the result of an accident, *i.e.*, of actuality. That in a comparison of Leviticus xxvi. with Jeremiah and Ezekiel, the former cannot claim priority, appears distinctly from the comparative use of the phrase *uncircumised heart*. That phrase originates in Jeremiah (iv. 4, ix. 24 seq.), but in Leviticus xxvi. it is used as a well-known set term. In the same way the phrase *pine away in their iniquity* is repeated by Ezekiel as he heard it in the mouth of the people. He is its originator in literature; in Leviticus xxvi. it is borrowed. *1*

*** 1. Horst tries to find a place for Leviticus xxvi. in the last years of king Zedekiah (op. cit. p. 65, 66), but in this he is merely working out his theory that the author was the youthful Ezekiel; and the theory is sufficiently condemned if it leads to this consequence. Delitzsch (Zeitschr. fur Kirchl. Wissench. 1880, p. 619) thinks it a piece of impertinence in me to read out of Ezekiel xxxiii. what that passage says. On Deuteronomy x. 16, xxx. 6, and generally on the color Hieremianus in Deuteronomy, see Jahrb. fur D. Thhcol., 1877, p. 464. ***

The criticism of Leviticus xvii. seq. leads us to the result, that a collection of laws which took form during the period of the exile was received into the Priestly Code, and there clothed with fresh life. We need not then tremble at Schrader's threatening us with "critical analysis," and Graf's hypothesis will not be thereby overturned.

IX.II.3. Two or three further important traces of the final priestly revision of the Hexateuch may here find mention. In the story of the flood the verses vii. 6-9 are an editorial addition, with the object of removing a contradiction between JE and Q; it shares the ideas and speaks the language of the Priestly Code. In the title of Deuteronomy the verse, "It came to pass in the fortieth year, in the eleventh [(#TY] month, on the first day of the month, that Moses spake unto the children of Israel according to all that Jehovah had given him in commandment unto them" (i. 3) is shown by the most undoubted signs to belong to the Priestly Code, and is intended to incorporate Deuteronomy in that work. We have already shown that the Priestly Code in the Book of Joshua is simply a filling-up of the Jehovistic-Deuteronomistic narrative.

That the Priestly Code consists of elements of two kinds, first of an independent stem, the Book of the Four Covenants (Q), and second, of innumerable additions and supplements which attach themselves principally to the Book of the Four Covenants, but not to it alone, and indeed to the whole of the Hexateuch—this assertion has not, strange to say, met with the opposition which might have been expected. Ryssel has even seen in the twofold nature of the Priestly Code a means to maintain the position of the Book of the Four Covenants before the exile: he sacrifices the additions, and places the necessary interval between them and the main body of the work. He thinks the close affinity between the two parts is sufficiently explained by the supposition that they both issued from the same circle, that of the priesthood of Jerusalem. Were it the case that the temple of Jerusalem was as autonomous and as solely legitimate in the days of Solomon as in those of the foreign domination, that the priests had as much to say under Ahaz, Hezekiah, and Josiah as after the exile, if it were allowable to represent them according as it suits one's views, and not according to the historical evidence, if, in short, there were no Israelite history at all, such an explanation might be allowed to stand. The secondary part of the Priestly Code of necessity draws the primary part with it. The similarity in matter and in form, the perfect agreement in tendencies and ideas, in expressions and ways of putting things, all compel us to think that the whole, if not a literary, is yet a historical, unity.

IX.III.

IX.III.1. It has lately been the fashion to regard the language of the Priestly Code as an insuperable barrier to the destructive efforts of tendency criticism. But it is unfortunate that this veto of language is left as destitute of detailed proof, by Delitzsch, Riehm, and Dillmann, as the veto of critical analysis by Schrader; and we cannot be called upon to show proof against a contention which is unsupported by evidence. But I take advantage of the opportunity to communicate some detached observations, which I may perhaps remark did not occur to me in connection with the investigation of the Pentateuch, but on a quite different occasion. In the passage 2Samuel vi. 12 I was exceedingly struck with L(MT, and not less with BR) in the two passages Isaiah iv. 5, Amos iv. 13, and while following out the distribution of these two words I came on the traces of similar phenomena.

The language of the pre-exilic historical books is in general much akin to that of the Jehovistic work; that of the Priestly Code, on the contrary, is quite different. It is common enough to interpret this fact, as if the latter belonged to an earlier period. But not to mention that in that case the Code must have been entirely without influence on the history of the language, it agrees ill with this view, that on going back to the oldest documents preserved to us of the historical literature of the Hebrews we find the difference increasing rather than diminishing. Take Judges v. and 2Samuel i.; the poetical pieces in JE may be compared with them, but in Q there is nothing like them. And on the other hand, it is in the narratives which were introduced very late into the history, such as Judges xix.-xxi.; 1Samuel vii. viii. x. 17 seq. xii.; 1Kings xiii., and the apocryphal additions in 1Kings vi.-viii. that we recognise most readily some linguistic approximation to the Priestly Code. And as in the historical so also in the prophetical literature. The speech of Amos, Isaiah, Micah, answers on the whole to that of the Jehovist, not to that of the priestly author.

Deuteronomy and the Book of Jeremiah first agree with the Priestly Code in certain important expressions. In Ezekiel such expressions are much more numerous, and the agreement is by no means with Leviticus xvii.-xxvi. alone. *1*

** I Especially noticeable is P)T NGB TYMNH in Ezekiel and the Priestly Code. In the latter Negeb, even when it refers to the actual Negeb, yet is used as denoting south (Numbers xxxiv. 3, xxv. 2-4),   *i.e.,*   it   has   completely   lost   its   original   meaning. **

In the subsequent post-exilic prophets down to Malachi the points of contact are limited to details, but do not cease to occur; they occur also in the Psalms and in Ecclesiastes. Reminiscences of the Priestly Code are found nowhere but in the Chronicles and some of the Psalms. For that Amos iv. 11 is borrowed from Genesis xix. 29 is not a whit more clear than that the original of Amos i. 2 must be sought in Joel iv. 19 [iii. 16].

The Priestly Code maintains its isolated literary character as against the later literature also. This is the result partly of the use of a number of technical terms, partly of the incessant repetition of the same formulae, and of its great poverty of language. But if we neglect what is due to the stiff and hard idiosyncrasy of the author, it is undoubtedly the case that he makes use of a whole series of characteristic expressions which are not found before the exile, but gradually emerge and come into use after it. The fact is not even denied, it is merely put aside. To show what weight is due to it we may find room here for a short statement of the interesting points for the history of language to be found in Genesis i.

Genesis i. 1, R)#YT means in the older Hebrew, not the COMMENCEMENT of a process which goes forward in time, but the FIRST (and generally the BEST) part of a thing. In the sense of a beginning in time, as the contrary to)XRYT, it is first found in a passage of Deuteronomy, xi. 12; then in the titles in the Book of Jeremiah, xxvi. 1, xxvii. 1, xxviii. 1, xlix. 34, and in Isaiah xlvi. 10, and lastly in the Hagiographa, Job viii. 7, xili. 12; Proverbs xvii. 14; Ecclesiastes vii. 8. In Genesis x. 10 R)#YT MMLKTW has a different meaning from that in Jeremiah xxvi. 1 in the one it is the principal part of the kingdom; in the other it is the beginning of the reign. *In the beginning* was in the early time, if absolute, BFR)#NH, BATTXLH; if relative, BTXLT TXLT. *1*

*** 1 The vocalisation B:R#YT is very curious: we should expect BFRA$YT. It has been attempted to do justice to it by translating: "In the beginning, when God created heaven and earth—but the earth was without form and void, and darkness lay upon the deep, and the spirit of God brooded over the water—then God spake: Let there be light." But this translation is desperate, and certainly not that followed by the punctuators, for the Jewish tradition (Septuagint, Aquila, Onkelos) is unanimous in translating: "In the beginning God created heaven and earth." In Aramaic, on the contrary, such adverbs take, as is well known, the form of the *status constructus*. Cf. RBT Psalm lxvv. 10, cxx. 6.
****

We have already spoken *VIII.I.1. "a special word"* of the word BR), a word remarkable for its specific theological import. Apart from Amos iv. 13 and Isaiah iv. 5 it is first found outside the Priestly Code in the Deuteronomist in Exodus xxxiv. 10, Numbers xvi. 30 (?), Deuteronomy iv. 32, and in the Book of Jeremiah, xxxi. 22: then in Ezekiel xxi. 35, xxviii. 13, 15; Malachi ii. 10; in Psalms li. 12, lxxxix. 13, 48, cii. 19, civ. 30, cxlviii. 5; Ecclesiastes xii. 1. It occurs, however, most frequently, 20 times in fact, in Isaiah xl.-lxvi.; and curiously enough, never in Job, where we should expect to find it. It has nothing to do with B"R") (cut down wood) and BRY) (fat). *2*

*** 2. I do not speak of the use of *Elohim* and the application of the names of God in the Priestly Code: the matter is not yet clear to me. Very curious is H#M, Leviticus xxiv. 11.
****

Genesis i. 2, THW WBHW occurs also in Jeremiah iv. 23; Isaiah xxxiv. 11. THW alone is not so rare, but it also occurs, Isaiah xxix. 21 excepted, only in the later literature Deuteronomy xxxii. 10; 1Samuel xii. 21; Isaiah xxiv. 10, xl. 17, 23, xli. 29, xliv. 9, xlv. 18 seq., xlix. 4, lix. 4; Job vi. 18, xii.24, xxvi. 7; Psalm cvii. 40. The verb RXP (brood), which is common in Aramaic, only recurs in a single passage in the Old Testament, and that a late one, Deuteronomy xxxii. 11. Yet the possibility must be conceded that there was no occasion for its more frequent employment.

Genesis i. 4, HBDYL and NBDL (divide and divide one's self), common in the Priestly Code, is first used by Deuteronomy and the Deuteronomist (Deuteronomy iv. 41, x.8, xix. 7, xxix. 10; 1Kings viii. 53), then by Ezekiel (xxii. 26, xxxix. 14, xlii. 10) and the author of Isaiah xl. seq. (lvi. 3, lix. 2). It is most used by the writer of Chronicles, (1Chronicles xii. 8, xxiii. 13, xxv. 1; 2Chronicles xxv. 10; Ezra vi. 21, viii.24, ix. 1, x. 8, 11, 16 ; Nehemiah x. 2, 29, xiii. 3). On YWM)XD Genesis i. 5 compare Josephus, Antiquities I. i. 1: "That now would be the FIRST day, but Moses says ONE day; I could give the reason of this here, but as I have promised (in the Introduction) to give such reasons for everything in a separate work, I shall defer the exposition till then." The Rabbis also, in Genesis Rabba, feel the difficulty of the expression, which, however, has its parallel in the)XD LXD#, which belongs to the later way of speaking. In Syriac the ordinary expression is XD B#B); hence in the New Testament MIA SABBATWN for the first day of the week.

Genesis i. 6, RQY((firmament) is found, outside the Priestly Code, only in Ezekiel (i. 22-26, x. 1), and in still later writers ; Psalms xix. 2, cl. 1 ; Daniel xii. 3; cf. Job xxxviii. 18. *1*

*** 1. It does not mean, as is generally assumed, that which is beaten out thin, is stretched out. For, firstly, the heaven is never considered to be made of sheet-metal; secondly, the meaning in question only belongs to the Piel, and the substantive derived from it is RIQQUA(. The Kal, with which RQY(must be connected, is found in Isaiah xiii. 5, xliv. 24; Psalms cxxxvi. 6. It is generally translated *spread out*, but quite unwarrantably. Parallel with it are YSD and KWNN (compare Psalms xxiv. 2 with cxxxvi. 6); the Septuagint translates in all three passages with stereoun, and accordingly renders RQY(with STEREWMA (firmamentum). This rendering, which alone is supported by tradition, and which is very satisfactory, is confirmed by the Syriac, where the verb   RQ(is   frequent   in   the   sense   of   *fortify*.
****

Genesis i. 10 YMYM (the sea, singular, see i. 22; Leviticus xi. 9, 10), is rare in older times, and belongs to lofty poetical language; it is, on the contrary, frequent in Ezekiel (ten times), and in the Psalms (seven times); and occurs besides in Job vi. 3; Nehemiah ix. 6 ; Jonah ii. 4 ; Daniel xi. 45. Genesis i. 11 MYN (kind), a very peculiar word, especially in the form *Jeminehu*, is found outside of this chapter and Leviticus xiv., Genesis vi. 20, vii. 14, only in Deuteronomy xiv. and Ezekiel xlvii. 10.

324

Genesis i. 26, DMWT (likeness, verses 1, 3) does not occur in the earlier literature. It first appears in 2Kings xvi. 10, in a post-Deuteronomic passage, for the writer is that of chapter xi. seq., xxi. seq. Then in Ezekiel (15 times), Isaiah xiii. 4, xl. 18; 2Chronicles iv. 3; Psalms lxviii. 5. It is a borrowed word from Aramaic; and the corresponding verb only came into use in the period when Aramaic began to find its way in.

Genesis i. 27 ZFKFR (male) is in earlier times ZFKW.R; for this is the vocalization in Exodus xxiii. 17, xxxiv. 23; Deuteronomy xvi. 16, xx. 13; and if it is right in these passages, as we cannot doubt it is, it must be introduced in Exodus xxxiv. 19; Deuteronomy xv. 19; 1Kings xi. 15 seq. as well. In the Priestly Code ZFKFR occurs with great frequency, and elsewhere only in the later literature, Deuteronomy iv. 16; Jeremiah xx. 15, xxx. 6; Ezekiel xvi. 17; Isaiah lxvi. 7; Malachi i. 14; Judges xxi. 11, 12; 2Chronicles xxxi. 16; Ezra viii. As for NQBH (female), matters are even worse. Outside the Priestly Code it is only found in Jeremiah (xxxi. 22) and the Deuteronomist (iv. 16). The Jehovist, it is well known, always says)Y#, W)Y#H even of the lower animals: the editor of the Hexateuch, on the contrary, always follows the usage of the Priestly Code.

Genesis i. 28 XYH HRM#T attracts attention by the omission of the article with the substantive and its being merely prefixed to the following adjective; as if one should say in Greek,)ANHR (O)AGATHOS instead of (O)ANER (O)AGATHOS. In the same way i. 21 YWM H##Y, and ii. 3 YWM H#BY(Y. In Arabic there are some analogies for this, but on seeking one in Hebrew we have to come down to the period when it was usual to say KNST HGDWLH. KB# and RDH are Aramaisms. In KBSHWH we find the only verbal suffix in Genesis i. Instead we have always the forms)TM)TW; this is so in the Priestly Code generally. In the Jehovistic main work, in J, these substitutes with)T are only used sometimes and for special reasons: it may be generally asserted that they are more used the later we come down. Parallel with this is the use of)nky in J and)ny in the Priestly Code; the latter form grows always more frequent in later times.

These remarks carry us beyond Genesis i.; for the Priestly Code generally I am now able to refer to F. Giesebrecht's essay on the criticism of the Hexateuch. Such words as QRBN, (CM, L(MT, (#TY are each, by itself, strong arguments for assuming a late date for the production of the Priestly Code. We cannot believe that such everyday words should never have come into use in the other literature before the exile, if they were in existence. They cannot be counted technical terms: QRBN used in Hebrew for sacrifice and offering is simply as if an English writer should say priere instead of worship. In such comparisons of the vocabulary we have, however, to consider first the working up and revision which has been at work in every part of the books of the Bible, and secondly the caprice of the writers in apparent trifles, such as)NKY and)NY, especially outside the Pentateuch. These two agencies have so dislocated the original facts in this matter, that in general we can only deal in proportions, and must be content with showing that a word occurs say 3 times in the other literature and 27 times in an equal extent of the later. *1*

1. Too much importance must not be attached to Aramaisms: even when they admit of clear demonstration they prove little while occurring merely in single instances. We early find remarkable phenomena, such as NDR for NZR (hence NZYR = vovens), N+R for NCR (Amos i. 11 , Y+R for Y+RP?), comp. Arabic *lata* for *laisa*, Sur. 38, 2. Hudh. 84, 1. And yet such an Aramaism as BT #NTH in Numbers xv. 27, or even QRBN, is very remarkable.

IX.III.2. The study of the history of language is still at a very elementary stage in Hebrew. In that which pertains to the lexicographer it would do well to include in its scope the proper names of the Old Testament; when it would probably appear that not only Parnach (Numbers xxxiv. 25) but also composite names such as Peda-zur, Peda-el, Nathana-el, Pazi-el, Eli-asaph, point less to the Mosaic than to the Persian period, and have their analogies in the Chronicles. On the other hand, the prepositions and particles would have to be examined the use of the prepositions Beth and Lamed in the Priestly Code is very peculiar. That would lead further, to syntax; or better still, to rhetoric and style—a diffcult and little cultivated field of study, but one of great importance and lending itself readily to comparative treatment. This treatment yields the most far-reaching results in the case of those parallels which have an undoubted and direct relation to each other. The dependence of the Priestly Code on the Jehovist cannot be more strikingly demonstrated than by comparing its CDYQ, Genesis vi. 9, with the CDYQ BDWR HZH, of Genesis vii. 1 (JE.). The plural DRWT is quite on a line with the MYNYM, and the (MY H)RC, of the Rabbis, and the SPERMATA of Galatians iii. 15; it does not denote the successive generations, but contemporaries, the contemporaneous individuals of one and the same generation.

From words we are brought back to things again by noting that the age of the word depends in many cases on the introduction of the thing. The name BTR in the Song of Songs, for example, presupposes the cultivation of the malobathron in Syria and Palestine. The Priestly Code enumerates colours, stuffs, goldsmiths' work and jewels, which nowhere occur in the older literature: along with the Book of Ezekiel it is the principal quarry in the Old Testament for the history of art; and this is the less likely to be due to chance, as the geographical horizon of the two works is also the same. There is also some contact in this respect, though to a less degree, between the Priestly Code and Isaiah xl.-lxvi., and this must doubtless receive a historical explanation in the circumstances of the Babylonian age. *l*

1. On Canticles cf. Schuerer's Theol. Lit. Z., 1879, p. 31. It also, by the names of plants and similar details mentioned in it, is an important source for the history of external civilisation. In Isaiah liv. 11, read with the Septuagint NPK: instead of the meaningless PWK:, and)DNYK instead of)BNYK.

CHAPTER X. THE ORAL AND THE WRITTEN TORAH.

What importance the written letter, the book of the law, possessed for the Jews, we all know from the New Testament. Of ancient Israel, again, it is said in the introductory poem of Goethe's West-Oestlicher Divan, that the word was so important there, because it was a spoken word. The contrast which Goethe evidently perceived is really characteristic, and deserves some further attention.

X.I.

X.I.1. Even if it be the case that Deuteronomy and the Priestly Code were only reduced to writing at a late period, still there remains the Jehovistic legislation (Exodus xx.-xxiii. xxxiv.) which might be regarded as the document which formed the starting-point of the religious history of Israel. And this position is in fact generally claimed for it; yet not for the whole of it, since it is commonly recognised that the Sinaitic Book of the Covenant (Exodus xx.-xxiii. 19) was given to a people who were settled and thoroughly accustomed to agriculture, and who, moreover, had passed somewhat beyond the earliest stage in the use of money. *1*

*** 1. Exodus xxi. 35: compare xxi. 33 with Judges ix. 4 ***

The Decalogue alone is commonly maintained to be in the strictest sense Mosaic. This is principally on account of the statement that it was written down on the two stone tables of the sacred ark. Yet of Deuteronomy also we read, both that it was written on twelve stones and that it was deposited in the sacred ark (Deuteronomy xxxi. 26). We cannot therefore place implicit reliance on such statements. What is attested in this way of the Decalogue seems to find confirmation in 1Kings viii. 9. But the authority of this statement is greatly weakened by the fact that it occurs in a passage which has undergone the Deuteronomistic revision, and has been, in addition to this, subjected to interpolation. The more weight must we therefore allow to the circumstance, which makes for a different conclusion, that the name "The Ark of the Covenant" (i.e., the box of the law) *1* is peculiar to the later writers,

*** 1. Compare 1Kings viii. 21, "the ark wherein is the covenant of Jehovah," and viii 9, "there was nothing in the ark save the two tables of stone, which Moses put there at Horeb, the tables of the covenant which Jehovah had made with the children of Israel." The Deuteronomistic expression "tables of the covenant", alternates in the Priestly Code with that of "tables of testimony"; i e., likewise of the law. For H(DWT, "the testimony," 2Kings xi. 12, read HC(DWT, "the bracelets," according to 2Samuel i. 10. ***

and, when it occurs in older narratives, is proved by its sporadic appearance, as well as by a comparison of the Septuagint with the Massoretic text, to be a correction. In early times the ark was not a mere casket for the law; the "the ark of Jehovah" was of itself important, as we see clearly enough from 1Samuel iv.-vi. Like the twelve maccebas which surrounded the altar on the holy hill of Shechem, and which only later assumed the character of monuments of the law, so the ark of the covenant no doubt arose by a change of meaning out of the old idol. If there were stones in it at all, they probably served some other purpose than that of writing materials, otherwise they would not have been hidden as a mystery in the darkness of the sanctuary; they must have been exposed to public view. Add to this that the tradition is not agreed as to the tenor of the ten words said to have been inserted on the two tables; two decalogues being preserved to us, Exodus xx. and Exodus xxxiv., which are quite different from each other. It results from this that there was no real or certain knowledge as to what stood on the tables, and further that if there were such stones in the ark—and probably there were—there was nothing written on them. This is not the place to decide which of the two versions is prior to the other; the negative result we have obtained is sufficient for our present purpose.

X.I.2. Ancient Israel was certainly not without God-given bases for the ordering of human life; only they were not fixed in writing. Usage and tradition were looked on to a large extent as the institution of the Deity. Thus, for example, the ways and rules of agriculture. Jehovah had instructed the husbandman and taught him the right way. He it was whose authority gave to the unwritten laws of custom their binding power. "It is never so done in Israel," "that is folly in Israel," and similar expressions of insulted public conscience are of frequent occurrence, and show the power of custom: the fear of God acts as a motive for respecting it. "Surely there is no fear of God in this place, and they will slay me for my wife's sake," so Abraham says to himself in Gerar. "How shall I do such great wrong and sin against God?" says Joseph to the woman in Egypt. "The people of Sodom were wicked and sinned grievously against Jehovah," we read in Genesis xiii. 13. Similarly Deuteronomy xxv. 18: "The Amalekites attacked Israel on the march, and killed the stragglers, all that were feeble and fell behind, and feared not God." We see that the requirements of the Deity are known and of force, not to the Israelites only, but to all the world; and accordingly they are not to be identified with any positive commands. The patriarchs observed them long before Moses. "I know Abraham," Jehovah says, xviii. 19, "that he will command his children to keep the way of Jehovah, to do justice and judgment."

Much greater importance is attached to the special Torah of Jehovah, which not only sets up laws of action of universal validity, but shows man the way in special cases of difficulty, where he is at a loss. This Torah is one of the special gifts with which Israel is endowed (Deuteronomy xxxiii. 4); and it is intrusted to the priests, whose influence, during the period of the Hebrew kings, of which we are now speaking, rested much more on this possession than on the privilege of sacrifice. The verb from which Torah is derived signifies in its earliest usage to give direction, decision. The participle signifies *giver of oracles* in the two, examples *gibeath moreh* and *allon moreh*. The latter expression is explained by another which alternates with it, "oak of the soothsayers." Now we know that the priests in the days of Saul and David gave divine oracles by the ephod and the lots connected with it, which answered one way or the other to a question put in an alternative form. Their Torah grew no doubt out of this practice. *1* The Urim and Thummim are regarded,

*********************************** 1. 1Sam xiv. xxiii. xxx. In connection with 1Samuel xxxi. 3 I have conjectured that the verb of which Torah is the abstract means originally to throw the lot-arrows. The Thummim have been compared in the most felicitous way by Freytag, and by Lagarde independently of him (Proph. Chald. p. xlvii.) with the Arabian Tamaim, which not only signifies children's amulets but any means of "averruncatio". Urim is probably connected with)RR "to curse" (cf. Iliad i. 11 and Numbers xxiii. 23): the two words of the formula seem mutually to supplement each other. ∗∗∗∗∗∗∗∗∗∗∗∗∗∗∗∗∗∗∗∗∗∗∗∗∗∗∗∗∗∗∗∗∗∗∗∗∗

according to Deuteronomy xxxiii. 8, as the true and universal insignia of the priesthood; the ephod is last mentioned in the historical books in 1Kings ii. 26, *1*

∗∗∗∗∗∗∗∗∗∗∗∗∗∗∗∗∗∗∗∗∗∗∗∗∗∗∗∗∗∗∗∗∗∗∗∗∗∗∗ 1 Bleek, Einleiung in das A. T., 1878, p. 642. ∗∗∗∗∗∗∗∗∗∗∗∗∗∗∗∗∗∗∗∗∗∗∗∗∗∗∗∗∗∗∗∗∗∗∗∗∗∗

but appears to have remained in use down to the time of Isaiah (Hosea iii. 4; Isaiah xxx. 22). The Torah freed itself in the process of time, following the general mental movement, from such heathenish media and vehicles (Hab. ii. 19). But it continued to be an oral decision and direction. As a whole it is only a power and activity of God, or of the priests. Of this subject there can be no abstract; the TEACHING; is only thought of as the action of the TEACHER. There is no torah as a ready-made product, as a system existing independently of its originator and accessible to every one: it becomes actual only in the various utterances, which naturally form by degrees the basis of a fixed tradition. "They preserve Thy word, and keep Thy law; they teach Jacob Thy judgments and Israel Thy statutes " (Deuteronomy xxxiii. 9, 10).

The Torah of the priests appears to have had primarily a legal character. In cases which there was no regular authority to decide, or which were too difficult for human decision, the latter was brought in the last instance before God, *i.e.*, before the sanctuary or the priests (Exodus xviii. 25 seq.). The priests thus formed a kind of supreme court, which, however, rested on a voluntary recognition of its moral authority, and could not support its decisions by force. "If a man sin against another, God shall judge him," 1Samuel ii. 25 says, very indefinitely. Certain legal transactions of special solemnity are executed before God (Exodus xxi. 6). Now in proportion as the executive gained strength under the monarchy, *jus*—civil justice— necessarily grew up into a separate existence from the older sacred *fas*. The knowledge of God, which Hosea (chapter iv.) regards as the contents of the torah, has as yet a closer connection with jurisprudence than with theology; but as its practical issue is that God requires of man righteousness, and faithfulness, and good-will, it is fundamentally and essentially morality, though morality at that time addressed its demands less to the conscience than to society. A ritual tradition naturally developed itself even before the exile (2Kings xvii. 27, 28). But only those rites were included in the Torah which the priests had to teach others, not those which they discharged themselves; even in Leviticus this distinction may be traced; the instructions characterised as toroth being chiefly those as to animals which might or might not be eaten, as to clean and unclean states, as to leprosy and its marks (cf. Deuteronomy xxiv. 8).

So it was in Israel, to which the testimony applies which we have cited: and so it was in Judah also. There was a common proverb in the days of Jeremiah and Ezekiel, "The Torah shall not perish from the priest, nor counsel from the ancient, nor the word from the prophet:" but no doubt the saying was not new in their time,

330

and at any rate it will apply to the earlier time as well. Not because they sacrifice but because they teach, do the priests here appear as pillars of the religious order of things; and their Torah is a living power, equal to the occasion and never-failing. Micah reproaches them with judging for reward (iii. 11), and this shows their wisdom to have been based on a tradition accessible to them alone; this is also shown by some expressions of Deuteronomy (xvii. 10 seq., xxiv. 8). We have the counterpart to the proverb above cited (Jeremiah xviii. 18; Ezekiel vii. 26) in the complaint in Lamentations (ii. 9): "Jerusalem is destroyed; her king and her princes are among the Gentiles: the Torah is no more; the prophets obtain no vision from Jehovah;" after the ruin of the sanctuary and the priests there is no longer any Torah; and if that be so, the axe is laid to the root of the life of the people. In the post-exile prophets the torah, which even in Deuteronomy (xvii. 11) was mainly legal in its nature, acquires a strong savour of ritual which one did not notice before; yet even here it is still an oral teaching of the priests (Haggai ii. 11).

The priests derived their Torah from Moses: they claimed only to preserve and guard what Moses had left (Deuteronomy xxxiii 4, 9 seq.). He counted as their ancestor (xxxiii. 8; Judges xviii. 30); his father in-law is the PRIEST of Midian at Mount Sinai, as Jehovah also is derived in a certain sense from the older deity of Sinai. But at the same time Moses was reputed to be the incomparable originator and practicer of PROPHECY (Numbers xii. 6 seq.; Deuteronomy xxxiv. 10; Hos. xii. 14), as his brother Aaron also is not only a Levite (Exodus iv. 14), but also a prophet (iv. 15; Numbers xii. 2). There is thus a close relation between priests and prophets, *i.e.*, seers; as with other peoples (1Samuel vi.,; 1Kings xviii. 19, compare with 2Kings x. 19), so also with the Hebrews. In the earliest time it was not knowing the technique of worship, which was still very simple and undeveloped, but being a man of God, standing on an intimate footing with God, that made a man a priest, that is one who keeps up the communication with heaven for others; and the seer is better qualified than others for the office (1Kings xviii. 30 seq.). There is no fixed distinction in early times between the two offices; Samuel is in 1Samuel i.-iii. an aspirant to the priesthood; in ix. x. he is regarded as a seer.

In later times also, when priests and prophets drew off and separated from each other, they yet remained connected, both in the kingdom of Israel (Host iv. 5) and in Judah. In the latter this was very markedly the case (2Kings xxiii. 2; Jeremiah xxvi. 7 seq., v. 31; Deuteronomy xviii. 1-8, 9-22; Zechariah vii. 3). What connected them with each other was the revelation of Jehovah which went on and was kept alive in both of them. It is Jehovah from whom the torah of the priest and the word of the prophet proceeds: He is the true DIRECTOR, as Isaiah calls Him in the passage xxx. 20 seq., where, speaking of the Messianic time, he says to the people, "Then thy director (MWRYK) is no more concealed, but thine eyes see thy director, and thine ears hear the words of One calling behind thee; this is the way, walk ye in it; when ye are turning to the right hand or to the left." TORAH and WORD are cognate notions, and capable of being interchanged (Deuteronomy xxxiii. 9; Isaiah i. 10, ii. 3, v. 24, viii. 16, 20). This explains how both priests and prophets claimed Moses for their order: he was not regarded as the founder of the cultus.

The difference, in the period when it had fully developed itself, may be said to be this: the Torah of the priests was like a spring which runs always, that of the prophets like a spring which is intermittent, but when it does break forth, flows with all the greater force. The priests take precedence of the prophets when both are named together; they obviously consolidated themselves earlier and more strongly. The order, and the tradition which propagates itself within the order, are essential to them: they observe and keep the torah (Deuteronomy xxxiii. 9). For this reason, that they take their stand so entirely on the tradition, and depend on it, their claim to have Moses for their father, the beginner and founder of their tradition, is in itself the better founded of the two. *l*

************************************* 1 It is also more firmly rooted in history; for if Moses did anything at all, he certainly founded the sanctuary at Kadesh and the torah there, which the priests of the ark carried on after him, thus continuing the thread of the history of Israel, which was taken up again in power by the monarchy. The prophets only appeared among the Hebrews from the time of Samuel onwards, but the seers were older than Moses, and can scarcely have had such a close connection with his tradition as the priests at the sanctuary of the ark of Jehovah. ***********************************

In the ordinary parlance of the Hebrews torah always meant first, and chiefly the Priestly Torah. The prophets have notoriously no father (1Samuel x. 12), their importance rests on the individuals; it is characteristic that only names and sketches of their lives have reached us. They do indeed, following the tendency of the times, draw together in corporations; but in doing so they really renounce their own distinctive characteristics: the representative men are always single, resting on nothing outside themselves. We have thus on the one side the tradition of a class, which suffices for the occasions of ordinary life, and on the other the inspiration of awakened individuals, stirred up by occasions which are more than ordinary. After the spirit of the oldest men of God, Moses at the head of them, had been in a fashion laid to sleep in institutions, it sought and found in the prophets a new opening; the old fire burst out like a volcano through the strata which once, too, rose fluid from the deep, but now were fixed and dead.

The element in which the prophets live is the storm of the world's history, which sweeps away human institutions; in which the rubbish of past generations with the houses built on it begins to shake, and that foundation alone remains firm, which needs no support but itself. When the earth trembles and seems to be passing away, then they triumph because Jehovah alone is exalted. They do not preach on set texts; they speak out of the spirit which judges all things and itself is judged of no man. Where do they ever lean on any other authority than the truth of what they say; where do they rest on any other foundation than their own certainty? It belongs to the notion of prophecy of true revelation, that Jehovah, overlooking all the media of ordinances and institutions, communicates Himself to the INDIVIDUAL, the called one, in whom that mysterious and irreducible rapport in which the deity stands with man clothes itself with energy. Apart from the prophet, *in abstracto*, there is no revelation; it lives in his divine-human ego. This gives rise to a synthesis of apparent

332

contradictions: the subjective in the highest sense, which is exalted above all ordinances, is the truly objective, the divine. This it proves itself to be by the consent of the conscience of all, on which the prophets count, just as Jesus does in the Gospel of John, in spite of all their polemic against the traditional religion. They are not saying anything new: they are only proclaiming old truth. While acting in the most creative way they feel entirely passive: the *homo tantum et audacia* which may with perfect justice be applied to such men as Elijah, Amos, and Isaiah, is with them equivalent to *deus tantum et servitus*. But their creed is not to be found in any book. It is barbarism, in dealing with such a phenomenon, to distort its physiognomy by introducing the law.

X.I.3. It is a vain imagination to suppose that the prophets expounded and applied the law. Malachi (circa 450 B.C.) says, it is true, iv. 4, "Remember ye the torah of Moses my servant;" but where shall we look for any second expression of this nature? Much more correctly than modern scholars did these men judge, who at the close of the preexilic history looked back on the forces which had moulded it, both the divine and those opposed to God. In their eyes the prophets are not the expounders of Moses, but his continuators and equals; the word of God in their mouth is not less weighty than in the mouth of Moses; they, as well as he, are organs of the spirit of Jehovah by which He is present in Israel. The immediate revelation to the people, we read in Deuteronomy xviii., ceased with the ten commandments: from that point onwards Jehovah uses the prophets as His mouth: "A prophet like unto thee," He says to Moses, "will I raise up to them from among their brethren, and will put my words in his mouth, and he shall speak unto them all that I shall command him; and whosoever shall not hearken unto my words which he shall speak in my name, I will require it of him." We find it the same in Jeremiah; the voice of the prophets, always sounding when there is need for it, occupies the place which, according to the prevailing view, should have been filled by the law: this living command of Jehovah is all he knows of, and not any testament given once for all. "This only I commanded your fathers when I brought them up out of Egypt: Obey my voice, and walk ye in all the ways that I will command you. Since the day that your fathers came forth out of Egypt, I have sent unto you all my servants the prophets, daily rising up early and sending them; but ye would not hear." And even after the exile we meet in Zechariah (520 B.C.) the following view of the significance of the prophets: "Thus spake Jehovah of hosts [to the fathers before the exile], Speak true judgment, and show mercy and compassions every man to his brother, and oppress not the widow nor the fatherless, the stranger nor the poor: and let none of you imagine evil against his brother in his heart. But they refused to hearken, and shrugged the shoulder, and stopped their ears, that they should not hear. Yea, they made their hearts as a flint, lest they should hear the Torah and the words which Jehovah Sebaoth hath sent by His Spirit through the old prophets: therefore came a great wrath from Jehovah Sebaoth. And as He cried and they would not hear, so now shall they cry and I will not hear, and I will blow them away among the peoples.... Thus saith Jehovah Sebaoth [after the exile to the present generation], As I thought to punish you without pity because your fathers provoked me to anger, so again have I thought in these days to do well to the house of Judah: fear ye not. These are the things that ye shall do: Speak ye every man the truth to his neighbour; execute the judgment of truth and peace in your gates; and let none of you imagine evil in your hearts against his neighbour, and love no false oath, for all these are things which I hate, saith Jehovah" (Zechariah vii. 9-11, viii. 14-16). The contents of the Torah, on obedience to which the theocracy is here based, are very suggestive, as also its derivation from the "old" prophets. Even Ezra can say (ix. 10, 11): "We have forsaken Thy commandments which Thou hast commanded by the servants the prophets, saying, The land unto which ye go to possess it is an unclean land with the filthiness of the people of the land, which have filled it from one end to another with their uncleanness." He is thinking of Deuteronomy, Ezekiel, and Leviticus xvii.-xxvi.

Of those who at the end reflected on the meaning of the development which had run its course, the writer of Isaiah xl.-lxvi. occupies the first place. The Torah, which he also calls *mishpat*, right (i.e., truth), appears to him to be the divine and imperishable element in Israel. With him, however, it is inseparable from its mouthpiece, the servant of Jehovah, xlii. 1-4, xlix. 1-6, l. 4-9, lii. 13-liii. 12. The name would denote the prophet, but here it stands for the people, a prophet on a large scale. Israel's calling is not that of the world-monarchies, to make sensation and noise in the streets (xiii. 1-4), but the greater one of promulgating the Torah and getting it received. This is to be done both in Israel and among the heathen. What makes Israel a prophet is not his own inner qualities, but his relation to Jehovah, his calling as the depository of divine truth: hence it involves no contradiction that the servant should begin his work in Israel itself. *1*

*********************************** 1. This is as if one were to say that there is much to be done before we Evangelicals are truly evangelical. Yet the distinction as worked out in Isaiah xl. seq. is certainly very remarkable, and speaks for a surprising degree of profound meditation. ***********************************

Till now he has spent his strength only in the bosom of his own people, which is always inclined to fall away from Jehovah and from itself: heedless of reproach and suffering he has laboured unweariedly in carrying out the behests of his Master and has declared His word. All in vain. He has not been able to avert the victory of heathenism in Israel, now followed by its victory over Israel. Now in the exile Jehovah has severed His relation with His people; the individual Hebrews survive, but the servant, the people of Jehovah, is dead. Then is the Torah to die with him, and truth itself to succumb to falsehood, to heathenism? That cannot be; truth must prevail, must come to the light. As to the Apostle Paul the Spirit is the earnest of the resurrection of those who are born again, so to our author the Torah is the pledge of the resurrection of Israel, the justification of the servant of Jehovah. The final triumph of the cause, which is God's, will surpass all expectations. Not only in Israel itself will the Torah, will the servant of Jehovah prevail and bring about a regeneration of the people: the truth will in the future shine forth from Israel into the whole world, and obtain the victory among all the Gentiles (xlix. 6). Then it will appear that the work of the servant, resultless as it seemed to be up to the exile, has yet not been in vain.

It is surely unnecessary for me to demonstrate how uncommonly vivid, I might say how uncommonly historical, the notion of the Torah is as here set forth, and how entirely incompatible that notion is with "the Torah of Moses." It might most fitly be compared with the Logos of the prologue of John, if the latter is understood in accordance with John x. 35, an utterance certainly authentic, and not according to Philo. As Jesus is the revelation of God made man, so the servant of Jehovah is the revelation of God made a people. The similarity of their nature and their significance involves the similarity of their work and of their sufferings, so that the Messianic interpretation of Isaiah lii. 13-liii. 12 is in fact one which could not fail to suggest itself. *1*

** 1. The personification is carried further in this passage than anywhere else, and it is possible that the colours of the sketch are borrowed from some actual instance of a prophet-martyr: yet the Ebed Jahve cannot have a different meaning here from that which it has everywhere else. It is to be noted that the sufferings and death of the servant are in the past, and his glorification in the future, a long pause lying between them in the present. A resurrection of the individual could not be in the mind of the writer of Isaiah xl seq., nor do the details of the description, lii. 12 seq., at all agree with such an idea. Moreover, it is clear that liv. 1-lvi. 8 is a kind of sermon on the text lii. 13-liii. 12; and there the prophecy of the glorification of the servant has reference to Zion. See Vatke, p. 528 seq. **

X.II.

X.II.1. In the 18th year of King Josiah (621 B.C) Deuteronomy was found and published. In the account of the discovery, 2Kings xxii. xxiii., it is always called simply *the book of the Torah*; it was accordingly the first, and in its time the only book of the kind. It is certainly the case that the prophets had written down some of their speeches before this, and the priests also may before this time have written down many of their precepts: it appears in fact, as Vatke surmises, that we have a monument of their spirit, *e.g.*, in the Sinaitic Book of the Covenant. Deuteronomy presupposes earlier attempts of this kind, and borrows its materials largely from them; but on the other hand it is distinguished from them not only by its greater compass but also by its much higher claims. It is written with the distinct intention not to remain a private memorandum, but to obtain public authority as a book. The idea of making a definite formulated written Torah the law of the land, is the important point *1*

** 1. Duhm, ap. Cil. p. 201.
****

it was a first attempt and succeeded at the outset beyond expectation. A reaction set in afterwards, it is true; but the Babylonian exile completed the triumph of the law. Extraordinary excitement was at that time followed by the deepest depression (Amos viii. 11 seq.). At such a time those who did not despair of the future clung anxiously to the religious acquisitions of the past. These had been put in a book just in time in Deuteronomy, with a view to practical use in the civil and religious life of the people . The book of the Torah did not perish in the general ruin, but remained in existence, and was the compass of those who were shaping their course for a new Israel. How thoroughly determined they were to use it as their rule we see from the revision of the Hexateuch and of the historical books which was taken in hand during the exile.

With the appearance of the law came to an end the old freedom, not only in the sphere of worship, now restricted to Jerusalem, but in the sphere of the religious spirit as well. There was now in existence an authority as objective as could be; and this was the death of prophecy.

For it was a necessary condition of prophecy that the tares should be at liberty to grow up beside the wheat. The signs given in Deuteronomy to distinguish the true from the false prophet, are no doubt vague and unpractical: still they show the tendency towards control and the introduction of uniformity; that is the great step which is new. *1*

** 1. The difference between Deuteronomy xviii. 22 and 1Kings xxii. 19-23 may be thought to throw light on the two positions. In the former passage we read that if a prophet says something in the name of Jehovah which does not come to pass, it is a word which Jehovah has not spoken. Here, on the contrary, Micaiah ben Imlah, when the prophets of Jehovah promise the king of Israel a happy issue of the campaign against the Syrians, regards the prediction as contrary to the truth, but as none the less on that account inspired by the spirit of prophecy; Jehovah, he said, had made his spirit a lying spirit in the mouth of all his prophets. It may be that this difference reflects to us the interval between two different ages: but on the whole Micaiah's view appears to be rather a piece of ingenuity which might have been resorted to in later times as well. In the seventh century the command, "every firstborn is mine," was held to apply to the human firstborn as well, the sacrifice of which Jehovah was thought to require: this appears from Jeremiah's protest, "I commanded them not, neither came it into my mind," vii. 31, xix. 5. With reference to this Ezekiel says that because the Israelites despised the wholesome commandments of Jehovah, He gave them laws which were not good and statutes by which they could not live. That is a similar ingenious escape from a difficulty, without deeper meaning. See the converse, Koran, Sura ii. 174. **

It certainly was not the intention of the legislator to encroach upon the spoken Torah or the free word. But the consequence, favoured by outward circumstances, was not to be avoided: the feeling that the prophets had come to an end did not arise in the Maccabean wars only. In the exile we hear the complaint that the instruction of the priests and the word of the prophets are silent (Lamentations ii. 9); it is asked, where he is who in former times put his spirit in Israel (Isa lxiii. 11); in Nehemiah's time a doubtful question is left unsettled, at least theoretically, till the priest with Urim and Thummim, *i.e.*, with a trustworthy prophecy, shall appear (Nehemiah vii. 69). We may call Jeremiah the last of the prophets: *2*

******************************** 2. In his early years Jeremiah had a share in the introduction of the law: but in later times he shows himself little edified by the effects it produced: the lying pen of the scribes, he says, has written for a lie. People despised the prophetic word because they had the Torah in black and white (viii. 7-9). ***********************************

those who came after him were prophets only in name. Ezekiel had swallowed a book (iii. 1-3), and gave it out again. He also, like Zechariah, calls the pre-exilic prophets the old prophets, conscious that he himself belongs to the epigoni: he meditates on their words like Daniel and comments on them in his own prophecy (xxxviii. 17, xxxix. 8). The writer of Isaiah xl. seq. might with much more reason be called a prophet, but he does not claim to be one; his anonymity, which is evidently intentional, leaves no doubt as to this. He is, in fact, more of a theologian: he is principally occupied in reflecting on the results of the foregoing development, of which prophecy had been the leaven; these are fixed possessions now secured; he is gathering in the harvest. As for the prophets after the exile, we have already seen how Zechariah speaks of the old prophets as a series which is closed, in which he and those like him are not to be reckoned. In the writing of an anonymous contemporary which is appended to his book we find the following notable expression: "In that (hoped-for) day, saith Jehovah, I will cut off the names of the idols out of the land, that they be no more remembered, and also I will cause to cease the prophets and the unclean spirit; and if a man will yet prophesy, his parents shall say unto him, Thou shalt not live, for thou speakest lies in the name of Jehovah, and his parents shall thrust him through when he prophesieth" (xiii. 2-3).

X.II.2. Deuteronomy was the programme of a reform, not of a restoration. It took for granted the existence of the cultus, and only corrected it in certain general respects. But the temple was now destroyed and the worship interrupted, and the practice of past times had to be written down if it was not to be lost. Thus it came about that in the exile the conduct of worship became the subject of the Torah, and in this process reformation was naturally aimed at as well as restoration. We have seen *II.II.1.*) that Ezekiel was the first to take this step which the circumstances of the time indicated. In the last part of his work he made the first attempt to record the ritual which had been customary in the temple of Jerusalem. Other priests attached themselves to him (Leviticus xvii.-xxvi.), and thus there grew up in the exile from among the members of this profession a kind of school of people who reduced to writing and to a system what they had formerly practiced in the way of their calling. After the temple was restored this theoretical zeal still continued to work, and the ritual when renewed was still further developed by the action and reaction on each other of theory and practice: the priests who had stayed in Babylon took as great a part, from a distance, in the sacred services, as their brothers at Jerusalem who had actually to conduct them. The latter indeed lived in adverse circumstances and do not appear to have conformed with great strictness or accuracy to the observances which had been agreed upon. The last result of this labour of many years is the Priestly Code. It has indeed been said that we cannot ascribe the creation of such a work to an age which was bent on nothing but repristination. Granted that this is a correct description of it, such an age is peculiarly fitted for an artificial systematising of given materials, and this is what the originality of the Priestly Code in substance amounts to. *1*

*** 1. Dillmann arrives at the conclusion that the assumption is the most natural one in the world, and still capable of proof from ACD (!) that the priesthood of the central sanctuary wrote down their toroth even in early times; and that it is absurd to suppose that the priestly and ceremonial laws were first written down, or even made, in the exile and in Babylon, where there was no worship. We will let it be absurd, if it is true. It is not progress, though it is a fact, that the kings were succeeded by the high-priests, and the prophets by the Rabbis. Yet it is a thing which is likely to occur, that a body of traditional practice should only be written down when it is threatening to die out, and that a book should be, as it were, the ghost of a life which is closed.
****

The Priestly Code, worked into the Pentateuch as the standard legislative element in it, became the definite "Mosaic law." As such it was published and introduced in the year 444 B.C., a century after the exile . In the interval, the duration of which is frequently under-estimated, Deuteronomy alone had been known and recognised as the written Torah, though as a fact the essays of Ezekiel and his successors may have had no inconsiderable influence in leading circles. The man who made the Pentateuch the constitution of Judaism was the Babylonian priest and scribe, Ezra.

He had come from Babylon to Jerusalem as early as the year 458 B.C., the seventh of Artaxerxes Longimanus, at the head of a considerable company of zealous Jews, provided it is said with a mandate from the Persian king, empowering him to reform according to the law the congregation of the temple, which had not yet been able to consolidate itself inwardly nor to shut itself off sufficiently from those without.

"Thou art sent of the king and of his seven counsellors to hold an inquiry concerning Judah and Jerusalem *according to the law of thy God which is in thine hand*....And thou Ezra, according to *the wisdom of thy God which is in thine hand*, set magistrates and judges which may judge all the people that are beyond the river, all such as acknowledge the laws of thy God, and teach ye them that know them not. And whosoever will not do the law of thy God and the law of the king, let him be prosecuted." So we read in the commission of the Persian king to Ezra, vii. 12-26; which, even should it be spurious, must yet reflect the views of his contemporaries. The expression taken from Ezra's own memoirs, vii. 27, leaves no doubt that he was assisted by Artaxerxes in the objects he had in view. *1*

** 1. With regard to his relation to the law, we have to consider the following points: he was a scribe (SWPR = literatus), at home in the Torah of Moses, vii. 6. He had directed his mind to study the Torah of Jehovah, and to do and to teach in Israel judgment and statute, vii. 10. "The priest Ezra, the master of the law of the God of heaven," vii. 21. The most important expression, however, is that which states that the law (the wisdom) of his God was in his hand: thus it was his private property, though it claimed authority for all Israel. With this agree the statements as to the object of the learned priest's mission. **

But Ezra did not, as we should expect, at once introduce the law on his arrival in Judah. In concert with the heads of the people, and proceeding on the existing Torah, that, namely, of Deuteronony, he ordained and relentlessly carried out a strict separation of the returned exiles from the heathen and half-heathen inhabitants of the land. This was done a few months after his arrival in Jerusalem. But a long time, at least fourteen years, elapsed before he produced the law which he had brought with him. Why he delayed so long we can at the best only surmise, as no accounts have reached us of what he did in the interval; there is a great gap in the narrative of the Books of Ezra and Nehemiah between the 7th and the 20th year of Artaxerxes. Perhaps the outward circumstances of the young community, which, probably in consequence of the repellent attitude taken up to the surrounding peoples, were not of the happiest, made it unadvisable at once to introduce a legislative innovation; perhaps, too, Ezra desired to wait to see the correcting influence of the practice of Jerusalem on the product of Babylonian scholarship, and moreover to train up assistants for the work. The principal reason, however, appears to have been, that in spite of the good-will of the king he did not enjoy the energetic support of the Persian authorities on the spot, and could not without it get the authority of the new law recognised.

But in the year 445 it came about that a Jew and a sympathiser of Ezra, Nehemiah ben Hakkelejah, cup-bearer and favourite of Artaxerxes, appeared in Judea as Persian governor. With straightforward earnestness he first addressed himself to the task of liberating the Jewish community from outward pressure and lifting them up from their depressed condition; and, this being accomplished, the time had come to go forward with the introduction of the Pentateuch. Ezra and Nehemiah were manifestly in concert as to this. On the 1st day of the 7th month—we do not know the year, but it cannot have been earlier than 444 B.C.—the whole people came together as one man before the water-gate, and Ezra was called on to produce the book of the law of Moses, which Jehovah had commanded Israel. The scribe mounted a wooden pulpit; seven priests stood beside him on the right hand, and seven on the left. When he opened the book all present stood up, both men and women; with loud Amen they joined in the opening blessing, lifted up their heads, and cast themselves on the ground. Then he read the book, from early morning till mid-day, in small sections, which were repeated and expounded by a number of Levites dispersed throughout the crowd. The effect was that a general weeping arose, the people being aware that they had not till then followed the commandments of God. Nehemiah and Ezra and the Levites had to allay the excitement, and said: "This day is holy unto Jehovah your God; mourn not nor weep. Go your way, eat the fat and drink the sweet, and give unto them that have brought nothing with them." The assembled people then dispersed and set on foot a "great mirth," because they had understood the words which had been communicated to them. The reading was continued the next day, but before the heads of families only, and a very appropriate section was read, *viz.*, the ordinances as to festivals, and particularly that about the feast of tabernacles, which was to be kept under branches of trees on the 15th day of the 7th month, the month then just beginning. The matter was taken up with the greatest zeal, and the festival, which had not been kept RITE *sic!* since the days of Joshua ben Nun, was now instituted in accordance with the precepts of Leviticus xxiii. and celebrated with general enthusiasm from the 15th to the 22nd of the month. *1*

*** 1. For eight days, according to
Leviticus   xxiii.   39:   as   against   Deuteronomy   xvi.   13-15.
****

On the 24th, however, a great day of humiliation was held, with sackcloth and ashes. On this occasion also the proceedings began with reading the law, and then followed a confession of sins spoken by the Levites in the name of the people, and concluding with a prayer for mercy and compassion. This was preparatory to the principal and concluding act, in which the secular and spiritual officials and elders, 85 in number, bound themselves in writing to the Book of the Law, published by Ezra, and all the rest undertook an obligation, with oath and curse, to walk in the Torah of God, given by His servant Moses, and to keep all the commandments of Jehovah and His statutes and laws. Special attention was directed to such provisions of the Pentateuch as were of immediate importance for the people in the circumstances of the day—the greater part of the whole work is about the ritual of the priests—and those were in particular insisted on which refer to the contributions of the laity to the priesthood, on which the very existence of the hierocracy depended. *1*

340

1. Nehemiah viii. 1-x. 40. The credibility of the narrative appears on the face of it. The writer of Chronicles did not write it himself, but took it from his main source, from which also he drew the fragments he gives us of the memoirs of Ezra and Nehemiah. This we see from the fact that while copying Nehemiah vii. in Ezra ii. he unconsciously goes on with the beginning of Nehemiah viii. (= Ezra iii. 1). That shows that he found Nehemiah vii. and viii. in their present connection, and did not write viii. seq. himself, as we might suppose. ***************************************

Lagarde expresses great surprise—and the surprise is reasonable— that so little importance is attributed to this narrative by Old Testament critics; only Kuenen had rightly appreciated its significance. *2*

** 2 Goettinger Gel. Anzeigen, 1870, p. 1557 seq. Kuenen, Religion of Israel, vol. ii. chapter viii. ***************************************

It is obvious that Nehemiah viii.-x. is a close parallel to 2Kings xxii. xxiii., especially to xxiii. 1-3. There we read that Josiah caused all the elders of Judah and Jerusalem to come together, and went up with the men of Judah and the inhabitants of Jerusalem, with the priests and the prophets and all the people, high and low, to the house of Jehovah; where he read to the assemblage all the words of the Book of the Law, and bound himself with all the people before Jehovah to keep all the words of the book. Just as it is in evidence that Deuteronomy became known in the year 621, and that it was unknown up to that date, so it is in evidence that the remaining Torah of the Pentateuch—for there is no doubt that the law of Ezra was the whole Pentateuch—became known in the year 444 and was unknown till then. This shows in the first place, and puts it beyond question, that Deuteronomy is the first, and the priestly Torah the second, stage of the legislation. But in the second place, as we are accustomed to infer the date of the composition of Deuteronomy from its publication and introduction by Josiah, so we must infer the date of the composition of the Priestly Code from its publication and introduction by Ezra and Nehemiah. It would require very strong internal evidence to destroy the probability, thus based on a most positive statement of facts, that the codification of the ritual only took place in the post-exile period. We have already seen of what nature the internal evidence is which is brought forward with this view. *1*

*** 1. It is not, however, necessary, and it can scarcely be correct, to make Ezra more than the editor, the real and principal editor, of the Hexateuch: and in particular he is not likely to have been the author of Q. Nor on the other hand is it meant to deny that many new features may have been added and alterations made after Ezra. A body of customs is a subject which can scarcely be treated quite exhaustively. There are no directions about the *nervus ischiadicus* ***sciatic nerve??***, about the priests having their feet bare, about shutting up before Jehovah (1Samuel xxi cf. Jeremiah xxxvi. 5), or about the stoning of adulterers. ***

X.II.3. Ezra and Nehemiah, and the eighty-five men of the great assembly (Nehemiah viii. seq.), who are named as signatories of the covenant, are regarded by later tradition as the founders of the canon. And not without reason: only King Josiah has a still stronger claim to this place of honour. The introduction of the law, first Deuteronomy, and then the whole Pentateuch, was in fact the decisive step, by which the written took the place of the spoken word, and the people of the word became a "people of the book." To THE BOOK were added in course of time THE BOOKS; the former was formally and solemnly introduced in two successive acts, the latter acquired imperceptibly a similar public authority for the Jewish church. The notion of the canon proceeds entirely from that of the written Torah; the prophets and the hagiographa are also called Torah by the Jews, though not Torah of Moses.

The origin of the canon thus lies, thanks to the two narratives 2Kings xxii. xxiii., Nehemiah viii.-x. in the full light of history; but the traditional science of Biblical introduction has no clear or satisfactory account to give of it. Josiah, the ordinary notion is, introduced the law, but not the canon; Ezra, on the other hand, the canon and not the law. An analogy drawn from the secondary part of the canon, the prophets and hagiographa, is applied without consideration to the primary part, the Torah of Moses. The historical and prophetical books were, in part at least, a long time in existence before they became canonical, and the same, it is thought, might be the case with the law. But the case of the law is essentially different. The law claims to have public authority, to be a book of the community; the difference between law and canon, does not exist. Hence it is easy to understand that the Torah, though as a literary product later than the historical and prophetical books, is yet as law older than these writings, which have originally and in their nature no legal character, but only acquired such a character in a sort of metaphorical way, through their association with the law itself.

When it is recognised that THE CANON is what distinguishes Judaism from ancient Israel, it is recognised at the same time that what distinguishes Judaism from ancient Israel is THE WRITTEN TORAH. The water which in old times rose from a spring, the Epigoni stored up in cisterns.

CHAPTER XI. THE THEOCRACY AS IDEA AND AS INSTITUTION.

Writers of the present day play with the expressions "theocracy," and "theocratic" without making it clear to themselves what these words mean and how far they are entitled to use them. But we know that the word theokratia was only coined by Josephus; *1*

** 1.)OUKOUN)APEIROI MEN (AI KATA MEROS TWN)ETHWN KAI TWN NOMWN PARA TOIS)APASIN)ANTHRWPOS DIAFORAI.)OI MEN GAR MONARXIAIS, (OI DE TAIS)OLIGWN DUNASTEIAIS,)ALLOI DE TOIS PLHTHESIN)EPETREPYAN THN 'ECOUSIAN TWN POLITEUMATWN. (O D' (HMETEROS NOMOQETHS)EIS MEN TOUTWN OUD' (OTIOUN)APEIDEN, (WS D')AN TIS)EIPOI BIASAMENOS TON LOGON QEOKRATIAN)APEDEICE TO POLITEUMA, QEW| THN)ARXHN KAI TO KRATOS)ANAQEIS (contra Apion ii. 17). (" There are innumerable differences in the particular customs and laws that are among mankind; some have intrusted the power of their states to monarchies, some to oligarchies, and some to democracies: but our legislator had no regard to any of these forms, *but he ordered our governmernt to be what I may call by a strained expression a theocracy*, attributing the power and the authority to God." Compare also, on this whole chapter, Die Pharisaer und die Sadducaer, Greifswald, 1874. **

and when this writer speaks of the Mosaic constitution, he has before his eyes, it is well known, the sacred community of his own day as it existed down to the year 70 A.D. In ancient Israel the theocracy never existed in fact as a form of constitution. The rule of Jehovah is here an ideal representation; only after the exile was it attempted to realise it in the shape of a Rule of the Holy with outward means. It is perhaps the principal merit of Vatke's Biblical Theology to have traced through the centuries the rise of the theocracy and the metamorphosis of the idea to an institution.

XI.I.

XI.I.1. The upholders of the prevailing view do not assert that Moses wrote the Pentateuch, but they maintain all the more firmly that he organised the congregation of the tabernacle in the wilderness after the fashion described in the Priestly Code. They seem to think that Moses had no importance further than this; as if it were an act of no moment to cast into the field of time a seed which the action and reaction thence arising bring an immeasurable time after to maturity (Mark iv. 26 seq.). In fact Moses is the originator of the Mosaic constitution in about the same way as Peter is the founder of the Roman hierarchy. Of the sacred organisation supposed to have existed from the earliest times, there is no trace in the time of the judges and the kings. It is thought to have been a sort of pedagogic strait-waistcoat, to subdue the ungovernable obstinacy of the Hebrews and to guard them from evil influences from without. But even should it be conceded that a constitution could come into existence in ancient times which was so utterly out of relation to the peculiar life and temper of the people, the history of the ancient Israelites shows us nothing so distinctly as the uncommon freshness and naturalness of their impulses. The persons who appear always act from the constraining impulse of their nature, the men of God not less than the murderers and adulterers: they are such figures as could only grow up in the open air. Judaism, which realised the Mosaic constitution and carried it out logically, left no free scope for the individual; but in ancient Israel the divine right did not attach to the institution but was in the Creator Spirit, in individuals. Not only did they speak like the prophets, they also acted like the judges and kings, from their own free impulse, not in accordance with an outward norm, and yet, or just because of this, in the Spirit of Jehovah. The different view of different times is seen very characteristically in the views taken of Saul by the two versions above sifted and compared *VII.II.2* .

XI.I.2. It is a simple and yet a very important remark of Vatke, that the sacred constitution of the congregation, so circumstantially described to us in the Priestly Code, is after all very defective, and presupposes the existence of that which it was the chief task of the age of Moses to bring about, namely the state, in the absence of which the church cannot have any subsistence either. To maintain an elaborate and expensive worship, and an immense swarm of clergy, must have required considerable rates and taxes: and to raise these, as well as to uphold the authority of the sacred persons and institutions, and most of all to enforce the strict centralization and uniformity of the legitimate worship, all this among a people not yet very civilised, must have required an executive power which embraced and was able to control, the whole people. But where is this central authority in the period of the judges? Judicial competence resided at that time chiefly in the smallest circles, the families and houses. These were but little controlled, as it appears, by the superior power of the tribe, and the very notion of the state or of the kingdom did not as yet exist. Houses related to each other sometimes united for common undertakings, as no doubt also did neighbouring tribes; but this was not on the basis of any constitutional order, but from necessity, when it happened that a well-known man came forward to take the command and his summons to the levy was obeyed. These transient combinations under generals were the forerunners of a permanent union under a king: and even at the time of the Midianite war an attempt seems to have been made in this direction, which, however, was not quite successful. In the severe and protracted struggle with the Philistines the necessity for a solid union of the tribes was cryingly manifest, and the man came forward to meet the hour. Saul, a distinguished Benjamite of Gibeah, was overcome by anger at the scornful challenge which even the Ammonites ventured at such a time to cast in the teeth of his people: he called his fellow-countrymen to battle, not in virtue of any office he held, but on the strength of his own impulses; his enthusiasm proved contagious, none dared to say him nay. He began his career just like one of the earlier judges, but after he had led his people to victory they did not let him retire again. The person sought for, the king, was found.

Out of such natural beginnings did the state at that time arise: it owed nothing to the pattern of the "Mosaic theocracy," but bears all the marks of a new creation. Saul and David first made out of the Hebrew tribes a real people in the political sense

344

(Deuteronomy xxxiii. 5). David was in the eyes of later generations inseparable from the idea of Israel: he was the king par excellence: Saul was thrown into the shade, but both together are the founders of the kingdom, and have thus a much wider importance than any of their successors. It was they who drew the life of the people together at a centre, and gave it an aim; to them the nation is indebted for its historical self-consciousness. All the order of aftertimes is built up on the monarchy; it is the soil out of which all the other institutions of Israel grow up. In the time of the judges, we read, every man did that which was right in his own eyes, not because the Mosaic constitution was not in force, but because there was no king in those days. The consequences were very important in the sphere of religion as well: since the political advance of the people brought the historic and national character of Jehovah to the front again. During the time of the judges the Canaanite festival cultus had gradually been coming to be embodied in the worship of Jehovah, a process which was certainly necessary; but in this process there was for some time a danger that Jehovah would become a God of husbandry and of cattle, like Baal-Dionysus. The festivals long continued to be a source of heathenism, but now they were gradually divested of their character as nature-festivals, and forced at length to have reference to the nation and to its history, if they were not to disappear completely. The relation of Jehovah to people and kingdom remained firm as a rock: even to the worst idolaters He was the God of Israel; in war no one thought of looking for victory and success to any other God. This was the result of Israel's becoming a kingdom: the kingship of Jehovah, in that precise sense which we associate with it, is the religious expression of the fact of the foundation of the kingdom by Saul and David. The theocracy was the state of itself; the ancient Israelites regarded the civil state as a miracle, or, in their own words, a help of God. When the later Jews thought or spoke of the theocracy, they took the state for granted as already there, and so they could build the theocracy on the top of it as a specially spiritual feature: just as we moderns sometimes see the divine element in settled ordinances, such as marriage, not in their own nature, but in the consecration added to them by the church.

XI.I.3. The kingdom of Saul and David did not long remain at its height. Decay set in even at the separation, and when once the Assyrians were heard at the door, it advanced with steps not to be arrested. But the memory of the period of glory and power was all the greener, and the hope arose of its return. From the contrast between the sorrowful present and the brilliant past there arose the picture of the state as it should be; when ruin was seen without and anarchy within, the prophets set against this the pattern of the theocracy. The theocracy as the prophets represent it to themselves is not a thing essentially different from the political community, as a spiritual differs from a secular power; rather, it rests on the same foundations and is in fact the ideal of the state. Isaiah gave this ideal its classical form in those pictures of the future which we are accustomed to call Messianic prophecies. These passages are not predictions of this or that occurrence, but announcements of the aims which, it is true, the prophet only expects the future to realise, but which are of force or ought to be of force in the present, and towards which the community, if true to its own nature, must strive.

The first feature of these Messianic descriptions is the expulsion of the Assyrians; but most emphasis is laid on the restoration of the inner bases of the state, the rottenness of which has brought about and rendered inevitable the present crisis. The collapse of the government, the paralysis fallen on the law, the spoliation of the weak by the strong, these are the evils that call for redress. "How is the honourable city become a harlot; it was full of judgment, righteousness lodged in it—but now murderers! Thy princes are rascals and companions of thieves, every one loveth gifts and followeth after bribes; they judge not the fatherless, neither cloth the cause of the widow come unto them. Therefore saith the Lord: Ah, I will ease me of mine adversaries, and avenge me of mine enemies! And I will turn my hand against thee, Zion, and as with lye I will purge away thy dross, and I will restore thy judges as at the first, and thy counsellors as at the beginning; afterwards thou shalt be called a righteous and honourable city. Zion shall be redeemed by judgment and her inhabitants by righteousness" (Isaiah i. 21-27). The state the prophet has before his eye is always the natural state as it exists, never a community distinguished by a peculiar holiness in its organisation. The kingdom of Jehovah is with him entirely identical with the kingdom of David; the tasks he sets before it are political in their nature, similar, we might say, to the demands one would address to the Turkish Empire in our own days. He is unconscious of any difference between human and divine law: law in itself, jurist's law in the proper juristic sense of the word, is divine, and has behind it the authority of the Holy One of Israel. In that day shall Jehovah of hosts be for a crown of glory and a diadem of beauty unto the residue of His people, and for a spirit of judgment to him that sitteth in judgment, and a spirit of strength to them that drive back the battle from the borders " (xxviii. 5, 6). Jehovah is a true and perfect King, hence justice is His principal attribute and His chief demand. And this justice is a purely forensic or social notion: the righteousness of the Sermon on the Mount can only come into consideration when civil justice and order have come to be a matter of course—which at that time they had not yet done.

The representative of Jehovah is the human king. The earthly ruler is not in the way of the heavenly: even the glorious kingdom of the future cannot dispense with him. "Then a king shall reign in righteousness and princes shall rule in judgment; each of them shall be as an hiding-place from the wind and as a covert from the tempest; as rivers of waters in a dry place, as the shadow of a great rock in a weary land" (xxxii. 1, 2). As the reigning king is in general unsatisfactory, Isaiah hopes for a new one who will answer the pattern of David of old, the Messiah. "There shall come forth a rod out of the stem of Jesse, and a branch shall grow out of his roots: and the spirit of Jehovah shall rest upon Him, the spirit of wisdom and understanding, the spirit of counsel and of warlike might, the spirit of knowledge and of the fear of the Lord; and His breath shall be drawn in the fear of Jehovah. And He shall not judge after the sight of His eyes, nor decide by hearsay: but with righteousness shall He judge the poor, and give sentence with equity for the meek of the earth; but He shall smite the scorners with the rod of His mouth, and with the breath of His lips shall He slay the wicked, so that righteousness shall be the girdle of His loins, and faithfulness the girdle of His reins. Then the wolf shall dwell with the lamb, and the leopard shall lie down with the kid: and the calf and the young lion together, and a little child shall lead them. And the cow and the bear shall feed, their young ones shall lie down together; and the lion shall eat straw like the ox: and the sucking child shall stroke the head of the adder, and the weaned child shall put his hand on the eye-ball of the basilisk. They shall not hurt nor destroy in all my holy mountain" (xi. 1-9) This is generally considered to be a prediction of a universal golden age on earth; but Isaiah only speaks of the holy mountain as the scene, meaning by this the whole city of David as the centre of his kingdom. The just and strict government of the descendant of David is to bring it about that righteousness and truth kiss each other, and that the strong do not dare to injure the weak. Fear of the severity of the law engenders general confidence; the lamb is no longer afraid of the wolf. The opposite of this ideal is lawlessness and anarchy within, not war without; the hope is not that of international peace, as we see both from verse 1-5 and from verse 9. The Messiah is adorned just with the virtues which befit a ruler; and this shows sufficiently what is the nature of the kingdom of which he is to be the head, *i.e.*, what is the notion of the theocracy.

The other prophets of this period agree with Isaiah (Lamentations iv. 20), only Hosea is peculiar in this as in other points. He appears to have regarded the kingdom as such as an evil; in more than one expression he makes it the antithesis of the rule of Jehovah. But we have to remember that this judgment of his is based entirely on his historical experience. In the kingdom of the ten tribes the supreme power was constantly being seized by usurpers, so that instead of being the pillar of order and law it was the plaything of parties and the occasion of incessant disturbances. It is this North-Israelite kingdom that Hosea has in view; and he reprobates it for no other reason than that, in the three hundred years of its existence, it has not approved itself, and does not approve itself in the present time of need. He does not proceed as on *a priori* theory, he does not apply as his rule a pattern of the theocratic constitution given antecedently to any historical development. There can be no doubt that it never entered his head that the form God desired the community to take was not a thing to be determined by circumstances, but had been revealed at Mount Sinai. *1*

************************************** 1. He even speaks with favour of David and the kingdom of Judah, but I consider all such references in Hosea (as well as in Amos) to, be interpolations. In i. 7 there is a reference to the deliverance of Jerusalem under Hezekiah. **

XI.I.4. Nor did the theocracy exist from the time of Moses in the form of the covenant, though that was afterwards a favourite mode of regarding it. The relation of Jehovah to Israel was in its nature and origin a natural one; there was no interval between Him and His people to call for thought or question. Only when the existence of Israel had come to be threatened by the Syrians and Assyrians, did such prophets as Elijah and Amos raise the Deity high above the people, sever the natural bond between them, and put in its place a relation depending on conditions, conditions of a moral character. To them Jehovah was the God of righteousness in the first place, and the God of Israel in the second place, and even that only so far as Israel came up to the righteous demands which in His grace He had revealed to him. They inverted the order of these two fundamental articles of faith. "If your sins are as scarlet, how should they be reckoned white as snow? If they are red like crimson, how should they be as wool? If ye be willing and obedient, ye shall eat the good of the land, but if ye refuse and rebel, ye must eat the sword, for the mouth of Jehovah hath spoken it." Thus the nature of the conditions which Jehovah required of His people came to the very front in considering His relations with them: the Torah of Jehovah, which originally, like all His dealings, fell under the category of divine aid, especially in the doing of justice, of divine guidance in the solution of difficult questions, was now conceived of as incorporating the demands on the fulfilment of which His attitude towards Israel entirely depended. In this way arose, from ideas which easily suggested it, but yet as an entirely new thing, the substance of the notion of covenant or treaty. The name Berith, however, does not occur in the old prophets, not even in Hosea, who certainly presents us as clearly as possible with the thing, in his figure of the marriage of Jehovah and Israel (Isaiah i. 21). That he was unacquainted with the technical usage of Berith is strikingly proved by ii. 20 and vi. 7; and these passages must decide the view we take of viii. 1, a passage which is probably interpolated.

The NAME Berith comes, it is likely, from quite a different quarter. The ancient Hebrews had no other conception of law nor any other designation for it than that of a treaty. A law only obtained force by the fact of those to whom it was given binding themselves to keep it. So it is in Exodus xxiv. 3-8, and in 2Kings xxiii. 1-3; so also in Jeremiah xxxiv. 8 seq.—curiously enough just as with the people of Mecca at the time of Mohammed (lbn Hisham, p. 230 seq.). Hence also the term Sepher Berith for the Deuteronomic as well as the Jehovistic Book of the Law.

This use of the phrase Berith (ie., treaty) for law, fitted very well with the great idea of the prophets, and received from it in turn an interpretation, according to which the relation of Jehovah to Israel was conditioned by the demands of His righteousness, as set forth in His word and instruction. In this view of the matter Jehovah and Israel came to be regarded as the contracting parties of the covenant by which the various representatives of the people had originally pledged each other to keep, say, the Deuteronomic law. *1*

** I This variation gained entrance the more easily as Berith is used in various applications, e.g:, of the capitulation, the terms of which are imposed by the stronger on the weaker party: that the contracting parties had equal rights was by no means involved in the notion of the Berith. See the wavering of the notion in Jeremiah xxxiv. 13-18.
****

After the solemn and far-reaching act by which Josiah introduced this law, the notion of covenant-making between Jehovah and Israel appears to have occupied the central position in religious thought: it prevails in Deuteronomy, in Jeremiah, Ezekiel, in Isaiah xl.-lxvi., Leviticus xvii.-xxvi., and most of all in the Book of the Four Covenants. The Babylonian exile no doubt helped, as the Assyrian exile had previously done, to familiarise the Jewish mind with the idea that the covenant depended on conditions, and might possibly be dissolved.

XI.II.

XI.II.1. The tabernacle of David fell at last, and no king was born to set it up again. The state suffered not a crisis, but destruction. And the result was that such of the religious hopes of the people as they still held fast, were no longer limited to existing political conditions, but now took a freer flight, became tinged with enthusiasm, and cast off all restrictions. In former times there was always an enemy threatening in the background, a danger really approaching, to give rise to the expectation of a great conflagration, the materials for which had long been collected in the nation itself: but after the exile fancy dealt in general coalitions of God knows what peoples against the New Jerusalem, vaticinations for which there was no ground whatever in reality. *1*

** 1 Ezekiel xxxviii. xxxix.; Isaiah lxvi. 18-24; Joel iv.; Zechariah xii. xiv. In Isaiah v. 26, on the other hand, we must, of course, read GWY, for GWYM, the singular instead of the plural. **

In earlier times the national state as it had existed under David was the goal of all wishes. Now a universal world empire was erected in imagination, which was to lift up its head at Jerusalem over the ruins of the heathen powers. Prophecy was no longer tied to history, nor supported by it.

But the extravagant hopes now built on Jehovah were balanced on the other side by sober and realisable aims which the course of history presented. Those who waited for the consolation of Israel were then confronted from the nature of their situation with practical tasks. The old prophets were satisfied with expressing their ideas, with criticising existing evils; as to practical points they had nothing to say, the leadership of the people was in other hands. But the old community being now gone and its heads having fallen with it, the godly both had the power and felt the obligation to place themselves at the head of the Israel now to be anew created, after which they had long been striving, and their faith in which was still unshaken. In former times the nation had not been so seriously threatened as that its continued existence, notwithstanding the dangerous crises it might have to pass through, should ever cease to be regarded as natural, as a thing of course. But now this was by no means a thing of course, the danger was a pressing one that the Jewish exiles, like the Samaritan exiles before them, would be absorbed by the heathens among whom they dwelt. In that case the Messianic hopes also would have lost their point of application, for, however true it was that the realising of them was Jehovah's concern, the men must still be there to whom they were to be fulfilled. Thus everything depended on getting the sacred remnant safe across this danger, and giving it so solid an organisation that it might survive the storms and keep alive the expectation of the promise.

But in the eyes of those whose words had weight in the restoration the old community, as it had existed formerly, was not in good repute. They could not but allow Jehovah's sentence of condemnation to be just which He had spoken by the mouth of His servants and through the voice of history. The utterances of the prophets, that fortresses and horses and men of war, that kings and princes, cannot help, were called to mind and turned into practical principles: the sole rule of Jehovah was to be carried out in earnest. Circumstances favoured the design, and this was the great point. As matters then were, the reconstitution of an actual state was not to be thought of, the foreign rule would not admit of it (Ezra iv. 19 seq.). What plan was to be taken, what materials to be used for such a building as the times allowed? The prophetic ideas would not serve as building stones; they were not sufficiently practical. Then appeared the importance of institutions, of traditional forms, for the conservation even of the spiritual side of the religion.

The Jewish royal temple had early overshadowed the other sanctuaries, and in the course of the seventh century they were extinct or verging on extinction. Under the shelter of the monarchy the priests of Jerusalem had grown great and had at last attained, as against their professional brethren elsewhere, a position of exclusive legitimacy. The weaker the state grew, the deeper it sank from the fall of Josiah onwards, the higher became the prestige of the temple in the eyes of the people, and the greater and the more independent grew the power of its numerous priesthood; how much more do we feel it in Jeremiah's time than in that of Isaiah! This advance of the priesthood indicates unmistakably the rise into prominence of the cultus in the seventh century, a rise rather helped than hindered by the long reign of Manasseh, evil as is the reputation of that reign. It shows itself not only in the introduction of more luxurious materials, incense, for example, but even more in the importance given to great and striking services, *e.g.*, the sacrifice of children, and the expiatory offering. Even after the abolition of the horrid atrocities of Manasseh's time, the bloody earnestness remained behind with which the performance of divine service was gone about.

So closely was the cultus of Jerusalem interwoven with the consciousness of the Jewish people, and so strongly had the priesthood established their order, that after the collapse of the kingdom the elements still survived here for the new formation of a "congregation" answering to the circumstances and needs of the time. Around the ruined sanctuary the community once more lifted up its head (1Kings viii.; Haggai i. seq.; Zechariah i. seq.). The usages and ordinances were, though everywhere changes in detail, yet not created afresh. Whatever creating there was lay in this, that these usages were bound together in a system and made the instruments of restoring an organisation of "the remnant."

Ezekiel first pointed out the way which was suited for the time. He is the connecting link between the prophets and the law. He claims to be a prophet, and starts from prophetic ideas: but they are not his own ideas, they are those of his predecessors which he turns into dogmas. He is by nature a priest, and his peculiar merit is that he enclosed the soul of prophecy in the body of a community which was not political, but founded on the temple and the cultus. The chapters xl.-xlviii. are the most important in his book, and have been called by J. Orth, not incorrectly, the key of the Old Testament.

Thus arose that artificial product, the sacred constitution of Judaism. In the Priestly Code we have the picture of it in detail. *1*

*** 1. It is not the case that the hierocracy is based on the Priestly Code: that code was only introduced after the hierocracy was already in existence, but helped, no doubt, to consolidate and legalise it. The written law afterwards undermined the rule of the priests; and the scriptures played into the hands of the scribes and Pharisees. (Compare the case of the Parsees and Sabians, and *the reference given here,... namely "p.157, note" is in error. There is no note on p. 157 and I do not know what is being referred to ...*) ***

The distinction, drawn with such pains between the Mosaic theocracy and the post-exilic hierocracy, is too fine. Theocracy as a constitution is hierocracy. If Moses founded such a constitution, he did it prophetically, with a view to circumstances which only arose a thousand years after his day, *V.II.1.; VII.II.4.*. Old Israel had not shrunk to a religious congregation, public life was not quite absorbed in the service of the sanctuary; the high priest and the dwelling of Jehovah were not the centre round which all revolved *p.170 is not correct; .* These great changes were wrought by the destruction of the political existence first of Samaria, then of Judah. In this way the people became "a kingdom of priests and a holy nation," as we read in a Deuteronomistic passage, Exodus xix. 6. If the divine rule was formerly a belief supporting the natural ordinances of human society, it was now set forth in visible form as a divine state, in an artificial sphere peculiar to itself and transcending the ordinary life of the people. The idea had formerly informed and possessed the natural body, but now, in order that it might be thoroughly realised, it was to have spiritual body of its own. There arose a material, external antithesis of a sacred and profane; men's minds came to be full of this, and it was their great endeavour to draw the line as sharply as possible and to repress the natural sphere more and more. Holiness is the ruling idea in Ezekiel, in Leviticus xvii.-xxvi., and in the Priestly Code. The notion is a somewhat empty one, expressing rather what a thing is not than what it is; at first it meant the same as divine, but now it is used mainly in the sense of spiritual, priestly, as if the divine could be distinguished from the worldly, the natural, by outward visible marks of that kind.

The Mosaic theocracy, the residuum of a ruined state, is itself not a state at all, but an unpolitical artificial product created in spite of unfavourable circumstances by the impulse of an ever-memorable energy: and foreign rule is its necessary counterpart. In its nature it is intimately allied to the old Catholic church, which was in fact its child. As a matter of taste it may be objectionable to speak of the Jewish church, but as a matter of history it is not inaccurate, and the name is perhaps preferable to that of theocracy, which shelters such confusion of ideas.

XI.II.2. The Mosaic theocracy appears to show an immense retrogression. The law of Jehovah should denote what is characteristic of His people over against the heathen. But this certainly did not consist in the cultus of Israel: it would be vain labour to seek in this and that slight variation between the Hebrew and the Greek ritual a difference of principle between them. The cultus is the heathen element in the Israelite religion— the word heathen not being understood, of course, in an ignoble or unworthy sense. If the Priestly Code makes the cultus the principal thing, that appears to amount to a systematic decline into the heathenism which the prophets incessantly combated and yet were unable to eradicate. It will be readily acknowledged that at the constitution of the new Jerusalem the prophetic impulses were deflected by a previously existing natural tendency of the mass on which they had to operate. Yet in every part of the legal worship we see the most decided traces of their influence. We have seen to what a large extent that worship is everywhere marked by a centralising tendency. This tendency is not connected in the Priestly Code with opposition to improper or foreign worship; yet it must be interpreted as a polemical measure; and if it be regarded as an axiom necessary in the Priestly Code from the nature of the case, that is only saving that the demands of the prophets had prevailed most completely in a field where they had the greatest obstacles to contend with. Exclusive monolatry is by no means innate in the cultus; it can only be deduced from considerations which are foreign to the nature of the cultus: it is the antitype of strict monotheism. The prohibition of images, too, in the worship of the Deity, is not expressly insisted on, as in Deuteronomy, but is a provision which is taken for granted; so little is this position in danger of question that even doubtful and repugnant elements are embodied in the worship and assimilated by it without hesitation. The golden ephod, denounced by Isaiah, has become an insignificant decoration of the high-priest: talismans, forbidden even by Ezekiel, are allowed (Numbers xv. 37-41), but the object of them is "that ye may look upon them and remember all the commandments of Jehovah, and do them, and that ye follow not after your own heart and your own eyes, after which ye used to go a whoring." The gross idolatry, with which the expression znh is always connected in other passages, is by this time out of the question: the heart itself with its lawless motions is the strange God, whose service is forbidden.

We may go further and say that by the cultus-legislation the cultus is estranged from its own nature, and overthrown in its own sphere. That is most unmistakably the case with regard to the festivals. They have lost their reference to harvest and cattle, and have become historical commemorations: they deny their birth from nature, and celebrate the institution of supernatural religion and the gracious acts of Jehovah therewith connected. The broadly human, the indigenous element falls away, they receive a statutory character and a significance limited to Israel. They no longer draw down the Deity into human life on all important occasions, to take part in its joys and its necessities: they are not HUMAN ATTEMPTS with such naïve means as are at command to please the Deity and render Him favourable. They are removed from the natural sphere, and made DIVINE MEANS OF GRACE, which Jehovah has instituted in Israel as sacraments of the theocracy. The worshipper no longer thinks that in his gift he is doing God a pleasure, providing Him with an enjoyment: what pleases Him and is effectual is only the strict observance of the rite. The sacrifices must be offered exactly according to prescription: at the right place, at the right time, by the right individuals, in the right way. They are not based on the inner value of what is done, on the impulse arising out of fresh occasions, but on the positive command of a will outside the worshipper, which is not explained, and which prescribes every particular. The bond between cultus and sensuality is

352

severed: no danger can arise of an admixture of impure immoral elements, a danger which was always present in Hebrew antiquity. Worship no longer springs from an inner impulse, it has come to be an exercise of religiosity. It has no natural significance; its significance is transcendental, incomparable, not to be defined; the chief effect of it, which is always produced with certainty, is atonement. For after the exile the consciousness of sin, called forth by the rejection of the people from the face of Jehovah, was to a certain extent permanent: even when the hard service of Israel was accomplished and the wrath really blown over, it would not disappear.

If then the value of the sacred offerings lay not in themselves but in obedience to the commandments of God, the centre of gravity of the cultus was removed from that exercise itself and transferred to another field, that of morality. The consequence was that sacrifices and gifts gave way to ascetic exerctses, which were more strictly and more simply connected with morality. Precepts given originally in reference to the consecration of the priests for their religious functions were extended to the laity: the observance of these laws of physical cleanliness was of much more radical importance in Judaism than the great public cultus, and led by the straightest road towards the theocratic ideal of holiness and of universal priesthood. The whole of life was compressed into a certain holy path; there was always a divine command to be fulfilled, and by thinking of it a man kept himself from following after the desires and lusts of his own heart. On the other hand this private cultus, which constantly required attention, kept alive and active the individual sense of sin.

The great pathologist of Judaism is quite right: in the Mosaic theocracy the cultus became a pedagogic instrument of discipline. It is estranged from the heart; its revival was due to old custom, it would never have blossomed again of itself. It no longer has its roots in childlike impulse, it is a dead work, in spite of all the importance attached to it, nay, just because of the anxious conscientiousness with which it was gone about. At the restoration of Judaism the old usages were patched together in a new system, which, however, only served as the form to preserve something that was nobler in its nature, but could not have been saved otherwise than in a narrow shell that stoutly resisted all foreign influences. That heathenism in Israel against which the prophets vainly protested was inwardly overcome by the law on its own ground; and the cultus, after nature had been killed in it, became the shield of supernaturalistic monotheism.

The end of the Prolegomena

ISRAEL

Reprinted from the "Encyclopædia Britannica"

ISRAEL.

1. THE BEGINNINGS OF THE NATION.

According to the Book of Genesis, Israel was the brother of Edom, and the cousin of Moab and Ammon. These four petty peoples, which may be classed together as the Hebrew group, must at one time have formed some sort of a unity and have passed through a common history which resulted in their settlement in south-eastern Palestine. The Israelites, or rather that section of the Hebrew group which afterwards developed into Israel, appear at first to have been the immediate neighbours of Edom, and to have extended westwards towards the border of Egypt. As regards the ethnological position of the Hebrews as a whole, tradition has it that they had connexions not only with the Aramaeans of Osrhoene (Nahor), but also with certain of the old half-Arab inhabitants of the Sinaitic peninsula (Kenites, Amalek, Midian). To the Canaanites, whose language they had adopted, their relation was that of foreign conquerors and lords to a subject race (Gen. ix, 26).

Some fifteen centuries before our era a section of the Hebrew group left its ancient seat in the extreme south of Palestine to occupy the not distant pasture lands of Egypt (Goshen), where they carried on their old calling, that of shepherds and goatherds. Although settled within the territory of the Pharaohs, and recognising their authority, they continued to retain all their old characteristics,—their language, their patriarchal institutions, their nomad habits of life.

But in course of time these foreign guests were subjected to changed treatment. Forced labour was exacted of them for the construction of new public works in Goshen, an exaction which was felt to be an assault upon their freedom and honour, and which in point of fact was fitted to take away all that was distinctive of their nationality. But they had no remedy at hand, and had submitted in despair, until Moses at last saw a favourable opportunity of deliverance. Reminding his oppressed brethren of the God of their fathers, and urging that their cause was His, he taught them to regard self-assertion against the Egyptians as an article of religion; and they became once more a united people in a determination to seek refuge from oppression in the wilderness which was the dwelling-place of their kindred and the seat of their God. At a time when Egypt was scourged by a grievous plague, the Hebrews broke up their settlement in Goshen one night in spring, and directed their steps towards their old home again. According to the accounts, the king had consented to the exodus, and latterly had even forced it on, but it was none the less a secret flight.

To a not very numerous pastoral people such an undertaking presented no great difficulty. Nevertheless its execution was not to be carried out unimpeded. The Hebrews, compelled to abandon the direct eastward road (Exod. xiii. 17, 18), turned towards the south-west and encamped at last on the Egyptian shore of the northern arm of the Red Sea, where they were overtaken by Pharaoh's army. The situation was a critical one; but a high wind during the night left the shallow sea so low that it became possible to ford it. Moses eagerly accepted the suggestion, and made the venture with success. The Egyptians, rushing after, came up with them on the further shore, and a struggle ensued. But the assailants fought at a disadvantage, the ground being ill suited for their chariots and horsemen; they fell into confusion and attempted a retreat. Meanwhile the wind had changed; the waters returned, apd the pursuers were annihilated./1/

*********************************** 1. Exod. xvi. 21, 24, 25, 27, 30, 31. According to the Old Testament the exodus took place 480 years before the building of Solomon's temple, and 960 years before the end of the Babylonian captivity. These figures are "systematic" or at least systematised, but even so they are certainly more trustworthy than the combinations of the Egyptologists.
****

After turning aside to visit Sinai as related in Exodus, the emigrants settled at Kadesh, eastwards from Goshen, on the southern borders of Palestine, 2

*********************************** 2. The site of Sinai (= Horeb?) hardly admits of ascertainment. The best datum would be the sanctuary of Jethro, if we could identify it with Midian (Jakut, iv. 451), which lies on the Arabian coast of the Red Sea obliquely facing the traditional Sinai. With regard to Qadesh, see Quarterly Statement of the Palestine Exploration Fund (1871), pp. 20, 21.
****

where they remained for many years, having at the well of Kadesh their sanctuary and judgment-seat only, while with their flocks they ranged over an extensive tract. In all probability their stay at Kadesh was no involuntary detention; rather was it this locality they had more immediately had in view in setting out. For a civilised community of from two to three millions such a settlement would, of course, have been impossible; but it was quite sufficient for the immediate requirements of the Goshen shepherds, few in number as they were and inured to the life of the desert. That attempts may have been made by them to obtain possession of the more fertile country to the north is very likely; but that from the outset they contemplated the conquest of the whole of Palestine proper, and that it was only in expiation of a fault that they were held back at the gate of the promised land until the whole generation of the disobedient had died out, is not historically probable.

We can assign a definite reason for their final departure from Kadesh. In the district to the east of Jordan the (Canaanite) Amorites had, sometime previously, driven the Ammonites from the lower Jabbok and deprived the Moabites of all their territory to the north of the Arnon; on the plateau opposite Jericho Heshbon had become the capital of Sihon, the Amorite king. This sovereign now set himself to subdue southern Moab also, and not without success. "Fire went out from Heshbon, flame from the stronghold of Sihon, devoured the cities of Moab upon the heights of Arnon. Woe to thee, O Moab! thou art undone, O people of Chemosh!" From these straits the Moabites were rescued by their cousins, the nomads of the wilderness of Kadesh. The Israelites came forward on behalf of what was at once the common Hebrew cause and their own particular interest; they took the field against the Amorites, vanquished them in battle, and broke up the kingdom of Sihon. The consequence was that the land to the south of the Arnon remained in the undisputed possession of Moab, while the victors themselves became masters of the territory immediately to the north. Settled thus between Moab and Ammon their kinsmen, the Israelites supplied the link that was wanting in the chain of petty Hebrew nationalities established in the south of eastern Palestine.

The army that went out against the Amorites from Kadesh was certainly not exclusively composed of men who, or whose fathers, had accomplished the passage of the Red Sea Israel was not a formed nation when it left Egypt; and throughout the whole period of its sojourn in the wilderness it continued to be in process of growth. Instead of excluding the kindred elements which offered themselves to it on its new soil, it received and assimilated them. The life they had lived together under Moses had been the first thing to awaken a feeling of solidarity among the tribes which afterwards constituted the nation; whether they had previously been a unity in any sense of the word is doubtful. On the other hand, the basis of the unification of the tribes must certainly have been laid before the conquest of Palestine proper; for with that it broke up, though the memory of it continued. At the same time it must not be supposed that all the twelve tribes already existed side be side in Kadesh. The sons of the concubines of Jacob—Dan and Naphtali, Gad and Asher—manifestly do not pertain to Israel in the same sense as do those of Leah and Rachel; probably they were late arrivals and of very mixed origin. We know, besides, that Benjamin was not born until afterwards, in Palestine. If this view be correct, Israel at first consisted of seven tribes, of which one only, that of Joseph, traced its descent to Rachel, though in point of numbers and physical strength it was the equal of all the others together, while in intellectual force it surpassed them. The remaining six were the sons of Leah:—Reuben, Simeon, Levi, Judah; Issachar, Zebulon. They are always enumerated in this order; the fact that the last two are also invariably mentioned apart from the rest and after Joseph has its explanation in geographical considerations.

The time of Moses is invariably regarded as the properly creative period in Israel's history, and on that account also as giving the pattern and norm for the ages which followed. In point of fact the history of Israel must be held to have begun then, and the foundations of a new epoch to have been laid. The prophets who came after gave, it is true, greater distinctness to the peculiar character of the nation, but they did not make it; on the contrary, it made them. Again, it is true that the movement which resulted in the establishment of the monarchy brought together for the first time into organic unity the elements which previously had existed only in an isolated condition; but Israel's sense of national personality was a thing of much earlier origin, which even in the time of the judges bound the various tribes and families together, and must have had a great hold on the mind of the nation, although there was no formal and binding constitution to give it support. When the Israelites settled in Palestine they found it inhabited by a population superior to themselves both in numbers and in civilisation, which they did not extirpate, but on the contrary gradually subdued and absorbed. The process was favoured by affinity of race and similarity of speech; but, however far it went, it never had the effect of making Israelites Canaanites; on the contrary, it made Canaanites Israelites. Notwithstanding their inferiority, numerical and otherwise, they maintained their

357

individuality, and that without the support of any external organisation. Thus a certain inner unity actually subsisted long before it had found any outward political expression; it goes back to the time of Moses, who is to be regarded as its author.

The foundation upon which, at all periods, Israel's sense of its national unity rested was religious in its character. It was the faith which may be summed up in the formula, Jehovah is the God of Israel, and Israel is the people of Jehovah. Moses was not the first discoverer of this faith, but it was through him that it came to be the fundamental basis of the national existence and history. *1*

*** 1. Jehovah is to be regarded as having originally been a family or tribal god, either of the family to which Moses belonged or of the tribe of Joseph, in the possession of which we find the ark of Jehovah, and within which occurs the earliest certain instance of a composite proper name with the word Jehovah for one of its elements (Jeho-shua, Joshua). No essential distinction was felt to exist between Jehovah and El, any more than between Asshur and El; Jehovah was only a special name of El which had become current within a powerful circle, and which on that account was all the more fitted to become the designation of a national god. ***

The exigencies of their position severe a number of kindred clans from their customary surroundings, and drove them into his arms. He undertook the responsibilities of their leader, and the confidence of success which he manifested was justified by the result. But it was not through any merit of his that the undertaking (of which he was the soul) prospered as it did; his design was aided in a wholly unlooked-for way, by a marvellous occurrence quite beyond his control, and which no sagacity could possibly have foreseen. One whom the wind and sea obeyed had given him His aid. Behind him stood One higher than he, whose spirit wrought in him and whose arm wrought for him,—not for his personal aggrandisement indeed, but for the weal of the nation. It was Jehovah. Alike what was done by the deliberate purpose of Moses and what was done without any human contrivance by nature and by accident came to be regarded in one great totality as the doing of Jehovah for Israel. Jehovah it was who had directed each step in that process through which these so diverse elements, brought together by the pressure of necessity, had been caused to pass, and in the course of which the first beginnings of a feeling of national unity had been made to grow.

This feeling Moses was the first to elicit; he it was also who maintained it in life and cherished its growth. The extraordinary set of circumstances which had first occasioned the new national movement continued to subsist, though in a less degree, throughout the sojourn of the people in the wilderness, and it was under their pressure that Israel continued to be moulded. To Moses, who had been the means of so brilliantly helping out of their first straits the Hebrews who had accompanied him out of Egypt, they naturally turned in all subsequent difficulties; before him they brought all affairs with which they were not themselves able to cope. The authority which his antecedents had secured for him made him as matter of course the great

358

national "Kadhi" in the wilderness. Equally as matter of course did he exercise his judicial functions, neither in his own interest nor in his own name, but in the interest of the whole community and in the name of Jehovah. By connecting them with the sanctuary of Jehovah, which stood at the well of Kadesh, he made these functions independent of his person, and thus he laid a firm basis for a consuetudinary law and became the originator of the Torah in Israel. In doing this he succeeded in inspiring the national being with that which was the very life of his own soul; through the Torah he gave a definite positive expression to their sense of nationality and their idea of God. Jehovah was not merely the God of Israel; as such he was the God at once of law and of justice, the basis, the informing principle, and the implied postulate of their national consciousness.

The relationship was carried on in precisely the same manner as that in which it had been begun. It was most especially in the graver moments of its history that Israel awoke to full consciousness of itself and of Jehovah. Now, at that time and for centuries afterwards, the highwater marks of history were indicated by the wars it recorded. The name "Israel" means "El does battle," and Jehovah was the warrior El, after whom the nation styled itself. The camp was, so to speak, at once the cradle in which the nation was nursed and the smithy in which it was welded into unity; it was also the primitive sanctuary. There Israel was, and there was Jehovah. If in times of peace the relations between the two had become dormant, they were at once called forth into fullest activity when the alarm of danger was raised; Israel's awakening was always preceded by the awakening of Jehovah. Jehovah awakened men who under the guidance of His spirit placed themselves at the nation's head; in them His proper leadership was visibly expressed. Jehovah went forth with the host to battle, and in its enthusiasm His presence was seen (Judges. v. 13, 23). With signs and wonders from heaven Jehovah decided the struggle carried on upon earth. In it He was always upon Israel's side; on Israel was His whole interest concentrated, although His power (for He was God) reached far beyond their local limits.

Thus Jehovah was in a very real sense a living God; but the manifestations of His life in the great crises of His people's history were of necessity separated by considerable intervals of time. His activity had something abrupt and tumultuary about it, better suited for extraordinary occasions than for ordinary daily life. Traces of this feeling appear very prominently in the later stages of the development. But although the relations between Israel and Israel's God came most strongly into prominence in times of excitement, yet it did not altogether die out in the periods of comparative repose. It was in the case of Jehovah just as in the case of the human leaders of the people, who did not in times of peace wholly lose the influence they had gained in war. Jehovah had His permanent court at the places of worship where in times of quietude men clung to Him that they might not lose Him in times of trouble. His chief, perhaps in the time of Moses His only, sanctuary was with the so-called ark of the covenant. It was a standard, adapted primarily to the requirements of a wandering and warlike life; brought back from the field, it became, as symbol of Jehovah's presence, the central seat of His worship. The cultus itself was more than a mere paying of court to Jehovah, more than a mere expedient for retaining His sympathies against times of necessity; the Torah of Jehovah, the holy administration of law, was conjoined with it. This had first of all been exercised, at the instance of the priest of Midian, by Moses at the well of Kadesh; it was continued after him, at the sanctuary, within the circle of those who had attached themselves to him and were spiritually his heirs. In cases where the wisdom or the competency of the ordinary judges failed, men turned direct to the Godhead, *i.e.*, to the sanctuary and those who served it. Their decisions, whether given according to their own lights or by lot (according to the character of the question), were not derived from any law, but were received direct from Jehovah. *1*

*** 1 They were consulted chiefly on points of law, but also on all sorts of difficulties as to what was right and to be done, or wrong and to be avoided. ***

The execution of their decisions did not lie with them; they could only advise and teach. Their authority was divine, or, as we should say, moral, in its character; it rested upon that spontaneous recognition of the idea of right which, though unexpressed, was alive and working among the tribes—upon Jehovah Himself, who was the author of this generally diffused sense of right, but revealed the proper determinations on points of detail only to certain individuals. The priestly Torah was an entirely unpolitical or rather prepolitical institution; it had an existence before the state had, and it was one of the invisible foundation pillars on which the state rested.

War and the administration of justice were regarded as matters of religion before they became matters of obligation and civil order; this is all that is really meant when a theocracy is spoken of. Moses certainly organised no formal state, endowed with specific holiness, upon the basis of the proposition "Jehovah is the God of Israel;" or, at all events, if he did so, the fact had not in the slightest degree any practical consequence or historical significance. The old patriarchal system of families and clans continued as before to be the ordinary constitution, if one can apply such a word as constitution at all to an unorganised conglomeration of homogeneous elements. What there was of permanent official authority lay in the hands of the elders and heads of houses; in time of war they commanded each his own household force, and in peace they dispensed justice each within his own circle. But this obviously imperfect and inefficient form of government showed a growing tendency to break down just in proportion to the magnitude of the tasks which the nation in the course of its history was called upon to undertake. Appeal to Jehovah was always in these circumstances resorted to; His court was properly that of last resort, but the ordinary authorities were so inadequate that it had often enough to be applied to. Theocracy, if one may so say, arose as the complement of anarchy. Actual and legal existence (in the modern sense) was predicable only of each of the many clans; the unity of the nation was realised in the first instance only through its religion. It was out of the religion of Israel that the commonwealth of Israel unfolded itself,—not a HOLY state, but THE state. And the state continued to be, consciously, rooted in religion, which prevented it from quitting or losing its rapport with the soil from which it had originally sprung. With the intermediate and higher stages of political organisation, with the building of the upper structure, however, religion had no concern; they were too far removed from the foundation. The derivative, which did not carry immediately in itself its own title to exist, was a matter of indifference to it;

what had come into being it suffered to go its own way as soon as it was capable of asserting its independence. For this reason it always turned by preference to the future, not in a utopian but in a thoroughly practical way; by a single step only did it keep ahead of the present. It prepared the way for such developments as are not derived from existing institutions, but spring immediately from the depths in which human society has its secret and mysterious roots.

The expression "Jehovah is the God of Israel," accordingly, meant that every tosk of the nation, internal as well as external, was conceived as holy. It certainly did not mean that the almighty Creator of heaven and earth was conceived of as having first made a covenant with this one people that by them He might be truly known and worshipped. It was not as if Jehovah had originally been regarded as the God of the universe who subsequently became the God of Israel; on the contrary, He was primarily Israel's God, and only afterwards (very long afterwards) did He come to be regarded as the God of the universe. For Moses to have given to the Israelites an "enlightened conception of God" would have been to have given them a stone instead of bread; it is in the highest degree probable that, with regard to the essential nature of Jehovah, as distinct from His relation to men, he allowed them to continue in the same way of thinking with their fathers. With theoretical truths, which were not at all in demand, He did not occupy himself, but purely with practical questions which were put and urged by the pressure of the times. The religious starting-point of the history of Israel was remarkable, not for its novelty, but for its normal character. In all ancient primitive peoples the relation in which God is conceived to stand to the circumstances of the nation—in other words, religion—furnishes a motive for law and morals; in the case of none did it become so with such purity and power as in that of the Israelites. Whatever Jehovah may have been conceived to be in His essential nature-God of the thunderstorm or the like—this fell more and more into the background as mysterious and transcendental; the subject was not one for inquiry. All stress was laid upon His activity within the world of mankind, whose ends He made one with His own. Religion thus did not make men partakers in a divine life, but contrariwise it made God a partaker in the life of men; life in this way was not straitened by it, but enlarged. The so-called "particularism" of Israel's idea of God was in fact the real strength of Israel's religion; it thus escaped from barren mythologisings, and became free to apply itself to the moral tasks which are always given, and admit of being discharged, only in definite spheres. As God of the nation, Jehovah became the God of justice and of right; as God of justice and right, He came to be thought of as the highest, and at last as the only, power in heaven and earth.

***** In the preceding sketch the attempt has been made to exhibit Mosaism as it must be supposed to have existed on the assumption that the history of Israel commenced with it, and that for centuries it continued to be the ideal root out of which that history continued to grow. This being assumed, we cannot treat the legislative portion of the Pentateuch as a source from which our knowledge of what Mosaism really was can be derived; for it cannot in any sense be regarded as the starting-point of the subsequent development. If it was the work of Moses, then we must suppose it to have remained a dead letter for centuries, and only through King Josiah and Ezra the scribe to have become operative in the national history (compare sections 8 and 10). The historical tradition which has reached us relating to the period of the judges and of the kings of Israel is the main source, though only of course in an indirect way, of our knowledge of Mosaism. But within the Pentateuch itself also the historical tradition about Moses (which admits of being distinguished, and must carefully be separated, from the legislative, although the latter often clothes itself in narrative form) is in its main features manifestly trustworthy, and can only be explained as resting on actual facts.

From the historical tradition, then, it is certain that Moses was the founder of the Torah. But the legislative tradition cannot tell us what were the positive contents of his Torah. In fact it can be shown that throughout the whole of the older period the Torah was no finished legislative code, but consisted entirely of the oral decisions and instructions of the priests, as a whole it was potential only; what actually existed were the individual sentences given by the priesthood as they were asked for. Thus Moses was not regarded as the promulgator once for all of a national constitution, but rather as the first to call into activity the actual sense for law and justice, and to begin the series of oral decisions which were continued after him by the priests. He was the founder of the nation out of which the Torah and prophecy came as later growths. He laid the basis of Israel's subsequent peculiar individuality, not by any one formal act, but in virtue of his having throughout the whole of his long life been the people's leader, judge, and centre of union.

A correct conception of the manner in which the Torah was made by him can be derived from the narrative contained in Exod. xviii., but not from the long section which follows, relating to the Sinaitic covenant (chap. xix. seq.). The giving of the law at Sinai has only a formal, not to say dramatic, significance. It is the product of the poetic necessity for such a representation of the manner in which the people was constituted Jehovah's people as should appeal directly and graphically to the imagination. Only so can we justly interpret those expressions according to which Jehovah with His own mouth thundered the ten commandments down from the mountain to the people below, and afterwards for forty days held a confidential conference with Moses alone on the summit. For the sake of producing a solemn and vivid impression, that is represented as having taken place in a single thrilling moment which in reality occurred slowly and almost unobserved. Why Sinai should have been chosen as the scene admits of ready explanation. It was the Olympus of the Hebrew peoples, the earthly seat of the Godhead, and as such it continued to be regarded by the Israelites even after their settlement in Palestine (Judges v. 4, 5). This immemorial sanctity of Sinai it was that led to its being selected as the ideal scene of the giving of the law, not conversely. If we eliminate from the historical narrative the long Sinaitic section which has but a loose connection with it, the wilderness of Kadesh becomes the locality of the preceding and subsequent events. It was during the sojourn of many years here that the organisation of the nation, in any historical sense, took place. "There He made for them statute and ordinance, and there He proved them," as we read in Exod. xv. 26 in a dislocated poetical fragment. "Judgment and trial," "Massa and Meribah," point to Kadesh as the place referred to; there at all events is the scene of the narrative immediately following (Exod. xvii. = Num. xx.), and doubtless also of Exod. xviii.

If the legislation of the Pentateuch cease as a whole to be regarded as an authentic source for our knowledge of what Mosaism was, it becomes a somewhat precarious matter to make any exception in favour of the Decalogue. In particular, the following arguments against its authenticity must be taken into account. (1) According to Exod. xxxiv. the commandments which stood upon the two tables were quite different. (2) The prohibition of images was during the older period quite unknown; Moses himself is said to have made a brazen serpent which down to Hezekiah's time continued to be worshipped at Jerusalem as an image of Jehovah. (3) The essentially and necessarily national character of the older phases of the religion of Jehovah completely disappears in the quite universal code of morals which is given in the Decalogue as the fundamental law of Israel; but the entire series of religious personalities throughout the period of the judges and the kings—from Deborah, who praised Jael's treacherous act of murder, to David, who treated his prisoners of war with the utmost cruelty—make it very difficult to believe that the religion of Israel was from the outset one of a specifically moral character. The true spirit of the old religion may be gathered much more truly from Judges v. than from Exod. xx. (4) It is extremely doubtful whether the actual monotheism which is undoubtedly pre-supposed in the universal moral precepts of the Decalogue could have formed the foundation of a national religion. It was first developed out of the national religion at the downfall of the nation, and thereupon kept its hold upon the people in an artificial manner by means of the idea of a covenant formed by the God of the universe with, in the first instance, Israel alone (compare sections 6-10).

As for the question regarding the historical presuppositions of Mosaism, there generally underlies it a misunderstanding arising out of theological intellectualism-an attribute found with special frequency among nontheologians. Moses gave no new idea of God to his people. The question whence he could have derived it therefore need not be raised. It could not possibly be worse answered, however, than by a reference to his relations with the priestly caste of Egypt and their wisdom. It is not to be believed that an Egyptian deity could inspire the Hebrews of Goshen with courage for the struggle against the Egyptians, or that an abstraction of esoteric speculation could become the national deity of Israel. It is not inconceivable indeed, although at the same time quite incapable of proof, that Moses was indebted to the Egyptian priests for certain advantages of personal culture, or that he borrowed from them on all hands in external details of organisation or in matters of ritual. But the origin of the germ which developed into Israel is not to be sought for in Egypt, and Jehovah has nothing in common with the colourless divinity of Penta-ur or with the God-forsaken dreariness of certain modern Egyptologists. That monotheism must have been a foreign importation, because it is contrary to that sexual dualism of Godhead which is the fundamental characteristic of Semitic religion, is an untenable exaggeration which has recently become popular out of opposition to the familiar thesis about the monotheistic instinct of the Semites (Noldeke, Literar. Centralbl., 1877, p. 365). Moab, Ammon, and Edom, Israel's nearest kinsfolk and neighbours, were monotheists in precisely the same sense in which Israel itself was; but it would be foolish surely in their case to think of foreign importation.

Manetho's statements about the Israelites are for the most part to be regarded as malicious inventions: whether any genuine tradition underlies them at all is a point much needing to be investigated. The story of Exod. ii. 1 seq. is a mythus of frequent recurrence elsewhere, to which no further significance is attached, for that Moses was trained in all the wisdom of the Egyptians is vouched for by no earlier authorities than Philo and the New Testament. According to the Old Testament tradition his connexion is with Jethro's priesthood or with that of the Kenites. This historical presupposition of Mosaism has external evidence in its favour, and is inherently quite probable. *******

2. THE SETTLEMENT IN PALESTINE.

The kingdom of Sihon did not permanently suffice the Israelites, and the disintegration of the Canaanites to the west of Jordan in an endless number of kingdoms and cities invited attack. The first essay was made by Judah in conjunction with Simeon and Levi, but was far from prosperous. Simeon and Levi were annihilated; Judah also, though successful in mastering the mountain land to the west of the Dead Sea, was so only at the cost of severe losses which were not again made up until the accession of the Kenite families of the south (Caleb). As a consequence of the secession of these tribes, a new division of the nation into Israel and Judah took the place of that which had previously subsisted between the families of Leah and Rachel; under Israel were included all the tribes except Simeon, Levi, and Judah, which three are no longer mentioned in Judges v., where all the others are carefully and exhaustively enumerated. This half-abortive first invasion of the west was followed by a second, which was stronger and attended with much better results. It was led by the tribe of Joseph, to which the others attached themselves, Reuben and Gad only remaining behind in the old settlements. The district to the north of Judah, inhabited afterwards by Benjamin, was the first to be attacked. It was not until after several towns of this district had one by one fallen into the hands of the conquerors that the Canaanites set about a united resistance. They were, however, decisively repulsed by Joshua in the neighbourhood of Gibeon; and by this victory the Israelites became masters of the whole central plateau of Palestine. The first camp, at Gilgal, near the ford of Jordan, which had been maintained until then, was now removed, and the ark of Jehovah brought further inland (perhaps by way of Bethel) to Shiloh, where henceforward the headquarters were fixed, in a position which seemed as if it had been expressly made to favour attacks upon the fertile tract lying beneath it on the north. The Bne Rachel now occupied the new territory which up to that time had been acquired,—Benjamin, in immediate contiguity with the frontier of Judah, then Ephraim, stretching to beyond Shiloh, and lastly Manasseh, furthest to the north, as far as to the plain of Jezreel. The centre of gravity, so to speak, already lay in Ephraim, to which belonged Joshua and that is mentioned as the last achievement of Joshua that at the waters of Merom he defeated Jabin, king of Hazor, and the allied princes of Galilee, thereby opening up the north for Israelitish settlers. It is quite what we should expect that a great and united blow had to be struck at the Canaanites of the north before the new comers could occupy it in peace; and King Jabin, who reappears at a later date, certainly does not suit the situation described in Judges iv. v.

******* The Book of Joshua represents the conquest of western Palestine as having been the common undertaking of all the tribes together, which, after the original inhabitants have been extirpated, are exhibited as laying the ownerless country at Joshua's feet in order that he may divide it by lot amongst them. But this is a "systematic" generalisation, contradicted by the facts which we otherwise know. For we possess another account of the conquest of Palestine, that of Judges i., which runs parallel with the Book of Joshua. It is shorter indeed and more superficial, yet in its entire mode of presenting the subject more historical. According to its narrative, it appears that Joshua was the leader of Joseph and Benjamin only, with whom indeed Issachar, Zebulon, Dan, Naphtali, and Asher made common cause. But before his time the tribe of Judah had already crossed the Jordan and effected a lodgment in the territory which lay between the earlier seat of the nation in the wilderness of Kadesh and its then settlement on the plateau of Moab, forming in some degree a link of connection between the two. It might be supposed that the tribe of Judah had not taken the longer route to the eastward of the Dead Sea at all, but had already at Kadesh broken off from the main body and thence turned its steps directly northward. But the representation actually given in Judges i., to the effect that it was from the direction of the Jordan and not from that of the Negeb that they came to take possession of their land, finds its confirmation in the fact that the southern portion of their territory was the last to come into their possession. The tradition is unwavering that Hebron was taken not by Judah but by Caleb, a family which stood in friendly relations with Israel, but had no connexion with it by blood. It was only through the policy of David that Caleb, Othniel, Jerachmeel, and the rest of the Kenites who had their homes in the Negeb became completely incorporated with Judah, so that Hebron became at last the capital of that tribe. Its oldest seats, however, lay further to the north, in the region of Tekoa, Bethlehem, Baal Judah.

It harmonises well with this view to suppose that Simeon and Levi must have made at the same time their attempt to effect a settlement in the hill country of Ephraim. One of their families, Dinah bath Leah, met with a favourable reception in the town of Shechem, and began to mix freely with its population, and thus the way was paved for the establishment of peaceable relations between the old inhabitants of the land and the new importations. But these relations were brought to an end by the two brothers who, in concert it must be supposed with their sister, fell upon the Shechemites and massacred them. The final result proved disastrous. The Canaanites of the surrounding country united against them and completely destroyed them. There can be no doubt as to the trustworthiness of the somewhat enigmatical records of those events which are given in Gen. xlix. and xxxiv.; in no other way is it possible to explain why Simeon and Levi, which originally came upon the stage of history on an equal footing with Reuben and Judah, should have already disappeared as independent tribes at the very beginning of the period of the judges. Now, that the destruction of Shechem by the Manassite Abimelech is quite distinct from the attack made by Simeon and Levi need hardly be said. On the other hand, the occurrence cannot be regarded as pre-Mosaic, but must be assigned to a time previous to the conquest of the hill country of Ephraim by Joseph; for after Joseph's settlement there the two sons of Leah had manifestly nothing more to hope for in that locality. We are shut up, therefore, to the conclusion that they crossed the Jordan at the same time as Judah separated himself from the main body in search of a suitable territory. That

Simeon accompanied Judah in the first westward attempt is expressly stated in Judges i. The fate of Levi, again, cannot be separated from that of Simeon (Gen. xlix. 5-7); that he is not expressly mentioned in Judges i. ought not to cause surprise, when it is considered that later generations which regarded Levi as neither more nor less than a priest would have some difficulty in representing him as a thoroughly secular tribe. Such nevertheless he must have been, for the poet in Genesis xlix. 5-7 puts him on a footing of perfect equality with Simeon, and attributes to both brothers a very secular and bloodthirsty character; he has no conception that Levi has a sacred vocation which is the reason of the dispersion of the tribe; the dispersion, on the contrary, is regarded as a curse and no blessing, an annihilation and not the means of giving permanence to its tribal individuality. The shattered remains of Simeon, and doubtless those of Levi also, became incorporated with Judah, which thenceforward was the sole representative of the three sons of Leah, who according to the genealogy had been born immediately after Reuben the first-born. Judah itself seems at the same time to have suffered severely. Of its three older branches, Er, Onan, and Shelah, one only survived, and only by the accession of foreign elements did the tribe regain its vigour,—by the fresh blood which the Kenites of the Negeb brought. For Zarah and Pharez, which took the place of Er and Onan after these had disappeared, belonged originally, not to Israel, but to Hezron or the Kenites; under this designation are included families like those of Othniel, Jerachmeel, and Caleb, and, as has been already remarked, even in David's time these were not reckoned as strictly belonging to Judah. Thus the depletion which the tribe had to suffer in the struggle with the Canaanites at the beginning of the period of the judges was the remote cause of the prominence which, according to 1Chronicles ii., the Bne Hezron afterwards attained in Judah. The survivors of Simeon also appear to have been forced back upon these Hezronites in the Negeb; the cities assigned to them in the Book of Joshua all belong to that region. *******

Even after the united resistance of the Canaanites had been broken, each individual community had still enough to do before it could take firm hold of the spot which it had searched out for itself or to which it had been assigned. The business of effecting permanent settlement was just a continuation of the former struggle, only on a diminished scale; every tribe and every family now fought for its own land after the preliminary work had been accomplished by a united effort. Naturally, therefore, the conquest was at first but an incomplete one. The plain which fringed the coast was hardly touched; so also the valley of Jezreel with its girdle of fortified cities stretching from Acco to Bethshean. All that was subdued in the strict sense of that word was the mountainous land, particularly the southern hill country of "Mount Ephraim;" yet, even here the Canaanites retained possession of not a few cities, such as Jebus, Shechem, Thebez. It was only after the lapse of centuries that all the lacunae were filled up, and the Canaanite enclaves made tributary.

The Israelites had the extraordinarily disintegrated state of the enemy to thank for the ease with which they had achieved success. The first storm subsided comparatively soon, and conquerors and conquered alike learned to accommodate themselves to the new circumstances. Then the Canaanites once more collected all their energies to strike a blow for freedom. Under the hegemony of Sisera a great league was formed, and the plain of Jezreel became the centre of the reorganised power which made itself felt by its attacks both northwards and southwards. The Israelites were strangely helpless; it was as if neither shield nor spear could be found among their 40,000 fighting men. But at last there came an impulse from above, and brought life and soul to the unorganised mass; Deborah sent out the summons to the tribes, Barak came forward as their leader against the kings of Canaan who had assembled under Sisera's command by the brook of Kishon. The cavalry of the enemy was unable to withstand the impetuous rush of the army of Jehovah, and Sisera himself perished in the flight. From that day the Canaanites, although many strong towns continued to be held by them, never again raised their heads.

After these occurrences some further changes of a fundamental character took place in the relations of the tribes. The Danites proved unable to hold against the forward pressure of the Philistines their territory on the coast to the west of Benjamin and Ephraim; they accordingly sought a new settlement, which was found in the north at the foot of Hermon. In this way all the secondary tribes westward of Jordan (Asher, Naphtali, Dan) came to have their seats beside each other in the northern division of the land. Eastward of Jordan, Reuben rapidly fell from his old prominence, sharing the fate of his next eldest brethren Simeon and Levi. When Eglon of Moab took Jericho, and laid Benjamin under tribute, it is obvious that he must previously have made himself master of Reuben's territory. This territory became thenceforward a subject of constant dispute between Moab and Israel; the efforts to recover it, however, did not proceed from Reuben himself, but from Gad, a tribe which knew how to assert itself with vigour against the enemies by which it was surrounded. But if the Hebrews lost ground in the south, they materially enlarged their borders in the north of the land eastward of Jordan. Various Manassite families, finding their holdings at home too small, crossed the Jordan and founded colonies at Bashan and northern Gilead. Although this colonisation, on account of the rivalry of the Aramaeans, who were also pressing forward in this direction, was but imperfectly successful, it nevertheless was of very great importance, inasmuch as it seemed to give new strength to the bonds that united the eastern with the western tribes. Not only was Gilead not lost; it even became a very vigorous member of the body politic.
1

*************************** 1. It is probable that Manasseh's migration to the territory eastward of Jordan took place from the west, and later than the time of Moses. The older portions of the Hexateuch speak not of two and a half but only of two trans-Jordanic tribes, and exclude Manasseh; according to them the kingdom of Sihon alone was subdued by Moses, not that of Og also, the latter, indeed, being a wholly legendary personage. In the song of Deborah, Machir is reckoned among the western tribes, and it was not until much later that this became the designation of the Manassites eastward of Jordan. It is also worth noticing that Jair's colonisation of northern Gilead did not take place until the time of the judges (Judges x. 3 seq.), but is related also in Num. xxxii. 39-42. ***************************

The times of agitation and insecurity which followed upon the conquest of Palestine invited attacks by the eastern nomads, and once more the Israelite peasantry showed all its old helplessness, until at last the indignation of a Manassite of good family,

Gideon or Jerubbaal, was roused by the Midianites, who had captured some of his brothers and put them to death. With his family, that of Abiezer, he gave pursuit, and, overtaking the enemy on the borders of the wilderness, inflicted on them such chastisement as put an end to these incursions. His heroism had consequences which reached far beyond the scope of his original purpose. He became the champion of the peasantry against the freebooters, of the cultivated land against the waste; social respect and predominance were his rewards. In his native town of Ophrah he kept up a great establishment, where also he built a temple with an image of Jehovah overlaid with the gold which he had taken from the Midianites. He transmitted to his sons an authority, which was not limited to Abiezer and Manasseh alone, but, however slightly and indirectly, extended over Ephraim as well.

On the foundations laid by Gideon Abimelech his son sought to establish a kingship over Israel, that is, over Ephraim and Manasseh. The predominance, however, which had been naturally accorded to his father in virtue of his personal merits, Abimelech looked upon as a thing seized by force and to be maintained with injustice; and in this way he soon destroyed those fair beginnings out of which even at that time a kingdom might have arisen within the house of Joseph. The one permanent fruit of his activity was that Shechem was destroyed as a Canaanite city and rebuilt for Israel. *1*

******************************** 1. On the narratives contained in the Book of Judges see Bleek, Einl. ins Alte Testament (4th ed.), 88-98, and especially the sections on Barak and Sisera, Gideon, Jephthah, Samson, the Danite migration, and the Benjamites of Gibeah (93-98). ********************************

The most important change of the period of the judges went on gradually and in silence. The old population of the country, which, according to Deuteronomy, was to have been exterminated, slowly became amalgamated with the new. In this way the Israelites received a very important accession to their numbers. In Deborah's time the fighting men of Israel numbered 40,000; the tribe of Dan when it migrated to Laish, counted 600 warriors; Gideon pursued the Midianites with 300. But in the reigns of Saul and David we find a population reckoned by millions. The rapid increase is to be accounted for by the incorporation of the Canaanites.

At the same time the Hebrews learned to participate in the culture of the Canaanites, and quietly entered into the enjoyment of the labours of their predecessors. From the pastoral they advanced to the agricultural stage; corn and wine, the olive and the fig, with them are habitually spoken of as the necessaries of life. It was not strange that this change in the manner of their everyday life should be attended with certain consequences in the sphere of religion also. It is inconceivable that the Israelites should have brought with them out of the desert the cultus they observed in the time of the kings (Exod. xxii. xxiii. xxiv.), which throughout presupposed the fields and gardens of Palestine; they borrowed it from the Canaanites. *1*

**************************** 1. In the earliest case where the feast of the ingathering, afterwards the chief feast of the Israelites, is mentioned, it is celebrated

368

by Canaanites of Shechem in honour of Baal (Judges ix. 27).
****

This is confirmed by the fact that they took over from these the "Bamoth" or "high places" also, notwithstanding the prohibition in Deuteronomy xii.

It was natural enough that the Hebrews should also appropriate the divinity worshipped by the Canaanite peasants as the giver of their corn, wine, and oil, the Baal whom the Greeks identified with Dionysus. The apostasy to Baal, on the part of the first generation which had quitted the wilderness and adopted a settled agricultural life, is attested alike by historical and prophetical tradition. Doubtless Baal, as the god of the land of Canaan, and Jehovah, as the God of the nation of Israel, were in the first instance co-ordinated. 2

***************************** 2. In Judges v. Jehovah retains his original abode in the wilderness of Sinai, and only on occasions of necessity quits it to come to Palestine. *****************************

But it was not to be expected that the divinity of the land should permanently be different from the God of the dominant people. In proportion as Israel identified itself with the conquered territory, the divinities also were identified. Hence arose a certain syncretism between Baal and Jehovah, which had not been got over even in the time of the prophet Hosea. At the same time the functions of Baal were more frequently transferred to Jehovah than conversely. Canaan and Baal represented the female, Israel and Jehovah the male, principle in this union.

Had the Israelites remained in the wilderness and in barbarism, the historical development they subsequently reached would hardly have been possible; their career would have been like that of Amalek, or, at best, like those of Edom, Moab, and Ammon. Their acceptance of civilisation was undoubtedly a step in the forward direction; but as certainly did it also involve a peril. It involved an overloading, as it were, of the system with materials which it was incapable of assimilating at once. The material tasks imposed threatened to destroy the religious basis of the old national life. The offensive and defensive alliances among the tribes gradually dissolved under the continuance of peace; the subsequent occupation of the country dispersed those whom the camp had united. The enthusiastic *elan* with which the conquest had been achieved gave way to the petty drudgery by which the individual families, each in its own circle, had to accommodate themselves to their new surroundings. Yet under the ashes the embers were still aglow; and the course of history ever fanned them anew into flame, bringing home to Israel the truths that man does not live by bread alone, and that there are other things of worth than those which Baal can bestow; it brought ever again into the foreground the divineness of heroical self sacrifice of the individual for the good of the nation.

3. THE FOUNDATION OF THE KINGDOM, AND THE FIRST THREE KINGS.

The Philistines were the means of arousing from their slumber Israel and Jehovah. From their settlements by the sea on the low-lying plain which skirts the mountains of Judah on the west, they pressed northwards into the plain of Sharon, and thence into the plain of Jezreel beyond, which is connected with that of Sharon by the upland valley of Dothan. Here, having driven out the Danites, they came into direct contact with the tribe of Joseph, the chief bulwark of Israel, and a great battle took place at Aphek, where the plain of Sharon merges into the valley of Dothan. The Philistines were victorious and carried off as a trophy the Israelite standard, the ark of Jehovah. Their further conquests included, not only the plain of Jezreel and the hill country bordering it on the south, but also the proper citadel of the country, "Mount Ephraim." The old sanctuary at Shiloh was destroyed by them; its temple of Jehovah thenceforward lay in ruins. Their supremacy extended as far as to Benjamin; the Philistines had a nec,ib in Gibeah. *1*

************************ 1. *nec,ib* is an Aramaic word of uncertain meaning. In the name of the town *Nec,ibin* (Nisibis) it certainly seems to mean "pillars;" according to 1Kings iv. 5 and xxii. 48 (where it is pointed niccab), "governor", seems the best translation, and this is the only rendering consistent with the expression in 1Samuel xiii. 3 ("Jonathan slew the *necib*," &c.). ***************************

But the assertion that they had confiscated all weapons and removed all smiths must be regarded as an unhistorical exaggeration; under their regime at all events it was possible for the messengers of a beleaguered city on the east of Jordan to summon their countrymen in the west to their relief.

The shame of the Israelites under the reproach of Philistine oppression led, in the first instance, to a widespread exaltation of religious feeling. Troops of ecstatic enthusiasts showed themselves here and there, and went about with musical accompaniments in processions which often took the shape of wild dances; even men of the most sedate temperament were sometimes smitten with the contagion, and drawn into the charmed circle. In such a phenomenon, occurring in the East, there was nothing intrinsically strange; among the Canaanites, such "Nebiim"—for so they were styled—had long been familiar, and they continued to exist in the country after the old fashion, long after their original character, so far as Israel was concerned, had been wholly lost. The new thing at this juncture was that this spirit passed over upon Israel, and that the best members of the community were seized by it. It afforded an outlet for the suppressed excitement of the nation.

The new-kindled zeal had for its object, not the abolition of Baal worship, but resistance to the enemies of Israel. Religion and patriotism were then identical. This spirit of the times was understood by an old man, Samuel ben Elkanah, who lived at Ramah in south-western Ephraim. He was not himself one of the Nebiim; on the contrary, he was a seer of that old type which had for a long time existed amongst the Hebrews much as we find it amongst the Greeks or Arabs. Raised by his foreseeing talent to a position of great prominence, he found opportunity to occupy himself with other questions besides those which he was professionally called on to answer. The national distress weighed upon his heart; the neighbouring peoples had taught him to recognise the advantages which are secured by the consolidation of families and tribes into a kingdom. But Samuel's peculiar merit lay, not in discovering what it was that the nation needed, but in finding out the man who was capable of supplying that need. Having come to know Saul ben Kish, a Benjamite of the town of Gibeah, a man of gigantic form, and swift, enthusiastic nature, he declared to him his destiny to become king over Israel.

Saul very soon had an opportunity for showing whether Samuel had been a true seer or no. The city of Jabesh in Gilead was besieged by the Ammonites, and the inhabitants declared themselves ready to surrender should they fail in obtaining speedy succour from their countrymen. Their messengers had passed through all Israel without meeting with anything more helpful than pity, until at last tidings of their case reached Saul as he was returning with a yoke of oxen from the field. Hewing his cattle in pieces, he caused the portions to be sent in all directions, with the threat that so should it be done with the oxen of every one who should refuse to help in relieving Jabesh. The people obeyed the summons, fell suddenly one morning upon the Ammonites, and delivered the beleaguered city.

Having thus found Saul the man for their need, they refused to let him go. In Gilgal, Joshua's old camp, they anointed him king. The act was equivalent to imposing upon him the conduct of the struggle against the Philistines, and so he understood it. The first signal for the attack was given by his son Jonathan, when he slew the *necib* of the Philistines at Gibeah. These in consequence advanced in force towards the focus of the revolt, and took up a position opposite Gibeah on the north, being divided from it only by the gorge of Michmash. Only a few hundred Benjamites ventured to remain with Saul. The struggle opened with a piece of genuine old heroic daring. While the Philistines were dispersed over the country in foraging expeditions, Jonathan, accompanied by his armour-bearer only, and without the knowledge of Saul, made an attack upon the weak post which they had left behind at the pass of Michmash. After the first had been surprised and overmastered, the others took to flight, no doubt in the belief that the two assailants were supported. They carried their panic with them into the half-deserted camp, whence it spread among the various foraging bands. The commotion was observed from Gibeah opposite, and, without pausing to consult the priestly oracle, King Saul determined to attack the camp. The attempt was completely successful, but involved no more than the camp and its stores; the Philistines themselves effected an unmolested retreat by the difficult road of Bethhoron.

Saul was no mere raw stripling when he ascended the throne; he already had a grown-up son at his side. Nor was he of insignificant descent, the family to which he belonged being a widespread one, and his heritage considerable. His establishment at Gibeah was throughout his entire reign the nucleus of his kingdom. The men on whom he could always reckon were his Benjamite kinsmen. He recognised as belonging to him no other public function besides that of war; the internal affairs of the country he permitted to remain as they had been before his accession. War was at once the business and the resource of the new kingdom. It was carried on against the Philistines without interruption, though for the most part not in the grand style but rather in a series of border skirmishes. *1*

As regards the position of Samuel in the theocracy and the relation in which the stood to Saul, the several narratives in the Book of Samuel differ widely. The preceding account, so far as it relates to Samuel, is based upon 1Samuel ix., x. 1-15, xi., where he appears simply as a Roeh at Ramah, and has nothing to do either with the administration of the theocracy or with the Nebiim.   Compare   Prolegomena   above,   chap.   VII.

It is not without significance that the warlike revival of the nation proceeded from Benjamin. By the battle of Aphek Ephraim had lost at once the hegemony and its symbols (the camp-sanctuary at Shiloh, the ark of the covenant). The centre of Israel gravitated southward, and Benjamin became the connecting link between Ephraim and Judah. It would appear that there the tyranny of the Philistines was not so much felt. Their attacks never were made through Judah, but always came from the north; on the other hand, people fled from them southwards, as is instanced by the priests of Shiloh, who settled in Nob near Jerusalem. Through Saul Judah entered definitely into the history of Israel; it belonged to his kingdom, and it more than most others supplied him with energetic and faithful supporters. His famous expedition against the Amalekites had been undertaken purely in the interests of Judah, for it only could possibly suffer from their marauding hordes.

Among the men of Judah whom the war brought to Gibeah, David ben Jesse of Bethlehem took a conspicuous place; his skill on the harp brought him into close relations with the king. He became Saul's armour-bearer, afterwards the most intimate friend of his son, finally the husband of his daughter. While he was thus winning the affections of the court, he at the same time became the declared favourite of the people, the more so because unexampled good fortune attended him in all he undertook. This excited the jealousy of Saul, naturally enough in an age in which the king always required to be the best man. Its first outburst admitted of explanation as occasioned by an attack of illness; but soon it became obtrusively clear that the king's love for his son-in-law had changed into bitter hatred. Jonathan warned his friend and facilitated his flight, the priests of Nob at the same time providing him with arms and food. He went into the wilderness of Judah, and became the leader of a miscellaneous band of outlaws who had been attracted by his name to lead a roving life under his leadership. His kinsmen from Bethlehem were of their number, but also Philistines and Hittites. Out of this band David's bodyguard subsequently grew, the nucleus of his army. They reckoned also a priest among them, Abiathar ben Ahimelech ben Ahitub ben Phinehas ben Eli, the solitary survivor of the massacre of the sons of Eli at Nob which Saul had ordered on account of suspected conspiracy with David. Through him David was able to have recourse to the sacred lot before the ephod. In the end he found it impossible to hold his own in Judah against Saul's persecutions, especially as his countrymen for the most part withheld their assistance. He therefore took the desperate step of placing his services at the disposal of Achish the Philistine king of Gath, by whom he was received with open arms, the town of Ziklag being assigned him as a residence. Here with his band he continued to follow his old manner of life as an independent prince, subject only to an obligation to render military service to Achish.

Meanwhile the Philistines had once more mustered their forces and marched by the usual route against Israel. Saul did not allow them to advance upon Gibeah, but awaited their attack in the plain of Jezreel. A disastrous battle on Mount Gilboa ensued; after seeing his three eldest sons fall one after another at his side, Saul threw himself upon his sword, and was followed by his armour-bearer. The defeat seemed to have undone the work of his life. The immediate consequence at least was that the Philistines regained their lost ascendancy over the country to the west of Jordan. Beyond Jordan, however, Abner, the cousin and generalissimo of Saul, made his son Ishbaal, still a minor, king in Mahanaim, and he was successful in again establishing the dominion of the house over Jezreel, Ephraim, and Benjamin, of course in uninterrupted struggle with the Philistines.

But he did not regain hold of Judah. David seized the opportunity to set up for himself, with the sanction of the Philistines, and, it may safely be presumed, as their vassal, a separate principality which had its centre of gravity in the south, which was inhabited, not by the tribe of Judah properly so called, but by the Calebites and Jerachmeelites. This territory Abner disputed with him in vain. In the protracted feud between the houses of Saul and David, the fortunes of war declared themselves ever increasingly for the latter. Personal causes at last brought matters to a crisis. Abner, by taking to himself a concubine of Saul's called Rizpah, had roused Ishbaal's suspicions that he was aiming at the inheritance, and was challenged on the point. This proved too much for his patience, and forthwith he abandoned the cause of his ward (the hopelessness of which had already perhaps become apparent), and entered into negotiations with David at Hebron. When about to set out on his return he fell by the hand of Joab in the gate of Hebron, a victim of jealousy and blood-feud. His plans nevertheless were realised. His death left Israel leaderless and in great confusion; Ishbaal was personally insignificant, and the people's homage continued to be rendered to him only out of grateful fidelity to his father's memory. At this juncture he also fell by assassins' hands. As he was taking his midday rest, and even the portress had gone to sleep over her task of cleaning wheat, two Benjamite captains introduced themselves into his palace at Mahanaim and murdered him in the vain hope of earning David's thanks. The elders of Israel no longer hesitated about offering David the crown, which he accepted.

His residence was immediately transferred from Hebron to Jebus, which until then had remained in possession of the Canaanites, and first derives historical importance from him. It lay on the border between Israel and Judah,—still within the territory of Benjamin, but not far from Bethlehem; near also to Nob, the old priestly city. David made it not only the political but also the religious metropolis by transferring thither from Kirjathjearim the ark of the covenant, which he placed within his citadel on what afterwards became the temple hill.

Still the crown was far from being a merely honorary possession; it involved heavy responsibilities, and doubtless what contributed more than anything else to David's elevation to the throne was the general recognition of the fact that he was the man best fitted on the whole to overtake the labour it brought with it, *viz.*, the prosecution of the war with the Philistines, a war which was as it were the forge in which the kingdom of Israel was welded into one. The struggle began with the transference of the seat of royalty to Jerusalem; unfortunately we possess only scanty details as to its progress, hardly anything more indeed than a few anecdotes about deeds of prowess by individual heroes. The result was in the end that David completed what Saul had begun, and broke for ever the Philistine yoke. This was undoubtedly the greatest achievement of his reign.

From the defensive against the Philistines David proceeded to aggressive war, in which he subjugated the three kinsfolk of Israel,—Moab, Ammon, and Edom. He appears to have come into conflict first with the Moabites, whom he vanquished and treated with savage atrocity. Not long afterwards the king of Ammon died, and David sent an embassy of condolence to Hanun his successor. Hanun suspected in this a sinister design,—a suspicion we can readily understand if David had already, as is probable, subjugated Moab,—and with the utmost contumely sent back the messengers to their master forthwith, at the same time making preparations for war by entering into alliance with various Syrian kings, and particularly with the powerful king of Soba *1*

** 1. Soba appears to have been situated somewhat to the north of Damascus, and to have bordered on the west with Hamath. The Aramaeans were beginning even at that period to press westwards; the Hittites, Phoenicians, and Israelites had common interests against them. To the kingdom of Soba succeeded afterwards that of Damascus.
****

David took the initiative, and sent his army under command of Joab against Rabbath-Ammon. The Syrians advanced to the relief of the besieged city; but Joab divided his forces, and, leaving his brother Abishai to hold the Ammonites in the town in check, proceeded himself against the Syrians and repulsed them. On their afterwards threatening to renew the attack in increased force, David went against them in strength and defeated them at Helam "on the river." It seems that as a result of this the kingdom of Soba was broken up and made tributary to Damascus. Rabbath-Ammon could not now hold out any longer, and the Ammonites shared the fate of their Moabite brethren. Finally, Edom was about the same time coerced and depopulated; and thus was fulfilled the vision of Balaam,—the youngest of the four Hebrew nationalities trod the three elder under his feet.

So far as external foes were concerned, David henceforward had peace; but new dangers arose at home within his own family. At once by ill-judged leniency and equally ill-timed severity he had completely alienated his son Absalom, who, after Amnon's death, was heir-apparent to the throne. Absalom organised a revolt against his father, and to foster it availed himself of a misunderstanding which had arisen

374

between David and the men of Judah, probably because they thought they were not treated with sufficient favour. The revolt had its focus in Hebron; Ahithophel, a man of Judah, was its soul; Amasa, also of Judah, its arm; but the rest of Israel was also drawn into the rebellion, and only the territory to the east of Jordan remained faithful. Thither David betook himself with precipitancy, for the outbreak had taken him completely by surprise. At Mahanaim, which had once before been the centre from which the kingdom was regained, he collected his faithful followers around him with his 600 Cherethites and Pelethites for a nucleus, Absalom against Ahithophel's advice allowing him time for this. In the neighbourbood of Mahanaim, in the wood of Ephraim, the decisive blow was struck. Absalom fell, and with his death the rebellion was at an end. It was Joseph that, in the first instance, penitently sent a deputation to the king to bring him back. Judah, on the other hand, continued to hold aloof. Ultimately a piece of finesse on the king's part had the effect of bringing Judah also to its allegiance, though at the cost of kindling such jealousy between Israel and Judah that Sheba the Benjamite raised a new revolt, this time of Israelites, which was soon, however, repressed by Joab.

David seems to have died soon afterwards. His historical importance is very great. Judah and Jerusalem were wholly his creation, and, though the united kingdom of Israel founded by him and Saul together soon fell to pieces, the recollection of it nevertheless continued in all time to be proudly cherished by the whole body of the people. His personal character has been often treated with undue disparagement. For this we must chiefly blame his canonisation by the later Jewish tradition which made a Levitical saint of him and a pious hymn-writer. It then becomes a strange inconsistency that he caused military prisoners to be treated with barbarity, and the bastard sons of Saul to be hanged up before the Lord in Gibeon. But if we take him as we find him, an antique king in a barbarous age, our judgment of him will be much more favourable. The most daring courage was combined in him with tender susceptibility; even after he had ascended the throne be continued to retain the charm of a pre-eminent and at the same time child-like personality. Even his conduct in the affair of Uriah is not by any means wholly to his discredit; not many kings can be mentioned who would have shown repentance public and deep such as he manifested at Nathan's rebuke. Least to his credit was his weakness in relation to his sons and to Joab. On the other hand, the testament attributed to him in 1Kings ii. cannot be justly laid to his charge; it is the libel of a later hand seeking to invest him with a fictitious glory. In like manner it is unjust to hold him responsible for the deaths of Abner and Amasa, or to attribute to him any conspiracy with the hierocracy for the destruction of Saul, and thus to deprive him of the authorship of the elegy in 2Samuel i, which certainly was not the work of a hypocrite.

Solomon had already reached the throne, some time before his father's death, not in virtue of hereditary right, but by palace intrigue which had the support of the bodyguard of the Six Hundred. His glory was not purchased on the battlefield. So far was he from showing military capacity that he allowed a new Syrian kingdom to arise at Damascus, a far more dangerous thing for Israel than that of Soba which had been destroyed, and which it succeeded. During this reign Edom also regained its independence, nothing but the port of Elath remaining in Solomon's hands. As regards Moab and Ammon we have no information; it is not improbable that they also revolted. But if war was not Solomon's forte, he certainly took much greater pains than either of his predecessors in matters of internal administration; according to tradition, the wisdom of the ruler and the judge was his special "gift." Disregarding the tribal system, he divided his kingdom into twelve provinces, over each of which he placed a royal governor, thus making a beginning of vigorous and orderly administration. *1*

************************************ 1. Very possibly the Canaanites, whose complete absorption falls within this period, were an element that helped to loosen the bonds of tribal unity, and consolidate a state in its place. ***********************************

Judah alone he exempted from this arrangement, as if to show special favour. For his aim was less the advantage of his subjects than the benefit of his exchequer, and the same object appears in his horse traffic (1Kings ix. 19), his Ophir trade (1Kings x. 11), and his cession of territory to Hiram (1Kings ix. 11). His passions were architecture, a gorgeous court, and the harem, in which he sought to rival other Oriental kings, as for example his Egyptian father-in-law. For this he required copious means-forced labour, tribute in kind, and money. He had especially at heart the extension and improvement of Jerusalem as a strong and splendid capital; the temple which he built was only a portion of his vast citadel, which included within its precincts a number of private and public buildings designed for various uses.

It is plain that new currents were introduced into the stream of the nation's development by such a king as this. As formerly, after the occupation, Canaanite culture had come in, so now, after the establishment of the kingdom, the floodgate was open for the admission of Oriental civilisation in a deeper and wider sense. Whatever the personal motives which led to it may have been, the results were very important, and by no means disadvantageous on the whole. On the basis of the firmer administration now introduced, stability and order could rest; Judah had no cause to regret its acceptance of this yoke. Closer intercourse with foreign lands widened the intellectual horizon of the people, and at the same time awakened it to a deeper sense of its own peculiar individuality. If Solomon imported Phoenician and Egyptian elements into the worship of Jehovah at his court temple, the rigid old Israelite indeed might naturally enough take offence (Exodus xx. 24-26), but the temple itself nevertheless ultimately acquired a great and positive importance for religion. It need not be denied that mischievous consequences of various kinds slipped in along with the good. The king, moreover, can hardly be blamed for his conduct in erecting in the neighbourhood of Jerusalem altars to deities of Ammon and Egypt. For those altars remained undisturbed until the time of Josiah, although between Solomon and him there reigned more than one pious king who would certainly have destroyed them had he found them as offensive as did the author of Deuteronomy.

4. FROM JEROBOAM I. TO JEROBOAM II.

After the death of Solomon the discontent which had been aroused by his innovations, and especially by the rigour of his government, openly showed itself against his successor; and when Rehoboam curtly refused the demands which had been laid before him by an assembly of the elders at Shechem, they withdrew from their allegiance and summoned to be their king the Ephraimite Jeroboam ben Nebat, who already had made an abortive attempt at revolt from Solomon, and afterwards had taken refuge in Egypt. Only Judah and Jerusalem remained faithful to the house of David. Among the causes of the revolt of the ten tribes, jealousy of Judah must certainly be reckoned as one. The power of Joseph had been weakened by the Philistines, and by the establishment of the monarchy the centre of gravity had been shifted from the north where it naturally lay. But now it was restored to its old seat; for once more it was situated, not in Judah, but in Joseph. Monarchy itself, however, was not abolished by the revolting tribes, conclusively showing how unavoidable and how advantageous that institution was now felt to be; but at the same time they did not refrain from attempts to combine its advantages with those of anarchy, a folly which was ultimately the cause of their ruin. As for their departure from the Mosaic cultus observed at Jerusalem on the other hand, it was first alleged against them as a sin only by the later Jews. At the time religion put no obstacle in the way of their separation; on the contrary, it actually suggested and promoted it (Ahijah of Shiloh). The Jerusalem cultus had not yet come to be regarded as the alone legitimate; that instituted by Jeroboam at Bethel and at Dan was recognised as equally right; images of the Deity were exhibited in all three places, and indeed in every place where a house of God was found. So far as the religious and intellectual life of the nation was concerned, there was no substantial difference between the two kingdoms, except indeed in so far as new displays of vigorous initiative generally proceeded from Israel. *1*

*********************************** 1. Even in the Deuteronomic redaction of the Book of Kings indeed, and still more by the Chronicler, the political rebellion of Israel is regarded as having been ecclesiastical and religious in its character. The Book of Chronicles regards Samaria as a heathen kingdom, and recognises Judah alone as Israel. But in point of fact Judah takes up the history of Israel only after the fall of Samaria; see ## 6, 7. ***********************************

Rehoboam did not readily accept the situation; he sought to reduce the revolt by force of arms, with what degree of success is shown by the fact that his rival found himself constrained to take up his residence at Peniel (near Mahanaim) on the other side of Jordan. The invasion of Shishak, however, who took Jerusalem and burnt it, gave Jeroboam at last a breathing space. The feud continued indeed, but Rehoboam could no longer dream of bringing back the ten tribes. The scale by and by turned in Israel's favour. King Baasha, who had seated himself on the throne in place of Nadab, Jeroboam's son, took the offensive, and Asa ben Rehoboam had no help for it but to call in Benhadad of Damascus against his adversary. In this way he gained his immediate purpose, it is true, but by the most dangerous of expedients.

Baasha's son Elah was supplanted by his vizier Zimri, who, however, was in his turn unable to hold his own against Omri, who had supreme command of the army. Against Omri there arose in another part of the country a rival, Tibni ben Ginath, who succeeded in maintaining some footing until his death, when Omri became supreme. Omri must be regarded as the founder of the first dynasty, in the proper sense of that word, in Israel, and as the second founder of the kingdom itself, to which he gave a permanent capital in Samaria. The Bible has hardly anything to tell us about him, but his importance is evident from the fact that among the Assyrians "the kingdom of Omri" / 1/

***************************** 1. Bit Humri, like)OIKOS *LUSANIOU, and similar territorial names in Syriac.* ******************************

was the ordinary name of Israel. According to the inscription of Mesha, it was he who again subjugated Moab, which had become independent at the death of David or of Solomon. He was not so successful against the Damascenes, to whom he had to concede certain privileges in his own capital (1 Kings xx. 34) *2*

***************************** 2. Omri's accession is to be placed somewhere about 900 B.C It is a date, and the first, that can be determined with some precision, if we place the battle of Karkar (854) near the end of Ahab's reign, and take the servitude of Moab, which lasted forty years and ended with Ahab's deatb, to begin in Omri's first decade. **************************************

Ahab, who succeeded Omri his father, seems during the greater part of his reign to have in some sort acknowledged Syrian suzerainty. In no other way can we account for the fact that in the battle of Karkar against the Assyrians (854 B.C.) a contingent was contributed by him. But this very battle made the political situation so clear that he was led to break off his relations with Damascus. With this began a series of ferocious attacks on Israel by Benhadad and Hazael. They were met by Ahab with courage and success, but in the third year of that fifty years' war he fell in the battle at Ramoth Gilead (c. 851).

***** After the events recorded in 1 Kings xx., a forced alliance with Damascus on the part of Samaria is incredible; but the idea of spontaneous friendly relations is also inadmissible. Schrader indeed finds support for the latter theory in 1 Kings xx. 34; but in that passage there is no word of any offensive or defensive alliance between the rival kings; all that is stated is that Ahab releases the captive Benhadad on condition (BBRYT) that the latter undertakes certain obligations, particularly those of keeping the peace and restoring the cities which had been taken. By this arrangement no change was made in the previously strained relations of the two kingdoms; and, moreover, the BRYT was not kept (xxii. 1 seq.). Not much nearer the truth than the preceding is the view that the danger threatened by Assyria drove the kings of Syria and Palestine into one another's arms, and so occasioned an alliance between Ahab and Benhadad also. For if feelings of hostility existed at all between the two last named, then Ahab could not do otherwise than congratulate himself that in the person of Shalmaneser II. there had arisen against Benhadad an enemy who would be able to keep him effectually in check. That Shalmaneser might prove dangerous to himself probably did not at that time occur to him; but if it had he would still have chosen the remote in preference to the immediately threatening evil. For it was the political existence of Israel that was at stake in the struggle with Damascus; in such circumstances every ally would of course be welcome, every enemy of the enemy would be hailed as a friend, and the political wisdom which Max Duncker attributes to Ahab would have been nothing less than unpardonable folly. The state of matters was at the outset in this respect just what it continued to be throughout the subsequent course of events; the Assyrian danger grew in subsequent years, and with it grew the hostility between Damascus and Samaria. This fact admits only of one explanation,—that the Israelites utilised to the utmost of their power for their own protection against the Syrians the difficulties into which the latter were thrown by Shalmaneser II., and that these in their turn, when the Assyrians gave them respite, were all the fiercer in their revenge. On the evidence of the monuments and the Bible we may even venture to assert that it was the Assyrian attacks upon Damascus which at that time preserved Israel from becoming Aramaic,—of course only because Israel made the most of them for her political advantage.

Assuming that Ahab the Israelite (Ahabu Sirlaai) fought in the battle of Karkar (854) on the side of the king of Damascus, it was only because he could not help himself; but if it is actually the case that he did so, the battle of Karkar must have taken place BEFORE the events recorded in 1Kings xx. ****

The Moabites took advantage of an accession under such critical circumstances to shake off the yoke imposed by Omri forty years before; an accurate account of their success, obviously written while the impression of it was still fresh, *1* has come down to

***************************** 1. It is obvious that Mesha's narrative is to be taken with 2Kings i. 1, and not with 2Kings iii. *****************************

us in the famous inscription of King Mesha. Ahaziah, Ahab's immediate successor, was obliged to accept the situation; after his early death a futile attempt again to subjugate them was made by his brother Joram. Such a campaign was possible to him only in the event of the Syrians keeping quiet, and in point of fact it would appear that they were not in a position to follow up the advantage they had gained at Ramoth; doubtless they were hampered by the inroads of the Assyrians in 850 and 849. As soon as they got a little respite, however, they lost no time in attacking Joram, driving him into his capital, where they besieged him. Samaria had already been brought to the utmost extremities of famine, when suddenly the enemy raised the siege on account of a report of an invasion of their own land by the "Egyptians and Hittites." Possibly we ought to understand by these the Assyrians rather, who in 846 renewed their attacks upon Syria; to ordinary people in Israel the Assyrians were an unknown quantity, for which it would be natural in popular story to substitute something more familiar. This turn of affairs relieved Joram from his straits; it would even seem that, favoured by a change of dynasty at Damascus, he had succeeded in taking from the Syrians the fortress of Ramoth in Gilead, which had been the object of Ahab's unsuccessful endeavours, when suddenly there burst upon the house of Omri the overwhelming catastrophe for which the prophets had long been preparing.

When the prophets first made their appearance, some time before the beginning of the Philistine war, they were a novel phenomenon in Israel; but in the interval they had become so naturalised that they now had a recognised and essential place in connection with the religion of Jehovah. They had in the process divested themselves of much that had originally characterised them, but they still retained their habit of appearing in companies and living together in societies, and also that of wearing a peculiar distinctive dress. These societies of theirs had no ulterior aims; the rabbinical notion that they were schools and academies in which the study of the Torah and of sacred history was pursued imports later ideas into an earlier time. First-rate importance on the whole cannot be claimed for the Nebiim, but occasionally there arose amongst them a man in whom the spirit which was cultivated within their circles may be said to have risen to the explosive pitch. Historical influence was exercised at no time save by these individuals, who rose above their order and even placed themselves in opposition to it, but always at the same time had their base of operations within it. The prototype of this class of exceptional prophets, whom we not unjustly have been accustomed to regard as the true, is Elijah of Thisbe, the contemporary of Ahab.

In compliment to Jezebel his wife, Ahab had set up in Samaria a temple with richly endowed religious services in honour of the Syrian Baal. In doing so he had no intention of renouncing Jehovah; Jehovah continued to be the national God after whom he named his sons Ahaziah and Jehoram. The destruction of Jehovah's altars or the persecution of His prophets was not at all proposed, or even the introduction of a foreign cultus elsewhere than in Samaria. Jehovah's sovereignty over Israel being thus only remotely if at all imperilled, the popular faith found nothing specially offensive in a course of action which had been followed a hundred years before by Solomon also. Elijah alone was strenuous in his opposition; the masses did not understand him, and were far from taking his side. To him only, but not to the nation, did it seem like a halting between two opinions, an irreconcilable inconsistency, that Jehovah should be worshipped as Israel's God and a chapel to Baal should at the same time be erected in Israel.

In solitary grandeur did this prophet tower conspicuously over his time; legend, and not history, could alone preserve the memory of his figure. There remains a vague impression that with him the development of Israel's conception of Jehovah entered upon a new stadium, rather than any data from which it can be ascertained wherein the contrast of the new with the old lay. After Jehovah, acting more immediately within the political sphere, had established the nation and kingdom, he now began in the spiritual sphere to operate against the foreign elements, the infusion of which previously had been permitted to go on almost unchecked. *1*

*** 1. It is worth noticing how much more frequent from this period onwards proper names compounded with the word Jehovah become. Among the names of the judges and of the kings before Ahab in Israel and Asa in Judah, not a single instance occurs; thenceforward they become the rule. ***

The Rechabites, who arose at that time, protested in their zeal for Jehovah altogether against all civilisation which presupposes agriculture, and in their fundamental principles aimed at a recurrence to the primitive nomadic life of Israel in the wilderness; the Nazarites abstained at least from wine, the chief symbol of Dionysiac civilisation. In this indeed Elijah was not with them; had he been so, he would doubtless have been intelligible to the masses. But, comprehending as he did the spirit from which these demonstrations proceeded, he thought of Jehovah as a great principle which cannot coexist in the same heart with Baal. To him first was it revealed that we have not in the various departments of nature a variety of forces worthy of our worship, but that there exists over all but one Holy One and one Mighty One, who reveals Himself not in nature but in law and righteousness in the world of man. The indignation he displayed against the judicial murder at Jezreel was as genuine and strong as that which he manifested against the worship of Baal in Samaria; the one was as much a crime against Jehovah as the other.

Elijah ascended to heaven before he had actually achieved much in the world. The idea which his successors took from him was that it was necessary to make a thorough clearance from Samaria of the Baal worship and of the house of Ahab as well. For this practical end Elisha made use of practical means. When Elijah, after the murder of Naboth, had suddenly appeared before Ahab and threatened him with a violent end, an officer of high command had been present, Jehu ben Nimshi, and he had never forgotten the incident. He now found himself at the head of the troops at Ramoth Gilead after the withdrawal to Jezreel of Joram ben Ahab from the field to be healed of his wound. To Elisha the moment seemed a suitable one for giving to Jehu in Jehovah's name the command now to carry out Elijah's threat against the house of Ahab. Jehu gained over the captains of the army, and carried out so well the task with which the prophet had commissioned him that not a single survivor of Ahab's dynasty or of his court was left. He next extirpated Baal and his worshippers in Samaria. From that date no worship of foreign gods seems ever to have recurred in Israel. Idolatry indeed continued to subsist, but the images, stones, and trees, even the seraphim apparently, belonged to the cultus of Jehovah, or were at least brought into relation with it.

Jehu founded the second and last dynasty of the kingdom of Samaria His inheritance from the house of Omri included the task of defending himself against the Syrians. The forces at his disposal being insufficient for this, he resorted to the expedient of seeking to urge the Assyrians to renew their hostilities against the Arameeans. For this end his ambassadors carried presents to Shalmaneser II.; these were not of a regular but only of an occasional character, but the vanity of the great king represents them as the tribute of a vassal. In the years 842 and 839 Assyrian campaigns against Hazael of Damascus actually took place; then they were intermitted for a long time, and the kings of Samaria, Jehu and his two successors, were left to their own resources. These were evil times for Israel. With a barbarity never intermitted the frontier war went on in Gilead, where Ammon and Moab showed themselves friendly to the Syrian cause (Amos i.); occasionally great expeditions took place, one of which brought King Hazael to the very walls of Jerusalem. It was only with the greatest difficulty that Israel's independence was maintained. Once more religion went hand in hand with the national cause; the prophet Elisha was the main stay of the kings in the struggle with the Syrians, "the chariot and horsemen of Israel." Joash ben Joahaz ben Jehu at last succeeded in inflicting upon Syria several blows which proved decisive. Thenceforward Israel had nothing to fear from that quarter. Under Joash's son, Jeroboam II., the kingdom even reached a height of external power which recalled the times of David. Moab was again subdued; southwards the frontier extended to the brook of the wilderness (Amos vi. 14), and northward to Hamath.

5. GOD, THE WORLD, AND THE LIFE OF MEN IN OLD ISRAEL.

Before proceeding to consider the rise of those prophets who were the makers of the new Israel, it will not be out of place here to cast a glance backwards upon the old order of things which perished with the kingdom of Samaria. With reference to any period earlier than the century 850-750 B.C., we can hardly be said to possess any statistics. For, while the facts of history admit of being handed down with tolerable accuracy through a considerable time, a contemporary literature is indispensable for the description of standing conditions. But it was within this period that Hebrew literature first flourished—after the Syrians had been finally repulsed, it would seem. Writing of course had been practiced from a much earlier period, but only in formal instruments, mainly upon stone. At an early period also the historical sense of the people developed itself in connection with their religion; but it found its expression in songs, which in the first instance were handed down by word of mouth only. Literature began with the collection and writing out of those songs; *the Book of the Wars of the Lord* and *the Book of Jashar* were the oldest historical books. The transition was next made to the writing of prose history with the aid of legal documents and family reminiscences; a large portion of this early historiography has been preserved to us in the Books of Judges, Samuel, and Kings. Contemporaneously also certain collections of laws and decisions of the priests, of which we have an example in Exodus xxi. xxii., were committed to writing. Somewhat later, perhaps, the legends about the patriarchs and primitive times, the origin of which cannot be assigned to a very early date, *1*

** 1. Even the Jehovistic narratives about the patriarchs belong to the time when Israel had already become a powerful kingdom; Moab, Ammon,, and Edom had been subjugated (Genesis xxvii. 29), and vigorous frontier wars were being carried on with the Syrians about Gilead (Genesis xxxi. 52). In Genesis xxvii. 40 allusion is made to the constantly repeated subjugations of Edom by Judah, alternating with successful revolts on the part of the former; see Delitzsch on K)$R;. **************************************

received literary shape. Specially remarkable is the rise of a written prophecy. The question why it was that Elijah and Elisha committed nothing to writing, while Amos a hundred years later is an author, hardly admits of any other answer than that in the interval a non-literary had developed into a literary age. How rapid the process was may be gathered from a comparison between the singularly broken utterances of the earlier oracle contained in Isaiah xv. xvi. with the orations of Isaiah himself.

We begin our survey with that of the family relations. Polygamy was rare, monogamy the rule; but the right of concubinage was unlimited. While a high position was accorded both by affection and custom to the married wife, traces still existed of a state of society in which she was regarded as property that went with the inheritance. The marriage of relations was by no means prohibited; no offence was taken at the circumstance that Abraham was the husband of his sister (by a different mother). Parents had full power over their children; they had the right to sell and even to sacrifice them. In this respect, however, the prevailing usage was mild, as also in regard to slaves, who socially held a position of comparative equality with their masters, and even enjoyed some measure of legal protection. Slavery, it is plain, had not the same political importance as with the Greeks and Romans; it could have been abolished without any shock to the foundations of the state.

Throughout this period agriculture and gardening continued to be regarded as man's normal calling (Genesis iii. iv.); the laws contained in Exod. xxi.-xxiii. rest entirely upon this assumption. To dwell in peace under his vine and under his fig-tree was the ideal of every genuine Israelite. Only in a few isolated districts, as in the country to the east of Jordan and in portions of Judah, did the pastoral life predominate. Art and industry were undeveloped, and were confined to the production of simple domestic necessaries.

Commerce was in old time followed exclusively by the Canaanite towns, so that the word "Canaanite" was used in the general sense of "trader." But by and by Israel began to tread in Canaan's footsteps (Hosea xii. 8, 9), *1*

*************************** 1. "Canaan (i.e., Ephraim Canaanised) has deceitful balances in his hand, and loves to overreach. Ephraim indeed saith, I am become rich, I have gained weealth; but all his profits will not suffice for (expiation of) the guilt which he has incurred." ***************************

The towns grew more influential than the country; money notably increased; and the zeal of piety was quite unable to arrest the progress of the change which set in. The kings themselves, from Solomon onwards, were the first to set the bad example; they eagerly sought to acquire suitable harbours, and in company or in competition with the Syrians entered upon large commercial transactions. The extortions of the corn-market, the formation of large estates, the frequency of mortgages, all show that the small peasant proprietorship was unable to hold its own against the accumulations of wealth. The wage-receiving class increased, and cases in which free Hebrews sold themselves into slavery were not rare.

On all hands the material progress of the commonwealth made itself felt, the old simplicity of manners disappeared, and luxury increased. Buildings of hewn stone began to be used even by private individuals. The towns, especially the chief ones, were fortified; and in time of war refuge was sought in them, and not as formerly in woods and caves. Even in the time of David the Israelites always fought on foot; but now horses and chariots were regarded as indispensable. The bow came to be the principal weapon of offence, and a military class appears to have sprung up.

The monarchy retained in the kingdom of the ten tribes its military character; the commander-in-chief was the first person in the kingdom. In internal affairs its interference was slight; with systematic despotism it had little in common, although of course within its narrow sphere it united executive and legislative functions. It was little more than the greatest house in Israel. The highest official was called "master of the household." The court ultimately grew into a capital, the municipal offices of which were held by royal officials. The provinces had governors who, however, in time of war withdrew to the capital (1Kings xx.); the presumption is that their sole charge was collection of the revenue.

The state was not charged with affairs of internal administration; all parties were left free to maintain their own interests. Only in cases in which conflicts had emerged in consequence could the king be approached. Ruling and judging were regarded as one and the same; there was but one word for both (2Kings xv. 5). Still, the king was not altogether the only judge; there were, in fact, a number of independent jurisdictions. Wherever within a particular circle the power lay, there the right of judging was also found, whether exercised by heads of families and communities or by warriors and powerful lords. It was only because the king was the most powerful that he was regarded as the judge of last resort; but it was equally permitted to apply to him from the first. Of method and rule in these things there was but little; a man was glad to find any court to receive his complaint. Of course without complaint one got no justice. The administration of justice was at best but a scanty supplement to the practice of self-help. The heir of the murdered man would not forego the right of blood revenge; but his family or the commune gave him aid, and in case of need took his place, for bloodshed had at all hazards to be atoned for.

The firm establishment of civil order was rendered all the more difficult by the continual wars and violent changes of dynasty which ever and anon made its very existence problematical. Power, which is more important than righteousness to a judicatory, was what the government was wanting in In the simpler social conditions of the earlier time a state which was adapted merely for purposes of war might easily be found to work satisfactorily enough, but a more complex order of things had now arisen. Social problems had begun to crop up; for the poor and the proletariat the protection of a thoughtful government had come to be required, but was not forthcoming.

But these defects did not check all progress. The weakness of the government, the want of political consolidation, were insufficient to arrest intellectual advance or to corrupt the prevailing moral tone and feeling for justice; in fact it was precisely in this period (the period in which the main part of the Jehovistic history must have been written) that the intellectual and moral culture of the people stood at its highest. Even when the machinery of the monarchy had got out of order, the organisation of the families and communes continued to subsist; the smaller circles of social life remained comparatively untouched by the catastrophes that shook the greater. Above all, the national religion supplied the spiritual life with an immovable basis.

The favourite illustrations of the power of religion in the Israel of that period are drawn from the instances of great prophets who raised kings out of the dust and smote them to it again. But the influence and importance of these is generally exaggerated in the accounts we have. That among them there occasionally occurred manifestations of such power as to give a new turn in history is indeed true; a figure like that of Elijah is no mere invention. But such a man as he was a prophecy of the future rather than an actual agent in shaping the present. On the whole, religion was a peaceful influence, conserving rather than assailing the existing order of things. The majority of the prophets were no revolutionists; rather in fact were they always too much inclined to prophesy in accordance with the wishes of the party in power. Besides, in ordinary circumstances their influence was inferior to that of the priests, who were servants of royalty at the chief sanctuaries, but everywhere attached to the established order.

The Torah of Jehovah still continued to be their special charge. It was not even now a code or law in our sense of the word; Jehovah had not yet made His Testament; He was still living and active in Israel. But the Torah appears during this period to have withdrawn itself somewhat from the business of merely pronouncing legal decisions and to have begun to move in a freer field. It now consisted in teaching the knowledge of God, in showing the right God-given way where men were not sure of themselves. Many of the counsels of the priests had become a common stock of moral convictions, which, indeed, were all of them referred to Jehovah as their author, yet had ceased to be matters of direct revelation. Nevertheless the Torah had still occupation enough, the progressive life of the nation ever affording matter for new questions.

Although in truth the Torah and the moral influence of Jehovah upon the national life were things much weightier and much more genuinely Israelitic than the cultus, yet this latter held on the whole a higher place in public opinion. To the ordinary man it was not moral but liturgical acts that seemed to be truly religious. Altars of Jehovah occurred everywhere, with sacred stones and trees—the latter either artificial (Asheras) or natural—beside them; it was considered desirable also to have water in the neighbourhood (brazen sea). In cases where a temple stood before the altar it contained an ephod and teraphim, a kind of images before which the lot was cast by the priest. Of the old simplicity the cultus retained nothing; at the great sanctuaries especially (Bethel, Gilgal, Beersheba) it had become very elaborate. Its chief seasons were the agricultural festivals—the passover, the feast of weeks, and most especially the feast of the ingathering at the close of the year. These were the only occasions of public worship properly so called, at which every one was expected to

385

attend; in other cases each worshipper sought the presence of God only in special circumstances, as for example at the beginning and at the end of particular undertakings. The cultus, as to place, time, matter, and form, belonged almost entirely to the inheritance which Israel had received from Canaan; to distinguish what belonged to the worship of Jehovah from that which belonged to Baal was no easy matter. *1*

** 1. The description of the cultus by the Prophet Hosea shows this very clearly. It is obvious enough, however, that the object was to serve Jéhovah, and not any foreign deity, by this worship. ***

It was the channel through which also paganism could and did ever anew gain admittance into the worship of Jehovah. Yet that publicity of the cultus which arose out of the very nature of Jehovah, and in consequence of which the teraphim even were removed from the houses to the temples, cannot but have acted as a corrective against the most fatal excesses.

As for the substance of the national faith, it was summed up principally in the proposition that Jehovah is the God of Israel. But "God" was equivalent to "helper;" that was the meaning of the word. "Help," assistance in all occasions of life,—that was what Israel looked for from Jehovah, not "salvation" in the theological sense. The forgiveness of sins was a matter of subordinate importance; it was involved in the "help," and was a matter not of faith but of experience. The relation between the people and God was a natural one as that of son to father; it did not rest upon observance of the conditions of a pact. But it was not on that account always equally lively and hearty; Jehovah was regarded as having varieties of mood. To secure and retain His favour sacrifices were useful; by them prayer and thanksgiving were seconded.

Another main article of faith was that Jehovah judges and recompenses, not after death (then all men were thought to be alike), but upon the earth. Here, however, but little account was taken of the individual; over him the wheel of destiny remorselessly rolled; his part was resignation and not hope. Not in the career of the individual but in the fate of families and nations did the righteousness of Jehovah find scope for its manifestation; and this is the only reason why the religion could dispense with the conceptions of heaven and hell. For the rest, it was not always easy to bring the second article into correlation with the first; in practice the latter received the superior place.

It need hardly be said that superstition of every kind also abounded. But the superstition of the Israelites had as little real religious significance as had that poetical view of nature which the Hebrews doubtless shared in greater or less degree with all the other nations of antiquity.

6. THE FALL OF SAMARIA.

386

Under King Jeroboam II., two years before a great earthquake that served ever after for a date to all who had experienced it, there occurred at Bethel, the greatest and most conspicuous sanctuary of Jehovah in Israel, a scene full of significance. The multitude were assembled there with gifts and offerings for the observance of a festival, when there stepped forward a man whose grim seriousness interrupted the joy of the feast. It was a Judaean, Amos of Tekoa, a shepherd from the wilderness bordering on the Dead Sea. Into the midst of the joyful tones of the songs which with harp and tabor were being sung at the sacred banquet he brought the discordant note of the mourner's wail. For over all the joyous stir of busy life his ear caught the sounds of death: "the virgin of Israel is fallen, never more to rise; lies prostrate in her own land with no one to lift her up." He prophesied as close at hand the downfall of the kingdom which just at that moment was rejoicing most in the consciousness of power, and the deportation of the people to a far-off northern land.

There was something rotten in the state of Israel in spite of the halcyon days it enjoyed under Jeroboam II. From the indirect results of war, from changes in the tenure and in the culture of the soil, from defective administration of justice, the humbler classes had much to suffer; they found that the times were evil. But it was not this that caused Amos to foresee the end of Israel, not a mere vague foreboding of evil that forced him to leave his flocks; the dark cloud that threatened on the horizon was plain enough—the Assyrians. Once already at an earlier date they had directed their course south-westwards, without, however, on that occasion becoming a source of danger to the Israelites. But now that the bulwark against the Assyrians, Aram of Damascus, was falling into ruins, a movement of these against Lebanon in the time of Jeroboam II. opened to Israel the alarming prospect that sooner or later they would have to meet the full force of the irresistible avalanche.

What then? The common man was in no position truly to estimate the danger; and, so far as he apprehended it, he lived in the firm faith that Jehovah would not abandon His people in their straits. The governing classes prided themselves on the military resources of Israel, or otherwise tried to dismiss from their minds all thought of the gravity of the situation. But Amos heard the question distinctly enough, and did not hesitate to answer it: the downfall of Israel is imminent. It was nothing short of blasphemy to utter anything of this kind, for everything, Jehovah Himself included, depended on the existence of the nation. But the most astounding thing has yet to come; not Asshur, but Jehovah Himself, is bringing about the overthrow of Israel; through Asshur it is Jehovah that is triumphing over Israel. A paradoxical thought— as if the national God were to cut the ground from under His own feet! For the faith in Jehovah as the God of Israel was a faith that He intervenes on behalf of His people against all enemies, against the whole World; precisely in times of danger was religion shown by staying oneself upon this faith. Jehovah might indeed, of course, hide His face for a time, but not definitively; in the end He ever arose at last against all opposing powers. "The day of the Lord" was an object of hope in all times of difficulty and oppression; it was understood as self-evident that the crisis would certainly end in favour of Israel. Amos took up the popular conception of that day; but how thoroughly did he change its meaning! "Woe to them who long for the day of the Lord!—What to you is the day of the Lord,? It is darkness, not light." His own opposition to the popular conception is formulated in a paradox which he prefixes as theme to the principal section of his book:—"Us alone does Jehovah know," say the Israelites, drawing from this the inference that He is on their side, and of course must take their part. "You only do I know," Amos represents Jehovah as saying, "therefore do I visit upon you all your sins."

If the question, Whereon did Jehovah's relation to Israel ultimately rest? be asked, the answer, according to the popular faith, must substantially be that it rested on the fact that Jehovah was worshipped in Israel and not among the heathen, that in Israel were His altars and His dwelling. His cultus was the bond between Him and the nation; when therefore it was desired to draw the bond still closer, the solemn services of religion were redoubled. But to the conception of Amos Jehovah is no judge capable of accepting a bribe; with the utmost indignation he repudiates the notion that it is possible to influence Him by gifts and offerings. Though Israel alone has served Him he does not on that account apply any other standard to it than to other nations (chaps. i. ii.). If Israel is better known to Him, it does not follow that on that account He shuts His eyes and blindly takes a side. Neither Jehovah nor His prophet recognises two moral standards; right is everywhere right, wrong always wrong, even though committed against Israel's worst enemies (ii. 1). What Jehovah demands is righteousness,—nothing more and nothing less; what He hates is injustice. Sin or offence to the Deity is a thing of purely moral character; with such emphasis this doctrine had never before been heard. Morality is that for the sake of which all other things exist; it is the alone essential thing in the world. It is no postulate, no idea, but at once a necessity and a fact, the most intensely living of personal powers-Jehovah the God of Hosts. In wrath, in ruin, this holy reality makes its existence known; it annihilates all that is hollow and false.

Amos calls Jehovah the God of Hosts, never the God of Israel. The nation as such is no religious conception to him; from its mere existence he cannot formulate any article of faith. Sometimes it seems as if he were denying Israel's prerogative altogether. He does not really do so, but at least the prerogative is conditional and involves a heavy responsibility. The saying in iii. 2 recalls Luke xii. 47. The proposition "Jehovah knows Israel" is in the mouth of Amos almost the same thing as "Israel knows Jehovah; " save only that this is not to be regarded as any merit on Israel's part, but as a manifestation of the grace of Jehovah, who has led His people by great deeds and holy men, and so made Himself known. Amos knows no other truth than that practical one which he has found among his own people and nowhere else, Iying at the foundation of life and morality, and which he regards as the product of a divine providential ordering of history. From this point of view, so thoroughly Israelitish, he pronounces Israel's condemnation. He starts from premises generally conceded, but he accentuates them differently and draws from them divergent conclusions.

Amos was the founder, and the purest type, of a new phase of prophecy. The impending conflict of Asshur with Jehovah and Israel, the ultimate downfall of Israel, is its theme. Until that date there had subsisted in Palestine and Syria a number of petty kingdoms and nationalities, which had their friendships and enmities with one another, but paid no heed to anything outside their own immediate environment, and revolved, each on its own axis, careless of the outside world, until suddenly the Assyrians burst in upon them. These commenced the work which was carried on by the Babylonians, Persians, and Greeks, and completed by the Romans. They introduced a new factor, the conception of the world,—the world of course in the historical sense of that expression. In presence of that conception the petty nationalities lost their centre of gravity, brute fact dispelled their illusions, they flung their gods to the moles and to the bats (Isaiah ii.). The prophets of Israel alone did not allow themselves to be taken by surprise by what had occurred, or to be plunged in despair; they solved by anticipation the grim problem which history set before them. They absorbed into their religion that conception of the world which was destroying the religions of the nations, even before it had been fully grasped by the secular consciousness. Where others saw only the ruin of everything that is holiest, they saw the triumph of Jehovah over delusion and error. Whatever else might be overthrown, the really worthy remained unshaken. They recognised ideal powers only, right and wrong truth and falsehood; second causes were matters of indifference to them, they were no practical politicians. But they watched the course of events attentively, nay, with passionate interest. The present, which was passing before them, became to them as it were the plot of a divine drama which they watched with an intelligence that anticipated the *denouement*. Everywhere the same goal of the development, everywhere the same laws. The nations are the *dramatis personae*, Israel the hero, Jehovah the poet of the tragedy. *1*

***************************** 1. In very much the same way the threatened and actual political annihilation of Ionia led to the rise of Greek philosophy (Xenophanes, Heraclitus). *****************************

The canonical prophets, the series of whom begins with Amos, were separated by an essential distinction from the class which had preceded them and which still continued to be the type of the common prophet. They did not seek to kindle either the enthusiasm or the fanaticism of the multitude; they swam not with but against the stream. They were not patriotic, at least in the ordinary acceptation of that word; they prophesied not good but evil for their people (Jer. xxviii. 8). Until their time the nation had sprung up out of the conception of Jehovah; now the conception of Jehovah was casting the nation into the shade. The natural bond between the two was severed, and the relation was henceforward viewed as conditional. As God of the righteousness which is the law of the whole universe, Jehovah could be Israel's God only in so far as in Israel the right was recognised and followed. The ethical element destroyed the national character of the old religion. It still addressed itself, to be sure, more to the nation and to society at large than to the individual; it insisted less upon a pure heart than upon righteous institutions; but nevertheless the first step towards universalism had been accomplished, towards at once the general diffusion and the individualisation of religion. Thus, although the prophets were far from originating a new conception of God, they none the less were the founders of what has been called "ethical monotheism." But with them this ethical monotheism was no product of the "self-evolution of dogma," but a progressive step which had been called forth simply by the course of events. The providence of God brought it about that this call came at an opportune period, and not too suddenly. The downfall of the nation did not take place until the truths and precepts of religion were already strong enough to be able to live on alone; to the prophets belongs the merit of having recognised the independence of these, and of having secured perpetuity to Israel by refusing to allow the conception of Jehovah to be involved in the ruin of the kingdom. They saved faith by destroying illusion.

The event which Amos had foreseen was not long in coming. The Israelites flew spontaneously, like "silly doves," into the net of the Assyrians. Zechariah ben Jeroboam was overthrown after a short reign, Shallum his murderer and successor was also unable to hold his own, and was followed after the horrors of a civil war by Menahem ben Gadi (745 B.C). But Menahem, in the presence of domestic (and perhaps also foreign) assailants, *1* had no other

******************************** 1. It is not inconceivable that the wars carried on by Tiglath-pileser II. against Hamath had some connection with his interventions in favour of Menahem. The kingdom of Hamath, which may have been threatened by Jeroboam II., may have availed itself of the state of matters which followed his death to secure its own aggrandisement at Israel's expense; in correspondence with this attack from the northern side another by Judah in concert with Hamath may well have been made from the south. In this way, though not without the aid of pure hypothesis, it might be possible to fit into the general historical connection the fragmentary Assyrian notices about Azariah of Judah and his relations to Hamath; the explanations suggested by the Assyriologists have hitherto been total failures. But in that case it would certainly be necessary to assume that the Assyrians were badly informed as to the nature of the relations between Hamath and Judah, and also as to the individual who at that time held the throne of Judah. Uzziah (= Azariah), who in his old age had become a leper, could only nominally at best have been king of Judah then. ******************************

resort than to purchase by payment of a great tribute the assistance of King Tiglath-pileser II., who at that time was giving new force to the Assyrian predominance in these regions. By such means he succeeded in attaining his immediate end, but the further consequence was that the rival party in the state turned for support to Egypt, and Palestine now became the arena of conflict between the two great world-powers.

Menahem transmitted his kingdom to Pekahiah; Pekahiah was murdered about 735 B.C. by Pekah, and Pekah himself shortly afterwards was overthrown. All this happened within a few years. It would have been possible to conjecture the state of the country in these circumstances, even if we had not been informed of it by means of the prophetical book of Hosea, which dates from the time when the Assyrians had begun indeed to tamper with the country, but had not yet shown their full design. After the death of Jeroboam II. there had been wild outbursts of partisan war; none of the kings who in quick succession appeared and disappeared had real power, none established order. It was as if the danger from without, which was only too obviously threatening the existence of the kingdom, had already dissolved all internal bonds; every one was at war with his neighbour. Assyrians and Egyptians were called in to support this or that government; by such expedients the external confusion was, naturally, only increased. Was there any other quarter in which help could yet be sought? The people, led by the priests, turned to the altars of Jehovah, and outdid itself in pious works, as if by any such illusory means, out of all relation to the practical problem in hand, the gangrene of anarchy could possibly be healed. Still more zealous than Amos against the cultus was Hosea, not merely on the ground that it had the absurd motive of forcing Jehovah's favour, but also because it was of heathenish character, nature-worship and idolatry. That Jehovah is the true and only helper is certainly not denied by Hosea. But His help is coupled with the condition that Israel shall undergo a complete change, and of such a change he sees no prospect. On this account the downfall of the state is in Hosea's view inevitable, but not final ruin, only such an overthrow as is necessary for the transition to a new and fair recommencement. In Hosea's prophecies the relation between Jehovah and Israel is conceived of as dissoluble, and as actually on the point of being dissolved, but it has struck its roots so deep that it must inevitably at last establish itself again.

The first actual collision between Israel and Assyria occurred in 734. Resin, king of Damascus, and Pekah, king of Samaria, had united in an expedition against Judah, where at that time Ahaz ben Jotham occupied the throne. But Ahaz parried the blow by placing himself under the protection of the Assyrians, who perhaps would in any case have struck in against the alliance between Aram and Israel. Tiglath-pileser made his first appearance in 734, first on the sea-coast of Palestine, and subsequently either in this or in the following year took up his quarters in the kingdom of the ten tribes. After he had ravaged Galilee and Gilead, he finally concluded a peace with Samaria conditionally on his receiving the head of King Pekah and a considerable yearly tribute. Hosea ben Elah was raised to the throne in Pekah's place and acknowledged by the Assyrian as a vassal For some ten years he held his position quietly, regularly paying his dues. But when at the death of Tiglath-pileser the Syro-Palestinian kingdoms rebelled *en masse*, Samaria also was seized with the delirium of patriotic fanaticism (Isaiah xxviii.). Relying upon the help of Seve, king of Ethiopia and Egypt, Hosea ventured on a revolt from Assyria. But the Egyptians left him in the lurch as soon as Shalmaneser IV., Tiglath-pileser's successor, invaded his territory. Before his capital had fallen, Hosea himself fell into the hands of the Assyrians. Samaria offered a desperate resistance, and succumbed only to Sargon, Shalmaneser's successor (72I). Energetic measures were adopted by the victor for the pacification of the country; he carried all the inhabitants of mark into captivity to Calachene, Gozanitis, and Armenia. Much light is thrown upon the conditions of the national religion then and upon its subsequent development by the single fact that the exiled Israelites were absorbed by the surrounding heathenism without leaving a trace behind them, while the population of Judah, who had the benefit of a hundred years respite, held their faith fast throughout the period of the Babylonian exile, and by means of it were able to maintain their own individuality afterwards in all the circumstances that arose. The fact that the fall of Samaria did not hinder but helped the religion of Jehovah is entirely due to the prophets. That they had foreseen the downfall of the state, and declared in the name of religion that it was inevitable, was a matter of much greater historical importance than the actual downfall itself.

7. THE DELIVERANCE OF JUDAH.

Hitherto the small kingdom of Judah had stood in the background. Its political history had been determined almost exclusively by its relation to Israel. Under the dynasty of Omri the original enmity had been changed into a close but perhaps not quite voluntary friendship. Judah found itself drawn completely into the train of the more powerful neighbouring state, and seems even to have rendered it military service. The fall of the house of Omri was an ominous event for Judah as well as Israel; Jehu, as he passed to the throne, put to death not only Ahaziah the king but also two and forty other members of the royal house of David who had fallen into his hands; and those who still survived, children for the most part, were murdered wholesale by the regent Athaliah for reasons that are unknown. Only one little boy, Joash, was concealed from her fury, and by a successful conspiracy six years afterwards was placed upon the throne of his ancestors. At that time the Syrians were extending their incursions to Judah and Philistia, and Joash bought them off from Jerusalem with the temple treasures. Perhaps it was this disgrace that he expiated with his death; in like manner perhaps the assassination of his successor Amaziah is to be accounted for by the discredit he had incurred by a reckless and unsuccessful war against Israel. Just as Israel was beginning to recover itself after the happy termination of the Syrian wars, Judah also experienced its period of highest prosperity. What Jeroboam II. was to the northern kingdom, Uzziah was to that of the south. He appears to have obtained possession of Edom, and for a considerable time to have held that one province of David's conquests which fell to Judah; and at the trading port of Elath he revived the commerce which Solomon had created. The prosperity of his long reign was uninterrupted till in his later years he was smitten with leprosy, and found it necessary to hand over the affairs of the kingdom to his son Jotham. But Jotham appears to have died about the same time as his father,—his successor, still in very early youth (Isaiah iii. 12), being Ahaz ben Jotham ben Uzziah.

If Judah could not compare with Israel in political and general historical importance, it nevertheless enjoyed more than one considerable advantage over the larger kingdom. It was much safer from foreign foes; for the Egyptians, as a rule, were not dangerous neighbours. But its chief advantage consisted in the stability of its dynasty. It was David who had elevated Judah and Jerusalem to a position of historical significance, and the prosperity of his house was most intimately connected with that of the town and territory, and even with that of religion. On two separate occasions it occurred that a king of Judah was murdered by subjects, but in both cases the "people of the land" rose up against the assassins and once more placed a member of the Davidic family upon the throne. The one actual recorded revolution was that against Athaliah, which had for its object the restoration of the throne to the legitimate heir. Under shelter of the monarchy the other institutions of the state also acquired a measure of permanency such as was not found at all in Israel, where everything depended on the character of individuals, and the existing order of things was ever liable to be subjected to fresh dispute. Life in Judah was a much more stable affair, though not so exciting or dramatic. Possibly the greater isolation of the little kingdom, its more intimate relations with the neighbouring wilderness, and the more primitive modes of life which resulted, were also factors which contributed to this general result.

392

In the capital of course the life was not primitive, and its influence was undoubtedly greater than that of the country. Successive kings exerted themselves for its external improvement, and in this respect Hezekiah ben Ahaz was specially distinguished. Above all they manifested sincere interest in the temple, which from an early period exerted a powerful force of attraction over the entire mass of the population. They regulated the cultus according to their individual tastes, added to it or curtailed it at their pleasure, and dealt with the sacred treasures as they chose. Although the priests had in a certain sense great power—the conspiracy against Athaliah was led not by a prophet but by a priest,—they were nevertheless subjects of the king, and had to act according to his orders. That the cultus of Jehovah at Jerusalem was purer than that at Bethel or at Samaria is an assertion which is contradicted by more than one well-attested fact. In this respect there was no essential difference between Israel and Judah. It was in Israel that the reaction against Baal-worship originated which afterwards passed over into Judah; the initiative in all such matters was Israel's. There the experiments were made from which Jerusalem learned the lesson. How deep was the interest felt in the affairs of the larger kingdom by the inhabitants even of one of the smaller provincial towns of Judah is shown in the instance of Amos of Tekoah.

Step by step with the decline of Israel after the death of Jeroboam II. did Judah rise in importance; it was already preparing to take the inheritance. The man through whom the transition of the history from Israel to Judah was effected, and who was the means of securing for the latter kingdom a period of respite which was fruitful of the best results for the consolidation of true religion, was the Prophet Isaiah. The history of his activity is at the same time the history of Judah during that period.

Isaiah became conscious of his vocation in the year of King Uzziah's death; his earliest discourses date from the beginning of the reign of Ahaz. In them he contemplates the imminent downfall of Samaria, and threatens Judah also with the chastisement its political and social sins deserve. In chapter ix., and also in chapters ii.-v., he still confines himself on the whole to generalities quite after the manner of Amos. But on the occasion of the expedition of the allied Syrians and Ephraimites against Jerusalem he interposed with bold decision in the sphere of practical politics. To the very last he endeavoured to restrain Ahaz from his purpose of summoning the Assyrians to his help; he assured him of Jehovah's countenance, and offered him a token in pledge. When the king refused this, the prophet recognised that matters had gone too far, and that the coming of the Assyrians could not be averted. He then declared that the dreaded danger would indeed be obviated by that course, but that another far more serious would be incurred. For the Egyptians would resist the westward movement of Assyria, and Judah as the field of war would be utterly laid waste; only a remnant would remain as the basis of a better future.

The actual issue, however, was not yet quite so disastrous. The Egyptians did not interfere with the Assyrians, and left Samaria and Damascus to their fate. Judah became indeed tributary to Assyria, but at the same time enjoyed considerable prosperity. Henceforward the prophet's most zealous efforts were directed to the object of securing the maintenance, at any price, of this condition of affairs. He sought by every means at his command to keep Judah from any sort of intervention in the politics of the great powers, in order that it might devote itself with undivided energies to the necessities of internal affairs. He actually succeeded in maintaining the peace for many years, even at times when in the petty kingdoms around the spirit of revolt was abroad. The ill success of all attempts elsewhere to shake off the yoke confirmed him in the conviction that Assyria was the rod of chastisement wielded by Jehovah over the nations, who had no alternative but to yield to its iron sway.

While thirty years passed thus peacefully away so far as foreign relations were concerned, internal changes of all the greater importance were taking place. Hezekiah ben Ahaz undertook for the first time a thoroughgoing reformation in the cultus of Jehovah. "He removed the high places, and brake the pillars, and cut down the Ashera, and brake in pieces the brazen serpent that Moses had made;" so we are told in 2Kings xviii. 4, with a mixture of the general and the special that does not inspire much confidence. For, *e.g.*, the "high places" which Solomon had raised on the Mount of Olives were not removed by Hezekiah, although they stood quite close to Jerusalem, and moreover were consecrated to foreign deities. But in every respect there must have been a wide difference between the objects and results of the reformations of Hezekiah and Josiah. Undoubtedly Hezekiah undertook his reforms in worship under the influence of Isaiah. Following in the footsteps of Hosea, who had been the first to take and to express offence at the use of images in the worship of Jehovah, this prophet, utilising the impression which the destruction of Samaria had produced in Jerusalem (Isaiah xvii., cf. Jeremiah iii.), strove to the utmost against the adoration of the work of men's hands in the holy places, against the Asheras and pillars (sun-pillars), and above all against the ephods, *i.e.*, the idols of silver and gold, of which the land was full. But against the high places in and by themselves, against the multiplicity of the altars of Jehovah, he made no protest. "(In the Messianic time) ye shall loathe and cast away as an unclean thing your graven images with silver coverings and your molten images overlaid with gold," he says (xxx. 22); and the inference is that he contemplated the purification of the high places from superstitious excesses, but by no means their abolition. To this one object *1*

***************************** 1. That is, to the abolition of the images. Jeremiah's polemic is directed no longer against the images, but against wood and stone, i.e, Asheras and pillars. The date of the reformation under Hezekiah is uncertain; perhaps it ought to be placed after Sennacherib's withdrawal from Jerusalem. ********************************

Hezekiah's reformation seems to have confined itself,—an object of much greater primary importance than the destruction of the altars themselves. Their destruction was a measure which arose simply out of despair of the possibility of cleansing them.

Sargon, king of Assyria, was succeeded in 705 by Sennacherib. The opportunity was seized by Merodach Baladan of Babylon to secure his independence; and by means of an embassy he urged Hezekiah also to throw off the yoke. The proposal was adopted, and the king of Judah was joined by other petty kingdoms, especially some of the Philistine towns. Relations with Egypt were established to secure its support in case of need. Sennacherib's more immediate and pressing business in Babylon enabled Palestine to gain some time; but the issue of that revolt made self-deception impossible as to the probable result of the other movement.

This was the period at which Isaiah, already far advanced in life, wielded his greatest influence. The preparations for revolt, the negotiations with Egypt, were concealed from him,-a proof how greatly he was feared at court. When he came to know of them, it was already too late to undo what had been done. But he could at least give vent to his anger. With Jerusalem, it seemed to him, the story of Samaria was repeating itself; uninstructed by that sad lesson, the capital was giving itself up to the mad intoxication of leaders who would inevitably bring her to ruin. "Quietness and rest" had been the motto given by Jehovah to Judah, powerless as it was and much in need of a period of peace; instead of this, defiance based on ignorance and falsehood expressed the prevailing temper. But those who refused to listen to the intelligible language of Jehovah would be compelled to hear Him speak in Assyrian speech in a way that would deafen and blind them. Isaiah shows himself no less indignant against the crowd that stupidly stared at his excitement than against the God-forsaken folly of the king, with his counsellors, his priests, and his prophets. They do not suffer themselves to be shaken out of their ordinary routine by the gravity of such a crisis as this; the living work of Jehovah is to them a sealed book, their piety does not extend beyond the respect they show for certain human precepts learnt by rote.

Meanwhile Sennacherib, at the head of a great army, was advancing against Philistia and Judah along the Phoenician coast (701). Having captured Ascalon, he next laid siege to Ekron, which, after the combined Egyptian and Ethiopian army sent to its relief had been defeated at Eltheke, fell into the enemy's hand, and was severely dealt with. Simultaneously various fortresses of Judah were occupied, and the level country was devastated (Isaiah i.). The consequence was that Hezekiah, in a state of panic, offered to the Assyrians his sub-mission, which was accepted on payment of a heavy penalty, he being permitted, however, to retain possession of Jerusalem. He seemed to have got cheaply off from the unequal contest.

The way being thus cleared, Sennacherib pressed on southwards, for the Egyptians were collecting their forces against him. The nearer he came to the enemy the more undesirable did he find it that he should leave in his rear so important a fortress as Jerusalem in the hands of a doubtful vassal. Notwithstanding the recently ratified treaty, therefore, he demanded the surrender of the city, believing that a policy of intimidation would be enough to secure it from Hezekiah. But there was another personality in Jerusalem of whom his plans had taken no account. Isaiah had indeed regarded the revolt from Assyria as a rebellion against Jehovah Himself, and therefore as a perfectly hopeless undertaking which could only result in the utmost humiliation and sternest chastisement for Judah. But still more distinctly than those who had gone before him did he hold firm as an article of faith the conviction that the kingdom would not be utterly annihilated; all his speeches of solemn warning closed with the announcement that a remnant should return and form the kernel of a new commonwealth to be fashioned after Jehovah's own heart. For him, in contrast to Amos, the great crisis had a positive character; in contrast to Hosea, he did not expect a temporary suspension of the theocracy, to be followed by its complete reconstruction, but in the pious and God-fearing individuals who were still to be met with in this Sodom of iniquity, he saw the threads, thin indeed yet sufficient, which formed the links between the Israel of the present and its better future. Over against the vain confidence of the multitude Isaiah had hitherto brought into prominence the darker obverse of his religious belief, but now he confronted their present depression with its bright reverse; faint-heartedness was still more alien to his nature than temerity. In the name of Jehovah he bade King Hezekiah be of good courage, and urged that he should by no means surrender. The Assyrians would not be able to take the city, not even to shoot an arrow into it nor to bring up their siege train against it. "I know thy sitting, thy going, and thy standing," is Jehovah's language to the Assyrian, "and also thy rage against me. And I will put my ring in thy nose, and my bridle in thy lips, and I will turn thee back by the way by which thou camest." And thus it proved in the issue. By a still unexplained catastrophe, the main army of Sennacherib was annihilated on the frontier between Egypt and Palestine, and Jerusalem thereby freed from all danger. The Assyrian king had to save himself by a hurried retreat to Nineveh; Isaiah was triumphant. A more magnificent close of a period of influential public life can hardly be imagined.

***** What Sennacherib himself relates of his expedition against his rebellious vassals in Palestine (George Smith, Assyrian Eponym Canon, p. 67, 68, 131-136) runs parallel with 2 Kings xviii. 14-16, but not with the rest of the Bible narrative. These three verses are peculiar, and their source is different from that of the context. After having captured various Phoenician cities, and received tribute from a number of kings, his first measure is forcibly to restore the Assyrian governor who had been expelled from Ascalon, and next he turns his arms against Ekron. This city had put in irons its own king, Padi (who remained loyal to the suzerain), and handed him over to Hezekiah, who appears as the soul of the rebellion in these quarters. The Egyptians, who as usual have a hand in the matter, advance with an army for the relief of the beleaguered city, but are defeated near Eltheke in the immediate neighbourhood; Ekron is taken, remorselessly chastised, and forced to take Padi back again as its king. For Hezekiah in the meantime has delivered up his prisoner, and, terrified by the fall of his fortresses and the devastation of his territory, has accepted the position of a vassal once more, paying at the same time a heavy fine, inclusive of 30 talents of gold and 800 of silver. Such is the Assyrian account. If we treat the 300 talents mentioned in 2Kings xviii. 14 as Syrian (=800 Babylonian), it completely fills in the vague outlines given in 2Kings xviii. 14-16, and, while confirming in their place immediately after ver. 13 these verses, unrelated as they are to the main connection of the Biblical narrative, corrects them only in one point, by making it probable that the subjection of Hezekiah (which is not equivalent to the surrender of his city) took place while Sennacherib was still before Ekron, and not at later date when he had gone further south towards Libnah. As regards his further advance towards Egypt, and the reasons of his sudden withdrawal (related by Herodotus also from Egyptian tradition), the great king is silent, having nothing to boast of in it. The battle of Eltheke, which is to be regarded only as an episode in the siege of Ekron, being merely the repulse of the Egyptian relieving army, was not an event of great historical importance, and ought not to be brought into any connection either with 2Kings xix. 7 or with xix. 35; Sennacherib's inscription speaks only of the first and prosperous stage of the expedition, not of the decisive one which resulted so disastrously for him, as must be clear from the words themselves to every unprejudiced reader.

8. THE PROPHETIC REFORMATION.

Isaiah was so completely a prophet that even his wife was called the prophetess after him. No such title could have been bestowed on the wife of either Amos or Hosea. But what distinguished him more than anything else from those predecessors was that his position was not, like theirs, apart from the government; he sat close to the helm, and took a very real part in directing the course of the vessel. He was more positive and practical than they; he wished to make his influence felt, and when for the moment he was unsuccessful in this so far as the great whole of the state was concerned, he busied himself in gathering round him a small circle of like-minded persons on whom his hope for the future rested. Now that Israel had been destroyed, he wished at all events to save Judah. The lofty ideality of his faith (ii. 1 seq.) did not hinder him from calling in the aid of practical means for this end. But the current of his activities was by the circumstances of the case directed into a channel in which after his death they continued to flow towards a goal which had hardly been contemplated by himself.

The political importance of the people of Jehovah was reduced to a minimum when Judah only was left. Already at an earlier period in that kingdom the sacred had come to be of more importance than the secular; much more was this the case under the suzerainty of Assyria. The circumstances of the time themselves urged that the religion of Israel should divest itself of all politico-national character; but Isaiah also did his best to further this end. It was his most zealous endeavour to hold king and people aloof from every patriotic movement; to him the true religious attitude was one of quietness and sitting still, non-intervention in political affairs, concentration on the problems of internal government. But he was compelled to leave over for the coming Messiah (xi. 1 seq.) that reformation in legal and social matters which seemed to him so necessary; all that he could bring the secular rulers of his country to undertake was a reform in worship. This was the most easily solved of the problems alluded to above, and it was also that which most closely corresponded to the character of the kingdom of Judah. Thus it came about that the reform of the theocracy which had been contemplated by Isaiah led to its transformation into an ecclesiastical state. No less influential in effecting a radical change in the old popular religion was Isaiah's doctrine which identified the true Israel with the holy remnant which alone should emerge from the crisis unconsumed. For that remnant was more than a mere object of hope; it actually stood before him in the persons of that little group of pious individuals gathered around him. Isaiah founded no "ecclesiola in ecclesia" indeed, but certainly an "ecclesia in civitate Dei." Now began that distinction between the true Israel and the Israel according to the flesh, that bipartite division of the nation which became so important in later times. As head and founder of the prophetic party in Judah, Isaiah was, involuntarily, the man who took the first steps towards the institution of the church.

The catastrophe which befell the army of Sennacherib had no very great effect upon the external affairs of Judah. Sennacherib indeed, being busy in the east, was unable to retrieve the loss he had sustained, but his son Esarhaddon, who succeeded him in 681, resumed the Egyptian war with better success. He made himself master of the Nile valley, and brought the Ethiopians into submission. That the petty kingdoms of Palestine returned to the old relations of dependence is to be taken as a matter of course. Judah appears to have resumed the yoke voluntarily, but the Samaritans only after force had been applied; they were afterwards deported, whereupon the deserted country was occupied by foreign colonists, who, however, accepted the cultus of the god of the land.

That Manasseh ben Hezekiah should have again come under Assyrian suzerainty appears at that time to have made but little impression; since the time of Ahaz Judah had been accustomed to this relation. The Book of Kings speaks only of internal affairs under the reign of Manasseh. According to it, he was a bad ruler, who permitted, and even caused, innocent blood to flow like water. But what was of greater consequence for the future, he took up an attitude of hostility towards the prophetic party of reform, and put himself on the side of the reaction which would fain bring back to the place of honour the old popular half-pagan conception of Jehovah, as against the pure and holy God whom the prophets worshipped. The revulsion manifested itself as the reform had done, chiefly in matters of worship. The old idolatrous furniture of the sanctuaries was reinstated in its place, and new frippery was imported from all quarters, especially from Assyria and Babylon, to renovate the old religion; with Jehovah was now associated a "queen of heaven." Yet, as usual, the restoration did more than merely bring back the old order of things. What at an earlier period had been mere naïveté now became superstition, and could hold its ground only by having imparted to it artificially a deeper meaning which was itself borrowed from the prophetical circle of ideas. Again, earnestness superseded the old joyousness of the cultus; this now had reference principally to sin and its atonement. Value was attached to services rendered to the Deity, just in proportion to their hardness and unnaturalness; at this period it was that the old precept to sacrifice to Jehovah the male that opens the matrix was extended to children. The counter-reformation was far from being unaffected by the preceding reformation, although it understood religious earnestness in quite another sense, and sought, not to eliminate heathenism from the cultus, but to animate it with new life. On the other hand, the reaction was, in the end, found to have left distinct traces of its influence in the ultimate issue of the reformation.

We possess one document dating from Manasseh's time in Micah vi. 1- vii. 6. Here, where the lawlessness and utter disregard of every moral restraint in Judah are set in a hideous light, the prophetic point of view, as contrasted with the new refinements in worship, attains also its simplest and purest expression. Perhaps to this period the Decalogue also, which is so eloquently silent in regard to cultus, is to be assigned.

Jehovah demands nothing for Himself, all that He asks is only for men; this is here the fundamental law of the theocracy.

Manasseh's life was a long one, and his son Amon walked in his ways. The latter died after a brief reign, and with his death a new era for Judah began. It was introduced by the great catastrophe in which the Assyrian empire came to an end. The sovereignty of the world was beginning to pass out of the hands of the Semites into those of the Aryans. Phraortes of Media indeed was unsuccessful in his attempt against the Assyrians, but Cyaxares beat them and proceeded to besiege their capital. The Scythian invasion of Media and Western Asia (c. 630) at this juncture gave them another respite of more than twenty years; but even it tended to break in pieces the great, loosely-compacted monarchy. The provinces became gradually disintegrated, and the kingdom shrivelled up till it covered no more than the land of Asshur. *1*

** 1. Our knowledge of the events of the second half of the 7th century has remained singularly imperfect hitherto, notwithstanding the importance of the changes they wrought on the face of the ancient world. The account given above is that of Herodotus (i. 103-106), and there the matter must rest until really authentic sources shall have been brought to light. With regard to the final siege of Nineveh, our chief informant is Ctesias as quoted by Diodorus (ii. 26, 27). Whether the prophecy of Nabum relates to the LAST siege is doubtful (in spite of ii. 7, and the oracle given in Diodorus, (OTI THN *NINON)OUDEIS (ELEI KATA KRATOS)EAN MH PROTERON (O POTAMOS TH| POLEI GENHTAI POLEMOS), inasmuch as Nahum (i. 9) expressly speaks of the siege alluded to by him as the first, saying, "the trouble shall not rise up the second time."*
****

The inroad of the Scythians aroused to energy again the voice of prophecy which had been dumb during the very sinful but not very animated period of Manasseh's reign. Zephaniah and Jeremiah threatened with the mysterious northern foe, just as Amos and Hosea had formerly done with the Assyrians. The Scythians actually did invade Palestine in 626 (the 13th year of Josiah), and penetrated as far as to Egypt; but their course lay along the shore line, and they left Judah untouched. This danger that had come so near and yet passed them by, this instance of a prophetic threatening that had come to pass and yet been mercifully averted, made a powerful impression upon the people of Judah; public opinion went through a revolution in favour of the reforming party which was able to gain for itself the support also of the young king Josiah ben Amon. The circumstances were favourable for coming forward with a comprehensive programme for a reconstruction of the theocracy. In the year 621 (the eighteenth of Josiah) Deuteronomy was discovered, accepted, and carried into effect.

The Deuteronomic legislation is designed for the reformation, by no means of the cultus alone, but at least quite as much of the civil relations of life. The social interest is placed above the cultus, inasmuch as everywhere humane ends are assigned for the rites and offerings. In this it is plainly seen that Deuteronomy is the progeny of the prophetic spirit. Still more plainly does this appear in the *motifs* of the legislation; according to these, Jehovah is the only God, whose service demands the whole heart and every energy; He has entered into a covenant with Israel, but upon fundamental conditions that, as contained in the Decalogue, are purely moral and of absolute universality. Nowhere does the fundamental religious thought of prophecy find clearer expression than in Deuteronomy,—the thought that Jehovah asks nothing for Himself, but asks it as a religious duty that man should render to man what is right, that His will lies not in any unknown height, but in the moral sphere which is known and understood by all. *1*

*************************************** 1. The commandments which I command thee are not unattainable for thee, neither are they far off; not in heaven so that one might say, Who can climb up into heaven and bring them down, and tell us them that we might do them! not beyond the sea so that one might say, Who shall go over the sea, and fetch them, and tell us them that we might do them!—but the matter lies very near thee, in thy mouth and in thy heart, so that thou canst do it (Deut. xxx. 11-14). ***

But the result of the innovation did not correspond exactly to its prophetic origin. Prophecy died when its precepts attained to the force of laws; the prophetic ideas lost their purity when they became practical. Whatever may have been contemplated, only provisional regulations actually admitted of being carried, and even these only in co-operation with the king and the priests, and with due regard to the capacity of the masses. The final outcome of the Deuteronomic reformation was principally that the cultus of Jehovah was limited to Jerusalem and abolished everywhere else,—such was the popular and practical form of prophetic monotheism. The importance of the Salomonic temple was thereby increased in the highest degree, and so also the influence of the priests of Jerusalem, the sons of Zadok, who now in point of fact got rid entirely of their rivals, the priests of the country districts.

9. JEREMIAH AND THE DESTRUCTION OF JERUSALEM.

Josiah lived for thirteen years after the accomplishment of his great work. It was a happy period of external and internal prosperity. The nation possessed the covenant, and kept it. It seemed as if the conditions had been attained on which, according to the prophets, the continuance of the theocracy depended; if their threatenings against Israel had been fulfilled, so now was Judah proving itself the heir of their promises. Already in Deuteronomy is the "extension of the frontier" taken into consideration, and Josiah actually put his hand to the task of seeking the attainment of this end.

Jehovah and Israel, religion and patriotism, once more went hand in hand. Jeremiah alone did not suffer himself to be misled by the general feeling. He was a second Amos, upon a higher platform— but, unlike his predecessor, a prophet by profession; his history, like Isaiah's, is practically the history of his time. In the work of introducing Deuteronomy he had taken an active part, and throughout his life he showed his zeal against unlawful altars and against the adoration of wood and stone (Asheras and pillars). But he was by no means satisfied with the efforts of the

400

reformation that had been effected; nothing appeared to him more sinful or more silly than the false confidence produced by it in Jehovah and in the inviolability of His one true temple. This confidence he maintained to be delusive; Judah was not a whit better than Israel had been, Jerusalem would be destroyed one day like the temple of Shiloh. The external improvements on which the people of Judah prided themselves he held to leave this severe judgment unaffected; what was needed was a quite different sort of change, a change of heart, not very easy positively to define.

An opportunity for showing his opposition presented itself to the prophet at the juncture when King Josiah had fallen at Megiddo in the battle with Pharaoh Necho (608), and when the people were seeking safety and protection by cleaving to Jehovah and His holy temple. At the instance of the priests and the prophets he had almost expiated with his blood the blasphemies he had uttered against the popular belief; but he did not suffer himself to be driven from his course. Even when the times had grown quiet again, he persisted, at the risk of his life and under universal reproach and ridicule, in his work as a prophet of evil. Moments of despair sometimes came to him; but that he had correctly estimated the true value of the great conversion of the nation was speedily proved by the facts. Although Deuteronomy was not formally abolished under Jehoiakim, who as the vassal of Egypt ascended the throne of his father Josiah, nevertheless it ceased to have practical weight, the battle of Megiddo having shown that in spite of the covenant with Jehovah the possibilities of non-success in war remained the same as before. Jehoiakim tended to return to the ways of Manasseh, not only as regarded idolatry, but also in his contempt for law and the private rights of his subjects;—the two things seem to stand in connection.

The course of events at last brought upon the theocracy the visible ruin which Jeremiah had been so long expecting. After the Egyptians had, with comparative ease, subjugated Syria at the time when the Medes and Chaldaeans were busied with the siege of Nineveh, Nebuchadnezzar, that task accomplished, came upon them from Babylon and routed them on the Euphrates near Carchemish (605-4). The people of Judah rejoiced at the fall of Nineveh, and also at the result of Carchemish; but they were soon undeceived when the prospect began to open on them of simply exchanging the Egyptian for the Chaldaean yoke. The power of the Chaldaeans had been quite unsuspected, and now it was found that in them the Assyrians had suddenly returned to life. Jeremiah was the only man who gained any credit by these events. His much ridiculed "enemy out of the north," of whom he had of old been wont to speak so much, now began to be talked of with respect, although his name was no longer "the Scythian" but "the Babylonian." It was an epoch,—the close of an account which balanced in his favour. Therefore it was that precisely at this moment he received the Divine command to commit to writing that which for twenty-three years he had been preaching, and which, ever pronounced impossible, had now showed itself so close at hand.

After the victory of Carchemish the Chaldaeans drove Pharaoh out of Syria, and also compelled the submission of Jehoiakim (c. 602). For three years he continued to pay his tribute, and then he withheld it; a mad passion for liberty, kindled by religious fanaticism, had begun to rage with portentous power amongst the influential classes, the grandees, the priests, and the prophets. Nebuchadnezzar satisfied himself in the first instance with raising against Judah several of the smaller nationalities around, especially the Edomites; not till 597 did he appear in person before Jerusalem. The town was compelled to yield; the more important citizens were carried into exile, amongst them the young king Jechoniah, son of Jehoiakim, who had died in the interval; Zedekiah ben Josiah was made king in his stead over the remnant left behind. The patriotic fanaticism that had led to the revolt was not broken even by this blow. Within four years afterwards new plans of liberation began to be again set on foot; but on this occasion the influence of Jeremiah proved strong enough to avert the danger. But when a definite prospect of help from Pharaoh Hophra (Apries) presented itself in 589, the craving for independence proved quite irrepressible. Revolt was declared; and in a very short time the Chaldaean army, with Nebuchadnezzar at its head, lay before Jerusalem. For a while everything seemed to move prosperously; the Egyptians came to the rescue, and the Chaleaeans were compelled to raise the siege in order to cope with them. At this there was great joy in Jerusalem; but Jeremiah continued to express his gloomy views. The event proved that he was right; the Egyptians were repulsed and the siege resumed. The city was bent on obstinate resistance; in vain did Jeremiah, at continual risk of his life, endeavour to bring it to reason. The king, who agreed with the prophet, did not venture to assert his opinion against the dominant terrorism. The town in these circumstances was at last taken by storm, and along with the temple, reduced to ruins. Cruel vengeance was taken on the king and grandees, and the pacification of the country was ensured by another and larger deportation of the inhabitants to Babylon. Thus terminated in 586 the kingdom of Judah.

The prophets had been the spiritual destroyers of the old Israel. In old times the nation had been the ideal of religion in actual realisation; the prophets confronted the nation with an ideal to which it did not correspond. Then to bridge over this interval the abstract ideal was framed into a law, and to this law the nation was to be conformed. The attempt had very important consequences, inasmuch as Jehovah continued to be a living power in the law, when He was no longer realised as present in the nation; but that was not what the prophets had meant to effect. What they were unconsciously labouring towards was that religious individualism which had its historical source in the national downfall, and manifested itself not exclusively within the prophetical sphere. With such men as Amos and Hosea the moral personality based upon an inner conviction burst through the limits of mere nationality; their mistake was in supposing that they could make their way of thinking the basis of a national life. Jeremiah saw through the mistake; the true Israel was narrowed to himself. Of the truth of his conviction he never had a moment's doubt; he knew that Jehovah was on his side, that on Him depended the eternal future. But, instead of the nation, the heart and the individual conviction were to him the subject of religion. On the ruins of Jerusalem he gazed into the future filled with joyful hope, sure of this that Jehovah would one day pardon past sin and renew the relation which had been broken off-though on the basis of another covenant than that laid down in Deuteronomy. "I will put my law upon their heart, and write it on their mind; none shall say to his neighbour, Know the Lord, for all shall have that knowledge within them."

10. THE CAPTIVITY AND THE RESTORATION

The exiled Jews were not scattered all over Chaldaea, but were allowed to remain together in families and clans. Many of them, notwithstanding this circumstance, must have lapsed and become merged in the surrounding heathenism; but many also continued faithful to Jehovah and to Israel. They laboured under much depression and sadness, groaning under the wrath of Jehovah, who had rejected His people and cancelled His covenant. They were lying under a sort of vast interdict; they could not celebrate any sacrifice or keep any feast; they could only observe days of fasting and humiliation, and such rites as had no inseparable connection with the holy land. The observance of the Sabbath, and the practice of the rite of circumcision, acquired much greater importance than they formerly possessed as signs of a common religion. The meetings on the Sabbath day out of which the synagogues were afterwards developed appear to have first come into use during this period; perhaps also even then it had become customary to read aloud from the prophetic writings which set forth that all had happened in the providence of God, and moreover that the days of adversity were not to last for ever.

Matters improved somewhat as Cyrus entered upon his victorious career. Was he the man in whom the Messianic prophecies had found their fulfilment? The majority were unwilling to think so. For it was out of Israel (they argued) that the Messiah was to proceed who should establish the kingdom of God upon the ruins of the kingdoms of the world; the restitution effected by means of a Persian could only be regarded as a passing incident in the course of an historical process that had its goal entirely elsewhere. This doubt was met by more than one prophetical writer, and especially by the great anonymous author to whom we are indebted for Isaiah xl.-lxvi. "Away with sorrow; deliverance is at the door! Is it a humiliating thing that Israel should owe its freedom to a Persian? Nay, is it not rather a proof of the world-wide sway of the God of Jacob that He should thus summon His instruments from the ends of the earth? Who else than Jehovah could have thus sent Cyrus? Surely not the false gods which he has destroyed? Jehovah alone it was who foretold and foreknew the things which are now coming to pass,—because long ago He had prearranged and predetermined them, and they are now being executed in accordance with his plan. Rejoice therefore in the prospect of your near deliverance; prepare yourselves for the new era; gird yourselves for the return to your homes." It is to be observed, as characteristic in this prophecy, how the idea of Jehovah as God alone and God over all—in constantly recurring lyrical parenthesis he is praised as the author of the world and of all nature—is yet placed in positive relation to Israel alone, and that upon the principle that Israel is in exclusive possession of the universal truth, which cannot perish with Israel, but must through the instrumentality of Israel, become the common possession of the whole world. "There is no God but Jehovah, and Israel is his prophet."

For many years the Persian monarch put the patience of the Jews to the proof; Jehovah's judgment upon the Chaldaeans, instead of advancing, seemed to recede. At length, however, their hopes were realised; in the year 538 Cyrus brought the empire of Babylon to an end, and gave the exiles leave to seek their fatherland once more. This permission was not made use of by all, or even by a majority. The number of those who returned is stated at 42,360; whether women and children are included in this figure is uncertain. On arriving at their destination, after the difficult march through the desert, they did not spread themselves over the whole of Judah, but settled chiefly in the neighbourhood of Jerusalem. The Calebites, for example, who previously had had their settlements in and around Hebron, now settled in Bethlehem and in the district of Ephrath. They found it necessary to concentrate themselves in face of a threatened admixture of doubtful elements. From all sides people belonging to the surrounding nations had pressed into the depopulated territory of Judah. Not only had they annexed the border territories—where, for example, the Edomites or Idumaeans held the whole of the Negeb as far as to Hebron; they had effected lodgments everywhere, and— as the Ammonites, Ashdodites, and especially the Samaritans—had amalgamated with the older Jewish population, a residue of which had remained in the country in spite of all that had happened. These half-breed "pagani" (Amme haarec 'oxloi) gave a friendly reception to the returning exiles (Bne haggola); particularly did the Samaritans show themselves anxious to make common cause with them. But they were met with no reciprocal cordiality. The lesson of religious isolation which the children of the captivity had learned in Babylon, they did not forget on their return to their home. Here also they lived as in a strange land. Not the native of Judaea, but the man who could trace his descent from the exiles in Babylon, was reckoned as belonging to their community.

The first decennia after the return of the exiles, during which they were occupied in adjusting themselves to their new homes, were passed under a variety of adverse circumstances and by no means either in joyousness or security. Were these then the Messianic times which, it had been foretold, were to dawn at the close of their captivity? They did not at all events answer the expectations which had been formed. A settlement had been again obtained, it was true, in the fatherland; but the Persian yoke pressed now more heavily than ever the Babylonian had done. The sins of God's people seemed still unforgiven, their period of bond-service not yet at an end. A slight improvement, as is shown by the prophecies of Haggai and Zechariah, followed when in the year 520 the obstacles disappeared which until then had stood in the way of the rebuilding of the temple; the work then begun was completed in 516. Inasmuch as the Jews were now nothing more than a religious community, based upon the traditions of a national existence that had ceased, the rebuilding of the temple, naturally, was for them an event of supreme importance.

The law of the new theocracy was the Book of Deuteronomy; this was the foundation on which the structure was to be built. But the force of circumstances, and the spirit of the age, had even before and during the exile exerted a modifying influence upon that legislative code; and it continued to do so still. At first a "son of David" had continued to stand at the head of the Bne haggola, but this last relic of the old monarchy soon had to give way to a Persian governor who was under the control of the satrap of trans-Euphratic Syria, and whose principal business was the collection of revenue. Thenceforward the sole national chief was Joshua the high priest, on whom, accordingly, the political representation also of the community naturally devolved. In the circumstances as they then were no other arrangement was possible. The way had been paved for it long before in so far as the Assyrians had destroyed the kingdom of Israel, while in the kingdom of Judah which survived it the religious cultus had greater importance attached to it than political affairs, and also inasmuch as in point of fact the practical issue of the prophetic reformation sketched in Deuteronomy had been to make the temple the national centre still more than formerly. The hierocracy towards which Ezekiel had already opened the way was simply inevitable. It took the form of a monarchy of the high priest, he having stepped into the place formerly occupied by the theocratic king. As his peers and at his side stood the members of his clan, the Levites of the old Jerusalem, who traced their descent from Zadok (Sadduk); the common Levites held a much lower rank, so far as they had maintained their priestly rank at all and had not been degraded, in accordance with Ezekiel's law (chapter xliv.), to the position of mere temple servitors. "Levite," once the title of honour bestowed on all priests, became more and more confined to members of the second order of the clergy.

Meanwhile no improvement was taking place in the condition of the Jewish colonists. They were poor; they had incurred the hostility of their neighbours by their exclusiveness; the Persian Government was suspicious; the incipient decline of the great kingdom was accompanied with specially unpleasant consequences so far as Palestine was concerned (Megabyzus). All this naturally tended to produce in the community a certain laxity and depression. To what purpose (it was asked) all this religious strictness, which led to so much that was unpleasant? Why all this zeal for Jehovah, who refused to be mollified by it? It is a significant fact that the upper ranks of the priesthood were least of all concerned to counteract this tendency. Their priesthood was less to them than the predominance which was based upon it; they looked upon the neighbouring ethnarchs as their equals, and maintained relations of friendship with them. The general community was only following their example when it also began to mingle with the Amme haarec.

The danger of Judaism merging into heathenism was imminent. But it was averted by a new accession from without. In the year 458 Ezra the scribe, with a great number of his compatriots, set out from Babylon, for the purpose of reinforcing the Jewish element in Palestine. The Jews of Babylon were more happily situated than their Palestinian brethren, and it was comparatively easy for them to take up a separatist attitude, because they were surrounded by heathenism not partial but entire. They were no great losers from the circumstance that they were precluded from participating directly in the life of the ecclesiastical community; the Torah had long ago become separated from the people, and was now an independent abstraction following a career of its own. Babylonia was the place where a further codification of the law had been placed alongside of Deuteronomy. Ezekiel had led the way in reducing to theory and to writing the sacred praxis of his time; in this he was followed by an entire school; in their exile the Levites turned scribes. Since then Babylon continued to be the home of the Torah; and, while in Palestine itself the practice was becoming laxer, their literary study had gradually intensified the strictness and distinctive peculiarities of Judaism. And now there came to Palestine a Babylonian scribe having the law of his God in his hand, and armed with authority from the Persian king to proceed upon the basis of this law with a reformation of the community.

Ezra did not set about introducing the new law immediately on his arrival in Judaea In the first instance he concentrated his attention on the task of effecting a strict separation between the Bne haggola and the heathen or half-heathen inhabitants. So much he could accomplish upon the basis of Deuteronomy, but it was long before he gave publicity to the law which he himself had brought. Why he hesitated so long it is impossible to say; between the seventh and the twentieth year of Artaxerxes Longimanus (458-445 B.C.) there is a great hiatus in the narrative of the books of Ezra and Nehemiah. The main reason appears to have been that, in spite of the good will of the Persian king, Ezra had not the vigorous support of the local authorities. But this was indispensably necessary in order to secure recognition for a new law.

At last, in 445, it fell to the lot of a Jew, who also shared the views of Ezra, Nehemiah ben Hakkelejah, *1*

*** 1. According to the present punctuation this name is Hakalja (Hachaljah), but such a pronunciation is inadmissible; it has no possible etymology, the language having no such word as *hakal.* The name in its correct form means "wait upon Jehovah." ***

the cupbearer and the favourite of Artaxerxes, to be sent as Persian governor to Judaea. After he had freed the community from external pressure with vigour and success, and brought it into more tolerable outward circumstances, the business of introducing the new law-book was next proceeded with; in this Ezra and Nehemiah plainly acted in concert.

On the first of Tisri—the year is unfortunately not given, but it cannot have been earlier than 444 B.C.—the promulgation of the law began at a great gathering in Jerusalem; Ezra, supported by the Levites, was present. Towards the end of the month, the concluding act took place, in which the community became solemnly bound by the contents of the law. Special prominence was given to those provisions with which the people were directly concerned, particularly those which related to the dues payable by the laity to the priests.

The covenant which hitherto had rested on Deuteronomy was thus expanded into a covenant based upon the entire Pentateuch. Substantially at least Ezra's law-book, in the form in which it became the Magna Charta of Judaism in or about the year 444, must be regarded as practically identical with our Pentateuch, although many minor amendments and very considerable additions may have been made at a later date.

The character of the post-Deuteronomic legislation (Priestly Code) is chiefly marked, in its external aspects, by the immense extension of the dues payable to the priests, and by the sharp distinction made between the descendants of Aaron and the common Levites; this last feature is to be traced historically to the circumstance that after the Deuteronomic reformation the legal equality between the Levites who until then had ministered at the "high places" and the priests of the temple at Jerusalem was not *de facto* recognised. Internally, it is mainly characterised by its ideal of

Levitical holiness, the way in which it everywhere surrounds life with purificatory and propitiatory ceremonies, and its prevailing reference of sacrifice to sin. Noteworthy also is the manner in which everything is regarded from the point of view of Jerusalem, a feature which comes much more boldly into prominence here than in Deuteronomy; the nation and the temple are strictly speaking identified. That externalisation towards which the prophetical movement, in order to become practical, had already been tending in Deuteronomy finally achieved its acme in the legislation of Ezra; a new artificial Israel was the result; but, after all, the old would have pleased an Amos better. At the same time it must be remembered that the kernel needed a shell. It was a necessity that Judaism should incrust itself in this manner; without those hard and ossified forms the preservation of its essential elements would have proved impossible. At a time when all nationalities, and at the same time all bonds of religion and national customs, were beginning to be broken up in the seeming cosmos and real chaos of the Graeco-Roman empire, the Jews stood out like a rock in the midst of the ocean. When the natural conditions of independent nationality all failed them, they nevertheless artificially maintained it with an energy truly marvellous, and thereby preserved for themselves, and at the same time for the whole world, an eternal good.

As regards the subsequent history of the Jewish community under the Persian domination, we have almost no information. The high priest in Nehemiah's time was Eliashib, son of Joiakim and grandson of Joshua, the patriarchal head of the sons of Zadok, who had returned from Babylon; he was succeeded in the direct line by Joiada, Johanan, and Jaddua (Nehemiah xii. 10, 11, 22); the last-named was in office at the time of Alexander the Great (Josephus, Antiquities, xi. 8). Palestine was the province which suffered most severely of all from the storms which marked the last days of the sinking Persian empire, and it is hardly likely that the Jews escaped their force; we know definitely, however, of only one episode, in which the Persian general Bagoses interfered in a disagreeable controversy about the high-priesthood (cir. 375).

To this period also (and not, as Josephus states, to the time of Alexander) belongs the constitution of the Samaritan community on an independent footing by Manasseh, a Jewish priest of rank. He was expelled from Jerusalem by Nehemiah in 432, for refusing to separate from his alien wife. He took shelter with his father-in-law Sanballat, the Samaritan prince, who built him a temple on Mount Gerizim near Shechem, where he organised a Samaritan church and a Samaritan worship, on the Jerusalem model, and on the basis of a but slightly modified Jerusalem Pentateuch. If the Samaritans had hitherto exerted, themselves to the utmost to obtain admission into the fellowship of the Jews, they henceforward were as averse to have anything to do with these as these were to have any dealings with them; the temple on Mount Gerizim was now the symbol of their independence as a distinct religious sect. For the Jews this was a great advantage, as they had no longer to dread the danger of syncretism. They could now quite confidently admit the Amme haarec into their communion, in the assurance of assimilating them without any risk of the opposite process taking place. The Judaizing process began first with the country districts immediately surrounding Jerusalem, and then extended to Galilee and many portions of Peraea. In connection with it, the Hebrew language, which hitherto had been firmly retained by the Bne haggola, now began to yield to the Aramaic, and to hold its own only as a sacred speech.

---

11. JUDAISM AND CHRISTIANITY.

The post-Deuteronomic legislation is not addressed to the people, but to the congregation; its chief concern is the regulation of worship. Political matters are not touched upon, as they are in the hands of a foreigner lord. The hierocracy is taken for granted as the constitution of the congregation. The head of the cultus is the head of the whole; the high priest takes the place of the king. The other priests, though his brothers or his sons, are officially subordinate to him, as bishops to the supreme pontiff. They, again, are distinguished from the Levites not only by their office but also by their noble blood, though the Levites belong by descent to the clergy, of which they form the lowest grade. The material basis of the hierarchical pyramid is furnished by the contributions of the laity, which are required on a scale which cannot be called modest. Such is the outward aspect of the rule of the holy in Israel. Inwardly, the ideal of holiness governs the whole of life by means of a net of ceremonies and observances which separate the Jew from the natural man. "Holy" means almost the same as "exclusive." Originally the term was equivalent to divine, but now it is used chiefly in the sense of religious, priestly, as if the divine were to be known from the worldly, the natural, by outward marks.

It had so fallen out, even before the exile, that the reform of the theocracy which the prophets demanded began in the cultus; and after the exile this tendency could not fail to be persisted in. The restoration of Judaism took place in the form of a restoration of the cultus. Yet this restoration was not a relapse into the heathen ways which the prophets had attacked. The old meaning of the festivals and of the sacrifices had long faded away, and after the interruption of the exile they would scarcely have blossomed again of themselves; they had become simply statutes, unexplained commands of an absolute will. The cultus had no longer any real value for the Deity; it was valuable only as an exercise of obedience to the law. If it had been at first the bond connecting Israel with heathenism, now, on the contrary, it was the shield behind which Judaism retreated to be safe from heathenism. There was no other means to make Judaism secure; and the cultus was nothing more than a means to that end. It was the shell around the faith and practice of the fathers, around the religion of moral monotheism, which it alone preserved until it could become the common property of the world. The great public worship gave the new theocracy a firm centre, thus keeping it one and undivided, and helped it to an organisation. But of more importance was the minor private cultus of pious exercises, which served to Judaize the whole life of every individual. For the centre of gravity of Judaism was in the individual. Judaism was gathered from scattered elements, and it depended on the labour of the individual to make himself a Jew. This is the secret of the persistence of Judaism, even in the diaspora. The initiatory act of circumcision, which conferred an indelible character, was not the only safeguard; the whole of the education which followed that act went to guard against the disintegrating effects of

408

individualism. This is the real significance of the incessant discipline, which consisted mainly in the observance of laws of purity and generally of regulations devised to guard against sin. For what holiness required was not to do good, but to avoid sin. By the sin and trespass offerings, and by the great day of atonement, this private cultus was connected with that of the temple; hence it was that all these institutions fitted so admirably into the system. The whole of life was directed in a definite sacred path; every moment there was a divine command to fulfil, and this kept a man from following too much the thoughts and desires of his own heart. The Jews trained themselves with an earnestness and zeal which have no parallel to create, in the absence of all natural conditions, a holy nation which should answer to the law, the concrete embodiment of the ideals of the prophets.

In the individualism thus moulded into uniformity lay the chief difference which separated the new period from the old. The aim was universal culture by the law, that the prophecy should be fulfilled which says: "They shall all be taught of God." This universal culture was certainly of a peculiar kind, and imposed more troublesome observances than the culture of our day. Yet the strange duties which the law imposed were not universally felt to be a heavy burden. Precepts which were plain and had to do with something outward were very capable of being kept; the harder they seemed at first, the easier were they when the habit had been formed. A man saw that he was doing what was prescribed, and did not ask what was the use of it. The ever-growing body of regulations even came to be felt as a sort of emancipation from self. Never had the individual felt himself so responsible for all he did and left undone, but the responsibility was oppressive, and it was well that there should be a definite precept for every hour of his life, thus diminishing the risk of his going astray. Nor must we forget that the Torah contained other precepts than those which were merely ceremonial. The kernel did not quite harden into wood inside the shell; we must even acknowledge that moral sentiment gained very perceptibly in this period both in delicacy and in power. This also is connected with the fact that religion was not, as before, the custom of the people, but the work of the individual. A further consequence of this was, that men began to reflect upon religion. The age in question saw the rise of the so-called "Wisdom," of which we possess examples in the Book of Job, in the Proverbs of Solomon and of the Son of Sirach, and in Ecclesiastes. This wisdom flourished not only in Judah, but also at the same time in Edom; it had the universalistic tendency which is natural to reflection. The Proverbs of Solomon would scarcely claim attention had they arisen on Greek or Arabian soil; they are remarkable in their pale generality only because they are of Jewish origin. In the Book of Job, a problem of faith is treated by Syrians and Arabians just as if they were Jews. In Ecclesiastes religion abandons the theocratic ground altogether, and becomes a kind of philosophy in which there is room even for doubt and unbelief. Speculation did not on the whole take away from depth of feeling; on the contrary, individualism helped to make religion more intense. This is seen strikingly in the Psalms, which are altogether the fruit of this period. Even the sacrificial practice of the priests was made subjective, being incorporated in the Torah, *i.e.*, made a matter for every one to learn. Though the laity could not take part in the ceremony, they were at least to be thoroughly informed in all the minutiae of the system; the law was a means of interesting every one in the great public sacrificial procedure. Another circumstance also tended to remove the centre of gravity of the temple service from the priests to the congregation. The service of song, though executed by choirs of singers, was yet in idea the song of the congregation, and came to be of more importance than the acts of worship which it accompanied and inspired. The Holy One of Israel sat enthroned, not on the smoke-pillars of the altar, but in the praises of the congregation pouring out its heart in prayer; the sacrifices were merely the external occasion for visiting the temple, the real reason for doing so lay in the need for the strength and refreshment to be found in religious fellowship.

By the Torah religion came to be a thing to be learned. Hence the need of teachers in the church of the second temple. As the scribes had codified the Torah, it was also their task to imprint it on the minds of the people and to fill their life with it; in this way they at the same time founded a supplementary and changing tradition, which kept pace with the needs of the time. The place of teaching was the synagogue; there the law and the prophets were read and explained on the Sabbath. The synagogue and the Sabbath were of more importance than the temple and the festivals; and the moral influence of the scribes transcended that of the priests, who had to be content with outward power and dignity. The rule of religion was essentially the rule of the law, and consequently the Rabbis at last served themselves heirs to the hierarchs. At the same time, while the government of the law was acknowledged in principle, it could at no time be said to be even approximately realised in fact. The high-born priests who stood at the head of the theocracy, cared chiefly, as was quite natural, for the maintenance of their own supremacy. And there were sheep in the flock not to be kept from breaking out, both in the upper and in the lower classes of society; the school could not suppress nature altogether. It was no trifle even to know the six hundred and thirteen commandments of the written law, and the incalculable number of the unwritten. Religion had to be made a profession of, if it was to be practiced aright. It became an art, and thereby at the same time a matter of party:, the leaders of the religious were of course the scribes. The division became very apparent in the time of the Hellenization which preceded the Maccabaean revolt; at that period the name of Pharisees, *i.e.*, the Separated, came into vogue for the party of the religious. But the separation and antipathy between the godly and the ungodly had existed before this, and had marked the life of the congregation after the exile from the very first.

It was the law that gave the Jewish religion its peculiar character. But, on the other hand, a hope was not wanting to that religion; the Jews cherished the prospect of a reward for the fulfilling of the law. This hope attached itself to the old prophecies, certainly in a very fantastic way. The Jews had no historical life, and therefore painted the old time according to their ideas, and framed the time to come according to their wishes. They stood in no living relation with either the past or the future; the present was not with them a bridge from the one to the other; they did not think of bestirring themselves with a view to the kingdom of God. They had no national and historical existence, and made no preparations to procure such a thing for themselves; they only hoped for it as a reward of faithful keeping of the law. Yet they dreamed not only of a restoration of the old kingdom, but of the erection of a universal world-monarchy, which should raise its head at Jerusalem over the ruins of the heathen empires. They regarded the history of the world as a great suit between

410

themselves and the heathen. In this suit they were in the right; and they waited for right to be done them. If the decision was delayed, their sins were the reason; Satan was accusing them before the throne of God, and causing the judgment to be postponed. They were subjected to hard trials, and if tribulation revived their hopes, with much greater certainty did it bring their sins into sorrowful remembrance. Outward circumstances still influenced in the strongest way their religious mood.

But the old belief in retribution which sought to justify itself in connection with the fortunes of the congregation proved here also unequal to the strain laid upon it. Even in Deuteronomy it is maintained that the race is not to suffer for the act of an individual. Jeremiah's contemporaries thought it monstrous that because the fathers had eaten sour grapes the teeth of the children should be set on edge. Ezekiel championed in a notable way the cause of individualism on this ground. He denounced the Jews who had remained in Palestine, and who regarded themselves as the successors of the people of Jehovah because they dwelt in the Holy Land and had maintained some sort of existence as a people. In his view only those souls which were saved from the dispersion of the exile were to count as heirs of the promise; the theocracy was not to be perpetuated by the nation, but by the individual righteous men. He maintained that each man lived because of his own righteousness, and died because of his own wickedness; nay more, the fate of the individual corresponded even in its fluctuations to his moral worth at successive times. The aim he pursued in this was a good one; in view of a despair which thought there was nothing for it but to pine and rot away because of former sins, he was anxious to maintain the freedom of the will, *ie.*, the possibility of repentance and forgiveness. But the way he chose for this end was not a good one; on his showing it was chance which ultimately decided who was good and who was wicked. The old view of retribution which allowed time for judgment to operate far beyond the limit of the individual life had truth in it, but this view had none. Yet it possessed one merit, that it brought up a problem which had to be faced, and which was a subject of reflection for a long time afterwards.

The problem assumed the form of a controversy as to the principle on which piety was rewarded—this controversy taking the place of the great contest between Israel and the heathen. Were the wicked right in saying that there was no God, *i.e.*, that He did not rule and judge on earth? Did He in truth dwell behind the clouds, and did He not care about the doings of men? In that case piety would be an illusion. Piety cannot maintain itself if God makes no difference between the godly and the wicked, and has nothing more to say to the one than to the other; for piety is not content to stretch out its hands to the empty air, it must meet an arm descending from heaven. It must have a reward, not for the sake of the reward, but in order to be sure of its own reality, in order to know that there is a communion of God with men and a road which leads to it. The usual form of this reward is the forgiveness of sins; that is the true motive of the fear of God. That is to say, as long as it is well with him, the godly man does not doubt, and so does not require any unmistakable evidence by which he may be justified and assured of the favour of God. But misfortune and pain destroy this certainty. They are accusers of sin, God's warnings and corrections. Now is the time to hold fast the faith that God leads the godly to repentance, and destroys the wicked, that He forgives the sin of the former, but punishes and avenges that of the latter. But this faith involves a hope of living to see better things; the justification of which the good man is sure must at last be attested by an objective judgment of God before the whole world, and the godly delivered from his sufferings. Hence the constant anxiety and restlessness of his conscience; the judgment passed upon him is ultimately to be gathered from the external world, and he can never be sure how it is to turn out. And a principle is also at stake the whole time, namely, the question whether godliness or ungodliness is right in its fundamental conviction. Each individual case at once affects the generality, the sufferings of one godly person touch all the godly. When he recovers and is saved, they triumph; when he succumbs, or seems to succumb, to death, they are cast down, unless in this case they should change their minds about him and hold him to be a hypocrite whom God has judged and unmasked. In the same way, they are all hurt at the prosperity of an ungodly man, and rejoice together at his fall, not from jealousy or pleasure in misfortune for its own sake, but because in the one case their faith is overturned, while in the other it is confirmed.

The tortures incident to this curious oscillation between believing and seeing are set forth in the most trenchant way in the Book of Job. Job, placed in an agonizing situation, condemned without hope to the death of sinners, and yet conscious of his godliness, demands vengeance for his blood unjustly shed. But the vengeance is to be executed on God, and in such a case who can be the avenger? There is no one but God Himself, and thus the striking thought arises, that God will be the champion against God of his innocence, after having first murdered it. From the God of the present he appeals to the God of the future; but the identity between these two is yet maintained, and even now the God who slays him is the sole witness of his innocence, in which the world and his friends have ceased to believe. God must be this now if He is to avenge him in the future. An inner antinomy is in this way impersonated; the view of the friends is one of which the sufferer himself cannot divest himself; hence the conflict in his soul. But, supported by the unconquerable power of his good conscience, he struggles till he frees himself from the delusion; he believes more firmly in the direct testimony of his conscience than in the evidence of facts and the world's judgment about him, and against the dreadful God of reality, the righteous God of faith victoriously asserts Himself.

Job in the end reaches the conclusion that he cannot understand God's ways. This is a negative expression of the position that he holds fast, in spite of all, to himself and to God; that is to say, that not outward experience, but inner feeling, is to decide. This inner feeling of the union of God with the godly meets us also in some of the Psalms, where, in spite of depression arising from untoward circumstances, it maintains itself as a reality which cannot be shaken, which temptations and doubts even tend to strengthen. It was a momentous step when the soul in its relations to God ventured to take its stand upon itself, to trust itself. This was an indirect product of prophecy, but one of not less importance than its direct product, the law. The prophets declared the revelation of God, which had authority for all, but along with this they had their own personal experience, and the subjective truth of which they thus became aware proved a more powerful solvent and emancipator than the objective one which formed the subject of their revelation. They preached the law to deaf ears, and laboured in vain to convert the people. But if their labour had produced no outward result, it had an inner result for them. Rejected by the people, they clung the more closely to Jehovah, in the conviction that the defeated cause was favoured by Him, that He was with them and not with the people. Especially with Jeremiah did prophecy, which is designed primarily to act on others, transform itself into an inner converse with the Deity, which lifted him above all the annoyances of his life. In this relation, however, there was nothing distinctively prophetical, just because it was a matter of the inner life alone, and was sufficient for itself; it was just the essence of the life of religion that the prophets thus brought to view and helped to declare itself. The experience of Jeremiah propagated itself and became the experience of religious Israel. This was the power by which Israel was enabled to rise again after every fall; the good conscience towards God, the profound sentiment of union with Him, proved able to defy all the blows of outward fortune. In this strength the servant, despised and slain, triumphed over the world; the broken and contrite heart was clothed and set on high with the life and power of the Almighty God. This divine spirit of assurance rises to its boldest expression in the 73rd Psalm: "Nevertheless I am continually with Thee; Thou holdest me by my right hand; Thou guidest me with Thy counsel, and drawest me after Thee by the hand. If I have Thee, I desire not heaven nor earth; if my flesh and my heart fail, Thou, God, art for ever the strength of my heart, and my portion."

The life surrendered is here found again in a higher life, without any expression of hope of a hereafter. In the Book of Job we do indeed find a trace of this hope, in the form that even after the death of the martyr, God may still find opportunity to justify him and pronounce him innocent; yet this idea is only touched on as a distant possibility, and is at once dropped. Certainly the position of that man is a grand one who can cast into the scale against death and devil his inner certainty of union with God— so grand indeed that we must in honesty be ashamed to repeat those words of the 73d Psalm. But the point of view is too high. The danger was imminent of falling from it down into the dust and seeking comfort and support in the first earthly experience that might offer, or, on the other hand, sinking into despair. Subjective feeling was not enough of itself to outbid the contradictions of nature; the feeling must take an objective form, a world other than this one, answering the demands of morality, must build itself up to form a contrast to the world actually existing. The merit of laying the foundations for this religious metaphysic which the time called for belongs, if not to the Pharisees themselves, at least to the circles from which they immediately proceeded. The main features of that metaphysic first appear in the Book of Daniel, where we find a doctrine of the last things. We have already spoken of the transition from the old prophecy to apocalypse. With the destruction of the nation and the cessation of historical life, hope was released from all obligation to conform to historical conditions; it no longer set up an aim to which even the present might aspire, but ran riot after an ideal, at the advent of which the historical development would be suddenly broken off. To be pious was all the Jews could do at the time; but it caused them bitter regret that they had no part in the government of the world, and in thought they anticipated the fulfilment of their wishes. These they raised to an ever-higher pitch in proportion as their antagonism to the heathen became more pronounced, and as the world became more hostile to them and they to the world. As the heathen empires stood in the way of the universal dominion of Israel, the whole of them together were regarded as one power, and this world-empire was then set over against the kingdom of God, *i.e.*, of Israel. The kingdom of God was entirely future; the fulfilling of the law did not prepare the way for it, but was only a statutory condition for its coming, not related to it inwardly as cause to effect. History was suddenly to come to a stop and cease. The Jews counted the days to the judgment; the judgment was the act by which God would at once realise all their wishes. The view thus taken of the world's history was a very comprehensive one and well worked out from its principle, yet of an entirely negative character; the further the world's history went wilfully away from its goal, the nearer did it unintentionally approach its goal. In this view, moreover, the earth always continued to be the place of hope; the kingdom of God was brought by the judgment into earthly history; it was on earth that the ideal was to be realised. A step further, and the struggle of the dualism of the earth was preluded in the skies by the angels, as the representatives of the different powers and nations. In this struggle a place was assigned to Satan; at first he was merely the accuser whom God Himself had appointed, and in this character he drew attention to the sins of the Jews before God's judgment-seat, and thereby delayed the judicial sentence in their favour; but ultimately (though this took place late, and is not met with in the Book of Daniel) he came to be the independent leader of the power opposed to God, God's cause being identified with that of the Jews. But as this prelude of the struggle took place in heaven, its result was also anticipated. The kingdom of God is on earth a thing of the future, but even now it is preserved in heaven with all its treasures, one day to descend from there to the earth. Heaven is the place where the good things of the future are kept, which are not and yet must be; that is its original and true signification. But the most important question came at last to be, how individuals were to have part in the glory of the future? How was it with the martyrs who had died in the expectation of the kingdom of God, before it came? The doctrine of the *zakuth* was formed: if their merit was not of service to themselves, it was yet of service to others. But this was a solution with which individualism could not rest content. And what of the ungodly? Were they to escape from wrath because they died before the day of judgment? It was necessary that the departed also should be allowed to take some part in the coming retribution. Thus there arose—it is remarkable how late and how slowly—the doctrine of the resurrection of the dead, that the kingdom of God might not be of service only to those who happened to be alive at the judgment. Yet at first this doctrine was only used to explain particularly striking cases. The Book of Daniel says nothing of a general resurrection, but speaks in fact only of a resurrection of the martyrs and a punishment of the wicked after death. With all this the resurrection is not the entrance to a life above the earth but to a second earthly life, to a world in which it is no longer the heathen but the Jews who bear rule and take the lead. Of a general judgment at the last day, or of heaven and hell in the Christian sense, the Jews know nothing, though these ideas might so easily have suggested themselves to them.

It is not easy to find points of view from which to pronounce on the character of Judaism. It is a system, but a practical system, which can scarcely be set forth in relation to one leading thought, as it is an irregular product of history. It lives on the stores of the past, but is not simply the total of what had been previously acquired; it is full of new impulses, and has an entirely different physiognomy from that of Hebrew antiquity, so much so that it is hard even to catch a likeness. Judaism is

414

everywhere historically comprehensible, and yet it is a mass of antinomies. We are struck with the free flight of thought and the deep inwardness of feeling which are found in some passages in the Wisdom and in the Psalms; but, on the other hand, we meet with a pedantic asceticism which is far from lovely, and with pious wishes the greediness of which is ill-concealed; and these unedifying features are the dominant ones of the system. Monotheism is worked out to its furthest consequences, and at the same time is enlisted in the service of the narrowest selfishness; Israel participates in the sovereignty of the One God. The Creator of heaven and earth becomes the manager of a petty scheme of salvation; the living God descends from His throne to make way for the law. The law thrusts itself in everywhere; it commands and blocks up the access to heaven; it regulates and sets limits to the understanding of the divine working on earth. As far as it can, it takes the soul out of religion and spoils morality. It demands a service of God, which, though revealed, may yet with truth be called a self-chosen and unnatural one, the sense and use of which are apparent neither to the understanding nor the heart. The labour is done for the sake of the exercise; it does no one any good, and rejoices neither God nor man. It has no inner aim after which it spontaneously strives and which it hopes to attain by itself, but only an outward one, namely, the reward attached to it, which might as well be attached to other and possibly even more curious conditions. The ideal is a negative one, to keep one's self from sin, not a positive one, to do good upon the earth; the morality is one which scarcely requires for its exercise the existence of fellow-creatures. Now pious exercises can dam up life and hold it in bounds, they may conquer from it more and more ground, and at last turn it into one great Sabbath, but they cannot penetrate it at the root. The occupation of the hands and the desire of the heart fall asunder. What the hands are doing has nothing in common with the earth, and bears no reference to earthly objects; but with the Jews the result of this is that their hope assumes a more worldly complexion. There is no connection between the Good One and goodness. There are exceptions, but they disappear in the system.

The Gospel develops hidden impulses of the Old Testament, but it is a protest against the ruling tendency of Judaism. Jesus understands monotheism in a different way from his contemporaries. They think in connection with it of the folly of the heathen and their great happiness in calling the true God their own; He thinks of the claims, not to be disputed or avoided, which the Creator makes on the creature. He feels the reality of God dominating the whole of life, He breathes in the fear of the Judge who requires an account for every idle word, and has power to destroy body and soul in hell. "No man can serve two masters; ye cannot serve God and Mammon; where your treasure is, there will your heart be also." This monotheism is not to be satisfied with stipulated services, how many and great soever; it demands the whole man, it renders doubleness of heart and hypocrisy impossible. Jesus casts ridicule on the works of the law, the washing of hands and vessels, the tithing of mint and cummin, the abstinence even from doing good on the Sabbath. Against unfruitful self-sanctification He sets up another principle of morality, that of the service of one's neighbour. He rejects that lofty kind of goodness, which says to father and mother, If I dedicate what I might give to you, that will be best even for you yourselves; He contends for the weightier matters in the law, for the common morality which sees its aim in the furtherance of the well-being of others, and which commends itself at once to the heart of every one. Just this natural morality of self-surrender does He call the law of God; that supernatural morality which thinks to outbid this, He calls the commandment of men. Thus religion ceases to be an art which the Rabbis and Pharisees understand better than the unlearned people which know nothing of the law. The arrogance of the school fares ill at the hands of Jesus; He will know nothing of the partisanship of piety or of the separateness of the godly; He condemns the practice of judging a man's value before God. Holiness shrinks from contact with sinners, but He helps the world of misery and sin; and there is no commandment on which He insists more than that of forgiving others their debts as one hopes for forgiveness himself from heaven. He is most distinctly opposed to Judaism in His view of the kingdom of heaven, not as merely the future reward of the worker, but as the present goal of effort, it being the supreme duty of man to help it to realise itself on earth, from the individual outwards. Love is the means, and the community of love the end.

Self-denial is the chief demand of the Gospel; it means the same thing as that repentance which must precede entrance into the kingdom of God. The will thereby breaks away from the chain of its own acts, and makes an absolutely new beginning not conditioned by the past. The causal nexus which admits of being traced comes here to an end, and the mutual action, which cannot be analysed, between God and the soul begins. Miracle does not require to be understood, only to be believed, in order to take place. With men it is impossible, but with God it is possible. Jesus not only affirmed this, but proved it in His own person. The impression of His personality convinced the disciples of the fact of the forgiveness of their sins and of their second birth, and gave them courage to believe in a new divine life and to live it. He had in fact lost His life and saved it; He could do as he would. He had escaped the limits of the race and the pains of self-seeking nature; He had found freedom and personality in God, who alone is master of Himself, and lifts those up to Himself who seek after Him.

Jesus works in the world and for the world, but with His faith He stands above the world and outside it. He can sacrifice Himself for the world because He asks nothing from the world, but has attained in retirement with God to equanimity and peace of soul. And further, the entirely supra-mundane position, at which Jesus finds courage and love to take an interest in the world, does not lead Him to anything strained or unnatural. He trusts God's Providence, and resigns Himself to His will, He takes up the attitude of a child towards Him, and loves best to call Him the Heavenly Father. The expression is simple, but the thing signified is new. He first knows Himself, not in emotion but in sober quietness, to be God's child; before Him no one ever felt himself to be so, or called himself so. He is the first-born of the Father, yet, according to His own view, a first-born among many brethren. For He stands in this relation to God not because His nature is unique, but because He is man; He uses always and emphatically this general name of the race to designate His own person. In finding the way to God for Himself He has opened it to all; along with the nature of God He has at the same time discovered in Himself the nature of man.

416

Eternity extends into the present with Him, even on earth He lives in the midst of the kingdom of God; even the judgment He sees inwardly accomplished here below in the soul of man. Yet He is far from holding the opinion that he who loves God aright does not desire that God should love him in return. He teaches men to bear the cross, but he does not teach that the cross is sweet and that sickness is sound. A coming reconciliation between believing and seeing, between morality and nature, everywhere forms the background of His view of the world; even if He could have done without it for His own person, yet it is a thing He takes for granted, as it is an objective demand of righteousness. So much is certain; for the rest the eschatology of the New Testament is so thoroughly saturated with the Jewish ideas of the disciples, that it is difficult to know what of it is genuine.

Jesus was so full of new and positive ideas that He did not feel any need for breaking old idols, so free that no constraint could depress Him, so unconquerable that even under the load of the greatest accumulations of rubbish He could still breathe. This ought ye to do, He said, and not to leave the other undone; He did not seek to take away one iota, but only to fulfil. He never thought of leaving the Jewish community. The Church is not His work, but an inheritance from Judaism to Christianity. Under the Persian domination the Jews built up an unpolitical community on the basis of religion. The Christians found themselves in a position with regard to the Roman Empire precisely similar to that which the Jews had occupied with regard to the Persian; and so they also founded, after the Jewish pattern, in the midst of the state which was foreign and hostile to them, and in which they could not feel themselves at home, a religious community as their true fatherland. The state is always the presupposition of the Church; but it was at first, in the case both of the Jewish and of the Christian Church, a foreign state. The original meaning of the Church thus disappeared when it no longer stood over against the heathen world-power, it having become possible for the Christians also to possess a natural fatherland in the nation. In this way it became much more difficult to define accurately the spheres of the state and the Church respectively, regarding the Church as an organisation, not as an invisible community of the faithful. The distinction of religious and secular is a variable one; every formation of a religious community is a step towards the secularisation of religion; the religion of the heart alone remains an inward thing. The tasks of the two competing organisations are not radically different in their nature; on the one side it may be said that had not the Christian religion found civil order already in existence, had it come, like Islam, in contact with the anarchy of Arabia instead of the Empire of Rome it must have founded not the Church, but the state; on the other side it is well known that the state has everywhere entered into possession of fields first reclaimed to cultivation by the Church. Now we must acknowledge that the nation is more certainly created by God than the Church, and that God works more powerfully in the history of the nations than in Church history. The Church, at first a substitute for the nation which was wanting, is affected by the same evils incident to an artificial cultivation as meet us in Judaism. We cannot create for ourselves our sphere of life and action; better that it should be a natural one, given by God. And yet it would be unjust to deny the permanent advantages of the differentiation of the two. The Church will always be able to work in advance for the state of the future. The present state unfortunately is in many respects only nothing more than a barrier to chaos; if the Church has still a task, it is that of preparing an inner unity of practical conviction, and awakening a sentiment, first in small circles, that we belong to each other.

Whether she is to succeed in this task is certainly the question. The religious individualism of the Gospel is, and must remain for all time, the true salt of the earth. The certainty that neither death nor life can separate us from the love of God drives out that fear which is opposed to love; an entirely supra-mundane faith lends courage for resultless self-sacrifice and resigned obedience on earth. We must succeed: *sursum corda*!

12. THE HELLENISTIC PERIOD.

Palestine fell into Alexander's possession in 332; after his death it had an ample share of the troubles arising out of the partition of his inheritance. In 320 it was seized by Ptolemy I., who on a Sabbath-day took Jerusalem; but in 3I5 he had to give way before Antigonus. Even before the battle of Ipsus, however, he recovered possession once more, and for a century thereafter Southern Syria continued to belong to the Egyptian crown, although the Seleucidae more than once sought to wrench it away.

In the priestly dynasty during the period of the Ptolemies, Onias I. ben Jaddua was succeeded by his son Simon I., after whom again came first his brothers Eleazar and Manasseh, and next his son Onias II.; the last-named was in his turn followed by his son Simon II., whose praises are sung by the son of Sirach (xlix. 14-16). At the side of the high priest stood the gerusia of the town of Jerusalem, as a council of state, including the higher ranks of the priesthood. The new sovereign power was at once stronger and juster than the Persian,—at least under the earlier Ptolemies; the power of the national government increased; to it was intrusted the business of raising the tribute.

As a consequence of the revolutionary changes which had taken place in the conditions of the whole East, the Jewish dispersion (diaspora) began vigorously to spread. It dated its beginning indeed from an earlier period,—from the time when the Jews had lost their land and kingdom, but yet, thanks to their religion, could not part with their nationality. They did not by any means all return from Babylon; perhaps the majority permanently settled abroad. The successors of Alexander (diadochi) fully appreciated this international element, and used it as a link between their barbarian and Hellenic populations. Everywhere they encouraged the settlement of Jews,—in Asia Minor, in Syria, and especially in Egypt. Alongside of the Palestinian there arose a Hellenistic Judaism which had its metropolis in Alexandria. Here, under Ptolemy I. and II., the Torah had already been translated into Greek, and around this sprung up a Jewish-Greek literature which soon became very extensive. At the court and in the army of the Ptolemies many Jews rose to prominent positions; everywhere they received the preference over, and everywhere they in consequence earned the hatred of, the indigenous population.

418

After the death of Ptolemy IV. (205) Antiochus III. attained the object towards which he and his predecessors had long been vainly striving; after a war protracted with varying success through several years, he succeeded at last in incorporating Palestine with the kingdom of the Seleucidae. The Jews took his side, less perhaps because they had become disgusted with the really sadly degenerate Egyptian rule, than because they had foreseen the issue of the contest, and preferred to attach themselves voluntarily to the winning side. In grateful acknowledgment, Antiochus confirmed and enlarged certain privileges of the "holy camp," *i.e.*, of Jerusalem (Josephus, Antiquities, xii. 3, 3). It soon, however, became manifest that the Jews had made but a poor bargain in this exchange. Three years after his defeat at Magnesia, Antiochus III. died (187), leaving to his son Seleucus IV. an immense burden of debt, which he had incurred by his unprosperous Roman war. Seleucus, in his straits, could not afford to be over-scrupulous in appropriating money where it was to be found: he did not need to be twice told that the wealth of the temple at Jerusalem was out of all proportion to the expenses of the sacrificial service. The sacred treasure accordingly made the narrowest possible escape from being plundered; Heliodorus, who had been charged by the king to seize it, was deterred at the last moment by a heavenly vision. But the Jews derived no permanent advantage from this.

It was a priest of rank, Simon by name, who had called the attention of the king to the temple treasure; his motive had been spite against the high priest Onias III., the son and successor of Simon II. The circumstance is one indication of a melancholy process of disintegration that was at that time going on within the hierocracy. The high-priesthood, although there were exceptional cases, such as that of Simon II., was regarded less as a sacred office than as a profitable princedom; within the ranks of the priestly nobility arose envious and jealous factions; personal advancement was sought by means of the favour of the overlord, who had something to say in the making of appointments. A collateral branch of the ruling family, that of the children of Tobias, had by means of the ill-gotten wealth of Joseph ben Tobias attained to a position of ascendancy, and competed in point of power with the high priest himself. It appears that the above-mentioned Simon, and his still more scandalous brother AIenelaus, also belonged to the Tobiadae, and, relying upon the support of their powerful party (Josephus, Antiquities, xii. 5, 1), cherished the purpose of securing the high-priesthood by the aid of the Syrian king.

The failure of the mission of Heliodorus was attributed by Simon to a piece of trickery on the part of Onias the high priest, who accordingly found himself called upon to make his own justification at court and to expose the intrigues of his adversary. Meanwhile Seleucus IV. died of poison (175), and Antiochus IV. Epiphanes did not confirm Onias in his dignity, but detained him in Antioch, while he made over the office to his brother Jason, who had offered a higher rent. Possibly the Tobiadae also had something to do with this arrangement; at all events, Menelaus was at the outset the right hand of the new high priest. To secure still further the favour of the king, Jason held himself out to be an enlightened friend of the Greeks, and begged for leave to found in Jerusalem a gymnasium and an ephebeum, and to be allowed to sell to the inhabitants there the rights of citizenship in Antioch,—a request which was readily granted.

The malady which had long been incubating now reached its acute phase. Just in proportion as Hellenism showed itself friendly did it present elements of danger to Judaism. From the periphery it slowly advanced towards the centre, from the diaspora to Jerusalem, from mere matters of external fashion to matters of the most profound conviction. *1* Especially did the upper and cultivated

*************************************** 1. The Hellenising fashion is amusingly exemplified in the Grecising of the Jewish names; *e.g.*, Alcimus = Eljakim, Jason = Jesus, Joshua; Menelaus = Menahem. **

classes of society begin to feel ashamed, in presence of the refined Greeks, of their Jewish singularity, and to do all in their power to tone it down and conceal it. In this the priestly nobility made itself conspicuous as the most secular section of the community, and it was the high priest who took the initiative in measures which aimed at a complete Hellenising of the Jews. He outdid every one else in paganism. Once he sent a considerable present for offerings to the Syrian Hercules on the occasion of his festival; but his messenger, ashamed to apply the money to such a purpose, set it apart for the construction of royal ships of war.

The friendship shown by Jason for the Greek king and for all that was Hellenic did not prevent Antiochus IV. from setting pecuniary considerations before all others. Menelaus, intrusted with the mission of conveying to Antioch the annual Jewish tribute, availed himself of the opportunity to promote his own personal interests by offering a higher sum for the high-priesthood, and having otherwise ingratiated himself with the king, gained his object (171). But though nominated, he did not find it quite easy to obtain possession of the post. The Tobiadae took his side, but the body of the people stuck to Jason, who was compelled to give way only when Syrian troops had been brought upon the scene. Menelaus had immediately, however, to encounter another difficulty, for he could not at once pay the amount of tribute which he had promised. He helped himself so far indeed by robbing the temple, but this landed him in new embarrassments. Onias III., who was living out of employment at Antioch, threatened to make compromising revelations to the king; he was, however, opportunely assassinated. The rage of the people against the priestly temple-plunderer now broke out in a rising against a certain Lysimachus, who at the instance of the absent Menelaus had made further inroads upon the sacred treasury. The Jews' defence before the king (at Tyre) on account of this uproar resolved itself into a grievous complaint against the conduct of Menelaus. His case was a bad one, but money again helped him out of his straits, and the extreme penalty of the law fell upon his accusers.

The feelings of the Jews with reference to this wolfish shepherd may easily be imagined. Nothing but fear of Antiochus held them in check. Then a report gained currency that the king had perished in an expedition against Egypt (170); and Jason, who meanwhile had found refuge in Ammanitis, availed himself of the prevailing current of feeling to resume his authority with the help of one thousand men. He was not able, however, to hold the position long, partly because he showed an unwise

420

vindictiveness against his enemies, partly (and chiefly) because the rumour of the death of Antiochus turned out to be false. The king was already, in fact, close at hand on his return from Egypt, full of anger at an insurrection which he regarded as having been directed against himself. He inflicted severe and bloody chastisement upon Jerusalem, carried off the treasures of the temple, and restored Menelaus, placing Syrian officials at his side. Jason fled from place to place, and ultimately died in misery at Lacedaemon.

The deepest despondency prevailed in Judaea; but its cup of sorrow was not yet full. Antiochus, probably soon after his last Egyptian expedition (168), sent Apollonius with an army against Jerusalem. He fell upon the unsuspecting city, disarmed the inhabitants and demolished the walls, but on the other hand fortified Acra, and garrisoned it strongly, so as to make it a standing menace to the whole country. Having thus made his preparations, he proceeded to carry out his main instructions. All that was religiously distinctive of Judaism was to be removed; such was the will of the king. The Mosaic cultus was abolished, Sabbath observance and the rite of circumcision prohibited, all copies of the Torah confiscated and burnt. In the desecrated and partially-destroyed temple pagan ceremonies were performed, and upon the great altar of burnt-offering a small altar to Jupiter Capitolinus was erected, on which the first offering was made on 25th Kislev 168. In the country towns also heathen altars were erected, and the Jews compelled, on pain of death, publicly to adore the false gods and to eat swine's flesh that had been sacrificed to idols.

The princes and grandees of the Jews had represented to Antiochus that the people were ripe for Hellenisation; and inasmuch as, apart from this, to reduce to uniformity the extremely motley constituents of his kingdom was a scheme that lay near his heart, he was very willing to believe them. That the very opposite was the case must of course have become quite evident very soon; but the resistance of the Jews taking the form of rebellious risings against his creatures, he fell upon the hopeless plan of coercion,—hopeless, for he could attain his end only by making all Judaea one vast graveyard. There existed indeed a pagan party; the Syrian garrison of Acra was partly composed of Jews who sold themselves to be the executioners of their countrymen. Fear also influenced many to deny their convictions; but the majority adhered firmly to the religion of their fathers. Jerusalem, the centre of the process of Hellenisation, was abandoned by its inhabitants, who made their escape to Egypt, or hid themselves in the country, in deserts and caves. The scribes in especial held fast by the law; and they were joined by the party of the Asidaeans (i.e., pious ones).

13. THE HASMONAEANS.

At first there was no thought of meeting violence with violence; as the Book of Daniel shows, people consoled themselves with thoughts of the immediate intervention of God which would occur in due time. Quite casually, without either plan or concert, a warlike opposition arose. There was a certain priest Mattathias, of the family of the Hasmonaeans, a man far advanced in life, whose home was in Modein, a little country town to the west of Jerusalem. Hither also the Syrian soldiers came to put the population to a positive proof of their change of faith; they insisted upon Mattathias leading the way. But he was steadfast in his refusal; and, when another Jew addressed himself before his eyes to the work of making the heathen offering, he killed him and the Syrian officer as well, and destroyed the altar. Thereupon he fled to the hill country, accompanied by his sons (Johannes Gaddi, Simon Thassi, Judas Maccabaeus, Eleazar Auaran, Jonathan Apphus) and other followers. But he resolved to defend himself to the last, and not to act as some other fugitives had done, who about the same time had allowed themselves to be surrounded and butchered on a Sabbath-day without lifting a finger. Thus he became the head of a band which defended the ancestral religion with the sword. They traversed the country, demolished the altars of the false gods, circumcised the children, and persecuted the heathen and heathenishly disposed. The sect of the Asidaeans also intrusted itself to their warlike protection (1Maccabees ii. 42).

Mattathias soon died and left his leadership to Judas Maccabaeus, by whom the struggle was carried on in the first instance after the old fashion; soon, however, it assumed larger dimensions, when regular armies were sent out against the insurgents. First Apollonius, the governor of Judaea, took the field; but he was defeated and fell in battle. Next came Seron, governor of Ccelesyria, who also was routed near Bethhoron (I66). Upon this Lysias, the regent to whom Antiochus IV., who was busied in the far east, had intrusted the government of Syria and the charge of his son, Antiochus Philopator, a minor, sent a strong force under the command of three generals. Approaching from the west, it was their design to advance separately upon Jerusalem, but Judas anticipated their plan and compelled them to quit the field (166). The regent now felt himself called on to interpose in person. Invading Judaea from the south, he encountered the Jews at Bethsur, who, however, offered an opposition that was not easily overcome; he was prevented from resorting to the last measures by the intelligence which reached him of the death of the king in Elymais (165).

The withdrawal of Lysias secured the fulfilment of the desires of the defenders of the faith in so far as it now enabled them to restore the Jerusalem worship to its previous condition. They lost no time in setting about the accomplishment of this. They were not successful indeed in wresting Acra from the possession of the Syrians, but they so occupied the garrison as to prevent it from interfering with the work of restoration. On 25th Kislev 165, the very day on which, three years before, "the abomination of desolation" had been inaugurated, the first sacrifice was offered on the new altar, and in commemoration of this the feast of the dedication was thenceforth celebrated.

As it was easy to see that danger still impended, the temple was put into a state of defence, as also was the town of Bethsur, where Lysias had been checked. But the favourable moment presented by the change of sovereign was made use of for still bolder attempts. Scattered over the whole of Southern Syria there were a number of Jewish localities on which the heathens now proceeded to wreak their vengeance.

For the purpose of rescuing these oppressed co-religionists, and of bringing them in safety to Judaea, the Maccabees made a series of excursions, extending in some cases as far as to Lebanon and Damascus. Lysias had his hands otherwise fully occupied, and perhaps did not feel much disposed to continue the fight on behalf of the cultus of Jupiter Capitolinus. Daily gaining in boldness, the Jews now took in hand also to lay regular siege to Acra. Then at last Lysias yielded to the pressure of Syrian and Jewish deputations and determined to take serious steps (162). With a large force he entered Judaea, again from the south, and laid siege to Bethsur. Judas vainly attempted the relief of the fortress; he sustained near Bethzachariah a defeat in which his brother Eleazar perished. Bethsur was unable to hold out, being short of provisions on account of the sabbatic year. The Syrians advanced next to Jerusalem and besieged the temple; it also was insufficiently provisioned, and would soon have been compelled to surrender, had not Lysias been again called away at the critical moment by other exigencies. A certain Philip was endeavouring to oust him from the regency; as it was necessary for him to have his hands free in dealing with this new enemy, he closed a treaty with the temple garrison and the people at large, in accordance with which at once the political subjection and the religious freedom of the Jews were to be maintained; Thus the situation as it had existed before Antiochus IV. was restored. Only no attempt was made to replace Menelaus as high priest and ethnarch; this post was to be filled by Alcimus.

The concessions thus made by Lysias were inevitable; and even King Demetrius I., son of Seleucus IV., who towards the end of 162 ascended the throne and caused both Lysias and his ward to be put to death, had no thought of interfering with their religious freedom. But the Maccabees desired something more than the *status quo ante*; after having done their duty they were disinclined to retire in favour of Alcimus, whose sole claim lay in his descent from the old heathenishly-disposed high-priestly family. Alcimus was compelled to invoke the assistance of the king, who caused him to be installed by Bacchides. He was at once recognised by the scribes and Asidaeans, for whom, with religious liberty, everything they wished had been secured; the claims to supremacy made by the Hasmonaeans were of no consequence to them. Doubtless the masses also would ultimately have quietly accepted Alcimus, who of course refrained from interference with either law or worship, had he not abused the momentary power he derived from the presence of Bacchides to take a foolish revenge. But the consequence of his action was that, as soon as Bacchides had turned his back, Alcimus was compelled to follow him. For the purpose of restoring him a Syrian army once more invaded Judaea under Nicanor (160), but first at Kapharsalama and afterwards at Bethhoron was defeated by Judas, and almost annihilated in the subsequent flight, Nicanor himself being among the slain (13th Adar = Nicanor's day). Judas was now at the acme of his prosperity; about this time he concluded his (profitless) treaty with the Romans. But disaster was impending. In the month of Nisan, barely a month after the defeat of Nicanor, a new Syrian army under Bacchides entered Judaea from the north; near Elasa, southward from Jerusalem, a decisive battle was fought which was lost by Judas, and in which he himself fell.

The religious war properly so called had already been brought once for all to an end by the convention of Lysias. If the struggle continued to be carried on, it was not for the faith but for the supremacy,—less in the interests of the community than in those of the Hasmonaeans. After the death of Judas the secular character which the conflict had assumed ever since 162 continually became more conspicuous. Jonathan Apphus fought for his house, and in doing so used thoroughly worldly means. The high-priesthood, *i.e.*, the ethnarchy, was the goal of his ambition. So long as Alcimus lived, it was far from his reach. Confined to the rocky fastnesses beside the Dead Sea, he had nothing for it but, surrounded by his faithful followers, to wait for better times. But on the death of Alcimus (159) the Syrians refrained from appointing a successor, to obviate the necessity of always having to protect him with military force. During the interregnum of seven years which followed, Jonathan again came more and more to the front, so that at last Bacchides concluded an armistice with him on the basis of the *status quo* (1Maccabees ix. 13). From his residence at Michmash Jonathan now exercised a *de facto* authority over the entire nation.

When accordingly Alexander Balas, a reputed son of Antiochus IV., rose against Demetrius, both rivals exerted themselves to secure the alliance of Jonathan, who did not fail to benefit by their competition. First of all, Demetrius formally recognised him as prince of Judah; in consequence of this he removed to Jerusalem, and expelled the heathen and heathenishly disposed, who continued to maintain a footing only in Acra and Bethsur. Next Alexander Balas conferred on him the title of "high priest of the nation and friend of the king;" in gratitude for which Jonathan went over to his side (152). He remained loyal, although Demetrius now made larger offers; he was justified by the event, for Demetrius I. had the worst of it and was slain (150). The victorious Balas heaped honours upon Jonathan, who maintained his fidelity, and fought successfully in his interests when in I47 Demetrius II., the son of Demetrius I., challenged a conflict. The high priest was unable indeed to prevent the downfall of Alexander in 145; but Demetrius II., won by presents, far from showing any hostility, confirmed him in his position in consideration of a tribute of 300 talents.

Jonathan was grateful to the king, as he showed by going with 3000 men to his aid against the insurgent Antiochenes. But when the latter drew back from his promise to withdraw the garrison from Acra, he went over to the side of Trypho, who had set up a son of Alexander Balas (Antiochus) as a rival. In the war which he now waged as Seleucid-strategus against Demetrius he succeeded in subduing almost the whole of Palestine. Meanwhile his brother Simon remained behind in Judaea, mastered the fortress of Bethsur, and resumed with great energy the siege of Acra. All this was done in the names of Antiochus and Trypho, but really of course in the interests of the Jews themselves. There were concluded also treaties with the Romans and Lacedaemonians, certainly not to the advantage of the Syrians.

Trypho sought now to get rid of the man whom he himself had made so powerful. He treacherously seized and imprisoned Jonathan in Ptolemais, and meditated an attack upon the leaderless country. But on the frontier Simon, the last remaining son of Mattathias, met him in force. All Trypho's efforts to break through proved futile; after skirting all Judaea from west to south, without being able to get clear of Simon, he at last withdrew to Peraea without having accomplished anything. On the person of Jonathan, whom he caused to be executed, he vented the spleen he felt on the discovery that the cause for which that prince had fought was able to gain the victory even when deprived of his help. Simon, in point of fact, was Jonathan's equal as a soldier and his superior as a ruler. He secured his frontier by means of fortresses, made himself master of Acra (141), and understood how to enable the people in time of peace to reap the advantages that result from successful war; agriculture, industry, and commerce (from the haven of Joppa) began to flourish vigorously. In grateful recognition of his services the high-priesthood and the ethnarchy were bestowed upon him as hereditary possessions by a solemn assembly of the people, "until a trustworthy prophet should arise."

Nominally the Seleucidae still continued to possess the suzerainty. Simon naturally had detached himself from Trypho and turned to Demetrius II., who confirmed him in his position, remitted all arrears of tribute, and waived his rights for the future (142). The friendship of Demetrius II. and of his successor Antiochus Sidetes with Simon, however, lasted only as long as Trypho still remained in the way. But, he once removed, Sidetes altered his policy. He demanded of Simon the surrender of Joppa, Gazara, and other towns, besides the citadel of Jerusalem, as well as payment of all tribute resting due. The refusal of these demands led to war, which in its earlier stages was carried on with success, but the scales were turned after the murder of Simon, when Sidetes in person took the field against John Hyrcanus, Simon's son and successor. Jerusalem capitulated; in the negotiations for peace the surrender of all the external possessions of the Jews was insisted upon; the suzerainty of the Syrians became once more a reality (135). But in 130 the powerful Antiochus Sidetes fell in an expedition against the Parthians, and the complications anew arising in reference to the succession to the Syrian throne placed Hyrcanus in a position to recover what he had lost and to make new acquisitions. He subjugated Samaria and Idumaea, compelling the inhabitants of the latter to accept circumcision. Like his predecessors, he too sought to secure the favour of the Romans, but derived no greater benefit from the effort than they had done. After a prosperous reign of thirty years he died in 105. By Josephus he is represented as a pattern of all that a pious prince ought to be; by the rabbins as representing a splendid high-priesthood. The darkness of the succeeding age lent a brighter colour to his image.

The external splendour of the Hasmonaean kingdom did not at once die away,—the downfall of the Seleucidae, which was its negative condition, being also a slow affair. Judah Aristobulus, the son of Hyrcanus, who reigned for only one year, was the first to assume the Greek title of royalty; Ituraea was subdued by him, and circumcision forced upon the inhabitants. His brother Jonathan (Jannaeus) Alexander (104-79), in a series of continual wars, which were never very prosperous, never-theless succeeded in adding the whole coast of Philistia (Gaza) as well as a great portion of Peraea to his hereditary dominions. 1

** 1. A number of half-independent towns and communes lay as tempting subjects of dispute between the Seleucidae, the Nabathaeans or Arabs of Petra, and the Jews. The background was

occupied   by   the   Parthians   and   the   Romans.
****

But the external enlargement of the structure was secured at the cost of its internal consistency.

From the time when Jonathan, the son of Mattathias, began to carry on the struggle no longer for the cause of God but for his own interests, the scribes and the Asidaeans, as we have seen, had withdrawn themselves from the party of the Maccabees There can be no doubt that from their legal standpoint they were perfectly right in contenting themselves, as they did, with the attainment of religious liberty, and in accepting Alcimus. The Hasmonaeans had no hereditary right to the high-priesthood, and their politics, which aimed at the establishment of a national monarchy, were contrary to the whole spirit and essence of the second theocracy. The presupposition of that theocracy was foreign domination; in no other way could its sacred—i.e., clerical— character be maintained. God and the law could not but be forced into the background if a warlike kingdom, retaining indeed the forms of a hierocracy, but really violating its spirit at every point, should ever grow out of a mere pious community. Above all, how could the scribes hope to retain their importance if temple and synagogue were cast into the shade by politics and clash of arms? But under the first great Hasmonaeans the zealots for the law were unable to force their way to the front; the enthusiasm of the people was too strong for them; they had nothing for it but to keep themselves out of the current and refuse to be swept along by it. Even under Hyrcanus, however, they gained more prominence, and under Jannaeus their influence upon popular opinion was paramount. For under the last-named the secularisation of the hierocracy no longer presented any attractive aspects; it was wholly repellent. It was looked upon as a revolting anomaly that the king, who was usually in the field with his army, should once and again assume the sacred mantle in order to perform the sacrifice on some high festival, and that his officers, profane persons as they were, should at the same time be holders of the highest spiritual offices. The danger which in all this threatened "the idea of Judaism" could not in these circumstances escape the observation of even the common people; for this idea was God and the law, not any earthly fatherland. The masses accordingly ranged themselves with ever-growing unanimity on the side of the Pharisees (i.e., the party of the scribes) as against the Sadducees (i.e., the Hasmonaean party). *1*

** 1. PRW# means "separated," and refers perhaps to the attitude of isolation taken by the zealots for the law during the interval between 162 and 105. CDWQY *(SADDOUKAIOS) comes from CDWQ* (SADDOUK, LXX.) the ancestor of the higher priesthood of Jerusalem (1Kings ii. 35; 1Samuel ii. 35; Ezekiel xliv. 15), and designates the governing nobility. The original character of the opposition, as it appeared under Jannaeus, changed entirely with the lapse of time, on account of the Sadducees' gradual loss of political power, till they fell at last to the condition of a sort of "fronde."

426

On one occasion, when Alexander Jannaeus had returned to Jerusalem at the feast of tabernacles, and was standing in his priestly vestments before the altar to sacrifice, he was pelted by the assembled crowd of worshippers with citrons from the green branches they carried. By the cruelty with which he punished this insult he excited the populace to the highest pitch, and, when he lost his army in the disaster of Gadara, rebellion broke out. The Pharisees summoned the Syrian king Demetrius Eucaerus; Jannaeus was worsted and fled into the desert. But as he wandered in helplessness there, the patriotism of the people and sympathy for the heir of the Maccabees suddenly awoke; nature proved itself stronger than that consistency which in the cause of the Divine honour had not shrunk from treason. The insurgents for the most part went over to the side of the fugitive king; the others he ultimately overpowered after a struggle which lasted through several years, Demetrius having withdrawn his intervention. The vengeance which he took on the Pharisees was a bloody one; their only escape was by voluntary exile. Thenceforward he had peace so far as they were concerned. His last years were occupied with the reacquisition of the conquests which he had been compelled to yield to the Arabs during the civil war. He died in the field at the siege of Ragaba in Peraea (79).

Under Queen Salome, his widow, matters were as if they had been specially arranged for the satisfaction of the Pharisees. The high-priesthood passed to Salome's son, Hyrcanus II.; she herself was only queen. In the management of external affairs her authority was absolute (Antiquities, xiii. 16, 6); in home policy she permitted the scribes to wield a paramount influence. The common assertion, indeed, that the synedrium was at that time practically composed of scribes, is inconsistent with the known facts of the case; the synedrium at that time was a political and not a scholastic authority. *1*

*********************************** 1. Kuenen, "Over de Samenstelling van het Sanhedrin," in Proceedings of Royal Netherl. Acad., 1866.
****

In its origin it was the municipal council of Jerusalem (so also the councils of provincial towns are called synedria, Mark xiii. 9), but its authority extended over the entire Jewish community; alongside of the elders of the city the ruling priests were those who had the greatest number of seats and votes. John Hyrcanus appears to have been the first to introduce some scribes into its composition; it is possible that Salome may have increased their number, but even so this high court was far from being changed into a college of scribes like that at Jamnia. If the domination of the Pharisees at this time is spoken of, the expression cannot be understood as meaning that they already held all the public offices, but only at most that the holders of those offices found it necessary to administer and to judge in their spirit and according to their fundamental principles.

The party of the Sadducees (consisting of the old Hasmonaean officers and officials, who were of priestly family indeed, but attached only slight importance to their priestly functions) at length lost all patience. Led by Aristobulus, the second son of

Jannaeus, the leaders of the party came to the palace, and begged the queen to dismiss them from the court and to send them into the provinces. There they were successful in securing possession of several fortresses 2 in preparation for insurrection, a favourable

** 2. Alexandrium, Coreae, and similar citadels, which were at that time of great importance for Palestine and Syria. **

opportunity for which they were watching. Such an opportunity occurred, it seemed to Aristobulus, as his mother lay on her death-bed. The commandants of the fortresses were at his orders, and by their assistance an army also, with which he accordingly advanced upon Jerusalem, and, on the death of Salome, made himself master of the situation (69). Hyrcanus was compelled to resign office. With this event the good understanding between the civil government and the Pharisees came to an end; the old antagonisms became active once more, and now began to operate for the advantage of a third party, the Idumaean Antipater, Hyrcanus's confidential friend. After the latter, aided by Antipater, had at length with great difficulty got himself into a position for asserting his rights against Aristobulus, the Pharisees could not do otherwise than rank themselves upon his side, and the masses joined them against the usurper. With the help of the Nabataean monarch the effort to restore the elder brother to the supreme authority would doubtless have succeeded had not the Romans procured relief for Aristobulus, besieged as he was in Jerusalem (65), though without thereby recognising his claims. Pompey continued to delay a decision on the controversy in 64 also when the rival claimants presented themselves before him at Damascus; he wished first to have the Nabataeans disposed of, and to have free access to them through Judaea. This hesitation roused the suspicions of Aristobulus; still he did not venture to take decisive action upon them. He closed the passes (to Mount Ephraim) against the Romans, but afterwards gave them up; he prepared Jerusalem for war, and then went in person to the Roman camp at Jericho, where he promised to open the gates of the city and also to pay a sum of money. But the Roman ambassadors found the gates barred, and had to return empty-handed. Aristobulus thereupon was arrested, and siege was laid to Jerusalem. The party of Hyrcanus, as soon as it had gained the upper hand, surrendered the town; but the supporters of Aristobulus took their stand in the temple, and defended it obstinately. In June 63 the place was carried by storm; Pompey personally inspected the Holy of Holies, but otherwise spared the religious feelings of the Jews. But he caused the chief promoters of the war to be executed, and carried Aristobulus and his family into captivity. He abolished the kingship, but restored the high-priestly dignity to Hyrcanus. The territory was materially reduced in area, and made tributary to the Romans; the city was occupied by a Roman garrison.

14. HEROD AND THE ROMANS.

Henceforward Roman intervention forms a constant disturbing factor in Jewish history. The struggle between the Pharisees and the Sadducees continued indeed to be carried on, but only because the momentum of their old feud was not yet

428

exhausted. The Pharisees in a sense had been victorious. While the two brothers were pleading their rival claims before Pompey, ambassadors from the Pharisees had made their appearance in Damascus to petition for the abolition of the kingship; this object had now to some extent been gained. Less ambiguous than the victory of the Pharisees was the fall of the Sadducees, who in losing the sovereignty of the Jewish state lost all real importance. But the intervention of the foreign element exercised its most powerful influence upon the temper of the lower classes. Though in times of peace the masses still continued to accept the guidance of the rabbins, their patriotism instantly burst into flame as soon as a pretender to the throne, belonging to the family of Aristobulus, appeared in Palestine. During the decennia which immediately followed, Jewish history was practically absorbed in vain attempts to restore the old Hasmonaean kingdom. Insurrections of steadily increasing dimensions were made in favour of Aristobulus, the representative of the national cause. For Hyrcanus was not regarded as a Hasmonaean at all, but merely as the creature of Antipater and the Romans. First, in the year 57, Alexander the son of Aristobulus broke into rebellion, then in 56 Aristobulus himself and his son Antigonus, and in 55 Alexander again. Antipater was never able to hold his own; Roman intervention was in every case necessary. The division of the Hasmonaean state into five "aristocracies" by Gabinius had no effect in diminishing the feeling of national unity cherished by the Jews of Palestine. Once again, after the battle of Carrhae, a rising took place, which Cassius speedily repressed.

In 49 the great Roman civil war broke out; Cæsar instigated Aristobulus against Antipater, who in common with the whole East had espoused the cause of Pompey. But Aristobulus was poisoned by the opposite party while yet in Italy, and about the same time his son Alexander was also put to death at Antioch; thus the danger to Antipater passed away. After the battle of Pharsalus he went over to Caesar's side, and soon after rendered him an important service by helping him out of his difficulties at Alexandria. By this means he earned the good-will of Cæsar towards the whole body of the Jews and secured for himself (or Hyrcanus) a great extension of power and of territory. The five "synedria" or "aristocracies" of Gabinius were superseded, the most important conquest of the Hasmonaeans restored, the walls of Jerusalem, which Pompey had razed, rebuilt.

However indisputable the advantages conferred by the rule of Antipater, the Jews could not forget that the Idumaean, in name of Hyrcanus, the rightful heir of the Hasmonaeans, was in truth setting up an authority of his own. The Sadducaean aristocracy in particular, which formerly in the synedrium had shared the supreme power with the high priest, endeavoured to restore reality once more to the nominal ascendancy which still continued to be attributed to the ethnarch and the synedrium. "When the authorities (hoi 'en telei) of the Jews saw how the power of Antipater and his sons was growing, their disposition towards him became hostile" (Josephus, Antiquities, xiv. 9, 3). They were specially jealous of the youthful Herod, to whom Galilee had been entrusted by his father. On account of the arbitrary execution of a robber chief Ezechias, who perhaps had originally been a Hasmonaean partisan, they summoned him before the synedrium, under the impression that it was not yet too late to remind him that he was after all but a servant. But the defiant demeanour of the culprit, and a threatening missive which at the same time arrived from Sextus

Cæsar demanding his acquittal, rendered his judges speechless, nor did they regain their courage until they had heard the stinging reproaches of Sameas the scribe. Yet the aged Hyrcanus, who did not comprehend the danger that was threatening himself, postponed judgment upon Herod, and gave him opportunity to withdraw. Having been appointed strategus of Coelesyria by Sextus Cæsar in the meanwhile he soon afterwards appeared before Jerusalem at the head of an army, and the authorities were compelled to address themselves in a conciliatory manner to his father and to Phasael his brother in order to secure his withdrawal.

The attempt to crush the serpent which had thus effected a lodgment in the Hasmonaean house came too late. The result of it simply was that the Herodians had now the advantage of being able to distinguish between Hyrcanus and his "evil counsellors." From that moment the downfall of the Sadducaean notables was certain. It was of no avail to them that after the battle of Philippi (42) they accused Herod and Phasael (Antipater having been murdered in 43) before Antony of having been helpful in every possible way to Cassius; Antony declared himself in the most decisive manner for the two brothers. In their despair—for properly speaking they were not national fanatics but only egoistic politicians—they ultimately made common cause with Antigonus the son of Aristobulus, and threw themselves into the arms of the Parthians, perceiving the interests of the Romans and of Herod to be inseparable (40). Fortune at first seemed to have declared in favour of the pretender. The masses unanimously took his side; Phasael committed suicide in prison; with a single blow Herod was stripped of all his following and made a helpless fugitive. He took refuge in Rome, however, where he was named king of Judaea by the senate, and after a somewhat protracted war he finally, with the help of the legions of Sosius, made himself master of Jerusalem (37). The captive Antigonus was beheaded at Antioch.

King Herod began his reign by reorganising the synedrium; he ordered the execution of forty-five of its noblest members, his most zealous opponents. These were the Sadducaean notables who long had headed the struggle against the Idumaean interlopers. Having thus made away with the leaders of the Jerusalem aristocracy, he directed his efforts to the business of corrupting the rest. He appointed to the most important posts obscure individuals, of priestly descent, from Babylon and Alexandria, and thus replaced with creatures of his own the old aristocracy. Nor did he rest content with this; in order to preclude the possibility of any independent authority ever arising alongside of his own, he abolished the life-tenure of the high-priestly office, and brought it completely under the control of the secular power. By this means he succeeded in relegating the Sadducees to utter insignificance. They were driven out of their native sphere—the political—into the region of theoretical and ecclesiastical discussion, where they continued, but on quite unequal terms, their old dispute with the Pharisees.

It was during the period of Herod's activity that the Pharisees, strictly speaking, enjoyed their greatest prosperity (Sameas and Abtalion, Hillel and Shammai); in the synedrium they became so numerous as almost to equal the priests and elders. Quite consistently with their principles they had abstained from taking any part in the life

430

and death struggle for the existence of the national state. Their leaders had even counselled the fanatical defenders of Jerusalem to open the gates to the enemy; for this service they were treated with the highest honour by Herod. He made it part of his general policy to favour the Pharisees (as also the sect of the Essenes, insignificant though it was), it being his purpose to restrict the national life again within those purely ecclesiastical channels of activity which it had abandoned since the Maccabaean wars. However reckless his conduct in other respects, he was always scrupulously careful to avoid wounding religious susceptibilities (Antiquities, xiv. 16, 3). But although the Pharisees might be quite pleased that the high-priesthood and the kingship were no longer united in one and the same person, and that interest in the law again overshadowed interest in politics, the populace for their part could never forgive Herod for overthrowing the old dynasty. That he himself, at least in religious profession, was a Jew did not improve his position, but rather made it worse. It was not easy for him to stifle the national feeling after it had once been revived among the Jews; they could not forget the recent past, and objected to being thrust back into the time when foreign domination was endured by them as a matter of course. The Romans were regarded in quite a different light from that in which the Persians and the Greeks had been viewed, and Herod was only the client of the Romans.

His greatest danger seemed to arise from the still surviving members of the Hasmonaean family, to whom, as is easily understood, the national hopes clung. In the course of the earlier years of his reign he removed every one of them from his path, beginning with his youthful brother-in-law Aristobulus (35), after whom came his old patron Hyrcanus II. (30), then Mariamne his wife (29), and finally his stepmother Alexandra (28), the daughter of Hyrcanus and the widow of Alexander Aristobuli. Subsequently, in 25, he caused Costobarus and the sons of Babas to be executed. While thus occupied with domestic affairs, Herod had constant trouble also in his external relations, and each new phase in his political position immediately made itself felt at home. In the first instance he had much to suffer from Cleopatra, who would willingly have seen Palestine reduced under Egyptian domination once more, and who actually succeeded in inducing Antony to take from Herod several fair and valuable provinces of his realm. Next, his whole position was imperilled by the result of the battle of Actium; he had once more ranged himself upon the wrong side. But his tact did not fail him in winning Octavianus, as before it had made Antony his friend. In fact he reaped nothing but advantage from the great overturn which took place in Roman affairs; it rid him of Cleopatra, a dangerous enemy, and gave him in the new imperator a much better master than before.

During the following years he had leisure to carry out those splendid works of peace by which it was his aim to ingratiate himself with the emperor. He founded cities and harbours (Antipatris, Caesarea), constructed roads, theatres, and temples, and subsidised far beyond his frontier all works of public utility. He taxed the Jews heavily, but in compensation promoted their material interests with energy and discretion, and built for them, from 20 or 19 B.C. onwards, the temple at Jerusalem. To gain their sympathies he well knew to be impossible. Apart from the Roman legions at his back his authority had its main support in his fortresses and in his system of espionage.

But just as the acme of his splendour had been reached, he himself became the instrument of a terrible vengeance for the crimes by which his previous years had been stained; as executioner of all the Hasmonaeans, he was now constrained to be the executioner of his own children also. His suspicious temper had been aroused against his now grown-up sons by Mariamne, whose claims through their mother to the throne were superior to his own; his brother Pheroras and his sister Salome made it their special business to fan his jealousy into flame. To show the two somewhat arrogant youths that the succession was not so absolutely secure in their favour as they were supposing, the father summoned to his court Antipater, the exiled son of a former marriage. Antipater, under the mask of friendship, immediately began to carry on infamous intrigues against his half brothers, in which Pheroras and Salome unconsciously played into his hands. For years he persevered alike in favouring and unfavouring circumstances with his part, until at last, by the machinations of a Lacedemonian, Eurycles, who had been bribed, Herod was induced to condemn the sons of Mariamne at Berytus, and cause them to be strangled (Samaria, 7-6 B.C.). Not long afterwards a difference between Antipater and Salome led to the exposure of the former. Herod was compelled to drain the cup to the dregs; he was not spared the knowledge that he had murdered his children without a cause. His remorse threw him into a serious illness, in which his strong constitution wrestled long with death. While he lay at Jericho near his end he gave orders for the execution of Antipater also; and to embitter the joy of the Jews at his removal he caused their elders to be shut up together in the hippodrome at Jericho with the injunction to butcher them as soon as he breathed his last, that so there might be sorrow throughout the land. The latter order, however, was not carried out.

His death (4 B.C.) gave the signal for an insurrection of small beginnings which gradually spread until it ultimately infected all the people; it was repressed by Varus with great cruelty. Meanwhile Herod's connexions were at Rome disputing about the inheritance. The deceased king (who was survived by several children of various marriages) had made a will, which was substantially confirmed by Augustus. By it his son Philip received the northern portion of the territory on the east of the Jordan along with the district of Paneas (Caesarea Philippi); his thirty-seven years' reign over this region was happy. Another son, Herod Antipas, obtained Galilee and Peraea; he beautified his domains with architectural works (Sepphoris, Tiberias; Livias, Machaerus), and succeeded by his fox-like policy in ingratiating himself with the emperors, particularly with Tiberius, for that very cause, however, becoming odious to the Roman provincial officials. The principal heir was Archelaus, to whom Idumaea, Judaea, and Samaritis were allotted; Augustus at first refused him the title of king. Archelaus had experienced the greatest difficulty in carrying through his claims before the emperor in face of the manifold oppositions of his enemies; the vengeance which he wreaked upon his subjects was so severe that in 6 A.D. a Jewish and Samaritan embassy besought the emperor for his deposition. Augustus assented, banishing Archelaus to Vienne, and putting in his place a Roman procurator. Thenceforward Judaea continued under procurators, with the exception of a brief interval (41-44 A.D.), during which Herod Agrippa I. united under his sway all the dominions of his grandfather. 1

1. Agrippa was the grandson of Mariamne through Aristobulus. Caligula, whose friendship he had secured in Rome, bestowed upon him in 37 the dominions of Philip with the title of king, and afterwards the tetrarchy of Antipas, whom he deposed and banished to Lugdunum (39). Claudius added the possessions of Archelaus. But the kingdom was again taken away from his son Agrippa II. (44), who, however, after the death of his uncle, Herod of Chalcis, obtained that principality for which at a later period (52) the tetrarchy of Philip was substituted. His sister Berenice is known as the mistress of Titus; another sister, Drusilla, was the wife of the procurator Felix. The descendants of Mariamne through Alexander held for some time an Armenian principality.

The termination of the vassal kingship resulted in manifest advantage to the Sadducees. The high priest and synedrium again acquired political importance; they were the responsible representatives of the nation in presence of the suzerain power, and conceived themselves to be in some sort lords of land and people (John xi. 48). For the Pharisees the new state of affairs appears to have been less satisfactory. That the Romans were much less oppressive to the Jews than the rulers of the house of Herod was a consideration of less importance to them than the fact that the heathen first unintentionally and then deliberately were guilty of the rudest outrages upon the law, outrages against which those sly half-Jews had well understood how to be on their guard. It was among the lower ranks of the people, however, that hatred to the Romans had its proper seat. On the basis of the views and tendencies which had long prevailed there, a new party was now formed, that of the Zealots, which did not, like the Pharisees, aim merely at the fulfilment of all righteousness, *i.e.*, of the law, and leave everything else in the hands of God, but was determined to take an active part in bringing about the realisation of the kingdom of God (Josephus, Antiquities, xviii. 1, 1).

As the transition to the new order of things was going on, the census of Quirinius took place (6-7 A.D.); it occasioned an immense excitement, which, however, was successfully allayed. On the withdrawal of Quirinius, Coponius remained behind as procurator of Judaea; he was followed, under Augustus, by Marcus Ambivius and Annius Rufus; under Tiberius, by Valerius Gratus (15-26 A.D.) and Pontius Pilatus (26-36 A.D.); under Caligula, by Marcellus (36-37) and Marullus (37-41 A.D.). The procurators were subordinate to the imperial legati of Syria; they resided in Caesarea, and visited Jerusalem on special occasions only. They had command of the military, and their chief business was the maintenance of the peace and the care of the revenue. They interested themselves in affairs of religion only in so far as these had a political side; the temple citadel Antonia was constantly garrisoned with a cohort. The administration of justice appears to have been left to a very considerable extent in the hands of the synedrium, but it was not allowed to give effect to any capital sentence. At the head of the native authorities stood at this time not so much the actual high priest as the college of the chief priests. The actual office of high priest had lost its political importance in consequence of the frequency with which its holders were changed; thus, for example, Annas had more influence than Caiaphas.

433

The principle of interfering as little as possible with the religious liberty of the Jews was rudely assailed by the Emperor Caius, who like a second Antiochus, after various minor vexations, gave orders that his image should be set up in the temple of Jerusalem as in others elsewhere. It was entirely through the courage and tact of the Syrian governor P. Petronius that the execution of these orders was temporarily postponed until the emperor was induced by Agrippa I. to withdraw them. Caius soon afterwards died, and under the rule of Agrippa I., to whom the government of the entire kingdom of his grandfather was committed by Claudius, the Jews enjoyed much prosperity; in every respect the king was all they could wish. This very prosperity seems, however, to have caused them fresh danger. For it made them feel the government by procurators, which was resumed after the death of Agrippa I., to be particularly hard to bear, whatever the individual characters of these might be. They were Cuspius Fadus (from 44, under whom Theudas), Tiberius Alexander (the Romanised nephew of Philo, till 48), Cumanus (48-52, under whom the volcano already began to give dangerous signs of activity), and Felix (52-60). Felix, who has the honour to be pilloried in the pages of Tacitus, contrived to make the dispeace permanent. The influence of the two older parties, both of which were equally interested in the maintenance of the existing order, and in that interest were being drawn nearer to each other, diminished day by day. The masses broke loose completely from the authority of the scribes; the ruling nobility adapted itself better to the times; under the circumstances which then prevailed, it is not surprising that they became thoroughly secular and did not shrink from the employment of directly immoral means for the attainment of their ends. The Zealots became the dominant party. It was a combination of noble and base elements; superstitious enthusiasts (Acts xxi. 38) and political assassins, the so-called sicarii, were conjoined with honest but fanatical patriots. Felix favoured the sicarii in order that he might utilise them; against the others his hostility raged with indiscriminating cruelty, yet without being able to check them. The anarchy which he left behind him as a legacy was beyond the control of his able successor Porcius Festus (60-62), and the last two procurators, Albinus (62-64) and Gessius Florus, acted as if it had been their special business to encourage and promote it. All the bonds of social order were dissolved; no property was secure; the assassins alone prospered, and the procurators went shares with them in the profits.

It was inevitable that deep resentment against the Romans should be felt in every honest heart. At last it found expression. During his visit to Jerusalem in May 66 Florus laid hands upon the temple treasure; the Jews allowed themselves to go so far as to make a joke about it, which he avenged by giving over a portion of the city to be plundered, and crucifying a number of the inhabitants. He next insisted upon their kissing the rod, ordering that a body of troops which was approaching should be met and welcomed. At the persuasion of their leaders the Jews forced themselves even to this; but a constant succession of fresh insults and cruelties followed, till patience was quite exhausted at last, and in a violent street fight the Romans were so handled that the procurator withdrew from the town, leaving only the cohort in Antonia. Once again was an attempt at pacification made by Agrippa II., who hastened from Alexandria with this purpose, but the Jews could not bring themselves to make submission to Gessius Florus. It so happened that at this juncture the fortress of Masada on the Dead Sea fell into the hands of the Zealots; the courage of the party of action rose, and at the instance of the hot-headed Eleazar the son of Ananias, a man, still young, of highest priestly family, the sacrifice on behalf of the emperor was discontinued, *ie.*, revolt was declared. But the native authorities continued opposed to a war. At their request King Agrippa sent soldiers to Jerusalem; at first they appeared to have some effect, but ultimately they were glad to make their escape in safety from the city. The cohort in Antonia was in like manner unable to hold its own; freedom was given it to withdraw; but, contrary to the terms of capitulation, it was put to the sword. The war party now signalised its triumph over all elements of opposition from within by the murder of the high priest Ananias.

A triumph was gained also over the outer foe. The Syrian legate, Cestius Gallus, appeared before Jerusalem in the autumn of 66, but after a short period raised the siege; his deliberate withdrawal was changed into a precipitate flight in an attack made by the Jews at Bethhoron. The revolt now spread irresistibly through all ranks and classes of the population, and the aristocracy found it expedient itself to assume the leadership. An autonomous government was organised, with the noblest members of the community at its head; of these the most important was the high priest Ananus.

Meanwhile Nero entrusted the conduct of the Jewish war to Vespasian, his best general. In the spring of 67 he began his task in Galilee, where the historian Josephus had command of the insurgents. The Jews entirely distrusted him and he them; in a short time the Romans were masters of Galilee, only a few strong places holding out against them. Josephus was besieged in Jotapata, and taken prisoner; the other places also were unable to hold out long. Such of the champions of freedom in Galilee as escaped betook themselves to Jerusalem; amongst these was the Zealot leader John of Giscala. There they told the story of their misfortunes, of which they laid the blame upon Josephus, and upon the aristocratic government as having no heart for the common cause and having treachery for their motto. The Zealots now openly aimed at the overthrow of the existing government, but Ananus bravely withstood them, and pressed so hard on them that they summoned the Idumaeans into the city to their aid. These honourable fanatics indeed withdrew again as soon as they had discovered that they were being used for sinister designs; but in the meanwhile they had accomplished the work of the Zealots. The old magistracy of Jerusalem was destroyed, Ananus with the heads of the aristocracy and very many other respectable citizens put to death. The radicals, for the most part not natives of the city, came into power; John of Giscala at their head tyrannized over the inhabitants.

While these events were taking place in Jerusalem, Vespasian had subdued the whole country, with the exception of one or two fortresses. But as he was setting about the siege of the capital, tidings arrived of the death of Nero, and the offensive was discontinued. For almost two years (June 68 to April 70), with a short break, war was suspended. When Vespasian at the end of this period became emperor, he entrusted to Titus the task of reducing Jerusalem. There in the interval the internal struggle had been going on, even after the radicals had gained the mastery. As a counterpoise to John of Giscala the citizens had received the guerilla captain Simon bar Giora into the city; the two were now at feud with each other, but were alike in their rapacity towards the citizens. John occupied the temple, Simon the upper city lying over against it on the west. For a short time a third entered into competition with the two rivals, a certain Eleazar who had separated from John and established himself in the inner temple. But just as Titus was beginning the siege (Easter, 70) John contrived to get rid of this interloper.

Titus attacked from the north. After the lower city had fallen into his hands, he raised banks with a view to the storm of the temple and the upper city. But the defenders, who were now united in a common cause, taught him by their vigorous resistance that his object was not to be so quickly gained. He therefore determined to reduce them by famine, and for this end completely surrounded the city with a strong wall. In the beginning of July he renewed the attack, which he directed in the first instance against the temple. The tower of Antonia fell on the 5th, but the temple continued to beheld notwithstanding; until the 17th the daily sacrifice continued to be offered. The Romans succeeded in gaining the outer court in August only. To drive them out, the Jews in the night of August 10-11 made a sortie, but were compelled to retire, the enemy forcing their way behind them into the inner court. A legionary flung a firebrand into an annexe of the temple, and soon the whole structure was in flames. A terrible slaughter of the defenders ensued, but John with a determined band succeeded in cutting his way out, and by means of the bridge over the Tyropceon valley made his escape into the upper city.

No attack had as yet been directed against this quarter; but famine was working terrible ravages among the crowded population. Those in command, however, refused to capitulate unless freedom to withdraw along with their wives and children were granted. These terms being withheld, a storm, after the usual preparations on the part of the Romans, took place. The resistance was feeble; the strong towers were hardly defended at all; Simon bar Giora and John of Giscala now thought only of their personal safety. In the unprotected city the Roman soldiers spread fire and slaughter unchecked (September 7, 70).

Of those who survived also some were put to death; the rest were sold or carried off to the mines and amphitheatres. The city was levelled with the ground; the tenth legion was left behind in charge. Titus took with him to Rome for his triumphal procession Simon bar Giora and John of Giscala, along with seven hundred other prisoners, also the sacred booty taken from the temple, the candlestick, the golden table, and a copy of the Torah. He was slightly premature with his triumph; for some time elapsed, and more than one bloody battle was necessary before the rebellion was completely stifled. It did not come wholly to an end until the fall of Masada (April 73).

I5. THE RABBINS.

Even now Palestine continued for a while to be the centre of Jewish life, but only in order to prepare the way for its transition into thoroughly cosmopolitan forms. The development of thought sustained no break on account of the sad events which had taken place, but was only directed once more in a consistent manner towards these objects which had been set before it from the time of the Babylonian exile. On the ruins of the city and of the temple the Pharisaic Judaism which rests upon the law and the school celebrated its triumph. National fanaticism indeed was not yet extinguished, but it burnt itself completely out in the vigorous insurrection led by Simeon bar Koziba (Bar Cochebas, 132-135). That a conspicuous rabbin, Akiba, should have taken part in it, and have recognised in Simeon the Messiah, was an inconsistency on his part which redounds to his honour.

Inasmuch as the power of the rabbins did not depend upon the political or hierarchical forms of the old commonwealth, it survived the fall of the latter. Out of what hitherto had been a purely moral influence something of an official position now grew. They formed themselves into a college which regarded itself as a continuation of the old synedrium, and which carried forward its name. At first its seat was at Jamnia, but it soon removed to Galilee, and remained longest at Tiberias. The presidency was hereditary in the family of Hillel, with the last descendants of whom the court itself came to an end. *1*

** 1. The following is the genealogy of the first Nasi:—Gamaliel ben Simeon (Josephus, Vita, 38) ben Gamaliel (Acts v. 34, xxii. 3) ben simeon ben Hillel. The name Gamaliel was that which occurred most frequently among the patriarchs; see Codex Theod. xvi. 8, 22. **

The respect in which the synedrial president was held rapidly increased; like Christian patriarchs under Mahometan rule, he was also recognised by the imperial government as the municipal head of the Jews of Palestine, and bore the secular title of the old high priests (nasi, ethnarch, patriarch). Under him the Palestinian Jews continued to form a kind of state within a state until the 5th century. From the non-Palestinian Jews he received offerings of money. (Compare Gothofredus on Codex Theod., xvi. 8, "De Judaeis;" and Morinus, Exer. Bibl., ii. exerc. 3, 4).

The task of the rabbins was so to reorganise Judaism under the new circumstances that it could continue to assert its distinctive character. What of external consistency had been lost through the extinction of the ancient commonwealth required to be compensated for by an inner centralisation proportionately stronger. The separation from everything heathenish became more pronounced than before; the use of the Greek language was of necessity still permitted, but at least the Septuagint was set aside by Aquila (Cod. Justinian., Nov. 146) inasmuch as it had now become the Christian Bible. For to this period also belongs the definitive separation between the synagogue and the church; henceforward Christianity could no longer figure as a Jewish sect. Intensified exclusiveness was accompanied by increased internal

437

stringency. What at an earlier period had still remained to some extent fluid now became rigidly fixed; for example, an authentic text of the canon was now established, and at the same time the distinction between canon and apocrypha sharply drawn. The old tendency of the scribes to leave as little as possible free to the individual conscience, but to bring everything within the scope of positive ordinance, now celebrated its greatest triumphs. It was only an apparent movement in the direction of liberty, if regulations which had become quite impossible were now modified or cancelled. The most influential of the rabbins were indeed the least solicitous about the maintenance of what was old, and had no hesitation in introducing numerous and thoroughgoing innovations; but the conservatives R. Eliezer ben Hyrcanus and R. Ishmael ben Elisha were in truth more liberal-minded than the leaders of the party of progress, notably than R. Akiba. Even the Ultramontanes have never hesitated at departures from the usage of the ancient and mediaeval church; and the Pharisaic rabbins were guided in their innovations by liberal principles no more than they. The object of the new determinations was simply to widen the domain of the law in a consistent manner, to bring the individual entirely under the iron rule of system. But the Jewish communities gave willing obedience to the hierarchy of the rabbins; Judaism had to be maintained, cost what it might. That the means employed were well adapted to the purpose of maintaining the Jews as a firmly compacted religious community even after all bonds of nationality had fallen away cannot be doubted. But whether the attainment of this purpose by incredible exertion was a real blessing to themselves and the world may very well be disputed.

One consequence of the process of intellectual isolation and of the effort to shape everything in accordance with hard and fast rules and doctrines was the systematisation and codification of juristic and ritual tradition, a work with which a beginning was made in the century following the destruction of Jerusalem. Towards the end of the 2nd century the Pharisaic doctrine of Hillel as it had been further matured by Akiba was codified and elevated to the position of statute law by the patriarch Rabban Judah the Holy (Mishna). *1*

************************************** 1. The Mishna succeeded almost, but not quite, in completely doing away with all conflicting tendencies. At first the heterodox tradition of that time was also committed to writing (R. Ishmael ben Elisha) and so handed down,—in various forms (col]ection of the Baraithas, that is, of old precepts which had not been received into the Mishna, in the Tosephtha). Nor did the active opposition altogether die out even at a later period; under favouring circumstances it awoke to new life in Karaism, the founder of which, Anan ben David, lived in Babylonia in the middle of the 8th century. **********************************

But this was only the first stage in the process of systematising and fixing tradition. The Mishna became itself the object of rabbinical comment and supplement; the Tannaim, whose work was registered in the Mathnetha (Mishna, DEUTERWSIS = doctrine), were followed by the Amoraim, whose work in turn took permanent shape in the Gemara (= doctrine). The Palestinian Gemara was reduced to writing in

438

perhaps the 4th or 5th century; unfortunately it has been preserved to us only in part, but appears to have reached the Middle Ages in a perfect state (compare Schiller-Szinessy in the Academy, 1878, p. 170 seq.). Even thus the process which issued in the production of the Talmud was not yet completed; the Babylonian Amoraim carried it forward for some time longer, until at last at the rise of Islam the Babylonian Gemara was also written down.

In the sth century Palestine ceased to be the centre of Judaism. Several circumstances conspired to bring this about. The position of the Jews in the Roman Empire had changed for the worse with the elevation of Christianity to be the religion of the state; the large autonomy which until then they had enjoyed in Palestine was now restricted; above all, the family of the Patriarchs, which had come to form a veritable dynasty, became extinct. *1*

** 1. Compare Gothofredus on Cod. Theod., xvi. 8, 29, ad voc. "post excessum patriarcharum."
****

But this did not make an end of what may be called the Jewish church-state; henceforward it had its home in Babylonia. From the period of the exile, a numerous and coherent body of Jews had continued to subsist there; the Parthians and Sassanidae granted them self-government; at their head was a native prince (Resh Galutha,—can be clearly traced from 2nd century A.D. onwards) who, when the Palestinian patriarchate came to an end, was left without a rival. This remarkable relic of a Jewish commonwealth continued to exist until the time of the Abassides. *2*

************************************* 2. See Noeldeke, Tabari; 68, 118, and Kremer, Culturgeschichte des Orients unter den Chalifen, i. 188, ii. 176.
****

Even as early as the beginning of the 3rd century A.D. certain rabbins, at their head Abba Areka (Rab), had migrated from Palestine and founded a settlement for learning in the law in Babylonia. The schools there (at Pumbeditha, Sora, Nahardea) prospered greatly, vied with those of Palestine, and continued to exist after the cessation of the latter, when the patriarchate became extinct; thus they had the last word in the settlement of doctrine.

Alongside of the settlement of tradition went another task, that of fixing the letters of the consonantal text of the Bible (by the Massora), its vowel pronunciation (by the punctuation), and its translation into the Aramaic vernacular (Targum). Here also the Babylonians came after the Palestinians, yet of this sort of erudition Palestine continued to be the headquarters even after the 5th century.

With this task—that of attaining to the greatest possible conformity to the letter and of continuing therein—the inner development of Jewish thought came to an end. *1*

*************************************** 1. Compare F. Weber, System der altsynagagalen palaestinischen Theologie, Leipsic, 1880.
****

The later Hebrew literature, which does not fall to be considered here, contributed very few new elements; in so far as an intellectual life existed at all among the Jews of the Middle Ages, it was not a growth of native soil but proceeded from the Mahometan or Latin culture of individuals. The Kabbala at most, and even it hardly with justice, can be regarded as having been a genuine product of Judaism. It originated in Palestine, and subsequently flourished chiefly in the later Middle Ages in Spain, and, like all other methodised nonsense, had strong attractions for Christian scholars.

16. THE JEWISH DISPERSION.

Something still remains to be said with reference to the diaspora. We have seen how it began; in spite of Josephus (Antiquities, xi. 5, 2), it is to be carried back not to the Assyrian but merely to the Babylonian captivity; it was not composed of Israelites, but solely of citizens of the southern kingdom. It received its greatest impulse from Alexander, and then afterwards from Cæsar. In the Graeco-Roman period Jerusalem at the time of the great festival presented the appearance of a veritable Babel (Acts ii. 9-11); with the Jews themselves were mingled the proselytes (Acts ii. 11), for even already that religion was gaining considerable conquests among the heathen; as King Agrippa I. writes to the Emperor Caius (Philo, Legat. ad Gaium, sec. 36), "Jerusalem is the metropolis not only of Judaea but of very many lands, on account of the colonies which on various occasions ('epi xairwn) it has sent out into the adjoining countries of Egypt, Phoenicia, Syria, and Coelesyria, and into the more remote Pamphylia, Cilicia, the greater part of Asia Minor as far as to Bithynia and the remotest parts of Pontus; likewise into Europe—Thessaly, Boeotia, Macedonia, AEtolia, Attica, Argos, Corinth, most parts (and these the fairest) of the Peloponnesus. Nor are the Jewish settlements confined to the mainland only; they are found also in the more important islands, Euboea, Cyprus, Crete. I do not insist on the countries beyond the Euphrates, for with few exceptions all of them, Babylon and the fertile regions around it, have Jewish inhabitants." In the west of Europe also they were not wanting; many thousands of them lived in Rome. In those cities where they were at all numerous they, during the imperial period, formed separate communities; Josephus has preserved a great variety of documents in which the Roman authorities recognise their rights and liberties (especially as regards the Sabbath rest and the observance of festivals). Of greatest importance was the community in Alexandria; according to Philo a million of Jews had their residence there under an ethnarch for whom a gerusia was afterwards substituted by Augustus (In Flac., secs. 6, 10). The extent to which this diaspora was helpful in the diffusion of Christianity, the manner in which the mission of the apostles everywhere attached itself to the synagogues and proseuchai, is well known from the New Testament. That the Christians of the 1st cenentury had much to suffer along with the Jews is also a familiar fact. For at this period, in other respects more favourable to them than any other had previously been, the Jews had occasionally to endure

440

persecution. The emperors, taking umbrage at their intrusiveness, more than once banished them from Rome (Acts xviii. 2). The good will of the native population they never secured; they were most hated in Egypt and Syria, where they were strongest. *1*

******************************* 1. Compare Schuerer, Neutest. Zeitgeschichte (1874), sec. 31. The place taken by the Jewish element in the world of that time is brilliantly set forth by Mommsen in his History of Rome (book v. chapter ii.; English translation iv. p. 538 seq., 1866):— "How numerous even in Rome the Jewish population was already before Caesar's time, and how closely at the same time the Jews even then kept together as fellow-countrymen, is shown by the remark of an author of this period, that it was dangerous for a governor to offend the Jews in his province, because he might then certainly reckon on being hissed after his return, by the populace of the capital. Even at this time the predominant business of the Jews was trade.... At this period too we encounter the peculiar antipathy of the Occidentals touards this so thoroughly Oriental race and their foreign opinions and customs. This Judaism, although not the most pleasing feature in the nowhere pleasing picture of the mixture of nations which then prevailed, was, nevertheless, an historical element developing itself in the natural course of things,... which Cæsar just like his predecessor Alexander fostered as far as possible....They did not, of course, contemplate placing the Jewish nationality on an equal footing with the Hellenic or Italo-Hellenic. But the Jew who has not, like the Occidental, received the Pandora's gift of political organisation, and stands substantially in a relation of indifference to the state, who, moreover, is as reluctant to give up the essence of his national idiosyncrasy as he is ready to clothe it with any nationality at pleasure and to adapt himself up to a certain degree to foreign habits—the Jew was, for this very reason, as it were, made for a state which was to be built on the ruins of a hundred living polities, and to be endowed with a somewhat abstract and, from the outset, weakened nationality. In the ancient world also Judaism was an effective leaven of cosmopolitanism and of national decomposition."
****

The position of the Jews in the Roman Empire was naturally not improved by the great risings under Nero, Trajan (in Cyrene, Cyprus, Mesopotamia), and Hadrian. The East strictly so called, became more and more their proper home. The Christianization of the empire helped still further in a very special way to detach them from the Western world. *1*

******************************* 1. For a brief time only were they again favoured by Julian the Apostate; compare Gibbon, chapter xxiii.
****

They sided with the Persians against the Byzantines; in the year 614 they were even put in possession of Jerusalem by Chosroes, but were not long able to hold their own against Heraclius. *2*

With Islam also they found themselves in greater sympathy than with Christianity, although they were cruelly treated by Mahomet in Arabia, and driven by Omar out of the Hejaz, and notwithstanding the facts that they were as matter of course excluded from citizenship, and that they were held by Moslems as a whole in greater contempt than the Christians. They throve especially well on what may be called the bridge between East and West, in Mauretania and Spain, where they were the intellectual intermediaries between the Arab and the Latin culture. In the Sephardim and Ashkenazim the distinction between the subtler Oriental and the more conservative Western Jews has maintained itself in Europe also. From the 8th century onwards Judaism put forth a remarkable side shoot in the Khazars on the Volga; if legend Is to he believed, but little was required at one time to have induced the Russians to accept the Jewish rather than the Christian faith.

In the West the equal civil rights which Caracalla had conferred on all free inhabitants of the empire came to an end, so far as the Jews were concerned, in the time of Constantine. The state then became the secular arm of the church, and took action, though with less severity, against Jews just as against heretics and pagans. As early as the year 315, Constantine made conversion from Christianity to Judaism a penal offence, and prohibited Jews, on pain of death, from circumcising their Christian slaves. These laws were re-enacted and made more severe by Constantius, who attached the penalty of death to marriages between Jews and Christians. Theodosius I. and Honorius, indeed, by strictly prohibiting the destruction of synagogues, and by maintaining the old regulation that a Jew was not to be summoned before a court of justice on a Sabbath-day, put a check upon the militant zeal of the Church, by which even Chrysostom, for example, allowed himself to be carried away at Antioch. But Honorius rendered them ineligible for civil or military service, leaving open to them only the bar and the decurionate, the latter being a *privilegiium odiosum.* Their liberty to try cases by their own law was curtailed; the cases between Jews and Christians were to be tried by Christian judges only. Theodosius II. prohibited them from building new synagogues, and anew enforced their disability for all state employments. Most hostile of all was the orthodox Justinian, who, however, was still more severe against Pagans and Samaritans. *1*

*** 1. Cod. Theod., xvi. 8: "De Judaeis, Coelicolis, et Samaritanis;" Cod. Just., i. 9: "De Judaeis et Coelicolis." With regard to these coelicolae, see Gothofredus on Cod. Theod., xvi. 8, 9, and also J. Bernays, "Ueber die Gottesfuerchtigen bei Juvenal," in the Comm. Philol in hon. Th. Mommsen, 1877, p. 163. ***

He harassed the Jews with a law enjoining them to observe Easter on the same day as the Christians, a law which it was of course found impossible to carry out. *2*

**   2.   Gibbon,   chapter   xlvii.
****

In the Germanic states which arose upon the ruins of the Roman empire, the Jews did not fare badly on the whole. It was only in cases where the state was dominated by the Catholic Church, as, for example; among the Spanish Visigoths, that they were cruelly oppressed; among the Arian Ostrogoths, on the other hand, they had nothing to complain of. One thing in their favour was the Germanic principle that the law to be applied depended not on the land but on the nationality, as now in the East Europeans are judged by the consuls according to the law of their respective nations. The autonomy of the Jewish communities, which had been curtailed by the later emperors, was now enlarged once more under the laxer political and legal conditions. The Jews fared remarkably well under the Frankish monarchy; the Carolingians helped them in every possible way, making no account of the complaints of the bishops. They were allowed to hold property in land, but showed no eagerness for it; leaving agriculture to the Germans, they devoted them selves to trade. The market was completely in their hands; as a specially lucrative branch of commerce they still carried on the traffic in slaves, which had engaged them even in ancient times. *1*

** 1. Agobardus Lugdunensis, Die Insolentia Judaeorum, De Judaicis superstitionibus. Agobard was no superstitious fanatic, but one of the weightiest and most enlightened ecclesiastics of the Middle Ages. **

Meanwhile the Church was not remiss in seeking constantly repeated re-enactments of the old imperial laws, in the framing of which she had had paramount influence, and which she now incorporated with her own canon law. *2*

** 2. Compare Decret. i., dist. 45, c. 3; Decr. ii., caus. 23, qaest. 8, c. 9, caus. 28, qu. 1, c. 10-12; Decr. iii., de consecr., dist. 4, c. 93; Decretal. Greg. 5, 6 ("De Judaeis, Sarracenis, et eorum servis"), 5, 19, 18; Extrav. commun 5, 2. **

Gradually she succeeded in attaining her object. In the later Middle Ages the position of the Jews in the Christian society deteriorated. Intercourse with them was shunned; their isolation from being voluntary became compulsory; from the I3th century onwards they were obliged to wear, as a distinctive mark (more necessary in the East than in the West), a round or square yellow badge on their breast. *3*

** 3. Compare Du Cange, s. v. "Judaei;" also Reuter, Gesch. d. Aufklaerung im Mittelalter, i. 154 seq. In spite of all the legal restrictions laid upon them, the Jews still continued to have great influence with the princes, and more especially with the popes, of the Middle Ages. **

The difference of religion elicited a well-marked religious hate with oft-repeated deadly outbreaks, especially during the period of the crusades, and afterwards when the Black Death was raging (1348-50). Practical consequences like these the Church of course did not countenance; the popes set themselves against persecutions of the Jews, *4*

*********************************** 4. Decr. ii. 23, 8, 9. Alexander II. omnibus episeopis Hispaniae: Dispar...est Judaeorum et Sarracenorum eausa; in illos enim, qui Christianos persequuntur et ex urbibus et propriis sedibus pellunt, juste pugnatur, hi vero ubique servire parati sunt.
****

but with imperfect success. The popular aversion rested by no means exclusively on religious considerations; worldly motives were also present. The Jews of that period had in a still higher degree than now the control of financial affairs in their hands; and they used it without scruple. The Church herself had unintentionally given them a monopoly of the money market, by forbidding Christians to take interest. *5*

*********************************** 5. Decretal. Greg. v. 19, 18. Innocent III. in name of the Lateran Council: Quanto amplius Christiana religio ab exactione compescitur usurarum, tanto gravisu super his Judaeorum perfidia insolescit, ita quod brevi tempore Christianorum exhauriunt facultates. Volentes igitur in hac parse prospicere Christianis, ne a Judaeis immaniter aggraventur, synodali decreto statuimus, ut, si de caetero quocunque praetextu Judaaei a Christianis graves immoderatasve usuras extorserint, Christianorum eis participium subtrahatur, donec de immoderato gravamine satisfecerint competenter.... Principibus autem injungimus, ut propter hoc non sint Christianis infesti, sed potius a tanto gravamine studeant cohibere Judaeos.
****

In this way the Jews became rich indeed, but at the same time made themselves still more repugnant to the Christian population than they previously were by reason of their religion.

Having, according to the later mediaeval system, no rights in the Christian state, the Jews were tolerated only in those territories where the sovereign in the exercise of free favour accorded them protection. This protection was granted them in many quarters, but never for nothing; numerous and various taxes, which could be raised or changed in a perfectly arbitrary way, were exacted in exchange. But in countries where the feeling of nationality attained to a vigorous development, the spirit of toleration was speedily exhausted; the Jews were expelled by the act of the state. England was the first kingdom in which this occurred (1290); France followed in 1395, Spain and Portugal in 1492 and 1495. In this way it came about that the Holy Roman Empire— Germany, Italy, and adjoining districts—became the chief abode of the Jews. *1* In the anarchy which here prevailed they could best

*********************************** 1. The Polish Jews are German Jews who migrated in the Middle Ages to Poland, but have maintained to the present day their German speech, a mediaeval South-Frankish dialect, of course greatly

corrupted. In Russian "German" and "Jew" mean the same thing.
****

maintain their separate attitude, and if they were expelled from one locality they readily found refuge in some other. The emperor had indeed the right of extirpating them altogether (with the exception of a small number to be left as a memorial); but, in the first place, he had in various ways given up this right to the states of the empire, and, moreover, his pecuniary resources were so small that he could not afford to want the tax which the Jews as his "servi camerae" paid him for protecting their persons and property. In spite of many savage persecutions the Jews maintained their ground, especially in those parts of Germany where the political confusion was greatest. They even succeeded in maintaining a kind of autonomy by means of an arrangement in virtue of which civil processes which they had against each other were decided by their own rabbins in accordance with the law of the Talmud. 2

*** 2. Stobbe, Die Juden in Deutschl. waehr. d. Mittelalt., Brunsw., 1866.
****

The Jews, through their having on the one hand separated theselves, and on the other hand been excluded on religious grounds from the Gentiles, gained an internal solidarity and solidity which has hitherto enabled them to survive all the attacks of time. The hostility of the Middle Ages involved them in no danger; the greatest peril has been brought upon them by modern times, along with permission and increasing inducements to abandon their separate position. It is worth while to recall on this point the opinion of Spinoza, who was well able to form a competent judgment (Tract. Theol. polit., c. 4, ad fin.):— "That the Jews have maintained themselves so long in spite of their dispersed and disorganised condition is not at all to be wondered at, when it is considered how they separated themselves from all other nationalities in such a way as to bring upon themselves the hatred of all, and that not only by external rites contrary to those of other nations, but also by the sign of circumcision, which they maintain most religiously. Experience shows that their conservation is due in a great degree to the very hatred which they have incurred. When the king of Spain compelled the Jews either to accept the national religion or to go into banishment, very many of them accepted the Roman Catholic faith, and in virtue of this received all the privileges of Spanish subjects, and were declared eligible for every honour; the consequence was that a process of absorption began immediately, and in a short time neither trace nor memory of them survived. Quite different was the history of those whom the king of Portugal compelled to accept the creed of his nation; although converted, they continued to live apart from the rest of their fellow-subjects, having been declared unfit for any dignity. So great importance do I attach to the sign of circumcision also in this connection, that I am persuaded that it is sufficient by itself to maintain the separate existence of the nation for ever." The persistency of the race may of course prove a harder thing to overcome than Spinoza has supposed; but nevertheless he will be found to have spoken truly in declaring that the so-called emancipation of the Jews must inevitably lead to the extinction of Judaism wherever the process is extended beyond the political to the social sphere. For the accomplishment of this centuries may be required.

Printed in France by Amazon
Brétigny-sur-Orge, FR

30432068R10252